# Śrī Bṛhad Bhāgavatāmṛta

# Śrī Bṛhad Bhāgavatāmṛta

### *of Śrīla Sanātana Gosvāmī*

**VOLUME THREE**

translated from the original Sanskrit,
with a summary of the author's
*Dig-darśinī* commentary,
by Gopīparāṇadhana Dāsa

THE BHAKTIVEDANTA BOOK TRUST
LOS ANGELES STOCKHOLM MUMBAI SYDNEY

Readers interested in the subject matter of this book
are invited to correspond with the publisher at
one of the following addresses:

The Bhaktivedanta Book Trust
P.O. Box 34074, Los Angeles, CA 90034, USA
Phone: +1-800-927-4152 • Fax: +1-310-837-1056
E-mail: bbt.usa@krishna.com

The Bhaktivedanta Book Trust
Korsnäs Gård, 147 92 Grödinge, Sweden
Phone: +46-8-53029800 • Fax: +46-8-53025062
E-mail: bbt.se@krishna.com

The Bhaktivedanta Book Trust
P.O. Box 380, Riverstone, NSW 2765, Australia
Phone: +61-2-96276306 • Fax: +61-2-96276052
E-mail: bbt.au@krishna.com

The Bhaktivedanta Book Trust
Hare Krishna Land, Juhu, Mumbai 400 049, India
Phone: +91-22-26206860 • Fax: +91-22-26205214
E-mail: bbt.in@krishna.com

www.krishna.com

Illustrations: Dīna-bandhu Dāsa
Design: Brāhma Muhūrta Dāsa, Govinda Dāsa



ISBN 0-89213-345-7 (*volume 1*)
ISBN 0-89213-346-5 (*volume 2*)
ISBN 0-89213-347-3 (*volume 3*)
ISBN 0-89213-348-1 (*set*)

Printed in Germany

*This book is a humble offering to the disciples and granddisciples of His Divine Grace A.C. Bhaktivedanta Swami Prabhupāda. By staying faithful to his instructions and his spirit of generosity, they can transform the world.*

# Contents

# Preface

I WOULD BE UNGRATEFUL not to express my thanks to all the thoughtful Vaiṣṇavas who have shared with me their words of appreciation for the first two volumes of this book. I cannot take much credit for this work, since I've only served as a middleman between Śrīla Sanātana Gosvāmī, who provided the exquisite original poetry and his definitive commentary on it, and our editors — Keśava Bhāratī Dāsa Goswāmī and Jayādvaita Swāmī — who made the English almost as delightful and elegant as the Sanskrit.

Gopīparāṇadhana Dāsa
at Girirāja Govardhana
Śrī Bahulāṣṭamī
November 5, 2004

# Part Two

# Śrī-goloka-māhātmya

## The Glories of Goloka

(CONCLUDED)

# FIVE

# *Prema: Love of God*

## TEXT 1

श्रीगोपकुमार उवाच
अथ तत्र गतो विप्रैः कियद्भिर्माथुरैः सह ।
यादवान्क्रीडतोऽद्राक्षं सङ्घशः सकुमारकान् ॥

*śrī-gopa-kumāra uvāca*
*atha tatra gato vipraiḥ*
*kiyadbhir māthuraiḥ saha*
*yādavān krīḍato 'drākṣaṁ*
*saṅghaśaḥ sa-kumārakān*

*śrī-gopa-kumāraḥ uvāca* — Śrī Gopa-kumāra said; *atha* — then; *tatra* — there; *gataḥ* — going; *vipraiḥ* — with *brāhmaṇas; kiyadbhiḥ* — a few; *māthuraiḥ* — belonging to Mathurā; *saha* — together; *yādavān* — the Yādavas; *krīḍataḥ* — enjoying; *adrākṣam* — I saw; *saṅghaśaḥ* — in groups; *sa-kumārakān* — with their children.

**Śrī Gopa-kumāra said: I then went to Dvārakā. There I saw various groups of Yādavas, along with their children. They were accompanied by some brāhmaṇas of Mathurā and were enjoying themselves.**

COMMENTARY: In this fifth chapter, Gopa-kumāra meets the Lord of Dvārakā and hears the glories of the earthly Gokula and the pastimes the Lord enacts there. By understanding the glories of that Gokula he comes to know the glories of Kṛṣṇa's planet Goloka in the spiritual sky.

Upon arriving in Dvārakā, Gopa-kumāra saw that the Yadus were completely free from anxiety and in fact were full of the most perfect ecstasy. They were constantly enjoying various kinds of pleasure. He saw large numbers of them, assembled in groups, and besides the adults he saw many children also.

TEXT 2

पुरा क्वापि न दृष्टा या सर्वतो भ्रमता मया ।
मधुरिम्णां परा काष्ठा सा तेष्वेव विराजते ॥

*purā kvāpi na dṛṣṭā yā*
*sarvato bhramatā mayā*
*madhurimṇāṁ parā kāṣṭhā*
*sā teṣv eva virājate*

*purā* — before; *kva api* — anywhere; *na* — not; *dṛṣṭā* — seen; *yā* — which; *sarvataḥ* — everywhere; *bhramatā* — who was traveling; *mayā* — by me; *madhurimṇām* — of all kinds of attractiveness; *parā kāṣṭhā* — ultimate perfection; *sā* — that; *teṣu* — among them; *eva* — only; *virājate* — was visible.

**I had wandered everywhere, but never before had I seen such a perfection of charm as that which shone in them.**

COMMENTARY: Not even in Vaikuṇṭha and Ayodhyā had Gopa-kumāra seen such handsome people.

TEXT 3

सर्वार्थो विस्मृतो हर्षान्मया तद्दर्शनोद्भवात् ।
तैस्त्वाकृष्य परिष्वक्तः सर्वज्ञप्रवरैरहम् ॥

*sarvārtho vismṛto harṣān*
*mayā tad-darśanodbhavāt*
*tais tv ākṛṣya pariṣvaktaḥ*
*sarva-jña-pravarair aham*

*sarva* — all; *arthaḥ* — my purposes; *vismṛtaḥ* — forgotten; *harṣāt* — out of the delight; *mayā* — by me; *tat* — of them; *darśana* — from the sight; *udbhavāt* — which arose; *taiḥ* — by them; *tu* — and; *ākṛṣya* — been drawn; *pariṣvaktaḥ* — embraced; *sarva-jña* — of all-knowing sages; *pravaraiḥ* — by the best; *aham* — I.

**Seeing them gave me such delight that I forgot everything I had in mind. And those Yādavas, the best of all-knowing sages, drew me into their company and embraced me.**

COMMENTARY: Gopa-kumāra had intended to bow down to offer the Yādavas his respects, but he was so enchanted by what he was seeing that he forgot. The Yādavas, who were as all-knowing as the most proficient mystics, knew at once that Gopa-kumāra was looking for Kṛṣṇa, and so they greeted him enthusiastically.

## TEXT 4

गोवर्धनाद्रिगोपालपुत्रबुद्ध्या प्रवेशितः ।
अन्तःपुरं करे धृत्वा स्नेहपूरार्द्रमानसैः ॥

*govardhanādri-gopāla-*
*putra-buddhyā praveśitaḥ*
*antaḥ-puraṁ kare dhṛtvā*
*sneha-pūrārdra-mānasaiḥ*

*govardhana-adri* — of Govardhana Hill; *gopāla* — of a cowherd; *putra* — the son; *buddhyā* — with the idea of my being; *praveśitaḥ* — brought inside; *antaḥ-puram* — the inner precincts of the city; *kare* — my hand; *dhṛtvā* — holding; *sneha-pūra* — in a flood of affection; *ārdra* — melting; *mānasaiḥ* — whose hearts.

**When they recognized me as the son of a cowherd from Govardhana Hill, their hearts melted in a flood of affection,**

**and they took me by the hand and brought me into the inner precincts of the city.**

TEXT 5

पश्यामि दूरात्सदसो महीयसो
मध्ये मणिस्वर्णमये वरासने ।
तूलीवरोपर्युपविश्य लीलया
विभ्राजमानो भगवान्स वर्तते ॥

*paśyāmi dūrāt sadaso mahīyaso*
*madhye maṇi-svarṇa-maye varāsane*
*tūlī-varopary upaviśya līlayā*
*vibhrājamāno bhagavān sa vartate*

*paśyāmi* — I saw; *dūrāt* — at a distance; *sadasaḥ* — of an assembly hall; *mahīyasaḥ* — vast; *madhye* — in the midst; *maṇi* — of jewels; *svarṇa* — and gold; *maye* — made; *vara* — excellent; *āsane* — on a throne; *tūlī* — a cushion; *vara* — excellent; *upari* — on; *upaviśya* — sitting; *līlayā* — playfully; *vibhrāja-mānaḥ* — resplendent; *bhagavān* — the Personality of Godhead; *saḥ* — He; *vartate* — was present.

**From a distance I saw the Personality of Godhead, brilliantly manifest. At leisure in a vast assembly hall, He sat on the excellent cushion of an excellent throne made of gold and jewels.**

COMMENTARY: The hall was known as Sudharmā.

TEXT 6

वैकुण्ठनाथस्य विचित्रमाधुरी-
सारेण तेनास्त्यखिलेन सेवितः ।
केनापि केनाप्यधिकाधिकेन सो
ऽमुष्मादपि श्रीभरसञ्चयेन च ॥

*vaikuṇṭha-nāthasya vicitra-mādhurī-*
*sāreṇa tenāsty akhilena sevitaḥ*
*kenāpi kenāpy adhikādhikena so*
*'muṣmād api śrī-bhara-sañcayena ca*

*vaikuṇṭha-nāthasya* — of the Lord of Vaikuṇṭha; *vicitra* — manifold; *mādhurī* — of the charm; *sāreṇa* — essence; *tena* — by that; *asti* — He was; *akhilena* — all; *sevitaḥ* — served; *kena api kena api* — by some various; *adhika-adhikena* — greater and greater; *saḥ* — He; *amuṣmāt* — than these; *api* — also; *śrī-bhara* — of splendors; *sañcayena* — by multitudes; *ca* — and.

**He was served by all the many quintessential charms of the Lord of Vaikuṇṭha, and by many different splendors, greater and greater, that even that Lord does not possess.**

COMMENTARY: Many of the attractive features of Lord Nārāyaṇa are also visible in Kṛṣṇa, the Lord of Dvārakā — a beautiful mouth, eyes, and so on, fine ornaments, opulent paraphernalia, and such pastimes as chewing *pān* and sitting on a throne. Kṛṣṇa displays these charms even more attractively than Lord Nārāyaṇa, and what to speak of Kṛṣṇa's own unique ways of attracting His devotees.

## TEXT 7

कैशोरशोभार्द्रितयौवनार्चितो
भक्तेष्वभिव्यञ्जितचारुदोर्युगः ।
माधुर्यभङ्गीह्रियमाणसेवक-
स्वान्तो महाश्चर्यविनोदसागरः ॥

*kaiśora-śobhārdrita-yauvanārcito*
*bhakteṣv abhivyañjita-cāru-dor-yugaḥ*
*mādhurya-bhaṅgī-hriyamāṇa-sevaka-*
*svānto mahāścarya-vinoda-sāgaraḥ*

*kaiśora* — of adolescence; *śobhā* — by the charm; *ārdrita* — softened; *yauvana* — by mature youth; *arcitaḥ* — worshiped; *bhakteṣu* — to the devotees; *abhivyañjita* — revealed; *cāru* — beautiful; *doḥ-yugaḥ* — two arms; *mādhurya* — of attractiveness; *bhaṅgī* — by gestures; *hriyamāṇa* — stealing; *sevaka* — of His servants; *sva-antaḥ* — the inner selves; *mahā-āścarya* — supremely wonderful; *vinoda* — of pastimes; *sāgaraḥ* — the ocean.

**Revealing His two beautiful arms for His devotees, Lord Kṛṣṇa, the ocean of supremely wonderful pastimes, was worshiped by youthful maturity softened by a touch of adolescent grace. His sublime gestures stole the hearts of His servants.**

COMMENTARY: Young adults are especially beautiful, but in Kṛṣṇa the mature beauty of youth is made even sweeter by traces of childlike innocence. Never leaving Him unattended, this special mixture of charm serves Him with pure devotion, like a faithful worshiper of His Deity form. Since the devotees in Dvārakā are Kṛṣṇa's dearest servants, they can enjoy seeing His beauty constantly. And whereas devotees of Viṣṇu see their Lord with four arms, the more intimate among the residents of Dvārakā generally see Him with only two. Gopa-kumāra saw how Kṛṣṇa's smiles, His pleasant words, His sidelong glances, and the movements of His eyebrows charmed the Dvārakā-vāsīs in the Sudharmā hall. Only devotees favored by the Lord can know how such gestures affect the heart, for it cannot be adequately described in words. Indeed, the eternally deep ocean of Kṛṣṇa's playful pastimes goes beyond the delimiting power of words and the mind. In this narration, Gopa-kumāra can only hint at such charms.

## TEXT 8

श्वेतातपत्रं विततं विराजते
तस्योपरिष्टाद्द्रचामरद्वयम् ।

पार्श्वद्वये विभ्रमदग्रतोऽस्य च
श्रीपादुके हाटकपीठमस्तके ॥

*śvetātapatraṁ vitataṁ virājate*
*tasyopariṣṭād vara-cāmara-dvayam*
*pārśva-dvaye vibhramad agrato 'sya ca*
*śrī-pāduke hāṭaka-pīṭha-mastake*

*śveta* — white; *ātapatram* — an umbrella; *vitatam* — broad; *virājate* — shone; *tasya* — Him; *upariṣṭāt* — above; *vara* — excellent; *cāmara-dvayam* — a pair of *cāmara* fans; *pārśva-dvaye* — at His two sides; *vibhramat* — waving; *agrataḥ* — in front; *asya* — of Him; *ca* — and; *śrī* — divine; *pāduke* — two slippers; *hāṭaka* — golden; *pīṭha* — of a stool; *mastake* — on the top.

**Above Him shone a broad white umbrella, at His two sides waved a pair of excellent yak-tail fans, and in front of Him upon a golden footstool sat His divine slippers.**

COMMENTARY: Gopa-kumāra's attention now turned to Śrī Kṛṣṇa's royal paraphernalia. The Lord's white umbrella, large and finely crafted, was held above His head. Similarly large and white were the *cāmaras* with which He was being adroitly fanned on either side.

TEXT 9

श्रीराजराजेश्वरतानुरूपा
परिच्छदाली परितो विभाति ।
निजानुरूपाः परिचारकाश्च
तथा महावैभवपङ्क्तयोऽपि ॥

*śrī-rāja-rājeśvaratānurūpā*
*paricchadālī parito vibhāti*
*nijānurūpāḥ paricārakāś ca*
*tathā mahā-vaibhava-paṅktayo 'pi*

*śrī* — divine; *rāja-rāja* — of kings of kings; *īśvaratā* — for being the ruler; *anurūpā* — befitting; *paricchada-ālī* — various paraphernalia; *paritaḥ* — on all sides; *vibhāti* — were visible; *nija* — for Himself; *anurūpāḥ* — suitable; *paricārakāḥ* — servants; *ca* — and; *tathā* — and; *mahā-vaibhava* — of transcendental opulences; *paṅktayaḥ* — rows; *api* — also.

**All around Him were various symbols of royalty befitting the ruler of kings among kings, and there were servants qualified to attend Him, and transcendental opulences standing in rows before Him.**

COMMENTARY: Various weapons and other symbols of royalty stood near the Lord. Of course, the opulences of the Lord of Dvārakā are all purely spiritual and even more sublime than those of the Lord of Vaikuṇṭha, but for the sake of poetic comparison they are described as befitting a worldly emperor. In a very real sense, moreover, Kṛṣṇa in Dvārakā is the king of all kings.

Before describing the principal devotees present in the assembly hall, Gopa-kumāra mentions the devotees tending the Lord at His side. The attendants who stood on the four sides of the Lord were *nijānurūpa* — "qualified to serve the Supreme Lord" because of being unequaled in splendor. The opulences arrayed in rows before the Lord included His chariot and horses, His *pārijāta* flower and other playthings, and the personified arts of song, dance, and so forth.

## TEXT 10

स्वस्वासने श्रीवसुदेवरामा-
क्रूरादयो दक्षिणतो निविष्टाः ।
वामेऽस्य पार्श्वे गदसात्यकी च
पुरो निधायाधिपमुग्रसेनम् ॥

*sva-svāsane śrī-vasudeva-rāmā-*
*krūrādayo dakṣiṇato niviṣṭāḥ*

*vāme 'sya pārśve gada-sātyakī ca*
*puro nidhāyādhipam ugrasenam*

*sva-sva* — each on his own; *āsane* — seat; *śrī-vasudeva* — Śrī Vasudeva; *rāma* — Balarāma; *akrūra* — Akrūra; *ādayaḥ* — and so on; *dakṣiṇataḥ* — on the right; *niviṣṭāḥ* — seated; *vāme* — left; *asya* — His; *pārśve* — on the side; *gada* — Gada; *sātyakī* — and Sātyaki; *ca* — also; *puraḥ* — in front; *nidhāya* — being placed; *adhipam* — the king; *ugrasenam* — Ugrasena.

**Śrī Vasudeva, Balarāma, Akrūra, and others sat to His right, each on his own seat, Gada and Sātyaki to His left, and just before Him King Ugrasena.**

COMMENTARY: Besides Kṛṣṇa's father, His elder brother, and His respected friend Akrūra, others also sat on His right, including His *gurus* Sāndīpani and Garga. Ugrasena sat on a throne directly in front of Kṛṣṇa because Ugrasena was the king.

## TEXT 11

मन्त्री विकद्रुः कृतवर्मणा समं
तत्रैव वृष्णिप्रवरैः परैरपि ।
श्रीनारदो नर्मसुगीतवीणा-
वाद्यैरमुं क्रीडति हासयन्सः ॥

*mantrī vikadruḥ kṛtavarmaṇā samaṁ*
*tatraiva vṛṣṇi-pravaraiḥ parair api*
*śrī-nārado narma-sugīta-vīṇā-*
*vādyair amuṁ krīḍati hāsayan saḥ*

*mantrī* — His minister; *vikadruḥ* — Vikadru; *kṛtavarmaṇā* — with Kṛtavarmā; *samam* — together; *tatra* — there; *eva* — indeed; *vṛṣṇi-pravaraiḥ* — with the best Vṛṣṇis; *paraiḥ* — others; *api* — also; *śrī-nāradaḥ* — Śrī Nārada; *narma* — with clever words; *su-gīta* — fine singing; *vīṇā-vādyaiḥ* — and the music of his *vīṇā; amum* — Him; *krīḍati* — played; *hāsayan* — making smile; *saḥ* — he.

**Also nearby was the Lord's minister Vikadru, with Kṛtavarmā and several other prominent Vṛṣṇis. Śrī Nārada was entertaining the Lord, making Him smile with clever words, fine singing, and the music of his vīṇā.**

COMMENTARY: Vikadru, the trusted advisor, and Kṛtavarmā, the head of the army, also had privileged seats near Kṛṣṇa's throne. The same Nārada whom Gopa-kumāra had seen in Vaikuṇṭha was wandering about the assembly, praising various Yādavas with good humor.

TEXT 12

तिष्ठन्पुरः श्रीगरुडोऽस्ति तं स्तुवन्
पादाब्जसंवाहनकृत्तथोद्धवः ।
रहस्यवार्ताभिरसौ प्रियाभिः
सन्तोषयन्नस्ति निजेश्वरं तम् ॥

*tiṣṭhan puraḥ śrī-garuḍo 'sti taṁ stuvan*
*pādābja-saṁvāhana-kṛt tathoddhavaḥ*
*rahasya-vārtābhir asau priyābhiḥ*
*santoṣayann asti nijeśvaraṁ tam*

*tiṣṭhan* — standing; *puraḥ* — in front; *śrī-garuḍaḥ* — Śrī Garuḍa; *asti* — was; *tam* — Him; *stuvan* — praising; *pāda-abja* — to His lotus feet; *saṁvāhana-kṛt* — giving a massage; *tathā* — and; *uddhavaḥ* — Uddhava; *rahasya* — confidential; *vārtābhiḥ* — with comments; *asau* — he; *priyābhiḥ* — affectionate; *santoṣayan* — gratifying; *asti* — was; *nija* — his; *īśvaram* — Lord; *tam* — Him.

**Śrī Garuḍa stood before the Lord, glorifying Him with prayers. And Uddhava massaged the Lord's lotus feet and pleased Him with affectionate intimate remarks.**

COMMENTARY: As Kṛṣṇa's dearest friend in Dvārakā, Uddhava has the privilege of massaging the Lord's feet in the Sudharmā assembly hall. Being so close to the Lord, he can say things that others present should not overhear. He is also a disciple of Bṛhaspati, the master of speech, so he is a perfect scholar and Kṛṣṇa's favorite advisor. Even if someone were to stand close enough to hear what he was telling Kṛṣṇa, his speech was so circumspect that its confidential gist was beyond guessing. Although the Lord to whom Uddhava was speaking had submitted Himself to Uddhava's influence, that Lord was *nijeśvaram,* the supreme controller, what to speak of being most clever and resourceful.

## TEXT 13

निरीक्ष्य दीर्घात्मदिदृक्षितास्पदं
दूरेऽपतं प्रेमभरेण मोहितः ।
स तूद्भटस्नेहरसेन पूरितो
मन्नायनायोद्धवमादिदेश ॥

*nirīkṣya dīrghātma-didṛkṣitāspadaṁ*
*dūre 'pataṁ prema-bhareṇa mohitaḥ*
*sa tūdbhaṭa-sneha-rasena pūrito*
*man-nāyanāyoddhavam ādideśa*

*nirīkṣya* — seeing; *dīrgha* — for a long time; *ātma* — my own; *didṛkṣita* — of the desire to see; *āspadam* — the goal; *dūre* — at a distance; *apatam* — I fell down; *prema-bhareṇa* — by the burden of love; *mohitaḥ* — made unconscious; *saḥ* — He; *tu* — and; *udbhaṭa* — exalted; *sneha* — of affection; *rasena* — with the transcendental mood; *pūritaḥ* — filled; *mat* — me; *nāyanāya* — to bring; *uddhavam* — Uddhava; *ādideśa* — instructed.

**Seeing from a distance the goal I had long desired to see, I fell unconscious, overburdened by love. Then the Lord, brimming with the exalted rasa of affection, told Uddhava to bring me close.**

## TEXT 14

मामुद्धवो गोपकुमारवेशम्
आलक्ष्य हृष्टो द्रुतमागतोऽसौ ।
उत्थाप्य यत्नादथ चेतयित्वा
पाण्योर्गृहीत्वानयदस्य पार्श्वम् ॥

*mām uddhavo gopa-kumāra-veśam*
*ālakṣya hṛṣṭo drutam āgato 'sau*
*utthāpya yatnād atha cetayitvā*
*pāṇyor gṛhītvānayad asya pārśvam*

*mām* — me; *uddhavaḥ* — Uddhava; *gopa-kumāra* — of a cowherd boy; *veśam* — in the dress; *ālakṣya* — seeing; *hṛṣṭaḥ* — delighted; *drutam* — quickly; *āgataḥ* — came; *asau* — he; *utthāpya* — raising; *yatnāt* — with endeavor; *atha* — and; *cetayitvā* — bringing to full awareness; *pāṇyoḥ* — in his two hands; *gṛhītvā* — taking; *anayat* — brought; *asya* — His; *pārśvam* — to the side.

**Uddhava quickly came forward, delighted to see me in the dress of a cowherd boy. He carefully lifted me from the ground, brought me back to full awareness, and led me to the Lord's side with both hands.**

COMMENTARY: Since Uddhava has a special attachment to the residents of Gokula, he at once recognized Gopa-kumāra's dress. And he quickly left his service of massaging Kṛṣṇa's feet to carry out the Lord's order.

## TEXT 15

निजान्तिके मन्नयनार्थमात्मनै-
वोत्थातुकामेन पुरोऽर्पितस्य ।
पादाम्बुजस्योपरि मच्छिरो बलात्
स्वपाणिनाकृष्य बतोद्धवो न्यधात् ॥

*nijāntike man-nayanārtham ātmanai-*
*votthātu-kāmena puro 'rpitasya*
*pādāmbujasyopari mac-chiro balāt*
*sva-pāṇinākṛṣya batoddhavo nyadhāt*

*nija* — to Himself; *antike* — close by; *mat* — me; *nayana-artham* — for the purpose of bringing; *ātmanā* — by Himself; *eva* — indeed; *utthātu* — to lift; *kāmena* — with the desire; *puraḥ* — filled; *arpitasya* — offered; *pāda-ambujasya* — of His lotus feet; *upari* — on; *mat* — my; *śiraḥ* — head; *balāt* — by force; *sva* — his own; *pāṇinā* — with the hand; *ākṛṣya* — pulling; *bata* — ah; *uddhavaḥ* — Uddhava; *nyadhāt* — placed.

**Then the Lord, wanting to lift me up and draw me to His side, placed His feet close to me. And—oh!—Uddhava, with his own hand, firmly touched my head to those lotus feet.**

COMMENTARY: In all of Gopa-kumāra's travels throughout the material and spiritual worlds, he had never experienced such mercy from the Supreme Lord.

## TEXT 16

स प्राणनाथः स्वकराम्बुजेन मे
स्पृशन्प्रतीकान्परिमार्जयन्निव ।
वंशीं ममादाय कराद्विलोकयंस्
तूष्णीं स्थितोऽश्रूणि सृजन्महार्तवत् ॥

*sa prāṇa-nāthaḥ sva-karāmbujena me*
*spṛśan pratīkān parimārjayann iva*
*vaṁśīṁ mamādāya karād vilokayaṁs*
*tūṣṇīṁ sthito 'śrūṇi sṛjan mahārta-vat*

*saḥ* — He; *prāṇa-nāthaḥ* — the Lord of my life; *sva* — His own; *kara-ambujena* — with the lotus hand; *me* — my; *spṛśan* — touching; *pratīkān* — limbs; *parimārjayan* — cleaning; *iva* —

as if; *vaṁśīm* — flute; *mama* — my; *ādāya* — taking; *karāt* — from my hand; *vilokayan* — looking; *tūṣṇīm* — silent; *sthitaḥ* — remained; *aśrūṇi* — tears; *sṛjan* — shedding; *mahā-ārta-vat* — as if very much distressed.

**The Lord of my life then stroked me with His lotus hand, as if to cleanse each of my limbs. He took the flute from my hand, looked at it, and, apparently in great distress, silently shed tears.**

COMMENTARY: Although Kṛṣṇa was in the august assembly of royalty, He was unable to check His emotions when Gopa-kumāra came near Him. Kṛṣṇa surely knows how to deal lovingly with His devotees, and in front of the Yādava princes He tried His best to control Himself, but it was obvious He was becoming agitated.

## TEXT 17

क्षणात्तव क्षेममनामयोऽसि किं
न तत्र कच्चित्प्रभवेदमङ्गलम् ।
एवं वदन्नेव दशां स कामपि
व्रजन्कृतो मन्त्रिवरेण धैर्यवान् ॥

*kṣaṇāt tava kṣemam anāmayo 'si kiṁ*
*na tatra kaccit prabhaved amaṅgalam*
*evaṁ vadann eva daśāṁ sa kām api*
*vrajan kṛto mantri-vareṇa dhairyavān*

*kṣaṇāt* — after a moment; *tava* — your; *kṣemam* — well-being; *anāmayaḥ* — healthy; *asi* — you are; *kim* — anything; *na* — not; *tatra* — there; *kaccit* — whether; *prabhavet* — has an influence; *amaṅgalam* — inauspicious; *evam* — thus; *vadan* — saying; *eva* — just; *daśām* — a state; *saḥ* — He; *kām api* — some; *vrajan* — obtaining; *kṛtaḥ* — made; *mantri-vareṇa* — by His chief advisor (Uddhava); *dhairya-vān* — calm.

**The next moment He asked, "Is all well with you? Is your health good? I hope the place you came from is free from any misfortune." While speaking this way, He again began to feel disturbed, and Uddhava had to calm Him.**

COMMENTARY: As soon as Uddhava saw ecstatic symptoms appear in Kṛṣṇa's body, such as tears and choking of the voice, he took steps to calm the Lord. Kṛṣṇa's agitation was caused by the questions He had asked about Gopa-kumāra's hometown. Strictly speaking, inauspicious forces cannot enter the Dvārakā of Vaikuṇṭha, where Gopa-kumāra was present; they can enter only the Vṛndāvana and Dvārakā on earth. But Śrī Kṛṣṇa is always in the mood of His abodes on earth, which are ultimately identical with His abodes in the spiritual sky. Śrī Nārada will later elaborate on this esoteric truth.

## TEXT 18

अग्रतो दर्शितास्तेन सङ्केतेन सभास्थिताः ।
यादवा वसुदेवाद्या नृपा देवास्तथर्षयः ॥

*agrato darśitās tena*
*saṅketena sabhā-sthitāḥ*
*yādavā vasudevādyā*
*nṛpā devās tatharṣayaḥ*

*agrataḥ* — in front; *darśitāḥ* — shown; *tena* — by him; *saṅketena* — with a gesture; *sabhā* — in the assembly; *sthitāḥ* — present; *yādavāḥ* — the Yādavas; *vasudeva* — Vasudeva; *ādyāḥ* — and so on; *nṛpāḥ* — kings; *devāḥ* — demigods; *tathā* — also; *ṛṣayaḥ* — sages.

**With a gesture, Uddhava indicated to the Lord those present before them in the assembly—Vasudeva and the other Yādavas and many kings and demigods and sages.**

COMMENTARY: Uddhava moved his eyebrows to remind Kṛṣṇa

of the presence not only of Vasudeva and the other Yadus but also of kings like Yudhiṣṭhira, demigods like Indra, and sages like Gargācārya. As we have understood from the philosophical explanation by Nārada, these kings, demigods, and sages are all eternal associates of the Lord who reside in the Dvārakā within Vaikuṇṭha, just as they reside in the Dvārakā on earth, to enhance the Lord's enjoyment of His pastimes. Gopa-kumāra will see many of these devotees again when he reaches Goloka.

TEXT 19

उन्मील्य पद्मनेत्रे तानालोक्याग्रे प्रयत्नतः ।
सोऽवष्टभ्येषदात्मानं पुरान्तर्गन्तुमुद्यतः ॥

*unmīlya padma-netre tān*
*ālokyāgre prayatnataḥ*
*so 'vaṣṭabhyeṣad ātmānaṁ*
*purāntar gantum udyataḥ*

*unmīlya* — opening; *padma-netre* — His lotus eyes; *tān* — at them; *ālokya* — glancing; *agre* — before Him; *prayatnataḥ* — with difficulty; *saḥ* — He; *avaṣṭabhya* — calming; *īṣat* — somewhat; *ātmānam* — Himself; *pura* — His quarters; *antaḥ* — inside; *gantum* — to go; *udyataḥ* — got up.

**The Lord opened His lotus eyes and glanced at the people in front of Him. With difficulty He somewhat calmed Himself and then got up to enter His inner quarters.**

TEXT 20

चिरादभीष्टं निजजीवितेशं
तथाभिलभ्य प्रमदाब्धिमग्नः ।
किमाचराणि प्रवदानि वा किम्
इति स्म जानामि न किञ्चनाहम् ॥

*cirād abhīṣṭaṁ nija-jīviteśaṁ*
*tathābhilabhya pramadābdhi-magnaḥ*
*kim ācarāṇi pravadāni vā kim*
*iti sma jānāmi na kiñcanāham*

*cirāt* — for a long time; *abhīṣṭam* — who was yearned for; *nija* — my own; *jīvita-īśam* — Lord of the life; *tathā* — thus; *abhilabhya* — obtaining; *pramada* — of great joy; *abdhi* — in an ocean; *magnaḥ* — immersed; *kim* — what; *ācarāṇi* — should I do; *pravadāni* — should I say; *vā* — or; *kim* — what; *iti* — thus; *sma jānāmi na* — did not know; *kiñcana* — at all; *aham* — I.

**Because I had now attained the Lord of my life, for whom I had yearned for so long, I was immersed in an ocean of joy. I had no idea what to say or what to do.**

## TEXT 21

ततो बहिर्निःसरतो यदूत्तमान्
सम्मान्य ताम्बूलविलेपनादिभिः ।
विधृत्य मां दक्षिणपाणिनाञ्जलौ
रामोद्धवाभ्यामविशत्पुरान्तरम् ॥

*tato bahir niḥsarato yadūttamān*
*sammānya tāmbūla-vilepanādibhiḥ*
*vidhṛtya māṁ dakṣiṇa-pāṇināñjalau*
*rāmoddhavābhyām aviśat purāntaram*

*tataḥ* — then; *bahiḥ* — out; *niḥsarataḥ* — who were going; *yadu-uttamān* — the chiefs of Yadus; *sammānya* — honoring; *tāmbūla* — with *pān; vilepana* — sandalwood paste; *ādibhiḥ* — and so on; *vidhṛtya* — taking; *mām* — me; *dakṣiṇa-pāṇinā* — by the right hand; *añjalau* — by the folded palms; *rāma* — with Balarāma; *uddhavābhyām* — and Uddhava; *aviśat* — He entered; *pura-antaram* — the inner palace.

**As the chiefs of the Yadus began leaving, the Lord honored them with items such as pān and sandalwood paste. Holding my joined palms in His right hand, He took me with Him as He entered the inner palace with Balarāma and Uddhava.**

COMMENTARY: Kṛṣṇa's standing up ended the official business of the assembly, so the Yadus all began to leave. Gopa-kumāra, however, was escorted by the Lord Himself into the Lord's private quarters. The Lord took hold of Gopa-kumāra's hand very firmly.

## TEXT 22

श्वश्रूं पुरस्कृत्य सरोहिणीकां
श्रीदेवकीं साष्टशतोत्तराणि ।
प्रभुं सहस्राण्यथ षोडशाग्रे
ऽभ्ययुः सभृत्याः प्रमुदा महिष्यः ॥

*śvaśrūṁ puras-kṛtya sa-rohiṇīkāṁ*
*śrī-devakīṁ sāṣṭa-śatottarāṇi*
*prabhuṁ sahasrāṇy atha ṣoḍaśāgre*
*'bhyayuḥ sa-bhṛtyāḥ pramudā mahiṣyaḥ*

*śvaśrūm* — the mother-in-law; *puraḥ* — in front; *kṛtya* — placing; *sa-rohiṇīkām* — along with Rohiṇī; *śrī-devakīm* — Śrī Devakī; *sa-aṣṭa* — plus eight; *śata-uttarāṇi* — plus one hundred; *prabhum* — the Lord; *sahasrāṇi* — thousands; *atha* — then; *ṣoḍaśa* — sixteen; *agre* — forward; *abhyayuḥ* — proceeded; *sa-bhṛtyāḥ* — with their maidservants; *pramudā* — happily; *mahiṣyaḥ* — the queens.

**The Lord's 16,108 queens happily followed their husband, along with their maidservants. And in front the queens placed their mothers-in-law, Śrī Devakī and Rohiṇī.**

COMMENTARY: Immediately after Kṛṣṇa entered His quarters,

His queens and their attendants followed Him. They showed proper respect to the mothers of Kṛṣṇa and Balarāma by having them enter first.

## TEXT 23

रुक्मिणी सत्यभामा सा देवी जाम्बवती तथा ।
कालिन्दी मित्रविन्दा च सत्या भद्रा च लक्ष्मणा ॥

*rukmiṇī satyabhāmā sā*
*devī jāmbavatī tathā*
*kālindī mitravindā ca*
*satyā bhadrā ca lakṣmaṇā*

*rukmiṇī* — Rukmiṇī; *satyabhāmā* — Satyabhāmā; *sā* — she; *devī* — the goddess; *jāmbavatī* — Jāmbavatī; *tathā* — also; *kālindī* — Kālindī; *mitravindā* — Mitravindā; *ca* — and; *satyā* — Satyā; *bhadrā* — Bhadrā; *ca* — and; *lakṣmaṇā* — Lakṣmaṇā.

**Among the queens were the goddesses Rukmiṇī, Satyabhāmā, and Jāmbavatī, and Kālindī and Mitravindā, and Satyā, Bhadrā, and Lakṣmaṇā.**

COMMENTARY: The word *devī,* "supreme ruling goddess," here refers specifically to Satyabhāmā, who is especially dear to Kṛṣṇa, but it also refers to all these queens.

## TEXT 24

अन्याश्च रोहिणीमुख्यास्तस्यैवोचिततां गताः ।
सर्वाः सर्वप्रकारेण तुल्यदासीगणार्चिताः ॥

*anyāś ca rohiṇī-mukhyās*
*tasyaivocitatāṁ gatāḥ*
*sarvāḥ sarva-prakāreṇa*
*tulya-dāsī-gaṇārcitāḥ*

*anyāḥ* — others; *ca* — and; *rohiṇī* — Rohiṇī; *mukhyāḥ* — headed by; *tasya* — for Him; *eva* — just; *ucitatām gatāḥ* — fit; *sarvāḥ* — all; *sarva-prakāreṇa* — in all ways; *tulya* — suitable; *dāsī* — of maidservants; *gaṇa* — by groups; *arcitāḥ* — honored.

**The Lord's other queens followed, headed by Rohiṇī, all of them fit in every way to be His consorts and all honored by groups of suitably qualified maidservants.**

COMMENTARY: This Rohiṇī is different from Lord Balarāma's mother. Śrī Śukadeva Gosvāmī confirms that Rohiṇī was the leading princess rescued from the fortress of Bhaumāsura. In *Śrīmad-Bhāgavatam* (10.61.18), after listing the sons of Kṛṣṇa's first eight queens, Śukadeva says, *dīptimāṁs tāmrataptādyā/ rohiṇyās tanayā hareḥ:* "Dīptimān, Tāmratapta, and others were the sons of Lord Kṛṣṇa and Rohiṇī."

All of Kṛṣṇa's queens, beginning with Śrī Rukmiṇī, are fully qualified to be His consorts. We can deduce, therefore, that they are superexcellent in all ways, just as He is. When the queens entered the inner palace, maidservants followed them, each maidservant exactly suited to her queen's personality. For the service of the queens, these attendants carried such items as palanquins, *cāmara* fans, and boxes containing *pān*.

## TEXT 25

ताभ्याममूभिश्च सलज्जमावृतः
कुमारवर्गैरपि शोभितोऽविशत् ।
प्रासादमात्मीयमथासनोत्तमे
निह्नुत्य भावं निषसाद हृष्टवत् ॥

*tābhyām amūbhiś ca sa-lajjam āvṛtaḥ*
*kumāra-vargair api śobhito 'viśat*
*prāsādam ātmīyam athāsanottame*
*nihnutya bhāvaṁ niṣasāda hṛṣṭa-vat*

*tābhyām* — by the two of them (His mothers); *amūbhiḥ* — and them (His queens); *ca* — and; *sa-lajjam* — shyly; *āvṛtaḥ* — surrounded; *kumāra-vargaiḥ* — by groups of sons; *api* — also; *śobhitaḥ* — further graced with splendor; *aviśat* — He entered; *prāsādam* — the palace; *ātmīyam* — His own; *atha* — then; *āsana-uttame* — on the best of thrones; *nihnutya* — concealing; *bhāvam* — His ecstasy; *niṣasāda* — He sat down; *hṛṣṭa-vat* — apparently pleased.

**With His two mothers and all these queens surrounding Him shyly, the Lord entered His palace, followed also by several groups of young sons, who added to the splendor of that procession. Within His palace, He concealed the emotions He was feeling, and with apparent pleasure He sat down on the best of thrones.**

COMMENTARY: Last in the procession that entered the Lord's quarters were His sons, led by Śrī Pradyumna and Sāmba. Upon entering, Kṛṣṇa hid the agitation He felt, brought on by vividly remembering Gokula, and sat down on His throne. To satisfy His mother Devakī and the queens, but especially to put Gopa-kumāra in a good mood, He outwardly appeared happy (*hṛṣṭa-vat*). In any case, having Gopa-kumāra with Him was almost as good as being back in Gokula, and so He had reason to be happy.

## TEXT 26

तं श्रीयशोदाखिलगोपसुन्दरी-
गोपार्भवर्गैरिव भूषितं त्वहम् ।
पश्यन्समक्षं धृतवेणुमात्मनो
ध्येयं पुनर्हर्षभरेण मोहितः ॥

*taṁ śrī-yaśodākhila-gopa-sundarī-*
*gopārbha-vargair iva bhūṣitaṁ tv aham*
*paśyan samakṣaṁ dhṛta-veṇum ātmano*
*dhyeyaṁ punar harṣa-bhareṇa mohitaḥ*

*tam* — Him; *śrī-yaśodā* — by Śrī Yaśodā; *akhila* — all; *gopa-sundarī* — of beautiful *gopīs; gopa-arbha* — of cowherd boys; *vargaiḥ* — and by groups; *iva* — as if; *bhūṣitam* — decorated; *tu* — but; *aham* — I; *paśyan* — seeing; *samakṣam* — before my eyes; *dhṛta* — holding; *veṇum* — the flute; *ātmanaḥ* — my own; *dhyeyam* — object of meditation; *punaḥ* — again; *harṣa-bhareṇa* — due to the excess of delight; *mohitaḥ* — fainted.

**But I saw the Lord appearing before me as if adorned by the company of Śrī Yaśodā and all the beautiful young gopīs and many young cowherd boys. Seeing the object of my meditation holding my flute in His hand, I again fainted, overwhelmed by delight.**

COMMENTARY: In his meditation, Gopa-kumāra had always worshiped Śrī Madana-gopāladeva, who unlike Lord Kṛṣṇa in Dvārakā always carries His flute. But now Kṛṣṇa had just taken Gopa-kumāra's flute in His hand and was still holding it. That peculiar circumstance set off a special ecstasy in Gopa-kumāra, a mood in which he saw Devakī as mother Yaśodā, Kṛṣṇa's queens as *gopīs,* and the Lord's sons like Pradyumna and Sāmba as young cowherd boys. In Gopa-kumāra's rapture, Kṛṣṇa's own beauty remained unchanged, and so did that of Śrī Balarāma's mother, Rohiṇī, who has the same personality in both Vṛndāvana and Dvārakā. The only feature of Kṛṣṇa's that differed here in Dvārakā was the sacred *yajñopavīta* thread given to Him by Sāndīpani Muni at the time of His initiation, but this thread was concealed by Kṛṣṇa's upper cloth.

## TEXT 27

कृपाभरव्यग्रमनाः ससम्भ्रमं
स्वयं समुत्थाय स नन्दनन्दनः ।
कराम्बुजस्पर्शबलेन मेऽकरोत्
प्रबोधमङ्गानि मुहुर्विमार्जयन् ॥

*kṛpā-bhara-vyagra-manāḥ sa-sambhramaṁ*
*svayaṁ samutthāya sa nanda-nandanaḥ*
*karāmbuja-sparśa-balena me 'karot*
*prabodham aṅgāni muhur vimārjayan*

*kṛpā-bhara* — by an excess of compassion; *vyagra* — agitated; *manāḥ* — His mind; *sa-sambhramam* — hastily; *svayam* — Himself; *samutthāya* — getting up; *saḥ* — He; *nanda-nandanaḥ* — the son of Mahārāja Nanda; *kara-ambuja* — of the lotus hand; *sparśa* — of the touch; *balena* — by the force; *me* — my; *akarot* — made; *prabodham* — return to consciousness; *aṅgāni* — my limbs; *muhuḥ* — again; *vimārjayan* — cleaning.

**Then Nanda-nandana Himself, His mind moved by abundant compassion, quickly got up. And by the powerful touch of His lotus hand He brought me back to consciousness and carefully cleaned the limbs of my body.**

COMMENTARY: Though He be a powerful prince in Dvārakā, Kṛṣṇa is always the same Nanda-nandana, the darling son of Nanda Mahārāja and all the cowherds of Vraja. His prime concern is always to keep the devotees of Vraja happy. Therefore He could not help but feel anxious for Gopa-kumāra. Although He could have brought Gopa-kumāra back to consciousness simply by His omnipotent desire, Kṛṣṇa wanted to take personal care of him.

## TEXT 28

वृत्ते भोजनकालेऽपि भोक्तुमिच्छामकुर्वता ।
मातॄणामाग्रहेणैव कृत्यं माध्याह्निकं कृतम् ॥

*vṛtte bhojana-kāle 'pi*
*bhoktum icchām akurvatā*
*mātṝṇām āgraheṇaiva*
*kṛtyaṁ mādhyāhnikaṁ kṛtam*

*vṛtte* — coming; *bhojana* — of eating; *kāle* — the time; *api* — and; *bhoktum* — to eat; *icchām* — the desire; *akurvatā* — by Him who did not have; *mātṝṇām* — of His mothers; *āgraheṇa* — by the insistence; *eva* — only; *kṛtyam* — His duties; *mādhya-ahnikam* — noontime; *kṛtam* — were performed.

**It was now lunchtime, but the Lord didn't feel like eating. Only at the insistence of His mothers did He perform His noontime duties.**

COMMENTARY: The pain of separation Kṛṣṇa felt from remembering Gokula spoiled His appetite. But His mothers, not only Devakī but also Vasudeva's several other wives, wouldn't let Him go without eating. First, however, He took His noontime bath and performed His other normal duties.

## TEXT 29

दैवकीनन्दनेनाथ तेन किञ्चित्स्वपाणिना ।
भोजितोऽहं स्वयं पश्चाद्भुक्तं सन्तोषणाय मे ॥

*daivakī-nandanenātha*
*tena kiñcit sva-pāṇinā*
*bhojito 'haṁ svayaṁ paścād*
*bhuktaṁ santoṣaṇāya me*

*daivakī* — of Devakī; *nandanena* — by the darling son; *atha* — then; *tena* — by Him; *kiñcit* — something; *sva-pāṇinā* — with His own hand; *bhojitaḥ* — fed; *aham* — I; *svayam* — Himself; *paścāt* — after; *bhuktam* — ate; *santoṣaṇāya* — for the satisfaction; *me* — my.

**That darling son of Devakī fed me something with His own hand and only then took something Himself, for my satisfaction.**

COMMENTARY: Devakī's dear son agreed to eat because He

wanted to please His mother. But He also wanted His friends to eat, which they would do only in His presence.

## TEXT 30

कुमारमण्डलीमध्ये निवेश्य निजमग्रजम् ।
परिवेशयता स्वेन पूर्ववद्बाल्यलीलया ॥

*kumāra-maṇḍalī-madhye*
*niveśya nijam agrajam*
*pariveśayatā svena*
*pūrva-vad bālya-līlayā*

*kumāra* — of boys; *maṇḍalī* — a circle; *madhye* — within; *niveśya* — seating; *nijam* — His; *agra-jam* — elder brother; *pariveśayatā* — serving; *svena* — Himself; *pūrva-vat* — as before; *bālya-līlayā* — in His childhood pastimes.

**The Lord sat His elder brother down within a circle of boys and fed them, just as He had before in His childhood pastimes.**

COMMENTARY: In the middle of the circle of young Yadus sat Lord Balarāma, like the whorl of a lotus in bloom. Previously Kṛṣṇa and Balarāma had enjoyed noon meals like this in Vṛndāvana in the company of the cowherd boys, amid clever conversation and laughter. The Tenth Canto of *Śrīmad-Bhāgavatam* (10.13.11) describes those pastimes:

*bibhrad veṇuṁ jaṭhara-paṭayoḥ śṛṅga-vetre ca kakṣe*
*vāme pāṇau masṛṇa-kavalaṁ tat-phalāny aṅgulīṣu*
*madhye tiṣṭhan sva-parisuhṛdo hāsayan narmabhiḥ svaiḥ*
*svarge loke miṣati bubhuje yajña-bhug bāla-keliḥ*

"Kṛṣṇa is *yajña-bhuk* — that is, He eats only offerings of *yajña* — but to exhibit His childhood pastimes He now sat with His flute tucked between His waist and His tight cloth on His right side and with His horn bugle and cow-driving stick on His left. Holding in His hand a very nice preparation of yogurt and rice, with pieces of suitable fruit between His fingers, He sat like the whorl of a lotus, looking forward toward all His friends, personally joking with them and creating jubilant laughter among them as He ate. At that time, the denizens of heaven were watching, struck with wonder at how the Personality of Godhead, who eats only in *yajña,* was now eating with His friends in the forest." In this portrait from the Tenth Canto, Kṛṣṇa eats with His friends instead of serving the meal, because on this day His elder brother, Balarāma, is not present.

### TEXT 31

महाप्रसादमुच्छिष्टं भुक्त्वा स्वगृहमानयत् ।
भगवद्भावविज्ञोऽसावुद्धवो मां बलादिव ॥

*mahā-prasādam ucchiṣṭaṁ*
*bhuktvā sva-gṛham ānayat*
*bhagavad-bhāva-vijño 'sāv*
*uddhavo māṁ balād iva*

*mahā-prasādam* — specially graced by having been eaten by the Lord; *ucchiṣṭam* — the remnants; *bhuktvā* — eating; *sva* — his own; *gṛham* — to the house; *ānayat* — led; *bhagavat* — of the Lord; *bhāva* — of the ecstasies; *vijñaḥ* — the expert knower; *asau* — he; *uddhavaḥ* — Uddhava; *mām* — me; *balāt* — by force; *iva* — as if.

**Uddhava knew the Lord's ecstasies very well. So he ate some of Kṛṣṇa's mahā-prasāda remnants and then took me somewhat by force to his own house.**

COMMENTARY: Kṛṣṇa was thinking that Gopa-kumāra would not feel completely at ease in a palace filled with royal opulence. Therefore He decided that it would be better for Gopa-kumāra to stay with Uddhava at his house, since Uddhava had a unique affinity with the residents of Vraja. Uddhava knew what the Lord was thinking without the Lord's having to say anything, so as soon as Uddhava ate some of Kṛṣṇa's remnants, he took Gopa-kumāra with him, without so much as a word. Since Gopa-kumāra was still dazed, Uddhava had to drag him away.

## TEXT 32

तदानीमेव यातोऽहं सम्यक्संज्ञां ततोऽखिलम् ।
तत्रानुभूतं विमृशन्मुहुर्नृत्यन्नमंस्यदः ॥

*tadānīm eva yāto 'haṁ*
*samyak saṁjñāṁ tato 'khilam*
*tatrānubhūtaṁ vimṛśan*
*muhur nṛtyann amaṁsy adaḥ*

*tadānīm* — at that time; *eva* — only; *yātaḥ* — came; *aham* — I; *samyak* — complete; *saṁjñām* — to consciousness; *tataḥ* — then; *akhilam* — everything; *tatra* — there; *anubhūtam* — experienced; *vimṛśan* — reflecting on; *muhuḥ* — repeatedly; *nṛtyan* — dancing; *amaṁsi* — I thought; *adaḥ* — as follows.

**Only then did I completely return to normal consciousness. Reflecting on what I had seen happen, I danced for a long time and then began to think.**

COMMENTARY: In the more normal situation of Uddhava's house, Gopa-kumāra was able to gather his thoughts. He was delighted to have the opportunity to be with Kṛṣṇa and His devotees there in Dvārakā.

## TEXT 33

मनोरथानां परमं किलान्तम्
अहो गतोऽद्यैव यदिष्टदेवम् ।
प्राप्तोऽपरोक्षं व्रजनागरं तं
हृद्धचायमानाखिलमाधुरीभिः ॥

*mano-rathānāṁ paramaṁ kilāntam*
*aho gato 'dyaiva yad iṣṭa-devam*
*prāpto 'parokṣaṁ vraja-nāgaraṁ taṁ*
*hṛd-dhyāyamānākhila-mādhurībhiḥ*

*manaḥ-rathānām* — of my desires; *paramam* — ultimate; *kila* — indeed; *antam* — the perfection; *aho* — oh; *gataḥ* — achieved; *adya* — today; *eva* — indeed; *yat* — since; *iṣṭa-devam* — my worshipable Deity; *prāptaḥ* — obtained; *aparokṣam* — visible to my eyes; *vraja-nāgaram* — the romantic hero of Vraja; *tam* — Him; *hṛt* — in my heart; *dhyāyamāna* — being meditated on; *akhila* — with all; *mādhurībhiḥ* — His charms.

**I said to myself, "Indeed, today I have achieved the ultimate perfection of all my desires, for with my very eyes I have seen the hero of Vraja with all His attractive charms, that same person upon whom I have always meditated in my heart!"**

COMMENTARY: This is the form of the Absolute Truth that for so long had filled Gopa-kumāra's heart in his meditations — the audacious enjoyer of Vraja-bhūmi who attracts His devotees in countless ways.

## TEXT 34

प्रस्थायोद्धवसङ्गत्या स्वप्रभुं तं विलोकयन् ।
नाशकं हर्षवैवश्यात्किञ्चित्कर्तुं परं ततः ॥

*prasthāyoddhava-saṅgatyā*
*sva-prabhuṁ taṁ vilokayan*
*nāśakaṁ harṣa-vaivaśyāt*
*kiñcit kartuṁ paraṁ tataḥ*

*prasthāya* — setting off; *uddhava-saṅgatyā* — in the company of Uddhava; *sva-prabhum* — my Lord; *tam* — Him; *vilokayan* — seeing; *na aśakam* — I was not able; *harṣa* — with delight;

*vaivaśyāt* — because of being beside myself; *kiñcit* — anything; *kartum* — to do; *param* — else; *tataḥ* — than that.

**The next day I went with Uddhava and saw my Lord, but I was so beside myself with delight that I was unable to do more than that.**

COMMENTARY: On this second day, Gopa-kumāra was still so disoriented by the ecstasy of the new state of affairs that he was unable to render any service other than taking *darśana* of Kṛṣṇa.

## TEXTS 35–36

विचित्रं तस्य कारुण्यभरं सन्ततमाप्नुवन् ।
वसंस्तत्र महानन्दपूराननुभवामि यान् ॥

तेषां निरूपणं कर्तुं वाचा चित्तेन वा जनः ।
ब्रह्मायुषापि कः शक्तो भगवद्भक्तिमानपि ॥

*vicitraṁ tasya kāruṇya-*
*bharaṁ santatam āpnuvan*
*vasaṁs tatra mahānanda-*
*pūrān anubhavāmi yān*

*teṣāṁ nirūpaṇaṁ kartuṁ*
*vācā cittena vā janaḥ*
*brahmāyuṣāpi kaḥ śakto*
*bhagavad-bhaktimān api*

*vicitram* — various; *tasya* — His; *kāruṇya* — of the mercy; *bharam* — the abundance; *santatam* — constantly; *āpnuvan* — receiving; *vasan* — residing; *tatra* — there; *mahā-ānanda* — of supreme ecstasy; *pūrān* — floods; *anubhavāmi* — I experienced; *yān* — which; *teṣām* — of them; *nirūpaṇam* — the description; *kartum* — to do; *vācā* — by words; *cittena* — by the mind; *vā* — or; *janaḥ* — a person; *brahma* — of Lord Brahmā; *āyuṣā* — with a duration of life; *api* — even; *kaḥ* — who; *śaktaḥ*

— capable; *bhagavat-bhakti-mān* — possessing pure devotion to the Supreme Lord; *api* — even.

**While residing there in Dvārakā I constantly, abundantly received Lord Kṛṣṇa's wonderful mercy. I tasted such a flood of supreme ecstasy that no one could tell of it in words, or even think of it within the mind, not even a pure devotee of the Lord with a lifetime of Brahmā.**

COMMENTARY: The glories of Kṛṣṇa in Dvārakā are surely beyond the comprehension of the greatest scholars and mystic *yogīs*. Only rarely can even surrendered devotees approach those glories with the mind or words.

TEXT 37

मोक्षे सुखं ननु महत्तममुच्यते यत्
तत्कोटिकोटिगुणितं गदितं विकुण्ठे ।
युक्त्या कयाचिदधिकं किल कोशलायां
यद्द्वारकाभवमिदं तु कथं निरूप्यम् ॥

*mokṣe sukhaṁ nanu mahat-tamam ucyate yat*
*tat koṭi-koṭi-guṇitaṁ gaditaṁ vikuṇṭhe*
*yuktyā kayācid adhikaṁ kila kośalāyāṁ*
*yad dvārakā-bhavam idaṁ tu kathaṁ nirūpyam*

*mokṣe* — in liberation; *sukham* — the happiness; *nanu* — perhaps; *mahat-tamam* — supreme; *ucyate* — is said; *yat* — which; *tat* — that; *koṭi-koṭi* — many millions of times; *guṇitam* — multiplied; *gaditam* — said; *vikuṇṭhe* — in Vaikuṇṭha; *yuktyā* — by a logic; *kayācit* — some; *adhikam* — greater; *kila* — indeed; *kośalāyām* — in Ayodhyā; *yat* — which; *dvārakā* — in Dvārakā; *bhavam* — born; *idam* — this; *tu* — but; *katham* — how; *nirūpyam* — describable.

**The happiness found in liberation is said to be supreme. Multiplied many millions of times, it might be said to equal**

**the joy in Vaikuṇṭha. And if any joy still greater can be conceived, it is that which is found in Ayodhyā. But the joy born in Dvārakā—how can anyone even begin to describe it?**

COMMENTARY: The devotees of impersonal liberation consider the nullifying of material existence the highest possible perfection, its happiness greater than any other. They are unaware of the existence of a transcendental world in which there is a happiness much greater, although the Vaiṣṇavas openly proclaim that happiness to anyone willing to hear. Among the Vaiṣṇavas, those with especially fine powers of discrimination know and describe an even greater happiness, which is found in Lord Rāmacandra's kingdom of Ayodhyā. But no one's power of logic can surmise the superexcellent degree of happiness relished by Kṛṣṇa and His companions in Dvārakā.

Powerful thinkers have studied the *Vedas* and pondered the supreme happiness of liberation. But thinkers with still finer intelligence recognize that the happiness of impersonal liberation is nothing but the absence of material misery and so there must be something greater, namely the happiness of Vaikuṇṭha. They presume, moreover, that the ultimate limit of happiness lies in Vaikuṇṭha, because otherwise they would face the logical flaw of an endless regress of different degrees of happiness. Be that as it may, in the spiritual abode of Ayodhyā the Supreme Lord's servants have such exclusive devotion for Him and such determination to satisfy Him with their service that the happiness there is palpably greater than that of Vaikuṇṭha. Even better, however, is the happiness of Dvārakā. No speculator can find a methodology to analyze it, but it exists nonetheless. It is not a mere creation of devotees' sentiments, for many reliable authorities have perceived it for themselves.

## TEXT 38

तत्रापि तच्चिरदिदृक्षितजीवितेश-
प्राप्त्या तदेकदयितस्य जनस्य यत्स्यात् ।

वृत्त्या कयास्तु वचसो मनसोऽपि वात्तं
तद्वै विदुस्तदुचितात्मनि तद्विदस्ते ॥

*tatrāpi tac-cira-didṛkṣita-jīviteśa-*
*prāptyā tad-eka-dayitasya janasya yat syāt*
*vṛttyā kayāstu vacaso manaso 'pi vāttaṁ*
*tad vai vidus tad-ucitātmani tad-vidas te*

*tatra* — in that (happiness); *api* — indeed, moreover; *tat* — of him; *cira* — for a long time; *didṛkṣita* — whom he has wanted to see; *jīvita-īśa* — the Lord of his life; *prāptyā* — by achieving; *tat* — to Him; *eka* — exclusively; *dayitasya* — dear; *janasya* — of the person; *yat* — which; *syāt* — can occur; *vṛttyā* — by a faculty; *kayā* — which; *astu* — can there be; *vacasaḥ* — of words; *manasaḥ* — of the mind; *api* — even; *vā* — or; *āttam* — grasped; *tat* — that (happiness); *vai* — certainly; *viduḥ* — understand; *tat* — for that; *ucita* — fit; *ātmani* — in their minds; *tat* — that; *vidaḥ* — who are fit to know; *te* — they.

**Indeed, no faculty of mind or speech can grasp the joy a resident of Dvārakā feels from having gained the only Lord of his life after a long time yearning to see Him. Only those whose minds are fit can know that joy.**

COMMENTARY: Persons with strong intelligence but weak faith in devotional service to Kṛṣṇa may doubt whether happiness greater than found in Ayodhyā can exist. But although such doubters may be unable to know the happiness of Dvārakā, what right do they have to declare it nonexistent? There are other, more qualified persons who know the taste of it. Even though words and the mind can hardly comprehend the transcendental bliss known by the Dvārakā-vāsīs, it has been described with logical supporting arguments for the benefit of Kṛṣṇa's aspiring worshipers to fortify their enthusiasm for unalloyed devotional service. Just as the devotees of Ayodhyā taste greater happiness in their intimate moods of service than the *nārāyaṇa-bhaktas* of Vaikuṇṭha, the devotees of Dvārakā enjoy happiness still greater because they are personally connected to Kṛṣṇa in the mood of friendship. And when we extend this thinking a step further, we can understand that the happiness of Goloka, resting as it does on the topmost *prema* known only there, is greater still — and no happiness is greater.

## TEXT 39

एवं वसन्तं मां तत्र श्रीमद्यादवपुङ्गवाः ।
विश्वबाह्यान्तरानन्ददिदृक्षार्द्रहृदोऽब्रुवन् ॥

*evaṁ vasantaṁ māṁ tatra*
*śrīmad-yādava-puṅgavāḥ*
*viśva-bāhyāntar-ānanda-*
*didṛkṣārdra-hṛdo 'bruvan*

*evam* — thus; *vasantam* — who was living; *mām* — to me; *tatra* — there; *śrīmat-yādava* — of the divine Yādavas; *puṅgavāḥ* — the best; *viśva* — for the whole world; *bāhya* — internal; *antaḥ* — and external; *ānanda* — bliss; *didṛkṣā* — with eagerness to see; *ārdra* — melted; *hṛdaḥ* — whose hearts; *abruvan* — spoke.

**After I had lived for some time there in Dvārakā, some of the best of the divine Yādavas said something to me, their hearts melted with eagerness to see everyone in the world happy within and without.**

COMMENTARY: What Gopa-kumāra is speaking to his disciple is not merely theoretical. While residing in Dvārakā Gopa-kumāra had tasted enough of Dvārakā's unique happiness to rightfully claim knowledge of it. On one occasion during his stay, he had been approached by some concerned residents who only wanted the greatest possible happiness for everyone, both externally in the form of good food, clothing, ornaments, and other means for enjoyment and internally in the form of the priceless treasure of *prema* and its ecstasies.

## TEXT 40

श्रीयादवा ऊचुः
वैकुण्ठतोऽप्युत्तमभूतिपूरिते
स्थाने त्वमेत्यात्र सखेऽस्मदन्वितः ।
यद्वन्यवेशेन सुदीनवद्वसेर्
मन्यामहे साधु न तत्कथञ्चन ॥

*śrī-yādavā ūcuḥ*
*vaikuṇṭhato 'py uttama-bhūti-pūrite*
*sthāne tvam etyātra sakhe 'smad-anvitaḥ*
*yad vanya-veśena sudīna-vad vaser*
*manyāmahe sādhu na tat kathañcana*

*śrī-yādavāḥ ūcuḥ* — the divine Yādavas said; *vaikuṇṭhataḥ* — compared with Vaikuṇṭha; *api* — even; *uttama* — supreme; *bhūti* — splendor; *pūrite* — which is full of; *sthāne* — to the place; *tvam* — you; *etya* — coming; *atra* — this; *sakhe* — O friend; *asmat* — of us; *anvitaḥ* — in the company; *yat* — the fact that; *vanya* — of the forest; *veśena* — in dress; *su-dīna-vat* — like a very wretched person; *vaseḥ* — you reside; *manyāmahe* — we think; *sādhu* — good; *na* — not; *tat* — that; *kathañcana* — at all.

**The divine Yādavas said: Dear friend, you have come to this place, which is more full in supreme splendor than even Vaikuṇṭha, and you are now our companion. We think it hardly fitting that you continue to dress like a miserable forest dweller.**

COMMENTARY: Of course, Gopa-kumāra was beyond material misery, as the Yādavas expressed by speaking of him as *sudīna-vat,* "as if very miserable" — not actually miserable. Still, they felt that Gopa-kumāra's incongruous dress and behavior were depriving him of many of the joys of residing in Dvārakā.

## TEXT 41

चित्ते दुःखमिवास्माकमपि किञ्चिद्भवेदतः ।
स्वतः सिद्धं तमस्माकमिव वेशादिकं तनु ॥

*citte duḥkham ivāsmākam*
*api kiñcid bhaved ataḥ*
*svataḥ siddhaṁ tam asmākam*
*iva veśādikaṁ tanu*

*citte* — in the mind; *duḥkham* — distress; *iva* — as if; *asmākam* — for us; *api* — also; *kiñcit* — some; *bhavet* — there is; *ataḥ* — therefore; *svataḥ-siddham* — automatically available; *tam* — that; *asmākam* — our; *iva* — like; *veśa-ādikam* — dress and so on; *tanu* — please assume.

**This troubles our minds, so please take on our type of dress and looks, which are naturally available to anyone who lives here.**

COMMENTARY: The citizens of Dvārakā know only the highest constant ecstasy, but these devotees felt a little unhappy to see Gopa-kumāra in an apparently wretched condition. By nature they were intolerant of even an outward semblance of misery. Gopa-kumāra should not wonder where to get the right dress and capabilities for enjoying like a Dvārakā-vāsī, because the very atmosphere of Dvārakā readily provides these to any resident who wants them.

## TEXT 42

श्रीगोपकुमार उवाच
तेषां तत्राग्रहेणापि स्वचित्तस्याच्युतस्य च ।
अलब्ध्वा स्वरसं तेषु नीचाकिञ्चनवत्स्थितः ॥

*śrī-gopa-kumāra uvāca*
*teṣāṁ tatrāgraheṇāpi*
*sva-cittasyācyutasya ca*
*alabdhvā sva-rasaṁ teṣu*
*nīcākiñcana-vat sthitaḥ*

*śrī-gopa-kumāraḥ uvāca* — Śrī Gopa-kumāra said; *teṣām* — their; *tatra* — there; *āgraheṇa* — with the insistence; *api* — even; *sva-cittasya* — of my mind; *acyutasya* — of Lord Acyuta; *ca* — and; *alabdhvā* — not obtaining; *sva-rasam* — the special taste; *teṣu* — among them; *nīca* — one who is poor; *akiñcana* — and without possessions; *vat* — like; *sthitaḥ* — remained.

**Śrī Gopa-kumāra said: Even though these Yādavas insisted, I stayed like a poor, simple devotee because in their dress I would not have been able to taste the special mood that appealed to my mind, and to Lord Acyuta's.**

COMMENTARY: Gopa-kumāra preferred to stay inferior to these prominent Yādavas. To him, more important than keeping up appearances was protecting his personal *rasa* with Kṛṣṇa.

## TEXT 43

आसीनस्य सभामध्ये सेवितस्य महर्द्धिभिः ।
पार्श्वे भगवतोऽथाहं गन्तुं लज्जे बिभेमि च ॥

*āsīnasya sabhā-madhye*
*sevitasya maharddhibhiḥ*
*pārśve bhagavato 'thāhaṁ*
*gantuṁ lajje bibhemi ca*

*āsīnasya* — who was seated; *sabhā-madhye* — in the midst of the assembly hall; *sevitasya* — served; *mahā-ṛddhibhiḥ* — by vast opulences; *pārśve* — to the side; *bhagavataḥ* — of the Personality of Godhead; *atha* — then; *aham* — I; *gantum* — to go; *lajje* — I was ashamed; *bibhemi* — I was afraid; *ca* — and.

**I then became shy and feared to go near the Personality of Godhead when He was seated in His court and being served by His transcendental opulences.**

COMMENTARY: To maintain his unbroken inner mood of service, Gopa-kumāra declined to follow the Yādavas' suggestion that he change his dress. But this further disturbed his heart. Now that the matter had been brought to his attention, he began to feel uncomfortable about appearing before Lord Kṛṣṇa in the assembly hall; he thought his own appearance incongruent and was apprehensive that he might do something wrong. Not only was he embarrassed, he was also daunted by the great opulence he saw in the Sudharmā hall and the huge crowds of kings, sages, and demigods. His uneasiness at coming before Kṛṣṇa while the Lord was seated on His throne in the royal court made Gopa-kumāra begin thinking again about going somewhere else.

## TEXT 44

चतुर्बाहुत्वमप्यस्य पश्येयं तत्र कर्हिचित् ।
न च क्रीडाविशेषं तं व्रजभूमिकृतं सदा ॥

*catur-bāhutvam apy asya*
*paśyeyaṁ tatra karhicit*
*na ca krīḍā-viśeṣaṁ taṁ*
*vraja-bhūmi-kṛtaṁ sadā*

*catuḥ-bāhutvam* — having four hands; *api* — also; *asya* — His; *paśyeyam* — I would see; *tatra* — there; *karhicit* — sometimes; *na* — not; *ca* — and; *krīḍā* — the pastimes; *viśeṣam* — special; *tam* — those; *vraja-bhūmi* — in Vraja-bhūmi; *kṛtam* — performed; *sadā* — always.

**Sometimes I would see the Lord with four hands. I couldn't always see the special pastimes He performs in Vraja-bhūmi.**

COMMENTARY: When devotees like Śrī Rukmiṇī were present, Gopa-kumāra found it difficult to envision Kṛṣṇa as He is in His Vṛndāvana pastimes. When the Lord was talking with Nārada Muni or Arjuna, Gopa-kumāra could hardly see Him tending His cows. Sometimes Gopa-kumāra could see Him as if in Vṛndāvana, but not often enough.

## TEXT 45

कदाचिदेष तत्रैव वर्तमानानदूरतः ।
पाण्डवानीक्षितुं गच्छेदेकाकी प्रियबान्धवान् ॥

*kadācid eṣa tatraiva*
*vartamānān adūrataḥ*
*pāṇḍavān īkṣituṁ gacched*
*ekākī priya-bāndhavān*

*kadācit* — sometimes; *eṣaḥ* — He; *tatra* — there; *eva* — indeed; *vartamānān* — who were staying; *adūrataḥ* — not far away; *pāṇḍavān* — the Pāṇḍavas; *īkṣitum* — to see; *gacchet* — would go; *ekākī* — alone; *priya* — dear; *bāndhavān* — His friends.

**Sometimes the Lord would go alone to visit His dear friends the Pāṇḍavas, who stayed nearby.**

COMMENTARY: On earth the Pāṇḍavas lived a good distance away from Dvārakā, in Hastināpura, so Kṛṣṇa had to make a long journey to meet them. In Vaikuṇṭha, however, the situation is different. Even if the residence of the Pāṇḍavas is physically distant from Dvārakā-purī, in the spiritual realm there are no limitations of time and space. By the power of the Lord's desire, any place to which He wishes to travel is at once nearby.

## TEXT 46

इत्थं चिरन्तनाभीष्टासम्पूर्त्या मे व्यथेत हृत् ।
तादृग्रूपगुणस्यास्य दृष्ट्वैवाथापि शाम्यति ॥

*itthaṁ cirantanābhīṣṭā-*
*sampūrtyā me vyatheta hṛt*
*tādṛg-rūpa-guṇasyāsya*
*dṛṣṭyaivāthāpi śāmyati*

*ittham* — thus; *cirantana* — long-sustained; *abhīṣṭa* — my desires; *asampūrtyā* — because of not being fulfilled; *me* — my; *vyatheta* — would be tormented; *hṛt* — heart; *tādṛk* — such; *rūpa* — of the beauty; *guṇasya* — and qualities; *asya* — His; *dṛṣṭyā* — by seeing; *eva* — only; *atha api* — however; *śāmyati* — it would be pacified.

**And so, because of desires long held but unfulfilled, my heart would feel tormented. But when I could see His beauty and qualities once again, my heart would again become peaceful.**

COMMENTARY: Being unable for even a short time to see Kṛṣṇa's beauty and His kind behavior would throw Gopa-kumāra into anxious turmoil. But as soon as Kṛṣṇa would return, Gopa-kumāra would recover his composure.

## TEXT 47

तस्य वागमृतैस्तैस्तैः कृपाभिव्यञ्जनैरपि ।
भवेत्सुखविशेषो यो जिह्वा स्पृशतु तं कथम् ॥

*tasya vāg-amṛtais tais taiḥ*
*kṛpābhivyañjanair api*
*bhavet sukha-viśeṣo yo*
*jihvā spṛśatu taṁ katham*

*tasya* — His; *vāk* — of speech; *amṛtaiḥ* — by the varieties of nectar; *taiḥ taiḥ* — them; *kṛpā* — compassion; *abhivyañjanaiḥ* — which revealed; *api* — also; *bhavet* — there would be; *sukha* — happiness; *viśeṣaḥ* — unique; *yaḥ* — which; *jihvā* — the tongue; *spṛśatu* — could touch; *tam* — this; *katham* — how.

**His nectarean words revealed His mercy. How can my tongue even touch the unique happiness they created?**

## TEXT 48

एवमुद्धवगेहे मे दिनानि कतिचिद्ययुः ।
यदि स्यात्कोऽपि शोकस्तं संवृणोम्यवहित्थया ॥

*evam uddhava-gehe me*
*dināni katicid yayuḥ*
*yadi syāt ko 'pi śokas taṁ*
*saṁvṛṇomy avahitthayā*

*evam* — thus; *uddhava* — of Uddhava; *gehe* — in the house; *me* — my; *dināni* — days; *katicit* — several; *yayuḥ* — passed; *yadi* — if; *syāt* — there would be; *kaḥ api* — any; *śokaḥ* — unhappiness; *tam* — that; *saṁvṛṇomi* — I would conceal; *avahitthayā* — by feigning.

**During the several days I spent this way in the house of Uddhava, if there were any unhappiness I would conceal it by feigning happiness.**

COMMENTARY: Besides Kṛṣṇa's occasional absence from Dvārakā, another cause of anxiety for Gopa-kumāra was the tendency to remember the land of his birth. Although being unable to see his worshipable Lord playing in the pastimes of Vraja made Gopa-kumāra unhappy, he tried hard to conceal this because he knew that the Dvārakā-vāsīs couldn't tolerate seeing anyone in pain and also because he was reluctant to make a show of his private ecstasies.

## TEXT 49

एकदा नारदं तत्रागतं वीक्ष्य प्रणम्य तम् ।
हर्षेण विस्मयेनापि वेष्टितोऽवोचमीदृशम् ॥

*ekadā nāradaṁ tatrā-*
*gataṁ vīkṣya praṇamya tam*
*harṣeṇa vismayenāpi*
*veṣṭito 'vocam īdṛśam*

*ekadā* — once; *nāradam* — Nārada; *tatra* — there; *āgatam* — who had come; *vīkṣya* — seeing; *praṇamya* — bowing down; *tam* — to him; *harṣeṇa* — with joy; *vismayena* — with amazement; *api* — although; *veṣṭitaḥ* — enveloped; *avocam* — I spoke; *īdṛśam* — in this way.

**One day I saw Nārada come. I bowed down to him, and in utter joy and amazement I spoke to him in the following way.**

COMMENTARY: To help Gopa-kumāra achieve his long-cherished goal, Nārada appeared at just the right moment to tell him about the glories of Śrī Goloka and how to achieve Goloka.

## TEXT 50

मुनीन्द्रवेश प्रभुपार्षदोत्तम
स्वर्गादिलोकेषु भवन्तमीदृशम् ।
वैकुण्ठलोकेऽत्र च हन्त सर्वतः
पश्याम्यहो कौतुकमावृणोति माम् ॥

*munīndra-veśa prabhu-pārṣadottama*
*svargādi-lokeṣu bhavantam īdṛśam*
*vaikuṇṭha-loke 'tra ca hanta sarvataḥ*
*paśyāmy aho kautukam āvṛṇoti mām*

*muni-indra* — of an exalted sage; *veśa* — whose dress; *prabhu* — of the Lord; *pārṣada* — of the associates; *uttama* — O best; *svarga-ādi* — of heaven and so on; *lokeṣu* — in the worlds; *bhavantam* — you; *īdṛśam* — like this; *vaikuṇṭha-loke* — in Vaikuṇṭha-loka; *atra* — here; *ca* — also; *hanta* — indeed; *sarvataḥ* — everywhere; *paśyāmi* — I see; *aho* — oh; *kautukam* — surprise; *āvṛṇoti* — is enveloping; *mām* — me.

**O Nārada, best of the Lord's associates in the guise of an exalted sage, I see you just everywhere—in the heavenly planets, in Vaikuṇṭha, and now here—looking just the same. How fascinated I am to see this!**

COMMENTARY: Inspired by the joy of seeing Nārada Muni, Gopa-kumāra wants to hear more about the sage's glories from his own mouth and hear further details about the special powers of the Supreme Lord's associates in Vaikuṇṭha, powers Nārada has briefly mentioned before:

*evaṁ vicitra-deśeṣu*
*svapnādāv apy anekadhā*
*dṛśyamānasya kṛṣṇasya*
*pārṣadānāṁ padasya ca*

*ekatvam apy anekatvaṁ*
*satyatvaṁ ca su-saṅgatam*

"Thus although Kṛṣṇa, His associates, and His abode are seen in various forms in different places, and in dreams and other special states of consciousness, they are with perfect consistency one although many, and they are always real." (*Bṛhad-bhāgavatāmṛta* 2.4.161–162)

Nārada dresses in saffron like a lifelong *brahmacārī,* but the true extent of his glories goes far beyond strict celibacy. In the words of Gopa-kumāra, Nārada is the best of the Supreme Lord's intimate associates. Gopa-kumāra is amazed that he meets Nārada almost everywhere and sees him always the same, with the same *vīṇā* in hand and the same unabashed humor. But as Gopa-kumāra has already heard from Nārada, even when Nārada expands himself to be present in many different locations he is still one and the same person.

TEXT 51

श्रीनारद उवाच
गोपबालक एवासि सत्यमद्यापि कौतुकी ।
पूर्वमेव मयोद्दिष्टमेतदस्ति न किं त्वयि ॥

*śrī-nārada uvāca*
*gopa-bālaka evāsi*
*satyam adyāpi kautukī*
*pūrvam eva mayoddiṣṭam*
*etad asti na kiṁ tvayi*

*śrī-nāradaḥ uvāca* — Śrī Nārada said; *gopa-bālaka* — O cowherd boy; *eva* — indeed; *asi* — you are; *satyam* — indeed; *adya* — now; *api* — even; *kautukī* — playful; *pūrvam* — before; *eva* — even; *mayā* — by me; *uddiṣṭam* — explained; *etat* — this; *asti na* — has not been; *kim* — whether; *tvayi* — to you.

**Śrī Nārada said: My dear young cowherd, surely you have always been a curious boy, and so you are even now. Haven't I explained all this to you before?**

COMMENTARY: Like Nārada, Gopa-kumāra has his own peculiar ways: he dresses and acts like a cowherd boy regardless of where he is. Moreover, it seems curious to Nārada that Gopa-kumāra still doubts the ability of powerful devotees of the Lord to expand themselves into multiple forms, especially since Nārada has explained this truth scientifically and Gopa-kumāra has seen tangible evidence of it with his own eyes. Gopa-kumāra may insist that he is honestly confused and not simply trying to make some game of expressing doubt, but Nārada reasserts that Gopa-kumāra, however briefly, has already heard him elucidate the subject.

TEXT 52

यथा हि भगवानेकः श्रीकृष्णो बहुमूर्तिभिः ।
बहुस्थानेषु वर्तेत तथा तत्सेवका वयम् ॥

*yathā hi bhagavān ekaḥ*
*śrī-kṛṣṇo bahu-mūrtibhiḥ*
*bahu-sthāneṣu varteta*
*tathā tat-sevakā vayam*

*yathā* — as; *hi* — certainly; *bhagavān* — the Supreme Lord; *ekaḥ* — one; *śrī-kṛṣṇaḥ* — Śrī Kṛṣṇa; *bahu* — with many; *mūrtibhiḥ* — forms; *bahu* — in many; *sthāneṣu* — places; *varteta* — can be present; *tathā* — so; *tat-sevakāḥ* — His servants; *vayam* — we.

**Just as the one Personality of Godhead Śrī Kṛṣṇa exists in many forms and many places, so also do we, His servants.**

TEXT 53

श्रीसुपर्णादयः सर्वे श्रीमद्धनूमदादयः ।
उद्धवोऽपि तथैवायं तादृशा यादवादयः ॥

*śrī-suparṇādayaḥ sarve*
*śrīmad-dhanūmad-ādayaḥ*
*uddhavo 'pi tathaivāyaṁ*
*tādṛśā yādavādayaḥ*

*śrī-suparṇa* — Śrī Garuḍa; *ādayaḥ* — and others; *sarve* — all; *śrīmat-hanūmat* — Śrīmān Hanumān; *ādayaḥ* — and others; *uddhavaḥ* — Uddhava; *api* — and; *tathā eva* — also; *ayam* — we; *tādṛśāḥ* — like this; *yādava* — the Yādavas; *ādayaḥ* — and others.

**So it is with all of us — Śrī Garuḍa and other attendants, devotees like Śrīmān Hanumān, and our friend Uddhava, and others too, like these Yādavas.**

COMMENTARY: Devotees like Garuḍa and Śeṣa are associates of the Lord of Vaikuṇṭha, whereas Hanumān, Jāmbavān, and others are servants of Lord Rāmacandra. Hanumān sings the glories of Lord Rāma in the Kimpuruṣa-loka of the Bhūloka region and simultaneously in the Ayodhyā of Vaikuṇṭha. And Uddhava, whom Gopa-kumāra can see right before him, is simultaneously one of the principal companions of Kṛṣṇa in Dvārakā on earth, along with the Yādavas, the Pāṇḍavas, and others. Considering the topic too confidential to bring up just now, Nārada chooses not to mention Kṛṣṇa's devotees in Śrī Goloka.

### TEXT 54

सर्वेऽपि नित्यं किल तस्य पार्षदाः
सेवापराः क्रीडनकानुरूपाः ।
प्रत्येकमेते बहुरूपवन्तो
ऽप्यैक्यं भजामो भगवान्यथासौ ॥

*sarve 'pi nityaṁ kila tasya pārṣadāḥ*
*sevā-parāḥ krīḍanakānurūpāḥ*
*praty-ekam ete bahu-rūpavanto*
*'py aikyaṁ bhajāmo bhagavān yathāsau*

*sarve* — all; *api* — even; *nityam* — always; *kila* — indeed; *tasya* — His; *pārṣadāḥ* — associates; *sevā* — to His service; *parāḥ* — fully dedicated; *krīḍanaka* — like playthings; *anurūpāḥ* — suitable; *prati-ekam* — each one; *ete* — they; *bahu* — many; *rūpa-vantaḥ* — possessing forms; *api* — although; *aikyam* — oneness; *bhajāmaḥ* — maintain; *bhagavān* — the Lord; *yathā* — as; *asau* — He.

**All the Lord's personal associates are at His hand like playthings. They are always fully dedicated to His service. Each assumes a variety of forms yet stays essentially one, just like the Lord Himself.**

COMMENTARY: As Śrī Kṛṣṇacandra, the original Supreme Person, expands Himself into innumerable forms of Godhead, when required for service to the Lord His eternal associates can also expand themselves into many forms. Perpetually dedicated to worshiping Him, they are willing instruments in the enactment of His pleasure pastimes. Whatever gives the Lord happiness is also their satisfaction. So when He expands Himself and His abode into all sorts of forms, they accompany Him in suitably corresponding forms. Gopa-kumāra should therefore not be amazed that Nārada appears in many places at once for the service of the Lord.

## TEXT 55

नानाविधास्तस्य परिच्छदा ये
नामानि लीलाः प्रियभूमयश्च ।
नित्यानि सत्यान्यखिलानि तद्वद्
एकान्यनेकान्यपि तानि विद्धि ॥

*nānā-vidhās tasya paricchadā ye*
*nāmāni līlāḥ priya-bhūmayaś ca*
*nityāni satyāny akhilāni tadvad*
*ekāny anekāny api tāni viddhi*

*nānā-vidhāḥ* — of various kinds; *tasya* — His; *paricchadāḥ* — paraphernalia; *ye* — which; *nāmāni* — names; *līlāḥ* — pastimes; *priya* — favorite; *bhūmayaḥ* — abodes; *ca* — and; *nityāni* — eternal; *satyāni* — real; *akhilāni* — all; *tadvat* — in that same way; *ekāni* — one; *anekāni* — many; *api* — even; *tāni* — them; *viddhi* — please understand.

**The Lord's names, His pastimes, and His favorite abodes and everything that has to do with His service can assume various forms. And you should know that just as all these are eternally real, each of them is simultaneously one and many.**

COMMENTARY: While still on the topic of multiple expansions, Nārada takes the opportunity to mention that the Personality of Godhead's pastimes, His dear abodes such as Śrī Mathurā, and

His paraphernalia like the Kaustubha gem and Sudarśana weapon display the same power of expansion. Here the word *bhūmi* refers not only to the earth but to any location, and so indicates other spiritual realms, such as Vaikuṇṭha. The Supreme Lord's personal property, His names, His pastimes, and the places of His appearance are all by nature pure *sac-cid-ānanda,* just as He is.

## TEXT 56

आश्चर्यमेतत्त्वमपीदृगेव सन्
पूर्वस्वभावं तनुषेऽत्र लीलया ।
परं महाश्चर्यमिहापि लक्ष्यसे
ऽतृप्तार्तचेता इव सर्वदा मया ॥

*āścaryam etat tvam apīdṛg eva san*
*pūrva-svabhāvaṁ tanuṣe 'tra līlayā*
*paraṁ mahāścaryam ihāpi lakṣyase*
*'tṛptārta-cetā iva sarvadā mayā*

*āścaryam* — amazing; *etat* — this; *tvam* — you; *api* — even; *īdṛk* — thus; *eva* — just; *san* — being; *pūrva* — former; *svabhāvam* — character; *tanuṣe* — you are maintaining; *atra* — here; *līlayā* — playfully; *param* — most; *mahā-āścaryam* — very astonishing; *iha* — here; *api* — even; *lakṣyase* — you appear; *atṛpta* — dissatisfied; *ārta* — and distressed; *cetāḥ* — in your heart; *iva* — as if; *sarvadā* — always; *mayā* — by me.

**What amazes me is that you still appear like this, playfully showing your same character as before. And even here you seem always discontent and distressed at heart. That is most astonishing to me.**

COMMENTARY: Gopa-kumāra too is spiritually potent, so he also should be able to assume different forms in different places. Instead, however, he always remains the same innocent cowherd boy, even in Vaikuṇṭha and Dvārakā. Nārada thinks that Gopa-kumāra is simply playing a game, pretending to be ignorant even though he knows the reality. This is very surprising to Nārada. And even more surprising is that everywhere they have met, Nārada has seen in Gopa-kumāra a persistent dissatisfaction, shown by his downturned face and distracted glance.

## TEXT 57

श्रीगोपकुमार उवाच
मया सपादग्रहमेष नत्वा
सदैन्यमुक्तो भगवंस्त्वमेव ।
जानासि तत्सर्वमितीदमाह
स्मित्वा निरीक्ष्याननमुद्धवस्य ॥

*śrī-gopa-kumāra uvāca*
*mayā sa-pāda-graham eṣa natvā*
*sa-dainyam ukto bhagavaṁs tvam eva*
*jānāsi tat sarvam itīdam āha*
*smitvā nirīkṣyānanam uddhavasya*

*śrī-gopa-kumāraḥ uvāca* — Śrī Gopa-kumāra said; *mayā* — by me; *sa-pāda-graham* — with taking hold of his feet; *eṣaḥ* — he; *natvā* — bowing down; *sa-dainyam* — with humility; *uktaḥ* — was addressed; *bhagavan* — O lord; *tvam* — you; *eva* — indeed; *jānāsi* — know; *tat* — that; *sarvam* — all; *iti* — thus; *idam* — this; *āha* — he said; *smitvā* — smiling; *nirīkṣya* — looking; *ānanam* — at the face; *uddhavasya* — of Uddhava.

**Śrī Gopa-kumāra said: Taking hold of Nārada's feet, I bowed down and humbly told him, "My lord, you know everything about this." Then Nārada smiled and spoke, looking at Uddhava's face.**

COMMENTARY: Gopa-kumāra was most grateful that Nārada fully understood the cause and scope of his mind's discontent.

Since Gopa-kumāra honestly recognized his own inferior, dependent position, he bowed down and touched Nārada's feet. Nārada was happy to see this because it meant that Gopa-kumāra was approaching perfection. So he smiled at Gopa-kumāra's eagerness to receive the most confidential truth and turned to Uddhava, who would properly reveal it.

## TEXTS 58–59

श्रीनारद उवाच
उद्धवायमहो गोपपुत्रो गोवर्धनोद्भवः ।
मादृशां त्वादृशानां च मृग्यन्वस्तु सुदुर्लभम् ॥

इतस्ततो भ्रमन्व्यग्रः कदाचिदपि कुत्रचित् ।
नातिक्रामति चित्तान्तर्लग्नं तं शोकमार्तिदम् ॥

*śrī-nārada uvāca*
*uddhavāyam aho gopa-*
*putro govardhanodbhavaḥ*
*mādṛśāṁ tvādṛśānāṁ ca*
*mṛgyan vastu su-durlabham*

*itas tato bhraman vyagraḥ*
*kadācid api kutracit*
*nātikrāmati cittāntar-*
*lagnaṁ taṁ śokam ārti-dam*

*śrī-nāradaḥ uvāca* — Śrī Nārada said; *uddhava* — O Uddhava; *ayam* — this; *aho* — ah; *gopa-putraḥ* — son of a cowherd; *govardhana-udbhavaḥ* — born at Govardhana; *mādṛśām* — by me; *tvādṛśānām* — by persons like you; *ca* — and; *mṛgyan* — seeking; *vastu* — an object; *su-durlabham* — very difficult to obtain; *itaḥ tataḥ* — here and there; *bhraman* — wandering; *vyagraḥ* — agitated; *kadācit api* — at any time; *kutracit* — anywhere; *na atikrāmati* — he does not rise above; *citta-antaḥ* —

inside his heart; *lagnam* — fix; *tam* — that; *śokam* — distress; *ārti-dam* — giving pain.

**Śrī Nārada said: Just see, Uddhava! This cowherd's son, born at Govardhana, is seeking something unachievable for persons like you and me. Greatly agitated, he wanders here and there, never anywhere transcending the painful distress that is fixed in his heart.**

COMMENTARY: This seeker, the son of a cowherd, has wandered all over the material and spiritual worlds, his heart full of indescribable pain, and now he has taken shelter in Uddhava's house. He has not been able to find peace, because his desired goal is beyond the reach of even great Vaiṣṇavas like Nārada and Uddhava. Why Gopa-kumāra has such an unlikely ambition Nārada explains with the phrase *govardhanodbhavaḥ* ("born at Govardhana").

## TEXT 60

तदेनं बत तत्रत्यलोकानुग्रहकातरः ।
भवानपि न पार्श्वस्थं प्रतिबोधयति क्षणम् ॥

*tad enaṁ bata tatratya-*
*lokānugraha-kātaraḥ*
*bhavān api na pārśva-sthaṁ*
*pratibodhayati kṣaṇam*

*tat* — therefore; *enam* — this person; *bata* — oh; *tatratya* — of that place; *loka* — for the people; *anugraha* — to favor; *kātaraḥ* — who are anxious; *bhavān* — your good self; *api na* — why not; *pārśva-stham* — present at your side; *pratibodhayati* — enlighten; *kṣaṇam* — for a moment.

**Indeed, Uddhava, you are always anxious to favor the residents of Vraja. Then why not spend a moment to enlighten this boy who is present right beside you?**

## TEXT 61

पदं दूरतरं तद्वै तत्सुखानुभवस्तथा ।
तत्साधनमपि प्रार्थ्यमस्माकमपि दुर्घटम् ॥

*padaṁ dūra-taraṁ tad vai*
*tat-sukhānubhavas tathā*
*tat-sādhanam api prārthyam*
*asmākam api durghaṭam*

*padam* — abode; *dūra-taram* — very far; *tat* — that; *vai* — indeed; *tat* — there; *sukha* — of happiness; *anubhavaḥ* — the experience; *tathā* — also; *tat* — it; *sādhanam* — the means to achieve; *api* — also; *prārthyam* — to be prayed for; *asmākam* — by us; *api* — also; *durghaṭam* — difficult to obtain.

**The abode of Goloka is very far away, and the happiness relished there is inaccessible to us. And even the means to achieve that abode is so rarely obtained that we can only pray for it.**

COMMENTARY: Although time and space do not exist in the spiritual realm, Goloka is still considered far away in the sense that the common residents of Vaikuṇṭha cannot approach it. Nor can they enjoy the pleasure of seeing Śrī Nanda-nandana and taking part in His childhood play. Even the intimate companions of Lord Nārāyaṇa worship the good fortune of the devotees in Goloka, a place they can approach only in prayer.

## TEXT 62

श्रीमदुद्धव उवाच
व्रजभूमावयं जातस्तस्यां गोपत्वमाचरत् ।
गोपालोपासनानिष्ठो विशिष्टोऽस्मन्महाशयः ॥

*śrīmad-uddhava uvāca*
*vraja-bhūmāv ayaṁ jātas*
*tasyāṁ gopatvam ācarat*
*gopālopāsanā-niṣṭho*
*viśiṣṭo 'sman mahāśayaḥ*

*śrīmat-uddhavaḥ uvāca* — Śrīmān Uddhava said; *vraja-bhūmau* — in Vraja-bhūmi; *ayam* — he; *jātaḥ* — born; *tasyām* — there; *gopatvam* — the occupation of a cowherd; *ācarat* — he carried out; *gopāla* — of Lord Gopāla; *upāsanā* — to the worship; *niṣṭhaḥ* — dedicated; *viśiṣṭaḥ* — special; *asmat* — compared to us; *mahā-āśayaḥ* — a great soul.

**Śrīmān Uddhava said: He was born in Vraja-bhūmi, and there he was engaged as a cowherd. And he is firmly established in the worship of Lord Gopāla. He is surely a much greater soul than you and I.**

COMMENTARY: Nārada has just told Uddhava that Śrī Goloka is a place that he and Uddhava can hardly approach. This statement somewhat disturbed Uddhava because he disliked the implication that he himself was better than everyone else in Vaikuṇṭha. Still, he wanted to please Nārada by enlightening Gopa-kumāra as requested. So he first gave his opinion that Gopa-kumāra was the most spiritually advanced person present, not himself or even Nārada. After all, Gopa-kumāra was a native of Govardhana, a lifelong tender of the cows in the holy *dhāma,* and a worshiper of Śrī Madana-gopāla and His ten-syllable *mantra.* Moreover, wherever Gopa-kumāra went he remained dissatisfied because he couldn't find his worshipable Lord.

## TEXT 63

सोत्साहमाह तं हर्षात्तच्छ्रुत्वाश्लिष्य नारदः ।
यथायं लभतेऽभीष्टं तथोपादिश सत्वरम् ॥

*sotsāham āha taṁ harṣāt*
*tac chrutvāśliṣya nāradaḥ*
*yathāyaṁ labhate 'bhīṣṭaṁ*
*tathopādiśa satvaram*

*sa-utsāham* — with enthusiasm; *āha* — said; *tam* — to him; *harṣāt* — with delight; *tat* — that; *śrutvā* — hearing; *āśliṣya* — embracing; *nāradaḥ* — Nārada; *yathā* — so that; *ayam* — he; *labhate* — obtains; *abhīṣṭam* — his desire; *tathā* — so; *upādiśa* — please give instruction; *satvaram* — quickly.

**Nārada was delighted to hear this. He embraced Uddhava and enthusiastically told him, "Please hurry and instruct him so that he may fulfill his desires."**

## TEXT 64

अब्रवीदुद्धवो जात्या क्षत्रियोऽहं महामुने ।
उपदेशप्रदाने तन्नाधिकारी त्वयि स्थिते ॥

*abravīd uddhavo jātyā*
*kṣatriyo 'haṁ mahā-mune*
*upadeśa-pradāne tan*
*nādhikārī tvayi sthite*

*abravīt* — said; *uddhavaḥ* — Uddhava; *jātyā* — by caste; *kṣatriyaḥ* — a warrior; *aham* — I; *mahā-mune* — O great sage; *upadeśa* — of instructions; *pradāne* — for giving; *tat* — thus; *na* — not; *adhikārī* — a qualified person; *tvayi* — you; *sthite* — being present.

**Uddhava replied, "O great sage, since I am a kṣatriya by birth, in your presence I have no right to instruct him."**

COMMENTARY: Uddhava considers himself second class by birth and character. Nonetheless, he might be reminded that *kṣatriyas* are also allowed to teach. According to the *dharma-śāstras, kṣatriyas* may engage in the same duties prescribed for *brāhmaṇas,* except for receiving charity. This is confirmed in the Seventh Canto of *Śrīmad-Bhāgavatam* (7.11.14):

*viprasyādhyayanādīni*
*ṣaḍ-anyasyāpratigrahaḥ*

"For a *brāhmaṇa* there are six occupational duties. A *kṣatriya* should not accept charity, but he may perform the other five."

Though not denying this authoritative statement, Uddhava is still reluctant to speak in the presence of Nārada, the *ādi-guru* for the process of devotional service.

## TEXT 65

नारदो नितरामुच्चैर्विहस्यावददुद्धवम् ।
न वैकुण्ठेऽप्यपेतास्मिन्क्षत्रियत्वमतिस्तव ॥

*nārado nitarām uccair*
*vihasyāvadad uddhavam*
*na vaikuṇṭhe 'py apetāsmin*
*kṣatriyatva-matis tava*

*nāradaḥ* — Nārada; *nitarām* — very; *uccaiḥ* — loudly; *vihasya* — laughing; *avadat* — said; *uddhavam* — to Uddhava; *na* — not; *vaikuṇṭhe* — in Vaikuṇṭha; *api* — even; *apetā* — stopped; *asmin* — in this place; *kṣatriyatva* — of being a *kṣatriya; matiḥ* — the mentality; *tava* — your.

**Nārada laughed very loudly and said to Uddhava, "Even here in Vaikuṇṭha you can't stop thinking yourself a kṣatriya!"**

COMMENTARY: In the material world, particularly within Bhārata-varṣa, the distinctions of caste and occupation are prevalent, but in Vaikuṇṭha these distinctions should not be considered, because everyone there has a purely spiritual body. The positions of *brāhmaṇa, kṣatriya,* and so on are designations of bodies that are limited and temporary, but Vaikuṇṭha bodies are never subject to the limits imposed by material nature.

## TEXT 66

उद्धवः सस्मितं प्राह किं ब्रूयां सा न मादृशाम् ।
अपेतेति किलास्माकं प्रभोरप्यपयाति न ॥

*uddhavaḥ sa-smitaṁ prāha*
*kiṁ brūyāṁ sā na mādṛśām*
*apeteti kilāsmākaṁ*
*prabhor apy apayāti na*

*uddhavaḥ* — Uddhava; *sa-smitam* — smiling; *prāha* — said; *kim* — what; *brūyām* — can I say; *sā* — that (mentality); *na* — not; *mādṛśām* — for those like me; *apetā* — gone away; *iti* — thus; *kila* — indeed; *asmākam* — our; *prabhoḥ* — for the Lord; *api* — even; *apayāti* — it goes away; *na* — not.

**Smiling, Uddhava told him, "What can I say? How can someone like me stop thinking himself a kṣatriya when even our Lord does not?**

## TEXT 67

यथा तत्र तथात्रापि सद्धर्मपरिपालनम् ।
गार्हस्थ्यारिजयज्येष्ठविप्रसम्माननादिकम् ॥

*yathā tatra tathātrāpi*
*sad-dharma-paripālanam*
*gārhasthyāri-jaya-jyeṣṭha-*
*vipra-sammānanādikam*

*yathā* — as; *tatra* — there; *tathā* — so; *atra* — here; *api* — also; *sat-dharma* — of civilized religious principles; *paripālanam* —

the maintenance; *gārhasthya* — the proper behavior of a family man; *ari* — over enemies; *jaya* — victory; *jyeṣṭha* — to elders; *vipra* — and *brāhmaṇas; sammānana* — showing respect; *ādikam* — and so on.

**"Here in Vaikuṇṭha the Lord maintains the religious principles of civilized people, just as He does on earth. He behaves like a proper family man, conquers His enemies, shows respect to elders and brāhmaṇas, and so on."**

COMMENTARY: In Dvārakā, both on earth and in Vaikuṇṭha, Śrī Kṛṣṇadeva thinks and acts like a proper householder and *kṣatriya*. He dutifully does everything expected of a responsible householder, goes forth with relish into battle to subdue opposing kings, and sincerely honors the *brāhmaṇas* and His spiritual masters and His elders like Balarāma. The word *ādi* ("and so on") implies other daily duties He performs as a *gṛhastha-kṣatriya,* such as rising during the early hours of the *brāhma-muhūrta.*

## TEXT 68

तदुक्त्या नारदो हर्षभराक्रान्तमना हसन् ।
उत्प्लुत्योत्प्लुत्य चाक्रोशन्निदमाह सुविस्मितः ॥

*tad-uktyā nārado harṣa-*
*bharākrānta-manā hasan*
*utplutyotplutya cākrośann*
*idam āha su-vismitaḥ*

*tat* — by those; *uktyā* — words; *nāradaḥ* — Nārada; *harṣa-bhara* — by an excess of joy; *ākrānta* — overcome; *manāḥ* — his mind; *hasan* — laughing; *utplutya utplutya* — jumping high again and again; *ca* — and; *akrośan* — shouting; *idam* — this; *āha* — said; *su-vismitaḥ* — very surprised.

**These words filled Nārada's mind with pleasure, and**

**he laughed, jumped up and down, and shouted in joy. Astonished, he spoke as follows.**

## TEXT 69

श्रीनारद उवाच
अहो भगवतो लीलामाधुर्यमहिमाद्भुतः ।
तदेकनिष्ठागाम्भीर्यं सेवकानां च तादृशम् ॥

*śrī-nārada uvāca*
*aho bhagavato līlā-*
*mādhurya-mahimādbhutaḥ*
*tad-eka-niṣṭhā-gāmbhīryaṁ*
*sevakānāṁ ca tādṛśam*

*śrī-nāradaḥ uvāca* — Śrī Nārada said; *aho* — oh; *bhagavataḥ* — of the Personality of Godhead; *līlā* — of the pastimes; *mādhurya* — the charm; *mahimā* — and glory; *adbhutaḥ* — amazing; *tat* — to Him; *eka-niṣṭhā* — of the exclusive commitment; *gāmbhīryam* — the seriousness; *sevakānām* — of His servants; *ca* — and; *tādṛśam* — such.

**Śrī Nārada said: Indeed, just see the amazing charm and glory of the Personality of Godhead's pastimes! And see in those pastimes how seriously committed His devotees are to serving Him, and Him alone!**

## TEXT 70

अहो अलं कौतुकमेतदीक्ष्यते
यथैष विक्रीडति मर्त्यलोकगः ।
तथैव वैकुण्ठपदोपरि स्थितो
निजप्रियाणां परितोषहेतवे ॥

*aho alaṁ kautukam etad īkṣyate*
*yathaiṣa vikrīḍati martya-loka-gaḥ*

*tathaiva vaikuṇṭha-padopari sthito*
*nija-priyāṇāṁ paritoṣa-hetave*

*aho* — oh; *alam* — very; *kautukam* — curious; *etat* — this; *īkṣyate* — is seen; *yathā* — how; *eṣaḥ* — He; *vikrīḍati* — plays; *martya-loka* — to the world of mortals; *gaḥ* — coming; *tathā* — so; *eva* — just; *vaikuṇṭha* — of Vaikuṇṭha; *pada* — the abode; *upari* — above; *sthitaḥ* — situated; *nija* — His own; *priyāṇām* — of the dear devotees; *paritoṣa* — of the satisfaction; *hetave* — for the purpose.

**Oh, how very curious that this Lord plays in the highest abode above Vaikuṇṭha the same way as in the world of mortals, just to satisfy His dear devotees!**

## TEXT 71

यल्लीलानुभवेनायं भ्रमः स्यान्मादृशामपि ।
वैकुण्ठद्वारकायां किं मर्त्ये वर्तामहेऽथ वा ॥

*yal-līlānubhavenāyaṁ*
*bhramaḥ syān mādṛśām api*
*vaikuṇṭha-dvārakāyāṁ kiṁ*
*martye vartāmahe 'tha vā*

*yat* — which; *līlā* — of the pastimes; *anubhavena* — by experiencing; *ayam* — this; *bhramaḥ* — bewilderment; *syāt* — arises; *mādṛśām* — for persons like me; *api* — even; *vaikuṇṭha* — in Vaikuṇṭha; *dvārakāyām* — and in Dvārakā; *kim* — whether; *martye* — in the material world; *vartāmahe* — we are present; *atha* — here; *vā* — or.

**Even experienced devotees like me are bewildered to see such pastimes, which make us wonder whether we are in the Dvārakā of Vaikuṇṭha or the Dvārakā of the material world.**

## TEXT 72

युक्तं तदेका प्रभुपादपद्मयोः
सप्रेमभक्तिर्भवतामपेक्षिता ।
भक्तप्रियस्यास्य च भक्तकामित-
प्रपूरणं केवलमिष्टमुत्तमम् ॥

*yuktaṁ tad ekā prabhu-pāda-padmayoḥ*
*saprema-bhaktir bhavatām apekṣitā*
*bhakta-priyasyāsya ca bhakta-kāmita-*
*prapūraṇaṁ kevalam iṣṭam uttamam*

*yuktam* — fitting; *tat* — that; *ekā* — only; *prabhu* — of the Lord; *pāda-padmayoḥ* — for the lotus feet; *sa-prema-bhaktiḥ* — loving devotional service; *bhavatām* — by you; *apekṣitā* — desired; *bhakta-priyasya* — who is affectionate to His dear devotees; *asya* — His; *ca* — and; *bhakta* — of the devotees; *kāmita* — the ambitions; *prapūraṇam* — fulfilling; *kevalam* — the only; *iṣṭam* — goal; *uttamam* — final.

**It is quite fitting that you devotees care only for prema-bhakti, pure loving devotional service to the Lord's lotus feet. Such prema-bhakti for the Lord, who is very affectionate to His devotees, fulfills all their ambitions and is alone their final goal.**

COMMENTARY: If Kṛṣṇa deals virtually the same way with His devotees in both the spiritual and material worlds, what is special then about Vaikuṇṭha? Nārada's answer is that in the quality of the relationships between the Lord and His devotees there is no practical difference between the material and spiritual worlds. In either realm the Lord and the devotees achieve the fulfillment of all their desires, so whatever they do is just apt for the time and place in which they happen to be. For devotees, nothing is as important as the opportunity to always serve His lotus feet in pure love. And likewise for the Personality of Godhead nothing is as important as satisfying His devotees.

Since nouns in Sanskrit may be either singular, dual, or plural and since the word *bhavatām* ("by you") is plural, here the word indicates that Nārada is speaking not only to Uddhava and Gopa-kumāra but to all the fully devoted servants of the Lord.

## TEXT 73

वैकुण्ठवासोचितमीहितं न वो
नो मर्त्यलोकस्थितियोग्यमप्यतः ।
ऐश्वर्ययोग्यं न हि लोकबन्धुता
युक्तं च तस्यापि भवेदपेक्षितम् ॥

*vaikuṇṭha-vāsocitam īhitaṁ na vo*
*no martya-loka-sthiti-yogyam apy ataḥ*
*aiśvarya-yogyaṁ na hi loka-bandhutā*
*yuktaṁ ca tasyāpi bhaved apekṣitam*

*vaikuṇṭha* — in Vaikuṇṭha; *vāsa* — for residence; *ucitam* — suitable; *īhitam* — activities; *na* — not; *vaḥ* — by you; *na u* — nor; *martya-loka* — in the material world; *sthiti* — for being situated; *yogyam* — suitable; *api* — even; *ataḥ* — thus; *aiśvarya* — for opulence; *yogyam* — fitting; *na* — not; *hi* — indeed; *loka* — worldly; *bandhutā* — friendship; *yuktam* — suitable; *ca* — and; *tasya* — by Him; *api* — even; *bhavet* — is; *apekṣitam* — desired.

**You have no great interest in acting as residents of Vaikuṇṭha or sojourners in the material world, and He has no great interest in showing His opulence or getting involved in mundane relationships.**

COMMENTARY: Because the Supreme Lord and His pure devotees are interested only in pleasing one another, it makes little difference to them where they happen to be. The devotees may be in Vaikuṇṭha, endowed with *sac-cid-ānanda* spiritual bodies and the corresponding powers and comforts to enjoy, or they may be *gṛhasthas* or whatever in the material world, with bodies made of the physical elements, and may worship the Lord in a form of His that also seems material. But in any case, the Lord and His devotees are never distracted from their pure loving exchanges of *rasas,* not even when the Lord fully expands His opulences or His complete self-satisfaction or seems to establish worldly affinities by becoming a father, a son, or some other relative of His devotees. Since the devotees are exclusively devoted to the Lord, their hearts are satisfied simply by relishing His pastimes and transcendental qualities. Similarly, the Lord is interested only in making His devotees happy. These ambitions of the Lord and His devotees can be fulfilled equally well in Vaikuṇṭha or in the material world, so for them there is no substantial difference between the two realms.

## TEXT 74

सप्रेमभक्तेः परमानुकूलं
 दैन्यं महापुष्टिकरं सदा वः ।
तस्यापि तत्प्रेमविभावनेऽलं
 भोगाकुलग्राम्यविहारजातम् ॥

*saprema-bhakteḥ paramānukūlaṁ*
*dainyaṁ mahā-puṣṭi-karaṁ sadā vaḥ*
*tasyāpi tat-prema-vibhāvane 'laṁ*
*bhogākula-grāmya-vihāra-jātam*

*sa-prema* — loving; *bhakteḥ* — of devotional service; *parama* — most; *anukūlam* — appropriate; *dainyam* — humility; *mahā* — greatly; *puṣṭi* — success; *karam* — producing; *sadā* — always; *vaḥ* — for you; *tasya* — for Him; *api* — also; *tat* — that; *prema* — of the pure love; *vibhāvane* — for evoking; *alam* — sufficient; *bhoga* — for obtaining sense gratification; *ākula* — of one who is agitated; *grāmya* — worldly; *vihāra* — in pastimes; *jātam* — born.

**You always live in utter humility, which most favorably nourishes devotion in pure love. And the Lord's pastimes**

**of seeming absorbed in worldly pleasure amply evoke such love.**

COMMENTARY: In Vaikuṇṭha the Lord and His devotees have purely spiritual bodies with which to enjoy transcendental reciprocations. But when Kṛṣṇa descends to the material world He seems to have the body of an ordinary human being, and that is even more conducive to the full blossoming of *prema-bhakti.* In Vaikuṇṭha Lord Nārāyaṇa expands unlimited opulence, but on earth Kṛṣṇa acts even more wonderfully by simply being the friend of His devotees and satisfying them in every possible way. Nārada here congratulates the Lord's devotees for their humility, which more than anything else helps them achieve all success in loving devotional service.

## TEXT 75

प्रेमोद्रेकपरीपाकमहिमा केन वर्ण्यताम् ।
यः कुर्यात्परमेशं तं सद्बन्धुमिव लौकिकम् ॥

*premodreka-parīpāka-*
*mahimā kena varṇyatām*
*yaḥ kuryāt parameśaṁ taṁ*
*sad-bandhum iva laukikam*

*prema* — of pure love; *udreka* — of the perfection; *parīpāka* — of the maturity; *mahimā* — the greatness; *kena* — by whom; *varṇyatām* — can be described; *yaḥ* — which; *kuryāt* — can make; *parama-īśam* — the Supreme Lord; *tam* — Him; *sat* — good; *bandhum* — a friend; *iva* — as if; *laukikam* — ordinary.

**Who can describe the greatness of the mature perfection of love of God, which makes the Supreme Lord act like an ordinary good friend?**

COMMENTARY: The Supreme Lord's appearance as a cowherd boy in Gokula is no false trick of Māyā. It is the highest truth, manifest in response to the purest forms of absolute love. The mature stage of *prema* shared by Kṛṣṇa and His devotees in Gokula is beyond the power of words to describe. It is so exalted that it impels the Lord to forget His supremacy and behave like an ordinary person to fulfill the desires of His devotees. This marvel cannot be an illusion created by Māyā, because the Māyā of the material world has no power to delude either Kṛṣṇa or His devotees.

## TEXT 76

अहो लौकिकसद्बन्धुभावं च स्तौमि येन हि ।
गौरवादेर्विलोपेन कृष्णे सत्प्रेम तन्यते ॥

*aho laukika-sad-bandhu-*
*bhāvaṁ ca staumi yena hi*
*gauravāder vilopena*
*kṛṣṇe sat-prema tanyate*

*aho* — oh; *laukika* — worldly; *sat-bandhu* — of a good friend; *bhāvam* — the mood; *ca* — and; *staumi* — I praise; *yena* — by which; *hi* — indeed; *gaurava* — of reverence; *ādeḥ* — and so on; *vilopena* — by the eclipse; *kṛṣṇe* — in Kṛṣṇa; *sat-prema* — pure love; *tanyate* — is expanded.

**Oh, let me praise Kṛṣṇa's mood as an ordinary friend, which does away with the respect and reverence of His devotees and expands their pure love for Him!**

COMMENTARY: After hearing what Nārada has just said, some Vaiṣṇavas may remain doubtful, thinking that love of God can develop to its full potential only by specific knowledge of the Supreme Lord's greatness, not by conceptions of Him in worldly relationships, such as that of a son. In fact, such devotees might argue that to view the Personality of Godhead in such relationships is a serious error. After all, in *Śrīmad-Bhāgavatam* (10.85.19) Kṛṣṇa's own father Śrī Vasudeva prayed:

*tat te gato 'smy araṇam adya padāravindam*
*āpanna-saṁsṛti-bhayāpaham ārta-bandho*
*etāvatālam alam indriya-lālasena*
*martyātma-dṛk tvayi pare yad apatya-buddhiḥ*

"Therefore, O friend of the distressed, I now approach Your lotus feet for shelter — the same lotus feet that dispel all fear of worldly existence for those who have surrendered to them. Enough! Enough with hankering for sense enjoyment, which makes me identify with this mortal body and think of You, the Supreme, as my child."

In this prayer, Vasudeva begs to be relieved of the delusion that compels him to imagine that God is his son. Vasudeva might be advised, "You are very happy, so why are you complaining?" But he counters this idea by describing his pitiable confusion, in which out of greed for sense enjoyment he thinks that he is the body and that the Supreme Lord is his son.

Vasudeva also tells Kṛṣṇa in the *Viṣṇu Purāṇa* (5.20.99):

*sāpahnavaṁ mama mano*
*yad etat tvayi jāyate*
*devakyāś cātmaja-prītyā*
*tad atyanta-viḍambanam*

"That both Devakī and I are bewildered into loving You like our own child is so absurd!" Vasudeva feels he should be the butt of jokes for daring to consider the Supreme Lord his son.

But here Nārada explains that this exceptional attitude and behavior, even though they appear to follow the pattern of mundane human relationships, expand the limits of the most perfect love for Kṛṣṇa. The key to understanding how this kind of devotional service works is to comprehend that it does away with the restrictions of respect, fear, and reverential faith toward the Supreme Lord. Awe and reverence may be indispensable in Vaikuṇṭha, but they only inhibit the expression of *prema* between Kṛṣṇa and His intimate devotees. This has already been discussed in *Śrī Bṛhad-bhāgavatāmṛta* and will be made even clearer later on.

Gopa-kumāra understands from what Nārada has said that the most beneficial and sensible thing to do is whatever will strengthen one's pure love for the Personality of Godhead. Śrī Vasudeva was lamenting because he had focused his attention on the idea that the Lord was his son, rather than simply act in affection for Him like Śrī Nanda and Yaśodā. Or alternatively, Vasudeva, as an extremely humble Vaiṣṇava, suffered from the self-dissatisfaction that naturally arises when *bhakti* becomes intense. He is of course a perfect devotee who has all the Lord's blessings.

## TEXT 77

श्रीगोपकुमार उवाच
एवं वदन्प्रेमभराभियन्त्रितो
विकारजातं विविधं भजन्मुनिः ।
तूष्णीमभूदार्तमथाह मां पुनः
सापेक्षमालक्ष्य निजोपदेशने ॥

*śrī-gopa-kumāra uvāca*
*evaṁ vadan prema-bharābhiyantrito*
*vikāra-jātaṁ vividhaṁ bhajan muniḥ*
*tūṣṇīm abhūd ārtam athāha māṁ punaḥ*
*sāpekṣam ālakṣya nijopadeśane*

*śrī-gopa-kumāraḥ uvāca* — Śrī Gopa-kumāra said; *evam* — thus; *vadan* — speaking; *prema* — of pure love; *bhara* — by the weight; *abhiyantritaḥ* — overwhelmed; *vikāra* — of ecstatic transformations; *jātam* — kinds; *vividham* — various; *bhajan* — assuming; *muniḥ* — the sage; *tūṣṇīm* — silent; *abhūt* — became; *ārtam* — troubled; *atha* — then; *āha* — he said; *mām* — to me; *punaḥ* — again; *sa-apekṣam* — interested; *ālakṣya* — noting; *nija* — his; *upadeśane* — for the instructions.

**Śrī Gopa-kumāra continued: After saying this, the sage was overwhelmed by the weight of love. Swept up in various**

**ecstatic transformations, he remained silent a while. Then he spoke to me again, because he saw that I was troubled and keen for his instructions.**

COMMENTARY: When Nārada stopped he felt ecstatic and showed symptoms like trembling, tears, and standing of the bodily hairs. But soon he noticed that Gopa-kumāra was ill at ease and waiting for further instructions.

## TEXT 78

श्रीनारद उवाच
गोपालदेवप्रिय गोपनन्दन
श्रीमानितो दूरतरो विराजते ।
गोलोकनामोपरि सर्वसीमगो
वैकुण्ठतो देशविशेषशेखरः ॥

*śrī-nārada uvāca*
*gopāla-deva-priya gopa-nandana*
*śrīmān ito dūra-taro virājate*
*goloka-nāmopari sarva-sīma-go*
*vaikuṇṭhato deśa-viśeṣa-śekharaḥ*

*śrī-nāradaḥ uvāca* — Śrī Nārada said; *gopāla-deva* — of Gopāladeva; *priya* — O dear devotee; *gopa-nandana* — O son of a cowherd; *śrīmān* — splendid; *itaḥ* — from here; *dūra-taraḥ* — far away; *virājate* — shines forth; *goloka-nāmā* — named Goloka; *upari* — higher; *sarva* — all; *sīma* — limits; *gaḥ* — crossing; *vaikuṇṭhataḥ* — than Vaikuṇṭha; *deśa* — of places; *viśeṣa* — special; *śekharaḥ* — the topmost.

**Śrī Nārada said: Dear devotee of Lord Gopāladeva, O son of a cowherd, far away from here lies the most exalted of all places, called Goloka. It is full of all splendor and beyond the borders of all other regions, including Vaikuṇṭha.**

COMMENTARY: Gopa-kumāra is *gopāla-deva-priya* in two ways: Lord Gopāla is dear to him, and he is dear to Lord Gopāla. This is because Gopa-kumāra is *gopa-nandana,* a young cowherd boy from Śrī Govardhana Hill.

Goloka stands above all the other spiritual planets because it is superior in every way. The *Brahma-saṁhitā* (5.43) states:

*goloka-nāmni nija-dhāmni tale ca tasya*
*devī-maheśa-hari-dhāmasu teṣu teṣu*
*te te prabhāva-nicayā vihitāś ca yena*
*govindam ādi-puruṣaṁ tam ahaṁ bhajāmi*

"Lowest of all lies Devī-dhāma [the mundane world], next above it is Maheśa-dhāma [the abode of Maheśa], above Maheśa-dhāma is Hari-dhāma [the abode of Hari], and above them all is Kṛṣṇa's own realm, named Goloka. I adore the primeval Lord Govinda, who has allotted their respective authorities to the rulers of those graded realms." The eight coverings of the universe over which Durgā presides, and the abode of Lord Śiva, and the Vaikuṇṭha kingdom of Lord Hari all stand below Goloka.

## TEXT 79

स माथुरश्रीव्रजभूमिरूपस्
तत्रैव देवी मथुरापुरी च ।
वृन्दावनादिव्रजभूमिमात्म-
सारं विना स्थातुमपारयन्ती ॥

*sa māthura-śrī-vraja-bhūmi-rūpas*
*tatraiva devī mathurā-purī ca*
*vṛndāvanādi-vraja-bhūmim ātma-*
*sāraṁ vinā sthātum apārayantī*

*saḥ* — it; *māthura* — in the district of Mathurā; *śrī-vraja-bhūmi* — of the blessed land of Vraja; *rūpaḥ* — having the form; *tatra* — there; *eva* — only; *devī* — divine; *mathurā-purī* — Mathurā

City; *ca* — and; *vṛndāvana* — of Vṛndāvana; *ādi* — and so on; *vraja-bhūmim* — Vraja-bhūmi; *ātma* — her (Mathurā's) own; *sāram* — essence; *vinā* — without; *sthātum* — to remain; *apārayantī* — unable.

**That same Goloka takes the form of the divine Vraja-bhūmi of the district of Mathurā. And the city of Mathurā is also there, unable to stay apart from her own essence—Vṛndāvana and the other forests of Vraja-bhūmi.**

COMMENTARY: According to this statement, Mathurā is not separate from Vraja-bhūmi like Ayodhyā and other abodes of the Lord. One might ask: "Although the district of Mathurā is nondifferent from Śrī Goloka, what about the city of Mathurā?" Mathurā City is *devī* in the sense that she is "effulgent" and "splendid," and she is included in Goloka. Even though Mathurā has her own distinct identity, she cannot bear to be apart from the forests of Vraja-bhūmi. According to the spiritual geography of Goloka, the Mathurā district includes Vṛndāvana and the other Vraja forests, which are the most essential parts of Mathurā.

## TEXT 80

सा गोप्रधानदेशत्वात्सर्वा श्रीमथुरोच्यते ।
गोलोक इति गूढोऽपि विख्यातः स हि सर्वतः ॥

*sā go-pradhāna-deśatvāt*
*sarvā śrī-mathurocyate*
*goloka iti gūḍho 'pi*
*vikhyātaḥ sa hi sarvataḥ*

*sā* — that; *go* — by cows; *pradhāna* — predominated; *deśatvāt* — because of being a region; *sarvā* — entire; *śrī-mathurā* — Śrī Mathurā; *ucyate* — is called; *golokaḥ* — Goloka; *iti* — thus; *gūḍhaḥ* — confidential; *api* — although; *vikhyātaḥ* — famous; *saḥ* — it; *hi* — certainly; *sarvataḥ* — everywhere.

**Because the entire region of Śrī Mathurā is a land of cows, it is called Goloka. Though a confidential place, it is famous everywhere.**

COMMENTARY: The transcendental abode that includes the city of Ayodhyā is also called Ayodhyā. Why then is the abode that includes the city of Mathurā called Goloka rather than Mathurā? The answer is that the entire Mathurā district, with its city, towns, and forests, is full of cows. Furthermore, the Goloka of the spiritual world is famous by that name. The intimate pastimes of the Personality of Godhead are a well-kept secret, but the name Goloka is known everywhere. Lord Indra, for example, refers to Goloka by name in his prayers to Śrī Kṛṣṇa in the *Hari-vaṁśa*. So there is no reason to doubt the glories of Goloka on the grounds that it is an obscure, unknown place.

## TEXT 81

स च तद्व्रजलोकानां श्रीमत्प्रेमानुवर्तिना ।
कृष्णे शुद्धतरेणैव भावेनैकेन लभ्यते ॥

*sa ca tad-vraja-lokānāṁ*
*śrīmat-premānuvartinā*
*kṛṣṇe śuddha-tareṇaiva*
*bhāvenaikena labhyate*

*saḥ* — that (Goloka); *ca* — and; *tat* — of that; *vraja* — Vraja; *lokānām* — of the residents; *śrīmat-prema* — the sublime love; *anuvartinā* — which follows; *kṛṣṇe* — to Kṛṣṇa; *śuddha-tareṇa* — purest; *eva* — indeed; *bhāvena* — by the ecstatic mood; *ekena* — only; *labhyate* — is obtained.

**That abode can be reached only through the purest sentiments, in which one follows the sublime love held for Kṛṣṇa by the residents of Vraja.**

COMMENTARY: Goloka can by reached only by *prema* free of

fault, untouched by *jñāna, karma,* or any other material endeavor, and concentrated on the son of Nanda Mahārāja. And to learn this kind of *prema,* one must carefully study the examples of Vraja-vāsīs like Śrī Nanda and Yaśodā, and especially the ideal example of Śrī Rādhā and Her companions.

## TEXT 82

तादृग्भगवति प्रेमा पारमैश्वर्यदृष्टितः ।
सदा सम्पद्यते नैव भयगौरवसम्भवात् ॥

*tādṛg bhagavati premā*
*pāramaiśvarya-dṛṣṭitaḥ*
*sadā sampadyate naiva*
*bhaya-gaurava-sambhavāt*

*tādṛk* — such; *bhagavati* — for the Personality of Godhead; *premā* — pure love; *pārama-aiśvarya* — of supreme power; *dṛṣṭitaḥ* — by a vision; *sadā* — always; *sampadyate na* — cannot be achieved; *eva* — indeed; *bhaya* — of fear; *gaurava* — and reverence; *sambhavāt* — because of the likelihood.

**One can never achieve such pure love for the Personality of Godhead by concentrating on His supreme power, because in that mood one invariably feels fear and reverence.**

## TEXT 83

केवलं लौकिकप्राणसुहृद्बुद्ध्या स सिध्यति ।
लोकालोकोत्तरो योऽसावतिलोकोत्तरोऽपि यः ॥

*kevalaṁ laukika-prāṇa-*
*suhṛd-buddhyā sa sidhyati*
*lokālokottaro yo 'sāv*
*ati-lokottaro 'pi yaḥ*

*kevalam* — only; *laukika* — ordinary; *prāṇa-suhṛt* — as dear friend; *buddhyā* — by thinking; *saḥ* — it; *sidhyati* — is achieved; *loka* — the material world; *aloka* — and the coverings of the universe; *uttaraḥ* — beyond; *yaḥ* — which; *asau* — that; *ati-loka* — the transcendental world; *uttaraḥ* — beyond; *api* — also; *yaḥ* — which.

**One achieves that love only by thinking of the Lord as one's ordinary dear friend. That love is higher than found in the material worlds and the outer coverings of the universe, and higher than in the spiritual kingdom beyond.**

COMMENTARY: Only by considering Kṛṣṇa one's lifelong friend in one of the spiritual relationships can a devotee rise to the level of the pure love known only in Vraja. This *vraja-prema* is not an inferior version of love of God; it is not love in the mode of worldly affection. It is in fact superior to any feeling known in *loka* (the fourteen worlds of the material universe), *aloka* (the elemental coverings of the universe), or *ati-loka* (the Vaikuṇṭha planets beyond those coverings). *Vraja-prema* is the essential nature of the highest of all worlds; the Lord who is its object is supreme, and the sweetness it embodies is also supreme.

## TEXT 84

लोकानुगापि सान्योन्यं प्रियतातीतलौकिका ।
मधुरात्यद्भुतैश्वर्यलौकिकत्वविमिश्रिता ॥

*lokānugāpi sānyonyaṁ*
*priyatātīta-laukikā*
*madhurāty-adbhutaiśvarya-*
*laukikatva-vimiśritā*

*loka* — the ordinary world; *anugā* — imitating; *api* — although; *sā* — that; *anyonyam* — mutual; *priyatā* — affection; *ātīta* —

beyond; *laukikā* — ordinary dealings; *madhurā* — sweet; *ati-adbhuta* — extremely wonderful; *aiśvarya* — with opulence; *laukikatva* — and worldly simplicity; *vimiśritā* — combined.

**Although that reciprocal affection seems to follow the ways of the ordinary world, it is beyond the world. It combines intimate sweetness, amazing opulence, and worldly simplicity.**

COMMENTARY: Goloka's Lord and its residents care for one another as do people of the material world, yet their *prema* transcends the limits of mundane love. The loving dealings of Vraja are like nothing ever seen in this world. When Mother Yaśodā simply remembers Kṛṣṇa, milk flows from her breasts. And Nanda Mahārāja is constantly drenched in a flood of his own tears of love for Kṛṣṇa. The cowherd men use everything they have, even their wives and children, only for Kṛṣṇa's pleasure, never their own. And some of the old ladies of Vraja adopt the mood of Yaśodā, while others disguise themselves as their own young daughters to please Kṛṣṇa. Kṛṣṇa's friends are constantly desirous of seeing Him, so much so that they cannot tolerate even the momentary obstruction caused by Kṛṣṇa's passing behind a tree. And the blessed cowherd girls have no interest in life other than Him; whether separated from Him, or going out to meet Him, or enjoying His company, they relish all sorts of extraordinary ecstasy.

In these ways the *prema* of Vraja is both amazing and sweet, combining within itself the majestic opulence of the spiritual world and the simple sweetness of the material world. The devotees of Vraja possess superworldly opulence, and at the same time they are the most simple people. By their opulent power they are expertly able to understand and take part in all the various aspects of the Lord's countless pastimes. And like ordinary people, the Vraja-vāsīs, as is well known from the accounts of their lives, enjoy food and drink, the company of friends and relatives, and so on. And even the Personality of Godhead, though showing His opulence, shows it in the pastimes of an ordinary child. During His infant pastimes, for example, Kṛṣṇa drank milk from the breast of Pūtanā and sucked out the life air from that powerful witch, who had never suspected He could do so. And in countless other ways also, the Lord, though showing His opulence, acted like an ordinary human being. As the narration of *Bṛhad-bhāgavatāmṛta* continues, this will all be thoroughly explained.

With such ideas in mind, Śrī Śukadeva Gosvāmī said:

*evaṁ nigūḍhātma-gatiḥ sva-māyayā*
*gopātmajatvaṁ caritair viḍambayan*
*reme ramā-lālita-pāda-pallavo*
*grāmyaiḥ samaṁ grāmya-vad īśa-ceṣṭitaḥ*

"In this way the Supreme Lord, whose soft lotus feet are personally attended by the goddess of fortune, concealed His transcendental opulences by His internal potency and acted like the son of a cowherd. Yet even while enjoying like a village boy in the company of other village residents, He often exhibited feats only God could perform." (*Bhāgavatam* 10.15.19)

The word *viḍambayan* in this Tenth Canto verse is a form of the verb *viḍamb* ("to imitate") as a present participle ("imitating"). This participial form, however, can also sometimes mean "for the purpose of," as it does here — "for the purpose of imitating." Thus the verse can be construed to say that Kṛṣṇa hides His supremacy (*nigūḍhātma-gatiḥ*) by His own special potencies (*sva-māyayā*) for the purpose of imitating or assuming the nature of a cowherd boy (*gopātmajatvam*). He hides His godly powers (*ātma-gati*) so that He can act like an ordinary human, but His absolute power is still discernible in the extreme limit of the perfect sweetness He displays in each of His pastimes. He enjoys having His feet massaged by the supreme goddess of fortune, and He does things only God can do (*īśa-ceṣṭitaḥ*), and yet He plays like an ordinary village boy (*grāmya-vat*) in the company of other villagers.

## TEXT 85

व्यवहारोऽस्य तेषां च सोऽन्योन्यं प्रेमवर्धनः ।
वैकुण्ठे परमैश्वर्यपदे न किल सम्भवेत् ॥

*vyavahāro 'sya teṣāṁ ca*
*so 'nyonyaṁ prema-vardhanaḥ*
*vaikuṇṭhe paramaiśvarya-*
*pade na kila sambhavet*

*vyavahāraḥ* — the dealings; *asya* — His; *teṣām* — their; *ca* — and; *saḥ* — it; *anyonyam* — mutual; *prema-vardhanaḥ* — increasing their love; *vaikuṇṭhe* — in Vaikuṇṭha; *parama* — supreme; *aiśvarya* — of opulence; *pade* — the abode; *na* — not; *kila* — indeed; *sambhavet* — is possible.

**In Goloka the dealings between the Lord and His devotees increase their mutual love in a way not possible in Vaikuṇṭha, the abode of supreme opulence.**

COMMENTARY: Nārada has said that Goloka lies far away from Vaikuṇṭha, and now he explains why. The Supreme Lord simply cannot behave with His devotees in Vaikuṇṭha with the same familiarity as in Goloka.

## TEXT 86

तादृशी साप्ययोध्येयं द्वारकापि ततोऽधिका ।
अतः स लोकः कृष्णेन दूरतः परिकल्पितः ॥

*tādṛśī sāpy ayodhyeyaṁ*
*dvārakāpi tato 'dhikā*
*ataḥ sa lokaḥ kṛṣṇena*
*dūrataḥ parikalpitaḥ*

*tādṛśī* — similar; *sā* — that; *api* — also; *ayodhyā* — Ayodhyā; *iyam* — this; *dvārakā* — Dvārakā; *api* — also; *tataḥ* — than them; *adhikā* — greater; *ataḥ* — therefore; *saḥ* — that; *lokaḥ* — planet; *kṛṣṇena* — by Kṛṣṇa; *dūrataḥ* — far away; *parikalpitaḥ* — located.

**Ayodhyā and Dvārakā resemble Vaikuṇṭha, but Goloka is even greater. Therefore Kṛṣṇa has arranged for it to be far away.**

COMMENTARY: Ayodhyā and Dvārakā are somewhat secret portions of Vaikuṇṭha, but as Gopa-kumāra has already seen, they retain the basic Vaikuṇṭha mood of reverence for the Personality of Godhead's supremacy. Dvārakā is far superior to Ayodhyā, which is superior to the other Vaikuṇṭha planets, but the superiority of both Ayodhyā and Dvārakā is due to their being even more opulent than the rest of Vaikuṇṭha. Therefore neither Lord Rāmacandra in Ayodhyā nor Lord Kṛṣṇa in Dvārakā is free to subordinate Himself fully to the control of His devotees' love.

## TEXT 87

सुखक्रीडाविशेषोऽसौ तत्रत्यानां च तस्य च ।
माधुर्यान्त्यावधिं प्राप्तः सिध्येत्तत्रोचितास्पदे ॥

*sukha-krīḍā-viśeṣo 'sau*
*tatratyānāṁ ca tasya ca*
*mādhuryāntyāvadhiṁ prāptaḥ*
*sidhyet tatrocitāspade*

*sukha-krīḍā* — pleasure pastimes; *viśeṣaḥ* — special; *asau* — those; *tatratyānām* — of the residents of that place; *ca* — and; *tasya* — His; *ca* — and; *mādhurya* — of the sweetness; *antya* — ultimate; *avadhim* — the limit; *prāptaḥ* — which have obtained; *sidhyet* — are realized; *tatra* — there; *ucita* — delightful; *āspade* — in the abode.

**In that most delightful abode, the residents share special pleasure pastimes with the Lord in which they all realize the ultimate limit of sweetness.**

COMMENTARY: Here Nārada does not get specific about what makes the pastimes of Goloka unique. He refers to them only by mentioning *sukha-krīḍā-viśeṣo 'sau* ("that special kind of enjoyment"). The pronoun *asau* ("that"), normally used to point out something visible but distant, indicates that those pastimes are beyond the power of words to delimit and also that they are the fixed goal of all of Gopa-kumāra's endeavors. Only in Goloka can the Lord and His devotees enjoy pastimes in which the servants and the served equally dominate one another.

## TEXT 88

अहो किल तदेवाहं मन्ये भगवतो हरेः ।
सुगोप्यभगवत्तायाः सर्वसारप्रकाशनम् ॥

*aho kila tad evāhaṁ*
*manye bhagavato hareḥ*
*sugopya-bhagavattāyāḥ*
*sarva-sāra-prakāśanam*

*aho* — oh; *kila* — indeed; *tat* — that; *eva* — indeed; *aham* — I; *manye* — consider; *bhagavataḥ* — of the Supreme Lord; *hareḥ* — Hari; *su-gopya* — most confidential; *bhagavattāyāḥ* — of the status of being God; *sarva* — complete; *sāra* — of the essence; *prakāśanam* — the displaying.

**Indeed that world, I think, displays the complete essence of Lord Hari's most confidential Godhood.**

COMMENTARY: Goloka is even more splendidly opulent than Vaikuṇṭha. Someone may doubt, then, how Goloka could appear like an ordinary place of the finite world. Despite this doubt, Śrī Goloka is factually the one spiritual realm where the Supreme Lord shows the essential perfection of His beauty, personality, and sporting pastimes. This highest perfection is also the most confidential mystery, which only a few fortunate souls are privileged to understand. Goloka holds the supreme position among all the Lord's abodes, for there the Lord constantly displays perfections never seen anywhere else. Goloka is greater than all other spiritual abodes, and Kṛṣṇa in Goloka is greater than all other forms of Godhead. Kṛṣṇa in Goloka is especially known as Hari, the Lord who steals the heart of everyone with His beauty, personality, and pastimes.

## TEXT 89

वैकुण्ठोपरिवृत्तस्य जगदेकशिरोमणेः ।
महिमा सम्भवेदेव गोलोकस्याधिकाधिकः ॥

*vaikuṇṭhopari-vṛttasya*
*jagad-eka-śiromaṇeḥ*
*mahimā sambhaved eva*
*golokasyādhikādhikaḥ*

*vaikuṇṭha-upari* — above Vaikuṇṭha; *vṛttasya* — which is situated; *jagat* — of the worlds; *eka* — one; *śiraḥ-maṇeḥ* — of the crest jewel; *mahimā* — the glories; *sambhavet* — can be possible; *eva* — only; *golokasya* — of Goloka; *adhika-adhikaḥ* — superlative.

**Standing above Vaikuṇṭha, only Goloka, the unique crest jewel of all worlds, can show such superlative glories.**

COMMENTARY: Why is Goloka so glorious? Because it is the most perfect of all worlds. And why is that? Because Goloka is even higher than Vaikuṇṭha. Goloka stands above Vaikuṇṭha because its excellences surpass those of Vaikuṇṭha.

## TEXT 90

मर्त्यलोकान्तरस्थस्य मथुरागोकुलस्य च ।
माहात्म्यं सर्वतः श्रेष्ठमाश्चर्यं केन वर्ण्यताम् ॥

*martya-lokāntara-sthasya*
*mathurā-gokulasya ca*
*māhātmyaṁ sarvataḥ śreṣṭham*
*āścaryaṁ kena varṇyatām*

*martya-loka-antara* — within the material world; *sthasya* — which is situated; *mathurā* — in Mathurā district; *gokulasya* — of Gokula; *ca* — and; *māhātmyam* — the greatness; *sarvataḥ* — compared to everything; *śreṣṭham* — supreme; *āścaryam* — wonder; *kena* — by whom; *varṇyatām* — can be described.

**And the Gokula of the Mathurā district within the material world is again so supremely great that no one can properly describe its astonishing glories.**

COMMENTARY: Gokula, Goloka's direct expansion on earth, is also greater than Vaikuṇṭha.

## TEXT 91

शृणु कण्डूयते जिह्वा ममेयं चपला सखे ।
रत्नमुद्घाटयाम्यद्य हृन्मञ्जुषार्पितं चिरात् ॥

*śṛṇu kaṇḍūyate jihvā*
*mameyaṁ capalā sakhe*
*ratnam udghāṭayāmy adya*
*hṛn-mañjuṣārpitaṁ cirāt*

*śṛṇu* — please listen; *kaṇḍūyate* — is itching; *jihvā* — tongue; *mama* — my; *iyam* — this; *capalā* — unsteady; *sakhe* — O friend; *ratnam* — a jewel; *udghāṭayāmi* — I will uncover; *adya* — now; *hṛt* — of my heart; *mañjuṣā* — in the treasure chest; *arpitam* — kept; *cirāt* — for a long time.

**Please listen, dear friend. My unsteady tongue is itching to speak. I shall now uncover a jewel I have long kept stored in the treasure chest of my heart.**

COMMENTARY: Nārada considers his tongue too bold, but in fact such eagerness to glorify Kṛṣṇa is an admirable quality, in him or anyone else. Nārada, in any case, cannot check his tongue from disclosing more, and so he is going to describe something he has kept hidden in his heart for a long time. He has not discussed this with anyone before.

## TEXT 92

तत्तन्महाप्रेमविहारकामः
कस्मिन्नपि द्वापरकालशेषे ।
गोलोकनाथो भगवान्स कृष्णः
कृत्स्नांशपूर्णोऽवतरत्यमुष्मिन् ॥

*tat-tan-mahā-prema-vihāra-kāmaḥ*
*kasminn api dvāpara-kāla-śeṣe*
*goloka-nātho bhagavān sa kṛṣṇaḥ*
*kṛtsnāṁśa-pūrṇo 'vataraty amuṣmin*

*tat-tat* — various; *mahā* — most exalted; *prema* — in pure love; *vihāra* — pastimes; *kāmaḥ* — desiring; *kasmin api* — a certain; *api* — indeed; *dvāpara-kāla* — of a Dvāpara age; *śeṣe* — at the end; *goloka-nāthaḥ* — the Lord of Goloka; *bhagavān* — the Personality of Godhead; *saḥ* — He; *kṛṣṇaḥ* — Kṛṣṇa; *kṛtsna* — all; *aṁśa* — with His partial expansions; *pūrṇaḥ* — complete; *avatarati* — descends; *amuṣmin* — in that place (the district of Mathurā on earth).

**When the Personality of Godhead Kṛṣṇa, Lord of Goloka, wants to enjoy His various pastimes of the highest pure love, at the end of a certain Dvāpara age He descends to the material world in that special place. He descends complete with all His partial expansions.**

COMMENTARY: Beginning with this verse and continuing through Text 172, Nārada now describes the most confidential glories of Bhauma-vṛndāvana, Goloka's manifestation on earth. To prepare the grounds for establishing these glories, in texts 92 through 101 he first demonstrates the superexcellence of the Lord of that abode.

The current verse explains why and when Lord Golokanātha appears on earth in Mathurā Gokula. The reason He descends is to satisfy His own desires; He is eager to taste the pleasures of supercharged *prema*. And the time He descends is during the final earthly years of Dvāpara-yuga, the age that from its dawn to its dusk lasts 2,400 years of the demigods. But as we know from authoritative scriptures, Kṛṣṇa comes to earth not at the end of every Dvāpara-yuga but only during the twenty-eighth Dvāpara-yuga of the seventh *manv-antara* in a day of Brahmā.

## TEXTS 93–94

नानात्वमाप्तैरिव वर्तमानैः
सर्वैः स्वरूपैः सममद्वयः सन् ।
वैकुण्ठलोकादिकमाशु हित्वा
नित्यांश्च तत्रत्यपरिच्छदादीन् ॥

स्वपारमैश्वर्यमपि प्रसक्तं
दूरादुपेक्ष्य श्रियमप्यनन्याम् ।
अस्मादृशोऽनन्यगतींश्च भृत्यान्
सर्वाननादृत्य स याति तत्र ॥

*nānātvam āptair iva vartamānaiḥ*
*sarvaiḥ svarūpaiḥ samam advayaḥ san*
*vaikuṇṭha-lokādikam āśu hitvā*
*nityāṁś ca tatratya-paricchadādīn*

*sva-pāramaiśvaryam api prasaktaṁ*
*dūrād upekṣya śriyam apy ananyām*
*asmādṛśo 'nanya-gatīṁś ca bhṛtyān*
*sarvān anādṛtya sa yāti tatra*

*nānātvam* — variegatedness; *āptaiḥ* — which have obtained; *iva* — as if; *vartamānaiḥ* — present; *sarvaiḥ* — all; *svarūpaiḥ* — with His personal expansions; *samam* — equal; *advayaḥ* — nondifferent; *san* — being; *vaikuṇṭha-loka-ādikam* — Vaikuṇṭha-loka and so on; *āśu* — suddenly; *hitvā* — abandoning; *nityān* — eternal; *ca* — and; *tatratya* — belonging to that place; *paricchada-ādīn* — paraphernalia and associates; *sva* — His own; *pārama-aiśvaryam* — supreme power; *api* — even; *prasaktam* — devoted; *dūrāt* — far away; *upekṣya* — neglecting; *śriyam* — His opulence; *api* — also; *ananyām* — exclusive; *asmādṛśaḥ* — like us; *ananya* — no other; *gatīn* — whose goal; *ca* — and; *bhṛtyān* — servants; *sarvān* — all; *anādṛtya* — disregarding; *saḥ* — He; *yāti* — goes; *tatra* — there.

**Though the Lord's personal expansions assume many different appearances, the Lord is one with them all. And that Lord suddenly abandons Vaikuṇṭha and His other abodes, He abandons His things and His people of those abodes, and His own supreme power, and He leaves far behind His consort and servants like us, who are exclusively devoted to Him and have no other shelter. Neglecting us all, He goes to the material world.**

COMMENTARY: All the expansions of Viṣṇu are included within the original Godhead Kṛṣṇa. Thus when Kṛṣṇa descends to Mathurā Gokula in the material world He takes all His expansions with Him. They are nondifferent from Him, yet each of them also has His own individual identity.

As indicated by the word *-ādikam* ("and so on") in the phrase *vaikuṇṭha-lokādikam,* when Kṛṣṇa comes to earth He leaves aside all His other abodes, from Indra's heaven up to Vaikuṇṭha. He abandons His paraphernalia of those abodes — His ornaments, palaces, weapons, thrones. And as indicated by the second "and so on," in the phrase *tatratya-paricchadādīn,* He also leaves behind His servants and attendants. He loses interest in His innate powers like self-satisfied renunciation and puts them aside too. He even neglects the goddess Mahā-lakṣmī and His eternal associates, not inviting them to accompany Him even though they are exclusively devoted to Him.

## TEXT 95

अन्यैः सहान्यत्र न लभ्यते यल्
लब्धुं सुखं श्रीमथुराव्रजे तत् ।
तत्रत्यलोकैरुचितस्वभावैः
साकं यथेच्छं नितरां विहृत्य ॥

*anyaiḥ sahānyatra na labhyate yal*
*labdhuṁ sukhaṁ śrī-mathurā-vraje tat*
*tatratya-lokair ucita-svabhāvaiḥ*
*sākaṁ yathecchaṁ nitarāṁ vihṛtya*

*anyaiḥ* — others; *saha* — with; *anyatra* — elsewhere; *na labhyate* — cannot be obtained; *yat* — which; *labdhum* — to obtain; *sukham* — the happiness; *śrī-mathurā* — in Śrī Mathurā; *vraje* — of Vraja; *tat* — that; *tatratya* — belonging to that place; *lokaiḥ* — with the people; *ucita* — suitable; *svabhāvaiḥ* — whose natures; *sākam* — together; *yathā-iccham* — as He desires; *nitarām* — freely; *vihṛtya* — sporting.

**To enjoy a happiness unobtainable in any other company, He sports freely in the Vraja of Śrī Mathurā with its residents, who have natures exactly suited to His own.**

COMMENTARY: The purpose of Kṛṣṇa's descent was mentioned in Text 92 as His "wanting to enjoy His various pastimes of the highest pure love" (*tat-tan-mahā-prema-vihāra-kāmaḥ*). This is further elaborated upon in the current verse. The devotees of Vraja-bhūmi are able to satisfy Kṛṣṇa by joining Him in His favorite pastimes. Thus the earthly Gokula sometimes displays perfections not found even in Goloka in the spiritual sky.

## TEXT 96

तदातनानां दृढभक्तिभाग्य-
विशेषभाजां जगतां हि साक्षात् ।
दृश्यो भवेन्नूनमनन्यकाल-
प्रादुष्कृतेनात्मकृपाभरेण ॥

*tadātanānāṁ dṛḍha-bhakti-bhāgya-*
*viśeṣa-bhājāṁ jagatāṁ hi sākṣāt*
*dṛśyo bhaven nūnam ananya-kāla-*
*prāduṣkṛtenātma-kṛpā-bhareṇa*

*tadātanānām* — of that time; *dṛḍha* — firm; *bhakti* — of devotion; *bhāgya* — the good fortune; *viśeṣa* — exceptional; *bhājām* — who possess; *jagatām* — of the people of the universe; *hi* — indeed; *sākṣāt* — directly; *dṛśyaḥ* — visible; *bhavet* — becomes; *nūnam* — indeed; *ananya* — at no other; *kāla* — time; *prāduṣkṛtena* — revealed; *ātma* — His own; *kṛpā* — of the mercy; *bhareṇa* — by the abundance.

**By an abundance of His mercy never disclosed before, He then becomes directly visible to the people of the universe who have the exceptional good fortune of firm devotion for Him.**

## TEXT 97

अतो वैकुण्ठनाथस्य वैकुण्ठेऽपि कदाचन ।
दर्शनं नैव लभ्येत भवताप्यन्वभावि तत् ॥

*ato vaikuṇṭha-nāthasya*
*vaikuṇṭhe 'pi kadācana*
*darśanaṁ naiva labhyeta*
*bhavatāpy anvabhāvi tat*

*ataḥ* — therefore; *vaikuṇṭha-nāthasya* — of the Lord of Vaikuṇṭha; *vaikuṇṭhe* — in Vaikuṇṭha; *api* — even; *kadācana* — sometimes; *darśanam* — the sight; *na* — not; *eva* — indeed; *labhyeta* — is obtained; *bhavatā* — by you; *api* — indeed; *anvabhāvi* — has been experienced; *tat* — that.

**And so it is that sometimes the Lord of Vaikuṇṭha is not seen in Vaikuṇṭha. You have found this out for yourself.**

COMMENTARY: Sometimes Lord Nārāyaṇa sneaks away from His abode to visit the material world, as Gopa-kumāra discovered when staying in Vaikuṇṭha.

## TEXT 98

अत एवर्षयस्तत्तल्लोकवृत्तान्ततत्पराः ।
वैकुण्ठनायकं केचित्सहस्रशिरसं परे ॥

*ata evarṣayas tat-tal-*
*loka-vṛttānta-tatparāḥ*
*vaikuṇṭha-nāyakaṁ kecit*
*sahasra-śirasaṁ pare*

*ataḥ eva* — thus; *ṛṣayaḥ* — sages; *tat-tat* — of various; *loka* — worlds; *vṛttānta* — in the history; *tat-parāḥ* — engrossed; *vaikuṇṭha-nāyakam* — the master of Vaikuṇṭha; *kecit* — some; *sahasra-śirasam* — the thousand-headed Lord; *pare* — others.

**Sages concerned with the history of various worlds therefore describe Lord Kṛṣṇa in different ways. Some say He is the master of Vaikuṇṭha and others the thousand-headed Puruṣa.**

## TEXTS 99–100

नारायणं नरसखं केऽपि विष्णुं च केचन ।
क्षीरोदशायिनं त्वन्ये केशवं मथुरापुरे ॥

अवतीर्णं वदन्त्यार्याः स्वस्वमत्यनुसारतः ।
निर्णीतेश्वरमाहात्म्यमाधुर्याद्यवलोचनात् ॥

*nārāyaṇaṁ nara-sakhaṁ*
*ke 'pi viṣṇuṁ ca kecana*
*kṣīroda-śāyinaṁ tv anye*
*keśavaṁ mathurā-pure*

*avatīrṇaṁ vadanty āryāḥ*
*sva-sva-maty-anusārataḥ*
*nirṇīteśvara-māhātmya-*
*mādhuryādy-avalocanāt*

*nārāyaṇam* — Nārāyaṇa; *nara-sakham* — the friend of Nara; *ke api* — some; *viṣṇum* — Viṣṇu; *ca* — and; *kecana* — some; *kṣīra-uda* — in the Ocean of Milk; *śāyinam* — He who lies; *tu* — and; *anye* — others; *keśavam* — Keśava; *mathurā-pure* — in Mathurā City; *avatīrṇam* — descended; *vadanti* — say; *āryāḥ* — the followers of progressive Vedic culture; *sva-sva* — each their own; *mati-anusārataḥ* — according to the understandings; *nirṇīta* — ascertained; *īśvara* — of the Supreme Lord; *māhātmya* — the supremacy; *mādhurya* — sweetness; *ādi* — and so on; *avalocanāt* — by having studied.

**Some sages think that the Lord who has descended in Mathurā City is Lord Nārāyaṇa, the friend of Nara, others think Him Lord Viṣṇu, and yet others Lord Keśava, who lies in the Ocean of Milk. Thus the followers of progressive Vedic culture describe Kṛṣṇa's descent, each in accord with his own understanding, from what they have ascertained about the Lord's supremacy and His sweetness and His other qualities.**

COMMENTARY: The great sages of the Vedic culture are all individuals, each with his own spiritual realizations and opinions, which are reflected in the *mantras* of the *Vedas*. In the Vedic hymns we hear the sages' various understandings of who Kṛṣṇa is. In accordance with such statements as *kṛṣṇas tu bhagavān svayam*—"Kṛṣṇa is the original Personality of Godhead" (*Śrīmad-Bhāgavatam* 1.3.28)—some think that it is the Lord of Vaikuṇṭha who incarnates in Mathurā City. Others quote *sahasra-śirasaṁ brahma-lokādhiṣṭhātāram*—"The Lord with thousands of heads rules over the planet of Brahmā"—and identify Kṛṣṇa with the thousand-headed form of Lord Viṣṇu. Still others, following their reading of a verse from the Fourth Canto of the *Bhāgavatam* (4.1.59), consider Kṛṣṇa an incarnation of Nara-Nārāyaṇa, the sons of Dharma and Mūrti:

*tāv imau vai bhagavato*
*harer aṁśāv ihāgatau*
*bhāra-vyayāya ca bhuvaḥ*
*kṛṣṇau yadu-kurūdvahau*

"These two partial expansions of Nara and Nārāyaṇa, the Supreme Personality of Godhead, have now appeared in the dynasties of Yadu and Kuru in the forms of Kṛṣṇa and Arjuna to mitigate the burden of the world."

Yet other sages say that Kṛṣṇa is the same Lord Keśava who lies on the Ocean of Milk. They cite as evidence for their understanding the words of the *Bhāgavatam* (2.7.26) *sita-kṛṣṇa-keśaḥ,* which some commentators explain to mean that Lord Kṣīrodaka-śāyī Viṣṇu created Balarāma and Kṛṣṇa from two strands of His own hair, one white (*sita*) and the other black (*kṛṣṇa*). Lord Kṣīrodaka-śāyī Viṣṇu is called Keśava because His hair is especially beautiful. And the *Viṣṇu Purāṇa* (5.1.60) states more explicitly, *ujjahārātmanaḥ keśau sita-kṛṣṇau mahā-mune:* "O great sage, the Lord pulled out two of His own hairs, one white and one black." Śrīla Rūpa Gosvāmī, however, in his *Laghu-bhāgavatāmṛta* (1.5.155–164), gives the definitive understanding of these passages about the hairs. He says that Kṛṣṇa has beautiful black hair (*kṛṣṇa-keśa*), which is always nicely combed (*sita*). And since the Lord has an eternally youthful form, He never appears old enough to have white hairs.

Each sage, having focused his attention on a particular aspect of the Supreme Lord's glories, has realized a particular form of the Lord in meditation. So the sages naturally describe as having descended to earth as Kṛṣṇa the particular form of the Lord they have realized. Since all the expansions of Godhead, with their individual features, are included within Kṛṣṇa, technically there is no fault in saying that one of Kṛṣṇa's expansions has come to earth and become Kṛṣṇa. In effect, however, what all this indicates is that Kṛṣṇa is the Supreme Personality of Godhead and all other forms of God emanate from Him.

One might ask how these all-knowing sages can have so many differing opinions about Kṛṣṇa's identity. This is not difficult to explain: the sages speak according to their own realizations, and authorities discuss whichever aspect of the Supreme Lord they understand. But shouldn't such knowers of the revealed scriptures be able to understand the full reality as it is? Yes, but they are *āryas,* which can be understood to mean "men of simple intelligence"; the subtle logic that analyzes the identity of Kṛṣṇa is too difficult for them to comprehend. Or, taking the idea of simplicity a different way: the sages know very well the truth about Kṛṣṇa, but they express their views as they do because they assume, thinking simply, that glorifying any one of the Lord's incarnations glorifies all His incarnations.

## TEXT 101

किन्तु स्वयं स एव श्रीगोलोकेशो निजं पदम् ।
भूर्लोकस्थमपि क्रीडाविशेषैर्भूषयेत्सदा ॥

*kintu svayaṁ sa eva śrī-*
*golokeśo nijaṁ padam*
*bhūr-loka-stham api krīḍā-*
*viśeṣair bhūṣayet sadā*

*kintu* — but; *svayam* — Himself; *saḥ* — He; *eva* — indeed; *śrī-goloka-īśaḥ* — the divine Lord of Goloka; *nijam* — His own; *padam* — abode; *bhūḥ-loka* — on the earth; *stham* — situated; *api* — even; *krīḍā* — by pastimes; *viśeṣaiḥ* — special; *bhūṣayet* — adorns; *sadā* — perpetually.

**But in truth the divine Lord of Goloka eternally adorns His own abode upon the earth, enjoying His own unique pastimes.**

COMMENTARY: After mentioning several other opinions about Kṛṣṇa's appearance on earth, Nārada now states his own.

### TEXT 102

नात्र कोऽप्यस्ति भिन्नो यत्तत्रत्यजनवल्लभः ।
उद्धवस्त्वं च तत्रत्यस्तद्गोप्यं किञ्चिदुच्यते ॥

*nātra ko 'py asti bhinno yat*
*tatratya-jana-vallabhaḥ*
*uddhavas tvaṁ ca tatratyas*
*tad gopyaṁ kiñcid ucyate*

*na* — not; *atra* — here; *kaḥ api* — anyone; *asti* — there is; *bhinnaḥ* — alien; *yat* — who; *tatratya* — who belong to that place; *jana* — to the people; *vallabhaḥ* — beloved; *uddhavaḥ* — Uddhava; *tvam* — you; *ca* — and; *tatratyaḥ* — a resident of that place; *tat* — so; *gopyam* — confidential; *kiñcit* — something; *ucyate* — can be said.

**No one in this house is an outsider. Uddhava is very dear to the residents of Vraja, and you are from Vraja yourself. Therefore I can say something confidential.**

COMMENTARY: In the previous verse Nārada referred to the glories of the Lord of Goloka, and in the next verse he begins elaborating on the supreme opulence the Lord displays there. In Text 88 Nārada mentioned this topic briefly when he said "Indeed that world, I think, displays the complete essence of Lord Hari's most confidential Godhood." Nārada can speak freely in Uddhava's house because everyone present is fit to hear such topics. Everyone sitting there has the right kind of special love for the Personality of Godhead.

## TEXT 103

काष्ठाममुत्रैव परां प्रभोर्गता
स्फुटा विभूतिर्विविधा कृपालुता ।
सुरूपताशेषमहत्त्वमाधुरी
विलासलक्ष्मीरपि भक्तवश्यता ॥

*kāṣṭhām amutraiva paraṁ prabhor gatā*
*sphuṭā vibhūtir vividhā kṛpālutā*
*su-rūpatāśeṣa-mahattva-mādhurī*
*vilāsa-lakṣmīr api bhakta-vaśyatā*

*kāṣṭhām* — the limit; *amutra* — there; *eva* — only; *parām* — ultimate; *prabhoḥ* — of the Lord; *gatā* — achieved; *sphuṭā* — visibly; *vibhūtiḥ* — opulence; *vividhā* — various; *kṛpālutā* — compassion; *su-rūpatā* — beauty; *aśeṣa* — of all; *mahattva* — His glories; *mādhurī* — the sweetness; *vilāsa* — of His pastimes; *lakṣmīḥ* — the splendor; *api* — and; *bhakta-vaśyatā* — His subservience to His devotees.

**In that Vraja-bhūmi the Lord's opulences have visibly achieved their final perfection, and so also, in many various ways, have His mercy, His beauty, the sweetness of all His excellent qualities, the splendor of His pastimes, and His subservience to His devotees.**

## TEXT 104

व्रजः स नन्दस्य गुणैः स्वकीयैर्
विलासभूरास महाविभूतेः ।
यस्याः कटाक्षेण जगद्विभूतिर्
वैकुण्ठनाथस्य गृहेश्वरी या ॥

*vrajaḥ sa nandasya guṇaiḥ svakīyair*
*vilāsa-bhūr āsa mahā-vibhūteḥ*

*yasyāḥ kaṭākṣeṇa jagad-vibhūtir*
*vaikuṇṭha-nāthasya gṛheśvarī yā*

*vrajaḥ* — the pasture; *saḥ* — that; *nandasya* — of Nanda; *guṇaiḥ* — with its qualities; *svakīyaiḥ* — own; *vilāsa-bhūḥ* — the place of pastimes; *āsa* — has become; *mahā-vibhūteḥ* — of topmost opulence; *yasyāḥ* — of which (opulence); *kaṭa-akṣeṇa* — by the sidelong glance; *jagat* — of the material world; *vibhūtiḥ* — the opulence; *vaikuṇṭha-nāthasya* — of the Lord of Vaikuṇṭha; *gṛha-īśvarī* — the mistress of its household; *yā* — who.

**The pastures of Nanda Mahārāja, unique in their features, have become the land in which the Lord's highest opulence personally sports, the opulence whose mere sidelong glance creates all the glories of the material world and who serves as mistress of the household for the Lord of Vaikuṇṭha.**

COMMENTARY: Nārada now begins to explain in detail each feature of Kṛṣṇa's glories in Gokula. In this verse and the next, Nārada talks about Kṛṣṇa's godly opulence. So attractive is the land of Vraja, where the *gopas* headed by Nanda graze their cows, that the supreme goddess of fortune Mahā-lakṣmī has chosen it as the place of her pastimes. Even though her mere sidelong glance empowers the great controllers of the universe, beginning with Brahmā and Rudra, the gentle charms of Vraja attract her. And if Gokula's opulences enchant Mahā-lakṣmī, who enchants everyone in the material world, then those opulences must be much greater than those of Brahmā, Rudra, and all the demigods. Moreover, since the same Mahā-lakṣmī who comes to Vraja on earth is also the wife of the Lord of Vaikuṇṭha, the opulences of Vraja must be even greater than those of Vaikuṇṭha.

In Vaikuṇṭha, Lakṣmī has many responsibilities in the household of Lord Nārāyaṇa, but in Vraja she is free to enjoy herself all the time. So the opulences of Lakṣmī are most fully manifest in Vraja. As Śukadeva Gosvāmī describes in the Tenth Canto of *Śrīmad-Bhāgavatam* (10.5.18):

*tata ārabhya nandasya*
*vrajaḥ sarva-samṛddhimān*
*harer nivāsātma-guṇai*
*ramākrīḍam abhūn nṛpa*

"O Mahārāja Parīkṣit, the home of Nanda Mahārāja is eternally the abode of the Supreme Personality of Godhead and His transcendental qualities and is therefore always naturally endowed with the opulence of all wealth. Yet beginning from Lord Kṛṣṇa's appearance there, it became the place for the pastimes of the goddess of fortune."

## TEXT 105

यस्यैकवृक्षोऽपि निजेन केनचिद्
द्रव्येण कामांस्तनुतेऽर्थिनोऽखिलान् ।
तथापि तत्तन्न सदा प्रकाशयेद्
ऐश्वर्यमीशः स्वविहारविघ्नतः ॥

*yasyaika-vṛkṣo 'pi nijena kenacid*
*dravyeṇa kāmāṁs tanute 'rthino 'khilān*
*tathāpi tat tan na sadā prakāśayed*
*aiśvaryam īśaḥ sva-vihāra-vighnataḥ*

*yasya* — of which (Vraja-bhūmi); *eka* — one; *vṛkṣaḥ* — tree; *api* — even; *nijena* — own; *kenacit* — by its own; *dravyeṇa* — substances; *kāmān* — the desires; *tanute* — supplies; *arthinaḥ* — of one who has desires; *akhilān* — all; *tathā api* — nonetheless; *tat tat* — all those; *na* — not; *sadā* — always; *prakāśayet* — He displays; *aiśvaryam* — His power; *īśaḥ* — the Lord; *sva* — His; *vihāra* — to the pastimes; *vighnataḥ* — because of obstruction.

**In the land of Vraja any tree with any of its parts can fulfill all the desires of anyone who asks. Yet the Lord does not always display His opulences in Vraja, because that might obstruct the enjoyment of His pastimes.**

COMMENTARY: As a simple example of how opulent is the land of Vraja, even the trees there can satisfy all desires with a single fruit, a single flower, or any part of their bodies. In other words, a person who approaches those trees has his life's ambitions fulfilled. This is described in *Śrīmad-Bhāgavatam* (10.22.34) by the Personality of Godhead Himself:

*patra-puṣpa-phala-cchāyā-*
*mūla-valkala-dārubhiḥ*
*gandha-niryāsa-bhasmāsthi-*
*tokmaiḥ kāmān vitanvate*

"These trees fulfill one's desires with their leaves, flowers and fruits, their shade, roots, bark, and wood, and also with their fragrance, sap, ashes, pulp, and shoots."

If even the trees in Vraja display such wonderful powers, how could the opulences of Vraja be kept secret? And how then could Vraja be a suitable place for the Supreme Lord to enjoy pastimes as an ordinary person? Vraja is suitable because the Lord reveals those opulences only in select instances, when they are useful for His purposes. If there is no special need for them He keeps them hidden. Thus the opulences of Godhead are only occasionally seen in Vraja, though the Lord's charming pastimes as the darling of the cowherds are always visibly expanding.

## TEXT 106

सद्वेषमात्रेण हि बालघातिनीं
तां राक्षसीं मातृगतिं निनाय सः ।
तद्बान्धवान्मुक्तिमघासुरादिकान्
साधुद्रुहस्तादृशलीलयानयत् ॥

*sad-veṣa-mātreṇa hi bāla-ghātinīṁ*
*tāṁ rākṣasīṁ mātṛ-gatiṁ nināya saḥ*
*tad-bāndhavān muktim aghāsurādikān*
*sādhu-druhas tādṛśa-līlayānayat*

*sat* — of a respectable person; *veṣa* — because of the dress; *mātreṇa* — merely; *hi* — indeed; *bāla-ghātinīm* — the child-killer; *tām* — her; *rākṣasīm* — the demoness (Pūtanā); *mātṛ* — of a mother; *gatim* — to the destination; *nināya* — brought; *saḥ* — He; *tat* — her; *bāndhavān* — family members; *muktim* — to liberation; *agha-asura* — the demon Agha; *ādikān* — and so on; *sādhu* — of pious devotees; *druhaḥ* — enemies; *tādṛśa* — similar; *līlayā* — by pastimes; *anayat* — brought.

**Simply because Pūtanā, the child-killing demoness, disguised herself as a respectable person, the Lord bestowed upon her the destination of being His mother. By similar pastimes He also gave liberation to her family members — Aghāsura and others — even though they were enemies of the pious devotees.**

COMMENTARY: In these pastimes Kṛṣṇa demonstrates the extent of His kindness. Pūtanā dressed herself very nicely, so that Yaśodā and the other ladies of Vraja would accept her as one of them, a cultured Vaiṣṇava. This was enough to satisfy Kṛṣṇa, who, even though Pūtanā was a most wicked demon, arranged for her to achieve an auspicious destination equal to that of Mother Yaśodā. Uddhava therefore declared in *Śrīmad-Bhāgavatam* (3.2.23):

*aho bakī yaṁ stana-kāla-kūṭaṁ*
*jighāṁsayāpāyayad apy asādhvī*
*lebhe gatiṁ dhātry-ucitāṁ tato 'nyaṁ*
*kaṁ vā dayāluṁ śaraṇaṁ vrajema*

"Alas, how shall I take shelter of one more merciful than Him who granted the position of mother to a she-demon [Pūtanā] although she was unfaithful and she prepared deadly poison to be sucked from her breast?"

Not only Pūtanā but also many of her demon friends and relatives, like Agha, Baka, and Kaṁsa, were liberated simply by being drawn to Kṛṣṇa's supremely charming childhood pastimes.

As described by Lord Brahmā in his prayers to Kṛṣṇa:

*sad-veṣād iva pūtanāpi sa-kulā tvām eva devāpitā*
*yad-dhāmārtha-suhṛt-priyātma-tanaya-prāṇāśayās tvat-kṛte*

"You have already arranged to give Yourself to Pūtanā and her family members in exchange for her disguising herself as a devotee. So what is left for You to give these devotees of Vṛndāvana, whose homes, wealth, friends, dear relations, bodies, children, and very lives and hearts are all dedicated only to You?" (*Śrīmad-Bhāgavatam* 10.14.35)

## TEXT 107

गोदामवीथीभिरुदूखलाङ्घ्रौ
स्वस्योदरे बन्धनमाददेऽसौ ।
प्रोत्साहनेन व्रजयोषितां तन्
नृत्यादिकं तां च निदेशवर्तिताम् ॥

*go-dāma-vīthībhir udūkhalāṅghrau*
*svasyodare bandhanam ādade 'sau*
*protsāhanena vraja-yoṣitāṁ tan*
*nṛtyādikaṁ tāṁ ca nideśa-vartitām*

*go* — of cows; *dāma* — for tying; *vīthībhiḥ* — by ropes; *udūkhala* — of a grinding mortar; *aṅghrau* — to the base; *svasya* — His; *udare* — by the abdomen; *bandhanam* — the binding; *ādade* — accepting; *asau* — He; *protsāhanena* — as the way of enlivening; *vraja-yoṣitām* — the women of Vraja; *tat* — that; *nṛtya-ādikam* — dancing and so on; *tām* — that; *ca* — and; *nideśa* — according to orders; *vartitām* — the acting.

**He allowed His belly to be tied to the base of a grinding mortar with ropes for tying cows. And to enliven the women of Vraja, He danced, entertained them in other ways, and carried out their orders.**

COMMENTARY: In Text 103, when Nārada listed Kṛṣṇa's excellences in Vraja-bhūmi, he placed Kṛṣṇa's subservience to His devotees last, but here he takes the opportunity to elaborate on this topic out of sequence, since it closely bears on the topic of Kṛṣṇa's mercy.

When Mother Yaśodā wanted to punish Kṛṣṇa by tying Him up, she joined all the ropes available, including the ones used for tying the cows at milking, but still she could not make a rope long enough to bind her son:

*evaṁ sva-geha-dāmāni*
*yaśodā sandadhaty api*
*gopīnāṁ su-smayantīnāṁ*
*smayantī vismitābhavat*

"Thus Mother Yaśodā joined whatever ropes were available in the household, but still she failed in her attempt to bind Kṛṣṇa. Mother Yaśodā's friends, the elderly *gopīs* in the neighborhood, were smiling and enjoying the fun. Similarly, Mother Yaśodā, although laboring in that way, was also smiling. All of them were struck with wonder." (*Bhāgavatam* 10.9.17)

Finally Kṛṣṇa agreed to let Himself be tied to the same grinding mortar He had climbed on to steal butter. In *Śrīmad-Bhāgavatam* (10.9.18–19) Śrī Śukadeva Gosvāmī narrates:

*sva-mātuḥ svinna-gātrāyā*
*visrasta-kabara-srajaḥ*
*dṛṣṭvā pariśramaṁ kṛṣṇaḥ*
*kṛpayāsīt sva-bandhane*

*evaṁ sandarśitā hy aṅga*
*hariṇā bhṛtya-vaśyatā*
*sva-vaśenāpi kṛṣṇena*
*yasyedaṁ seśvaraṁ vaśe*

"Because of Mother Yaśodā's hard labor, her whole body became covered with perspiration, and the flowers and comb were falling from her hair. When child Kṛṣṇa saw His mother thus fatigued, He became merciful to her and agreed to be bound. O Mahārāja Parīkṣit, this entire universe, with its great, exalted demigods like Lord Śiva, Lord Brahmā, and Lord Indra, is under the control of the Supreme Personality of Godhead. Yet the Supreme Lord has one special transcendental attribute: He comes under the control of His devotees. This was now exhibited by Kṛṣṇa in this pastime."

The ladies of Vraja delighted in witnessing these pastimes, and Kṛṣṇa further encouraged their love for Him by performing antics for their pleasure and by submitting to their commands. This too is described by Śukadeva Gosvāmī:

*gopībhiḥ stobhito nṛtyan*
*bhagavān bāla-vat kvacit*
*udgāyati kvacin mugdhas*
*tad-vaśo dāru-yantra-vat*

"The *gopīs* would say, 'If You dance, my dear Kṛṣṇa, then I shall give You half a sweetmeat.' By saying these words or by clapping their hands, all the *gopīs* encouraged Kṛṣṇa in different ways. At such times, although He was the supremely powerful Personality of Godhead, He would smile and dance according to their desire, as if He were a wooden doll in their hands. Sometimes He would sing very loudly, at their bidding. In this way, Kṛṣṇa came completely under the control of the *gopīs*.

*bibharti kvacid ājñaptaḥ*
*pīṭhakonmāna-pādukam*
*bāhu-kṣepaṁ ca kurute*
*svānāṁ ca prītim udvahan*

"Sometimes Mother Yaśodā and her *gopī* friends would tell Kṛṣṇa, 'Bring this article' or 'Bring that article.' Sometimes they would order Him to bring a wooden plank, wooden shoes, or a wooden measuring pot, and Kṛṣṇa, when thus ordered by the mothers, would try to bring them. Sometimes, however, as if unable to raise these things, He would touch them and stand there. Just to invite the pleasure of His relatives, He would strike His body with His arms to show that He had sufficient strength.

*darśayaṁs tad-vidāṁ loka*
*ātmano bhakta-vaśyatām*
*vrajasyovāha vai harṣaṁ*
*bhagavān bāla-ceṣṭitaiḥ*

"To pure devotees throughout the world who could understand His activities, the Supreme Personality of Godhead, Kṛṣṇa, exhibited how much He can be subdued by His devotees, His servants. In this way He increased the pleasure of the Vraja-vāsīs by His childhood activities." (*Bhāgavatam* 10.11.7–9)

By these pastimes Lord Kṛṣṇa sent a clear message to the *jñānīs* who think they know Him very well as the Absolute Truth: "To achieve Me through the process of knowledge is not at all easy. Only by *bhakti* am I readily obtained."

## TEXT 108

रूपस्य तस्य महिमानमलं न कोऽपि
वक्तुं तथापि कथयामि यथात्मशक्ति ।
तस्यापि विस्मयकरं यदुदीक्ष्य भावं
तं गोद्विजद्रुमलतातरवोऽप्यगच्छन् ॥

*rūpasya tasya mahimānam alaṁ na ko 'pi*
*vaktuṁ tathāpi kathayāmi yathātma-śakti*
*tasyāpi vismaya-karaṁ yad udīkṣya bhāvaṁ*
*taṁ go-dvija-druma-latā-taravo 'py agacchan*

*rūpasya* — of the beauty; *tasya* — His; *mahimānam* — the glories; *alam* — capable; *na kaḥ api* — no one; *vaktum* — to describe; *tathā api* — nonetheless; *kathayāmi* — I speak; *yathā* — as far as; *ātma-śakti* — my power; *tasya* — to Him; *api* — even; *vismaya* — amazement; *karam* — causing; *yat* — which; *udīkṣya* — seeing; *bhāvam* — ecstasy; *tam* — that; *go* — the cows; *dvija*

— birds; *druma* — bushes; *latā* — creepers; *taravaḥ* — trees; *api* — and; *agacchan* — attained.

**No one can describe the glories of His beauty, but still I shall speak about them as far as I am able. His beauty amazes even Him. Seeing Him, the cows, birds, bushes, creepers, and trees all became ecstatic.**

COMMENTARY: Beauty is next in the list of the Supreme Lord's opulences in Gokula. In texts 108 through 111, Nārada speaks of that beauty. Because the beauty Kṛṣṇa showed during His appearance in Vṛndāvana had never before been seen in this world, no one was able to explain it in terms of previous experience. Uddhava describes that astounding beauty in the Third Canto of *Śrīmad-Bhāgavatam* (3.2.12):

*yan martya-līlaupayikaṁ sva-yoga-*
*māyā-balaṁ darśayatā gṛhītam*
*vismāpanaṁ svasya ca saubhagarddheḥ*
*paraṁ padaṁ bhūṣaṇa-bhūṣaṇāṅgam*

"Lord Krsna in His eternal form, just suitable for His pastimes, appeared in the mortal world by His internal potency, Yogamāyā. His pastimes were wonderful for everyone, even for those proud of their own opulence, including Kṛṣṇa Himself in His form as the Lord of Vaikuṇṭha. Thus Śrī Kṛṣṇa's transcendental body is the ornament of all ornaments."

Upon seeing Kṛṣṇa, the moving and nonmoving creatures of Vṛndāvana would show the symptoms of *prema,* including the *sāttvika* ecstasies of horripilation, floods of tears, and so on. As the young *gopīs* told Kṛṣṇa at the beginning of their *rāsa-līlā:*

*kā stry aṅga te kala-padāyata-veṇu-gīta-*
*sammohitārya-caritān na calet tri-lokyām*
*trailokya-saubhagam idaṁ ca nirīkṣya rūpaṁ*
*yad go-dvija-druma-mṛgāḥ pulakāny abibhran*

"Dear Kṛṣṇa, what woman in all the three worlds wouldn't deviate from religious behavior when bewildered by the sweet, drawn-out melody of Your flute? Your beauty makes all three worlds auspicious. Indeed, even the cows, birds, trees, and deer manifest the ecstatic symptom of bodily hair standing on end when they see Your beautiful form." (*Bhāgavatam* 10.29.40)

## TEXT 109

यत्तात तासामपि धैर्यमोषकं
या वै कुलस्त्रीकुलपूजिताङ्घ्रयः ।
रूपेण शीलेन गुणेन कर्मणा
श्रैष्ठ्यं गता हन्त महाश्रियोऽपि याः ॥

*yat tāta tāsām api dhairya-moṣakaṁ*
*yā vai kula-strī-kula-pūjitāṅghrayaḥ*
*rūpeṇa śīlena guṇena karmaṇā*
*śraiṣṭhyaṁ gatā hanta mahā-śriyo 'pi yāḥ*

*yat* — which (beauty); *tāta* — my dear boy; *tāsām* — of those women; *api* — also; *dhairya* — of the soberness; *moṣakam* — the robber; *yāḥ* — who; *vai* — indeed; *kula* — of respectable families; *strī-kula* — by hordes of women; *pūjita* — worshipable; *aṅghrayaḥ* — whose feet; *rūpeṇa* — by their beauty; *śīlena* — by their behavior; *guṇena* — by their virtues; *karmaṇā* — by their activities; *śraiṣṭhyam gatā* — excelling; *hanta* — oh; *mahā-śriyaḥ* — the supreme goddess of fortune; *api* — even; *yāḥ* — who.

**My dear boy, in beauty, character, virtues, and behavior the women of Vraja excelled even the supreme goddess of fortune. All women of respectable families worshiped their feet. Yet even so, Kṛṣṇa's beauty robbed the women of Vraja of their sobriety.**

COMMENTARY: To inspire Gopa-kumāra to listen carefully to

this important narration, Nārada here uses the affectionate word *tāta* ("my dear boy").

Kṛṣṇa's beauty shook the *gopīs'* determination to uphold their religious principles, but not because the *gopīs* were simply women, who by nature are supposedly unsteady. The *gopīs* of Vraja were reputable cultured ladies in a respectable society, so they were not inclined to careless behavior. They were equal to Lakṣmī, the best of women, and even better: They were more beautiful, and more sublime in their gravity and shyness, they were more capable of making proper decisions, maintaining firm determination, and expertly dealing with all kinds of situations, and they were more competent in the various activities of worshiping their beloved. Nārada therefore uses the interjection *hanta* ("indeed") to express his surprise and delight.

## TEXT 110

यद्दर्शने पक्ष्मकृतं शपन्ति
विधिं सहस्राक्षमपि स्तुवन्ति ।
वाञ्छन्ति दृक्त्वं सकलेन्द्रियाणां
कां कां दशां वा न भजन्ति लोकाः ॥

*yad-darśane pakṣma-kṛtaṁ śapanti*
*vidhiṁ sahasrākṣam api stuvanti*
*vāñchanti dṛktvaṁ sakalendriyāṇāṁ*
*kāṁ kāṁ daśāṁ vā na bhajanti lokāḥ*

*yat* — which (beauty); *darśane* — while seeing; *pakṣma* — of eyelids; *kṛtam* — the creator; *śapanti* — they curse; *vidhim* — Brahmā; *sahasra-akṣam* — the thousand-eyed (Indra); *api* — and; *stuvanti* — they praise; *vāñchanti* — they hanker for; *dṛktvam* — the power of seeing; *sakala* — on the part of all; *indriyāṇām* — the senses; *kām kām* — which various; *daśām* — states; *vā* — and; *na bhajanti* — they would not achieve; *lokāḥ* — the people.

**Seeing His beauty, people would curse Brahmā, the creator of eyelids, and praise Indra, who has a thousand eyes, and hanker for all their senses to become eyes. What extraordinary states would anyone not attain upon seeing His beauty?**

COMMENTARY: Śrī Gopāladeva's beauty not only stole the sobriety of the *gopīs,* His dearmost girlfriends, but also drove other people to extraordinary states of consciousness. The Vraja-vāsīs cursed Brahmā for creating lids on their eyes that made it more difficult to see Kṛṣṇa constantly. And even though Indra had committed many offenses against Kṛṣṇa and was deformed because of Gautama Ṛṣi's curse, the Vraja-vāsīs glorified him, for they admired his having a thousand eyes on his body, eyes with which he could enjoy seeing Kṛṣṇa that much more. The Vraja-vāsīs prayed that all their own senses change into eyes so that with those eyes they could see Kṛṣṇa even more and no competing senses would distract their eyes from the sight of Kṛṣṇa's beauty.

## TEXT 111

किं वर्ण्यतां व्रजभुवो महिमा स तस्या
यत्रैव तत्स भगवान्वितनोति रूपम् ।
यत्तादृशप्रकृतिनाप्यमुना समेता
नान्यत्रिका दधति भावमिमेऽपि तद्वत् ॥

*kiṁ varṇyatāṁ vraja-bhuvo mahimā sa tasyā*
*yatraiva tat sa bhagavān vitanoti rūpam*
*yat tādṛśa-prakṛtināpy amunā sametā*
*nānyatrikā dadhati bhāvam ime 'pi tadvat*

*kim* — how; *varṇyatām* — can be described; *vraja-bhuvaḥ* — of Vraja-bhūmi; *mahimā* — glories; *saḥ* — those; *tasyāḥ* — of it (Vraja); *yatra* — where; *eva* — only; *tat* — that (beauty); *saḥ* — He; *bhagavān* — the Personality of Godhead; *vitanoti* — expands; *rūpam* — beauty; *yat* — which (glories and beauty);

*tādṛśa* — same; *prakṛtinā* — who has the nature; *api* — although; *amunā* — of Him; *sametāḥ* — in the company; *na* — do not; *anyatrikāḥ* — persons of other places; *dadhati* — have; *bhāvam* — ecstasy; *ime* — they; *api* — even; *tadvat* — such.

**How can I describe the greatness of the land of Vraja, where the Personality of Godhead displayed His own beautiful form? He may possess the same transcendental nature everywhere, but even in His company the devotees in other places don't feel the same ecstasy.**

COMMENTARY: The beauty Śrī Kṛṣṇa displays in Vraja-bhūmi is never seen anywhere else. No matter where He goes His transcendental nature is changeless, and He is always the same person; but devotees in other places, like Vaikuṇṭha and Dvārakā, do not taste from seeing Him and being with Him the same exquisite feelings of love as the Vraja-vāsīs. Thus we should understand that the Personality of Godhead reveals selected aspects of His special greatness in particular times and places — and Vraja-bhūmi is supremely glorious. For one reason or another, Kṛṣṇa chooses in some instances to show His eternal glories and in others to allow His personal energies to conceal them. Nārada's sentiment to this effect was closely paralleled by the words Gopa-kumāra had earlier heard on Janaloka from Pippalāyana Ṛṣi:

*ānandaka-svabhāvo 'pi*
*bhakti-māhātmya-darśanāt*
*bhaktān harṣayituṁ kuryād*
*durghaṭaṁ ca sa īśvaraḥ*

"The Supreme Lord, by nature the bestower of ecstasy, creates such unlikely situations to delight His devotees by showing them the greatness of devotional service." (*Bṛhad-bhāgavatāmṛta* 2.2.100)

Nārada has now concluded his description of Kṛṣṇa's special beauty in Vṛndāvana.

### TEXT 112

वयश्च तच्छैशवशोभयाश्रितं
सदा तथा यौवनलीलयादृतम् ।
मनोज्ञकैशोरदशावलम्बितं
प्रतिक्षणं नूतननूतनं गुणैः ॥

*vayaś ca tac chaiśava-śobhayāśritaṁ*
*sadā tathā yauvana-līlayādṛtam*
*manojña-kaiśora-daśāvalambitaṁ*
*prati-kṣaṇaṁ nūtana-nūtanaṁ guṇaiḥ*

*vayaḥ* — age; *ca* — and; *tat* — that; *śaiśava* — of childhood (the *kaumāra* age); *śobhayā* — by the charm; *āśritam* — sheltered; *sadā* — always; *tathā* — also; *yauvana* — of mature youth; *līlayā* — by the pastimes; *ādṛtam* — honored; *manojña* — attractive; *kaiśora-daśā* — adolescence; *avalambitam* — partaking of; *prati-kṣaṇam* — at every moment; *nūtana-nūtanam* — newer and newer; *guṇaiḥ* — by His qualities.

**Whatever age He appears to be, He always maintains the special charm of childhood, He accepts service from the pastimes of mature youth, and He also partakes of the attractiveness of adolescence. And at every moment His personal qualities appear newer and newer.**

COMMENTARY: Since youth is a cause of beauty, Nārada now takes the liberty to discuss the variety of ages in which Kṛṣṇa performs His pastimes. No matter how old Kṛṣṇa may be, He always has the special qualities of childhood — extreme gentleness, naughty behavior, absence of facial hair, and so on. Still, Kṛṣṇa is always clever and skillful like a mature young adult, and yet He always displays the qualities of a fifteen-year-old adolescent. With such an extraordinary combination of attractive features from all stages of young life, Kṛṣṇa enchants His devotees more and more at every moment. Thus, attraction to Kṛṣṇa never becomes stale, and those who see Him are never satiated.

Although Nārada here mentions mature youth (*yauvana*), Krsna doesn't appear in that age until after He leaves Vraja. In Vraja Kṛṣṇa appears in three ages — *kaumāra* (from birth till the end of the fifth year), *paugaṇḍa* (after five years up to the end of the tenth), and *kaiśora* (after ten years until the end of the fifteenth). In both of the two earlier ages, He performs pastimes more appropriate to the later, *kaiśora* age, and then, after killing the demon Keśī, He actually enters that age. For this reason, and because Nārada is particularly attracted to Kṛṣṇa at the *kaiśora* age, Nārada especially describes it.

## TEXT 113

यद्यन्न पूर्वं कृतमस्ति केनचित्
स्वयं च तेनापि कथञ्चन क्वचित् ।
तत्तत्कृतं सुन्दरबाल्यचेष्टया
तत्र व्रजे यच्च पुरास दुष्करम् ॥

*yad yan na pūrvaṁ kṛtam asti kenacit*
*svayaṁ ca tenāpi kathañcana kvacit*
*tat tat kṛtaṁ sundara-bālya-ceṣṭayā*
*tatra vraje yac ca purāsa duṣkaram*

*yat yat* — what various things; *na* — not; *pūrvam* — before; *kṛtam* — done; *asti* — were; *kenacit* — by anyone; *svayam* — Himself; *ca* — and; *tena* — by Him; *api* — even; *kathañcana* — in any way; *kvacit* — anywhere; *tat tat* — all that; *kṛtam* — done; *sundara* — beautiful; *bālya* — of childhood; *ceṣṭayā* — by His activity; *tatra* — there; *vraje* — in Vraja; *yat* — which; *ca* — and; *purā* — previously; *āsa* — was; *duṣkaram* — impossible to do.

**What no one before had ever done, what He Himself had never done under any pretext or in any circumstance, and what till then had been impossible for anyone — all this He did in Vraja during His all-attractive childhood pastimes.**

COMMENTARY: Of the topics listed in Text 103, two remain to be discussed: *aśeṣa-mahattva-mādhurī* ("the sweetness of all His excellent qualities") and *vilāsa-lakṣmī* ("the splendor of His pastimes"). Following the principle of *madhureṇa samāpayet* ("One should end on a sweet note"), Śrīla Sanātana prefers to save his description of *aśeṣa-mahattva-mādhurī* for last. Thus he now enters the topic of *vilāsa-lakṣmī*.

No person of the material world, not even Lord Brahmā, Rudra, or any demigod, has ever done anything similar to the wonderful deeds Kṛṣṇa performed in Vṛndāvana. Not even the Supreme Lord's other incarnations, including Śrī Nṛsiṁhadeva and Śrī Rāmacandra, have pastimes that can compare to Kṛṣṇa's. In Vaikuṇṭha the Supreme Lord has never enacted these pastimes or even tried to make a show of imitating them. Before the Lord unveiled in Vṛndāvana His all-attractive childhood activities, He never so easily killed demons and distributed His pure devotional service.

## TEXT 114

तत्तद्विनोदामृतसागरान्तरं
बिभेत्यलं मे रसनावगाहितुम् ।
सदैव तत्तन्मधुरप्रियापि यत्
कर्मण्यशक्ये न जनः प्रवर्तते ॥

*tat-tad-vinodāmṛta-sāgarāntaraṁ*
*bibhety alaṁ me rasanāvagāhitum*
*sadaiva tat-tan-madhura-priyāpi yat*
*karmaṇy aśakye na janaḥ pravartate*

*tat-tat* — all those; *vinoda* — of the pastimes; *amṛta* — of the nectar; *sāgara* — the ocean; *antaram* — within; *bibheti* — is afraid; *alam* — alas; *me* — my; *rasanā* — tongue; *avagāhitum* — to delve deeply; *sadā* — always; *eva* — indeed; *tat-tat* — of those (pastimes); *madhura* — to the sweetness; *priyā* — fondly disposed; *api* — although; *yat* — which; *karmaṇi* — in an activity; *aśakye* — impossible; *na* — not; *janaḥ* — a person; *pravartate* — proceeds.

**All those pastimes are an ocean of nectar, and though my tongue is always eager to relish their sweetness, it is terrified of drowning in them. A person should never proceed with something impossible.**

COMMENTARY: Here Nārada shifts the blame for his rash eagerness to his uncontrollable tongue, but in fact the greed to relish the *rasa* of Kṛṣṇa's *vṛndāvana-līlā* is his own. Nārada may think that his tongue is fearful of saying too much, either because it is incapable of speaking properly or because it is embarrassed to speak in front of others. Either way, in fact it would be perfectly proper for his tongue to drown in the nectar ocean of Kṛṣṇa's pastimes. Nārada's speech is but poetic irony. His tongue is not at all ashamed of what it is about to do.

## TEXT 115

पीतं सकृत्कर्णपुटेन तत्तल्-
लीलामृतं कस्य हरेन्न चेतः ।
प्रवर्तितुं वाञ्छति तत्र तस्माल्
लज्जां न रक्षेत्किल लोलता हि ॥

*pītaṁ sakṛt karṇa-puṭena tat-tal-*
*līlāmṛtaṁ kasya haren na cetaḥ*
*pravartituṁ vāñchati tatra tasmāl*
*lajjāṁ na rakṣet kila lolatā hi*

*pītam* — drunk; *sakṛt* — just once; *karṇa-puṭena* — by the earholes; *tat-tat* — of those various; *līlā* — pastimes; *amṛtam* — the nectar; *kasya* — whose; *haret na* — fails to steal; *cetaḥ* — mind; *pravartitum* — to proceed; *vāñchati* — it wants; *tatra* — there; *tasmāt* — therefore; *lajjām* — humility; *na rakṣet* — will not maintain; *kila* — indeed; *lolatā* — restlessness; *hi* — certainly.

**Whose heart would not be stolen when he has drunk even once through his earholes the nectar of all those pastimes? My tongue therefore wants to proceed. And its restlessness no longer lets me maintain my shyness.**

TEXT 116

त्रैमासिको यः शकटं बभञ्ज
स्थूलं शयानो मृदुना पदेन ।
स्तन्याय रोदित्युत यः प्रसूं द्वि-
वारौ मुखे दर्शयति स्म विश्वम् ॥

*trai-māsiko yaḥ śakaṭaṁ babhañja*
*sthūlaṁ śayāno mṛdunā padena*
*stanyāya rodity uta yaḥ prasūṁ dvi-*
*vārau mukhe darśayati sma viśvam*

*trai-māsikaḥ* — three months old; *yaḥ* — who; *śakaṭam* — a cart; *babhañja* — broke; *sthūlam* — large; *śayānaḥ* — lying; *mṛdunā* — tender; *padena* — with His foot; *stanyāya* — for breast milk; *roditi* — cried; *uta* — and then; *yaḥ* — who; *prasūm* — to His mother; *dvi-vārau* — two times; *mukhe* — in His mouth; *darśayati sma* — showed; *viśvam* — the universe.

**At the age of three months, Kṛṣṇa lay under a large cart and broke it with His tender foot, and then He cried for breast milk. On two occasions He showed His mother the whole universe within His mouth.**

COMMENTARY: In texts 116 through 137, Nārada summarizes many of the pastimes of Kṛṣṇa described in the Tenth Canto of *Śrīmad-Bhāgavatam*. Anyone who wants more details about these pastimes can consult that greatest of scriptures.

The first major pastime, the deliverance of Pūtanā, Nārada has already mentioned while glorifying Kṛṣṇa's merciful nature. The summary begins, therefore, with the breaking of the cart. The cart that infant Kṛṣṇa was lying under was a large one, as indicated here by the word *sthūlam.* As Śukadeva Gosvāmī describes, it was so big that several strong cowherd men were needed to lift it up again after Kṛṣṇa had knocked it down:

*pūrva-vat sthāpitaṁ gopair*
*balibhiḥ sa-paricchadam*

"The strong, stout cowherd men assembled the pots and paraphernalia on the handcart and set it up as before." (*Bhāgavatam* 10.7.12)

After His miraculous deed of knocking down the cart, Kṛṣṇa cried for His mother to come and feed Him her milk. It is amazing to contemplate that a person with such unequaled power can also cry for His mother's breast milk. And from another point of view, it is amazing also that Kṛṣṇa dared ask His mother for milk after destroying the cart that was virtually the most valuable possession of the household. Baby Kṛṣṇa twice showed Mother Yaśodā the universe within His mouth: once while drinking from her breast and again after she accused Him of eating dirt. How much more amazing it is, then, that a person who can perform such miracles can also cry for His mother's milk.

Although after the killing of the Tṛṇāvarta demon Mother Yaśodā had visions of the universal form within Kṛṣṇa's mouth on two different occasions, they are mentioned together in this verse to highlight how wonderful it is that this powerful Kṛṣṇa was crying helplessly for milk. Kṛṣṇa's Gokula Vṛndāvana pastimes are supremely splendid and charming because they combine the ultimate display of God's power with the ultimate display of His sweetness.

## TEXT 117

या सा तृणावर्तवधेन लीला
तस्याथ या रिङ्गणभङ्गिकाभिः ।
त्वां पातु गोपीगणतोषणाय
कृता च या गोरसमोषणेन ॥

*yā sā tṛṇāvarta-vadhena līlā*
*tasyātha yā riṅgaṇa-bhaṅgikābhiḥ*
*tvāṁ pātu gopī-gaṇa-toṣaṇāya*
*kṛtā ca yā go-rasa-moṣaṇena*

*yā* — which; *sā* — that; *tṛṇāvarta-vadhena* — by the killing of Tṛṇāvarta; *līlā* — pastime; *tasya* — His; *atha* — and; *yā* — which; *riṅgaṇa* — of crawling; *bhaṅgikābhiḥ* — by the charming sports; *tvām* — you; *pātu* — may it protect; *gopī-gaṇa* — of the *gopīs; toṣaṇāya* — for the satisfaction; *kṛtā* — done; *ca* — and; *yā* — which; *go-rasa* — of milk products; *moṣaṇena* — by the stealing.

**May you be protected by His pastimes of killing Tṛṇāvarta and crawling around in charming ways and stealing butter and yogurt to satisfy the gopīs.**

COMMENTARY: The pronouns *yā sā* ("those very same") imply that these pastimes are extremely famous, extremely amazing, and extremely attractive. Śrī Nārada prays that these pastimes protect Gopa-kumāra — protect him from all kinds of fear, and perhaps from becoming too bewildered by the ecstasy that arises from hearing the pastimes of Kṛṣṇa's infancy.

Nārada Muni's presentation now focuses on the sweetness of Kṛṣṇa's pastimes in Vṛndāvana. He skips mentioning pastimes that do not highlight this sweetness, such as the name-giving ceremony performed by Garga Ṛṣi. Kṛṣṇa did not do anything special in that pastime, in which Garga told Nanda and Yaśodā of Kṛṣṇa's glories.

## TEXT 118

गोपीगणाक्रोशनतो जनन्याः
साक्षाद्भयालोकनचातुरी सा ।
मां पातु मृद्भक्षणकौतुकं तत्
क्रीडा च मातुर्दधिमन्थने सा ॥

*gopī-gaṇākrośanato jananyāḥ*
*sākṣād-bhayālokana-cāturī sā*
*māṁ pātu mṛd-bhakṣaṇa-kautukaṁ tat*
*krīḍā ca mātur dadhi-manthane sā*

*gopī-gaṇa* — of the *gopīs; ākrośanataḥ* — because of the complaints; *jananyāḥ* — at his mother; *sākṣāt* — directly; *bhaya* — fearful; *ālokana* — of glancing; *cāturī* — cleverness; *sā* — that; *mām* — me; *pātu* — may it protect; *mṛt-bhakṣaṇa* — of eating dirt; *kautukam* — entertainment; *tat* — that; *krīḍā* — games; *ca* — and; *mātuḥ* — by His mother; *dadhi* — of yogurt; *manthane* — during the churning; *sā* — those.

**May I be protected by the clever glances He cast at His mother in apparent fear when the gopīs complained to her, by the delight He showed in eating dirt, and by the games He played while His mother churned yogurt.**

COMMENTARY: Like an ordinary child, Kṛṣṇa exposed His fear by glancing quickly from side to side. Śrī Nārada has already described that when Mother Yaśodā rebuked Kṛṣṇa for eating dirt, He showed her the universe within His mouth. After that pastime, *Śrīmad-Bhāgavatam* continues with a glorification of Nanda and Yaśodā's good fortune, but in that narration Kṛṣṇa is not active, so Nārada does not refer to it. Next comes the all-auspicious *dāmodara-līlā,* described in this and the following two texts. Nārada did mention this pastime earlier, but only briefly to help illustrate how Kṛṣṇa submits Himself to the control of His devotees.

While Mother Yaśodā churned yogurt, baby Kṛṣṇa would play such pranks as holding on to the churning rod.

## TEXT 119

तद्रोदनं तद्दधिभाण्डभञ्जनं
तच्छिक्यपात्रान्नवनीतमोषणम् ।

तन्मातृभीतिद्रवणं भयाकुला-
लोकेक्षणत्वं च महाद्भुतं प्रभोः ॥

*tad rodanaṁ tad dadhi-bhāṇḍa-bhañjanaṁ*
*tac chikya-pātrān nava-nīta-moṣaṇam*
*tan mātṛ-bhīti-dravaṇaṁ bhayākulā-*
*lokekṣaṇatvaṁ ca mahādbhutaṁ prabhoḥ*

*tat* — that; *rodanam* — crying; *tat* — that; *dadhi-bhāṇḍa* — of yogurt pots; *bhañjanam* — breaking; *tat* — that; *śikya* — on ropes suspended from the ceiling; *pātrāt* — from vessels; *nava-nīta* — of newly churned butter; *moṣaṇam* — stealing; *tat* — that; *mātṛ* — of His mother; *bhīti* — in fear; *dravaṇam* — running; *bhaya* — with fear; *ākula* — distraught; *āloka* — look; *īkṣaṇatvam* — in whose eyes; *ca* — and; *mahā-adbhutam* — very wonderful; *prabhoḥ* — of the Lord.

**The Lord's crying, His breaking the yogurt pots, His stealing fresh butter from storage pots hanging from the ceiling, His running away in fear of His mother, and His restlessly looking about with fear in His eyes are all very wonderful.**

## TEXT 120

आकर्षणं यत्तदुलूखलस्य
बद्धस्य पाशैर्जठरे जनन्या ।
चेतो हरेन्मेऽर्जुनभञ्जनं तत्
तस्यां दशायां च वरप्रदानम् ॥

*ākarṣaṇaṁ yat tad ulūkhalasya*
*baddhasya pāśair jaṭhare jananyā*
*ceto haren me 'rjuna-bhañjanaṁ tat*
*tasyāṁ daśāyāṁ ca vara-pradānam*

*ākarṣaṇam* — dragging; *yat* — which; *tat* — that; *ulūkhalasya* — of the grinding mortar; *baddhasya* — who was bound; *pāśaiḥ*

— by ropes; *jaṭhare* — to His belly; *jananyā* — by His mother; *cetaḥ* — the mind; *haret* — may it steal; *me* — my; *arjuna* — of the *arjuna* trees; *bhañjanam* — breaking; *tat* — that; *tasyām* — in that; *daśāyām* — condition; *ca* — and; *vara* — of a benediction; *pradānam* — bestowing.

**May my mind be enchanted by His dragging the mortar to which His mother had tied Him with ropes around His belly, by His felling the arjuna trees, and by His bestowing a benediction even while tied in that way.**

COMMENTARY: While still bound tightly to the mortar with the strong ropes used to bind cows, Kṛṣṇa graciously blessed the reformed sons of Kuvera:

*tad gacchataṁ mat-paramau*
*nalakūvara sādanam*
*sañjāto mayi bhāvo vām*
*īpsitaḥ paramo 'bhavaḥ*

"O Nalakūvara and Maṇigrīva, now you may both return home. Since you desire to be always absorbed in My devotional service, your desire to develop love and affection for Me will be fulfilled, and now you will never fall from that platform." (*Bhāgavatam* 10.10.42)

TEXT 121

वृन्दावने तर्णकचारणेन
क्रीडन्नहन्वत्सबकौ तथा यः ।
मां वेणुवाद्यादिगुरुः स वन्य-
वेशोऽवताज्जन्तुरुतानुकारी ॥

*vṛndāvane tarṇaka-cāraṇena*
*krīḍann ahan vatsa-bakau tathā yaḥ*
*māṁ veṇu-vādyādi-guruḥ sa vanya-*
*veśo 'vatāj jantu-rutānukārī*

*vṛndāvane* — in Vṛndāvana; *tarṇaka* — the calves; *cāraṇena* — while grazing; *krīḍan* — playing; *ahan* — killed; *vatsa-bakau* — the demons Vatsa and Baka; *tathā* — and; *yaḥ* — who; *mām* — me; *veṇu-vādya* — of flute playing; *ādi-guruḥ* — the first of *gurus; saḥ* — He; *vanya* — of the forest; *veśaḥ* — whose dress; *avatāt* — may protect; *jantu* — of the animals; *ruta* — of the sounds; *anukārī* — the imitator.

**While tending the calves and playing in the Vṛndāvana forest, He killed Vatsa and Baka. He adorns Himself in forest dress and imitates the sounds of the animals. May that first guru in the art of flute-playing protect me.**

COMMENTARY: Kṛṣṇa performed His earliest pastimes, just described by Nārada, in the forest called Mahāvana. This verse begins the description of His pastimes in the largest of Vraja's twelve forests, Vṛndāvana. Nārada calls Kṛṣṇa the *ādi-guru* of flute-players because it was during these pastimes that Kṛṣṇa perfected the art of playing the flute. While in the forest, Kṛṣṇa and His friends would collect the peacock feathers, *guñjā* berries, and other items with which Kṛṣṇa would be decorated.

## TEXT 122

प्रातः सवत्सः सखिभिः प्रविष्टो
वृन्दावनं यानकरोद्विहारान् ।
तत्तत्परामर्शमहाहिवक्त्र-
प्रवेशनादीन्सरसान्भजे तान् ॥

*prātaḥ sa-vatsaḥ sakhibhiḥ praviṣṭo*
*vṛndāvanaṁ yān akarod vihārān*
*tat-tat-parāmarśa-mahāhi-vaktra-*
*praveśanādīn sa-rasān bhaje tān*

*prātaḥ* — early in the morning; *sa-vatsaḥ* — with His calves; *sakhibhiḥ* — and the cowherd boys; *praviṣṭaḥ* — entered;

*vṛndāvanam* — Vṛndāvana; *yān* — which; *akarot* — did; *vihārān* — pastimes; *tat-tat* — in various ways; *parāmarśa* — pondering; *mahā-ahi* — of the giant serpent; *vaktra* — the mouth; *praveśana* — entering; *ādīn* — and so on; *sa-rasān* — relishable; *bhaje* — I worship; *tān* — them.

**I worship the pastimes He performed in the early mornings when He entered the Vṛndāvana forest with His calves and friends — most relishable pastimes, such as entering the mouth of a great serpent after pondering in various ways.**

COMMENTARY: On what began as a typical cow-grazing morning, the mighty demon Agha in the form of a gigantic snake confronted Kṛṣṇa's cowherd friends. The boys, having decorated themselves with festive forest attire, were in a very playful mood. After amusing themselves by stealing one another's lunch bags and teasing the monkeys and other animals, they were looking for another game when they spotted Agha lying on the path with his gaping mouth inviting them to enter. Kṛṣṇa watched helplessly as they marched into the demon's mouth, and He began to think:

*kṛtyaṁ kim atrāsya khalasya jīvanaṁ*
*na vā amīṣāṁ ca satāṁ vihiṁsanam*
*dvayaṁ kathaṁ syād iti saṁvicintya*
*jñātvāviśat tuṇḍam aśeṣa-dṛg ghariḥ*

" 'Now what is to be done? How can both the killing of this demon and the saving of the devotees be performed simultaneously?' Kṛṣṇa, being unlimitedly potent, decided to wait for an intelligent means by which He could simultaneously save the boys and kill the demon. Then He entered the mouth of Aghāsura." (*Bhāgavatam* 10.12.28)

These pastimes are filled with all the different *rasas* of loving exchange, and thus they enchant the heart of whoever hears them.

## TEXT 123

सरस्तटे शाद्वलजेमने या
लीला समाकर्षति सा मनो मे ।
तथा प्रभोस्तर्णकमार्गणे या
दध्योदनग्रासविलासिपाणेः ॥

*saras-taṭe śādvala-jemane yā*
*līlā samākarṣati sā mano me*
*tathā prabhos tarṇaka-mārgaṇe yā*
*dadhy-odana-grāsa-vilāsi-pāṇeḥ*

*saraḥ* — of a lake; *taṭe* — along the shore; *śādvala* — on the grass; *jemane* — while eating; *yā* — which; *līlā* — pastime; *samākarṣati* — totally enchants; *sā* — it; *manaḥ* — the mind; *me* — my; *tathā* — and; *prabhoḥ* — of the Lord; *tarṇaka* — for the calves; *mārgaṇe* — while searching; *yā* — which; *dadhi* — of yogurt; *odana* — and rice; *grāsa* — with a morsel; *vilāsi* — adorned; *pāṇeḥ* — whose hand.

**My mind is utterly enchanted by the Lord's pastime of taking lunch on the grassy shore of a lake and then going off to search for the calves, His hand adorned with a lump of rice mixed with yogurt.**

COMMENTARY: Lord Brahmā wanted to test Kṛṣṇa's greatness, so when Kṛṣṇa left His friends during lunch to go into the dense forest to find the wandering calves, Brahmā took the opportunity to kidnap the calves and the cowherd boys as well. Kṛṣṇa had just taken from a friend's plate a lump of yogurt rice and was still carrying it when He went looking for the calves. Śukadeva Gosvāmī says:

*vāme pāṇau masṛṇa-kavalaṁ tat-phalāny aṅgulīṣu*

"He was holding in His left hand a very nice preparation of yogurt and rice, with pieces of suitable fruit between His fingers." (*Bhāgavatam* 10.13.11)

*ity uktvādri-darī-kuñja-*
*gahvareṣv ātma-vatsakān*
*vicinvan bhagavān kṛṣṇaḥ*
*sapāṇi-kavalo yayau*

"'Let Me go and search for the calves,' Kṛṣṇa said. 'Don't disturb your enjoyment.' Then, carrying His yogurt and rice in His hand, the Supreme Personality of Godhead, Kṛṣṇa, immediately went out to search for the calves of His friends. To please His friends, He began searching in all the mountains, bushes, mountain caves, and narrow passages." (*Bhāgavatam* 10.13.14)

In fact, Kṛṣṇa was still holding that morsel in His hand a year later, when Brahmā came to apologize. Lord Brahmā said:

*naumīḍya te 'bhra-vapuṣe taḍid-ambarāya*
*guñjāvataṁsa-paripiccha-lasan-mukhāya*
*vanya-sraje kavala-vetra-viṣāṇa-veṇu-*
*lakṣma-śriye mṛdu-pade paśupāṅgajāya*

"My dear Lord, You are the only worshipable Lord, the Supreme Personality of Godhead, and therefore I offer my humble obeisances and prayers just to please You. O son of the king of the cowherds, Your transcendental body is dark blue like a new cloud, Your garment is brilliant like lightning, and the beauty of Your face is enhanced by Your *guñjā* earrings and the peacock feather on Your head. Wearing garlands of various forest flowers and leaves, and equipped with a herding stick, a buffalo horn, and a flute, You stand beautifully with a morsel of food in Your hand." (*Bhāgavatam* 10.14.1)

## TEXT 124

ब्रह्मापि यां वीक्ष्य विलासमाधुरीं
मुमोह तां वर्णयितुं नु कोऽर्हति ।
क्व सात्मवत्सार्भकरूपधारिता
क्व मुग्धवत्तत्सखिवत्समार्गणम् ॥

*brahmāpi yāṁ vīkṣya vilāsa-mādhurīṁ*
*mumoha tāṁ varṇayituṁ nu ko 'rhati*
*kva sātma-vatsārbhaka-rūpa-dhāritā*
*kva mugdha-vat tat sakhi-vatsa-mārgaṇam*

*brahmā* — Lord Brahmā; *api* — even; *yām* — which; *vīkṣya* — seeing; *vilāsa* — of pastimes; *mādhurīm* — the charm; *mumoha* — became bewildered; *tām* — them; *varṇayitum* — to describe; *nu* — indeed; *kaḥ* — who; *arhati* — is able; *kva* — where; *sā* — that; *ātma* — by His own power; *vatsa* — of the calves; *arbhaka* — and boys; *rūpa* — of the forms; *dhāritā* — the assuming; *kva* — where; *mugdha-vat* — like an innocent child; *tat* — that; *sakhi* — for His friends; *vatsa* — and calves; *mārgaṇam* — searching.

**Who can describe the charm of those pastimes, which bewildered even Brahmā when he saw them? Kṛṣṇa Himself assumed the forms of the calves and cowherd boys, and yet He went to search for His friends and calves like an innocent child.**

COMMENTARY: This pastime is doubly bewildering: Kṛṣṇa does something possible only for the supreme mystic, yet He acts like a naive child. Nārada Muni feels so charmed by this pastime that he doubts his ability to describe it.

## TEXT 125

तत्तद्विलासास्पदगोकुलस्य स
ब्रह्मैव माहात्म्यविशेषवित्तमः ।
अस्तौत्तथा यो भगवन्तमादरान्
मूर्तो महाप्रेमरसो व्रजस्य यः ॥

*tat-tad-vilāsāspada-gokulasya sa*
*brahmaiva māhātmya-viśeṣa-vittamaḥ*
*astaut tathā yo bhagavantam ādarān*
*mūrto mahā-prema-raso vrajasya yaḥ*

*tat-tat* — all those; *vilāsa* — of the pastimes; *āspada* — the abode; *gokulasya* — of Gokula; *saḥ* — he; *brahmā* — Lord Brahmā; *eva* — indeed; *māhātmya* — of the glories; *viśeṣa* — special; *vit-tamaḥ* — the best knower; *astaut* — praised; *tathā* — also; *yaḥ* — who; *bhagavantam* — the Supreme Lord; *ādarāt* — with reverence; *mūrtaḥ* — embodied; *mahā-prema* — of pure love; *rasaḥ* — the taste; *vrajasya* — of Vraja; *yaḥ* — who.

**Lord Brahmā came to understand better than anyone else the special glories of Gokula, the abode of all those pastimes, so with great respect he praised the Supreme Lord who embodies the exalted tastes of pure love in Vraja.**

COMMENTARY: Brahmā's defeat by Kṛṣṇa in their match of wits not only humbled Brahmā but also elevated him in understanding of Kṛṣṇa's pastimes in Gokula, so much so that Nārada calls him *māhātmya-viśeṣa-vittama,* "the best of those who know the special glories of Gokula." We find evidence of Brahmā's understanding in his solemn prayer to Kṛṣṇa:

*tad bhūri-bhāgyam iha janma kim apy aṭavyāṁ*
*yad gokule 'pi katamāṅghri-rajo-'bhiṣekam*
*yaj-jīvitaṁ tu nikhilaṁ bhagavān mukundas*
*tv adyāpi yat-pada-rajaḥ śruti-mṛgyam eva*

"My greatest possible good fortune would be to take any birth whatever in this forest of Gokula and have my head bathed by the dust falling from the lotus feet of any of its residents. Their entire life and soul is the Supreme Personality of Godhead, Mukunda, the dust of whose lotus feet is still being searched for in the Vedic *mantras.*" (*Bhāgavatam* 10.14.34)

Brahmā became qualified to praise Kṛṣṇa suitably by realizing Him as the reservoir of all the ecstatic moods of *vraja-prema.* In many verses of *Śrīmad-Bhāgavatam* Śrī Śukadeva Gosvāmī expertly describes those varieties of *rasa.* For example:

*tan-mātaro veṇu-rava-tvarotthitā*
*utthāpya dorbhiḥ parirabhya nirbharam*

*sneha-snuta-stanya-payaḥ-sudhāsavaṁ*
*matvā paraṁ brahma sutān apāyayan*

"The mothers of the boys, upon hearing the sounds of the flutes and bugles being played by their sons, immediately rose from their household tasks, lifted their boys onto their laps, embraced them with both arms, and began to feed them with their breast milk, which flowed forth because of extreme love specifically for Kṛṣṇa. Actually Kṛṣṇa is everything, but at that time, expressing extreme love and affection, they took special pleasure in feeding Kṛṣṇa, the Para-brahman, and Kṛṣṇa drank the milk from His respective mothers as if it were a nectarean beverage." (*Bhāgavatam* 10.13.22)

Brahmā himself also very competently described these *rasas* in his prayers:

*aho 'ti-dhanyā vraja-go-ramaṇyaḥ*
*stanyāmṛtaṁ pītam atīva te mudā*
*yāsāṁ vibho vatsatarātmajātmanā*
*yat-tṛptaye 'dyāpi na cālam adhvarāḥ*

"O almighty Lord, how greatly fortunate are the cows and ladies of Vṛndāvana, the nectar of whose breast-milk You have happily drunk to Your full satisfaction, taking the form of their calves and children! All the Vedic sacrifices performed from time immemorial up to the present day have not given You as much satisfaction." (*Bhāgavatam* 10.14.31)

## TEXT 126

गोपालनेनाग्रजमाननेन
वृन्दावनश्रीस्तवनेन चासौ ।
तेनालिगानाभिनयादिनापि
प्रभुर्व्यधाद्यां भज तां सुलीलाम् ॥

*gopālanenāgraja-mānanena*
*vṛndāvana-śrī-stavanena cāsau*

*tenāli-gānābhinayādināpi*
*prabhur vyadhād yāṁ bhaja tāṁ su-līlām*

*go-pālanena* — by tending the cows; *agra-ja* — His elder brother; *mānanena* — by honoring; *vṛndāvana* — of Vṛndāvana; *śrī* — the beauty; *stavanena* — by praising; *ca* — and; *asau* — He; *tena* — by that; *ali* — of the bees; *gāna* — of the son; *abhinaya* — by imitating; *ādinā* — and so on; *api* — also; *prabhuḥ* — the Lord; *vyadhāt* — enacted; *yām* — which; *bhaja* — you should worship; *tām* — those; *su-līlām* — wonderful pastimes.

**Please worship the wonderful pastimes the Lord enacted, such as tending the cows, honoring His elder brother, glorifying the beauty of Vṛndāvana, and imitating the singing of the bees.**

COMMENTARY: This verse begins the recounting of Kṛṣṇa's *pauganḍa-līlā,* the pastimes of years six through ten. Besides imitating the bees, Kṛṣṇa and His friends would also imitate the chattering of parrots, call out in deep voices to the distant cows, and enjoy naps on beds of soft leaves.

## TEXT 127

तालीवने याविरभूच्च लीला
या धेनुकज्ञातिविमर्दने च ।
सायं व्रजस्त्रीगणसङ्गमेऽपि
स्तोतुं न शक्नोम्यभिवादये ताम् ॥

*tālī-vane yāvirabhūc ca līlā*
*yā dhenuka-jñāti-vimardane ca*
*sāyaṁ vraja-strī-gaṇa-saṅgame 'pi*
*stotuṁ na śaknomy abhivādaye tām*

*tālī-vane* — in the Tālavana forest; *yā* — which; *āvirabhūt* — was exhibited; *ca* — and; *līlā* — pastime; *yāḥ* — which; *dhenuka*

— of the ass Dhenuka; *jñāti* — the friends; *vimardane* — in killing; *ca* — and; *sāyam* — at dusk; *vraja* — of Vraja; *strī-gaṇa* — the women; *saṅgame* — in the meeting; *api* — and; *stotum* — to praise; *na śaknomi* — I am not able; *abhivādaye* — I offer my respects; *tām* — to them.

**The Lord disposed of Dhenuka and his relatives in the Tālavana and met at dusk with the women of Vraja. These pastimes I cannot adequately praise; I can only offer them my respects.**

COMMENTARY: Because the cowherd boys wanted to eat the fruits of the *tāla* trees and play with them as balls, they asked Kṛṣṇa and Balarāma to rid the Tālavana forest of the ass demons who refused to allow anyone to enter, and Kṛṣṇa and Balarāma did so. After such sports, when Kṛṣṇa came home in the evening, at the entrance of Nanda Mahārāja's village He would be greeted by His family and friends, including the young *gopīs:*

*taṁ go-rajaś-churita-kuntala-baddha-barha-*
*vanya-prasūna-rucirekṣaṇa-cāru-hāsam*
*veṇuṁ kvaṇantam anugair upagīta-kīrtiṁ*
*gopyo didṛkṣita-dṛśo 'bhyagaman sametāḥ*

"Lord Kṛṣṇa's hair, powdered with the dust raised by the cows, was decorated with a peacock feather and forest flowers. The Lord glanced charmingly and smiled beautifully, playing upon His flute while His companions chanted His glories. The *gopīs,* all together, came forward to meet Him, their eyes very eager to see Him.

*pītvā mukunda-mukha-sāragham akṣi-bhṛṅgais*
*tāpaṁ jahur viraha-jaṁ vraja-yoṣito 'hni*
*tat sat-kṛtiṁ samadhigamya viveśa goṣṭhaṁ*
*savrīḍa-hāsa-vinayaṁ yad apāṅga-mokṣam*

"With their beelike eyes, the women of Vṛndāvana drank the honey of the beautiful face of Lord Mukunda, and thus they gave up the distress they had felt during the day because of separation from Him. The young Vṛndāvana ladies cast sidelong glances at the Lord — glances filled with bashfulness, laughter, and submission — and Śrī Kṛṣṇa, completely accepting these glances as a proper offering of respect, entered the cowherd village." (*Bhāgavatam* 10.15.42–43)

Nārada feels unable to describe such intimate exchanges between Kṛṣṇa and His devotees, either because words are incapable of capturing the essence of these pastimes or because Nārada fears that if he says more than a few words about each pastime he will become too ecstatic and lose control of himself. Now, therefore, unable to freely offer elaborate service to these pastimes, he simply offers them obeisances with his words.

## TEXT 128

यो वै विहारोऽजनि कालियस्य
ह्रदे यशोदातनयस्य तस्य ।
तं स्मर्तुमीशो न भवामि शोक-
प्रहर्षवेगात्कथमालपानि ॥

*yo vai vihāro 'jani kāliyasya*
*hrade yaśodā-tanayasya tasya*
*taṁ smartum īśo na bhavāmi śoka-*
*praharṣa-vegāt katham ālapāni*

*yaḥ* — which; *vai* — indeed; *vihāraḥ* — sport; *ajani* — occurred; *kāliyasya* — of Kāliya; *hrade* — in the lake; *yaśodā-tanayasya* — of the son of Yaśodā; *tasya* — Him; *tam* — that; *smartum* — to remember; *īśaḥ* — capable; *na bhavāmi* — I am not; *śoka* — of sorrow; *praharṣa* — and joy; *vegāt* — due to the force; *katham* — how; *ālapāni* — can I speak.

**The sport that the son of Yaśodā enjoyed in the lake of Kāliya disturbs me so much with both sorrow and joy that I can't bear to remember it. How then can I recount it to you?**

COMMENTARY: Remembering the violence done by Kāliya made Nārada sad, but remembering how Kṛṣṇa tamed Kāliya by dancing on his hoods enlivened him.

## TEXT 129

क्व दुष्टचेष्टस्य खलस्य तस्य
दण्डस्तदा क्रोधभरेण कार्यः ।
क्व चोन्नते तत्फणवर्गरङ्गे
नृत्योत्सवो हर्षभरेण तादृक् ॥

*kva duṣṭa-ceṣṭasya khalasya tasya*
*daṇḍas tadā krodha-bhareṇa kāryaḥ*
*kva connate tat-phaṇa-varga-raṅge*
*nṛtyotsavo harṣa-bhareṇa tādṛk*

*kva* — where; *duṣṭa* — evil; *ceṣṭasya* — whose behavior; *khalasya* — cruel; *tasya* — of him (Kāliya); *daṇḍaḥ* — the punishment; *tadā* — then; *krodha* — of anger; *bhareṇa* — by the swelling; *kāryaḥ* — caused; *kva* — where; *ca* — and; *unnate* — which was upraised; *tat* — his; *phaṇa-varga* — of the row of hoods; *raṅge* — on the stage; *nṛtya* — of dancing; *utsavaḥ* — the festival; *harṣa* — of joy; *bhareṇa* — with an abundance; *tādṛk* — similar.

**When the Lord's anger swelled, what a punishment He gave to that wicked, cruel-hearted creature! And what joy the Lord felt when He performed His festival of dancing on the stage of that serpent's upraised hoods!**

COMMENTARY: Kāliya had the arrogance to grasp with his filthy coils the divine body of the Supreme Person, thus causing great anxiety to the Lord's devotees. Kāliya's heart was full of wicked pride, and he felt no shame raising his hoods high in the air. Therefore Kṛṣṇa gave him a fitting punishment: He turned

Kāliya's hoods into a dancing stage and gleefully pummeled the serpent into submission.

## TEXT 130

क्व निग्रहस्तादृगनुग्रहः क्व वा
शेषोऽपि यं वर्णयितुं न शक्नुयात् ।
तन्नागपत्नीनिवहाय मे नमः
स्तुत्यर्चने योऽकृत कालियाय च ॥

*kva nigrahas tādṛg anugrahaḥ kva vā*
*śeṣo 'pi yaṁ varṇayituṁ na śaknuyāt*
*tan nāga-patnī-nivahāya me namaḥ*
*stuty-arcane yo 'kṛta kāliyāya ca*

*kva* — where; *nigrahaḥ* — punishment; *tādṛk* — such; *anugrahaḥ* — mercy; *kva* — where; *vā* — and; *śeṣaḥ* — Ananta Śeṣa; *api* — even; *yam* — which; *varṇayitum* — to describe; *na śaknuyāt* — is not able; *tat* — that; *nāga-patnī* — of wives of the serpent; *nivahāya* — to the crowd; *me* — my; *namaḥ* — obeisances; *stuti* — prayers; *arcane* — and worship; *yaḥ* — who; *akṛta* — offered; *kāliyāya* — to Kāliya; *ca* — and.

**Even Ananta Śeṣa is unable to describe such punishment and mercy! To the serpent's many wives, who offered Kṛṣṇa prayers and worship, and to Kāliya himself, I bow down.**

COMMENTARY: Kāliya received the severe punishment of having his heads crushed by the Supreme Lord's heels, and simultaneously the exquisite mercy of obtaining the dust of Kṛṣṇa's lotus feet on those same heads. The dust of Kṛṣṇa's feet is the rarest treasure. Even the original thousand-headed serpent, Ananta Śeṣa, has difficulty, therefore, expressing the glories of the mercy Kāliya received. But Kāliya's wives managed to describe it in their humble prayers.

## TEXT 131

तीरे ह्रदस्यास्य दवानलेन या
क्रीडाद्भुता मुञ्जवनेऽप्यतोऽधिका ।
भाण्डीरसंक्रीडनचातुरी च सा
ज्येष्ठस्य कीर्त्यै रचिता तनोतु शम् ॥

*tīre hradasyāsya davānalena yā*
*krīḍādbhutā muñja-vane 'py ato 'dhikā*
*bhāṇḍīra-saṅkrīḍana-cāturī ca sā*
*jyeṣṭhasya kīrtyai racitā tanotu śam*

*tīre* — on the shore; *hradasya* — of the lake; *asya* — His; *dava-analena* — with the forest fire; *yā* — which; *krīḍā* — pastime; *adbhutā* — wonderful; *muñja-vane* — in the Muñja forest; *api* — also; *ataḥ* — than that; *adhikā* — even greater; *bhāṇḍīra* — in the Bhāṇḍīra forest; *saṅkrīḍana* — of sporting; *cāturī* — the clever arrangement; *ca* — and; *sā* — which; *jyeṣṭhasya* — of His elder brother; *kīrtyai* — for the glory; *racitā* — created; *tanotu* — may it expand; *śam* — good fortune.

**The pastime of the forest fire took place on the shore of that same lake, and a pastime with an even greater fire took place in the forest known as Muñja. In the Bhāṇḍīra forest the clever arrangements for sporting magnified the glories of Balarāma, the Lord's elder brother. May all these pastimes expand our good fortune.**

COMMENTARY: Kṛṣṇa twice saved the cowherd boys from a forest fire, but the second fire was even more amazing than the first. In that emergency Kṛṣṇa told His friends to simply close their eyes and He would save them, and then suddenly they found themselves transported to Bhāṇḍīravana. While the boys played in that forest, Lord Balarāma especially showed His glories. Kṛṣṇa, defeated in wrestling, carried Śrīdāma on His back, and victorious Balarāma was carried by Pralambāsura, whom Balarāma then killed.

### TEXT 132

मनोहरा प्रावृषि या हि लीला
महीरुहाङ्काश्रयणादिका सा ।
जीयाद्व्रजस्त्रीस्मरतापदात्री
शरद्वनश्रीभरवर्धिता च ॥

*manoharā prāvṛṣi yā hi līlā*
*mahīruhāṅkāśrayaṇādikā sā*
*jīyād vraja-strī-smara-tāpa-dātrī*
*śarad-vana-śrī-bhara-vardhitā ca*

*manaḥ-harā* — enchanting; *prāvṛṣi* — in the rainy season; *yā* — which; *hi* — indeed; *līlā* — pastimes; *mahī-ruha* — of trees; *aṅka* — at the base; *āśrayaṇa* — resting; *ādikā* — and so on; *sā* — these; *jīyāt* — should be glorified; *vraja* — of Vraja; *strī* — to the women; *smara* — of Cupid; *tāpa* — the torment; *dātrī* — which give; *śarat* — autumnal; *vana* — of the forests; *śrī-bhara* — by the great beauty; *vardhitā* — enhanced; *ca* — and.

**All glories to His pastimes in the rainy season, like His resting at the feet of trees, and to His autumnal pastimes—enhanced by the beauty of the forests—which heaped the pain of Cupid's torment on the women of Vraja.**

COMMENTARY: During the rains, Kṛṣṇa enjoyed such seasonal pastimes as sitting at the bases of trees, eating white radishes, and joining His friends on the tops of big rocks to feast on yogurt rice. When the next season commenced, the beauty of the forest increased luxuriantly, expanding the pleasure of Kṛṣṇa's pastimes and increasing the disturbance the girls of Vraja felt from the arrows of Cupid. As described by Śukadeva Gosvāmī in *Śrīmad-Bhāgavatam* (10.20.45):

*āśliṣya sama-śītoṣṇaṁ*
*prasūna-vana-mārutam*
*janās tāpaṁ jahur gopyo*
*na kṛṣṇa-hṛta-cetasaḥ*

"The people could forget their suffering by embracing the wind coming from the flower-filled forest, a wind neither hot nor cold. But the *gopīs* could not, for their hearts had been stolen by Kṛṣṇa."

## TEXT 133

सा वन्यभूषा स च वेणुवाद्य-
माधुर्यपूरोऽखिलचित्तहारी ।
तद्गोपयोषिद्गणमोहनं च
मया कदास्यानुभविष्यतेऽद्धा ॥

*sā vanya-bhūṣā sa ca veṇu-vādya-*
*mādhurya-pūro 'khila-citta-hārī*
*tad gopa-yoṣid-gaṇa-mohanaṁ ca*
*mayā kadāsyānubhaviṣyate 'ddhā*

*sā* — that; *vanya* — of the forest; *bhūṣā* — adornment; *saḥ* — that; *ca* — and; *veṇu-vādya* — of flute playing; *mādhurya* — of sweetness; *pūraḥ* — the flood; *akhila* — of everyone; *citta* — the hearts; *hārī* — which steals; *tat* — that; *gopa-yoṣit-gaṇa* — of all the cowherd women; *mohanam* — the enchanting; *ca* — and; *mayā* — by me; *kadā* — when; *asya* — His; *anubhaviṣyate* — will be experienced; *addhā* — directly.

**When will I see with my own eyes the way He dresses in forest attire, steals everyone's heart with the downpour of sweetness from the music of His flute, and enchants all the cowherd girls?**

COMMENTARY: About the Personality of Godhead's forest dress, Śukadeva Gosvāmī says:

*barhāpīḍaṁ naṭa-vara-vapuḥ karṇayoḥ karṇikāraṁ*
*bibhrad vāsaḥ kanaka-kapiśaṁ vaijayantīṁ ca mālām*
*randhrān veṇor adhara-sudhayāpūrayan gopa-vṛndair*
*vṛndāraṇyaṁ sva-pada-ramaṇaṁ prāviśad gīta-kīrtiḥ*

"Wearing a peacock-feather ornament upon His head, blue *karṇikāra* flowers on His ears, a yellow garment as brilliant as gold, and the Vaijayantī garland, Lord Kṛṣṇa exhibited His transcendental form as the greatest of dancers as He entered the forest of Vṛndāvana, beautifying it with the marks of His footprints. He filled the holes of His flute with the nectar of His lips, and the cowherd boys sang His glories." (*Bhāgavatam* 10.21.5)

The most expert analysts of the glories of Kṛṣṇa's flute are the *gopīs,* and many of their authoritative statements about those glories are recorded in the Tenth Canto of *Śrīmad-Bhāgavatam* — for example, in the Twenty-first Chapter, in the eight texts beginning with this one (Text 9):

*gopyaḥ kim ācarad ayaṁ kuśalaṁ sma veṇur*
*dāmodarādhara-sudhām api gopikānām*
*bhuṅkte svayaṁ yad avaśiṣṭa-rasaṁ hradinyo*
*hṛṣyat-tvaco 'śru mumucus taravo yathāryāḥ*

"My dear *gopīs,* what auspicious activities must the flute have performed to enjoy the nectar of Kṛṣṇa's lips independently and leave only a taste for us *gopīs,* for whom that nectar is actually meant! The forefathers of the flute, the bamboo trees, shed tears of pleasure. His mother, the river on whose bank the bamboo was born, feels jubilation, and therefore her blooming lotus flowers are standing like hair on her body."

The *gopīs,* in their constant praise of Kṛṣṇa, frequently return to the theme of the enchanting power of His flute:

*gā gopakair anu-vanaṁ nayator udāra-*
*veṇu-svanaiḥ kala-padais tanu-bhṛtsu sakhyaḥ*
*aspandanaṁ gati-matāṁ pulakas tarūṇāṁ*
*niryoga-pāśa-kṛta-lakṣaṇayor vicitram*

"My dear friends, as Kṛṣṇa and Balarāma pass through the forest with Their cowherd friends, leading Their cows, They carry ropes to bind the cows' rear legs at the time of milking. When Lord Kṛṣṇa plays on His flute, the sweet music makes the moving living entities become stunned and the nonmoving trees tremble with ecstasy. These things are certainly very wonderful." (*Bhāgavatam* 10.21.19)

More than anything else, the sound of Kṛṣṇa's flute most fully expresses the essence of His sweetness (*mādhurya*), so the wonders of Kṛṣṇa's flute-playing will be elaborated even more in the description of "the sweetness of all of Kṛṣṇa's excellent qualities" (*aśeṣa-mahattva-mādhurī*).

It was particularly in the autumn that Kṛṣṇa stole the hearts of the *gopīs* by playing the flute. While speaking about the arrival of autumn in Vṛndāvana, Śrī Śukadeva Gosvāmī says:

*tad vraja-striya āśrutya*
*veṇu-gītaṁ smarodayam*
*kāścit parokṣaṁ kṛṣṇasya*
*sva-sakhībhyo 'nvavarṇayan*

"When the young ladies in the cowherd village of Vraja heard the song of Kṛṣṇa's flute, which arouses the influence of Cupid, some of them privately began describing Kṛṣṇa's qualities to their intimate friends." (*Bhāgavatam* 10.21.3)

## TEXT 134

क्वाहो स कन्याम्बरमोषणोत्सवः
सा नीपमूर्धन्यधिरोहणत्वरा ।
नर्माणि तान्यञ्जलिवन्दनार्थनं
तत्स्वांसनीतांशुकदातृता च सा ॥

*kvāho sa kanyāmbara-moṣaṇotsavaḥ*
*sā nīpa-mūrdhany adhirohaṇa-tvarā*
*narmāṇi tāny añjali-vandanārthanaṁ*
*tat svāṁsa-nītāṁśuka-dātṛtā ca sā*

*kva* — where; *aho* — oh; *saḥ* — that; *kanyā* — of the girls; *ambara* — of the clothing; *moṣaṇa* — of stealing; *utsavaḥ* —

the festival; *sā* — that; *nīpa* — of the *kadamba* tree; *mūrdhani* — to the top; *adhirohaṇa* — in climbing; *tvarā* — the speed; *narmāṇi* — joking words; *tāni* — those; *añjali* — with joined palms; *vandana* — a gesture of respect; *arthanam* — and requests; *tat* — that; *sva-aṁsa* — on His own shoulder; *nīta* — placed; *aṁśuka* — of the garments; *dātṛtā* — giving; *ca* — and; *sā* — that.

**How wonderfully He enjoyed the festival of stealing the clothes of the young girls! He climbed quickly to the top of a kadamba tree and spoke joking words to the girls. And after they offered respects with joined palms and submitted their requests, He gave back the garments He had placed on His shoulder.**

COMMENTARY: In the festival of stealing the *gopīs'* clothes, Kṛṣṇa had the opportunity to share with the *gopīs* some humorous words:

*atrāgatyābalāḥ kāmaṁ*
*svaṁ svaṁ vāsaḥ pragṛhyatām*
*satyaṁ bruvāṇi no narma*
*yad yūyaṁ vrata-karśitāḥ*

"My dear girls, you may each come here as you wish and take back your garments. I'm telling you the truth and am not joking with you, since I see you're fatigued from executing austere vows." (*Bhāgavatam* 10.22.10)

Kṛṣṇa ordered the girls to come forward one by one and ask for their garments:

*bhagavān āhatā vīkṣya*
*śuddha-bhāva-prasāditaḥ*
*skandhe nidhāya vāsāṁsi*
*prītaḥ provāca sa-smitam*

"When the Supreme Lord saw how the *gopīs* were struck with embarrassment, He was satisfied by their pure loving affection.

Putting their clothes on His shoulder, the Lord smiled and spoke to them affectionately.

*yūyaṁ vivastrā yad apo dhṛta-vratā*
*vyagāhataitat tad u deva-helanam*
*baddhāñjaliṁ mūrdhny apanuttaye 'ṁhasaḥ*
*kṛtvā namo 'dho-vasanaṁ pragṛhyatām*

"You girls bathed naked while executing your vow, and that is certainly an offense against the demigods. To counteract your sin you should offer obeisances while placing your joined palms above your heads. Then you should take back your lower garments." (*Bhāgavatam* 10.22.18–19)

## TEXT 135

तां यज्वविप्रौदनयाचनां च
तत्पत्नीगणाकर्षणमप्यमुष्य ।
तान्भूषणावस्थितिवाक्प्रसादान्
ईडे तदन्नादनपाटवं च ॥

*tāṁ yajva-vipraudana-yācanāṁ ca*
*tat patnī-gaṇākarṣaṇam apy amuṣya*
*tān bhūṣaṇāvasthiti-vāk-prasādān*
*īḍe tad annādana-pāṭavaṁ ca*

*tām* — them; *yajva-vipra* — from the sacrificial *brāhmaṇas; odana* — of rice; *yācanām* — begging; *ca* — and; *tat* — that; *patnī-gaṇa* — of their wives; *ākarṣaṇam* — attraction; *api* — also; *amuṣya* — by Him; *tān* — those; *bhūṣaṇa* — His ornaments; *avasthiti* — their placement; *vāk* — His speech; *prasādān* — and His mercy; *īḍe* — I glorify; *tat* — that; *anna* — the food; *adana* — in eating; *pāṭavam* — the expertise; *ca* — and.

**I glorify His pastimes of begging food from the sacrificial brāhmaṇas, attracting the brāhmaṇas' wives, and gracefully**

**eating the food the wives offered. I glorify how He decorated Himself and how He stood, spoke, and bestowed His mercy.**

COMMENTARY: In the course of Śukadeva Gosvāmī's vivid description of Kṛṣṇa's pastimes, he highlights several of Kṛṣṇa's special attractive features. He tells of Kṛṣṇa's ornaments:

*śyāmaṁ hiraṇya-paridhiṁ vana-mālya-barha-*
*dhātu-pravāla-naṭa-veśam anuvratāṁse*
*vinyasta-hastam itareṇa dhunānam abjaṁ*
*karṇotpalālaka-kapola-mukhābja-hāsam*

"Wearing a peacock feather, colored minerals, sprigs of flower buds, and a garland of forest flowers and leaves, He was dressed just like a dramatic dancer. His complexion was dark blue and His garment golden. He rested one hand upon the shoulder of a friend and with the other twirled a lotus. Lilies graced His ears, His hair hung down over His cheeks, and His lotuslike face was smiling." (*Bhāgavatam* 10.23.22).

Śukadeva Gosvāmī also describes how Kṛṣṇa spoke:

*svāgataṁ vo mahā-bhāgā*
*āsyatāṁ karavāma kim*
*yan no didṛkṣayā prāptā*
*upapannam idaṁ hi vaḥ*

"Welcome, O most fortunate ladies. Please sit down and make yourselves comfortable. What can I do for you? That you have come here to see Me is most appropriate." (*Bhāgavatam* 10.23.25)

We also hear about the special mercy Kṛṣṇa showed the *brāhmaṇas'* wives by blessing them:

*patayo nābhyasūyeran*
*pitṛ-bhrātṛ-sutādayaḥ*
*lokāś ca vo mayopetā*
*devā apy anumanyate*

"Rest assured that your husbands will not be inimical toward you, nor will your fathers, brothers, or sons, your other relatives, or the general populace. I will personally advise them of the situation. Indeed, even the demigods will express their approval." (*Bhāgavatam* 10.23.31)

The love the wives of those Vedic *brāhmaṇas* had for Kṛṣṇa far exceeded the standards of worldly affection. Even the *brāhmaṇas* themselves recognized this. As Śukadeva Gosvāmī tells us:

*dṛṣṭvā strīṇāṁ bhagavati*
*kṛṣṇe bhaktim alaukikīm*
*ātmānaṁ ca tayā hīnam*
*anutaptā vyagarhayan*

"Taking note of their wives' pure, transcendental devotion for Lord Kṛṣṇa, the Supreme Personality of Godhead, and seeing their own lack of devotion, the *brāhmaṇas* felt most sorrowful and began to condemn themselves." (*Bhāgavatam* 10.23.39) The remorseful *brāhmaṇas* were unable to lovingly approach Kṛṣṇa as did their wives, but they did learn to admire their wives' Kṛṣṇa consciousness:

*aho paśyata nārīṇām*
*api kṛṣṇe jagad-gurau*
*duranta-bhāvaṁ yo 'vidhyan*
*mṛtyu-pāśān gṛhābhidhān*

"Just see the unlimited love these women have developed for Lord Kṛṣṇa, the spiritual master of the entire universe! That love has broken for them the very bonds of death — their attachments to family life." (*Bhāgavatam* 10.23.42)

Kṛṣṇa also demonstrated noble grace in accepting food as charity from the *brāhmaṇas'* wives:

*bhagavān api govindas*
*tenaivānnena gopakān*

*catur-vidhenāśayitvā*
*svayaṁ ca bubhuje prabhuḥ*

"Govinda, the Supreme Personality of Godhead, fed the cowherd boys with that food of four varieties. Then the all-powerful Lord Himself partook of the preparations." (*Bhāgavatam* 10.23.36)

## TEXT 136

गोवर्धनाद्रे रुचिरार्चनां तथा
स्ववामहस्तेन महाद्रिधारणम् ।
तद्गोपसन्तोषणमिन्द्रसान्त्वनं
वन्देऽस्य गोविन्दतयाभिषेचनम् ॥

*govardhanādre rucirārcanāṁ tathā*
*sva-vāma-hastena mahādri-dhāraṇam*
*tad gopa-santoṣaṇam indra-sāntvanaṁ*
*vande 'sya govindatayābhiṣecanam*

*govardhana-adreḥ* — of Govardhana Hill; *rucira* — all-attractive; *arcanām* — worship; *tathā* — and; *sva* — His; *vāma* — left; *hastena* — with the hand; *mahā-adri* — of the great mountain; *dhāraṇam* — holding; *tat* — that; *gopa* — of the cowherds; *santoṣaṇam* — satisfying; *indra* — of Indra; *sāntvanam* — pacifying; *vande* — I offer homage; *asya* — His; *govindatayā* — as Govinda; *abhiṣecanam* — to the royal ceremonial bath.

**I offer my homage to His all-attractively worshiping Govardhana Hill, His holding up the great hill with His left hand, His satisfying the cowherds, consoling Indra, and accepting coronation as Govinda, the Lord of the cows.**

COMMENTARY: Kṛṣṇa's intention is always to please His devotees. After He held Govardhana Hill aloft for seven days just for their benefit, their satisfaction knew no bounds:

*taṁ prema-vegān nirbhṛtā vrajaukaso*
*yathā samīyuḥ parirambhaṇādibhiḥ*
*gopyaś ca sa-sneham apūjayan mudā*
*dadhy-akṣatādbhir yuyujuḥ sad-āśiṣaḥ*

"All the residents of Vṛndāvana were overwhelmed with ecstatic love, and they came forward and greeted Śrī Kṛṣṇa according to their individual relationships with Him — some embracing Him, others bowing down to Him, and so forth. The cowherd women presented water mixed with yogurt and unbroken barleycorns as a token of honor, and they showered auspicious benedictions upon Him." (*Bhāgavatam* 10.25.29)

Kṛṣṇa's miraculous feat of lifting Govardhana Hill left the Vraja-vāsīs confused about who Kṛṣṇa really was. But Nanda Mahārāja was able to dispel their bewilderment and give them great satisfaction by repeating what Garga Muni had said at Kṛṣṇa's name-giving ceremony about Kṛṣṇa's identity.

*iti nanda-vacaḥ śrutvā*
*garga-gītaṁ vrajaukasaḥ*
*muditā nandam ānarcuḥ*
*kṛṣṇaṁ ca gata-vismayāḥ*

"Having heard Nanda Mahārāja relate the statements of Garga Muni, the residents of Vṛndāvana became enlivened. Their perplexity was gone, and they worshiped Nanda and Lord Kṛṣṇa with great respect." (*Bhāgavatam* 10.26.24)

As we hear from Śrī Parāśara Ṛṣi in the *Viṣṇu Purāṇa* (5.13.10–12), after Kṛṣṇa lifted Govardhana He also satisfied the Vraja-vāsīs with encouraging words:

*mat-sambandhena vo gopā*
*yadi lajjā na jāyate*
*ślāghyo 'haṁ vai tataḥ kiṁ vo*
*vicāreṇa prayojanam*

*yadi vo 'sti mayi prītiḥ*
*ślāghyo 'haṁ bhavatāṁ yadi*

*tadātma-bandhu-sadṛśī*
*buddhir vaḥ kriyatāṁ mayi*

*nāhaṁ devo na gandharvo*
*na yakṣo na ca dānavaḥ*
*ahaṁ vo bāndhavo jāto*
*nātaś cintyam ato 'nyathā*

"My dear cowherds, if you are not embarrassed to be related to Me and if I deserve praise, then why get perplexed? If you have affection for Me and I'm worthy of your praise, then just think of Me as your dear relative. I am no god or Gandharva or Yakṣa or Dānava, but am simply your family member. You should not think otherwise."

## TEXT 137

व्रजस्य वैकुण्ठपदानुदर्शनं
लोकाच्च नन्दानयनं प्रचेतसः ।
न वक्तुमर्हामि परान्तसीमगां
वक्ष्ये कथं तां भगवत्त्वमाधुरीम् ॥

*vrajasya vaikuṇṭha-padānudarśanaṁ*
*lokāc ca nandānayanaṁ pracetasaḥ*
*na vaktum arhāmi parānta-sīma-gāṁ*
*vakṣye kathaṁ tāṁ bhagavattva-mādhurīm*

*vrajasya* — to the people of Vraja; *vaikuṇṭha-pada* — the abode of Vaikuṇṭha; *anudarśanam* — showing; *lokāt* — from the world; *ca* — and; *nanda* — of Nanda Mahārāja; *ānayanam* — bringing back; *pracetasaḥ* — of Varuṇa; *na* — not; *vaktum* — to speak; *arhāmi* — I am able; *para-anta* — final; *sīma* — to its limit; *gām* — gone; *vakṣye* — I should speak; *katham* — how; *tām* — about that; *bhagavattva* — of Godhood; *mādhurīm* — the sweetness.

**I am unable to properly describe His superexcellent pastimes of showing the abode of Vaikuṇṭha to the residents of Vraja and rescuing Nanda Mahārāja from Varuṇa's realm. And how can I ever express in words the sweet way He showed Himself to be the Supreme Godhead?**

COMMENTARY: Kṛṣṇa proved Himself God in one way when He revealed Vaikuṇṭha to the Vraja-vāsīs and another way when He commanded the powerful demigod Varuṇa to release His father. But Kṛṣṇa displayed His supremacy in the greatest way when He conducted the all-attractive pastimes of charming the *gopīs* with His flute-song and enjoying with them in the *rāsa* dance. This will be discussed later on, under the topic of *aśeṣa-mahattva-mādhurī* ("the sweetness of all of Kṛṣṇa's excellent qualities").

## TEXT 138

वाच्यः किमेषां व्रजचेष्टितानां
यः सर्वतः श्रैष्ठ्यभरो विचारैः ।
तदक्षराणां श्रवणे प्रवेशाद्
उदेति हि प्रेमभरः प्रकृत्या ॥

*vācyaḥ kim eṣāṁ vraja-ceṣṭitānāṁ*
*yaḥ sarvataḥ śraiṣṭhya-bharo vicāraiḥ*
*tad-akṣarāṇāṁ śravaṇe praveśād*
*udeti hi prema-bharaḥ prakṛtyā*

*vācyaḥ* — possible to be described; *kim* — whether; *eṣām* — of these; *vraja* — of Vraja; *ceṣṭitānām* — activities; *yaḥ* — which; *sarvataḥ* — all-around; *śraiṣṭhya* — of excellence; *bharaḥ* — the expanse; *vicāraiḥ* — with careful thought; *tat* — those; *akṣarāṇām* — of the syllables; *śravaṇe* — in the ears; *praveśāt* — by the entering; *udeti* — arises; *hi* — certainly; *prema* — of love; *bharaḥ* — a flood; *prakṛtyā* — naturally.

**What can I say about these activities of the Lord in Vraja?**

**One who carefully thinks about them will conclude they are supreme in all respects. As soon as words describing those pastimes enter the ears, a flood of pure love spontaneously arises in the heart.**

COMMENTARY: This verse and the next summarize the topic of *vilāsa-lakṣmī* ("the splendor of Kṛṣṇa's pastimes"). Anyone who gives thoughtful attention to the pastimes of Vraja will conclude that they are more wonderful than the deeds of all the other incarnations of the Supreme Lord. Even the mere words that narrate those Vraja pastimes, beginning with the deliverance of Pūtanā, have a magical power to awaken *prema* in the heart. *Prema* begins to awaken when those narrations simply enter one's ears, what to speak of what happens when a thoughtful devotee contemplates them with attention. Without doubting, we should accept that such an effect is possible by the innate potency of the words themselves (*prakṛtyā*). Certain combinations of words have a natural power to evoke spiritual emotions, just as fire has its natural inalienable potencies of heat and light.

## TEXT 139

कृष्णेहितानामखिलोत्तमं यस्
तर्कैः प्रकर्षं तनुते स धन्यः ।
तेषां दराकर्णनमात्रतो यः
स्यात्प्रेमपूर्णस्तमहं नमामि ॥

*kṛṣṇehitānām akhilottamaṁ yas*
*tarkaiḥ prakarṣaṁ tanute sa dhanyaḥ*
*teṣāṁ darākarṇana-mātrato yaḥ*
*syāt prema-pūrṇas tam ahaṁ namāmi*

*kṛṣṇa-īhitānām* — of Kṛṣṇa's activities; *akhila-uttamam* — supermost; *yaḥ* — who; *tarkaiḥ* — by logical arguments; *prakarṣam* — the excellence; *tanute* — disseminates; *saḥ* — he; *dhanyaḥ* — very fortunate; *teṣām* — of them; *dara* — a little;

*ākarṇana* — by hearing; *mātrataḥ* — simply; *yaḥ* — who; *syāt* — becomes; *prema-pūrṇaḥ* — full of ecstatic love; *tam* — to him; *aham* — I; *namāmi* — bow down.

**Very fortunate is one who uses logical arguments to make known the supreme glories of Kṛṣṇa's pastimes. And to one who becomes full of prema simply by hearing a few words about those pastimes, I offer my humble obeisances.**

COMMENTARY: It is wonderful when pure love of God is inspired by thoughtful analysis of the meaning of Kṛṣṇa's pastimes. Much more wonderful, however, is the spontaneous response of pure devotees who are overcome by a flood of *prema* as soon as they hear the bare syllables of those pastimes. Such devotees need only hear the name Pūtanā or a few words from *Śrīmad-Bhāgavatam* for a sequence of ecstatic memories to arise in their hearts. Nārada considers those devotees his worshipable superiors, for they have the priceless treasure of natural responsiveness to *kṛṣṇa-kathā*.

## TEXT 140

अहो किलाशेषविलक्षणस्य
तदेकयोग्यस्य सदा कराब्जे ।
विक्रीडतस्तत्प्रियवस्तुनोऽपि
स्प्रष्टुं महत्त्वं रसना किमीष्टे ॥

*aho kilāśeṣa-vilakṣaṇasya*
*tad-eka-yogyasya sadā karābje*
*vikrīḍatas tat-priya-vastuno 'pi*
*spraṣṭuṁ mahattvaṁ rasanā kim īṣṭe*

*aho* — oh; *kila* — indeed; *aśeṣa* — from everything else; *vilakṣaṇasya* — which is distinct; *tat* — for Him; *eka* — only; *yogyasya* — suitable; *sadā* — always; *kara-abje* — in His lotus hand; *vikrīḍataḥ* — resting playfully; *tat* — that; *priya* — dear;

*vastunaḥ* — of the possession; *api* — even; *spraṣṭum* — to touch; *mahattvam* — the greatness; *rasanā* — my tongue; *kim* — how; *īṣṭe* — can desire.

**How can my tongue dare try to touch the greatness of Kṛṣṇa's dearmost possession, which stands out from all else, which befits only Him, and which always rests playfully in His lotus hands?**

COMMENTARY: The sound of Kṛṣṇa's flute attracted the young *gopīs* to join Kṛṣṇa in the *rāsa* dance, and after the *rāsa* dance that sound lingered in their memory. In *Śrīmad-Bhāgavatam,* Chapter Thirty-five, the *gopīs'* remembrance of that flute-song is captured in eleven pairs of verses, of which this pair is the first:

*śrī-gopya ūcuḥ*
*vāma-bāhu-kṛta-vāma-kapolo*
*valgita-bhrur adharārpita-veṇum*
*komalāṅgulibhir āśrita-mārgaṁ*
*gopya īrayati yatra mukundaḥ*

*vyoma-yāna-vanitāḥ saha siddhair*
*vismitās tad upadhārya sa-lajjāḥ*
*kāma-mārgaṇa-samarpita-cittāḥ*
*kaśmalaṁ yayur apasmṛta-nīvyaḥ*

"The *gopīs* said: When Mukunda vibrates the flute He has placed to His lips, stopping its holes with His tender fingers, He rests His left cheek on His left arm and makes His eyebrows dance. At that time the demigoddesses traveling in the sky with their husbands, the Siddhas, become amazed. As those ladies listen, they are embarrassed to find their minds yielding to the pursuit of lusty desires, and in their distress they are unaware that the belts of their garments are loosening." (*Bhāgavatam* 10.35.2–3)

Glorifying Kṛṣṇa's flute, Śrīla Sanātana Gosvāmī here begins a seventeen-verse discussion of the next topic, *aśeṣa-mahattva-mādhurī* ("the sweetness of all of Kṛṣṇa's excellent qualities").

Texts 140 through 149 specifically glorify Kṛṣṇa's flute. Everything about Kṛṣṇa's flute is exceptional. Since there is no other object like it in the entire world, there is nothing to compare it to. One can understand the greatness of that flute only by studying the amazing effects its sound produces. No one but Kṛṣṇa could own such a flute, and indeed Kṛṣṇa never lets it out of His hands; rather, He takes every opportunity to allow the flute to drink the nectar of His lips.

## TEXT 141

अथापि तत्प्रसादस्य प्रभावेणैव किञ्चन ।
यथाशक्ति तदाख्यामि भवत्ववहितो भवान् ॥

*athāpi tat-prasādasya*
*prabhāveṇaiva kiñcana*
*yathā-śakti tad ākhyāmi*
*bhavatv avahito bhavān*

*atha api* — nonetheless; *tat* — His; *prasādasya* — of the mercy; *prabhāveṇa* — by the power; *eva* — only; *kiñcana* — something; *yathā-śakti* — according to my capability; *tat* — that; *ākhyāmi* — I will say; *bhavatu* — please try to be; *avahitaḥ* — attentive; *bhavān* — your good self.

**Still, by the power of the Lord's mercy I will say something about it, as far as I am able. Please listen carefully.**

## TEXT 142

न श्रीमुखेनोपनिषन्मुखैः कृतं
यद्वेदवाक्यैरपरैर्वचोऽमृतैः ।
तत्तस्य बिम्बाधरयोगमात्रतः
सा दारवी मोहनवंशिकाकरोत् ॥

*na śrī-mukhenopaniṣan-mukhaiḥ kṛtaṁ*
*yad veda-vākyair aparair vaco-'mṛtaiḥ*
*tat tasya bimbādhara-yoga-mātrataḥ*
*sā dāravī mohana-vaṁśikākarot*

*na* — not; *śrī* — divine; *mukhena* — by the mouth; *upaniṣat* — by the *Upaniṣads; mukhaiḥ* — headed; *kṛtam* — created; *yat* — which; *veda* — of the *Vedas; vākyaiḥ* — by the words; *aparaiḥ* — other; *vacaḥ* — of speech; *amṛtaiḥ* — by the nectar; *tat* — that; *tasya* — His; *bimba-adhara* — of the lips like *bimba* fruit; *yoga-mātrataḥ* — simply by the contact; *sā* — that; *dāravī* — wooden object; *mohana* — enchanting; *vaṁśikā* — the little bamboo flute; *akarot* — created.

**The words of the Upaniṣads and the other Vedic texts come forth from the Lord's own divine mouth. But simply by contact with His bimba-red lips, that wooden object, the all-enchanting little bamboo flute, has created a sound more nectarean than the words of the Vedas and any other form of speech.**

COMMENTARY: Nārada has great admiration for Kṛṣṇa's flute, and so he calls it by the affectionate diminutive name *vaṁśikā* ("little bamboo flute"). At the same time, however, he cannot help but feel jealous of the flute's intimate relationship with Kṛṣṇa, which someone like himself can never have; therefore he also uses the somewhat derogatory term *dāravī* ("wooden object").

## TEXT 143

विमानयानाः सुरसिद्धसङ्घाः
समं वधूभिः प्रणयादमुह्यन् ।
महेन्द्ररुद्रद्रुहिणादयस्तु
मुग्धा गता विस्मृततत्त्वतां ते ॥

*vimāna-yānāḥ sura-siddha-saṅghāḥ*
*samaṁ vadhūbhiḥ praṇayād amuhyan*
*mahendra-rudra-druhiṇādayas tu*
*mugdhā gatā vismṛta-tattvatāṁ te*

*vimāna* — in airplanes; *yānāḥ* — traveling; *sura* — of demigods; *siddha* — and perfected mystics; *saṅghāḥ* — hordes; *samam* — along with; *vadhūbhiḥ* — their wives; *praṇayāt* — out of loving affection; *amuhyan* — became bewildered; *mahā-indra* — Lord Indra; *rudra* — Lord Śiva; *druhiṇa* — Lord Brahmā; *ādayaḥ* — and others; *tu* — and; *mugdhāḥ* — bewildered; *gatāḥ* — became; *vismṛta* — forgetful; *tattvatām* — about reality; *te* — they.

**Hearing that sound of the flute, all the demigods and perfected mystics flying in their airplanes were bewildered in divine love, and so were their wives. Indra, Śiva, Brahmā, and other demigods were so confused they could no longer tell fact from illusion.**

COMMENTARY: Flying over the earthly Vṛndāvana, the demigods and sages in their *vimānas,* the subtle vehicles that carry them all over the universe by the power of air, were helplessly attracted by Kṛṣṇa's flute, and their wives succumbed to the charms of Cupid. In *Śrīmad-Bhāgavatam* (10.21.12) the *gopīs* describe that scene:

*kṛṣṇaṁ nirīkṣya vanitotsava-rūpa-śīlaṁ*
*śrutvā ca tat-kvaṇita-veṇu-vicitra-gītam*
*devyo vimāna-gatayaḥ smara-nunna-sārā*
*bhraśyat-prasūna-kabarā mumuhur vinīvyaḥ*

"Kṛṣṇa's beauty and character create a festival for all women. Indeed, when the demigods' wives flying in airplanes with their husbands catch sight of Him and hear His resonant flute-song, their hearts are shaken by Cupid, and they become so bewildered that the flowers fall out of their hair and their belts loosen."

When the demigods and sages in their *vimānas* approached Vṛndāvana, they first heard the faint sound of Kṛṣṇa's flute from a distance. Then, as they came closer and the sound became more audible, even Brahmā, Śiva, and Indra were bewildered:

*vividha-gopa-caraṇeṣu vidagdho*
*veṇu-vādya urudhā nija-śikṣāḥ*
*tava sutaḥ sati yadādhara-bimbe*
*datta-veṇur anayat svara-jātīḥ*

*savanaśas tad upadhārya sureśāḥ*
*śakra-śarva-parameṣṭhi-purogāḥ*
*kavaya ānata-kandhara-cittāḥ*
*kaśmalaṁ yayur aniścita-tattvāḥ*

"O pious Mother Yaśodā, your son, who is expert in all the arts of herding cows, has invented many new styles of flute-playing. When He takes His flute to His *bimba*-red lips and sends forth harmonious tones in variegated melodies, Brahmā, Śiva, Indra, and other chief demigods become confused upon hearing the sound. Although they are the most learned authorities, they cannot ascertain the essence of that music, and thus they bow down their heads and hearts." (*Bhāgavatam* 10.35.14–15) The principal demigods and sages were so confused they couldn't even remember their own identities. They thought, "Now we can no longer be certain whether the Brahman we know from the *Upaniṣads* is actually the Absolute Truth. Perhaps the sound of this flute is the Absolute Truth instead, because it seems to be the supreme embodiment of pure ecstasy."

### TEXT 144

समाधिभङ्गोऽथ महामुनीनां
विकारजातस्य च जन्म तेषु ।
तत्कालचक्रभ्रमणानुवर्ति-
चन्द्रादिनित्याशुगतेर्निरोधः ॥

*samādhi-bhaṅgo 'tha mahā-munīnāṁ*
*vikāra-jātasya ca janma teṣu*
*tat-kāla-cakra-bhramaṇānuvarti-*
*candrādi-nityāśu-gater nirodhaḥ*

*samādhi* — of the meditation; *bhaṅgaḥ* — disruption; *atha* — and; *mahā-munīnām* — of the great sages; *vikāra-jātasya* — of various transformations; *ca* — and; *janma* — development; *teṣu* — in them; *tat* — that; *kāla* — of time; *cakra* — of the wheel; *bhramaṇa* — rotation; *anuvarti* — who follow; *candra-ādi* — of the moon and other planets; *nitya* — perpetual; *āśu* — swift; *gateḥ* — of the motion; *nirodhaḥ* — cessation.

**The great sages, their meditations breaking, felt transformations of ecstasy arising within themselves. And the motions of the moon and other planets, swift and unceasing, which strictly follow the whirling wheel of time, just stopped.**

COMMENTARY: Not only the faithful theists among the demigods and sages but also the self-contented impersonalists were enchanted by Kṛṣṇa's flute. Those impersonalists also experienced the *sāttvika-bhāvas* of love of God — trembling, horripilation, floods of tears, and so on — which they could never have dreamt of while philosophizing on the bliss of Brahman. And apart from those independent sages, also overcome by *prema* were the planets in space, whose motions are normally dictated by the rule of time. The planets felt the *sāttvika-bhāva* of being stunned, as indicated by the words of the *gopīs:* "Brahmā, Śiva, Indra, and other chief demigods become confused upon hearing the sound." (*Bhāgavatam* 10.35.15) The "other chief demigods" referred to include Candra, Sūrya, and the other rulers of the planets. Śrīla Śukadeva Gosvāmī also mentions the ecstasy of the planets in his account of the *rāsa-līlā:*

*kṛṣṇa-vikrīḍitaṁ vīkṣya*
*mumuhuḥ khe-cara-striyaḥ*

*kāmārditāḥ śaśāṅkaś ca*
*sa-gaṇo vismito 'bhavat*

"The wives of the demigods, observing Kṛṣṇa's playful activities from their airplanes, were entranced and became agitated with lust. Indeed, even the moon and his entourage, the stars, became astonished." (*Bhāgavatam* 10.33.18)

## TEXT 145

गोपाश्च कृष्णेऽर्पितदेहदैहिका-
त्मनो निजाचारविचारचञ्चलाः ।
लोकद्वयार्थेष्वनपेक्षितादृता
भार्यामपि स्वस्य नमन्ति तत्प्रियाम् ॥

*gopāś ca kṛṣṇe 'rpita-deha-daihikā-*
*tmano nijācāra-vicāra-cañcalāḥ*
*loka-dvayārtheṣv anapekṣitādṛtā*
*bhāryām api svasya namanti tat-priyām*

*gopāḥ* — the cowherds; *ca* — and; *kṛṣṇe* — to Kṛṣṇa; *arpita* — dedicated; *deha* — whose bodies; *daihika* — families; *ātmanaḥ* — and souls; *nija* — their own; *ācāra* — about the customs; *vicāra* — and personal concerns; *cañcalāḥ* — indifferent; *loka-dvaya* — of the two worlds (this life and the next); *artheṣu* — to the goals; *anapekṣita-ādṛtāḥ* — paying no respect; *bhāryām* — to their wives; *api* — even; *svasya* — own; *namanti* — they offer obeisances; *tat* — to Him; *priyām* — who are dear.

**The cowherds dedicated to Kṛṣṇa everything they had—their bodies, families, and property and their very selves. Those cowherds, indifferent to their own customs and needs, paying no regard to success in this world or the next, had so much respect for Kṛṣṇa that they even bowed down to their own wives, because those wives were dear to Him.**

COMMENTARY: Persons unfamiliar with Kṛṣṇa were not the only ones bewildered by His charms; even His own close friends and family members were confused. The *gopas* of Vraja offered everything they had to Kṛṣṇa, including their children and wives. Thus in the *Hari-vaṁśa* (2.12.46) the *gopas* tell Śrī Nanda Mahārāja:

*adya-prabhṛti gopānāṁ*
*gavāṁ goṣṭhasya cānagha*
*āpatsu śaraṇaṁ kṛṣṇaḥ*
*prabhuś cāyata-locanaḥ*

"From today onward, O sinless one, in dangerous situations broad-eyed Kṛṣṇa will be the shelter for the cowherds, the cows, and our whole community. He will be the master of us all." The phrase "our whole community" implies that the *gopas* meant to include in their statement the young *gopīs* but were too embarrassed to mention Kṛṣṇa's relationship with them directly. As the *gopas* well know, even their own wives belong to Kṛṣṇa; therefore, when the *gopas* refer to them as *bhāryā,* the women they are responsible to maintain, they mean for Kṛṣṇa's enjoyment, not their own.

## TEXT 146

तद्बालकाः सङ्गरता हि तस्य
छाया इवामुं क्षणमप्यदृष्ट्वा ।
दूरे गतं कौतुकतः कदाचिद्
आर्ता रमन्ते त्वरया स्पृशन्तः ॥

*tad-bālakāḥ saṅga-ratā hi tasya*
*chāyā ivāmuṁ kṣaṇam apy adṛṣṭvā*
*dūre gataṁ kautukataḥ kadācid*
*ārtā ramante tvarayā spṛśantaḥ*

*tat* — of them (the cowherds); *bālakāḥ* — the sons; *saṅga-ratāḥ* — attached to the association; *hi* — indeed; *tasya* — His; *chāyā*

— His shadow; *iva* — like; *amum* — Him; *kṣaṇam* — for a moment; *api* — even; *adṛṣṭvā* — not seeing; *dūre* — to a distance; *gatam* — gone; *kautukataḥ* — on a whim; *kadācit* — sometime; *ārtāḥ* — distressed; *ramante* — they delighted; *tvarayā* — rapidly; *spṛśantaḥ* — touching.

**So attached to Kṛṣṇa's company were the cowherds' little sons that they acted just like His shadow. If even for a moment they couldn't see Him—if He sometimes went away on a whim—they were filled with distress. And when He returned they would rejoice and rush to touch Him.**

COMMENTARY: Kṛṣṇa's cowherd friends were with Him constantly. Sometimes, however, Kṛṣṇa would leave them for a short while to pursue some other interest, like seeing the beautiful sights of Vṛndāvana. In *Śrīmad-Bhāgavatam* (10.12.6) Śukadeva Gosvāmī describes how when Kṛṣṇa returned from those excursions His friends would greet Him:

*yadi dūraṁ gataḥ kṛṣṇo*
*vana-śobhekṣaṇāya tam*
*ahaṁ pūrvam ahaṁ pūrvam*
*iti saṁspṛśya remire*

"Sometimes Kṛṣṇa would go to a somewhat distant place to see the beauty of the forest. Then all the other boys would run to meet Him, each one saying, 'I shall be the first to run and touch Kṛṣṇa! I shall touch Kṛṣṇa first!' In this way they enjoyed life by repeatedly touching Kṛṣṇa."

## TEXT 147

राधाद्यास्ताः परमभगवत्यस्तु पत्यात्मजादीन्
लोकान्धर्मान् ह्रियमपि परित्यज्य भावं तमाप्ताः ।
येनाजस्रं मधुरकटुकैर्व्याकुलास्तद्विकारैर्
मुग्धाः किञ्चित्तरुगतिमिता नानुसन्धातुमीशाः ॥

*rādhādyās tāḥ parama-bhagavatyas tu paty-ātmajādīn*
*lokān dharmān hriyam api parityajya bhāvaṁ tam āptāḥ*
*yenājasraṁ madhura-kaṭukair vyākulās tad-vikārair*
*mugdhāḥ kiñcit taru-gatim itā nānusandhātum īśāḥ*

*rādhā-ādyāḥ* — Śrī Rādhā and the others; *tāḥ* — they; *parama* — supremely; *bhagavatyaḥ* — fortunate; *tu* — and; *pati* — their husbands; *ātmaja* — sons; *ādīn* — and so on; *lokān* — destinations in the next life; *dharmān* — religious duties; *hriyam* — shyness; *api* — also; *parityajya* — abandoned; *bhāvam tam* — that ecstatic love; *āptāḥ* — attained; *yena* — by which; *ajasram* — constantly; *madhura* — sweet; *kaṭukaiḥ* — with plaintive cries; *vyākulāḥ* — distressed; *tat* — of that (ecstatic love); *vikāraiḥ* — by the transformations; *mugdhāḥ* — bewildered; *kiñcit* — anything; *taru-gatim* — the fate of trees; *itāḥ* — attaining; *na* — not; *anusandhātum* — to understand; *īśāḥ* — capable.

**Śrī Rādhā and the other supremely fortunate gopīs abandoned their husbands, children, and other relatives, their goals for the next life, their religious principles, and even their shyness; and the states of ecstatic love they attained left them always distraught. In such states they complained pitifully in sweet voices and went through upheavals in which they sometimes lost consciousness, stunned like trees, unable to understand anything.**

COMMENTARY: Śrī Rukmiṇī and the other queens of Dvārakā are the consorts of Bhagavān, the Personality of Godhead, but the *gopīs* headed by Śrīmatī Rādhārāṇī are the favorite devotees of Parama-bhagavān, the Personality of Godhead in His highest feature. Their love for Kṛṣṇa drives them to extreme states of ecstasy, as they tell in their own words:

*nija-padābja-dalair dhvaja-vajra-*
*nīrajāṅkuśa-vicitra-lalāmaiḥ*

*vraja-bhuvaḥ śamayan khura-todaṁ*
*varṣma-dhurya-gatir īḍita-veṇuḥ*

*vrajati tena vayaṁ sa-vilāsa-*
*vīkṣaṇārpita-manobhava-vegāḥ*
*kuja-gatiṁ gamitā na vidāmaḥ*
*kaśmalena kavaraṁ vasanaṁ vā*

"As Kṛṣṇa strolls through Vraja with His lotus-petal feet, marking the ground with the distinctive emblems of flag, thunderbolt, lotus, and elephant goad, He relieves the distress the ground feels from the cows' hooves. As He plays His renowned flute, His body moves with the grace of an elephant. Thus we *gopīs,* who become agitated by Cupid when Kṛṣṇa playfully glances at us, stand as still as trees, unaware that our hair and garments are becoming loose." (*Śrīmad-Bhāgavatam* 10.35.16–17)

Nārada speaks of the *gopīs'* complaints as *madhura-kaṭukaiḥ,* bittersweet, for those who hear them are overwhelmed both by joy and by sorrow. Everyone living in Vraja during Kṛṣṇa's presence was constantly immersed in intense *prema,* but when Kṛṣṇa played His flute the ecstasy of that *prema* grew unlimitedly, affecting not only those already in love with Kṛṣṇa, but all beings, living and inert.

## TEXT 148

आश्चर्यं वै शृणु पशुगणा बुद्धिहीनत्वमाप्ता
गावो वत्सा वृषवनमृगाः पक्षिणो वृक्षवासाः ।
दूरे क्रीडारतजलखगाः स्थावरा ज्ञानशून्या
नद्यो मेघा अपि निजनिजं तत्यजुस्तं स्वभावम् ॥

*āścaryaṁ vai śṛṇu paśu-gaṇā buddhi-hīnatvam āptā*
*gāvo vatsā vṛṣa-vana-mṛgāḥ pakṣiṇo vṛkṣa-vāsāḥ*
*dūre krīḍā-rata-jala-khagāḥ sthāvarā jñāna-śūnyā*
*nadyo meghā api nija-nijaṁ tatyajus taṁ svabhāvam*

*āścaryam* — wonder; *vai* — indeed; *śṛṇu* — please hear; *paśu-gaṇāḥ* — the many animals; *buddhi* — of intelligence; *hīnatvam* — lack; *āptāḥ* — who had; *gāvaḥ* — cows; *vatsāḥ* — calves; *vṛṣa* — bulls; *vana* — of the forest; *mṛgāḥ* — and beasts; *pakṣiṇaḥ* — birds; *vṛkṣa* — in the trees; *vāsāḥ* — whose residence; *dūre* — at a distance; *krīḍā-rata* — absorbed in sporting; *jala-khagāḥ* — waterfowl; *sthāvarāḥ* — living beings unable to move; *jñāna-śūnyāḥ* — unconscious; *nadyaḥ* — rivers; *meghāḥ* — clouds; *api* — even; *nija-nijam* — each their own; *tatyajuḥ* — would abandon; *tam* — that; *svabhāvam* — specific nature.

**Listen, and I will tell you the most wonderful thing: Upon hearing Kṛṣṇa's flute, the many animals, born without intelligence, abandoned their own natures. The cows did, and the bulls and calves, and the wild beasts of the forest, and the birds living in the trees, and the water birds sporting in distant lakes, and so too did the trees and plants and even the inanimate beings like rivers and clouds.**

COMMENTARY: One would expect the Vraja-vāsīs, expert in the arts of *rasa,* to respond ecstatically to the sound of Kṛṣṇa's flute. What is amazing is that dull animals and even lesser beings shared that ecstasy.

The creatures of Vṛndāvana mentioned in this verse are listed in order of decreasing intelligence. Along with the cows, bulls, and calves, the village animals also included buffaloes, sheep, and goats. Those domestic animals kept company with Kṛṣṇa every day. The deer and other forest animals saw Him less often, but even they tasted the ecstasies of *prema* when they heard Kṛṣṇa's flute. The birds frequenting the Vṛndāvana forest, who knew Kṛṣṇa from the times He had rested beneath their trees, and even the birds who lived in lakes far away, had the divine intelligence to come nearby when Kṛṣṇa played His flute. The unmoving creatures — the trees, bushes, and vines — and even the nonliving rivers also joined this festival of ecstasy initiated by Kṛṣṇa's flute song. And apart from all the beings present in Vraja on the surface of the earth, those who joined in that festival included even the clouds in the sky.

TEXT 149

चराः स्थिरत्वं चरतां स्थिरा गताः
सचेतना मोहमचेतना मतिम् ।
निमज्जिताः प्रेमरसे महत्यहो
विकारजाताक्रमिताः सदाभवन् ॥

*carāḥ sthiratvaṁ caratāṁ sthirā gatāḥ*
*sa-cetanā moham acetanā matim*
*nimajjitāḥ prema-rase mahaty aho*
*vikāra-jātākramitāḥ sadābhavan*

*carāḥ* — mobile creatures; *sthiratvam* — immobility; *caratām* — mobility; *sthirāḥ* — unmoving beings; *gatāḥ* — attained; *sa-cetanāḥ* — conscious beings; *moham* — unconsciousness; *acetanāḥ* — senseless beings; *matim* — consciousness; *nimajjitāḥ* — drowned; *prema-rase* — in the blissful nectar of pure love; *mahati* — vast; *aho* — oh; *vikāra-jāta* — by many kinds of transformations; *ākramitāḥ* — overcome; *sadā* — always; *abhavan* — they were.

**The moving creatures became immobile, the inanimate beings moved; the conscious beings lost consciousness, and the unconscious gained it. Constantly, indeed, these creatures and objects were submerged in a vast flood of prema-rasa, overwhelmed by many transformations of ecstasy.**

COMMENTARY: Animals, stunned by ecstasy, lost their power to move. Trees and other plants became mobile, trembling and erupting with new leaves. Conscious creatures no longer showed external expressions of life, and unconscious logs and stones appeared to come alive by sprouting leaves and rolling about in the wind. All these extraordinary phenomena were signs of the ecstasy evoked by the song of Kṛṣṇa's flute. In the words of the *gopīs:*

*gā gopakair anu-vanaṁ nayator udāra-*
*veṇu-svanaiḥ kala-padais tanu-bhṛtsu sakhyaḥ*
*aspandanaṁ gati-matāṁ pulakas tarūṇāṁ*
*niryoga-pāśa-kṛta-lakṣaṇayor vicitram*

"Dear friends, as Kṛṣṇa and Balarāma pass through the forest with Their cowherd friends, leading Their cows, They carry ropes to bind the cows' rear legs at the time of milking. When Lord Kṛṣṇa plays on His flute, the sweet music causes the moving living entities to become stunned and the nonmoving trees to tremble with ecstasy. These things are certainly very wonderful." (*Bhāgavatam* 10.21.19)

## TEXT 150

रासो हि तस्य भगवत्त्वविशेषगोप्यः
सर्वस्वसारपरिपाकमयो व्यनक्ति ।
उत्कृष्टतामधुरिमापरसीमनिष्ठां
लक्ष्म्या मनोरथशतैरपि यो दुरापः ॥

*rāso hi tasya bhagavattva-viśeṣa-gopyaḥ*
*sarvasva-sāra-paripāka-mayo vyanakti*
*utkṛṣṭatā-madhurimāpara-sīma-niṣṭhāṁ*
*lakṣmyā manoratha-śatair api yo durāpaḥ*

*rāsaḥ* — the *rāsa* dance; *hi* — indeed; *tasya* — His; *bhagavattva* — the status of God; *viśeṣa* — unique; *gopyaḥ* — and most confidential; *sarva-sva* — of everything He possesses; *sāra* — of the essence; *paripāka-mayaḥ* — comprising the perfection; *vyanakti* — reveals; *utkṛṣṭatā* — of His superexcellence; *madhurimā* — and of His sweetness; *apara-sīma-niṣṭhām* — the final limit; *lakṣmyā* — by the goddess Lakṣmī; *manoratha* —

with aspirations; *śataiḥ* — hundreds; *api* — even; *yaḥ* — which; *durāpaḥ* — impossible to obtain.

**The Lord's rāsa dance discloses the most confidential essence of His Godhood. It embodies the perfection of everything most dear to Him. It reveals the final limit of His supremacy and sweetness. The goddess Lakṣmī couldn't enter that dance, even after aspiring to do so in hundreds of attempts.**

COMMENTARY: Lakṣmī, the consort of Lord Nārāyaṇa, desired with all her heart to join the *rāsa* dance, but all the austerities she performed to gain this privilege proved futile. As Uddhava sings in *Śrīmad-Bhāgavatam* (10.47.60):

*nāyaṁ śriyo 'ṅga u nitānta-rateḥ prasādaḥ*
*svar-yoṣitāṁ nalina-gandha-rucāṁ kuto 'nyāḥ*
*rāsotsave 'sya bhuja-daṇḍa-gṛhīta-kaṇṭha-*
*labdhāśiṣāṁ ya udagād vraja-sundarīṇām*

"When Lord Śrī Kṛṣṇa was dancing with the *gopīs* in the *rāsa-līlā,* the *gopīs* were embraced by the arms of the Lord. This transcendental favor was never bestowed upon the goddess of fortune or other consorts in the spiritual world. Indeed, never was such a thing even imagined by the most beautiful girls in the heavenly planets, whose bodily luster and aroma resemble those of the lotus. And what to speak of worldly women who are very beautiful by mundane estimation?" The *gopīs* who enjoy Kṛṣṇa's embraces in the *rāsa* dance are clearly much more fortunate than Lakṣmī, and the *rāsa* dance is clearly the most glorious of the Supreme Lord's pastimes.

## TEXT 151

अहो वैदग्धी सा मधुरमधुरा श्रीभगवतः
समाकर्षत्युच्चैर्जगति कृतिनः कस्य न मनः ।

कुलस्त्रीणां तासां वनभुवि तथाकर्षणमथो
तथा वाक्चातुर्यं सपदि रुदितं ताभिरपि यत् ॥

*aho vaidagdhī sā madhura-madhurā śrī-bhagavataḥ*
*samākarṣaty uccair jagati kṛtinaḥ kasya na manaḥ*
*kula-strīṇāṁ tāsāṁ vana-bhuvi tathākarṣaṇam atho*
*tathā vāk-cāturyaṁ sapadi ruditaṁ tābhir api yat*

*aho* — oh; *vaidagdhī* — skill; *sā* — that; *madhura* — than the sweetest; *madhurā* — sweeter; *śrī-bhagavataḥ* — of the Supreme Lord; *samākarṣati* — attracts; *uccaiḥ* — powerfully; *jagati* — in this world; *kṛtinaḥ* — of the pious person; *kasya* — which; *na* — not; *manaḥ* — the mind; *kula-strīṇām* — of the women of good families; *tāsām* — them; *vana-bhuvi* — in the region of the forest; *tathā* — thus; *ākarṣaṇam* — the attracting; *atha u* — and thus; *tathā* — thus; *vāk* — of speech; *cāturyam* — the cleverness; *sapadi* — at once; *ruditam* — the crying; *tābhiḥ* — by them; *api* — and; *yat* — which.

**Oh, this most sweet skill of the Lord in loving dealings! What pious mind would not be utterly entranced by Kṛṣṇa's attracting women of good families to join Him in the forest, by the clever words He spoke to them, and by the way they responded by at once breaking into tearful sobs?**

COMMENTARY: Texts 151 through 156 elaborate on the glories of Kṛṣṇa's *rāsa-līlā,* following Śrī Śukadeva Gosvāmī's description in the five chapters of *Śrīmad-Bhāgavatam* called *rāsa-pañcādhyāya.*

## TEXT 152

श्लाघेऽवहित्थाकृतितां हरेस्तां
तत्काकुजाताद्यदि सा स्थिता स्यात् ।
व्यक्तात्मभावः क्षणतः स रेमे
ता मोहयन्कामकलावलीभिः ॥

*ślāghe 'vahitthā-kṛtitāṁ hares tāṁ*
*tat-kāku-jātād yadi sā sthitā syāt*
*vyaktātma-bhāvaḥ kṣaṇataḥ sa reme*
*tā mohayan kāma-kalāvalībhiḥ*

*ślāghe* — I praise; *avahitthā* — in concealing; *kṛtitām* — the expertise; *hareḥ* — of Lord Hari; *tām* — that; *tat* — of them (the *gopīs*); *kāku* — from the complaints; *jātāt* — born; *yadi* — if; *sā* — that; *sthitā* — steady; *syāt* — would be; *vyakta* — revealed; *ātma* — His own; *bhāvaḥ* — true feelings; *kṣaṇataḥ* — at once; *saḥ* — He; *reme* — enjoyed; *tāḥ* — them; *mohayan* — enchanting; *kāma* — of Cupid; *kalā-avalībhiḥ* — with all the arts.

**I could praise the Lord's expertise in concealing His mind from the gopīs had He been able to keep it concealed after they pitifully complained. But once they began to cry He showed them His true feelings and enjoyed with those gopīs, enchanting them with all the arts of Cupid.**

COMMENTARY: Pure worship of the Supreme Personality of Godhead has the power to awaken the transcendental Cupid sleeping in the hearts of all conditioned souls. To introduce such worship was Kṛṣṇa's main purpose for coming into the material world, and so it is that His pastimes on earth resemble the activities of ordinary people. But in the course of performing His intimate pastimes, He also displays His complete opulences. As mentioned by Śrī Śukadeva at the very end of the Tenth Canto (*Bhāgavatam* 10.90.48), *su-smita-śrī-mukhena/ vraja-pura-vanitānāṁ vardhayan kāma-devam:* His blissful smiling face always increases the lusty desires of the *gopīs* of Vṛndāvana. Commenting on this verse, Śrīla Śrīdhara Svāmī notes, "This Cupid is effulgent (*deva*) in the sense that He intends to conquer the material world. In other words, He bestows liberation by means of transcendental sense enjoyment."

Śukadeva Gosvāmī also discloses this transcendental pleasure in the Tenth Canto of *Śrīmad-Bhāgavatam,* chapters 29 through 33, which are dedicated to the *rāsa-līlā:*

*bāhu-prasāra-parirambha-karālakoru-*
*nīvī-stanālabhana-narma-nakhāgra-pātaiḥ*
*kṣvelyāvaloka-hasitair vraja-sundarīṇām*
*uttambhayan rati-patiṁ ramayāṁ cakāra*

"Kṛṣṇa threw His arms around the *gopīs* and embraced them. He aroused Cupid in the beautiful young ladies of Vraja by touching their hands, hair, thighs, belts, and breasts, by playfully scratching them with His fingernails, and also by joking with them, glancing at them, and laughing with them. In this way the Lord enjoyed His pastimes." (*Bhāgavatam* 10.29.46)

## TEXT 153

अन्तर्धानं तस्य तद्विप्रलम्भ-
लीलादक्षस्यानिशं को न गायेत् ।
यत्तास्तादृग्धैर्यगाम्भीर्यभाजो
ऽनैषीत्तां तामुक्तिमीहां दशां च ॥

*antardhānaṁ tasya tad vipralambha-*
*līlā-dakṣasyāniśaṁ ko na gāyet*
*yat tās tādṛg-dhairya-gāmbhīrya-bhājo*
*'naiṣīt tāṁ tām uktim īhāṁ daśāṁ ca*

*antardhānam* — disappearance; *tasya* — His; *tat* — that; *vipralambha* — of separation; *līlā* — in pastimes; *dakṣasya* — who is expert; *aniśam* — constantly; *kaḥ* — who; *na gāyet* — will not sing about; *yat* — which; *tāḥ* — them (the *gopīs*); *tādṛk* — such; *dhairya* — of composure; *gāmbhīrya* — and sobriety; *bhājaḥ* — possessors; *anaiṣīt* — brought; *tām tām* — to all these; *uktim* — speech; *īhām* — behavior; *daśām* — states of consciousness; *ca* — and.

**Who can avoid constantly chanting the glories of the Lord's disappearance from the rāsa dance? He is so expert in pastimes of separation. Though the gopīs were endowed**

**with great composure and sobriety, that separation transported them to extraordinary ways of speaking and acting and extraordinary states of heart.**

COMMENTARY: Kṛṣṇa is especially skillful in making His devotees feel agony in separation from Him. More than once He subjected the *gopīs* to such sorrow by abandoning them. When He disappeared from the *rāsa* dance, the *gopīs* apparently went insane and inquired from the animals and plants whether they knew where Kṛṣṇa had gone:

*dṛṣṭo vaḥ kaccid aśvattha*
*plakṣa nyagrodha no manaḥ*
*nanda-sūnur gato hṛtvā*
*prema-hāsāvalokanaiḥ*

"O *aśvattha* tree, O *plakṣa,* O *nyagrodha,* have you seen Kṛṣṇa? That son of Nanda Mahārāja has gone away after stealing our minds with His loving smiles and glances." (*Bhāgavatam* 10.30.5) Speaking thus, the intimate *gopīs* began to act out Kṛṣṇa's pastimes, and they reached the highest limits of *mahā-bhāva,* the devotional ecstasy known only by Śrīmatī Rādhārāṇī and Her most intimate associates.

## TEXT 154

बिभेम्यस्माद्धन्त दुर्बोधलीलात्
क्व तत्तस्याः सारसौभाग्यदानम् ।
क्व सद्योऽन्तर्धानतो रोदनाब्धाव्
अनाथाया यातनैकाकिनी या ॥

*bibhemy asmād dhanta durbodha-līlāt*
*kva tat tasyāḥ sāra-saubhāgya-dānam*
*kva sadyo 'ntardhānato rodanābdhāv*
*anāthāyā yātanaikākinī yā*

*bibhemi* — I am frightened; *asmāt* — by Him; *hanta* — alas; *durbodha* — unfathomable; *līlāt* — whose pastimes; *kva* — whereas; *tat* — that; *tasyāḥ* — to them (the *gopīs*); *sāra* — essential; *saubhāgya* — of good fortune; *dānam* — the granting; *kva* — whereas; *sadyaḥ* — sudden; *antardhānataḥ* — by His disappearance; *rodana* — of lamentation; *abdhau* — in an ocean; *anāthāyāḥ* — of a person who has lost her master; *yātanā* — the torment; *ekākinī* — exclusive; *yā* — which.

**So inconceivable are His pastimes that they frighten me! How could He grant the gopīs the very essence of all good fortune and then suddenly cast them into an ocean of grief, a torment known only to a woman deprived of her life and soul?**

COMMENTARY: Nārada considers Kṛṣṇa's *rāsa-līlā* beyond his comprehension. As hard as he tries, he cannot fully understand it. He can only offer respects to Kṛṣṇa, who graced Śrīmatī Rādhārāṇī with His greatest favor by taking Her away alone from the *rāsa* dance but who then suddenly disappeared, abandoning Her to Her own lamentation. At that moment even Her girlfriends, too far away to hear Her cries, were unable to help Her.

## TEXT 155

तासामार्त्या गीतवद्रोदनाद्यः
प्रादुर्भूयानन्दपूरं व्यधत्त ।
यः प्रश्नानामुत्तरं तद्ददौ च
स्वस्यर्णित्वस्थापकं सोऽवतु त्वाम् ॥

*tāsām ārtyā gīta-vad-rodanād yaḥ*
*prādurbhūyānanda-pūraṁ vyadhatta*
*yaḥ praśnānām uttaraṁ tad dadau ca*
*svasyarṇitva-sthāpakaṁ so 'vatu tvām*

*tāsām* — their; *ārtyā* — in distress; *gīta-vat* — songlike; *rodanāt*

— because of the crying; *yaḥ* — who (Kṛṣṇa); *prādurbhūya* — appearing; *ānanda* — of bliss; *pūram* — in an inundation; *vyadhatta* — placed them (the *gopīs*); *yaḥ* — who; *praśnānām* — of their questions; *uttaram* — the answer; *tat* — that; *dadau* — gave; *ca* — and; *svasya* — His; *ṛṇitva* — indebtedness; *sthāpakam* — which established; *saḥ* — He; *avatu* — may protect; *tvām* — you.

**Their sorrowful songlike crying made Kṛṣṇa reappear, to flood them with pure ecstasy. The answer He then gave to their questions proved His indebtedness. May that Lord protect you.**

COMMENTARY: Moved by their cries of trepidation, Kṛṣṇa returned to the *rāsa* dance and immersed all the *gopīs* in a flood of indescribable bliss. The *gopīs* then asked Kṛṣṇa about the mystery of His attitude toward them:

*bhajato 'nubhajanty eka*
*eka etad-viparyayam*
*nobhayāṁś ca bhajanty eka*
*etan no brūhi sādhu bhoḥ*

"Some people reciprocate the affection only of those who are affectionate toward them, while others show affection even to those who are indifferent or inimical. And yet others will not show affection toward anyone. Dear Kṛṣṇa, please properly explain this matter to us." (*Bhāgavatam* 10.32.16) In response to this question, Kṛṣṇa told the *gopīs:*

*na pāraye 'haṁ niravadya-saṁyujāṁ*
*sva-sādhu-kṛtyaṁ vibudhāyuṣāpi vaḥ*
*yā mābhajan durjara-geha-śṛṅkhalāḥ*
*saṁvṛścya tad vaḥ pratiyātu sādhunā*

"I am not able to repay My debt for your spotless service, even within a lifetime of Brahmā. Your connection with Me is beyond reproach. You have worshiped Me, cutting off all domestic ties, which are difficult to break. Therefore please let your own glorious deeds be your compensation." (*Bhāgavatam* 10.32.22)

The full purport of this statement will be discussed toward the end of *Śrī Bṛhad-bhāgavatāmṛta*.

## TEXT 156

सा मण्डलीबन्धनचातुरी प्रभोः
सा नृत्यगीतादिकलासु दक्षता ।
सापूर्वशोभाधिकतापरम्परा
मुष्णाति चेतो मम विश्वमोहिनी ॥

*sā maṇḍalī-bandhana-cāturī prabhoḥ*
*sā nṛtya-gītādi-kalāsu dakṣatā*
*sāpūrva-śobhādhikatā-paramparā*
*muṣṇāti ceto mama viśva-mohinī*

*sā* — that; *maṇḍalī* — of circles; *bandhana* — in forming; *cāturī* — cleverness; *prabhoḥ* — of the Lord; *sā* — that; *nṛtya* — of dance; *gīta-ādi* — song and so on; *kalāsu* — in the arts; *dakṣatā* — expertise; *sā* — that; *apūrva* — unprecedented; *śobhā* — of splendor; *adhikatā* — kinds of abundance; *paramparā* —one after another; *muṣṇāti* — steals away; *cetaḥ* — mind; *mama* — my; *viśva* — the universe; *mohinī* — which enchant.

**The Lord's cleverness at expertly arranging the gopīs in a circle, His expertise in arts like dance and song—the perfections of splendor, one after another, that were never seen before—those wonders steal away my heart and enchant the entire world.**

COMMENTARY: As expressed by the word *ādi* ("and so on") in the phrase *nṛtya-gītādi-kalāsu,* Kṛṣṇa not only artistically danced and sang with the *gopīs* but also played wonderful water sports with them in the Yamunā. These pastimes enchant great sages like Nārada — and enchant everyone in the world.

## TEXT 157

कृष्णाङ्घ्रिपद्ममकरन्दनिपानलुब्धो
जानाति तद्रसलिहां परमं महत्त्वम् ।
ब्रह्मैव गोकुलभुवामयमुद्धवोऽपि
गोपीगणस्य यदिमौ लषतः स्म तत्तत् ॥

*kṛṣṇāṅghri-padma-makaranda-nipāna-lubdho*
*jānāti tad-rasa-lihāṁ paramaṁ mahattvam*
*brahmaiva gokula-bhuvām ayam uddhavo 'pi*
*gopī-gaṇasya yad imau laṣataḥ sma tat tat*

*kṛṣṇa* — of Kṛṣṇa; *aṅghri-padma* — at the lotus feet; *makaranda* — the sweet sap; *nipāna* — for drinking; *lubdhaḥ* — one who is greedy; *jānāti* — knows; *tat* — that; *rasa* — nectar; *lihām* — of those who lick; *paramam* — supreme; *mahattvam* — the greatness; *brahmā* — Lord Brahmā; *eva* — indeed; *gokula-bhuvām* — of those born in Gokula; *ayam* — this person; *uddhavaḥ* — Uddhava; *api* — also; *gopī-gaṇasya* — of the *gopīs; yat* — inasmuch as; *imau* — these two (Brahmā and Uddhava); *laṣataḥ sma* — hankered; *tat tat* — for all of that.

**One who is greedy to drink the nectar at Kṛṣṇa's lotus feet knows how exalted are the devotees who relish it. Lord Brahmā therefore longs to come in touch with the greatness of those born in Gokula, and our friend Uddhava with the special greatness of the gopīs.**

COMMENTARY: While describing the glories of Śrī Mathurā Gokula, Nārada has already pointed out the glories of the Vraja-vāsīs, but now he wants to discuss their greatness in more detail. First he dispels all doubts about the Vraja-vāsīs' exaltedness. In the opinion of wise spiritual authorities like Brahmājī and Uddhava, the residents of Vraja are the most fortunate persons.

Brahmā showed in his prayers to Kṛṣṇa in Vṛndāvana that he is eager not only to become Kṛṣṇa's servant but more specifically to be given a little of the good fortune possessed by the Vraja-vāsīs. Brahmā said:

*tad bhūri-bhāgyam iha janma kim apy aṭavyāṁ*
*yad gokule 'pi katamāṅghri-rajo-'bhiṣekam*
*yaj-jīvitaṁ tu nikhilaṁ bhagavān mukundas*
*tv adyāpi yat-pada-rajaḥ śruti-mṛgyam eva*

"My greatest possible good fortune would be to take any birth whatever in this forest of Gokula and have my head bathed by the dust falling from the lotus feet of any of its residents. Their entire life and soul is the Supreme Personality of Godhead, Mukunda, the dust of whose lotus feet is still being searched for in the Vedic *mantras*." (*Bhāgavatam* 10.14.34)

When Uddhava visited Vṛndāvana he spoke similar praise of the *gopīs:*

*āsām aho caraṇa-reṇu-juṣām ahaṁ syāṁ*
*vṛndāvane kim api gulma-latauṣadhīnām*
*yā dustyajaṁ sva-janam ārya-pathaṁ ca hitvā*
*bhejur mukunda-padavīṁ śrutibhir vimṛgyām*

"The *gopīs* of Vṛndāvana have given up the association of their husbands, sons, and other family members, who are very difficult to give up, and have forsaken the path of chastity to take shelter of the lotus feet of Mukunda, Kṛṣṇa, which one should search for by Vedic knowledge. Oh, let me be fortunate enough to be one of the bushes, creepers, or herbs in Vṛndāvana, because the *gopīs* trample them and bless them with the dust of their lotus feet." (*Bhāgavatam* 10.47.61)

One should not think that Brahmā's aspiration for any birth at all in Vṛndāvana is better than Uddhava's specific desire for a birth in which he can have on his head the dust from the *gopīs'* feet. Brahmā, after all, is the appointed ruler of the material world, and simply to become a pure servant of Kṛṣṇa would be a great success for him. Uddhava, however, being already Kṛṣṇa's intimate servant and friend, will be satisfied only by becoming one of Kṛṣṇa's dearmost devotees. As a general rule, people desire what they lack. The prayers of both Brahmā and Uddhava, each in their own way, are completely fitting.

## TEXT 158

येषां हि यद्वस्तुनि भाति लोभस्
ते तद्वतां भाग्यबलं विदन्ति ।
गोप्यो मुकुन्दाधरपानलुब्धा
गायन्ति सौभाग्यभरं मुरल्याः ॥

*yeṣāṁ hi yad-vastuni bhāti lobhas*
*te tadvatāṁ bhāgya-balaṁ vidanti*
*gopyo mukundādhara-pāna-lubdhā*
*gāyanti saubhāgya-bharaṁ muralyāḥ*

*yeṣām* — of whom; *hi* — indeed; *yat* — for which; *vastuni* — the object; *bhāti* — is manifest; *lobhaḥ* — greed; *te* — they; *tadvatām* — of those who possess it; *bhāgya* — of the good fortune; *balam* — the strength; *vidanti* — understand; *gopyaḥ* — the *gopīs; mukunda* — of Kṛṣṇa; *adhara* — the lips; *pāna* — for drinking; *lubdhāḥ* — greedy; *gāyanti* — sing; *saubhāgya* — of good fortune; *bharam* — about the abundance; *muralyāḥ* — of His flute.

**Those who yearn for something understand the good luck of those who have it. So the gopīs sing of the extreme good fortune of Mukunda's flute because they too are greedy to drink the nectar of His lips.**

COMMENTARY: Here Nārada mentions that the *gopīs* admired Kṛṣṇa's flute because it had what they wanted:

*gopyaḥ kim ācarad ayaṁ kuśalaṁ sma veṇur*
*dāmodarādhara-sudhām api gopikānām*
*bhuṅkte svayaṁ yad avaśiṣṭa-rasaṁ hradinyo*
*hṛṣyat-tvaco 'śru mumucus taravo yathāryāḥ*

"Dear *gopīs,*" they said, "what auspicious activities must the flute have performed to enjoy the nectar of Kṛṣṇa's lips independently and leave only a taste for us *gopīs,* for whom that nectar is actually meant! The forefathers of the flute, the bamboo trees, shed tears of pleasure. His mother, the river on whose bank the bamboo was born, feels jubilation, and therefore her blooming lotus flowers are standing like hair on her body." (*Bhāgavatam* 10.21.9)

## TEXT 159

तद्गोष्ठलोकेषु महाद्भुतास्या-
सक्तिः सदा प्रेमभरेण तेषु ।
यया गतं ज्येष्ठसुतं स्तुवन्तं
विधिं नमन्तं न दिदृक्षतेऽपि ॥

*tad-goṣṭha-lokeṣu mahādbhutāsyā-*
*saktiḥ sadā prema-bhareṇa teṣu*
*yayā gataṁ jyeṣṭha-sutaṁ stuvantaṁ*
*vidhiṁ namantaṁ na didṛkṣate 'pi*

*tat* — His; *goṣṭha-lokeṣu* — for the company of friends; *mahā-adbhutā* — most amazing; *asya* — His; *āsaktiḥ* — affection; *sadā* — constant; *prema* — of love; *bhareṇa* — with an excess; *teṣu* — for them; *yayā* — due to which; *gatam* — who had come; *jyeṣṭha* — eldest; *sutam* — the son; *stuvantam* — offering prayers; *vidhim* — Brahmā; *namantam* — bowing down; *na didṛkṣate* — He does not care to notice; *api* — even.

**Kṛṣṇa is always so profoundly attached to His dearmost companions for their overwhelming love that He doesn't**

**even care to notice His eldest son, Brahmā, offering prayers to Him and bowing down.**

COMMENTARY: In Vṛndāvana Kṛṣṇa gives Himself entirely to His dear friends and family. So when great demigods and sages come to visit He hardly pays them any attention. After Brahmā was defeated in his attempt to steal the boys and calves and humbly approached Kṛṣṇa to beg forgiveness, Kṛṣṇa wasn't even interested in looking at him, what to speak of acknowledging his eloquent prayers or starting a conversation with him. Later, after Indra tried to destroy Vṛndāvana and then came with the Surabhi cow to apologize, Kṛṣṇa chose to speak to him, but only because Indra was terrified of losing his heavenly post. Another reason Kṛṣṇa agreed to pay attention to Indra is that Kṛṣṇa was pleased with being anointed Lord of the cows and given two new names, Govinda and Upendra. Kṛṣṇa was further pleased because Surabhi, the ancestor of all cows, accompanied Indra; because the great devotee Surabhi requested Kṛṣṇa to forgive the penitent demigod's offenses, Kṛṣṇa dealt kindly with Indra.

## TEXT 160

तत्पादपद्मैकगतींश्च मादृशान्
सम्भाषितुं नोत्सहतेऽपि स क्षणम् ।
तैर्मोहितोऽसौ किल गोष्ठनागरो
वन्यैर्विचित्रौषधिमन्त्रवित्तमैः ॥

*tat-pāda-padmaika-gatīṁś ca mādṛśān*
*sambhāṣituṁ notsahate 'pi sa kṣaṇam*
*tair mohito 'sau kila goṣṭha-nāgaro*
*vanyair vicitrauṣadhi-mantra-vittamaiḥ*

*tat*—His; *pāda-padma*—lotus feet; *eka*—only; *gatīn*—whose goal in life; *ca*—and; *mādṛśān*—persons like me; *sambhāṣitum*—to converse with; *na utsahate*—has no enthusiasm; *api*—even; *saḥ*—He; *kṣaṇam*—for a moment; *taiḥ*—

by them; *mohitaḥ* — enchanted; *asau* — He; *kila* — indeed; *goṣṭha* — of the cowherd community; *nāgaraḥ* — the romantic hero; *vanyaiḥ* — belonging to the forest; *vicitra* — various; *oṣadhi* — of herbs; *mantra* — and incantations; *vit-tamaiḥ* — the best knowers.

**Not even for a moment is Kṛṣṇa keen to talk with persons like me whose only goal in life is His lotus feet. Indeed, that romantic hero of the cowherds is enchanted by some forest-dwellers who know all sorts of herbs and mantras.**

COMMENTARY: Kṛṣṇa might not care much about demigods with official status like Brahmā, but what about Nārada, who is a simple devotee with no material position? Nārada has no shelter other than Kṛṣṇa, yet he laments that Kṛṣṇa is too busy with the Vraja-vāsīs even to say hello to him, what to speak of offering the proper greeting for a respectable sage. Nārada's jealousy impels him to suspect that the Vraja-vāsīs are controlling Kṛṣṇa with herbs and *mantras*. The Supreme Personality of Godhead, of course, can never succumb to such material influences, but Nārada in his ecstasy thinks like that. The only power that can subdue Kṛṣṇa is the Vraja-vāsīs' pure love. Another indication of Nārada's jealousy is his ironically speaking of Kṛṣṇa as *goṣṭha-nāgara,* "the romantic hero of the cowherd village." This name also implies that although Kṛṣṇa is very clever, the Vraja-vāsīs are even more clever, since they have Him under their control.

## TEXT 161

तेषां तदासक्तिरपि क्व वाच्या
ये नन्दगोपस्य कुमारमेनम् ।
प्रेम्णा विदन्तो बहु सेवमानाः
सदा महार्त्यैव नयन्ति कालम् ॥

*teṣāṁ tad-āsaktir api kva vācyā*
*ye nanda-gopasya kumāram enam*

*premṇā vidanto bahu sevamānāḥ*
*sadā mahārtyaiva nayanti kālam*

*teṣām* — their; *tat* — for Him; *āsaktiḥ* — the attachment; *api* — and; *kva* — how; *vācyā* — can be described; *ye* — who; *nanda-gopasya* — of the cowherd Nanda; *kumāram* — as the young son; *enam* — Him; *premṇā* — in pure love; *vidantaḥ* — know; *bahu* — fully; *sevamānāḥ* — being served; *sadā* — always; *mahā-ārtyā* — in great distress; *eva* — only; *nayanti* — they spend; *kālam* — their time.

**Who can describe the Vraja-vāsīs' attachment to Kṛṣṇa? In their pure love they know Him only as the young son of Nanda Gopa. And though fully blessed with that love, they spend all their time in great distress.**

COMMENTARY: The previous verses have described Kṛṣṇa's affection for the Vraja-vāsīs, and now we hear about their attachment to Him. The residents of Vraja are the greatest Vaiṣṇavas because they are motivated only by absolutely pure love, undiluted by reverence. Such intense love shows unique symptoms that to untrained eyes appear to be signs of unhappiness. This has already been discussed in previous chapters of *Bṛhad-bhāgavatāmṛta,* and later it will be analyzed even more explicitly.

## TEXT 162

कालातीता ज्ञानसम्पत्तिभाजाम्
अस्माकं ये पूज्यपादाः समन्तात् ।
वैकुण्ठस्यानुत्तमानन्दपूर-
भाजामेषां यादवानामपीज्याः ॥

*kālātītā jñāna-sampatti-bhājām*
*asmākaṁ ye pūjya-pādāḥ samantāt*
*vaikuṇṭhasyānuttamānanda-pūra-*
*bhājām eṣāṁ yādavānām apījyāḥ*

*kāla-atītāḥ* — transcendental to time; *jñāna* — of knowledge; *sampatti* — the asset; *bhājām* — who possess; *asmākam* — of us; *ye* — who; *pūjya* — worshipable; *pādāḥ* — whose feet; *samantāt* — in all respects; *vaikuṇṭhasya* — of Vaikuṇṭha; *anuttama* — unexcelled; *ānanda* — of ecstasy; *pūra* — of the flood; *bhājām* — who possess; *eṣām* — for these; *yādavānām* — Yādavas; *api* — also; *ijyāḥ* — worshipable.

**The residents of Vraja have transcended time. For those of us blessed with the opulence of wisdom their feet are deserving of worship in every way. Even the Yādavas here, who know the unexcelled flood of the ecstasy of Vaikuṇṭha, worship those residents of Vraja.**

COMMENTARY: It would be wrong to think that the Vraja-vāsīs consider Kṛṣṇa one of their own because they are ignorant of His absolute position as God. The devotees of Vraja are not ignorant, nor do they ever suffer or waste time. They act as they do only because of their pure *prema,* for which the exalted Vaiṣṇavas of Dvārakā, including Uddhava, hold them in the highest regard.

## TEXT 163

कृष्णेन न व्रजजनाः किल मोहितास्ते
तैः स व्यमोहि भगवानिति सत्यमेव ।
गत्वा मयैव स हि विस्मृतदेवकार्यो
ऽनुस्मारितः किमपि कृत्यमहो कथञ्चित् ॥

*kṛṣṇena na vraja-janāḥ kila mohitās te*
*taiḥ sa vyamohi bhagavān iti satyam eva*
*gatvā mayaiva sa hi vismṛta-deva-kāryo*
*'nusmāritaḥ kim api kṛtyam aho kathañcit*

*kṛṣṇena* — by Kṛṣṇa; *na* — not; *vraja-janāḥ* — the people of Vraja; *kila* — indeed; *mohitāḥ* — bewildered; *te* — they; *taiḥ* — by them; *saḥ* — He; *vyamohi* — has been bewildered;

*bhagavān* — the Personality of Godhead; *iti* — thus; *satyam* — true; *eva* — only; *gatvā* — having gone to Him; *mayā* — by me; *eva* — indeed; *saḥ* — He; *hi* — indeed; *vismṛta* — forgotten; *deva* — for the demigods; *kāryaḥ* — duty to be done; *anusmāritaḥ* — reminded; *kim api* — something; *kṛtyam* — to be done; *aho* — oh; *kathañcit* — somehow.

**The people of Vraja are not bewildered by Kṛṣṇa—the truth is that He is bewildered by them. When He forgot what He had to do for the demigods, I had to go to Him myself and somehow remind Him, "Oh, You have some unfinished business!"**

COMMENTARY: After Kṛṣṇa killed the demon Keśī, Nārada Muni went to Vṛndāvana and convinced Kṛṣṇa that He had to leave for Mathurā to slay Kaṁsa and other enemies of His devotees. With clever praise and arguments, Nārada reminded Kṛṣṇa that Kṛṣṇa had promised the demigods led by Brahmā to rid the earth of its burden of demonic kings:

*sa tvaṁ bhūdhara-bhūtānāṁ*
*daitya-pramatha-rakṣasām*
*avatīrṇo vināśāya*
*sādhūnāṁ rakṣaṇāya ca*

"You, the creator, have now descended to earth to annihilate the Daitya, Pramatha, and Rākṣasa demons who are posing as kings, and also to protect the godly."

*cāṇūraṁ muṣṭikaṁ caiva*
*mallān anyāṁś ca hastinam*
*kaṁsaṁ ca nihataṁ drakṣye*
*paraśvo 'hani te vibho*

"In just two days, O almighty Lord, I will see the deaths of Cāṇūra, Muṣṭika, and other wrestlers, and of the elephant Kuvalayāpīḍa and King Kaṁsa — all by Your hand." (*Bhāgavatam* 10.37.13, 15)

### TEXT 164

कथं कथमपि प्राज्ञेनाक्रूरेण बलादिव ।
व्रजान्मधुपुरीं नीतो यदूनां हितमिच्छता ॥

*kathaṁ katham api prājñe-*
*nākrūreṇa balād iva*
*vrajān madhu-purīṁ nīto*
*yadūnāṁ hitam icchatā*

*katham katham api* — somehow or other; *prājñena* — wise; *akrūreṇa* — by Akrūra; *balāt* — by force; *iva* — as if; *vrajāt* — from Vraja; *madhu-purīm* — to Mathurā City; *nītaḥ* — brought; *yadūnām* — of the Yadus; *hitam* — the benefit; *icchatā* — who desired.

**Somehow or other the wise Akrūra, desiring to promote the welfare of the Yadus, took Him from Vraja to Madhupurī as if by force.**

COMMENTARY: By telling Kṛṣṇa about the suffering of His parents, Vasudeva and Devakī, Akrūra convinced Him to come to Mathurā:

*vṛddhau tavādya pitarau*
*para-bhṛtyatvam āgatau*
*bhartsyete tvat-kṛte tena*
*kaṁsenāśubha-buddhinā*

"Your elderly parents have now become dependent servants, and because of You they are being harassed by evil-minded Kaṁsa." (*Hari-vaṁśa* 2.26.16)

### TEXT 165

स तान्व्रजजनान् हातुं शक्नुयान्न कदाचन ।
अभीक्ष्णं याति तत्रैव वसति क्रीडति ध्रुवम् ॥

*sa tān vraja-janān hātuṁ*
*śaknuyān na kadācana*
*abhīkṣṇaṁ yāti tatraiva*
*vasati krīḍati dhruvam*

*saḥ* — He; *tān* — them; *vraja-janān* — the people of Vraja; *hātum* — to abandon; *śaknuyāt na* — is not able; *kadācana* — ever; *abhīkṣṇam* — again and again; *yāti* — goes; *tatra* — there; *eva* — indeed; *vasati* — resides; *krīḍati* — sports; *dhruvam* — certainly.

**Kṛṣṇa can never abandon the people of Vraja. He surely returns there again and again to reside and enjoy His pastimes.**

COMMENTARY: In His eternal pastimes, Kṛṣṇa again and again goes to Mathurā to help the Yadus, and again and again returns home to Vṛndāvana. And when He comes back to Vṛndāvana He resumes His Vṛndāvana pastimes. With the word *dhruvam* ("certainly"), Nārada assures Gopa-kumāra that there is no reason to doubt these words.

## TEXT 166

परं परमकौतुकी विरहजातभावोर्मितो
व्रजस्य विविधेहितं निजमनोरमं वीक्षितुम् ।
निकुञ्जकुहरे यथा भवति नाम सोऽन्तर्हितस्
तथा विविधलीलयापसरति छलात्कर्हिचित् ॥

*paraṁ parama-kautukī viraha-jāta-bhāvormito*
*vrajasya vividhehitaṁ nija-manoramaṁ vīkṣitum*
*nikuñja-kuhare yathā bhavati nāma so 'ntarhitas*
*tathā vividha-līlayāpasarati chalāt karhicit*

*param* — but; *parama* — most; *kautukī* — curious; *viraha* — from separation; *jāta* — born; *bhāva* — of ecstasy; *ūrmitaḥ* —

due to the waves; *vrajasya* — of the devotees of Vraja; *vividha* — various; *īhitam* — the behavior; *nija* — to Himself; *manoramam* — charming; *vīkṣitum* — to see; *nikuñja* — of a grove; *kuhare* — in a cave; *yathā* — as; *bhavati* — is; *nāma* — indeed; *saḥ* — He; *antarhitaḥ* — hidden; *tathā* — so; *vividha* — various; *līlayā* — as pastimes; *apasarati* — goes away; *chalāt* — on a pretext; *karhicit* — sometimes.

**But Kṛṣṇa is most curious to see how the devotees of Vraja respond to the waves of ecstasy born of separation. Indeed, seeing this gives Him great pleasure. So just as He sometimes hides in a cave in the forest groves, on some pretext He sometimes goes away from Vraja while playing in His various pastimes.**

COMMENTARY: If Kṛṣṇa never abandons the Vraja-vāsīs, how is it they experience separation from Him? The answer is that although Kṛṣṇa is always with them He sometimes hides from them for a while just to see the extreme ecstasies found only in separation. He does this to increase both their pleasure and His own.

## TEXT 167

मन्येऽहमेवं परमप्रियेभ्यस्
तेभ्यः प्रदेयस्य सुदुर्लभस्य ।
द्रव्यस्य कस्यापि समर्पणार्हो
वदान्यमौलेर्व्यवहार एषः ॥

*manye 'ham evaṁ parama-priyebhyas*
*tebhyaḥ pradeyasya su-durlabhasya*
*dravyasya kasyāpi samarpaṇārho*
*vadānya-mauler vyavahāra eṣaḥ*

*manye* — consider; *aham* — I; *evam* — thus; *parama-priyebhyaḥ* — to the most dear friends; *tebhyaḥ* — them; *pradeyasya* —

worth presenting; *su-durlabhasya* — rarely obtained; *dravyasya* — of an object; *kasya api* — certain; *samarpaṇa* — the presentation; *arhaḥ* — befitting; *vadānya* — of magnanimous persons; *mauleḥ* — of the crest jewel; *vyavahāraḥ* — behavior; *eṣaḥ* — this.

**This way of acting, I think, just befits the most generous, the most magnanimous person, for He presents to His dearmost friends the most desirable object, the most rarely obtained.**

COMMENTARY: No one should criticize Kṛṣṇa for His behavior with the devotees of Vṛndāvana, who cannot tolerate His absence even for a fraction of a second. Here Nārada says he has no such complaint against Kṛṣṇa, although some persons may. Nārada understands that Kṛṣṇa's leaving is actually His way of giving the Vraja-vāsīs the most rare treasure of *vipralambha-bhāva*. No one else in creation is worthy of that gift, so the Vraja-vāsīs are greatly distinguished to be its recipients. Thus in *Śrīmad-Bhāgavatam* (10.47.27) Uddhava told Kṛṣṇa's girlfriends:

*sarvātma-bhāvo 'dhikṛto*
*bhavatīnām adhokṣaje*
*viraheṇa mahā-bhāgā*
*mahān me 'nugrahaḥ kṛtaḥ*

"You have rightfully claimed the privilege of unalloyed love for the transcendental Lord, O most glorious *gopīs*. Indeed, by exhibiting your love for Kṛṣṇa in separation from Him, you have shown me great mercy." Although Kṛṣṇa is the transcendental Godhead, Adhokṣaja, imperceptible to the material senses, the *gopīs* of Vraja have conquered Him by their exclusive devotion. Thus in no way can He ever abandon them. Uddhava recognized the *gopīs* to be the most fortunate and generous souls, who felt the pangs of imminent separation from Kṛṣṇa even while enjoying with Him face to face.

## TEXT 168

यथा क्रीडति तद्भूमौ गोलोकेऽपि तथैव सः ।
अधऊर्ध्वतया भेदोऽनयोः कल्प्येत केवलम् ॥

*yathā krīḍati tad-bhūmau*
*goloke 'pi tathaiva saḥ*
*adha-ūrdhvatayā bhedo*
*'nayoḥ kalpyeta kevalam*

*yathā* — as; *krīḍati* — plays; *tat* — in that; *bhūmau* — land; *goloke* — in Goloka; *api* — also; *tathā eva* — just so; *saḥ* — He; *adhaḥ-ūrdhvatayā* — in terms of being below and above; *bhedaḥ* — the difference; *anayoḥ* — between the two; *kalpyeta* — is imagined; *kevalam* — only.

**Just as Kṛṣṇa plays in this Vraja-bhūmi on earth, so also does He play on Goloka. The two realms are only imagined to be different, one above the other.**

COMMENTARY: The whole purpose of this discourse has been to enlighten Gopa-kumāra about the glories of Śrī Goloka, the topmost spiritual world. What Nārada has said about Gokula on earth is also true of the original Goloka. The difference between the two is slight: Although one is located on a planet in the middle of the material universe and the other is above Vaikuṇṭha, there is no substantial difference between them.

## TEXT 169

किन्तु तद्व्रजभूमौ स न सर्वैर्दृश्यते सदा ।
तैः श्रीनन्दादिभिः सार्धमश्रान्तं विलसन्नपि ॥

*kintu tad-vraja-bhūmau sa*
*na sarvair dṛśyate sadā*

*taiḥ śrī-nandādibhiḥ sārdham*
*aśrāntaṁ vilasann api*

*kintu* — but; *tat* — that; *vraja-bhūmau* — in Vraja-bhūmi; *saḥ* — He; *na* — not; *sarvaiḥ* — by all; *dṛśyate* — is seen; *sadā* — always; *taiḥ* — by them; *śrī-nanda-ādibhiḥ* — with Śrī Nanda and others; *sārdham* — together; *aśrāntam* — incessantly; *vilasan* — playing; *api* — even though.

**But in this earthly Vraja-bhūmi not everyone can see Him all the time, even though He forever enjoys in the company of Śrī Nanda and others.**

COMMENTARY: Only once in a day of Brahmā, at the end of a certain Dvāpara-yuga, can everyone see Kṛṣṇa in Gokula. At other times He is visible only occasionally, and only to a few. In Goloka, however, everyone can see Him all the time.

## TEXT 170

श्रीसुपर्णादयो यद्वद्वैकुण्ठे नित्यपार्षदाः ।
गोलोके तु तथा तेऽपि नित्यप्रियतमा मताः ॥

*śrī-suparṇādayo yadvad*
*vaikuṇṭhe nitya-pārṣadāḥ*
*goloke tu tathā te 'pi*
*nitya-priyatamā matāḥ*

*śrī-suparṇa-ādayaḥ* — Śrī Garuḍa and others; *yadvat* — just as; *vaikuṇṭhe* — in Vaikuṇṭha; *nitya* — eternal; *pārṣadāḥ* — associates; *goloke* — in Goloka; *tu* — and; *tathā* — so; *te* — they; *api* — also; *nitya* — eternally; *priya-tamāḥ* — most dear; *matāḥ* — considered.

**Just as in Vaikuṇṭha devotees like Śrī Garuḍa are the Lord's eternal associates, in Goloka the devotees of Vraja, we understand, are His eternal dear companions.**

COMMENTARY: Nanda Mahārāja and the other Vraja-vāsīs live with Kṛṣṇa not only on earth but also in the eternal kingdom of Goloka.

## TEXT 171

ते हि स्वप्राणनाथेन समं भगवता सदा ।
लोकयोरेकरूपेण विहरन्ति यदृच्छया ॥

*te hi sva-prāṇa-nāthena*
*samaṁ bhagavatā sadā*
*lokayor eka-rūpeṇa*
*viharanti yadṛcchayā*

*te* — they; *hi* — indeed; *sva-prāṇa* — of their own lives; *nāthena* — with the Lord; *samam* — together; *bhagavatā* — with the Personality of Godhead; *sadā* — always; *lokayoḥ* — in both worlds; *eka-rūpeṇa* — in the same one way; *viharanti* — enjoy; *yadṛcchayā* — as they desire.

**They enjoy pastimes with the Lord of their lives, the Personality of Godhead, in the same way in both worlds — Vraja-bhūmi on earth and Goloka in the spiritual realm — according to their pleasure.**

## TEXT 172

श्रीगोलोकं गन्तुमर्हन्त्युपायैर्
यादृग्भिस्तं साधकास्तादृशैः स्युः ।
द्रष्टुं शक्ता मर्त्यलोकेऽपि तस्मिंस्
तादृक्क्रीडं सुप्रसन्नं प्रभुं तम् ॥

*śrī-golokaṁ gantum arhanty upāyair*
*yādṛgbhis taṁ sādhakās tādṛśaiḥ syuḥ*
*draṣṭuṁ śaktā martya-loke 'pi tasmiṁs*
*tādṛk-krīḍaṁ su-prasannaṁ prabhuṁ tam*

*śrī-golokam* — to Śrī Goloka; *gantum* — to go; *arhanti* — are able; *upāyaiḥ* — by disciplines; *yādṛgbhiḥ* — by which; *tam* — to it; *sādhakāḥ* — practicing devotees; *tādṛśaiḥ* — of that sort; *syuḥ* — would be; *draṣṭum* — to see; *śaktāḥ* — able; *martya-loke* — in the material world; *api* — although; *tasmin* — in that; *tādṛk* — of the same kind; *krīḍam* — with pastimes; *su-prasannam* — completely satisfied; *prabhum* — the Lord; *tam* — Him.

**The disciplines by which devotees in practice can reach Śrī Goloka—those very same disciplines let them see the Lord performing pastimes like those of Goloka, completely satisfied, in Vraja-bhūmi in the mortal world.**

COMMENTARY: To search out his Lord, Gopa-kumāra need not go down to Gokula on earth, but he does need to learn the *sādhana,* the special practices, for attaining Kṛṣṇa's personal abode. For intimate associates like Nanda Mahārāja no spiritual practice is needed, because they are eternal Vraja-vāsīs. But for everyone else, careful endeavor is required.

On this path, not everyone attains the same level of success. A devotee may develop Kṛṣṇa consciousness to the point of being able to see Kṛṣṇa but may not be able to see Him busily enjoying the special pastimes of Vṛndāvana (*tādṛk-krīḍam*) with His intimate devotees. When more advanced, a Vaiṣṇava may occasionally see Kṛṣṇa engaging in His Vṛndāvana pastimes but not displaying the full scope of His blissful enjoyment (*su-prasannam*). And even such a Vaiṣṇava may not be fortunate enough to enter Kṛṣṇa's eternal pastimes and play with Kṛṣṇa in absolute freedom. The highest perfection of Kṛṣṇa consciousness is rarely achieved.

## TEXT 173

तात तादृशगोपालदेवपादसरोजयोः ।
विनोदमाधुरीं तां तामुत्सुकोऽसीक्षितुं कथम् ॥

*tāta tādṛśa-gopāla-*
*deva-pāda-sarojayoḥ*
*vinoda-mādhurīṁ tāṁ tām*
*utsuko 'sīkṣituṁ katham*

*tāta* — dear boy; *tādṛśa* — such; *gopāla-deva* — of Gopāladeva; *pāda-sarojayoḥ* — of the two lotus feet; *vinoda* — of the pastimes; *mādhurīm* — the sweetness; *tām tām* — of various kinds; *utsukaḥ* — eager; *asi* — you are; *īkṣitum* — to see; *katham* — how.

**My dear boy, how is it that you are so eager to take shelter of the lotus feet of this Gopāladeva and see all those sweet pastimes?**

COMMENTARY: Nārada's mind is perplexed by the thought that this simple boy Gopa-kumāra is intent on gaining the realization most rarely achieved.

## TEXT 174

सत्यं जानीहि रे भ्रातस्तत्प्राप्तिरतिदुर्घटा ।
तत्साधनं च नितरामेष मे निश्चयः परः ॥

*satyaṁ jānīhi re bhrātas*
*tat-prāptir ati-durghaṭā*
*tat-sādhanaṁ ca nitarām*
*eṣa me niścayaḥ paraḥ*

*satyam* — certainly; *jānīhi* — you should know; *re bhrātaḥ* — O brother; *tat* — of that; *prāptiḥ* — the attainment; *ati-durghaṭā* — very difficult; *tat* — for that; *sādhanam* — the discipline; *ca* — and; *nitarām* — especially; *eṣaḥ* — this; *me* — my; *niścayaḥ* — conviction; *paraḥ* — total.

**Dear brother, you must understand that to attain Him is**

**exceedingly difficult, especially because of the devotional discipline required. Of this I am fully convinced.**

COMMENTARY: Gopa-kumāra may argue that with the blessings of pure saints like Nārada, nothing is impossible. But Nārada warns him: so difficult is the goal that even Nārada's mercy will not be of much help. By saying this, Nārada hopes to increase Gopa-kumāra's eagerness to reach Goloka.

## TEXT 175

प्राणिनः प्रायशः शून्या हिताहितविवेचनैः ।
नरा वा कतिचित्तेषु सन्त्वाचारविचारिणः ॥

*prāṇinaḥ prāyaśaḥ śūnyā*
*hitāhita-vivecanaiḥ*
*narā vā katicit teṣu*
*santv ācāra-vicāriṇaḥ*

*prāṇinaḥ* — living entities; *prāyaśaḥ* — for the most part; *śūnyāḥ* — devoid; *hita-ahita* — between good and bad; *vivecanaiḥ* — of discrimination; *narāḥ* — human beings; *vā* — or; *katicit* — a few; *teṣu* — among them; *santu* — there may be; *ācāra* — proper behavior; *vicāriṇaḥ* — who can ascertain.

**Most living entities have no ability to discern good from bad. Only a few human beings can ascertain the proper way to behave.**

COMMENTARY: The vast majority of conditioned *jīvas* live in subhuman forms of life. In the bodies of lower species like animal, bird, and insect, they have no higher intelligence with which to judge ethical values. Human beings normally have some concept of right and wrong, but only a few apply that understanding consistently in how they act.

## TEXT 176

दृश्यन्तेऽथापि बहवस्तेऽर्थकामपरायणाः ।
स्वर्गसाधकधर्मेषु रतास्तु कतिचित्किल ॥

*dṛśyante 'thāpi bahavas*
*te 'rtha-kāma-parāyaṇāḥ*
*svarga-sādhaka-dharmeṣu*
*ratās tu katicit kila*

*dṛśyante* — are seen; *atha api* — nonetheless; *bahavaḥ* — many; *te* — of them; *artha* — to wealth; *kāma* — and sense gratification; *parāyaṇāḥ* — devoted; *svarga* — of heaven; *sādhaka* — which cause the achievement; *dharmeṣu* — about the principles of religion; *ratāḥ* — serious; *tu* — but; *katicit* — some few; *kila* — only.

**Among them, most are seen devoted to wealth and enjoyment. Only very few are serious about religious life for entering into heaven.**

COMMENTARY: Most people who regulate the way they act are driven by desires for wealth, power, and sense gratification, not by true respect for religion (*dharma*). Of the few who follow *dharma,* most do so merely for the sake of public esteem. And even fewer desire elevation to Svarga-loka.

## TEXT 177

तेषां कतिपये स्युर्वा रता निष्कामकर्मसु ।
तथाप्यरागिणस्तेषां केचिदेव मुमुक्षवः ॥

*teṣāṁ katipaye syur vā*
*ratā niṣkāma-karmasu*
*tathāpy arāgiṇas teṣāṁ*
*kecid eva mumukṣavaḥ*

*teṣām* — of them; *katipaye* — a few; *syuḥ* — are; *vā* — or; *ratāḥ* — serious; *niṣkāma-karmasu* — about duties performed without selfish desires; *tathā api* — moreover; *arāgiṇaḥ* — selfless workers; *teṣām* — among them; *kecit* — a few; *eva* — only; *mumukṣavaḥ* — eager for liberation.

**Of those candidates for heaven, only a few are intent upon working without selfish desire, and among them fewer still want liberation.**

COMMENTARY: Although it is true that the process of *niṣkāma-karma* — working without attachment to the fruits of work — encourages the spirit of renunciation, just how effectively it does so varies among individuals. Only a few *niṣkāma-karma-yogīs* are renounced in their hearts and therefore eager for liberation.

## TEXT 178

तेषां परमहंसा ये मुक्ताः स्युः केचिदेव ते ।
केचिन्महाशयास्तेषु भगवद्भक्तितत्पराः ॥

*teṣāṁ parama-haṁsā ye*
*muktāḥ syuḥ kecid eva te*
*kecin mahāśayās teṣu*
*bhagavad-bhakti-tatparāḥ*

*teṣām* — among them; *parama-haṁsāḥ* — self-realized persons; *ye* — who; *muktāḥ* — liberated; *syuḥ* — are; *kecit* — a few; *eva* — only; *te* — they; *kecit* — some; *mahā-āśayāḥ* — wise transcendentalists; *teṣu* — among them; *bhagavat-bhakti* — to the devotional service of the Supreme Lord; *tatparāḥ* — dedicated.

**Of the aspirants for liberation, hardly a few are transcendental, liberated souls, and of those exalted transcendentalists only a few are dedicated to the devotional service of the Lord.**

COMMENTARY: Persons firmly fixed in the practice of *yoga* are called *haṁsas,* and those who have factually realized the self are called *paramahaṁsas. Paramahaṁsas* are liberated, but even most of them are still enjoying the remnants of their accumulated *karma.* Among all *paramahaṁsas,* only a few are completely perfect, and of those perfected beings fewer still have no desire other than the selfless devotional service of the Personality of Godhead. Those most rare persons have the sharpest intelligence and gravest purpose; by the grace of the Supreme Lord they understand how insignificant liberation is. They are called *mahā-śayas,* wise souls, by virtue of their unbounded and unalloyed enthusiasm for *bhakti-rasa.*

As Śrī Parīkṣit Mahārāja told Śukadeva Gosvāmī in the Sixth Canto of *Śrīmad-Bhāgavatam* (6.14.3–5):

*rajobhiḥ sama-saṅkhyātāḥ*
*pārthivair iha jantavaḥ*
*teṣāṁ ye kecanehante*
*śreyo vai manujādayaḥ*

"In this material world there are as many living entities as atoms. Among these living entities, a very few are human beings, and among them, few are interested in following religious principles.

*prāyo mumukṣavas teṣāṁ*
*kecanaiva dvijottama*
*mumukṣūṇāṁ sahasreṣu*
*kaścin mucyeta sidhyati*

"O best of the *brāhmaṇas,* Śukadeva Gosvāmī, out of many persons who follow religious principles, only a few desire liberation from the material world. Among many thousands who desire liberation, one may actually achieve liberation, giving up material attachment to society, friendship, love, country, home, wife, and children. And among many thousands of such liberated persons, one who can understand the true meaning of liberation is very rare.

*muktānām api siddhānāṁ*
*nārāyaṇa-parāyaṇaḥ*
*su-durlabhaḥ praśāntātmā*
*koṭiṣv api mahā-mune*

"O great sage, among many millions who are liberated and perfect in knowledge of liberation, one may be a devotee of Lord Nārāyaṇa, or Kṛṣṇa. Such devotees, who are fully peaceful, are extremely rare." To call the Vaiṣṇavas *praśāntātmā,* "persons of peaceful mind," is an understatement because the satisfaction of Kṛṣṇa consciousness reaches far beyond ordinary ideas of "peace."

## TEXT 179

श्रीमन्मदनगोपालपादपद्मैकसौहृदे ।
रतात्मानो हि नितरां दुर्लभास्तेष्वपि ध्रुवम् ॥

*śrīman-madana-gopāla-*
*pāda-padmaika-sauhṛde*
*ratātmāno hi nitarāṁ*
*durlabhās teṣv api dhruvam*

*śrīmat-madana-gopāla* — of Śrīmān Madana-Gopāla; *pāda-padma* — to the lotus feet; *eka-sauhṛde* — in exclusive friendship; *rata* — absorbed; *ātmānaḥ* — whose hearts; *hi* — indeed; *nitarām* — extremely; *durlabhāḥ* — rare; *teṣu* — among them; *api* — also; *dhruvam* — without a doubt.

**And even among the Supreme Lord's devotees, those eager to give their hearts in exclusive friendship to the lotus feet of Śrīmān Madana-gopāla are by far the most rare, without a doubt.**

COMMENTARY: As mentioned above, Parīkṣit Mahārāja also confirmed that among great souls devotees of Kṛṣṇa are the most rare. He therefore said:

*vṛtras tu sa kathaṁ pāpaḥ*
*sarva-lokopatāpanaḥ*
*itthaṁ dṛḍha-matiḥ kṛṣṇa*
*āsīt saṅgrāma ulbaṇe*

"Vṛtrāsura was situated in the blazing fire of battle and was an infamous, sinful demon, always engaged in giving troubles and anxieties to others. How could such a demon become so greatly Kṛṣṇa conscious?" (*Bhāgavatam* 6.14.6)

## TEXT 180

एवं तत्तत्साधनानां रीतिरप्यवगम्यताम् ।
तज्ज्ञापकानां शास्त्राणां वचनानां च तादृशी ॥

*evaṁ tat-tat-sādhanānāṁ*
*rītir apy avagamyatām*
*taj-jñāpakānāṁ śāstrāṇāṁ*
*vacanānāṁ ca tādṛśī*

*evam* — thus; *tat-tat* — of the various; *sādhanānām* — disciplines for achieving success; *rītiḥ* — the methodology; *api* — indeed; *avagamyatām* — should be understood; *tat* — of this (methodology); *jñāpakānām* — which are teachers; *śāstrāṇām* — of the scriptures; *vacanānām* — of the statements; *ca* — and; *tādṛśī* — likewise.

**The methods of discipline and the scriptural statements that teach them should be understood to differ according to the different goals to be achieved.**

COMMENTARY: Because some goals of life are more popular than others, the disciplines the Vedic scriptures recommend for various ambitions vary in prominence. The *śāstras* teach more about economic development, somewhat less about sense gratification, still less about religiosity, less again about liberation, and the least about devotional service. For *artha* and *kāma* there are numerous engagements of the body, speech, and mind; for *dharma,* fewer practices, involving charity, pilgrimages, proper behavior, and vows of austerity; and for liberation only a few methods, such as *aṣṭāṅga-yoga.* And still fewer and lesser known are the simple *sādhanas* of *bhakti-yoga,* beginning with hearing and chanting.

Thus we can understand that pure devotional service, especially service given exclusively to the lotus feet of Śrī Madana-gopāladeva, is difficult to achieve. And so too, therefore, is the spiritual realm of Goloka; it is obtainable only by unalloyed devotion to Madana-gopāla.

## TEXT 181

तत्रापि यो विशेषोऽन्यः केषाञ्चित्कोऽपि वर्तते ।
लोकानां किल तस्याहमाख्याने नाधिकारवान् ॥

*tatrāpi yo viśeṣo 'nyaḥ*
*keṣāñcit ko 'pi vartate*
*lokānāṁ kila tasyāham*
*ākhyāne nādhikāravān*

*tatra api* — moreover; *yaḥ* — which; *viśeṣaḥ* — distinction; *anyaḥ* — other; *keṣāñcit* — among some; *kaḥ api* — whatever; *vartate* — exists; *lokānām* — among persons; *kila* — indeed; *tasya* — that; *aham* — I; *ākhyāne* — in describing; *na* — not; *adhikāra-vān* — qualified.

**Among some of the devotees of Śrī Madana-gopāla there are further distinctions still, but I am unfit to describe them.**

COMMENTARY: Here Nārada hints at the superexcellent devotion to Śrī Madana-gopāla found in the devotees whose service follows in the mood of the blessed *gopīs.* Nārada considers Uddhava more qualified than himself to talk about this most confidential topic.

## TEXT 182

श्रीगोपकुमार उवाच
इत्युक्त्वोद्धवमालिंग्य सदैन्यं काकुचाटुभिः ।
ययाचे नारदस्तस्य किञ्चित्त्वं कथयेति सः ॥

*śrī-gopa-kumāra uvāca*
*ity uktvoddhavam āliṅgya*
*sa-dainyaṁ kāku-cāṭubhiḥ*
*yayāce nāradas tasya*
*kiñcit tvaṁ kathayeti saḥ*

*śrī-gopa-kumāraḥ uvāca* — Śrī Gopa-kumāra said; *iti* — thus; *uktvā* — speaking; *uddhavam* — Uddhava; *āliṅgya* — embracing; *sa-dainyam* — with great humility; *kāku-cāṭubhiḥ* — with a plaintive and prayerful voice; *yayāce* — implored; *nāradaḥ* — Nārada; *tasya* — about this; *kiñcit* — something; *tvam* — you; *kathaya* — please tell; *iti* — thus; *saḥ* — he.

**Śrī Gopa-kumāra said: Having spoken thus, Nārada embraced Uddhava and begged him with great humility, in a plaintive and prayerful voice, "Please tell us something about this."**

## TEXT 183

जगौ प्रेमातुरः शीर्ष्णोद्धवो नीचैर्मुहुर्नमन् ।
वन्दे नन्दव्रजस्त्रीणां पादरेणुमभीक्ष्णशः ॥

*jagau premāturaḥ śīrṣṇo-*
*ddhavo nīcair muhur naman*
*vande nanda-vraja-strīṇāṁ*
*pāda-reṇum abhīkṣṇaśaḥ*

*jagau* — spoke; *prema-āturaḥ* — agitated by pure love; *śīrṣṇā* — with his head; *uddhavaḥ* — Uddhava; *nīcaiḥ* — bending it low; *muhuḥ* — repeatedly; *naman* — paying respects; *vande* — I offer obeisances; *nanda-vraja* — of Nanda's cow pastures; *strīṇām* — of the women; *pāda* — from the feet; *reṇum* — to the dust; *abhīkṣṇaśaḥ* — constantly.

**Uddhava, moved by pure love, bowed his head low again and again. He then said: "At every instant, I offer my respects to the dust from the feet of the women of Nanda's Vraja."**

COMMENTARY: Uddhava knew exactly what Nārada was referring to. With intense feeling, he bowed his head to the floor and then lifted his head and began to sing the glories of the *gopīs*. The words he speaks in this verse appear in the Tenth Canto of *Śrīmad-Bhāgavatam* (10.47.63).

## TEXT 184

क्षणान्महार्तितो व्यग्रो गृहीत्वा यवसं रदैः ।
नारदस्य पदौ धृत्वा हरिदासोऽवदत्पुनः ॥

*kṣaṇān mahārtito vyagro*
*gṛhītvā yavasaṁ radaiḥ*
*nāradasya padau dhṛtvā*
*hari-dāso 'vadat punaḥ*

*kṣaṇāt* — after a short moment; *mahā-ārtitaḥ* — very distressed; *vyagraḥ* — excited; *gṛhītvā* — holding; *yavasam* — a blade of grass; *radaiḥ* — by his teeth; *nāradasya* — of Nārada; *padau* — the feet; *dhṛtvā* — taking hold of; *hari-dāsaḥ* — Uddhava, the great servant of Hari; *avadat* — spoke; *punaḥ* — again.

**For a moment that servant of Hari appeared agitated and greatly distressed. Placing between His teeth a blade of grass and taking hold of Nārada's feet, he spoke again.**

COMMENTARY: Uddhava expected that his touching Nārada's feet would assure the success of his own prayer.

## TEXT 185

आसामहो चरणरेणुजुषामहं स्यां
वृन्दावने किमपि गुल्मलतौषधीनाम् ।
या दुस्त्यजं स्वजनमार्यपथं च हित्वा
भेजुर्मुकुन्दपदवीं श्रुतिभिर्विमृग्याम् ॥

*āsām aho caraṇa-reṇu-juṣām ahaṁ syāṁ*
*vṛndāvane kim api gulma-latauṣadhīnām*
*yā dustyajaṁ sva-janam ārya-pathaṁ ca hitvā*
*bhejur mukunda-padavīṁ śrutibhir vimṛgyām*

*āsām* — of the *gopīs; aho* — oh; *caraṇa-reṇu* — the dust of the lotus feet; *juṣām* — devoted to; *aham syām* — let me become; *vṛndāvane* — in Vṛndāvana; *kim api* — any one; *gulma-latā-oṣadhīnām* — among the bushes, creepers, and herbs; *yāḥ* — they who; *dustyajam* — very difficult to give up; *sva-janam* — family members; *ārya-patham* — the path of chastity; *ca* — and; *hitvā* — giving up; *bhejuḥ* — worshiped; *mukunda-padavīm* — the lotus feet of Mukunda, Kṛṣṇa; *śrutibhiḥ* — by the *Vedas; vimṛgyām* — to be searched for.

**"The gopīs of Vṛndāvana have given up the association of husbands, sons, and other family members, who are very difficult to give up, and have forsaken the path of chastity, to take shelter of the lotus feet of Mukunda, Kṛṣṇa, which one should search for by Vedic knowledge. Oh, let me be fortunate enough to be one of the bushes, creepers, or herbs in Vṛndāvana, because the gopīs trample them and bless them with the dust of their lotus feet."**

COMMENTARY: This is a verse spoken by Uddhava in the Tenth

Canto of *Śrīmad-Bhāgavatam* (10.47.61). Uddhava will now explain this verse briefly, and later more elaborately.

## TEXT 186

अथ प्रेमपरीपाकविकारैर्विविधैर्वृतः ।
सचमत्कारमुत्प्लुत्य सोऽगायत्पुनरुद्धवः ॥

*atha prema-parīpāka-*
*vikārair vividhair vṛtaḥ*
*sa-camatkāram utplutya*
*so 'gāyat punar uddhavaḥ*

*atha* — then; *prema-parīpāka* — of fully blossomed *prema; vikāraiḥ* — with emotional transformations; *vividhaiḥ* — various; *vṛtaḥ* — filled; *sa-camatkāram* — full of astonishment; *utplutya* — jumping up; *saḥ* — he; *agāyat* — sang; *punaḥ* — again; *uddhavaḥ* — Uddhava.

**Then Uddhava, filled with all sorts of emotions of fully blossomed love, jumped up and continued to sing, full of wonder.**

## TEXT 187

नायं श्रियोऽङ्ग उ नितान्तरतेः प्रसादः
स्वर्योषितां नलिनगन्धरुचां कुतोऽन्याः ।
रासोत्सवेऽस्य भुजदण्डगृहीतकण्ठ-
लब्धाशिषां य उदगाद्व्रजसुन्दरीणाम् ॥

*nāyaṁ śriyo 'ṅga u nitānta-rateḥ prasādaḥ*
*svar-yoṣitāṁ nalina-gandha-rucāṁ kuto 'nyāḥ*
*rāsotsave 'sya bhuja-daṇḍa-gṛhīta-kaṇṭha-*
*labdhāśiṣāṁ ya udagād vraja-sundarīṇām*

*na* — not; *ayam* — this; *śriyaḥ* — of the goddess of fortune; *aṅge* — on the chest; *u* — alas; *nitānta-rateḥ* — who is very intimately related; *prasādaḥ* — the favor; *svaḥ* — of the heavenly planets; *yoṣitām* — of women; *nalina* — of the lotus flower; *gandha* — having the aroma; *rucām* — and bodily luster; *kutaḥ* — much less; *anyāḥ* — others; *rāsa-utsave* — in the festival of the *rāsa* dance; *asya* — of Lord Śrī Kṛṣṇa; *bhuja-daṇḍa* — by the arms; *gṛhīta* — embraced; *kaṇṭha* — their necks; *labdha-āśiṣām* — who achieved such a blessing; *yaḥ* — which; *udagāt* — became manifest; *vraja-sundarīṇām* — of the beautiful *gopīs,* the transcendental girls of Vraja-bhūmi.

**"When Lord Śrī Kṛṣṇa was dancing with the gopīs in the rāsa-līlā, the gopīs were embraced by the arms of the Lord. This transcendental favor was never bestowed upon the goddess of fortune or other consorts in the spiritual world. Indeed, never was such a thing even imagined by the most beautiful girls in the heavenly planets, girls whose bodily luster and aroma resemble the beauty and fragrance of the lotus. And what to speak of worldly women who are very beautiful by mundane estimation?"**

COMMENTARY: This is another verse from the forty-seventh chapter of the Tenth Canto (10.47.60). In the next few verses, Nārada will explain this verse. Uddhava cites these texts from *Śrīmad-Bhāgavatam* to give his words more authority.

## TEXT 188

ततोऽतिविस्मयाविष्टो नारदो भगवान्पुनः ।
निरीक्षमाणो मामार्तं ससम्भ्रममिदं जगौ ॥

*tato 'ti-vismayāviṣṭo*
*nārado bhagavān punaḥ*
*nirīkṣamāṇo mām ārtaṁ*
*sa-sambhramam idaṁ jagau*

*tataḥ* — then; *ati-vismaya* — in extreme surprise; *āviṣṭaḥ* — immersed; *nāradaḥ* — Nārada; *bhagavān* — the great personality;

*punaḥ* — again; *nirīkṣamāṇaḥ* — looking; *mām* — at me; *ārtam* — who was distressed; *sa-sambhramam* — with great respect; *idam* — this; *jagau* — sang.

**Then the great Nārada, immersed in utter surprise, looked at me again in my distress and spoke to me with great respect.**

COMMENTARY: After hearing from Uddhava, Nārada could understand even better how difficult it would be for a less qualified person like himself to attain the *prema* of Goloka. He therefore felt somewhat discouraged.

## TEXT 189

श्रीनारद उवाच
श्रेयस्तमो निखिलभागवतव्रजेषु
यासां पदाम्बुजरजो बहु वन्दमानः ।
यासां पदाब्जयुगलैकरजोऽभिमर्श-
सौभाग्यभाक्तृणजनिमुत याचतेऽयम् ॥

*śrī-nārada uvāca*
*śreyas-tamo nikhila-bhāgavata-vrajeṣu*
*yāsāṁ padāmbuja-rajo bahu vandamānaḥ*
*yāsāṁ padābja-yugalaika-rajo-'bhimarśa-*
*saubhāgya-bhāk-tṛṇa-janim uta yācate 'yam*

*śrī-nāradaḥ uvāca* — Śrī Nārada said; *śreyaḥ-tamaḥ* — the topmost; *nikhila* — of all; *bhāgavata-vrajeṣu* — the devotees of the Lord; *yāsām* — of which (*gopīs*); *pada-ambuja* — of the lotus feet; *rajaḥ* — the dust; *bahu* — much; *vandamānaḥ* — glorifying; *yāsām* — whose; *pada-abja* — of the lotus feet; *yugala* — two; *eka-rajaḥ* — a single particle of dust; *abhimarśa* — by touching; *saubhāgya* — good fortune; *bhāk* — attaining; *tṛṇa* — as a blade of grass; *janim* — birth; *uta* — even; *yācate* — prays for; *ayam* — he.

**Śrī Nārada said: Uddhava is the very best among all the devotees of the Personality of Godhead because He is so much absorbed in glorifying the dust of the gopīs' lotus feet. Indeed, to have the good fortune of being touched by a single particle of dust from those feet, he has prayed for birth as a blade of grass.**

TEXT 190

सौभाग्यगन्धं लभते न यासां
सा रुक्मिणी या हि हरिप्रियेति ।
ख्याताच्युताशास्तकुलीनकन्या-
धर्मैकनर्मोक्तिभिया मृतेव ॥

*saubhāgya-gandhaṁ labhate na yāsāṁ*
*sā rukmiṇī yā hi hari-priyeti*
*khyātācyutāśāsta-kulīna-kanyā-*
*dharmaika-narmokti-bhiyā mṛteva*

*saubhāgya* — of the good fortune; *gandham* — a trace; *labhate na* — does not attain; *yāsām* — whose; *sā* — she; *rukmiṇī* — Rukmiṇī; *yā* — who; *hi* — indeed; *hari-priyā* — dear to Lord Hari; *iti* — thus; *khyātā* — renowned; *acyuta* — of Kṛṣṇa; *āśā* — by the desire; *asta* — abandoned; *kulīna-kanyā* — of an aristocratic maiden; *dharmā* — whose religious principles; *eka* — only; *narma* — joking; *ukti* — caused by some words; *bhiyā* — out of fear; *mṛtā* — dead; *iva* — as if.

**Rukmiṇī is renowned as the dearest queen of Hari, but despite having abandoned the religious principles of an aristocratic maiden just to satisfy Lord Acyuta's desire, and despite having once almost died of fear from a few of His joking words, she cannot obtain a trace of the gopīs' good fortune.**

COMMENTARY: In the previous verse, Nārada commented on two of Uddhava's statements (texts 183 and 185): "At every instant,

I offer my respects to the dust from the feet of the women of Nanda's Vraja" and "Oh, let me be fortunate enough to be one of the bushes, creepers, or herbs in Vṛndāvana." Now, in this verse and the next, he comments on the statement (made in Text 187) "This transcendental favor was never bestowed upon the goddess of fortune." The name Śrī in that text (*nāyaṁ śriyo 'ṅga*) can be understood to refer either to the consort of Lord Nārāyaṇa or to Rukmiṇī, Kṛṣṇa's first queen in Dvārakā. When Uddhava first spoke this verse, during his visit to Gokula, Rukmiṇī and Kṛṣṇa were not yet married, but in the present context, because Uddhava is reciting this verse again in the Dvārakā of Vaikuṇṭha, the name Śrī may fittingly indicate Rukmiṇī. Or perhaps when Uddhava first spoke this verse he had the mystic foresight to know that Rukmiṇī would be Kṛṣṇa's wife. In any case, Mahālakṣmī is Rukmiṇī's expansion, so Lakṣmī and Rukmiṇī are nondifferent. Both of them, therefore, may be called Hari-priyā. And because Śrīmatī Rukmiṇī is a greater devotee than Lakṣmī, that the *gopīs* are much greater than Lakṣmī is implied.

Rukmiṇī abandoned the standards of behavior acceptable for unmarried girls, just because Kṛṣṇa wanted her to. Ignoring the rule that an aristocratic girl should be offered in marriage by her father, she invited Kṛṣṇa to kidnap her. And when Kṛṣṇa once teased her, she almost died of fear that He was rejecting her. On that occasion Lord Kṛṣṇa had said:

*athātmano 'nurūpaṁ vai*
*bhajasva kṣatriyarṣabham*
*yena tvam āśiṣaḥ satyā*
*ihāmutra ca lapsyase*

"Now you should definitely accept a more suitable husband, a first-class man of the royal order who can help you achieve everything you want, both in this life and in the next." (*Bhāgavatam* 10.60.17) And Śrī Śukadeva Gosvāmī describes:

*tasyāḥ su-duḥkha-bhaya-śoka-vinaṣṭa-buddher*
*hastāc chlathad-valayato vyajanaṁ papāta*

*dehaś ca viklava-dhiyaḥ sahasaiva muhyan*
*rambheva vāyu-vihatā pravikīrya keśān*

"Rukmiṇī's mind was overwhelmed with unhappiness, fear, and grief. Her bangles slipped from her hand, and her fan fell to the ground. In her bewilderment she suddenly fainted, her hair scattering all about as her body fell to the ground like a plantain tree blown over by the wind." (*Bhāgavatam* 10.60.24)

## TEXT 191

क्व स्वर्देव्य इव स्त्रीणां मध्ये श्रेष्ठतमा अपि ।
कालिन्दीसत्यभामाद्याः क्व चान्या रोहिणीमुखाः ॥

*kva svar-devya iva strīṇāṁ*
*madhye śreṣṭha-tamā api*
*kālindī-satyabhāmādyāḥ*
*kva cānyā rohiṇī-mukhāḥ*

*kva* — where; *svaḥ-devyaḥ* — the women of heaven; *iva* — like; *strīṇām* — ladies; *madhye* — among; *śreṣṭha-tamāḥ* — the best; *api* — even; *kālindī* — Kālindī; *satyabhāmā* — Satyabhāmā; *ādyāḥ* — and others; *kva* — where; *ca* — and; *anyāḥ* — others; *rohiṇī-mukhāḥ* — headed by Rohiṇī.

**Though as attractive as the women of heaven, how can even the best of Kṛṣṇa's queens compare to the gopīs? Even the main queens—like Kālindī and Satyabhāmā—or the others, headed by Rohiṇī, can't compare.**

COMMENTARY: Despite possessing all heavenly beauty and good character, Kṛṣṇa's eight principal queens cannot hope for even a slight trace of the *gopīs'* good fortune. So what to speak of Kṛṣṇa's other 16,100 queens? Indeed, *svar-yoṣitāṁ nalina-gandha-rucāṁ kuto 'nyāḥ:* "Never was such good fortune even imagined by the most beautiful girls in the heavenly planets, girls whose bodily luster and aroma resemble the beauty and fragrance of the lotus."

(*Bhāgavatam* 10.47.60) The supreme goddess of fortune, Śrī Rukmiṇī, sometimes embraces Kṛṣṇa, but she cannot achieve the same favor Kṛṣṇa bestows upon the *gopīs*. Therefore, since Kālindī and the other queens are inferior to Rukmiṇī, how can those queens expect such favor?

## TEXT 192

अहं वराकः को नु स्यां तासां माहात्म्यवर्णने ।
तथापि चपला जिह्वा मम धैर्यं न रक्षति ॥

*ahaṁ varākaḥ ko nu syāṁ*
*tāsāṁ māhātmya-varṇane*
*tathāpi capalā jihvā*
*mama dhairyaṁ na rakṣati*

*aham* — I; *varākaḥ* — an insignificant person; *kaḥ* — what; *nu* — indeed; *syām* — am; *tāsām* — of them; *māhātmya* — the glories; *varṇane* — in describing; *tathā api* — even so; *capalā* — ill-mannered; *jihvā* — tongue; *mama* — my; *dhairyam* — sobriety; *na rakṣati* — does not maintain.

**I am just an insignificant creature. What right do I have to even try to describe the glories of the gopīs? Even so, my ill-mannered tongue cannot stay still.**

## TEXT 193

भो गोपपुत्र व्रजनाथमित्र हे
तत्प्रेमभक्तप्रवरोऽयमुद्धवः ।
तत्सारकारुण्यविशेषभाग्यतस्
तासां व्रजे प्रेमभरं तमैक्षत ॥

*bho gopa-putra vraja-nātha-mitra he*
*tat-prema-bhakta-pravaro 'yam uddhavaḥ*

*tat-sāra-kāruṇya-viśeṣa-bhāgyatas*
*tāsāṁ vraje prema-bharaṁ tam aikṣata*

*bhoḥ gopa-putra* — O son of a cowherd; *vraja-nātha* — of the Lord of Vṛndāvana; *mitra he* — O friend; *tat* — His (Kṛṣṇa's); *prema-bhakta* — of the devotees in pure love; *pravaraḥ* — most exalted; *ayam* — this; *uddhavaḥ* — Uddhava; *tat* — His; *sāra* — essential; *kāruṇya* — of mercy; *viśeṣa* — special; *bhāgyataḥ* — by the good fortune; *tāsām* — of them; *vraje* — in Vraja; *prema-bharam* — the fullness of love; *tam* — that; *aikṣata* — he saw.

**O son of a cowherd, dear friend of the Lord of Vraja, among Kṛṣṇa's devotees in pure love this Uddhava is the most exalted. By his good fortune he has attained the essence of the Lord's mercy: In Vraja he has seen the extent of the gopīs' love for Kṛṣṇa.**

## TEXT 194

तासां प्रसादातिशयस्य गोचरस्
तत्सङ्गतो विस्मृतकृष्णसङ्गमः ।
निर्धारमेतं व्यवहारमीदृशं
कुर्वन्वदेद्यत्तदतीव सम्भवेत् ॥

*tāsāṁ prasādātiśayasya gocaras*
*tat-saṅgato vismṛta-kṛṣṇa-saṅgamaḥ*
*nirdhāram etaṁ vyavahāram īdṛśaṁ*
*kurvan vaded yat tad atīva sambhavet*

*tāsām* — of them (the *gopīs*); *prasāda* — of the mercy; *atiśayasya* — extreme; *gocaraḥ* — a recipient; *tat* — their; *saṅgataḥ* — by association; *vismṛta* — forgotten; *kṛṣṇa-saṅgamaḥ* — his association with Kṛṣṇa; *nirdhāram* — conclusion in his mind; *etam* — this; *vyavahāram* — and behavior; *īdṛśam* — like this; *kurvan* — doing; *vadet* — would speak; *yat* — what; *tat* — that; *atīva* — very much; *sambhavet* — is feasible.

**Uddhava received from the gopīs such mercy that in their company he even forgot about his companionship with Kṛṣṇa. So whatever he concludes about them, and whatever he does or says, will be altogether right.**

COMMENTARY: Uddhava, being the best *prema-bhakta* of Lord Vrajanātha, is blessed with Kṛṣṇa's exceptional mercy. Kṛṣṇa has drawn Uddhava very close to Him because the Lord considers Uddhava especially worthy of His kindness. Uddhava attained this perfection by seeing in Vṛndāvana the exalted love the *gopīs* have for Kṛṣṇa and by obtaining the *gopīs'* blessings. The *gopīs* disclosed to Uddhava their most confidential ecstasies. In Uddhava's own words:

*sarvātma-bhāvo 'dhikṛto*
*bhavatīnām adhokṣaje*
*viraheṇa mahā-bhāgā*
*mahān me 'nugrahaḥ kṛtaḥ*

"O most glorious *gopīs,* you have rightfully claimed the privilege of unalloyed love for the transcendental Lord. Indeed, by exhibiting your ecstasy of separation from Him, you have shown me great mercy." (*Bhāgavatam* 10.47.27) Śrīla Śrīdhara Svāmī, in his commentary on this verse, gives his paraphrase, *bhagavat-prema-sukha-pradarśanena mamaiva mahān anugrahaḥ kṛtaḥ:* "By showing the joy of your love for the Supreme Lord, you have greatly favored me." Being in the company of the *gopīs* and staying in Gokula for a long time strongly affected Uddhava, so much so that he forgot his association with Kṛṣṇa, with whom he had been friends since childhood.

TEXT 195

श्वफल्कपुत्रो भगवत्पितृव्यः
स नीरसज्ञानविशुष्कचेताः ।
वृद्धो दयार्द्रान्तरताविहीनः
कंसस्य दौत्येऽभिरतो व्रजे यन् ॥

*śvaphalka-putro bhagavat-pitṛvyaḥ*
*sa nīrasa-jñāna-viśuṣka-cetāḥ*
*vṛddho dayārdrāntaratā-vihīnaḥ*
*kaṁsasya dautye 'bhirato vraje yan*

*śvaphalka-putraḥ* — son of Śvaphalka; *bhagavat-pitṛvyaḥ* — paternal uncle of the Supreme Lord; *saḥ* — he (Akrūra); *nīrasa* — tasteless; *jñāna* — by knowledge; *viśuṣka* — dried up; *cetāḥ* — whose heart; *vṛddhaḥ* — an old man; *dayā* — by mercy; *ārdra* — melted; *antaratā* — the state of having one's heart; *vihīnaḥ* — devoid of; *kaṁsasya* — of Kaṁsa; *dautye* — in the service as a messenger; *abhirataḥ* — diligently engaged; *vraje* — to Vraja; *yan* — going.

**Akrūra, son of Śvaphalka and paternal uncle of Lord Kṛṣṇa, was an old man whose heart had dried up from lifeless knowledge. His heart was so devoid of the softness of mercy that he came to Vraja as the diligent order-carrier of Kaṁsa.**

COMMENTARY: Akrūra's name means "not cruel," but by taking Kṛṣṇa away from Vṛndāvana he committed cruel offenses against the Vraja-vāsīs. He may have been Kṛṣṇa's uncle, but according to Uddhava his heart was completely dried up by knowledge untouched by the *rasas* of devotional service. Being an old man, Akrūra couldn't even make an outward show of being a connoisseur of *rasas*. And therefore, because he had no appreciation for the ecstatic mood of *vraja-prema,* he accepted the task of dragging Kṛṣṇa away from Vraja.

TEXT 196

सञ्चिन्तयन्कृष्णपदाम्बुजद्वयं
तस्य प्रकर्षातिशयं न्यवर्णयत् ।
गोपीमहोत्कर्षभरानुवर्णनैस्
तल्लोलितो धाष्टर्यमभावयन् हृदि ॥

*sañcintayan kṛṣṇa-padāmbuja-dvayaṁ*
*tasya prakarṣātiśayaṁ nyavarṇayat*
*gopī-mahotkarṣa-bharānuvarṇanais*
*tal-lolito dhārṣṭyam abhāvayan hṛdi*

*sañcintayan* — thinking; *kṛṣṇa* — of Kṛṣṇa; *pada-ambuja* — of the lotus feet; *dvayam* — about the pair; *tasya* — His; *prakarṣa-atiśayam* — superexcellence; *nyavarṇayat* — he described; *gopī* — of the *gopīs; mahā-utkarṣa* — the glories; *bhara* — extensive; *anuvarṇanaiḥ* — by describing; *tat* — by them; *lolitaḥ* — unsettled; *dhārṣṭyam* — his audacity; *abhāvayan* — unaware of; *hṛdi* — in his heart.

**Yet while meditating on the two lotus feet of Kṛṣṇa, he began to speak of Kṛṣṇa's supremacy. And with his heart tossing and turning from describing the superexcellent glories of the gopīs, he was blind to his own audacity.**

## TEXT 197

यदर्चितं ब्रह्मभवादिभिः सुरैः
श्रिया च देव्या मुनिभिः ससात्वतैः ।
गोचारणायानुचरैश्चरद्वने
यद्गोपिकानां कुचकुंकुमाचितम् ॥

*yad arcitaṁ brahma-bhavādibhiḥ suraiḥ*
*śriyā ca devyā munibhiḥ sa-sātvataiḥ*
*go-cāraṇāyānucaraiś carad vane*
*yad gopikānāṁ kuca-kuṅkumācitam*

*yat* — which (lotus feet); *arcitam* — worshiped; *brahma-bhava* — by Brahmā and Śiva; *ādibhiḥ* — and other; *suraiḥ* — demigods; *śriyā* — by Śrī; *ca* — also; *devyā* — the goddess of fortune; *munibhiḥ* — by the sages; *sa-sātvataiḥ* — along with the devotees; *go* — the cows; *cāraṇāya* — for tending; *anucaraiḥ* — together with His companions; *carat* — moving about; *vane* — in the forest; *yat* — which; *gopikānām* — of the cowherd girls; *kuca* — from the breasts; *kuṅkuma* — by the red *kuṅkuma* powder; *ācitam* — marked.

**[Akrūra thought:] "Those lotus feet are worshiped by Brahmā, Śiva, and all the other demigods, by the goddess of fortune, and also by the great sages and Vaiṣṇavas. Upon those lotus feet the Lord walks about the forest while herding the cows with His companions, and those feet are smeared with the kuṅkuma from the gopīs' breasts."**

COMMENTARY: This verse from *Śrīmad-Bhāgavatam* (10.38.8) expresses one of the thoughts Akrūra had while on the road to Vṛndāvana. The persons of whom Akrūra speaks he mentions one after another in order of their increasing greatness. Were he not to mention them in this way, his praise would be as ridiculous as praise given to the same person first for being a great *brāhmaṇa* and then a great king. Competent poets disapprove of such awkward sequences; such poets generally glorify related subjects in order, from the least significant to the most.

That Brahmā and other demigods worship Kṛṣṇa's lotus feet indicates that those feet are the supreme worshipable Deity and that Kṛṣṇa is the supreme controller. The goddess Lakṣmī, who bestows all riches simply by her sidelong glance, also worships Kṛṣṇa's feet, which indicates that Kṛṣṇa's feet possess the extreme limit of good fortune. Mystics who are self-satisfied (*ātmārāma*) are indifferent to the favor of the goddess of fortune, yet they also worship Kṛṣṇa's lotus feet. This means that to obtain Kṛṣṇa's feet is the highest goal of life. And apart from great mystics, also worshiping Kṛṣṇa's feet are the devotees interested only in pure devotional service to the Supreme Person. Such devotees are much greater than the *ātmārāma* mystics because pure devotees do not care even for liberation. This also implies that Kṛṣṇa is the most generous giver of charity because to such pure devotees He gives away even His very self.

Sages busy in the cultivation of *karma* and *jñāna* have no time to worship the Personality of Godhead's lotus feet. They lack the special knowledge that would inspire them to begin such worship, and they also lack the spiritual strength needed for devotional service. But *karmī* and *jñānī* sages who associate with pure Vaiṣṇavas can receive the Vaiṣṇavas' mercy and thus acquire the requisite knowledge and strength. In other words, the devotees of the Supreme Lord are superior to nondevotee sages.

By referring to the goddess Śrī as *devī* ("demigoddess") rather than *bhagavatī* ("beloved of Bhagavān"), Akrūra indicates that he is talking not about Lord Nārāyaṇa's wife Mahā-lakṣmī but about the partial expansion of Mahā-lakṣmī who rules the opulences of the material world. Vaiṣṇavas worship the original Mahā-lakṣmī as the dearmost consort of the Supreme Lord, which means that the Vaiṣṇavas accept her as greater than themselves.

Akrūra contemplates Kṛṣṇa going to the forest with His companions, the young cowherd boys, and in this way thinks of Kṛṣṇa's absolute affection and compassion for His devotees. The forest is Vṛndāvana, the place of Kṛṣṇa's greatest pleasure pastimes, and the purpose of His entering that forest is to tend His cows, a pastime of supreme happiness.

It is not precisely right to think that the words *arcitam* and *anucaraiḥ* together mean "worshiped by His companions." There may be some grammatical justification for such an understanding, but because the cowherd boys are Kṛṣṇa's intimate friends, their "worship" of His lotus feet differs from the worship usually indicated by the word *arcitam*.

Akrūra says that Kṛṣṇa's lotus feet are smeared with *kuṅkuma* from the breasts of the *gopīs*. This not only points toward an uncommon mode of worshiping the Supreme Lord but also indicates how Kṛṣṇa sports romantically and bestows the highest form of His mercy by coming under the control of pure love. The *gopīs* are mentioned last in this comparative sequence because they are the greatest of all of Kṛṣṇa's worshipers, and the word *yad* is repeated a second time in the last line to highlight the special nature of their worship. The sweetness invoked by the image of Kṛṣṇa's feet smeared with the *gopīs' kuṅkuma* suggests that His loving exchanges with the *gopīs* are the most important purpose for which He descended as an *avatāra;* His favoring the *gopīs* by submitting to their love is the most glorious thing He ever does.

In this way Akrūra compares various worshipers of Kṛṣṇa's lotus feet in exactly the fitting order: Lord Brahmā is greater than the demigods, Lord Śiva greater than Brahmā, the goddess Śrī greater than Śiva, the self-contented sages greater than Śrī, the pure Vaiṣṇavas greater than the sages, and Kṛṣṇa's cowherd friends and finally the *gopīs* greater than all others. Thus Akrūra became ecstatic as he approached Vṛndāvana, thinking:

*athāvarūḍhaḥ sapadīśayo rathāt*
*pradhāna-puṁsoś caraṇaṁ sva-labdhaye*
*dhiyā dhṛtaṁ yogibhir apy ahaṁ dhruvaṁ*
*namasya ābhyāṁ ca sakhīn vanaukasaḥ*

"Then I will at once alight from my chariot and bow down to the lotus feet of Kṛṣṇa and Balarāma, the Supreme Personalities of Godhead. Theirs are the same feet that great mystic *yogīs* striving for self-realization bear within their minds. I will also offer my obeisances to the Lords' cowherd boyfriends and to all the other residents of Vṛndāvana." (*Bhāgavatam* 10.38.15)

## TEXT 198

अप्यङ्घ्रिमूले पतितस्य मे विभुः
शिरस्यधास्यन्निजहस्तपङ्कजम् ।
दत्ताभयं कालभुजाङ्गरंहसा
प्रोद्वेजितानां शरणैषिणां नृणाम् ॥

*apy aṅghri-mūle patitasya me vibhuḥ*
*śirasy adhāsyan nija-hasta-paṅkajam*
*dattābhayaṁ kāla-bhujāṅga-raṁhasā*
*prodvejitānāṁ śaraṇaiṣiṇāṁ nṛṇām*

*api* — furthermore; *aṅghri* — of His feet; *mūle* — at the base; *patitasya* — who have fallen; *me* — of me; *vibhuḥ* — the almighty Lord; *śirasi* — upon the head; *adhāsyat* — will place; *nija* — His own; *hasta* — hand; *paṅkajam* — lotuslike; *datta* — which grants; *abhayam* — fearlessness; *kāla* — time; *bhuja-aṅga* — of the serpent; *raṁhasā* — by the swift force; *prodvejitānām* — who are greatly disturbed; *śaraṇa* — shelter; *eṣiṇām* — searching for; *nṛṇām* — to persons.

**"And when I have fallen at His feet, the almighty Lord will place His lotus hand upon my head. For those who seek shelter in Him because they are greatly disturbed by the swift, powerful serpent of time, that hand removes all fear.**

COMMENTARY: Akrūra also speaks this verse and the next in the Tenth Canto of *Śrīmad-Bhāgavatam* (10.38.16–17). The words *kāla-bhujāṅga* suggest that persons who are serious about achieving liberation fear the force of time. In another sense, however, the words *kāla-bhujāṅga* refer to liberation itself, comparing it to an all-devouring python or (still another meaning of *bhujāṅga*) a profligate man. A profligate man may boldly enter another person's house and refuse to leave, even if the owner tries to expel him; similarly, even though by the strength of Vaiṣṇava association a liberated soul may come to understand the paltriness of liberation and try to reject it, liberation may still persist in its hold on him.

## TEXT 199

समर्हणं यत्र निधाय कौशिकस्
तथा बलिश्चाप जगत्त्रयेन्द्रताम् ।
यद्वा विहारे व्रजयोषितां श्रमं
स्पर्शेन सौगन्धिकगन्ध्यपानुदत् ॥

*samarhaṇaṁ yatra nidhāya kauśikas*
*tathā baliś cāpa jagat-trayendratām*
*yad vā vihāre vraja-yoṣitāṁ śramaṁ*
*sparśena saugandhika-gandhy apānudat*

*samarhaṇam* — the respectful offering; *yatra* — into which; *nidhāya* — by placing; *kauśikaḥ* — Purandara; *tathā* — as well as; *baliḥ* — Bali Mahārāja; *ca* — also; *āpa* — attained; *jagat* — of the worlds; *traya* — three; *indratām* — rulership (as Indra, the king of heaven); *yat* — which (lotus hand of the Lord); *vā* — and; *vihāre* — during the pastimes (of the *rāsa* dance); *vraja-yoṣitām* — of the ladies of Vraja; *śramam* — the fatigue; *sparśena* — by their contact; *saugandhika* — like an aromatic flower; *gandhi* — fragrant; *apānudat* — wiped away.

**"By offering charity to that lotus hand, Purandara and Bali earned the status of Indra, king of heaven, and during the pleasure pastimes of the rāsa dance, when the Lord wiped away the gopīs' perspiration and removed their fatigue, the touch of their faces made that hand as fragrant as a sweet flower."**

COMMENTARY: Having described how Kṛṣṇa removes all fear from persons who take shelter of Him, Akrūra now describes how Kṛṣṇa awards His devotees success in life, whether or not they still have material desires, and how He gives Himself away to His most surrendered devotees.

Both Indra, while performing sacrifice, and Bali, while fulfilling Lord Vāmana's request for charity, sanctified their acts by placing items of worship in the Supreme Lord's hand. That was the right way for them to proceed, because no one can have a fruitful ritualistic performance without making some offering to the Supreme Lord.

Here the word *kauśika* refers to Indra Purandara, who is called Kauśika because he is a descendant of Kuśika Ṛṣi, but Kauśika is also another name of the sage Viśvāmitra. During the pastimes of Lord Rāmacandra, Viśvāmitra made various offerings to the Lord, such as teachings in *śāstra* and *mantras,* and various items of hospitality in his *āśrama,* including sanctified food. It is well known how Viśvāmitra thus became great in several ways, especially by attaining intense devotion to the Lord's lotus feet.

Thus Viśvāmitra became as prominent among the sages as Indra among the demigods.

Kṛṣṇa blessed the *gopīs* with the highest joy and became subservient to the dictates of their love because they considered Him their very life and soul. The word *vihāra* ("sport") indicates that Kṛṣṇa's pastimes with the *gopīs* were very enjoyable. The words *vraja-yoṣitām* ("of the women of Vraja") suggest that it was fitting for Kṛṣṇa to grant them His favor because these women of Vraja — the *gopīs* — were so affectionate to Him. The word *śramam* ("fatigue") implies that Kṛṣṇa reciprocated with the *gopīs* very skillfully, giving them the greatest pleasure, which compensated for the effort the *gopīs* spent in singing and dancing. That He removed their fatigue "by His touch" (*sparśena*) implies the coolness of His touch, and that His hand is *saugandhika-gandhi* ("fragrant like a flower") implies that His hand is supremely attractive and has the power to create happiness. In the same way that the subtle fragrance of a flower may be perceivable only by certain people, Kṛṣṇa's beauty and charm are fully relished only by devotees as dear to Him as the Vraja *gopīs*.

## TEXT 200

पितामहोऽसौ कुरुपाण्डवानां
बृहद्व्रतो धर्मपरोऽपि भीष्मः ।
व्रजाङ्गनोत्कर्षनिरूपणेन
तमन्तकाले भगवन्तमस्तौत् ॥

*pitāmaho 'sau kuru-pāṇḍavānāṁ*
*bṛhad-vrato dharma-paro 'pi bhīṣmaḥ*
*vrajāṅganotkarṣa-nirūpaṇena*
*tam anta-kāle bhagavantam astaut*

*pitāmahaḥ* — the grandfather; *asau* — he; *kuru* — of the Kurus; *pāṇḍavānām* — of the Pāṇḍavas; *bṛhat-vrataḥ* — the executor of the "great vow" of lifelong celibacy; *dharma-paraḥ* — devoted to the principles of religion; *api* — also; *bhīṣmaḥ* —

Bhīṣma; *vraja-aṅganā* — of the young women of Vraja; *utkarṣa* — the excellence; *nirūpaṇena* — by describing; *tam* — Him; *anta-kāle* — at the time of passing away; *bhagavantam* — the Personality of Godhead; *astaut* — praised.

**[Nārada continued:] The grandfather of the Kurus and Pāṇḍavas—Bhīṣma himself, sworn to the great vow of lifelong celibacy and strictly true to the principles of religion —at the time of passing away, praised the Personality of Godhead by telling of the excellence of the young women of Vraja.**

COMMENTARY: As wonderful as it is that Akrūra appreciated the *gopīs,* it is even more amazing that Bhīṣma, a warrior and lifelong celibate who should know nothing about such things, also glorified these young girls. As Bhīṣma lay on a bed of arrows on the Kurukṣetra battlefield, just before he left his body, he sang the glories of Kṛṣṇa's girlfriends in Vṛndāvana. This was the same Bhīṣma who was a strict *naiṣṭhika-brahmacārī,* a *kṣatriya* more interested in warfare than romantic concerns, the same Bhīṣma who dueled with his own *guru,* Paraśurāma, the Supreme Lord's incarnation, and shot cruel arrows at Kṛṣṇa, Arjuna's chariot driver. Such a great authority is Bhīṣma that if he considers the *gopīs* so elevated, surely they must be.

## TEXT 201

ललितगतिविलासवल्गुहास-
प्रणयनिरीक्षणकल्पितोरुमानाः ।
कृतमनुकृतवत्य उन्मदान्धाः
प्रकृतिमगन्किल यस्य गोपवध्वः ॥

*lalita-gati-vilāsa-valgu-hāsa-*
*praṇaya-nirīkṣaṇa-kalpitoru-mānāḥ*
*kṛtam anukṛtavatya unmadāndhāḥ*
*prakṛtim agan kila yasya gopa-vadhvaḥ*

*lalita* — attractive; *gati* — by His movements; *vilāsa* — fascinating gestures; *valgu-hāsa* — sweet smiling; *praṇaya* — loving; *nirīkṣaṇa* — and glances; *kalpita* — thinking themselves; *uru-mānāḥ* — highly glorified; *kṛtam* — His activities; *anukṛta-vatyaḥ* — copying; *unmada-andhāḥ* — gone mad in ecstasy; *prakṛtim* — characteristics; *agan* — assumed; *kila* —certainly; *yasya* — whose; *gopa-vadhvaḥ* — the cowherd damsels.

**"Let my mind be fixed upon Lord Śrī Kṛṣṇa, whose motions, gestures, sweet smiles, and loving glances made the gopīs of Vraja-dhāma feel greatly honored. Those gopīs, in blind ecstasy, imitated the activities of Kṛṣṇa and became just like Him."**

COMMENTARY: This verse from *Śrīmad-Bhāgavatam* (1.9.40) is among those that impart Bhīṣma's final words. The Supreme Personality of Godhead Kṛṣṇa favored the *gopīs* with the highest honor by worshiping them with His own graceful movements and gestures during His *rāsa-līlā* and other pastimes. Therefore the *gopīs* should be understood to be the greatest devotees of the Supreme Lord, greater than all the recipients of the Lord's gifts of sense enjoyment, power, liberation, and devotion, and greater even than Mahā-lakṣmī.

When Kṛṣṇa left the *gopīs* at the beginning of the *rāsa* dance, in their ecstatic madness they became as if blind; in other words, they lost their ability to see the means and ends of happiness in this world and the next. In that state they acted out His pastimes, like the lifting of Govardhana Hill, and became just like Him. That is to say, they entered a special kind of trance in which their bodies assumed many of His excellent qualities (*prakṛtim agan*). The *gopīs,* fixed in the *sac-cid-ānanda* spiritual nature, then appeared worthy of worship by the entire world, able to deliver the universe, and full of compassion for everyone.

Or, taking the meaning of the word *prakṛti* to be "mind" and *agan* to be "entered," when Kṛṣṇa was away from the *rāsa* dance the *gopīs* deeply entered His mind, and because of their extreme devotion while feeling His absence they became the object of His deep meditation. Therefore the *gopīs* are glorified in this way:

*viyoginīnām api paddhatiṁ vo*
*na yogino gantum api kṣamante*
*yad dhyeya-rūpasya parasya puṁso*
*yūyaṁ gatā dhyāna-padaṁ durāpam*

"Even great *yogīs* are not able to pursue your method of worshiping the Supreme Lord with the feeling of His absence. He is the proper object of meditation, but you have become the object of His. This is a perfection nearly impossible to attain." (*Padyāvalī* of Śrīla Rūpa Gosvāmī, 351)

Though Kṛṣṇa is the supreme goal, rarely achieved, of powerful lords of the universe like Brahmā and other demigods, of self-satisfied *yogīs* like Sanaka and his brothers, of pure devotees like Nārada, and of beloved consorts like the goddess Lakṣmī, Kṛṣṇa truly worships the *gopīs,* endeavoring to attract them with His unprecedented and splendid pastimes. When the *gopīs* are maddened in the height of their love in separation, they cannot discern right from wrong. And so they imitate Kṛṣṇa's activities and invade Kṛṣṇa's own mind. Thus they are surely the greatest of all Vaiṣṇavas, and to be the only object of desire for these greatest of Vaiṣṇavas, Kṛṣṇa must be the Supreme Person.

Thinking like this, Bhīṣma, filled with ecstasy at the time of his passing away, prayed that Śrī Gopīnātha be present before his eyes as he left his body.

## TEXT 202

तास्तथैवाहुरन्योन्यं कौरवेन्द्रपुरस्त्रियः ।
पश्यन्त्यो भगवन्तं तं गच्छन्तं स्वपुरं ततः ॥

*tās tathaivāhur anyonyaṁ*
*kauravendra-pura-striyaḥ*
*paśyantyo bhagavantaṁ taṁ*
*gacchantaṁ sva-puraṁ tataḥ*

*tāḥ* — they; *tathā eva* — in the same way; *āhuḥ* — spoke; *anyonyam* — to one another; *kaurava-indra* — of the king of the Kauravas; *pura* — of the capital city; *striyaḥ* — the ladies; *paśyantyaḥ* — watching; *bhagavantam* — the Supreme Lord; *tam* — Him; *gacchantam* — leaving; *sva* — His; *puram* — for the city; *tataḥ* — thus.

**The ladies of the capital of King Yudhiṣṭhira spoke the same way among themselves while watching that very Personality of Godhead leave for His own capital:**

COMMENTARY: Since the greatly learned Bhīṣma knew about the glories of the Personality of Godhead, it is understandable that he should have spoken such praise of the *gopīs*. More surprising, however, is that women without such specialized knowledge could glorify the *gopīs* in the same way, as did the women of Hastināpura. As described in the First Canto of *Śrīmad-Bhāgavatam* (1.10.20):

*anyonyam āsīt sañjalpa*
*uttama-śloka-cetasām*
*kauravendra-pura-strīṇāṁ*
*sarva-śruti-manoharaḥ*

"Absorbed in the thought of the transcendental qualities of the Lord, who is glorified in select poetry, the ladies on the roofs of all the houses of Hastināpura began to talk of Him. This talk was more attractive than the hymns of the *Vedas*."

Śrīla Śrīdhara Svāmī explains: "The prayers of the ladies in Hastināpura attracted the attention of all the *Vedas*, and thus the personified *Upaniṣads* congratulated those ladies. Because the ladies belonged to the capital of Śrī Yudhiṣṭhira, the Kaurava king, it is implied that by their connection with him they certainly could have spoken such realizations."

What is more, the women of Hastināpura expressed those realizations at a moment of painful crisis for them, when Kṛṣṇa was leaving the Kaurava capital for His own city, Dvārakā. Kṛṣṇa's influence is so wonderful that even while Kṛṣṇa was abandoning them they could glorify their rivals in Dvārakā and Vṛndāvana.

## TEXT 203

नूनं व्रतस्नानहुतादिनेश्वरः
समर्चितो ह्यस्य गृहीतपाणिभिः ।
पिबन्ति याः सख्यधरामृतं मुहुर्
व्रजस्त्रियः सम्मुमुहुर्यदाशयाः ॥

*nūnaṁ vrata-snāna-hutādineśvaraḥ*
*samarcito hy asya gṛhīta-pāṇibhiḥ*
*pibanti yāḥ sakhy adharāmṛtaṁ muhur*
*vraja-striyaḥ sammumuhur yad-āśayāḥ*

*nūnam* — certainly; *vrata* — by vows; *snāna* — bathing; *huta* — sacrifices in the fire; *ādinā* — and so on; *īśvaraḥ* — the Personality of Godhead; *samarcitaḥ* — perfectly worshiped; *hi* — certainly; *asya* — His; *gṛhīta-pāṇibhiḥ* — by the married wives; *pibanti* — relish; *yāḥ* — who; *sakhi* — O friend; *adhara-amṛtam* — the nectar from His lips; *muhuḥ* — again and again; *vraja-striyaḥ* — the damsels of Vraja-bhūmi; *sammumuhuḥ* — often fainted; *yat-āśayāḥ* — expecting to be favored in that way.

**"O friends, just think of His wives, whose hands He has accepted. How they must have undergone vows, baths, fire sacrifices, and perfect worship of the Lord of the universe to constantly relish now the nectar from His lips [by kissing]. The damsels of Vraja-bhūmi would often faint just by expecting such favors."**

COMMENTARY: This verse appears in the song by the Hastināpura ladies in the First Canto of *Śrīmad-Bhāgavatam* (1.10.28). In the opinion of these ladies, Śrī Kṛṣṇa's queens in Dvārakā must in previous lives have disciplined themselves and worshiped Him in many ways to have gained Him as their husband, for those queens can regularly taste the nectar of Kṛṣṇa's lips. But the *gopīs* of Vṛndāvana are even greater because they always think about that nectar within their hearts. The nectar of Kṛṣṇa's lips must be exceedingly pleasant, since the *gopīs,* those most respectable girls, are enchanted by it. Thus it is proven once again that Kṛṣṇa is the Supreme Person and that because of the extreme love the divine *gopīs* of Vraja have for Him they are superior even to Śrī Rukmiṇī and Kṛṣṇa's other wives.

Surely the *gopīs* also had the privilege of drinking the *adharāmṛta,* the nectar from Kṛṣṇa's lips; but beyond even that, they would become bewildered just by remembering it.

Although one can also achieve Śrī Goloka by developing love in the mood of Mother Yaśodā, Nanda Mahārāja, and other Vraja-vāsīs, it is mainly by developing love that follows the mood of the *gopīs* that one can attain the special perfection in which all one's ambitions are fulfilled.

Śrī Uddhava speaks another verse glorifying the *gopīs* in the Third Canto of *Śrīmad-Bhāgavatam* (3.2.14):

*yasyānurāga-pluta-hāsa-rāsa-*
*līlāvaloka-pratilabdha-mānāḥ*
*vraja-striyo dṛgbhir anupravṛtta-*
*dhiyo 'vatasthuḥ kila kṛtya-śeṣāḥ*

"The damsels of Vraja, after pastimes of laughter, humor, and exchanges of glances, were anguished when Kṛṣṇa left them. They used to follow Him with their eyes, and thus they sat down with stunned intelligence and couldn't finish their household duties." Nārada, however, chose to forgo reciting this verse, because he wished to avoid making the pure devotees who were present remember the pain the *gopīs* felt after Kṛṣṇa left Vṛndāvana.

## TEXT 204

श्रीगोपकुमार उवाच
एवं वदन्स भगवान्परिरब्धवान्मां
प्रेमाब्धिकम्पपुलकाश्रुतरङ्गमग्नः ।

दष्ट्वा रदैस्तदनुवर्णनलोलजिह्वां
नृत्यन्विचित्रमगमद्विविधामवस्थाम् ॥

*śrī-gopa-kumāra uvāca*
*evaṁ vadan sa bhagavān parirabdhavān māṁ*
*premābdhi-kampa-pulakāśru-taraṅga-magnaḥ*
*daṣṭvā radais tad-anuvarṇana-lola-jihvāṁ*
*nṛtyan vicitram agamad vividhām avasthām*

*śrī-gopa-kumāraḥ uvāca* — Śrī Gopa-kumāra said; *evam* — thus; *vadan* — saying; *saḥ* — he (Nārada); *bhagavān* — the spiritually potent person; *parirabdhavān* — embraced; *mām* — me; *prema-abdhi* — in an ocean of love of God; *kampa* — of trembling; *pulaka* — horripilation; *aśru* — and tears; *taraṅga* — in the waves; *magnaḥ* — immersed; *daṣṭvā* — biting; *radaiḥ* — with the teeth; *tat* — that (topic); *anuvarṇana* — for describing; *lola* — eager; *jihvām* — his tongue; *nṛtyan* — dancing; *vicitram* — wonderfully; *agamat* — assumed; *vividhām* — various; *avasthām* — ecstatic states.

**Śrī Gopa-kumāra said: After speaking thus, the great sage Nārada embraced me. Immersed in waves of an ocean of love of Godhead, he trembled and wept, and his hairs stood on end. He bit his tongue, a tongue uncontrollably eager to keep speaking. And he danced wonderfully and showed many symptoms of ecstasy.**

COMMENTARY: Nārada wanted to hold back from elaborating any further on the many-faceted glories of the *gopīs* because he was afraid of losing control of himself in ecstasy. As it was, he was already beginning to lose control; in fact, right in front of Gopa-kumāra and Uddhava he rolled on the ground, jumped about, and shouted and cried like a madman.

## TEXT 205

क्षणात्स्वास्थ्यमिवासाद्य दृष्ट्वा मां दीनमानसम् ।
सान्त्वयन् श्लक्ष्णया वाचा मुनीन्द्रः पुनराह सः ॥

*kṣaṇāt svāsthyam ivāsādya*
*dṛṣṭvā māṁ dīna-mānasam*
*sāntvayan ślakṣṇayā vācā*
*munīndraḥ punar āha saḥ*

*kṣaṇāt* — after a moment; *svāsthyam* — normal consciousness; *iva* — as if; *āsādya* — obtaining; *dṛṣṭvā* — seeing; *mām* — me; *dīna* — discouraged; *mānasam* — in my mind; *sāntvayan* — consoling; *ślakṣṇayā* — sweet; *vācā* — with words; *muni-indraḥ* — the best of sages; *punaḥ* — again; *āha* — spoke; *saḥ* — he.

**A moment later, he came back to more or less normal. Seeing me feeling discouraged, that best of sages spoke again, consoling me with sweet words.**

COMMENTARY: Seeing Nārada go mad in ecstasy made Gopakumāra worry that his own goal might be difficult to achieve.

## TEXT 206

श्रीनारद उवाच
इदं तु वृत्तं सर्वत्र गोपनीयं सदा सताम् ।
विशेषतो महैश्वर्यप्राकट्यभरभूमिषु ॥

*śrī-nārada uvāca*
*idaṁ tu vṛttaṁ sarvatra*
*gopanīyaṁ sadā satām*
*viśeṣato mahaiśvarya-*
*prākaṭya-bhara-bhūmiṣu*

*śrī-nāradaḥ uvāca* — Śrī Nārada said; *idam* — this; *tu* — but; *vṛttam* — subject matter; *sarvatra* — everywhere; *gopanīyam* — to be kept private; *sadā* — always; *satām* — for saintly persons; *viśeṣataḥ* — especially; *mahā-aiśvarya* — of supreme opulences; *prākaṭya-bhara* — of extensive display; *bhūmiṣu* — in the places.

**Śrī Nārada said: This subject should always be kept private, to be spoken only among saintly devotees. And it should especially be avoided in places where the Lord's supreme opulence is displayed.**

COMMENTARY: Thus Nārada asked Gopa-kumāra never to repeat in an unsuitable place what Nārada had just told him about various topics, beginning with the position of Goloka and ending with the glories of the *gopīs.*

TEXT 207

अतस्तदानीं वैकुण्ठे न मया ते प्रकाशितम् ।
परं त्वद्भावमाधुर्यलोलितोऽत्रावदं कियत् ॥

*atas tadānīṁ vaikuṇṭhe*
*na mayā te prakāśitam*
*paraṁ tvad-bhāva-mādhurya-*
*lolito 'trāvadaṁ kiyat*

*ataḥ* — so; *tadānīm* — at that time; *vaikuṇṭhe* — in Vaikuṇṭha; *na* — not; *mayā* — by me; *te* — these matters; *prakāśitam* — revealed; *param* — only; *tvat* — your; *bhāva* — of the ecstatic love; *mādhurya* — by the charm; *lolitaḥ* — driven; *atra* — here; *avadam* — I have spoken; *kiyat* — a little.

**That is why I didn't reveal these things to you in Vaikuṇṭha. Only here, moved by the charm of your ecstatic love for the Lord, have I spoken of them a little.**

COMMENTARY: Not in Vaikuṇṭha but only here in Dvārakā in Uddhava's house had it been appropriate to tell Gopa-kumāra something about Goloka and its devotees.

TEXT 208

स्वस्योद्धवस्य तेऽप्येष कृत्वाहं शपथं ब्रुवे ।
दुःसाध्यं तत्पदं ह्यत्र तत्साधनमपि ध्रुवम् ॥

*svasyoddhavasya te 'py eṣa*
*kṛtvāhaṁ śapathaṁ bruve*
*duḥsādhyaṁ tat padaṁ hy atra*
*tat-sādhanam api dhruvam*

*svasya* — on behalf of myself; *uddhavasya* — and Uddhava; *te* — to you; *api* — and; *eṣaḥ* — this; *kṛtvā* — making; *aham* — I; *śapatham* — vow; *bruve* — say; *duḥsādhyam* — very difficult to achieve; *tat* — that; *padam* — abode; *hi* — indeed; *atra* — here; *tat* — for achieving that; *sādhanam* — the discipline; *api* — also; *dhruvam* — certainly.

**On my own behalf and that of Uddhava I testify to you that from here that abode of the Lord is in fact most difficult to achieve—and so too is the discipline that leads to it.**

COMMENTARY: By using the words *hy atra* ("indeed here"), Nārada hints at the confidential truth that one can achieve this most difficult goal by residing in Mathurā Vraja-bhūmi on earth.

## TEXT 209

किन्तूपदेशं हितमेकमेतं
मत्तः शृणु श्रीपुरुषोत्तमाख्यम् ।
क्षेत्रं तदत्रापि विभात्यदूरे
पूर्वं त्वया यद्भुवि दृष्टमस्ति ॥

*kintūpadeśaṁ hitam ekam etaṁ*
*mattaḥ śṛṇu śrī-puruṣottamākhyam*
*kṣetraṁ tad atrāpi vibhāty adūre*
*pūrvaṁ tvayā yad bhuvi dṛṣṭam asti*

*kintu* — but; *upadeśam* — piece of advice; *hitam* — beneficial; *ekam* — one; *etam* — this; *mattaḥ* — from me; *śṛṇu* — please hear; *śrī-puruṣottama-ākhyam* — named Śrī Puruṣottama; *kṣetram* — the holy abode; *tat* — it; *atra* — here; *api* — also; *vibhāti* — is present; *adūre* — not far; *pūrvam* — previously;

*tvayā* — by you; *yat* — which; *bhuvi* — on earth; *dṛṣṭam* — seen; *asti* — was.

**But please hear from me this one piece of advice: Not far from here lies the Lord's holy abode known as Śrī Puruṣottama-kṣetra, which you visited before on earth.**

COMMENTARY: The transcendental abode of Lord Jagannātha on earth is also present in Vaikuṇṭha.

### TEXT 210

तस्मिन्सुभद्राबलरामसंयुतस्
तं वै विनोदं पुरुषोत्तमो भजेत् ।
चक्रे स गोवर्धनवृन्दकाटवी-
कलिन्दजातीरभुवि स्वयं हि यम् ॥

*tasmin subhadrā-balarāma-saṁyutas*
*taṁ vai vinodaṁ puruṣottamo bhajet*
*cakre sa govardhana-vṛndakāṭavī-*
*kalindajā-tīra-bhuvi svayaṁ hi yam*

*tasmin* — there; *subhadrā* — by Subhadrā; *balarāma* — and Balarāma; *saṁyutaḥ* — joined; *tam* — He; *vai* — indeed; *vinodam* — in sports; *puruṣottamaḥ* — Lord Puruṣottama; *bhajet* — engages; *cakre* — performed; *saḥ* — He; *govardhana* — of Govardhana; *vṛndakā-aṭavī* — the forest of Vṛndāvana; *kalinda-jā* — of the Yamunā; *tīra* — along the shores; *bhuvi* — on the land; *svayam* — Himself; *hi* — certainly; *yam* — which.

**There, in the company of Subhadrā and Balarāma, Lord Puruṣottama enjoys the same sports He enacted at Govardhana and in the Vṛndāvana forest and on the shores of the Yamunā.**

COMMENTARY: Lord Jagannātha is Kṛṣṇa Himself. By visiting Puruṣottama-kṣetra in Vaikuṇṭha, Gopa-kumāra will be able to see the object of his worship, Lord Kṛṣṇa, enjoying His favorite pastimes.

TEXT 211

सर्वावतारैकनिधानरूपस्
तत्तच्चरित्राणि च सन्तनोति ।
यस्मै च रोचेत यदस्य रूपं
भक्ताय तस्मै खलु दर्शयेत्तत् ॥

*sarvāvatāraika-nidhāna-rūpas*
*tat-tac-caritrāṇi ca santanoti*
*yasmai ca roceta yad asya rūpaṁ*
*bhaktāya tasmai khalu darśayet tat*

*sarva* — all; *avatāra* — of incarnations; *eka-nidhāna* — the one source; *rūpaḥ* — whose form; *tat-tat* — all the various; *caritrāṇi* — pastimes; *ca* — and; *santanoti* — He expands; *yasmai* — to whom; *ca* — and; *roceta* — is attractive; *yat* — which; *asya* — His; *rūpam* — form; *bhaktāya* — to that devotee; *tasmai* — him; *khalu* — indeed; *darśayet* — will show; *tat* — that.

**His transcendental form, the one source of all incarnations, expands all of His various pastimes. Whichever of His forms a devotee finds attractive, that form the Lord shows him.**

COMMENTARY: Within Lord Jagannātha, Gopa-kumāra will be able to see all the different forms of the Supreme Lord, for Lord Jagannātha shows Himself as one incarnation of Viṣṇu or another, at suitable times and places, by displaying that incarnation's pastimes. Gopa-kumāra may doubt whether all his desires can be fulfilled by Lord Jagannātha, whose form differs from that of Madana-gopāla. After all, Gopa-kumāra's heart belongs only to Madana-gopāla, who alone can attract him. To remove this doubt, Nārada speaks the second half of this verse.

Lord Jagannātha will surely respond to Gopa-kumāra's particular mood of devotion by appearing as his worshipable Lord Gopāla.

## TEXT 212

श्रीकृष्णदेवस्य सदा प्रियं तत्
क्षेत्रं यथा श्रीमथुरा तथैव ।
तत्पारमैश्वर्यभरप्रकाश-
लोकानुसारिव्यवहाररम्यम् ॥

*śrī-kṛṣṇa-devasya sadā priyaṁ tat*
*kṣetraṁ yathā śrī-mathurā tathaiva*
*tat-pāramaiśvarya-bhara-prakāśa-*
*lokānusāri-vyavahāra-ramyam*

*śrī-kṛṣṇa-devasya* — of Śrī Kṛṣṇadeva; *sadā* — eternally; *priyam* — dear; *tat* — that; *kṣetram* — holy abode; *yathā* — just as; *śrī-mathurā* — Śrī Mathurā; *tathā eva* — so; *tat* — His; *pārama-aiśvarya* — of His supreme opulence; *bhara* — completeness; *prakāśa* — with the display; *loka* — the ordinary world; *anusāri* — following; *vyavahāra* — with behavior; *ramyam* — charming.

**Eternally as dear to Śrī Kṛṣṇadeva as His beautiful Mathurā-dhāma is that Puruṣottama-kṣetra. There the Lord displays His supreme opulence and yet charms His devotees by acting like an ordinary person of the world.**

COMMENTARY: Gopa-kumāra may still insist that Kṛṣṇa reveals Himself in full sweetness only in His favorite abode, Vraja-bhūmi. And Gopa-kumāra may therefore not want to go anywhere else. But here Nārada explains that in Puruṣottama-kṣetra, nondifferent from Vraja, Kṛṣṇa also manifests all His powers of Godhead and all His sweetness.

Lord Jagannātha's being the complete, omnipotent Personality of Godhead is confirmed in *Śrī Śiva Purāṇa:*

*āste 'nanto 'vyayo viṣṇuḥ*
*purāṇa-puruṣottamaḥ*
*muktiṁ dadāti yo devaḥ*
*saptadhā bhakta-vatsalaḥ*

*smaraṇād bhakṣaṇād yānāt*
*tathā nāmānukīrtanāt*
*kṣetre vāsād asu-tyāgād*
*darśanāc ca yathā tathā*

"The unlimited, imperishable Viṣṇu, the primeval Supreme Person, abides there [in Purī]. That Lord, who is very kind to His devotees, bestows liberation in seven ways: His devotees in Purī are liberated by remembering Him, by eating remnants of His food, by making a pilgrimage, by repeatedly chanting His names, by living in that abode, by giving up their life airs, or by seeing Him."

*Śrī Skanda Purāṇa* confirms:

*yasmād arthāj jagad idaṁ*
*sambhūtaṁ sa-carācaram*
*so 'rtho dāru-svarūpeṇa*
*kṣetre jīva iva sthitaḥ*

"The same being who created this universe with all its moving and nonmoving creatures is present in Śrī-kṣetra in a form of wood, like the living soul of that abode."

Therefore, since Kṛṣṇa enjoys with the same freedom in Purī as in Vraja-bhūmi, Gopa-kumāra should be able to achieve in Purī everything he desires.

## TEXT 213

गतस्तत्र न सन्तृप्येस्तस्य दर्शनतोऽपि चेत् ।
तदा तत्रानुतिष्ठेस्त्वं निजेष्टप्राप्तिसाधनम् ॥

*gatas tatra na santṛpyes*
*tasya darśanato 'pi cet*

*tadā tatrānutiṣṭhes tvaṁ*
*nijeṣṭa-prāpti-sādhanam*

*gataḥ* — having gone; *tatra* — there; *na santṛpyeḥ* — you are not satisfied; *tasya* — His; *darśanataḥ* — by the seeing; *api* — even; *cet* — if; *tadā* — then; *tatra* — there; *anutiṣṭheḥ* — should remain; *tvam* — you; *nija-iṣṭa* — your own goal; *prāpti* — for achieving; *sādhanam* — as the means.

**And if you are still not fully satisfied after going there and seeing Him, then at least stay there some time as the means to achieve your desired goal.**

TEXT 214

तच्च श्रीबल्लवीप्राणनाथपादसरोजयोः ।
प्रेमैव तद्व्रजप्रेमसजातीयं न चेतरत् ॥

*tac ca śrī-ballavī-prāṇa-*
*nātha-pāda-sarojayoḥ*
*premaiva tad-vraja-prema-*
*sajātīyaṁ na cetarat*

*tat* — that (goal); *ca* — and; *śrī-ballavī* — of the divine *gopīs;* *prāṇa-nātha* — of the life and soul; *pāda-sarojayoḥ* — for the lotus feet; *prema* — pure love; *eva* — only; *tat* — His; *vraja* — of Vraja; *prema-sajātīyam* — in the mood of the love; *na* — not; *ca* — and; *itarat* — any other.

**Of course, your ultimate goal is pure love for the lotus feet of Kṛṣṇa, the divine gopīs' life and soul—love that follows the mood of the Lord's own Vraja-bhūmi. You seek no other goal than that.**

COMMENTARY: Here Nārada defines both Gopa-kumāra's desired goal and the correct means for achieving it. The only effective means of achieving Kṛṣṇa in Goloka is pure love. And the only proper objects of that love are the two lotus feet of Śrī Gopīnātha.

## TEXT 215

निदानं तु परं प्रेम्णः श्रीकृष्णकरुणाभरः ।
कस्याप्युदेत्यकस्माद्वा कस्यचित्साधनक्रमात् ॥

*nidānaṁ tu paraṁ premṇaḥ*
*śrī-kṛṣṇa-karuṇā-bharaḥ*
*kasyāpy udety akasmād vā*
*kasyacit sādhana-kramāt*

*nidānam*—the cause; *tu*—moreover; *param*—prime; *premṇaḥ*—of pure love; *śrī-kṛṣṇa*—of Śrī Kṛṣṇa; *karuṇā-bharaḥ*—the complete mercy; *kasya api*—for someone; *udeti*—it arises; *akasmāt*—causelessly; *vā*—or; *kasyacit*—for someone; *sādhana*—of practice; *kramāt*—by gradual development.

**But the prime cause of pure love for Śrī Kṛṣṇa is Kṛṣṇa's full mercy, which in someone may arise spontaneously and in someone else by gradual practice of devotional service.**

## TEXT 216

यथोदारान् मिलत्यन्नं पक्वं वा पाकसाधनम् ।
साधकस्योच्यते शास्त्रगत्यायं साधनक्रमः ॥

*yathodārān milaty annaṁ*
*pakvaṁ vā pāka-sādhanam*
*sādhakasyocyate śāstra-*
*gatyāyaṁ sādhana-kramaḥ*

*yathā*—as; *udārāt*—from a generous donor; *milati*—one receives; *annam*—food; *pakvam*—cooked; *vā*—or; *pāka-*

*sādhanam* — the means of cooking; *sādhakasya* — of a practitioner; *ucyate* — is said; *śāstra-gatyā* — according to the opinions of scripture; *ayam* — this; *sādhana* — of devotional practice; *kramaḥ* — step-by-step procedure.

**Just as from a generous donor one might receive food already cooked or the means and ingredients for cooking food oneself, so according to the opinions of scripture one receives Kṛṣṇa's mercy through a method of devotional practice [either regulative or spontaneous].**

COMMENTARY: Though all perfection in *bhakti* comes only by Kṛṣṇa's mercy, there is still a need for different methods of *sādhana*. To illustrate the point, we may consider the hungry people who should receive charity. Some should be given food already cooked and offered to the Supreme Lord. Others, like strict *brāhmaṇas* who eat only what they have cooked themselves and offered to their own Deities, should be given rice, other ingredients, and pots and fuel for cooking. Similarly, most aspiring Vaiṣṇavas need to be purified from material contamination by regulative devotional practice; only a few souls, already pure, can enter directly into spontaneous loving service.

## TEXT 217

तत्तु लौकिकसद्बन्धुबुद्ध्या प्रेम भयादिजम् ।
विघ्नं निरस्य तद्गोपगोपीदास्येप्सयार्जयेत् ॥

*tat tu laukika-sad-bandhu-*
*buddhyā prema bhayādi-jam*
*vighnaṁ nirasya tad-gopa-*
*gopī-dāsyepsayārjayet*

*tat* — that (goal); *tu* — and; *laukika* — ordinary; *sat-bandhu* — of a close friend; *buddhyā* — with the idea; *prema* — pure love; *bhaya-ādi* — fear and so on; *jam* — born out of; *vighnam* — obstacles; *nirasya* — dismissing; *tat* — His; *gopa* — of the cowherd boyfriends; *gopī* — and cowherd girlfriends; *dāsya* — the service attitude; *īpsayā* — with the desire of attaining; *arjayet* — one can earn.

**Once one has overcome the obstacles on the path that arise from frailties like fear, one can then achieve pure love in which one thinks of the Lord like a close friend in the ordinary world. For this one must have a strong desire to serve the Lord in the manner of His gopas and gopīs.**

COMMENTARY: When a serious devotee first sets his aim on following in the footsteps of the Goloka-vāsīs, the goal may seem far away. He may begin his endeavor still encumbered by many material desires. But the more he carefully studies the transcendental reality, the more he renounces his unsuitable desires. He then rises above the misgivings born of fear, reverence, distrust, and shame. The real beginning of spiritual life, therefore, is to become free from material desires.

Until the obstacles are overcome, the devotee sees the object of his devotion only as the supreme powerful and so remains too fearful and respectful to have any real love for Him. But later, when the devotee swims in the vast ocean of *bhakti,* the superficial waves of contrary impulses recede, and he is granted the superintelligence for friendship with the Supreme. The devotee then approaches the Lord with such apparently worldly moods as that of a consort or a son and serves His lotus feet accordingly. He renders pure devotional service, as defined in the *Padma Purāṇa:*

*ananya-mamatā viṣṇau*
*mamatā prema-saṁyutā*
*bhaktir ity ucyate bhīṣma-*
*prahlādoddhava-nāradaiḥ*

"When one develops an unflinching sense of ownership or possessiveness in relation to Lord Viṣṇu, or, in other words, when one thinks Viṣṇu and no one else to be the only object of love, such an awakening is called *bhakti* by exalted persons like Bhīṣma, Prahlāda, Uddhava, and Nārada."

## TEXT 218

तद्धि तत्तद्व्रजक्रीडाध्यानगानप्रधानया ।
भक्त्या सम्पद्यते प्रेष्ठनामसङ्कीर्तनोज्ज्वलम् ॥

*tad dhi tat-tad-vraja-krīḍā-*
*dhyāna-gāna-pradhānayā*
*bhaktyā sampadyate preṣṭha-*
*nāma-saṅkīrtanojjvalam*

*tat* — that; *hi* — indeed; *tat-tat* — various; *vraja-krīḍā* — the pastimes in Vraja; *dhyāna* — meditation on; *gāna* — and singing about; *pradhānayā* — consisting primarily of; *bhaktyā* — by devotional service; *sampadyate* — develops; *preṣṭha* — which are beloved; *nāma* — of the names; *saṅkīrtana* — by the ecstatic chanting; *ujjvalam* — made brilliant.

**One develops that love by practicing the devotional service whose main ways are meditation on and singing about the many Vraja pastimes of the Lord. That service becomes brilliant by saṅkīrtana of the Lord's most beloved holy names.**

COMMENTARY: *Vaidhī-sādhana-bhakti,* which consists of nine basic devotional practices, beginning with hearing, chanting, and remembering, prepares a devotee's heart for the awakening of *prema,* love of God. *Dhyāna* and *gāna* — the general methods of remembering and chanting about the Supreme Lord and His pastimes — transform, in the advanced stages of *sādhana,* into *preṣṭha-nāma-saṅkīrtana,* ecstatic absorption in the nectarean names of one's worshipable Lord. This *saṅkīrtana* is the most essential means for achieving *prema*. By *nāma-saṅkīrtana* one easily realizes the full glories of Kṛṣṇa and His pleasure potency.

## TEXT 219

तदेकरसलोकस्य सङ्गेऽभिव्यक्ततां स्वतः ।
प्रयास्यदपि तद्वस्तु गोपनीयं प्रयत्नतः ॥

*tad-eka-rasa-lokasya*
*saṅge 'bhivyaktatāṁ svataḥ*
*prayāsyad api tad vastu*
*gopanīyaṁ prayatnataḥ*

*tat* — that; *eka* — only; *rasa* — relishing the taste; *lokasya* — of people; *saṅge* — in the association; *abhivyaktatām* — manifestation; *svataḥ* — naturally; *prayāsyat* — coming to be obtained; *api* — and; *tat* — that; *vastu* — object (pure love); *gopanīyam* — meant to be concealed; *prayatnataḥ* — with effort.

**In the company of people whose only taste is for devotional service in pure love, that love appears of its own accord. Yet one must try hard to keep it concealed.**

COMMENTARY: The quickest way to achieve *prema* is to stay in the company of those who know its value. The association of first-class pure Vaiṣṇavas has the power to evoke *prema* in an aspirant's heart. But when love for Kṛṣṇa begins to mature, a devotee must be careful not to make a public show of his ecstasy. There is a saying, *gopayet mātṛ-jāra-vat:* "One should keep *prema* hidden, as one would conceal that one's mother has a paramour." A devotee actually experiencing *prema* would never divulge his inner ecstasies just to establish a reputation for himself among Vaiṣṇavas. Still, as indicated here by the word *svataḥ* ("of its own accord"), the situation of an ecstatic devotee is like that of an ordinary person separated from a loved one long enough for time to have covered the pain yet not so long that meeting friends of his beloved won't suddenly plunge him again into agony. The word *prāyasyat* is in a future tense, which implies that the injunction to keep *prema* hidden applies only before *prema* has fully appeared. Once fully developed, *prema* cannot be checked from showing itself whenever it wants.

## TEXT 220

तद्वै तस्य प्रियक्रीडावनभूमौ सदा रहः ।
निवसंस्तनुयादेवं सम्पद्येताचिराद् ध्रुवम् ॥

*tad vai tasya priya-krīḍā-*
*vana-bhūmau sadā rahaḥ*
*nivasaṁs tanuyād evaṁ*
*sampadyetācirād dhruvam*

*tat* — that (*prema*); *vai* — indeed; *tasya* — His; *priya* — favorite; *krīḍā-vana* — of the pastime forests; *bhūmau* — in the land; *sadā* — always; *rahaḥ* — in seclusion; *nivasan* — residing; *tanuyāt* — will develop; *evam* — thus; *sampadyeta* — will be fully achieved; *acirāt* — soon; *dhruvam* — certainly.

**When one resides always in seclusion in the land of the Lord's favorite pastime forests, surely such love will soon develop and mature.**

COMMENTARY: *Sādhana-bhakti* performed in Kṛṣṇa's holy *dhāma* is especially conducive to the awakening of *prema.*

## TEXT 221

तत्कर्मज्ञानयोगादिसाधनाद् दूरतः स्थितम् ।
सर्वत्र नैरपेक्ष्येण भूषितं दैन्यमूलकम् ॥

*tat karma-jñāna-yogādi-*
*sādhanād dūrataḥ sthitam*
*sarvatra nairapekṣyeṇa*
*bhūṣitaṁ dainya-mūlakam*

*tat* — that; *karma-jñāna-yoga-ādi* — such as *karma, jñāna,* and *yoga; sādhanāt* — from disciplines; *dūrataḥ* — by far differently; *sthitam* — situated; *sarvatra* — in all stages; *nairapekṣyeṇa*

— with indifference to other things; *bhūṣitam* — decorated; *dainya* — utter humility; *mūlakam* — having as its foundation.

**That loving devotional service is far different from disciplines such as karma, jñāna, and yoga. At every stage it is decorated by indifference to them, and its root is dainya, utter humility.**

COMMENTARY: The question here is whether prescribed duties and other methods of purification should be continued along with devotional service. Should one keep on with *karma* (the following of *varṇāśrama* regulations) or *jñāna* (the cultivating of discrimination between spirit and matter)? What about the eightfold practice of *yoga* and meditation in *samādhi*? And what about renunciation, chanting *mantras,* and other disciplines? Here Nārada answers that although these disciplines, starting with *karma,* may all assist in the *sādhana* of love of God, only in the very early stages of devotional practice are they of much use. Once *sādhana-bhakti* has yielded its fruit — *rāgānuga-bhakti,* spontaneous devotion — and especially once *prema* has appeared, the fruit of *rāgānuga-bhakti,* there is no longer any place in a devotee's life for those other practices.

The fact is that *prema* is not achievable by other methods, such as *karma* and *jñāna*. Devotees should therefore disregard those methods and simply busy themselves with the devotional service of hearing, chanting, remembering, and so on. This point has already been discussed in detail at the end of the Second Chapter of this part of *Bṛhad-bhāgavatāmṛta,* in the context of the glories of *bhakti.*

Great authorities have said:

*kāyena dūre vrajinaṁ tyajantī*
*japantam antaḥ-karaṇe hasantī*
*samādhi-yoge ca bahir bhavantī*
*sandṛśyate kāpi mukunda-bhaktiḥ*

"Devotional service to Lord Mukunda can be seen personified as it runs far away from those who perform fruitive rituals, and laughs at those who chant silent *mantras* in their minds, and avoids those who practice meditational *yoga.*"

*Bhakti-yoga* in all its phases of practice and achievement, in this life and the next, is always decorated with the ornament of indifference to material desires. This holds true whether *bhakti* is performed internally with the subtle body or externally with one's physical body and senses and the body's external possessions. When one allows secondary means and goals to become prominent, one deviates from *bhakti.* The most essential support — and a candidate for pure *bhakti* must always take help from it — is utter humility.

TEXT 222

येनासाधारणाशक्ताधमबुद्धिः सदात्मनि ।
सर्वोत्कर्षान्वितेऽपि स्याद् बुधैस्तद्दैन्यमिष्यते ॥

*yenāsādhāraṇāśaktā-*
*dhama-buddhiḥ sadātmani*
*sarvotkarṣānvite 'pi syād*
*budhais tad dainyam iṣyate*

*yena* — by which; *asādhāraṇa* — exceptional; *aśakta* — of being incapable; *adhama* — and fallen; *buddhiḥ* — the mentality; *sadā* — always; *ātmani* — in oneself; *sarva* — with all; *utkarṣa* — excellences; *anvite* — endowed; *api* — even; *syāt* — is; *budhaiḥ* — by the wise men; *tat* — that; *dainyam* — utter humility; *iṣyate* — is called.

**Wise men define dainya as the state in which one always thinks oneself exceptionally incapable and low, even when endowed with all excellences.**

COMMENTARY: Nārada's own definition of *dainya* distinguishes his use of the word from other possible meanings, such as "poverty," "becoming selfless by not accepting charity," and "being free from egotism." Someone might say that the quality of thinking oneself very fallen may also be seen in persons who are simply lazy or those who abandon auspicious work or indulge in sinful acts. Therefore Nārada specifies that one who actually has *dainya* is endowed with all good qualities; for instance, such a person observes positive and negative regulations, he is free of false ego, and he has a healthy fear of material life. Furthermore, though Nārada doesn't say so, transcendental *dainya* is a state of extreme agitation that can lead to tears and other ecstatic outbreaks.

## TEXT 223

यया वाचेहया दैन्यं मत्या च स्थैर्यमेति तत् ।
तां यत्नेन भजेद्विद्वांस्तद्विरुद्धानि वर्जयेत् ॥

*yayā vācehayā dainyaṁ*
*matyā ca sthairyam eti tat*
*tāṁ yatnena bhajed vidvāṁs*
*tad-viruddhāni varjayet*

*yayā*—by which; *vācā*—language; *īhayā*—and behavior; *dainyam*—utter humility; *matyā*—by which mode of thinking; *ca*—and; *sthairyam*—firmness; *eti*—attains; *tat*—it; *tām*—that; *yatnena*—with endeavor; *bhajet*—should cultivate; *vidvān*—an intelligent person; *tat*—to that; *viruddhāni*—obstacles; *varjayet*—he should avoid.

**An intelligent person should carefully cultivate speech, behavior, and thinking that fix him in utter humility, and anything that stands in the way of it he should avoid.**

## TEXT 224

दैन्यं तु परमं प्रेम्णः परीपाकेण जन्यते ।
तासां गोकुलनारीणामिव कृष्णवियोगतः ॥

*dainyaṁ tu paramaṁ premṇaḥ*
*parīpākeṇa janyate*
*tāsāṁ gokula-nārīṇām*
*iva kṛṣṇa-viyogataḥ*

*dainyam* — utter humility; *tu* — and; *paramam* — the highest degree; *premṇaḥ* — of pure love; *parīpākeṇa* — with the full maturity; *janyate* — is generated; *tāsām* — those; *gokula* — of Gokula; *nārīṇām* — of the women; *iva* — as; *kṛṣṇa-viyogataḥ* — in separation from Kṛṣṇa.

**Dainya at its most exalted comes forth when prema, pure love of God, reaches full maturity, as it did in the women of Gokula when they were separated from Kṛṣṇa.**

COMMENTARY: Ordinary *dainya* can be developed by human effort, but there is also a type of *dainya,* beyond the mundane, that comes from receiving the Supreme Lord's favor. The word *tu* in this verse contrasts these distinct kinds of *dainya.* Almost everyone in the material world is separated from Kṛṣṇa, but most people never experience *dainya* because they have no *prema.* Therefore they can never become free from suffering and attain true happiness. To achieve transcendental *dainya,* one must learn to love Kṛṣṇa in the mood felt by the *gopīs,* led by Śrī Rādhā, when Kṛṣṇa left them to go to Mathurā. We can understand from the example of the *gopīs' viraha-bhāva,* their feelings of love in separation, that this special *dainya* arises only when, by Śrī Kṛṣṇa's exceptional mercy, a devotee who has realized Kṛṣṇa's sweetness develops extraordinary *prema* in his heart in the mood of separation. As *prema* appears in degrees of excellence, so does *dainya.*

TEXT 225

परिपाकेण दैन्यस्य प्रेमाजस्रं वितन्यते ।
परस्परं तयोरित्थं कार्यकारणतेक्ष्यते ॥

*paripākeṇa dainyasya*
*premājasraṁ vitanyate*
*parasparaṁ tayor itthaṁ*
*kārya-kāraṇatekṣyate*

*paripākeṇa* — by the maturity; *dainyasya* — of *dainya; prema* — pure love; *ajasram* — without limit; *vitanyate* — develops; *parasparam* — mutual; *tayoḥ* — of both (*dainya* and *prema*); *ittham* — in this way; *kārya-kāraṇatā* — the relationship of cause and effect; *īkṣyate* — is seen.

**When dainya fully matures, prema unfolds without limit. And so we see dainya and prema acting in a relationship in which each is both cause and effect.**

COMMENTARY: If *prema* is supposed to be the final result of all devotional endeavors, how can *dainya* be a consequence of *prema*? In answer: Yes, *prema* is the final goal, but *dainya* is not altogether different from *prema. Dainya* is an integral component of *prema,* and both foster one another.

It is a misunderstanding to think that because there is always another level of perfection to achieve, one can never reach the supreme goal of life. What the progressive development of *prema* shows is not that there is no goal but that in spiritual life there is endless variety. By pure love for the lotus feet of Śrī Gopīnātha, the fruit one achieves is the attainment of Śrī Goloka; by that attainment, the direct sight of Śrī Gopīnātha; by that direct vision, His special mercy; by that mercy, the highest ecstasies of *viraha-bhāva,* and so on. This endless sequence is not a fault but simply the unfolding of spiritual variety. Even in Vaikuṇṭha, what to speak of Goloka, the bliss of devotional service unfolds in an infinite variety that puts the happiness of liberation to shame.

## TEXT 226

भ्रातः प्रेम्णः स्वरूपं यत्तद्धि जानन्ति तद्विदः ।
यस्य चित्तार्द्रताजातं बाह्यं कम्पादिलक्षणम् ॥

*bhrātaḥ premṇaḥ svarūpaṁ yat*
*tad dhi jānanti tad-vidaḥ*
*yasya cittārdratā-jātaṁ*
*bāhyaṁ kampādi-lakṣaṇam*

*bhrātaḥ* — dear brother; *premṇaḥ* — of love of God; *svarūpam* — the essential nature; *yat* — which; *tat* — that; *hi* — indeed; *jānanti* — know; *tad-vidaḥ* — those who have realized it; *yasya* — whose; *citta* — of the heart; *ardratā* — from the condition of melting; *jātam* — born; *bāhyam* — externally; *kampa* — trembling; *ādi* — and so on; *lakṣaṇam* — whose symptoms.

**Dear brother, those who know the essence of prema recognize its presence when the melting of a devotee's heart gives rise to trembling and other such outward signs.**

COMMENTARY: This statement settles a possible doubt over the nature of *prema*. Since *prema* develops from feelings of utter helplessness (*dainya*), is *prema* a mood of wretchedness? Or since *prema* is considered the greatest of all goals, is it a special mood of bliss that comes from getting free from all causes of wretchedness? According to Nārada, only those who have realized *prema* can distinguish its real nature. The essence of *prema* cannot be defined in mere words. At best it can be recognized by its secondary characteristics (*taṭastha-lakṣaṇa*). Thus we can understand the presence of *prema* by its external symptoms like trembling, floods of tears, and standing erect of the bodily hair. Softening of the heart (*cittārdratā*) also counts as an external symptom because it is knowable by the mind, even though it is also said to be internal because it is not a directly visible object.

## TEXT 227

दवानलार्चिर्यमुनामृतं भवेत्
तथा तदप्यग्निशिखेव यद्गताम् ।
विषं च पीयुषमहो सुधा विषं
मृतिः सुखं जीवनमार्तिवैभवम् ॥

*davānalārcir yamunāmṛtaṁ bhavet*
*tathā tad apy agni-śikheva yadvatām*
*viṣaṁ ca pīyuṣam aho sudhā viṣaṁ*
*mṛtiḥ sukhaṁ jīvanam ārti-vaibhavam*

*dāva-anala* — of a forest fire; *arciḥ* — the flames; *yamunā* — of the Yamunā; *amṛtam* — the nectar; *bhavet* — becomes; *tathā* — that; *tat* — that; *api* — also; *agni* — of a fire; *śikhā* — the flames; *iva* — as if; *yat-vatām* — for those who possess that (*prema*); *viṣam* — poison; *ca* — and; *pīyuṣam* — nectar; *aho* — oh; *sudhā* — nectar; *viṣam* — poison; *mṛtiḥ* — death; *sukham* — happiness; *jīvanam* — life; *ārti-vaibhavam* — an expansion of misery.

**For those who have prema, the blazing conflagration of their agony is like the nectarean water of the Yamunā and yet like the burning flames of a fire. To them poison is like nectar, and nectar like poison, death is happiness, and life but an expansion of misery.**

COMMENTARY: In the intoxication of *prema,* sources of pleasure seem like those of pain, and vice versa. In other words, the difference between pleasure and pain becomes blurred. Things one should accept as auspicious and beneficial one abhors because they remind one of the very beloved one is trying to forget; and things that help one forget one's beloved one welcomes as auspicious.

## TEXT 228

यतो विवेक्तुं न हि शक्यतेऽद्धा
भेदः स सम्भोगवियोगयोर्यः ।
तथेदमानन्दभरात्मकं वा-
थ वा महाशोकमयं हि वस्तु ॥

*yato vivektuṁ na hi śakyate 'ddhā*
*bhedaḥ sa sambhoga-viyogayor yaḥ*

*tathedam ānanda-bharātmakaṁ vā-*
*tha vā mahā-śoka-mayaṁ hi vastu*

*yataḥ* — because; *vivektum* — to be distinguished; *na* — not; *hi* — indeed; *śakyate* — is possible; *addhā* — clearly; *bhedaḥ* — difference; *saḥ* — that; *sambhoga* — of union; *viyogayoḥ* — and separation; *yaḥ* — which; *tathā* — thus; *idam* — this; *ānanda-bhara* — an abundance of ecstasy; *ātmakam* — consisting of; *vā* — either; *atha vā* — or else; *mahā-śoka-mayam* — full of great suffering; *hi* — indeed; *vastu* — object.

**Indeed, because one cannot clearly tell between coming together with the object of prema and being separated from it, prema is full of both the greatest ecstasy and the worst anguish.**

COMMENTARY: A devotee under the influence of *prema* loses the power to discriminate between ecstasy and misery. For example, in the final chapter of *Śrīmad-Bhāgavatam's* Tenth Canto we find that Kṛṣṇa's queens, after enjoying water sports with Kṛṣṇa, lamented the pain of their separation from Him even though He was still present with them. The nature of *bhakti* is such that it generates all varieties of emotions, especially as it develops towards its extreme limits. Even in ordinary life, things taken to their extremes can seem to change into their opposites: the coldest ice may feel hot to the touch like fire.

Devotees advanced in *prema* enjoy the company of the Personality of Godhead, the embodiment of supreme bliss. They delight in the special joy derived from taking part in His wonderful pastimes. But by the extraordinary nature of *bhakti,* in the very midst of that enjoyment appears the pain of separation. The ecstasy of separation, indeed, is the ripe fruit of fully developed *prema* and is one of its essential components, just as hunger is an essential part of the complete enjoyment of eating.

However it may appear superficially, the happiness of *prema* in separation is the rarest treasure. In previous chapters of *Bṛhad-*

*bhāgavatāmṛta* this has already been discussed, and in the last two chapters it will be clarified still further.

### TEXT 229

भवन्ति सम्पत्त्युदयेन यस्य
सदा महोन्मत्तविचेष्टितानि ।
न यद्विना सञ्जनयेत्सुखं सा
नवप्रकारापि मुकुन्दभक्तिः ॥

*bhavanti sampatty-udayena yasya*
*sadā mahonmatta-viceṣṭitāni*
*na yad vinā sañjanayet sukhaṁ sā*
*nava-prakārāpi mukunda-bhaktiḥ*

*bhavanti* — are; *sampatti* — of the opulences; *udayena* — by the manifesting; *yasya* — of which (*prema*); *sadā* — always; *mahā-unmatta* — of a person utterly insane; *viceṣṭitāni* — various kinds of behavior; *na* — not; *yat* — which; *vinā* — without; *sañjanayet* — produces; *sukham* — happiness; *sā* — that; *nava-prakārā* — ninefold; *api* — even; *mukunda-bhaktiḥ* — devotional service to Lord Mukunda.

**When prema matures, one inevitably acts from time to time in the ways of an utter madman. And without such prema not even the nine kinds of devotional service to Lord Mukunda can bring real happiness.**

COMMENTARY: The purpose of devotional service in regulative practice is to bring one to the stage of *prema*. Only by realizing the fullness of *prema* can one truly become happy. The symptoms of this *prema* are obvious and altogether different from those of any other kind of success:

*evaṁ-vrataḥ sva-priya-nāma-kīrtyā*
*jātānurāgo druta-citta uccaiḥ*

*hasaty atho roditi rauti gāyaty*
*unmāda-van nṛtyati loka-bāhyaḥ*

"By chanting the holy name of the Supreme Lord, one comes to the stage of love of Godhead. Then the devotee is fixed in his vow as an eternal servant of the Lord, and he gradually becomes very much attached to a particular name and form of the Supreme Personality of Godhead. As his heart melts with ecstatic love, he laughs very loudly or cries or shouts. Sometimes he sings and dances like a madman, for he is indifferent to public opinion." (*Bhāgavatam* 11.2.40)

## TEXT 230

यथा हि शाको लवणं विनैव
क्षुधां विना भोग्यचयो यथा च ।
विनार्थबोधादिव शास्त्रपाठः
फलं विनारामगणो यथैव ॥

*yathā hi śāko lavaṇaṁ vinaiva*
*kṣudhāṁ vinā bhogya-cayo yathā ca*
*vinārtha-bodhād iva śāstra-pāṭhaḥ*
*phalaṁ vinārāma-gaṇo yathaiva*

*yathā* — like; *hi* — certainly; *śākaḥ* — vegetables; *lavaṇam* — salt; *vinā* — without; *eva* — indeed; *kṣudhām* — hunger; *vinā* — without; *bhogya-cayaḥ* — many eatables; *yathā* — like; *ca* — and; *vinā* — without; *artha-bodhāt* — understanding of the meaning; *iva* — as if; *śāstra-pāṭhaḥ* — study of the scriptures; *phalam* — fruit; *vinā* — without; *ārāma-gaṇaḥ* — gardens; *yathā* — like; *eva* — indeed.

**Indeed, without prema the nine kinds of devotional service are like vegetables without salt, an elaborate meal without hunger, scriptural study without understanding, or gardens without fruit.**

## TEXT 231

सामान्यतः किञ्चिदिदं मयोक्तं
वक्तुं विशेषेण न शक्यते तत् ।
प्रेमा तु कृष्णे व्रजयोषितां यस्
तत्तत्त्वमाख्यातुमलं कथं स्याम् ॥

*sāmānyataḥ kiñcid idaṁ mayoktaṁ*
*vaktuṁ viśeṣeṇa na śakyate tat*
*premā tu kṛṣṇe vraja-yoṣitāṁ yas*
*tat tattvam ākhyātum alaṁ kathaṁ syām*

*sāmānyataḥ* — in general; *kiñcit* — something; *idam* — this; *mayā* — by me; *uktam* — said; *vaktum* — to speak; *viśeṣeṇa* — in detail; *na śakyate* — is not possible; *tat* — that; *premā* — the pure love; *tu* — but; *kṛṣṇe* — for Kṛṣṇa; *vraja-yoṣitām* — of the women of Vraja; *yaḥ* — which; *tat* — that; *tattvam* — truth; *ākhyātum* — able to explain; *alam* — properly; *katham* — how; *syām* — I can be.

**I am saying something general about this love, but it cannot be described in full detail. How can I adequately tell of the nature of the pure love the women of Vraja have for Kṛṣṇa?**

COMMENTARY: The general characteristics of *prema* can be seen in devotees of some of Kṛṣṇa's *avatāras* and in the servants of Śrī Vaikuṇṭhanātha. But the love that Śrī Rādhikā and Her followers offer to Śrī Nanda-nandana is so exceptional that Nārada feels he has no authority to speak about it.

## TEXT 232

कृष्णे गते मधुपुरीं बत बल्लवीनां
भावोऽभवत्सपदि यो लयवह्नितीव्रः ।

प्रेमास्य हेतुरुत तत्त्वमिदं हि तस्य
मा तद्विशेषमपरं बत बोद्धुमिच्छ ॥

*kṛṣṇe gate madhu-purīṁ bata ballavīnāṁ*
*bhāvo 'bhavat sapadi yo laya-vahni-tīvraḥ*
*premāsya hetur uta tattvam idaṁ hi tasya*
*mā tad-viśeṣam aparaṁ bata boddhum iccha*

*kṛṣṇe* — Kṛṣṇa; *gate* — when He went; *madhu-purīm* — to Mathurā; *bata* — alas; *ballavīnām* — of the cowherd women; *bhāvaḥ* — the state; *abhavat* — was; *sapadi* — at once; *yaḥ* — which; *laya* — of universal annihilation; *vahni* — like the fire; *tīvraḥ* — acute; *prema* — *prema; asya* — of this; *hetuḥ* — the cause; *uta* — indeed; *tattvam* — truth; *idam* — this; *hi* — indeed; *tasya* — of this matter; *mā* — not; *tat* — about that; *viśeṣam* — detail; *aparam* — further; *bata* — alas; *boddhum* — to learn; *iccha* — you should desire.

**When Kṛṣṇa went to Mathurā City, the cowherd women were plunged at once into a state more intense than the fire of universal annihilation. The simple truth is that the cause of this state was prema. Please, I beg you, do not try to delve into this any deeper.**

COMMENTARY: Feeling himself unqualified to explain the essence of the *gopīs' prema,* Nārada here again says only a little about this *prema* in terms of its secondary characteristics. He is fearful of proceeding further because a further description might make both Gopa-kumāra and himself lose control of their ecstasy.

TEXT 233

सा राधिका भगवती क्वचिदीक्ष्यते चेत्
प्रेमा तदानुभवमृच्छति मूर्तिमान्सः ।
शक्येत चेद्वदितुमेष तया तदैव
श्रूयेत तत्त्वमिह चेद्भवति स्वशक्तिः ॥

*sā rādhikā bhagavatī kvacid īkṣyate cet*
*premā tadānubhavam ṛcchati mūrtimān saḥ*
*śakyeta ced gaditum eṣa tayā tadaiva*
*śrūyeta tattvam iha ced bhavati sva-śaktiḥ*

*sā* — She; *rādhikā* — Rādhikā; *bhagavatī* — the divine goddess; *kvacit* — somehow; *īkṣyate* — is seen; *cet* — if; *premā* — love; *tadā* — then; *anubhavam* — realization; *ṛcchati* — will reach; *mūrti-mān* — in person; *saḥ* — it; *śakyeta* — it will be possible; *cet* — if; *gaditum* — to be spoken about; *eṣaḥ* — this (*prema*); *tayā* — by Her; *tadā* — then; *eva* — only; *śrūyeta* — one may hear; *tattvam* — the truth; *iha* — in this matter; *cet* — if; *bhavati* — there is; *sva* — in you; *śaktiḥ* — capacity.

**If ever you meet the divine goddess Rādhikā, then you will see prema in person. And if ever She speaks about prema, only then can you hear the truth about it, if you are able to understand it.**

COMMENTARY: Nārada can hardly describe the nature of the *gopīs'* pure love, and even if with great endeavor he could, that love is something Gopa-kumāra's heart is not yet prepared to realize. But if Gopa-kumāra were to meet a person who in truth possesses that love, then he would be able to perceive it directly. Of all the Lord's *gopīs,* Śrīmatī Rādhārāṇī is famous as the most dear to the Lord. If Gopa-kumāra could meet Her, She could explain the truth about Her love for Kṛṣṇa — how supremely ecstatic it is, how supremely painful and distressing, and so on. Even if Nārada could receive such instructions from Śrīmatī Rādhārāṇī, he would not be able to repeat them to Gopa-kumāra, because those instructions would render Nārada completely bewildered, like a madman. Thus Gopa-kumāra will only be able to learn the mysteries of this most exalted science by seeing them for himself in the person of its original teacher, Śrīmatī Rādhārāṇī.

## TEXT 234

चेत्कृष्णचन्द्रस्य महावतारस्
तादृग्निजप्रेमवितानकारी ।
स्याद्वा कदाचिद्यदि राधिकायाः
प्रेमानुभूतिं तदुपैत्यथापि ॥

*cet kṛṣṇa-candrasya mahāvatāras*
*tādṛg nija-prema-vitāna-kārī*
*syād vā kadācid yadi rādhikāyāḥ*
*premānubhūtiṁ tad upaity athāpi*

*cet* — if; *kṛṣṇa-candrasya* — of Kṛṣṇacandra; *mahā-avatāraḥ* — a complete incarnation; *tādṛk* — such; *nija* — His own; *prema* — of the pure love; *vitāna* — the distribution; *kārī* — doing; *syāt* — there were; *vā* — or; *kadācit* — sometime; *yadi* — if; *rādhikāyāḥ* — of Rādhikā; *prema-anubhūtim* — the experience of *prema; tat* — that; *upaiti* — attains; *atha api* — or else.

**Or should there ever be a full incarnation of Śrī Kṛṣṇa-candra to distribute pure kṛṣṇa-prema, or to experience the kṛṣṇa-prema of Śrīmatī Rādhikā, you might be able to understand it.**

COMMENTARY: Since Śrīmatī Rādhārāṇī is rarely seen by ordinary souls in this world, Gopa-kumāra might doubt whether a modern person like himself could ever get Her favor and understand Her glories. But if She were not the only source of *prema* in this world, the conditioned souls would not need to be hopeless. To protect the hope of Gopa-kumāra and other devotees to obtain love at the lotus feet of Śrī Rādhikā and the Lord of Her heart, here Nārada hints at the future appearance of Śrī Caitanya Mahāprabhu, the combined form of Śrī Śrī Rādhā and Kṛṣṇa. For even subtly alluding to the merciful descent of Lord Caitanya, Nārada is all-glorious.

## TEXT 235

तद्गच्छ शीघ्रं तत्क्षेत्रं माथुरं व्रजभूभव ।
निजार्थसिद्धये त्वं हि न मादृक् तद्दयालयः ॥

*tad gaccha śīghraṁ tat kṣetraṁ*
*māthuraṁ vraja-bhū-bhava*
*nijārtha-siddhaye tvaṁ hi*
*na mādṛk tad-dayālayaḥ*

*tat* — therefore; *gaccha* — please go; *śīghram* — quickly; *tat* — to that; *kṣetram* — holy place; *māthuram* — the replica of Mathurā; *vraja-bhū* — in Vraja-bhūmi; *bhava* — you who were born; *nija* — your; *artha* — of the desires; *siddhaye* — for the fulfillment; *tvam* — you; *hi* — indeed; *na mādṛk* — unlike me; *tat* — His; *dayā* — of mercy; *ālayaḥ* — a repository.

**So, dear son of Vraja-bhūmi, to fulfill your desires go quickly to Lord Jagannātha's abode, the holy place that is an image of Mathurā. Unlike me, you are surely a person in whom the Lord has reposed His mercy.**

COMMENTARY: Gopa-kumāra should not be discouraged that Nārada has declared the *prema* of Vraja extremely difficult to achieve. Nārada himself may not expect to attain such *prema,* but Gopa-kumāra, born in Vraja and blessed with so much of Kṛṣṇa's mercy, is more fortunate.

## TEXT 236

श्रीमदुद्धव उवाच
क्षेत्रं यथा तत्पुरुषोत्तमं प्रभोः
प्रियं तथैतत्पुरमप्यदो यथा ।
परेशतालौकिकतोचितेहितैर्
विभूषितं तस्य तथेदमप्यृतम् ॥

*śrīmad-uddhava uvāca*
*kṣetraṁ yathā tat puruṣottamaṁ prabhoḥ*
*priyaṁ tathaitat puram apy ado yathā*
*pareśatā-laukikatocitehitair*
*vibhūṣitaṁ tasya tathedam apy ṛtam*

*śrīmat-uddhavaḥ uvāca* — Śrīmān Uddhava said; *kṣetram* — the holy abode; *yathā* — as; *tat* — that; *puruṣottamam* — Jagannātha Purī; *prabhoḥ* — to the Lord; *priyam* — dear; *tathā* — so; *etat* — this; *puram* — transcendental city; *api* — also; *adaḥ* — that (Purī); *yathā* — as; *para-īśatā* — for the capacity of the supreme controller; *laukikatā* — and for the capacity of an ordinary person; *ucita* — appropriate; *īhitaiḥ* — by activities; *vibhūṣitam* — beautified; *tasya* — His; *tathā* — so; *idam* — this; *api* — also; *ṛtam* — real.

**Śrīmān Uddhava said: Certainly as dear to our Lord as that Puruṣottama-kṣetra is this Dvārakā-purī. Dvārakā is as fully beautified by the deeds the Lord performs, both as the supreme controller and as an ordinary person of the world.**

COMMENTARY: As a loyal devotee of Kṛṣṇa in His form of Śrī Dvārakānātha, Uddhava cannot agree with Nārada's depiction of Dvārakā as inferior to Puruṣottama-kṣetra, Jagannātha Purī. That the glories of Dvārakā are real (*ṛta*) has been verified by the personal experience of countless reputable Vaiṣṇavas.

## TEXT 237

श्रीदैवकीनन्दन एष नः प्रभुस्
तद्रूपधारी पुरुषोत्तमे स्वयम् ।
स्थैर्यं भजन्क्रीडति तन्निवासिनां
तत्प्रेमपूरार्द्रहृदां सदा मुदे ॥

*śrī-daivakī-nandana eṣa naḥ prabhus*
*tad-rūpa-dhārī puruṣottame svayam*
*sthairyaṁ bhajan krīḍati tan-nivāsināṁ*
*tat-prema-pūrārdra-hṛdāṁ sadā mude*

*śrī-daivakī-nandanaḥ* — the son of Devakī; *eṣaḥ* — this; *naḥ* — our; *prabhuḥ* — Lord; *tat* — that; *rūpa* — form; *dhārī* — who assumes; *puruṣottame* — in Puruṣottama-kṣetra; *svayam* — Himself; *sthairyam* — immobility; *bhajan* — assuming; *krīḍati* — He sports; *tat* — of that place; *nivāsinām* — of the residents; *tat* — for Him; *prema-pūra* — in a flood of love; *ārdra* — melting; *hṛdām* — whose hearts; *sadā* — eternally; *mude* — for the pleasure.

**It is our own master, Śrī Devakī-nandana, who in Puruṣottama-kṣetra assumes the form of Lord Jagannātha. Standing motionless, He sports eternally for the pleasure of its residents, whose hearts melt in a flood of love for Him.**

COMMENTARY: The same son of Devakī whom the Yadus consider their master appears as *dāru-brahma,* the Absolute Truth in wood, in His abode of Puruṣottama-kṣetra. Why does He do this? One reason is to give joy to the residents of that abode.

## TEXT 238

यत्तत्र संसिध्यति वस्त्विहापि
सम्पद्यते तत्किल नास्ति भेदः ।
किन्त्वस्य तत्र व्रजभूचरित्र-
दृष्टिश्रुतिभ्यां भविता स शोकः ॥

*yat tatra saṁsidhyati vastv ihāpi*
*sampadyate tat kila nāsti bhedaḥ*
*kintv asya tatra vraja-bhū-caritra-*
*dṛṣṭi-śrutibhyāṁ bhavitā sa śokaḥ*

*yat* — which; *tatra* — there; *saṁsidhyati* — is available; *vastu* — reality; *iha* — here; *api* — also; *sampadyate* — is manifest; *tat* — that; *kila* — indeed; *na asti* — there is no; *bhedaḥ* — difference; *kintu* — but; *asya* — His; *tatra* — there; *vraja-bhū* — of Vraja-bhūmi; *caritra* — the pastimes; *dṛṣṭi* — by hearing; *śrutibhyām* — and by seeing; *bhavitā* — there will be; *saḥ* — some; *śokaḥ* — unhappiness.

**The same reality shown there is also found here, without any difference. But there, by seeing and hearing about His pastimes in Vraja-bhūmi, you will feel a certain kind of sorrow.**

COMMENTARY: Since both in Purī and in Dvārakā the same Kṛṣṇa rules, Uddhava says, there is no reason to make the effort to travel from one place to the other. And being in Purī will have one disadvantage: There Gopa-kumāra will see plays of Kṛṣṇa's Gokula pastimes and hear those pastimes depicted in songs and recitations. Being reminded about his worshipable Lord yet being unable to see Him directly will cause Gopa-kumāra pain.

## TEXT 239

तस्मिञ्जगन्नाथमुखाब्जदर्शनान्
महाप्रसादावलिलाभतः सदा ।
यात्रोत्सवौघानुभवादपि स्फुरत्य्
उल्लास एवात्मनि नैव दीनता ॥

*tasmiñ jagannātha-mukhābja-darśanān*
*mahā-prasādāvali-lābhataḥ sadā*
*yātrotsavaughānubhavād api sphuraty*
*ullāsa evātmani naiva dīnatā*

*tasmin* — there; *jagannātha* — of Lord Jagannātha; *mukha-abja* — the lotus face; *darśanāt* — from seeing; *mahā-prasāda* — of His *mahā-prasādam; āvali* — heaps; *lābhataḥ* — from receiving; *sadā* — always; *yātra* — of excursions; *utsava* — and festivals; *ogha* — the huge number; *anubhavāt* — from experiencing; *api* — also; *sphurati* — is experienced; *ullāsaḥ* — delight; *eva* — certainly; *ātmani* — in your heart; *na* — not; *eva* — at all; *dīnatā* — the feeling of lowliness.

**And by seeing Lord Jagannātha's lotus face there, by getting plenty of His mahā-prasādam, and by enjoying His frequent festivals and processions, you will certainly feel delight in your heart as well—but not humility.**

COMMENTARY: In Uddhava's opinion, the environment of Purī will be at once so disturbing and so enjoyable that Gopa-kumāra will neither realize the happiness of *kṛṣṇa-prema* nor obtain his objective, Goloka.

## TEXT 240

तां विनोदेति न प्रेम गोलोकप्रापकं हि यत् ।
न च तल्लोकलाभेन विनास्य स्वास्थ्यमुद्भवेत् ॥

*tāṁ vinodeti na prema*
*goloka-prāpakaṁ hi yat*
*na ca tal-loka-lābhena*
*vināsya svāsthyam udbhavet*

*tām* — that (*dainya*); *vinā* — without; *udeti na* — does not develop; *prema* — the pure love; *goloka-prāpakam* — leading to entrance into Goloka; *hi* — indeed; *yat* — which; *na* — not; *ca* — and; *tat* — that; *loka* — of the world; *lābhena* — the attainment; *vinā* — without; *asya* — of that; *svāsthyam* — peacefulness; *udbhavet* — arises.

**Without utter humility, the pure love that leads to entrance into Goloka will never arise. And until you attain that world, you will never be at peace.**

## TEXT 241

पुनस्ततोऽसौ परदुःखकातरः
प्रहेष्यति श्रीपुरुषोत्तमस्त्विमम् ।
स्वगोकुले श्रीमथुराविभूषणे
तदेष तत्रैव कथं न चाल्यते ॥

*punas tato 'sau para-duḥkha-kātaraḥ*
*praheṣyati śrī-puruṣottamas tv imam*
*sva-gokule śrī-mathurā-vibhūṣaṇe*
*tad eṣa tatraiva kathaṁ na cālyate*

*punaḥ* — furthermore; *tataḥ* — from there; *asau* — He; *para* — of others; *duḥkha* — by the distress; *kātaraḥ* — feeling disturbed; *praheṣyati* — will send away; *śrī-puruṣottamaḥ* — Lord Jagannātha; *tu* — but; *imam* — this place; *sva* — His own; *gokule* — in Gokula; *śrī-mathurā* — of Mathurā; *vibhūṣaṇe* — which is the ornament; *tat* — there; *eṣaḥ* — this (Gokula); *tatra* — there (in Mathurā); *eva* — just; *katham* — why; *na cālyate* — should not be gone to.

**What's more, Lord Puruṣottama, who feels sympathy for the distress of others, will surely send you from Jagannātha Purī to His own Gokula, the ornament of Śrī Mathurā. Then why not just go there directly?**

COMMENTARY: Lord Jagannātha cannot tolerate seeing anyone suffer, especially not His very dear devotees. So just as before, He will again send Gopa-kumāra to Vṛndāvana.

## TEXTS 242–243

तत्रैवोत्पद्यते दैन्यं तत्प्रेमापि सदा सताम् ।
तत्तच्छून्यमिवारण्यसरिद्गिर्यादि पश्यताम् ॥

सदा हाहारवाक्रान्तवदनानां तथा हृदि ।
महासन्तापदग्धानां स्वप्रियं परिमृग्यताम् ॥

*tatraivotpadyate dainyaṁ*
*tat-premāpi sadā satām*
*tat tac chūnyam ivāraṇya-*
*sarid-giry-ādi paśyatām*

*sadā hāhā-ravākrānta-*
*vadanānāṁ tathā hṛdi*
*mahā-santāpa-dagdhānāṁ*
*sva-priyaṁ parimṛgyatām*

*tatra* — there; *eva* — indeed; *utpadyate* — arises; *dainyam* — utter humility; *tat* — for Him; *prema* — pure love; *api* — also; *sadā* — always; *satām* — of the devotees; *tat tat* — all these; *śūnyam* — empty; *iva* — as if; *araṇya* — the forests; *sarit* — rivers; *giri* — mountains; *ādi* — and so on; *paśyatām* — who are seeing; *sadā* — always; *hāhā-rava* — with cries of "alas!"; *ākrānta* — overtaken; *vadanānām* — whose mouths; *tathā* — similarly; *hṛdi* — in their hearts; *mahā-santāpa* — by the intense burning; *dagdhānām* — who are scorched; *sva* — their own; *priyam* — beloved; *parimṛgyatām* — who are seeking.

**There in Gokula the pure devotees always feel humility and pure love for the Lord. In that mood, they see the forests, rivers, and hills as if an empty wilderness. Those devotees, their mouths filled with cries of lamentation, their hearts burning in absolute grief, are always searching for their beloved.**

COMMENTARY: The mood of Gokula will assist Gopa-kumāra in quickly achieving his desired goal. After all, humility and pure love are abundant in Gokula, where the forests like Śrī Vṛndāvana, the rivers like Śrī Yamunā, the mountains like Śrī Govardhana, and the lakes and meadows are all decorated with the sports of Nanda-nandana.

The devotees who live in Gokula are always in agony, searching for Śrī Nanda-nandana and the nectar of seeing Him. All the ingredients of humility, therefore, are readily at hand, and this means that pure love can quickly grow to maturity. By achieving that pure love in Gokula, Gopa-kumāra will very soon reach Goloka. Therefore he should depart for Gokula at once.

## TEXT 244

श्रीगोपकुमार उवाच
मन्त्रिप्रवरवाक्यं तत्स्वहृद्यं न्यायबृंहितम् ।
निशम्य नितरां प्रीतो भगवान्नारदोऽब्रवीत् ॥

*śrī-gopa-kumāra uvāca*
*mantri-pravara-vākyaṁ tat*
*sva-hṛdyaṁ nyāya-bṛṁhitam*
*niśamya nitarāṁ prīto*
*bhagavān nārado 'bravīt*

*śrī-gopa-kumāraḥ uvāca* — Śrī Gopa-kumāra said; *mantri-pravara* — of the best of counselors; *vākyam* — the statement; *tat* — that; *sva* — to himself; *hṛdyam* — congenial; *nyāya* — with good reason; *bṛṁhitam* — filled; *niśamya* — hearing; *nitarām* — extremely; *prītaḥ* — pleased; *bhagavān* — the great personality; *nāradaḥ* — Nārada; *abravīt* — spoke.

**Śrī Gopa-kumāra said: The statements of that best of counselors were all reasonable, and they accorded with Nārada's own heart. So when the great Nārada heard them he was extremely pleased. He then spoke in reply.**

COMMENTARY: Though Uddhava's statement differed from Nārada's, it reverberated sympathetically in Nārada's heart. Nārada was happy to hear what he himself had not quite been able to say.

## TEXT 245

श्रीनारद उवाच
सत्यमुद्धव तद्भूमिलोकेषु प्रीतिमानसि ।
यदस्याश्विष्टसिद्ध्यर्थमात्थ मन्त्रमिमं हितम् ॥

*śrī-nārada uvāca*
*satyam uddhava tad-bhūmi-*
*lokeṣu prītimān asi*
*yad asyāśv-iṣṭa-siddhy-artham*
*āttha mantram imaṁ hitam*

*śrī-nāradaḥ uvāca* — Śrī Nārada said; *satyam* — truly; *uddhava* — O Uddhava; *tat* — of that; *bhūmi* — land; *lokeṣu* — for the residents; *prīti-mān* — possessing great affection; *asi* — you are; *yat* — since; *asya* — of him (Gopa-kumāra); *āśu* — quick; *iṣṭa* — of what he wants; *siddhi-artham* — for the achievement; *āttha* — you have spoken; *mantram* — advice; *imam* — this; *hitam* — beneficial.

**Śrī Nārada said: O Uddhava! You truly must have great affection for the residents of that land, for you have spoken your good advice to help this boy quickly achieve what he desires.**

COMMENTARY: Nārada admits that Vraja-bhūmi is the best place for Gopa-kumāra to advance further. In Śrī Puruṣottama-kṣetra the same perfection could be achieved, but only gradually.

## TEXT 246

तस्या व्रजभुवो वेत्ति भवानेव महिष्ठताम् ।
निजेष्टदैवतं कृष्णं त्यक्त्वा यत्रावसच्चिरम् ॥

*tasyā vraja-bhuvo vetti*
*bhavān eva mahiṣṭhatām*

*nijeṣṭa-daivataṁ kṛṣṇaṁ*
*tyaktvā yatrāvasac ciram*

*tasyāḥ* — of that; *vraja-bhuvaḥ* — of Vraja-bhūmi; *vetti* — knows; *bhavān* — your good self; *eva* — indeed; *mahiṣṭhatām* — the supreme greatness; *nija* — your own; *iṣṭa-daivatam* — worshipable Deity; *kṛṣṇam* — Lord Kṛṣṇa; *tyaktvā* — leaving; *yatra* — here; *avasat* — you remained; *ciram* — for a long time.

**You know the supreme greatness of that Vraja-bhūmi. You left Lord Kṛṣṇa, your worshipable Deity, and resided there a long time.**

COMMENTARY: For not first recommending that Gopa-kumāra return to Gokula on earth, Nārada excuses himself on the grounds that he doesn't know the special glories of Gokula as well as Uddhava.

## TEXT 247

श्रीगोपकुमार उवाच
परितः पुनरालोक्य लक्षणानि शुभानि सः ।
हृष्टो मामाह सर्वज्ञो नारदो वैष्णवप्रियः ॥

*śrī-gopa-kumāra uvāca*
*paritaḥ punar ālokya*
*lakṣaṇāni śubhāni saḥ*
*hṛṣṭo māṁ āha sarva-jño*
*nārado vaiṣṇava-priyaḥ*

*śrī-gopa-kumāraḥ uvāca* — Śrī Gopa-kumāra said; *paritaḥ* — on all sides; *punaḥ* — again; *ālokya* — seeing; *lakṣaṇāni* — signs; *śubhāni* — auspicious; *saḥ* — he; *hṛṣṭaḥ* — joyfully; *mām* — to me; *āha* — said; *sarva-jñaḥ* — the all-knowing; *nāradaḥ* — Nārada; *vaiṣṇava-priyaḥ* — the dear friend of the Vaiṣṇavas.

**Śrī Gopa-kumāra said: Nārada again looked all around. Beholding auspicious signs, that all-knowing sage and dear friend of the Vaiṣṇavas addressed me joyfully.**

COMMENTARY: Before taking the liberty to speak again, Nārada looked around him and noticed birds chirping and other auspicious omens. He wanted only the best for Gopa-kumāra.

## TEXT 248

श्रीनारद उवाच
व्रजवीरप्रिय श्रीमन्स्वार्थं विद्ध्याशु साधितम् ।
एतच्चास्ति महाभाग पुरैवानुमितं मया ॥

*śrī-nārada uvāca*
*vraja-vīra-priya śrīman*
*svārthaṁ viddhy āśu sādhitam*
*etac cāsti mahā-bhāga*
*puraivānumitaṁ mayā*

*śrī-nāradaḥ uvāca* — Śrī Nārada said; *vraja-vīra* — of the hero of Vraja; *priya* — O beloved; *śrīman* — O glorious one; *sva-artham* — your goal; *viddhi* — please understand; *āśu* — soon; *sādhitam* — achieved; *etat* — this; *ca* — and; *asti* — was; *mahā-bhāga* — O most fortunate one; *purā* — before; *eva* — even; *anumitam* — surmised; *mayā* — by me.

**Śrī Nārada said: O glorious one, beloved of the hero of Vraja, please know that soon your purpose will be achieved! Long ago, greatly fortunate one, I concluded that this would happen.**

## TEXT 249

श्रीवैकुण्ठेऽतुलसुखभरप्रान्तसीमास्पदेऽस्या-
योध्यापुर्यां तदधिकतरे द्वारकाख्ये पुरेऽस्मिन् ।

आयातस्यापि तव बलते दुर्घटं चित्तदुःखं
स्वर्गादौ च प्रभुवरपदाब्जेक्षणेनाप्यबोधः ॥

*śrī-vaikuṇṭhe 'tula-sukha-bhara-prānta-sīmāspade 'syā-*
*yodhyā-puryāṁ tad-adhika-tare dvārakākhye pure 'smin*
*āyātasyāpi tava balate durghaṭaṁ citta-duḥkhaṁ*
*svargādau ca prabhu-vara-padābjekṣaṇenāpy abodhaḥ*

*śrī-vaikuṇṭhe* — in Śrī Vaikuṇṭha; *atula* — incomparable; *sukha-bhara* — great happiness; *prānta-sīma* — of the limit; *āspade* — in the abode; *asya* — His; *ayodhyā-puryām* — in the transcendental city Ayodhyā; *tat* — than that (Vaikuṇṭha); *adhika-tare* — much greater; *dvārakā-ākhye* — named Dvārakā; *pure* — in the city; *asmin* — this; *āyātasya* — who have come; *api* — indeed; *tava* — of you; *balate* — increases in force; *durghaṭam* — in an unlikely way; *citta* — of your mind; *duḥkham* — the distress; *svarga* — in heaven; *ādau* — and so on; *ca* — and; *prabhu-vara* — of the Lord; *pada-abja* — lotus feet; *īkṣaṇena* — while seeing; *api* — even; *abodhaḥ* — ignorance.

**Even when you came to Śrī Vaikuṇṭha, the Lord's abode of limitless, incomparable joy, and to His transcendental city of Ayodhyā, and to this city of Dvārakā, even greater than both, your heart's distress only multiplied in a most unlikely way. On Svarga and the other material planets you remained naive, even though seeing the lotus feet of your Lord.**

COMMENTARY: It seems contrary that the dissatisfaction Gopakumāra felt in Vaikuṇṭha, Ayodhyā, and Dvārakā was in fact a sign of his approaching the highest extreme of spiritual happiness, just as it seems contrary that on each planet in his earlier travels in the material worlds he had the personal association of Lord Viṣṇu in His various expansions and yet was unaware of higher realms.

## TEXT 250

तच्चामुं च स्वदयितवरस्वामिपादारविन्द-
द्वन्द्वे दृश्ये प्रणयपटलीवर्धनायैव मन्ये ।
अस्मिलँ लोके कथमितरथा सम्भवेद्दुःखहेतुस्
तस्मिंस्तस्मिन्नपि मतिपदे तत्र तत्राज्ञता वा ॥

*tac cāmuṁ ca sva-dayita-vara-svāmi-pādāravinda-*
*dvandve dṛśye praṇaya-paṭalī-vardhanāyaiva manye*
*asmil̐ loke katham itarathā sambhaved duḥkha-hetus*
*tasmiṁs tasminn api mati-pade tatra tatrājñatā vā*

*tat* — that (misery); *ca* — and; *amum* — this (ignorance); *ca* — and; *sva* — your own; *dayita-vara* — most beloved; *svāmi* — of the master; *pāda-aravinda* — of the lotus feet; *dvandve* — for the pair; *dṛśye* — visible; *praṇaya* — of love; *paṭalī* — of the abundance; *vardhanāya* — for expanding; *eva* — only; *manye* — I consider; *asmin* — in this; *loke* — world; *katham* — how; *itarathā* — otherwise; *sambhavet* — there could be; *duḥkha* — for distress; *hetuḥ* — cause; *tasmin tasmin* — in these various; *api* — even; *mati* — of wisdom; *pade* — in the realms; *tatra tatra* — in those other (realms); *ajñatā* — ignorance; *vā* — or.

**I think all this occurred just to deepen your great love for the supreme object of your sight, those two lotus feet of your own dearest Lord. How else could there be any reason for distress in this realm, or ignorance in any of those abodes of knowledge?**

COMMENTARY: The lotus feet of Śrī Madana-gopāla have long been visible in the core of Gopa-kumāra's heart, and he hopes that he will soon be able to see them with his very eyes. Other than to deepen his attraction to his Lord's lotus feet, there would be no intelligible purpose for his sorrow in the spiritual world or his ignorance on the planets of the all-knowing sages.

## TEXT 251

यया हृत्क्षोभराहित्यान्महाकौतुकतोऽपि ते ।
वृत्तं भावविशेषेण तत्तल्लोकेऽच्युतेक्षणम् ॥

*yayā hṛt-kṣobha-rāhityān*
*mahā-kautukato 'pi te*
*vṛttaṁ bhāva-viśeṣeṇa*
*tat-tal-loke 'cyutekṣaṇam*

*yayā* — by which (ignorance); *hṛt* — of the heart; *kṣobha* — of agitation; *rāhityāt* — because of absence; *mahā-kautukataḥ* — due to the acute curiosity; *api* — indeed; *te* — your; *vṛttam* — occurred; *bhāva* — with ecstasy; *viśeṣeṇa* — special; *tat-tat* — in each; *loke* — world; *acyuta* — of Lord Acyuta; *īkṣaṇam* — the discovering.

**Your naiveté let you feel the piqued curiosity of a simple heart free from agitation. Thus you enjoyed the special ecstasy of discovering Lord Acyuta on every planet.**

COMMENTARY: Misery may sometimes intensify affection, but what is the use of ignorance? Nārada answers that on Maharloka and other planets Gopa-kumāra's simplicity allowed him to see in a very pure loving mood the Personality of Godhead. A mind filled with all kinds of knowledge becomes easily agitated by critical thoughts and is not free to enjoy enthusiasm like the mind of a simple person. Had Gopa-kumāra been more sophisticated, he would not have been able to discover the Supreme Lord in His various aspects with as much sincere affection and would not have derived as much joy from the Lord's *darśana*.

Dec 2/1/14

## TEXT 252

तद्गच्छतु भवान् शीघ्रं स्वदीर्घाभीष्टसिद्धये ।
माथुरीं व्रजभूमिं तां धराश्रीकीर्तिवर्धिनीम् ॥

*tad gacchatu bhavāñ śīghraṁ*
*sva-dīrghābhīṣṭa-siddhaye*
*māthurīṁ vraja-bhūmiṁ tāṁ*
*dharā-śrī-kīrti-vardhinīm*

*tat* — therefore; *gacchatu* — should go; *bhavān* — your good self; *śīghram* — quickly; *sva* — your; *dīrgha* — long-held; *abhīṣṭa* — of the desire; *siddhaye* — for the attainment; *māthurīm* — of Mathurā district; *vraja-bhūmim* — to Vraja-bhūmi; *tām* — that; *dharā* — of the earth; *śrī* — the splendor; *kīrti* — and fame; *vardhinīm* — which increases.

**So now go quickly to the Vraja-bhūmi of Mathurā district, which enhances the fame and splendor of the earth. Go fulfill the desire you have held for so long.**

COMMENTARY: In Vṛndāvana on earth Gopa-kumāra will finally see the lotus feet of Śrī Madana-gopāla. How Vṛndāvana increases the earth's beauty and reputation is described by the *gopīs* of Vṛndāvana:

*vṛndāvanaṁ sakhi bhuvo vitanoti kīrtiṁ*
*yad devakī-suta-padāmbuja-labdha-lakṣmi*
*govinda-veṇum anu matta-mayūra-nṛtyaṁ*
*prekṣyādri-sānv-avaratānya-samasta-sattvam*

"O friend, Vṛndāvana is spreading the glory of the earth, having obtained the treasure of the lotus feet of Kṛṣṇa, the son of Devakī. The peacocks dance madly when they hear Govinda's flute, and upon seeing them from the hilltops other creatures all become stunned." (*Bhāgavatam* 10.21.10)

## TEXT 253

तत्रैव साधनं सत्यं साधु सम्पद्यतेऽचिरात् ।
वैकुण्ठोपरि विभ्राजच्छ्रीमद्गोलोकयापकम् ॥

*tatraiva sādhanaṁ satyaṁ*
*sādhu sampadyate 'cirāt*
*vaikuṇṭhopari vibhrājac*
*chrīmad-goloka-yāpakam*

*tatra* — there; *eva* — indeed; *sādhanam* — spiritual practice; *satyam* — truly; *sādhu* — properly; *sampadyate* — is executed; *acirāt* — without delay; *vaikuṇṭha-upari* — above Vaikuṇṭha; *vibhrājat* — shining; *śrīmat-goloka* — to Śrī Goloka; *yāpakam* — bringing.

**There, without delay, you will surely succeed in the spiritual practice that will bring you to the brilliant world above Vaikuṇṭha—Śrī Goloka.**

TEXT 254

श्रीगोपकुमार उवाच
तस्य वाक्सुधया प्रीतस्तत्राहं गन्तुमुत्सुकः ।
अन्तर्भगवदाज्ञार्थी संलक्ष्योक्तो महात्मना ॥

*śrī-gopa-kumāra uvāca*
*tasya vāk-sudhayā prītas*
*tatrāhaṁ gantum utsukaḥ*
*antar bhagavad-ājñārthī*
*saṁlakṣyokto mahātmanā*

*śrī-gopa-kumāraḥ uvāca* — Śrī Gopa-kumāra said; *tasya* — his (Nārada's); *vāk* — of the words; *sudhayā* — by the nectar; *prītaḥ* — pleased; *tatra* — there; *aham* — I; *gantum* — to go; *utsukaḥ* — eager; *antaḥ* — within; *bhagavat* — from the Supreme Lord; *ājñā* — permission; *arthī* — anxious to obtain; *saṁlakṣya* — perceiving; *uktaḥ* — was addressed; *mahā-ātmanā* — by the magnanimous soul (Uddhava).

**Śrī Gopa-kumāra said: Pleased by Nārada's nectarean words,**

**I was eager to go to Vraja-bhūmi. But Uddhava perceived that within my heart I was anxious first to take permission from the Lord, and so the magnanimous Uddhava said something to me.**

COMMENTARY: Uddhava could tell by looking at Gopa-kumāra that he was anxious to ask permission from Śrī Dvārakānātha before going anywhere.

## TEXT 255

श्रीमदुद्धव उवाच
तदैव यादवेन्द्राज्ञापेक्ष्या स्याद्यदि गम्यते ।
कुत्रापि भवतान्यत्र सा भूर्ह्यस्य महाप्रिया ॥

*śrīmad-uddhava uvāca*
*tadaiva yādavendrājñā-*
*pekṣyā syād yadi gamyate*
*kutrāpi bhavatānyatra*
*sā bhūr hy asya mahā-priyā*

*śrīmat-uddhavaḥ uvāca* — Śrīmān Uddhava said; *tadā* — then; *eva* — just; *yādava-indra* — of the Lord of the Yādavas; *ājñā* — the order; *apekṣyā* — to be honored; *syāt* — is; *yadi* — if; *gamyate* — would be going; *kutra api* — somewhere; *bhavatā* — you; *anyatra* — else; *sā* — that; *bhūḥ* — land; *hi* — but; *asya* — His; *mahā-priyā* — most dear.

**Śrīmān Uddhava said: If you were going anywhere else, the proper thing would be to take permission from the Lord of the Yādavas. But that land of His is most dear to Him.**

COMMENTARY: As implied here by the word *mahā-priyā* ("most dear"), earthly Vṛndāvana is Kṛṣṇa's favorite abode. He favors it even more than His Dvārakā in Vaikuṇṭha.

21.12.14 rM



## TEXT 256

न साक्षात्सेवया तस्य या प्रीतिरिह जायते ।
तद्व्रजस्थानवासेन सा हि सम्पद्यते दृढा ॥

*na sākṣāt sevayā tasya*
*yā prītir iha jāyate*
*tad-vraja-sthāna-vāsena*
*sā hi sampadyate dṛḍhā*

*na* — not; *sākṣāt* — directly; *sevayā* — by the service; *tasya* — of Him; *yā* — which; *prītiḥ* — love; *iha* — here (in Dvārakā); *jāyate* — is born; *tat* — that; *vraja-sthāna* — in the land of Vraja; *vāsena* — by residing; *sā* — that; *hi* — just; *sampadyate* — develops; *dṛḍhā* — solidly.

**Not even by direct service to the Lord here in Dvārakā does the love arise that firmly develops if one merely lives in the land of Vraja.**

## TEXT 257

अत एवोषितं तस्यां व्रजभूमौ चिरं मया ।
तत्रत्यतत्प्रियप्राणिवर्गस्याश्वासनच्छलात् ॥

*ata evoṣitaṁ tasyāṁ*
*vraja-bhūmau ciraṁ mayā*
*tatratya-tat-priya-prāṇi-*
*vargasyāśvāsana-cchalāt*

*ataḥ* — therefore; *eva* — only; *uṣitam* — residing was done; *tasyām* — in that; *vraja-bhūmau* — land of Vraja; *ciram* — for a long time; *mayā* — by me; *tatratya* — who live in that place; *tat* — His; *priya* — beloved; *prāṇi-vargasya* — of those (devotees) left with only their lives; *āśvāsana* — of the consoling; *chalāt* — on the pretext.

**Therefore I spent a long time in Vraja-bhūmi, on the pretext of consoling the Lord's dear devotees, who lived there with nothing left but their lives.**

COMMENTARY: In spending so much time in Vraja-bhūmi, wasn't Uddhava's purpose to console the Vraja-vāsīs in their plight of having been abandoned by Kṛṣṇa? Externally it may have appeared so, but comforting the cowherd men and women was in fact only a pretext for Uddhava's visit. From his point of view there was no question of consoling the Vraja-vāsīs. He went to Vṛndāvana to learn from them how to love Kṛṣṇa.

### TEXT 258

मन्ये मदीश्वरोऽवेत्य काममेतं तवोत्कटम् ।
तां नेष्यत्येष भूमिं त्वां स्वयं स्वस्य प्रियां प्रियम् ॥

*manye mad-īśvaro 'vetya*
*kāmam etaṁ tavotkaṭam*
*tāṁ neṣyaty eṣa bhūmiṁ tvāṁ*
*svayaṁ svasya priyāṁ priyam*

*manye* — I think; *mat* — my; *īśvaraḥ* — Lord; *avetya* — knowing; *kāmam* — desire; *etam* — this; *tava* — your; *utkaṭam* — powerful; *tām* — to that; *neṣyati* — will bring; *eṣaḥ* — He; *bhūmim* — land; *tvām* — you; *svayam* — Himself; *svasya* — His own; *priyām* — dear (land); *priyam* — (you who are) dear.

**I am sure my Lord already knows of your powerful desire. So He will personally bring you, His dear friend, to His dearest abode.**

COMMENTARY: Gopa-kumāra might concede that to travel he need not ask the Lord's permission; but still, before leaving, he might simply want to have the Lord's auspicious *darśana*. Uddhava therefore tells Gopa-kumāra that Kṛṣṇa will go with him on his journey. Vṛndāvana is very dear to Kṛṣṇa, and so is

21.12.14. jf



Gopa-kumāra. Therefore Kṛṣṇa Himself will surely take Gopa-kumāra to Vṛndāvana.

## TEXT 259

श्रीगोपकुमार उवाच
तद्वागमृतपानेन परमानन्दपूरितः ।
गतो मोहमिवामुत्र क्षणं दृष्टी न्यमीलयम् ॥

*śrī-gopa-kumāra uvāca*
*tad-vāg-amṛta-pānena*
*paramānanda-pūritaḥ*
*gato moham ivāmutra*
*kṣaṇaṁ dṛṣṭī nyamīlayam*

*śrī-gopa-kumāraḥ uvāca* — Śrī Gopa-kumāra said; *tat* — his; *vāk* — of the words; *amṛta* — the nectar; *pānena* — by drinking; *parama-ānanda* — with topmost ecstasy; *pūritaḥ* — filled; *gataḥ moham* — I became unconscious; *iva* — as if; *amutra* — there (in Dvārakā); *kṣaṇam* — for a moment; *dṛṣṭī* — my eyes; *nyamīlayam* — I closed.

**Śrī Gopa-kumāra said: Filled with the highest ecstasy from drinking the immortal nectar of Uddhava's words, I seemed to lose consciousness. There in Dvārakā, for a moment I closed my eyes.**

COMMENTARY: Here the word *iva* implies that Gopa-kumāra did not actually faint; he only lost his external vision for a moment because of closing his eyes.

## TEXT 260

केनचिन्नीयमानोऽस्मि कुत्रापीति वितर्कयन् ।
दृशावुन्मील्य पश्यामि कुञ्जेऽस्मिन्नस्मि सङ्गतः ॥

*kenacin nīyamāno 'smi*
*kutrāpīti vitarkayan*
*dṛśāv unmīlya paśyāmi*
*kuñje 'sminn asmi saṅgataḥ*

*kenacit*—by someone; *nīyamānaḥ*—being carried; *asmi*—I was; *kutra api*—somewhere; *iti*—thus; *vitarkayan*—guessing; *dṛśau*—my eyes; *unmīlya*—opening; *paśyāmi*—I saw; *kuñje*—to the grove; *asmin*—this; *asmi*—I have been; *saṅgataḥ*—brought.

**Sensing that someone had taken me elsewhere, I then opened my eyes and saw that I had been brought to this grove.**

COMMENTARY: With his eyes closed, Gopa-kumāra couldn't see who was carrying him. Had he seen that it was Kṛṣṇa taking him to earth to leave him in Gokula, he would never have been able to give up the company of his Lord in Dvārakā to attain Goloka, the ultimate destination. Uddhava had also discouraged Gopa-kumāra from seeing Kṛṣṇa before leaving Dvārakā because if Gopa-kumāra had met Kṛṣṇa, to leave for Gokula Vṛndāvana would have been impossible. Kṛṣṇa and His devotees were conspiring to assure Gopa-kumāra's ultimate success.

*Thus ends the fifth chapter of Part Two of Śrīla Sanātana Gosvāmī's Bṛhad-bhāgavatāmṛta, entitled "Prema: Love of God."*

SIX

# Ābhīṣṭa-lābha: The Attainment of All Desires

TEXTS 1–2

श्रीगोपकुमार उवाच
तां नारदीयामनुसृत्य शिक्षां
श्रीकृष्णनामानि निजप्रियाणि ।
सङ्कीर्तयन्सुस्वरमत्र लीलास्
तस्य प्रगायन्ननुचिन्तयंश्च ॥

तदीयलीलास्थलजातमेतद्
विलोकयन्भावदशे गतो ये ।
तयोः स्वचित्ते करणेन लज्जे
कथं परस्मिन्कथयान्यहं ते ॥

*śrī-gopa-kumāra uvāca*
*tāṁ nāradīyām anusṛtya śikṣāṁ*
*śrī-kṛṣṇa-nāmāni nija-priyāṇi*
*saṅkīrtayan su-svaram atra līlās*
*tasya pragāyann anucintayaṁś ca*

*tadīya-līlā-sthala-jātam etad*
*vilokayan bhāva-daśe gato ye*
*tayoḥ sva-citte karaṇena lajje*
*kathaṁ parasmin kathayāny ahaṁ te*

*śrī-gopa-kumāraḥ uvāca* — Śrī Gopa-kumāra said; *tām* — those; *nāradīyām* — of Nārada; *anusṛtya* — following; *śikṣām* — instructions; *śrī-kṛṣṇa* — of Śrī Kṛṣṇa; *nāmāni* — the names;

*nija* — to myself; *priyāṇi* — dear; *saṅkīrtayan* — chanting; *su-svaram* — in a melodious voice; *atra* — here; *līlāḥ* — the pastimes; *tasya* — His; *pragāyan* — singing loudly; *anucintayan* — remembering; *ca* — and; *tadīya* — His; *līlā-sthala-jātam* — many places of pastimes; *etat* — these; *vilokayan* — seeing; *bhāva* — an ecstatic mood; *daśe* — and state of excitement; *gataḥ* — obtaining; *ye* — which; *tayoḥ* — of them; *sva-citte* — in my own mind; *karaṇena* — by expressing; *lajje* — I become embarrassed; *katham* — how; *parasmin* — to another; *kathayāni* — can describe; *aham* — I; *te* — them.

**Śrī Gopa-kumāra said: Following Nārada's instructions, here in Vraja I went to see the many places of Śrī Kṛṣṇa's pastimes. I sang His names most dear to me, I sang about His pastimes loudly and sweetly, I focused my mind upon them — and I attained such a state of ecstasy and became so emotional that it embarrasses me even to think of it. How then can I describe this to anyone else?**

COMMENTARY: In this sixth chapter, Gopa-kumāra goes to Goloka and meets Śrī Kṛṣṇa. Kṛṣṇa shows him special mercy, and Gopa-kumāra joins the pastimes of that world.

The first five verses show the good fortune Gopa-kumāra gained by following the instructions of Śrī Nārada. This good fortune will be his means of achieving Goloka. While visiting Śrī Vṛndāvana on earth, Gopa-kumāra saw with his own eyes Kṛṣṇa performing His cowherd pastimes. As a result, Gopa-kumāra's mind reached a rare level of ecstasy and manifested such exceptional states as *unmāda* ("divine madness").

## TEXT 3

सदा महार्त्या करुणस्वरै रुदन्
नयामि रात्रीर्दिवसांश्च कातरः ।
न वेद्मि यद्यत्सुचिरादनुष्ठितं
सुखाय वा तत्तदुतार्तिसिन्धवे ॥

*sadā mahārtyā karuṇa-svarai rudan*
*nayāmi rātrīr divasāṁś ca kātaraḥ*
*na vedmi yad yat su-cirād anuṣṭhitaṁ*
*sukhāya vā tat tad utārti-sindhave*

*sadā* — constantly; *mahā-ārtyā* — in great distress; *karuṇa* — pitiful; *svaraiḥ* — in tones; *rudan* — crying; *nayāmi* — I spent; *rātrīḥ* — the nights; *divasāḥ* — days; *ca* — and; *kātaraḥ* — distressed; *na vedmi* — I did not know; *yat yat* — all of which; *su-cirāt* — for a long time; *anuṣṭhitam* — practiced; *sukhāya* — for happiness; *vā* — or; *tat tat* — of that; *uta* — otherwise; *ārti* — of distress; *sindhave* — for (obtaining) an ocean.

**I spent my days and nights in great distress, always crying in a pitiful voice, not knowing whether the practice I had so long been following would lead me to happiness or cast me into an ocean of distress.**

COMMENTARY: It is difficult for Gopa-kumāra to describe his embarrassing state, but because of his special affection for the Mathurā *brāhmaṇa* he will try to explain it to some extent. Gopa-kumāra began his spiritual practice the day he left home as a young boy, and now all his practice seems to be reaching its culmination. But now he is uncertain whether the final result will be happy. Gopa-kumāra expresses himself here in a narrative present tense. Thus he says *na vedmi* — literally, "I do not know." But this clearly implies that this doubt has been with him for a long time and will continue for some time more.

## TEXT 4

कथञ्चिदप्याकलयामि नैतत्
किमेष दावाग्निशिखान्तरेऽहम् ।
वसामि किं वा परमामृताच्छ-
सुशीतलश्रीयमुनाजलान्तः ॥

*kathañcid apy ākalayāmi naitat*
*kim eṣa dāvāgni-śikhāntare 'ham*
*vasāmi kiṁ vā paramāmṛtāccha-*
*su-śītala-śrī-yamunā-jalāntaḥ*

*kathañcit* — somehow; *api* — although; *ākalayāmi na* — I could not distinguish; *etat* — this; *kim* — whether; *eṣaḥ* — this; *dāva-agni* — of a forest fire; *śikhā* — the flames; *antare* — within; *aham* — I; *vasāmi* — was living; *kim vā* — or whether; *parama* — supreme; *amṛta* — of the nectar; *accha* — clear; *su-śītala* — and very cool; *śrī-yamunā* — of Śrī Yamunā; *jala-antaḥ* — in the water.

**I couldn't tell whether I was living in the flames of a forest fire or in the supreme nectar of the clear, cool waters of Śrī Yamunā.**

## TEXT 5

कदाचिदेवं किल निश्चिनोम्यहं
शठस्य हस्ते पतितोऽस्मि कस्यचित् ।
सदा न्यमज्जं बहुदुःखसागरे
सुखस्य गन्धोऽपि न मां स्पृशेत्क्वचित् ॥

*kadācid evaṁ kila niścinomy ahaṁ*
*śaṭhasya haste patito 'smi kasyacit*
*sadā nyamañjaṁ bahu-duḥkha-sāgare*
*sukhasya gandho 'pi na māṁ spṛśet kvacit*

*kadācit* — sometimes; *evam* — thus; *kila* — indeed; *niścinomi* — thought; *aham* — I; *śaṭhasya* — of a cheater; *haste* — in the hand; *patitaḥ* — fallen; *asmi* — I was; *kasyacit* — a certain one; *sadā* — constantly; *nyamañjam* — I was being submerged; *bahu-duḥkha* — of great misery; *sāgare* — in an ocean; *sukhasya* — of happiness; *gandhaḥ* — a trace; *api* — even; *na* — not; *mām* — me; *spṛśet* — would touch; *kvacit* — ever.

**Sometimes I thought I had fallen into the hands of some great deceiver. I was always submerged in a vast ocean of misery. Not even a drop of happiness ever touched me.**

TEXT 6

इत्थं वसन्निकुञ्जेऽस्मिन्वृन्दावनविभूषणे ।
एकदा रोदनाम्भोधौ निमग्नो मोहमव्रजम् ॥

*itthaṁ vasan nikuñje 'smin*
*vṛndāvana-vibhūṣaṇe*
*ekadā rodanāmbhodhau*
*nimagno moham avrajam*

*ittham* — in this manner; *vasan* — residing; *nikuñje* — in the grove; *asmin* — this; *vṛndāvana-vibhūṣaṇe* — an ornament of Vṛndāvana; *ekadā* — one day; *rodana* — of crying; *ambhodhau* — in an ocean; *nimagnaḥ* — drowning; *moham* — unconsciousness; *avrajam* — I obtained.

**In such a way I lived in this grove, this most attractive ornament of Vṛndāvana. And one day, while immersed in an ocean of weeping, I fell unconscious.**

TEXT 7

दयालुचूडामणिनामुनैव
स्वयं समागत्य कराम्बुजेन ।
वंशीरतेनामृतशीतलेन
मद्गात्रतो मार्जयता रजांसि ॥

*dayālu-cūḍāmaṇināmunaiva*
*svayaṁ samāgatya karāmbujena*
*vaṁśī-ratenāmṛta-śītalena*
*mad-gātrato mārjayatā rajāṁsi*

*dayālu* — of merciful persons; *cūḍā-maṇinā* — the crown jewel; *amunā* — that; *eva* — only; *svayam* — in person; *samāgatya* — who approached; *kara-ambujena* — with His lotus hand; *vaṁśī* — to the flute; *ratena* — which was fondly attracted; *amṛta* — like nectar; *śītalena* — cool; *mat-gātrataḥ* — from my limbs; *mārjayatā* — who was wiping; *rajāṁsi* — the dust.

**Then the crest jewel of all who are merciful appeared before me. With His own lotus hand, a hand cool like nectar and always pleased to hold His flute, He wiped the dust from my limbs.**

## TEXT 8

नीतोऽस्मि सञ्चाल्य मुहुः सलीलं
संज्ञां महाधूर्तवरेण यत्नात् ।
नासाप्रविष्टैरपुरानुभूतैर्
आपूर्य सौरभ्यभरैः स्वकीयैः ॥

*nīto 'smi sañcālya muhuḥ sa-līlaṁ*
*saṁjñāṁ mahā-dhūrta-vareṇa yatnāt*
*nāsā-praviṣṭair apurānubhūtair*
*āpūrya saurabhya-bharaiḥ svakīyaiḥ*

*nītaḥ* — brought; *asmi* — I was; *sañcālya* — being stirred; *muhuḥ* — again; *sa-līlam* — playfully; *saṁjñām* — to consciousness; *mahā-dhūrta* — of great cheats; *vareṇa* — by the best; *yatnāt* — with some endeavor; *nāsā* — my nose; *praviṣṭaiḥ* — which entered; *apurā* — never before; *anubhūtaiḥ* — experienced; *āpūrya* — filling; *saurabhya* — of fragrances; *bharaiḥ* — with the abundance; *svakīyaiḥ* — His own.

**It wasn't easy, but that greatest of cheats playfully stirred me back to consciousness by filling my nostrils with His unique heady fragrances, which I had never known before.**

COMMENTARY: Śrī Madana-gopāla-deva appeared in person before Gopa-kumāra to award him the highest perfection. Gopa-kumāra was in a deep swoon, oblivious to everything around him, but Kṛṣṇa's presence awakened one of his senses, namely the sense of smell. Because Kṛṣṇa, the most expert enchanter, knows very well how to stir the senses of even an unconscious person, Gopa-kumāra wants to acknowledge Kṛṣṇa's omniscience by speaking of Him as *mahābhijña-vara* ("the best of those who know everything"), but the ecstasy of his love transforms that original idea, and it comes out from his mouth as *mahā-dhūrta-vara* ("the greatest of cheats"). Gopa-kumāra's ecstasy forces him to reason, "Although Kṛṣṇa may now be wiping my body with His own hands, soon enough that same Kṛṣṇa is just as likely to abandon me."

## TEXT 9

तदीयवक्त्राब्जमथावलोक्य
ससम्भ्रमं सत्वरमुत्थितोऽहम् ।
अमुं विधर्तुं वरपीतवस्त्रे
समुद्यतो हर्षभराचितात्मा ॥

*tadīya-vaktrābjam athāvalokya*
*sa-sambhramaṁ satvaram utthito 'ham*
*amuṁ vidhartuṁ vara-pīta-vastre*
*samudyato harṣa-bharācitātmā*

*tadīya* — His; *vaktra-abjam* — lotus face; *atha* — then; *avalokya* — seeing; *sa-sambhramam* — in perplexity; *satvaram* — quickly; *utthitaḥ* — standing up; *aham* — I; *amum* — Him; *vidhartum* — to take hold of; *vara* — splendid; *pīta* — yellow; *vastre* — the garment; *samudyataḥ* — attempting; *harṣa* — of joy; *bhara* — a burden; *ācita* — accumulating; *ātmā* — in my heart.

**Then, seeing His lotus face, I quickly stood up. Not**

**knowing what I was doing, my heart filling with joy, I tried to catch hold of His splendid yellow cloth.**

TEXT 10

स नागरेन्द्रोऽपससार पृष्ठतो
निनादयंस्तां मुरलीं स्वलीलया ।
अभूच्च कुञ्जान्तरितः सपद्यसौ
मया न लब्धो बत धावताप्यलम् ॥

*sa nāgarendro 'pasasāra pṛṣṭhato*
*ninādayaṁs tāṁ muralīṁ sva-līlayā*
*abhūc ca kuñjāntaritaḥ sapady asau*
*mayā na labdho bata dhāvatāpy alam*

*saḥ* — He; *nāgara* — of heroes; *indraḥ* — the king; *apasasāra* — escaped; *pṛṣṭhataḥ* — behind me; *ninādayan* — vibrating; *tām* — that; *muralīm* — flute; *sva-līlayā* — in His playful way; *abhūt* — He was; *ca* — and; *kuñja* — a grove; *antaritaḥ* — within; *sapadi* — suddenly; *asau* — He; *mayā* — by me; *na* — not; *labdhaḥ* — attained; *bata* — ah; *dhāvatā* — running; *api* — although; *alam* — a lot.

**That king of charming heroes blew His flute in His own playful way and escaped behind me. Suddenly He stepped into a grove. And — alas! — though I ran about looking, I couldn't find Him.**

TEXT 11

अन्तर्हितं तं त्वविलोक्य मूर्च्छां
प्राप्तोऽपतं श्रीयमुनाप्रवाहे ।
एतस्य वेगेन समुह्यमानो
लब्ध्वेव संज्ञां व्यकिरं स्वदृष्टी ॥

*antarhitaṁ taṁ tv avilokya mūrcchāṁ*
*prāpto 'pataṁ śrī-yamunā-pravāhe*
*etasya vegena samuhyamāno*
*labdhveva saṁjñāṁ vyakiraṁ sva-dṛṣṭī*

*antarhitam* — who had disappeared; *tam* — Him; *tu* — and; *avilokya* — not seeing; *mūrcchām* — unconsciousness; *prāptaḥ* — obtaining; *apatam* — I fell; *śrī-yamunā* — of Śrī Yamunā; *pravāhe* — in the swift current; *etasya* — its; *vegena* — by the force; *samuhyamānaḥ* — being carried; *labdhvā* — regaining; *iva* — as if; *saṁjñām* — normal consciousness; *vyakiram* — I cast; *sva-dṛṣṭī* — my glance.

**He had disappeared. Unable to see Him, I fainted and fell into the swift current of the Yamunā. And as it forcefully carried me away, I seemed to regain normal awareness and looked around.**

COMMENTARY: Gopa-kumāra says that he "seemed to regain consciousness" (*labdhvā iva saṁjñām*) because he had not actually lost his awareness; his fainting was not a material disturbance but an external symptom of ecstasy. His recovery of normal consciousness was also only apparent, because the abnormal bewilderment of his *prema* had still not subsided. Two verses later he will describe his "collecting his wits" (*cittam samādhāya*), which shows that now, at this earlier moment, he was still disoriented.

## TEXT 12

पश्याम्यतिक्रान्तमनोजवेन
यानेन केनापि महोर्धगेन ।
केनापि मार्गेण महाद्भुतेन
देशान्तरे कुत्रचिदागतोऽस्मि ॥

*paśyāmy atikrānta-mano-javena*
*yānena kenāpi mahordha-gena*

*kenāpi mārgeṇa mahādbhutena*
*deśāntare kutracid āgato 'smi*

*paśyāmi* — I saw; *atikrānta* — which superseded; *manaḥ-javena* — the speed of the mind; *yānena* — by a vehicle; *kena api* — some; *mahā-ūrdha* — way above; *gena* — which was going; *kena api* — by some; *mārgeṇa* — path; *mahā-adbhutena* — most wonderful; *deśa-antare* — to another place; *kutracit* — somewhere; *āgataḥ* — come; *asmi* — I was.

**I saw myself being transported to another place, along some wonderful path, by a vehicle flying faster than the mind and higher than one could imagine.**

COMMENTARY: Gopa-kumāra couldn't identify the vehicle that took him away, so he refers to it simply as "a certain vehicle" (*yānena kenāpi*). He could only say that it was moving upward at a speed greater than that of the mind. The path the vehicle took was also unfamiliar and not able to be identified, so Gopa-kumāra could only describe it as "most amazing." It was utterly different from any road he had ever traveled before.

## TEXT 13

चित्तं समाधाय मृशामि यावद्
वैकुण्ठलोकं तमितोऽस्मि तावत् ।
तं विस्मितो वीक्ष्य वहन्प्रहर्षं
पश्यन्नयोध्यादिकमत्यगां तत् ॥

*cittaṁ samādhāya mṛśāmi yāvad*
*vaikuṇṭha-lokaṁ tam ito 'smi tāvat*
*taṁ vismito vīkṣya vahan praharṣaṁ*
*paśyann ayodhyādikam atyagāṁ tat*

*cittam* — my mind; *samādhāya* — collecting; *mṛśāmi* — I noticed; *yāvat* — while; *vaikuṇṭha-lokam* — world of Vaikuṇṭha;

*tam* — that; *itaḥ* — from there; *asmi* — I reached; *tāvat* — then; *tam* — that; *vismitaḥ* — amazed; *vīkṣya* — seeing; *vahan* — experiencing; *praharṣam* — delight; *paśyan* — watching; *ayodhyā-ādikam* — Ayodhyā and other regions; *atyagām* — I passed; *tat* — them.

**Collecting my wits, I was amazed to see I was passing through Vaikuṇṭha-loka, and going beyond. I watched with great delight as I passed Ayodhyā and other realms.**

COMMENTARY: Without delay, the vehicle sped past the domain of Lord Nārāyaṇa, in which Gopa-kumāra had previously resided, and then past other supreme abodes, including Ayodhyā and Dvārakā.

## TEXT 14

श्रीगोलोकं तं चिराशावलम्बं
प्राप्तो भान्तं सर्वलोकोपरिष्टात् ।
आस्ते श्रीमन्माथुरे मण्डलेऽस्मिन्
यादृक्सर्वं तत्र वै तादृगेव ॥

*śrī-golokaṁ taṁ cirāśāvalambaṁ*
*prāpto bhāntaṁ sarva-lokopariṣṭāt*
*āste śrīman-māthure maṇḍale 'smin*
*yādṛk sarvaṁ tatra vai tādṛg eva*

*śrī-golokam* — at Śrī Goloka; *tam* — that; *cira* — long-held; *āśā* — of my desires; *avalambam* — the resort; *prāptaḥ* — I arrived; *bhāntam* — shining; *sarva-loka* — all worlds; *upariṣṭāt* — above; *āste* — was; *śrīmat* — divine; *māthure maṇḍale* — in Mathurā-maṇḍala; *asmin* — this; *yādṛk* — as; *sarvam* — everything; *tatra* — there; *vai* — indeed; *tādṛk* — so; *eva* — just.

**I arrived at the shining world above all others — Śrī Goloka, which I had long aspired to reach. Everything**

**there appeared the same as in this divine Mathurā-maṇḍala of the material world.**

COMMENTARY: Gopa-kumāra had long desired to attain Goloka, the land where his worshipable Lord, Śrī Kṛṣṇa, eternally enjoys His pastimes. The Mathurā *brāhmaṇa,* Gopa-kumāra's disciple, lacks the spiritual vision to understand Goloka properly, but to give him some idea of the glories of Goloka, Gopa-kumāra compares it to the transcendental abode where the two of them now sit. Goloka's resemblance to the earthly Gokula is the very reason why Goloka does without the mood of reverence for God's supremacy and displays instead the priceless treasure of superexcellent *prema.*

TEXT 15

तस्मिञ्श्रीमथुरारूपे गत्वा मधुपुरीमहम् ।
अत्रत्यामिव तां दृष्ट्वा विस्मयं हर्षमप्यगाम् ॥

*tasmiñ śrī-mathurā-rūpe*
*gatvā madhu-purīm aham*
*atratyām iva tāṁ dṛṣṭvā*
*vismayaṁ harṣam apy agām*

*tasmin* — that; *śrī-mathurā* — of Śrī Mathurā; *rūpe* — in the prototype; *gatvā* — coming; *madhu-purīm* — to Mathurā City; *aham* — I; *atratyām* — located here (on earth); *iva* — as if; *tām* — it; *dṛṣṭvā* — seeing; *vismayam* — surprise; *harṣam* — joy; *api* — and; *agām* — I experienced.

**In that original land of Mathurā, I visited Mathurā City. I was surprised and happy to see that it resembled the Mathurā here on earth.**

COMMENTARY: Gopa-kumāra was astonished to see that even above Vaikuṇṭha things appeared as in the mortal world. He was pleased to find such advantages for fulfilling his spiritual desires.

## TEXT 16

तस्यामशृणवं चेदं निगृह्य पितरं स्वयम् ।
देवकीं वसुदेवं च कंसो राज्यं करोति सः ॥

*tasyām aśṛṇavaṁ cedaṁ*
*nigṛhya pitaraṁ svayam*
*devakīṁ vasudevaṁ ca*
*kaṁso rājyaṁ karoti saḥ*

*tasyām* — there; *aśṛṇavam* — I heard; *ca* — and; *idam* — these; *nigṛhya* — arresting; *pitaram* — his father; *svayam* — on his own initiative; *devakīm* — Devakī; *vasudevam* — Vasudeva; *ca* — and; *kaṁsaḥ* — Kaṁsa; *rājyam karoti* — was ruling; *saḥ* — he.

**In that original Mathurā, I heard that Kaṁsa had taken it upon himself to arrest his father and Kṛṣṇa's parents, Devakī and Vasudeva, and was ruling the kingdom.**

COMMENTARY: Kaṁsa needed no introduction, especially to a person who hailed from Mathurā City. The *brāhmaṇa* must at least have read about him in the *Purāṇas* and other scriptures. Later in this narration we will discover how persons like wicked Kaṁsa, who in the material world had died long ago, could still be active in Śrī Goloka.

## TEXT 17

तस्य प्रियसुरामित्रपरिवारस्य शङ्कया ।
नोत्सहन्ते यथाकामं विहर्तुं यादवाः सुखम् ॥

*tasya priya-surāmitra-*
*parivārasya śaṅkayā*
*notsahante yathā-kāmaṁ*
*vihartuṁ yādavāḥ sukham*

*tasya* — of him; *priya* — were dear; *sura-amitra* — and were enemies of the demigods; *parivārasya* — whose family and friends; *śaṅkayā* — out of fear; *na utsahante* — did not dare; *yathā-kāmam* — as they might desire; *vihartum* — to enjoy; *yādavāḥ* — the Yādavas; *sukham* — freely.

**Out of fear of Kaṁsa, whose family and friends were enemies of the demigods, the Yādavas dared not enjoy themselves freely.**

TEXT 18

तस्माद्बहुविधां बाधामपि विन्दन्ति तेऽनिशम् ।
कुत्राप्यपसृताः केचित्सन्ति केऽपि तमाश्रिताः ॥

*tasmād bahu-vidhāṁ bādhām*
*api vindanti te 'niśam*
*kutrāpy apasṛtāḥ kecit*
*santi ke 'pi tam āśritāḥ*

*tasmāt* — on account of him; *bahu-vidhām* — of many kinds; *bādhām* — affliction; *api* — also; *vindanti* — experienced; *te* — they; *aniśam* — constantly; *kutra api* — somewhere; *apasṛtāḥ* — fled; *kecit* — some; *santi* — were; *ke api* — some; *tam* — of him; *āśritāḥ* — under the shelter.

**Because of him they constantly suffered all sorts of affliction. Some of the Yādavas escaped elsewhere, and others took shelter of him.**

COMMENTARY: Uddhava and other Yādavas went into exile in other districts. And some, like Akrūra, became Kaṁsa's order-carriers. As described in *Śrīmad-Bhāgavatam* (10.2.1–4):

*pralamba-baka-cāṇūra-*
*tṛṇāvarta-mahāśanaiḥ*
*muṣṭikāriṣṭa-dvivida-*
*pūtanā-keśī-dhenukaiḥ*

*anyaiś cāsura-bhūpālair*
*bāṇa-bhaumādibhir vṛtaḥ*
*yadūnāṁ kadanaṁ cakre*
*balī māgadha-saṁśrayaḥ*

"Under the protection of Magadharāja [Jarāsandha], the powerful Kaṁsa began persecuting the kings of the Yadu dynasty. In this he had the cooperation of demons like Pralamba, Baka, Cāṇūra, Tṛṇāvarta, and Aghāsura, and still others—Muṣṭika, Ariṣṭa, Dvivida, Pūtanā, Keśī, and Dhenuka, as well as Bāṇāsura and Narakāsura and many other demonic kings on the surface of the earth.

*te pīḍitā nivivisuḥ*
*kuru-pañcāla-kekayān*
*śālvān vidarbhān niṣadhān*
*videhān kośalān api*
*eke tam anurundhānā*
*jñātayaḥ paryupāsate*

"Persecuted by the demonic kings, the Yādavas left their own kingdom and entered various others, like those of the Kurus, Pañcālas, and Kekayas, the Śālvas, Vidarbhas, and Niṣadhas, and the Videhas and Kośalas. Some of the Yādavas, however, began to follow Kaṁsa's principles and act in his service."

The Supreme Lord arranges for His pleasure pastimes to occur in Goloka just as on earth. Were this not so, the hearts of His unalloyed devotees would not be fully satisfied.

## TEXT 19

ततोऽहमपि भीतः सन्कृतविश्रान्तिमज्जनः ।
निःसृत्य त्वरयागच्छं श्रीमद्वृन्दावनं ततः ॥

*tato 'ham api bhītaḥ san*
*kṛta-viśrānti-majjanaḥ*
*niḥsṛtya tvarayāgacchaṁ*
*śrīmad-vṛndāvanaṁ tataḥ*

*tataḥ* — so; *aham* — I; *api* — also; *bhītaḥ* — afraid; *san* — being; *kṛta* — having done; *viśrānti* — at Viśrāma-ghāṭa; *majjanaḥ* — bathing; *niḥsṛtya* — leaving; *tvarayā* — quickly; *agaccham* — I went; *śrīmat-vṛndāvanam* — to Śrīmad Vṛndāvana; *tataḥ* — then.

**I too was afraid of Kaṁsa. So as soon as I finished bathing at Viśrānti-ghāṭa I hurriedly left Mathurā and went to glorious Vṛndāvana.**

COMMENTARY: It was very good for Gopa-kumāra that he was already assuming the character of the Goloka-vāsīs, for that would lead him to his final perfection.

## TEXTS 20–21

तस्मिन्नगम्येऽखिलदेवतानां
लोकेश्वराणामपि पार्षदानाम् ।
एतस्य भूभारतवर्षकीया-
र्यावर्तदेशस्य निरूप्य रीतिम् ॥

दिव्यां दिनेशोद्गमनादिनैतां
भौमीं नृभाषाचरितादिनापि ।
महाचमत्कारभरेण रुद्धो
न्यमज्जमानन्दरसाम्बुराशौ ॥

*tasminn agamye 'khila-devatānāṁ*
*lokeśvarāṇām api pārṣadānām*
*etasya bhū-bhārata-varṣakīyā-*
*ryāvarta-deśasya nirūpya rītim*

*divyāṁ dineśodgamanādinaitāṁ*
*bhaumīṁ nṛ-bhāṣā-caritādināpi*

*mahā-camatkāra-bhareṇa ruddho*
*nyamajjam ānanda-rasāmbu-rāśau*

*tasmin* — there; *agamye* — inaccessible; *akhila* — all; *devatānām* — to the demigods; *loka-īśvarāṇām* — to the rulers of the planets; *api* — also; *pārṣadānām* — to the Lord's personal associates; *etasya* — of this (the Āryāvarta country); *bhū* — on earth; *bhārata-varṣakīya* — of Bhārata-varṣa; *āryāvarta-deśasya* — of the Āryāvarta country; *nirūpya* — noticing; *rītim* — the ways; *divyām* — in the sky; *dina-īśa* — of the sun (ruler of the days); *udgamana* — by the rising; *ādinā* — and so on; *etām* — this; *bhaumīm* — on the ground; *nṛ* — of humans; *bhāṣā* — by the language; *carita* — behavior; *ādinā* — and so on; *api* — also; *mahā-camatkāra* — of extreme astonishment; *bhareṇa* — by an excess; *ruddhaḥ* — stunned; *nyamajjam* — I drowned; *ānanda-rasa* — of ecstatic *rasa; ambu-rāśau* — in an ocean.

**In that realm, beyond the reach of all the demigods, planetary rulers, and personal attendants of the Supreme Lord, I saw that life was going on just as here in this Āryāvarta country in Bhārata-varṣa on earth. The sun was rising and the other natural events were taking place every day in the sky, and on the land the people were speaking and behaving the same way as here. I was stunned by astonishment — extreme astonishment — and immersed in an ocean of ecstatic rasa.**

COMMENTARY: Demigods like Sūrya and Candra, planetary rulers like Indra and Brahmā, and even associates of Lord Nārāyaṇa like Śrī Garuḍa cannot enter Goloka. Gopa-kumāra, preparing his student for descriptions of life there, now gives him a glimpse of how Goloka resembles Vṛndāvana on earth. Gopa-kumāra saw for himself that the environment and culture of Goloka were just like those of Āryāvarta, north central India, refined in civilization, where Vraja-bhūmi is located. What he saw in the sky (*divyām*) and on the ground (*bhaumīm*) could hardly be distinguished from the common experience of life on earth. This sight amazed him. He could now perceive the spiritual reality of *rasa* as something tangible, and the ecstasy of that *rasa* at once filled his heart and overflowed and left him swimming in an ocean of the nectar of devotion.

### TEXT 22

क्षणादपश्यं भ्रमतो गोपानिव वने नरान् ।
पुष्पाणि चिन्वतीर्वृद्धा गोपीवेशवतीस्तथा ॥

*kṣaṇād apaśyaṁ bhramato*
*gopān iva vane narān*
*puṣpāṇi cinvatīr vṛddhā*
*gopī-veśa-vatīs tathā*

*kṣaṇāt* — after a few moments; *apaśyam* — I saw; *bhramataḥ* — wandering; *gopān* — cowherds; *iva* — as if; *vane* — in the forest; *narān* — men; *puṣpāṇi* — flowers; *cinvatīḥ* — collecting; *vṛddhāḥ* — elderly women; *gopī-veśa-vatīḥ* — dressed as cowherdesses; *tathā* — and.

**After a few moments I saw some men, who might have been cowherds, wandering in the forest with some ladies, advanced in years and also wearing cowherd dress, who were picking flowers.**

COMMENTARY: Gopa-kumāra says that the men appeared "as if cowherds" (*gopān iva*). They certainly could not have been ordinary cowherds of the material world. Nor could he assume that the old women he saw were what they appeared. They were dressed as cowherd women, but what they actually were, Gopa-kumāra leaves for his student to find out later. The younger *gopīs* were not there picking flowers, either because their feelings of separation from Kṛṣṇa disenabled them from such useful service or else because they were not allowed to leave the cowherd village. In any case, Gopa-kumāra saw clearly that even the old people of Goloka had very special love for the Supreme Lord.

## TEXT 23

ते च सर्वे जनाः पूर्वदृष्टसर्वविलक्षणाः ।
केनापि हृतहृद्वित्तास्तद्भावव्याकुला इव ॥

*te ca sarve janāḥ pūrva-*
*dṛṣṭa-sarva-vilakṣaṇāḥ*
*kenāpi hṛta-hṛd-vittās*
*tad-bhāva-vyākulā iva*

*te* — they; *ca* — and; *sarve* — all; *janāḥ* — the people; *pūrva-dṛṣṭa* — seen before; *sarva* — from everyone; *vilakṣaṇāḥ* — different; *kena api* — by someone; *hṛta* — stolen; *hṛt* — of their hearts; *vittāḥ* — the wealth; *tat* — for him; *bhāva* — by love; *vyākulāḥ* — disturbed; *iva* — as if.

**The people there were different from anyone I had ever seen. Someone, it appeared, had stolen the wealth of their hearts and left them helplessly in love with him.**

COMMENTARY: Since the beauty and good character of Goloka's people were not to be found anywhere else, Gopa-kumāra could hardly think of an adequate metaphor by which these people could be described. They seemed distracted, as if someone had stolen their hearts. The actual cause of this strange behavior was that they suffered from divine madness. They seemed distraught because a thief had stolen the treasure of their hearts. Or at least that was how things appeared on the surface (*vyākulā iva*); because Gopa-kumāra had just been introduced to life in Goloka, he preferred to hold off on making a final judgment.

## TEXT 24

तेषां दर्शनमात्रेण तादृशं भावमाप्नुवन् ।
यत्नाद्धैर्यमिवासृत्यापृच्छं तानिदमादरात् ॥

*teṣāṁ darśana-mātreṇa*
*tādṛśaṁ bhāvam āpnuvan*

*yatnād dhairyam ivāsṛtyā-*
*pṛccham tān idam ādarāt*

*teṣām* — them; *darśana* — by seeing; *mātreṇa* — only; *tādṛśam* — of the same kind; *bhāvam* — loving affection; *āpnuvan* — obtaining; *yatnāt* — with endeavor; *dhairyam* — composure; *iva* — as if; *āsṛtya* — assuming; *apṛccham* — I asked; *tān* — them; *idam* — this; *ādarāt* — with respect.

**Simply by seeing them, I felt the same kind of loving affection. Trying hard, I composed myself and respectfully asked them the following questions.**

COMMENTARY: The mere sight of these devotees made Gopakumāra feel the same turbulent feelings they did. He managed to bring himself back to a condition almost sober (*dhairyam iva āsṛtya*), but not completely sober, otherwise he wouldn't have asked questions he could already answer.

## TEXT 25

परमहंसमनोरथदुर्लभैः
परमहर्षभरैः परिषेविताः ।
प्रणयभक्तजनैः कमलापतेः
परमयाच्यतदीयदयालयाः ॥

*paramahaṁsa-manoratha-durlabhaiḥ*
*parama-harṣa-bharaiḥ pariṣevitāḥ*
*praṇaya-bhakta-janaiḥ kamalā-pateḥ*
*parama-yācya-tadīya-dayālayāḥ*

*parama-haṁsa* — of the topmost sages; *manoratha* — in the imagination; *durlabhaiḥ* — rarely obtainable; *parama* — supreme; *harṣa* — of happiness; *bharaiḥ* — by the abundance; *pariṣevitāḥ* — served; *praṇaya* — loving; *bhakta-janaiḥ* — by the devotees; *kamalā-pateḥ* — of the husband of the goddess of fortune; *parama* — supreme; *yācya* — which is the object of prayer; *tadīya* — His; *dayā* — of the mercy; *ālayāḥ* — reservoirs.

**"O good people, you are served by a happiness so vast that the greatest sages can't obtain it even in dreams! You are reservoirs of the mercy of the Lord, the husband of the goddess of fortune, mercy for which His loving devotees always pray.**

COMMENTARY: Before placing his questions, Gopa-kumāra addresses the Goloka-vāsīs in this way because he cannot comprehend how the hearts of such supremely fortunate devotees could be disturbed. The kind of happiness these pure souls know cannot be imagined by sages fixed in the conception of Brahman, for the devotees of Goloka are much greater than liberated sages and even greater than the servants of the Lord of Vaikuṇṭha, who love Lord Nārāyaṇa with pure intent. Though the devotees of Nārāyaṇa admire and pray for the same mercy bestowed upon the Goloka-vāsīs, they never actually obtain it.

## TEXT 26

परमदीनमिमं शरणागतं
करुणया बत पश्यत पश्यत ।
कथयतास्य नृपो विषयस्य को
गृहममुष्य कुतोऽस्य च वर्त्म किम् ॥

*parama-dīnam imaṁ śaraṇāgataṁ*
*karuṇayā bata paśyata paśyata*
*kathayatāsya nṛpo viṣayasya ko*
*gṛham amuṣya kuto 'sya ca vartma kim*

*parama-dīnam* — most wretched person; *imam* — this; *śaraṇa* — for shelter; *āgatam* — who has come; *karuṇayā* — with kindness; *bata* — oh; *paśyata* — please look; *paśyata* — please look; *kathayata* — please tell; *asya* — of this; *nṛpaḥ* — the king; *viṣayasya* — of the region; *kaḥ* — who; *gṛham* — the residence; *amuṣya* — his; *kutaḥ* — where; *asya* — to it; *ca* — and; *vartma* — the road; *kim* — which.

**"Please, please look with kindness upon this most wretched person, who has come to you for shelter. Tell me, who is the king of this region? Where is his residence? Which road leads there?**

TEXT 27

भो भोः सकाकु पृच्छन्तं धन्याः कृपयतात्र माम् ।
दत्त प्रत्युत्तरं किञ्चित्सङ्केतेनापि सुव्रताः ॥

*bho bhoḥ sa-kāku pṛcchantaṁ*
*dhanyāḥ kṛpayatātra mām*
*datta pratyuttaraṁ kiñcit*
*saṅketenāpi su-vratāḥ*

*bhoḥ bhoḥ* — dear people; *sa-kāku* — in pitiful tones; *pṛcchantam* — inquiring; *dhanyāḥ* — O most fortunate persons; *kṛpayata* — please be merciful; *atra* — here; *mām* — to me; *datta* — please give; *pratyuttaram* — an answer; *kiñcit* — some; *saṅketena* — by a gesture; *api* — even; *su-vratāḥ* — O faithful ones.

**"Dear, dear most fortunate people, please be merciful to me, who am asking you with mournful cries. Please give me some answer, O faithful devotees, if even only by gesture!**

COMMENTARY: Not receiving an answer, Gopa-kumāra first guesses that perhaps these Goloka-vāsīs are nearly deaf. He therefore repeats his address more distinctly, saying loudly *bho bhoḥ* ("dear people, dear people"). He then realizes they are not deaf but simply paying no attention to him, so he tries to impress on them the sincerity of his request. He praises them as *dhanyāḥ* ("most fortunate") and *su-vratāḥ* ("faithful followers of regulative principles"). And if these devotees are following a vow of silence, at least they can answer him by hand signals.

## TEXT 28

अहो बत महार्तस्य शृणुतापि वचांसि मे ।
नूनं तस्यैव धूर्तस्य यूयं भावेन मोहिताः ॥

*aho bata mahārtasya*
*śṛṇutāpi vacāṁsi me*
*nūnaṁ tasyaiva dhūrtasya*
*yūyaṁ bhāvena mohitāḥ*

*aho* — oh; *bata* — alas; *mahā* — very much; *ārtasya* — of one who is tormented; *śṛṇuta* — please hear; *api* — and; *vacāṁsi* — the words; *me* — my; *nūnam* — certainly; *tasya* — for him; *eva* — indeed; *dhūrtasya* — the deceiver; *yūyam* — you; *bhāvena* — by the behavior; *mohitāḥ* — bespelled.

**"Oh, please hear the words of this tormented soul! Alas, you must be under the spell of that clever cheat."**

COMMENTARY: Even after Gopa-kumāra's fervent plea, the Goloka-vāsīs didn't respond. They didn't even look at him. But Gopa-kumāra, rather than become angry with them for their neglect, placed the blame on the enchanting Kṛṣṇa, who, after all, had deceived Gopa-kumāra just as He had them. Kṛṣṇa is indeed the most expert cheat; only He (*tasyaiva*) could bewilder them like this, and no one else.

## TEXT 29

इत्थं मुहुः सकातर्यं सम्पृच्छंस्तानितस्ततः ।
दृश्यमानान्पुरो भूत्वा व्रजस्थानान्यवाप्नुवम् ॥

*ittham muhuḥ sa-kātaryaṁ*
*sampṛcchaṁs tān itas tataḥ*
*dṛśyamānān puro bhūtvā*
*vraja-sthānāny avāpnuvam*

*ittham* — in this manner; *muhuḥ* — repeatedly; *sa-kātaryam* — anxiously; *sampṛcchan* — asking; *tān* — them; *itaḥ tataḥ* — here and there; *dṛśyamānān* — whom I saw; *puraḥ* — forward; *bhūtvā* — going; *vraja-sthānāni* — the pasturing grounds; *avāpnuvam* — I reached.

**In this way I moved here and there, anxiously questioning each person I met. And as I made my way forward, I came to the pasturing grounds of the cowherds.**

COMMENTARY: The anxiety Gopa-kumāra felt upon His arrival in Goloka was actually a symptom of *dainya,* the transcendental, unconditional humility that is the most important prerequisite for gaining eternal residence in Goloka.

## TEXT 30

परितश्चालयंश्चक्षुः पुरीमेकां विदूरतः ।
अद्राक्षं माधुरीसारपरीपाकेण सेविताम् ॥

*paritaś cālayaṁś cakṣuḥ*
*purīm ekāṁ vidūrataḥ*
*adrākṣaṁ mādhurī-sāra-*
*parīpākeṇa sevitām*

*paritaḥ* — around; *cālayan* — moving; *cakṣuḥ* — my eyes; *purīm* — a town; *ekām* — one; *vidūrataḥ* — far away; *adrākṣam* — I saw; *mādhurī* — of sweetness; *sāra* — of the essence; *parīpākeṇa* — with the mature perfection; *sevitām* — adorned.

**Looking around in all directions, I spotted in the distance a town adorned with the essence of all sweetness.**

COMMENTARY: The other realms Gopa-kumāra had visited in the material and spiritual worlds were each great in their own way, but none of them, not even Vaikuṇṭha, was as attractive as this.

## TEXT 31

तत्पार्श्वे चाभितोऽश्रौषं गोपीनां गीतमद्भुतम् ।
दध्नां मथनघोषाढ्यं कान्तं भूषणसिञ्जितैः ॥

*tat-pārśve cābhito 'śrauṣaṁ*
*gopīnāṁ gītam adbhutam*
*dadhnāṁ mathana-ghoṣāḍhyaṁ*
*kāntaṁ bhūṣaṇa-siñjitaiḥ*

*tat* — of it (the town); *pārśve* — on a side; *ca* — and; *abhitaḥ* — all around; *aśrauṣam* — I heard; *gopīnām* — of cowherd women; *gītam* — singing; *adbhutam* — wonderful; *dadhnām* — of yogurt; *mathana* — of churning; *ghoṣa* — by the sound; *āḍhyam* — enhanced; *kāntam* — attractive; *bhūṣaṇa* — of ornaments; *siñjitaiḥ* — along with the jingling.

**On one side of that town, all about I heard wonderful songs, sung by cowherd women, and the charming sound of the churning of butter, and the jingling of bangles.**

COMMENTARY: Nowhere had Gopa-kumāra ever heard such wonderful songs. Even though he was a liberated soul, with no interest in material sense gratification, he was attracted by the jingling sound of these women's bangles.

## TEXTS 32–34

प्रहर्षाकुलमात्मानं विष्टभ्य पुरतो व्रजन् ।
प्राप्नुवं कृष्ण कृष्णेति सवैयग्र्यं निरन्तरम् ॥

कीर्तयन्तं रुदन्तं च निविष्टं वृद्धमेकलम् ।
तस्मात्प्रयत्नचातुर्यैरश्रौषं गद्गदाक्षरात् ॥

गोपराजस्य नन्दस्य तच्छ्रीकृष्णपितुः पुरम् ।
तच्छब्दश्रुतिमात्रेण व्यमुह्यं हर्षवेगतः ॥

*praharṣākulam ātmānaṁ*
*viṣṭabhya purato vrajan*
*prāpnuvaṁ kṛṣṇa kṛṣṇeti*
*sa-vaiyagryaṁ nirantaram*

*kīrtayantaṁ rudantaṁ ca*
*niviṣṭaṁ vṛddham ekalam*
*tasmāt prayatna-cāturyair*
*aśrauṣaṁ gadgadākṣarāt*

*gopa-rājasya nandasya*
*tac chrī-kṛṣṇa-pituḥ puram*
*tac-chabda-śruti-mātreṇa*
*vyamuhyaṁ harṣa-vegataḥ*

*praharṣa* — by joy; *ākulam* — agitated; *ātmānam* — myself; *viṣṭabhya* — bringing under control; *purataḥ* — forward; *vrajan* — walking; *prāpnuvam* — I found; *kṛṣṇa kṛṣṇa* — O Kṛṣṇa! Kṛṣṇa!; *iti* — thus; *sa-vaiyagryam* — with intense emotion; *nirantaram* — incessantly; *kīrtayantam* — chanting; *rudantam* — crying; *ca* — and; *niviṣṭam* — seated; *vṛddham* — an old man; *ekalam* — one; *tasmāt* — from him; *prayatna* — by endeavors; *cāturyaiḥ* — skillful; *aśrauṣam* — I heard; *gadgada* — choking; *akṣarāt* — in syllables; *gopa-rājasya* — of the king of the cowherds; *nandasya* — Nanda; *tat* — it; *śrī-kṛṣṇa-pituḥ* — of Kṛṣṇa's father; *puram* — the town; *tat* — those; *śabda* — words; *śruti-mātreṇa* — just by hearing; *vyamuhyam* — I fainted; *harṣa* — of my joy; *vegataḥ* — by the force.

**Trying to subdue my agitated joy, I walked forward and came across a seated elderly gentleman, sobbing profusely,**

**incessantly chanting "Kṛṣṇa! Kṛṣṇa!" With some skillful effort I made him speak, and I heard him say, in a choked voice, that this town belonged to Nanda, the king of the cowherds, Śrī Kṛṣṇa's father. As soon as I heard those words I fainted, overcome with delight.**

COMMENTARY: From this verse we can understand that Nanda Mahārāja was officially the ruler of the district.

TEXT 35

क्षणात्तेनैव वृद्धेन चेतितोऽहं दयालुना ।
धावन्नग्रेऽभिसृत्यास्या न्यषीदं गोपुरे पुरः ॥

*kṣaṇāt tenaiva vṛddhena*
*cetito 'haṁ dayālunā*
*dhāvann agre 'bhisṛtyāsyā*
*nyaṣīdaṁ gopure puraḥ*

*kṣaṇāt* — after a moment; *tena* — by him; *eva* — indeed; *vṛddhena* — the old man; *cetitaḥ* — brought back to consciousness; *aham* — I; *dayālunā* — who was compassionate; *dhāvan* — running; *agre* — ahead; *abhisṛtya* — approaching; *asyāḥ* — of that; *nyaṣīdam* — I sat down; *gopure* — in a gateway; *puraḥ* — of the town.

**After a moment that compassionate old man revived me, and I ran ahead and approached a gateway of the town and sat there in the gate.**

TEXT 36

अदृष्टमश्रुतं चान्यैरसम्भाव्यं व्यलोकयम् ।
बहुप्रकारमाश्चर्यं लक्षशस्तत्र कोटिशः ॥

*adṛṣṭam aśrutaṁ cānyair*
*asambhāvyaṁ vyalokayam*

*bahu-prakāram āścaryaṁ*
*lakṣaśas tatra koṭiśaḥ*

*adṛṣṭam* — unseen; *aśrutam* — unheard of; *ca* — and; *anyaiḥ* — by others; *asambhāvyam* — unimaginable; *vyalokayam* — I saw; *bahu-prakāram* — of many kinds; *āścaryam* — wonders; *lakṣaśaḥ* — by the hundreds of thousands; *tatra* — there; *koṭiśaḥ* — and by the tens of millions.

**And there I saw, by the hundreds of thousands and tens of millions, all sorts of wonders, unseen, unheard of, unimaginable by anyone of this world.**

COMMENTARY: About the amazing things he saw, Gopa-kumāra cannot say much to someone like the Mathurā *brāhmaṇa,* who has not seen anything comparable. But being kindly disposed toward this disciple, Gopa-kumāra will try to help him understand something.

## TEXT 37

निश्चेतुं नाशकं किं ते परमानन्दनिर्वृताः ।
किं वा दुःखभरग्रस्ता जनाः सर्वे द्विजोत्तम ॥

*niścetuṁ nāśakaṁ kiṁ te*
*paramānanda-nirvṛtāḥ*
*kiṁ vā duḥkha-bhara-grastā*
*janāḥ sarve dvijottama*

*niścetum* — to determine; *na aśakam* — I was not able; *kim* — whether; *te* — they; *parama* — the highest; *ānanda* — bliss; *nirvṛtāḥ* — enjoying; *kim vā* — or whether; *duḥkha-bhara* — by terrible misery; *grastāḥ* — gripped; *janāḥ* — the people; *sarve* — all; *dvija-uttama* — O best of *brāhmaṇas.*

**O best of brāhmaṇas, I couldn't discern whether the people there were all enjoying the highest bliss or suffering in the grip of terrible misery.**

## TEXT 38

गोपिकानां च यद्गीतं श्रूयते रोदनान्वितम् ।
तत्तोषस्य शुचो वान्त्यकाष्ठयेति न बुध्यते ॥

*gopikānāṁ ca yad gītaṁ*
*śrūyate rodanānvitam*
*tat-toṣasya śuco vāntya-*
*kāṣṭhayeti na budhyate*

*gopikānām* — by the cowherd women; *ca* — and; *yat* — what; *gītam* — was sung; *śrūyate* — was heard; *rodana-anvitam* — accompanied by crying; *tat* — that; *toṣasya* — of satisfaction; *śucaḥ* — of lamentation; *vā* — or; *antya-kāṣṭhayā* — as the extreme limit; *iti* — thus; *na budhyate* — was not understood.

**I heard the gopīs' songs, coupled with their crying, but were they songs of the greatest contentment or the greatest sorrow? I couldn't tell.**

COMMENTARY: The behavior of the Goloka-vāsīs, arising as the culmination of their wonderful love for Kṛṣṇa, puzzled Gopa-kumāra. Such exalted *prema* is beyond the understanding of all but a few most fortunate persons.

## TEXTS 39–40

पदं तत्पश्यता मर्त्यलोकेऽस्मीत्येव मन्यते ।
यदा तु पूर्वपूर्वानुसन्धानं क्रियते बहु ॥

तदाखिलानां लोकानामलोकानामुपर्यपि ।
तथा लोकातिलोकानां वर्तेयेत्यवगम्यते ॥

*padaṁ tat paśyatā martya-*
*loke 'smīty eva manyate*

*yadā tu pūrva-pūrvānu-*
*sandhānaṁ kriyate bahu*

*tadākhilānāṁ lokānām*
*alokānām upary api*
*tathā lokāti-lokānāṁ*
*varteyety avagamyate*

*padam* — abode; *tat* — that; *paśyatā* — observing; *martya-loke* — in the mortal world; *asmi* — I am; *iti* — thus; *eva* — indeed; *manyate* — he would consider; *yadā* — if; *tu* — however; *pūrva-pūrva* — on various previous experiences; *anusandhānam* — reflection; *kriyate* — is done; *bahu* — sufficient; *tadā* — then; *akhilānām* — all; *lokānām* — material planets; *alokānām* — nonplanetary regions; *upari* — above; *api* — also; *tathā* — and; *loka-ati-lokānām* — transcendental abodes; *varteya* — I am present; *iti* — thus; *avagamyate* — would be understood.

**A person seeing that place might think he was in the material world. But by carefully reflecting on whatever he had seen before, he would understand he was now somewhere above all material planets, all higher nonplanetary regions, and all the transcendental realms of the spiritual world.**

COMMENTARY: Because Goloka in the spiritual sky and Mathurā-maṇḍala here on earth are nondifferent, at first Gopa-kumāra mistook one for the other. Reflecting back on his travels, however, he reconsidered. He had been to Vaikuṇṭha, Ayodhyā, and Dvārakā, and where he was now had all the signs of being even more exalted. Evidently this place was greater than the fourteen planetary systems of the material world (*lokānām*), the outer coverings of the material universe (*alokānām*), and the transcendent spiritual realms of Vaikuṇṭha (*lokāti-lokānām*). His present location, therefore, must be above all other worlds.

## TEXT 41

अथ तत्रागतामेकां वृद्धां नत्वातिकाकुभिः ।
अपृच्छं विहरत्यद्य क्वासौ श्रीनन्दनन्दनः ॥

*atha tatrāgatām ekāṁ*
*vṛddhāṁ natvāti-kākubhiḥ*
*apṛcchaṁ viharaty adya*
*kvāsau śrī-nanda-nandanaḥ*

*atha* — then; *tatra* — there; *āgatām* — who came; *ekām* — an; *vṛddhām* — old lady; *natvā* — bowing down to; *ati-kākubhiḥ* — in an extremely plaintive voice; *apṛccham* — I asked; *viharati* — plays; *adya* — today; *kva* — where; *asau* — He; *śrī-nanda-nandanaḥ* — Śrī Nanda-nandana.

**Then an elderly lady came by. I bowed down to her and asked in a plaintive voice where Śrī Nanda-nandana was playing today.**

COMMENTARY: Gopa-kumāra was still sitting inside the gateway of Nanda Mahārāja's cowherd village.

## TEXT 42

श्रीवृद्धोवाच
प्रातर्विहर्तुं गहनं प्रविष्टो
गोभिर्वयस्यैश्च महाग्रजेन ।
प्राणप्रदाता व्रजवासिनां नः
सायं समायास्यति सोऽधुनैव ॥

*śrī-vṛddhovāca*
*prātar vihartuṁ gahanaṁ praviṣṭo*
*gobhir vayasyaiś ca mahāgrajena*

*prāṇa-pradātā vraja-vāsināṁ naḥ*
*sāyaṁ samāyāsyati so 'dhunaiva*

*śrī-vṛddhā uvāca* — the elderly lady said; *prātaḥ* — in the morning; *vihartum* — to play; *gahanam* — the dense forest; *praviṣṭaḥ* — entered; *gobhiḥ* — with His cows; *vayasyaiḥ* — young friends; *ca* — and; *mahā* — respected; *agra-jena* — with His elder brother; *prāṇa-pradātā* — the bestower of life; *vraja-vāsinām* — to the Vraja-vāsīs; *naḥ* — us; *sāyam* — in the evening; *samāyāsyati* — will return; *saḥ* — He; *adhunā* — today; *eva* — indeed.

**The elderly lady said: "This morning that giver of life to us Vraja-vāsīs went into the dense forest to play, with His cows and friends and His respected elder brother. Later, at dusk, He will return.**

COMMENTARY: This old *gopī* anticipates that when Kṛṣṇa returns home (*samāyāsyati*) He will expertly fulfill the individual expectations of each Vraja-vāsī. "And if He doesn't come home on time," she further implies, "we will all die from disappointment."

## TEXT 43

तिष्ठन्ति यस्मिन्व्रजवासिनो जना
न्यस्तेक्षणा वर्त्मनि यामुनेऽखिलाः ।
एते नगा यस्य तदीक्षणोन्मुखाः
सन्त्युच्छदैरेष्यति नन्वनेन सः ॥

*tiṣṭhanti yasmin vraja-vāsino janā*
*nyastekṣaṇā vartmani yāmune 'khilāḥ*
*ete nagā yasya tad-īkṣaṇonmukhāḥ*
*santy ucchadair eṣyati nanv anena saḥ*

*tiṣṭhanti* — stand; *yasmin* — where; *vraja-vāsinaḥ* — residing in Vraja; *janāḥ* — the people; *nyasta* — fixed; *īkṣaṇā* — whose eyes; *vartmani* — on the path; *yāmune* — along the Yamunā; *akhilāḥ* — all; *ete* — these; *nagāḥ* — trees; *yasya* — whose; *tat* — Him; *īkṣaṇa* — for seeing; *unmukhāḥ* — eager; *santi* — are; *ucchadaiḥ* — with erect leaves; *eṣyati* — will come; *nanu* — certainly; *anena* — by this (path); *saḥ* — He.

**"All the Vraja-vāsīs are waiting on this path along the Yamunā, their eyes transfixed on the road. These trees stand with leaves erect, eagerly awaiting the chance to see Him. Surely He will come along this path."**

COMMENTARY: Discussing Kṛṣṇa's imminent return has obviously enlivened the elderly *gopī*.

## TEXT 44

श्रीगोपकुमार उवाच
परमामृतधाराभिरभिषिक्त इवाभवम् ।
तया तं दर्शितं मार्गमेकदृष्ट्या व्यलोकयम् ॥

*śrī-gopa-kumāra uvāca*
*paramāmṛta-dhārābhir*
*abhiṣikta ivābhavam*
*tayā taṁ darśitaṁ mārgam*
*eka-dṛṣṭyā vyalokayam*

*śrī-gopa-kumāraḥ uvāca* — Śrī Gopa-kumāra said; *parama-amṛta* — of most refined nectar; *dhārābhiḥ* — by a downpour; *abhiṣiktaḥ* — anointed; *iva* — as if; *abhavam* — I became; *tayā* — by her; *tam* — that; *darśitam* — shown; *mārgam* — at the path; *eka-dṛṣṭyā* — with one-pointed attention; *vyalokayam* — I looked.

**Śrī Gopa-kumāra said: As if anointed by a downpour of the purest nectar, I gazed with one-pointed attention down the path the old lady had pointed out.**

## TEXT 45

परमानन्दभारेण स्तम्भितोरुः कथञ्चन ।
यत्नेनाग्रे भवन्दूरेऽशृणवं कमपि ध्वनिम् ॥

*paramānanda-bhāreṇa*
*stambhitoruḥ kathañcana*
*yatnenāgre bhavan dūre*
*'śṛṇavaṁ kam api dhvanim*

*parama-ānanda* — of the highest ecstasy; *bhāreṇa* — by the force; *stambhita* — frozen; *ūruḥ* — my thighs; *kathañcana* — somehow; *yatnena* — with effort; *agre* — ahead; *bhavan* — going; *dūre* — at a distance; *aśṛṇavam* — I heard; *kam api* — a certain; *dhvanim* — sound.

**The sheer force of my ecstasy had frozen my thighs. But with some effort I moved on, and I heard from afar a certain sound.**

## TEXT 46

गवां हाम्बारावैः सुललिततरं मोहमुरली-
कलं लीलागीतस्वरमधुररागेण कलितम् ।
जगद्वैलक्षण्याचितविविधभङ्गीविलसितं
व्रजस्थानां तेषां सपदि परमाकर्षबलितम् ॥

*gavāṁ hāmbā-rāvaiḥ su-lalita-taraṁ moha-muralī-*
*kalaṁ līlā-gīta-svara-madhura-rāgeṇa kalitam*
*jagad-vailakṣaṇyācita-vividha-bhaṅgī-vilasitaṁ*
*vraja-sthānāṁ teṣāṁ sapadi paramākarṣa-balitam*

*gavām* — of the cows; *hāmbā* — of mooing; *rāvaiḥ* — by the loud sound; *su-lalita-taram* — most attractive; *moha* — enchanting; *muralī* — of the flute; *kalam* — the reverberation; *līlā* — sportingly; *gīta* — played; *svara* — with musical tones; *madhura*

— sweet; *rāgeṇa* — by a melody; *kalitam* — enhanced; *jagat* — from the entire world; *vailakṣaṇya* — by distinction; *ācita* — marked; *vividha* — various; *bhaṅgī* — with embellishments; *vilasitam* — decorated; *vraja-sthānām* — of those present in the cowherd village; *teṣām* — them; *sapadi* — at once; *parama* — supreme; *ākarṣa* — with attractive force; *balitam* — empowered.

**Mixed with the mooing of cows, it was the supremely attractive murmur of Kṛṣṇa's enchanting flute. That sound — sweet melodies of sportingly played notes, diverse with musical embellishments — was like nothing ever heard in the material world. Its attractive force at once overwhelmed everyone in the cowherd village.**

COMMENTARY: The first sounds Gopa-kumāra heard from Kṛṣṇa's flute were sweet but not very clear. Such an indistinct musical sound is called *kala*. Then Gopa-kumāra began to discern the different notes of the scale, and then coherent melodies like the *mallāra-rāga*. And then, as the sound came even closer, he could hear subtle embellishments known as *mūrcchanā* (chromatic modulations). Meditating on the sound absorbed Gopa-kumāra's attention, and indeed that of everyone present.

## TEXT 47

यस्मात्सस्रुस्तरुविततितो दीर्घधारा रसानां
घोषस्थानामपि तनुभृतां नेत्रतोऽश्रुप्रवाहाः ।
तन्मातॄणामपि विवयसां क्षीरपूराः स्तनेभ्यः
कालिन्द्याश्च प्रचलपयसां ते न्यवर्तन्त वेगाः ॥

*yasmāt sasrus taru-vitatito dīrgha-dhārā rasānāṁ*
*ghoṣa-sthānām api tanu-bhṛtāṁ netrato 'śru-pravāhāḥ*
*tan-mātṝṇām api vivayasāṁ kṣīra-pūrāḥ stanebhyaḥ*
*kālindyāś ca pracala-payasāṁ te nyavartanta vegāḥ*

*yasmāt* — because of which; *sasruḥ* — there flowed; *taru* — of trees; *vitatitaḥ* — from the rows; *dīrgha* — long; *dhārāḥ* — downpours; *rasānām* — of the various kinds of sap; *ghoṣa* — in the cowherd village; *sthānām* — who were situated; *api* — just; *tanu-bhṛtām* — of the embodied beings; *netrataḥ* — from the eyes; *aśru* — of tears; *pravāhāḥ* — a mighty current; *tat* — His (Kṛṣṇa's); *mātṝṇām* — of the mothers; *api* — although; *vivayasām* — elderly; *kṣīra* — with milk; *pūrāḥ* — filled; *stanebhyaḥ* — from the breasts; *kālindyāḥ* — of the Yamunā; *ca* — and; *pracala* — rapidly moving; *payasām* — from the water; *te* — it; *nyavartanta* — stopped; *vegāḥ* — the forceful currents.

**By the power of that sound, sap flowed in a downpour from the long rows of trees, a flood of tears fell from the eyes of every embodied being in the village of the cowherds, a shower of milk rained from the breasts of all of Kṛṣṇa's mothers, even the elderly, and the rapid currents of the Yamunā suddenly stood still.**

COMMENTARY: As the living beings in the forest had all enjoyed the association of Kṛṣṇa during the day, now in the evening everyone who lived in the village delighted in seeing Him again. Not only Mother Yaśodā but many other mothers of Kṛṣṇa, including His aunts and nurses, responded ecstatically to the sound that promised His return. All the mothers of the cowherd boys and calves had in fact become Kṛṣṇa's mothers when Kṛṣṇa had expanded Himself to replace the boys and calves stolen by Brahmā.

Normally, nothing can stop the current of Śrī Yamunā, but the sound of Kṛṣṇa's flute is no ordinary force.

## TEXT 48

न जाने सा वंश्युद्गिरति गरलं वामृतरसं
न जाने तन्नादोऽप्यशनिपरुषो वाम्बुमृदुलः ।

न जाने चात्युष्णो ज्वलितदहनाद्वेन्दुशिशिरो
यतो जातोन्मादा मुमुहुरखिलास्ते व्रजजनाः ॥

*na jāne sā vaṁśy udgirati garalaṁ vāmṛta-rasaṁ*
*na jāne tan-nādo 'py aśani-paruṣo vāmbu-mṛdulaḥ*
*na jāne cāty-uṣṇo jvalita-dahanād vendu-śiśiro*
*yato jātonmādā mumuhur akhilās te vraja-janāḥ*

*na jāne* — I did not know; *sā* — that; *vaṁśī* — flute; *udgirati* — emits; *garalam* — poison; *vā* — or; *amṛta-rasam* — the nectar of immortality; *na jāne* — I did not know; *tat* — its; *nādaḥ* — sound; *api* — also; *aśani* — like a thunderbolt; *paruṣaḥ* — hard; *vā* — or; *ambu* — like water; *mṛdulaḥ* — soft; *na jāne* — I did not know; *ca* — and; *ati-uṣṇaḥ* — very hot; *jvalita* — blazing; *dahanāt* — more than a fire; *vā* — or; *indu* — like the moon; *śiśiraḥ* — cooling; *yataḥ* — because of which; *jāta* — becoming; *unmādāḥ* — insane; *mumuhuḥ* — became bewildered; *akhilāḥ* — all; *te* — they; *vraja-janāḥ* — the inhabitants of Vṛndāvana.

**I didn't know whether that flute gave out poison or the nectar of immortality, whether its sound was harsh like thunder or soft like water, hotter than blazing fire or cooler than the moon. I couldn't tell. But that sound drove all the Vraja-vāsīs mad. All of them were utterly bewildered.**

## TEXT 49

अथानुपश्यामि गृहाद्विनिःसृतास्
तदीयनीराजनवस्तुपाणयः ।
प्रयान्ति काश्चिद्व्रजयोषितोऽपराः
शिरोऽर्पितालङ्करणोपभोग्यकाः ॥

*athānupaśyāmi gṛhād viniḥsṛtās*
*tadīya-nīrājana-vastu-pāṇayaḥ*

*prayānti kāścid vraja-yoṣito 'parāḥ*
*śiro-'rpitālaṅkaraṇopabhogyakāḥ*

*atha* — then; *anupaśyāmi* — I saw; *gṛhāt* — from the houses; *viniḥsṛtāḥ* — coming out; *tadīya* — of Him; *nīrājana* — for worshipful greeting; *vastu* — with items; *pāṇayaḥ* — in their hands; *prayānti* — go forth; *kāścit* — some; *vraja-yoṣitaḥ* — women of Vraja; *aparāḥ* — others; *śiraḥ* — on their heads; *arpita* — held; *alaṅkaraṇa* — ornaments for decorating; *upabhogyakāḥ* — and food for offering.

**Then I saw some women of Vraja come out of their homes, bearing in their hands the things needed to greet Kṛṣṇa with worship. Others who passed by held ornaments and offerings of food on their heads.**

COMMENTARY: Some of the ladies carried lamps, flowers, mustard seeds, and other articles for offering *ārati* to Kṛṣṇa. Other ladies carried pots of butter on their heads and carried garlands and fragrant sandalwood pulp and sweet and spicy yogurt, all meant for Kṛṣṇa's enjoyment.

## TEXT 50

किञ्चिच्च काश्चित्त्वनपेक्षमाणाः
सम्भ्रान्तिविघ्नाकलिताः स्खलन्त्यः ।
धावन्ति तस्यां दिशि यत्र धेनु-
हाम्बारवा वेणुनिनादमिश्राः ॥

*kiñcic ca kāścit tv anapekṣamāṇāḥ*
*sambhrānti-vighnākalitāḥ skhalantyaḥ*
*dhāvanti tasyāṁ diśi yatra dhenu-*
*hāmbā-ravā veṇu-ninādā-miśrāḥ*

*kiñcit* — anything; *ca* — and; *kāścit* — some ladies; *tu* — but; *anapekṣamāṇāḥ* — not paying attention to; *sambhrānti* — of their frenzy of affection; *vighna* — by the obstacle; *ākalitāḥ* — weakened; *skhalantyaḥ* — stumbling; *dhāvanti* — they ran; *tasyām* — in that; *diśi* — direction; *yatra* — where; *dhenu* — of the cows; *hāmbā-ravāḥ* — the sounds of the mooing; *veṇu* — of the flute; *nināda* — with the vibration; *miśrāḥ* — mixed.

**Other ladies, ignoring everything around them, ran toward the mingled sounds of the mooing of the cows and the song of the flute. In the frenzy of love for Kṛṣṇa, the ladies stumbled down the path.**

COMMENTARY: When these *gopīs* attempted to run forward, nothing could interfere but their own eagerness. This was evidence of how purely they loved Kṛṣṇa.

## TEXT 51

काश्चिद्विपर्यग्धृतभूषणा ययुः
काश्चिच्च नीवीकचबन्धनाकुलाः ।
अन्या गृहान्तस्तरुभावमाश्रिताः
काश्चिच्च भूमौ न्यपतन्विमोहिताः ॥

*kāścid viparyag-dhṛta-bhūṣaṇā yayuḥ*
*kāścic ca nīvī-kaca-bandhanākulāḥ*
*anyā gṛhāntas taru-bhāvam āśritāḥ*
*kāścic ca bhūmau nyapatan vimohitāḥ*

*kāścit* — some ladies; *viparyak* — in disarray; *dhṛta* — wearing; *bhūṣaṇāḥ* — their ornaments; *yayuḥ* — went; *kāścit* — some; *ca* — and; *nīvī* — their belts; *kaca-bandhana* — and the braiding of their hair; *ākulāḥ* — disordered; *anyāḥ* — others; *gṛha-antaḥ* — inside their houses; *taru* — of trees; *bhāvam* — the condition; *āśritāḥ* — resorted to; *kāścit* — some; *ca* — and; *bhūmau* — to the ground; *nyapatan* — fell; *vimohitāḥ* — unconscious.

**Some ladies ran with their ornaments in disarray, some could hardly keep their belts and hair tied, some stayed in their homes, stunned like trees, and others fell unconscious to the ground.**

TEXT 52

मोहं गताः काश्चन नीयमाना
धृत्वाश्रुलालार्द्रमुखाः सखीभिः ।
यान्तीतराः प्रेमभराकुलास्तं
पश्यैतमित्यालिभिरुच्यमानाः ॥

*mohaṁ gatāḥ kāścana nīyamānā*
*dhṛtvāśru-lālārdra-mukhāḥ sakhībhiḥ*
*yāntītarāḥ prema-bharākulās taṁ*
*paśyaitam ity ālibhir ucyamānāḥ*

*moham gatāḥ* — who fainted; *kāścana* — some; *nīyamānāḥ* — while being carried; *dhṛtvā* — being held; *aśru* — with tears; *lāla* — and saliva; *ārdra* — wet; *mukhāḥ* — their faces; *sakhībhiḥ* — by girlfriends; *yānti* — went; *itarāḥ* — others; *prema-bhara* — by the force of their love; *ākulāḥ* — distressed; *tam* — Him; *paśya* — come see; *etam* — this; *iti* — thus; *ālibhiḥ* — by their friends; *ucyamānāḥ* — being told.

**Some of the women who had fainted, their faces wet with tears and saliva, were carried forward by their girlfriends. Other ladies, pained by the urges of their love for Kṛṣṇa, went ahead pressed on by their friends — "Come see Him!"**

COMMENTARY: The *gopīs* had no need to specify to one another who the object of their attraction was. They simply referred to Kṛṣṇa as *tam etam* (Him, "this person"). Without any explicit description, they all knew whom they were talking about — Kṛṣṇa, the Lord of their life.

## TEXT 53

तदीयनामेहितगानतत्परा
विचित्रवेशाम्बरकान्तिभूषिताः ।
रमातिसौभाग्यमदप्रहारिका
जवेन कृष्णातटमाश्रयन्त ताः ॥

*tadīya-nāmehita-gāna-tatparā*
*vicitra-veśāmbara-kānti-bhūṣitāḥ*
*ramāti-saubhāgya-mada-prahārikā*
*javena kṛṣṇā-taṭam āśrayanta tāḥ*

*tadīya* — His; *nāma* — about the names; *īhita* — and activities; *gāna* — in singing; *tatparāḥ* — fully absorbed; *vicitra* — various; *veśa* — with ornaments; *ambara* — dress; *kānti* — and complexions; *bhūṣitāḥ* — adorned; *ramā* — of Ramā, the goddess of fortune; *ati-saubhāgya* — in her extreme good fortune; *mada* — the pride; *prahārikāḥ* — who derided; *javena* — swiftly; *kṛṣṇā-taṭam* — to the side of the Yamunā; *āśrayanta* — went to take shelter; *tāḥ* — they.

**The ladies, so diverse in complexion and adorned with diverse ornaments and dress, put to shame the good fortune of the goddess of fortune herself. Swiftly the ladies ran to the bank of the Yamunā, absorbed in singing His names and pastimes.**

## TEXT 54

ततोऽहमपि केनाप्याकृष्यमाण इवाग्रतः ।
धावन्तीभिः समन्ताभिर्धावन्नभ्यसरं रयात् ॥

*tato 'ham api kenāpyā-*
*kṛṣyamāṇa ivāgrataḥ*
*dhāvantībhiḥ samantābhir*
*dhāvann abhyasaraṁ rayāt*

*tataḥ* — then; *aham* — I; *api* — also; *kena api* — by someone; *ākṛṣyamāṇaḥ* — being pulled; *iva* — as if; *agrataḥ* — forward; *dhāvantībhiḥ* — along with the women who were running; *samantābhiḥ* — on all sides; *dhāvan* — running; *abhyasaram* — I went forward; *rayāt* — quickly.

**I too went forward, as if pulled by someone. Joining the throng of gopīs rushing forward on all sides, I too began to run quickly.**

COMMENTARY: The young *gopīs* came out of their houses and rushed in groups to the path along the Yamunā by which Kṛṣṇa was expected to return. These *gopīs* were more fortunate and more beautiful than even Mahā-lakṣmī, the wife of Lord Nārāyaṇa.

## TEXT 55

अथापश्यं दूरान्मधुरमुरलीराजितकरो
जवान्निःसृत्यासौ सखिपशुगणाद्धावनपरः ।
अये श्रीदामंस्त्वत्कुलकमलभास्वानयमितः
सरूपः प्राप्तो मे सुहृदिति वदन्नेति ललितम् ॥

*athāpaśyaṁ dūrān madhura-muralī-rājita-karo*
*javān niḥsṛtyāsau sakhi-paśu-gaṇād dhāvana-paraḥ*
*aye śrīdāmaṁs tvat-kula-kamala-bhāsvān ayam itaḥ*
*sarūpaḥ prāpto me suhṛd iti vadann eti lalitam*

*atha* — then; *apaśyam* — I saw; *dūrāt* — from a distance; *madhura* — sweet; *muralī* — His flute; *rājita* — shining; *karaḥ* — in His hand; *javāt* — quickly; *niḥsṛtya* — coming out; *asau* — He; *sakhi* — of His friends; *paśu* — and animals; *gaṇāt* — from the group; *dhāvana-paraḥ* — running; *aye śrīdāman* — O Śrīdāmā; *tvat* — your; *kula* — of the family; *kamala* — on the lotus; *bhāsvān* — the shining sun; *ayam* — this; *itaḥ* — here; *sarūpaḥ* — Sarūpa; *prāptaḥ* — obtained; *me* — My; *suhṛt* — dear friend; *iti* — thus; *vadan* — speaking; *eti* — He approached; *lalitam* — sweetly.

**Then from a distance I saw Him, His charming flute in hand. Running quickly, He emerged from among His friends and animals and approached me, saying in a sweet voice, "Look, Śrīdāmā! Here is My dear friend Sarūpa, the sun who shines on the lotus of your family!"**

COMMENTARY: In texts 55 through 59, Gopa-kumāra describes his first impression upon seeing Kṛṣṇa in Goloka. Because Kṛṣṇa recognized Gopa-kumāra as His friend Sarūpa, Kṛṣṇa left behind the cowherd boys and the cows and ran forward to greet him.

## TEXT 56

अरण्यवेशो विचलत्कदम्ब-
मालावतंसाम्बरबार्हमौलिः ।
सौरभ्यसंवासितदिक्तटान्तो
लीलास्मितश्रीविकसन्मुखाब्जः ॥

*araṇya-veśo vicalat-kadamba-*
*mālāvataṁsāmbara-bārha-mauliḥ*
*saurabhya-saṁvāsita-dik-taṭānto*
*līlā-smita-śrī-vikasan-mukhābjaḥ*

*araṇya-veśaḥ* — forest dress; *vicalat* — trembling; *kadamba* — of *kadamba* flowers; *mālā* — His garland; *avataṁsa* — earrings; *ambara* — dress; *bārha-mauliḥ* — and peacock-feather crown; *saurabhya* — by His fragrance; *saṁvāsita* — perfumed; *dik* — of the directions; *taṭa-antaḥ* — the remote extremes; *līlā* — playfully; *smita* — smiling; *śrī* — beautifully; *vikasat* — expanding; *mukha-abjaḥ* — His lotus face.

**Kṛṣṇa was dressed for the forest. His garments, earrings, and peacock-feather crown all swayed to and fro, and so**

**did His garland of kadamba flowers. His fragrance perfumed all directions, and His beautiful lotus face blossomed with a playful smile.**

## TEXT 57

कृपावलोकोल्लसदीक्षणाम्बुजो
विचित्रसौन्दर्यभरैकभूषणः ।
गोधूलिकालंकृतचञ्चलालक-
श्रेण्यावृतिव्यग्रकराम्बुजाङ्गुलिः ॥

*kṛpāvalokollasad-īkṣaṇāmbujo*
*vicitra-saundarya-bharaika-bhūṣaṇaḥ*
*go-dhūlikālaṅkṛta-cañcalālaka-*
*śreṇy-āvṛti-vyagra-karāmbujāṅguliḥ*

*kṛpā* — of mercy; *avaloka* — a glance; *ullasat* — beaming; *īkṣaṇa-ambujaḥ* — His lotus eyes; *vicitra* — various; *saundarya-bhara* — assets of beauty; *eka* — unique; *bhūṣaṇaḥ* — whose ornaments; *go* — from the cows; *dhūlikā* — with the dust; *alaṅkṛta* — decorated; *cañcala* — moving; *alaka* — of hair; *śreṇī* — whose locks; *āvṛti* — in pushing back; *vyagra* — busy; *kara-ambuja* — of whose lotus hand; *aṅguliḥ* — the fingers.

**His lotus eyes beamed with a merciful glance, and the varied assets of beauty decorated Him in a singular way. The fingers of His lotus hand busily pushed back the locks of His hair, which flew about, adorned with the dust raised by the cows.**

## TEXT 58

धरातलश्रीभरदानहेतुना
भूमिस्पृशोर्नृत्यविलासगामिनोः ।

सुजातयोः श्रीपदपद्मयोर्जवाद्
उच्चालनोल्लासभरैर्मनोहरः ॥

*dharā-tala-śrī-bhara-dāna-hetunā*
*bhūmi-spṛśor nṛtya-vilāsa-gāminoḥ*
*sujātayoḥ śrī-pada-padmayor javād*
*uccālanollāsa-bharair manoharaḥ*

*dharā-tala* — the surface of the earth; *śrī-bhara* — of supreme splendor; *dāna* — the gift; *hetunā* — with the purpose of granting; *bhūmi* — the earth; *spṛśoḥ* — which were touching; *nṛtya* — of dance; *vilāsa* — with the play; *gāminoḥ* — which were moving; *sujātayoḥ* — tender; *śrī* — divine; *pada-padmayoḥ* — of His lotus feet; *javāt* — quickly; *uccālana* — for walking with large steps; *ullāsa* — of eagerness; *bharaiḥ* — by the abundance; *manaḥ-haraḥ* — stealing the heart.

**His tender, divine lotus feet touched the surface of the earth just to grant her the gift of supreme splendor. Playfully dancing as they moved, they attracted everyone's heart with their great eagerness to walk quickly with large steps.**

## TEXT 59

कैशोरमाधुर्यभरोल्लसच्छ्री-
गात्राभ्रकान्त्युज्ज्वलिताखिलाशः ।
तत्रत्यनित्यप्रियलोकचित्त-
ग्राह्याद्भुतानेकमहत्त्वसिन्धुः ॥

*kaiśora-mādhurya-bharollasac-chrī-*
*gātrābhra-kānty-ujjvalitākhilāśaḥ*
*tatratya-nitya-priya-loka-citta-*
*grāhyādbhutāneka-mahattva-sindhuḥ*

*kaiśora* — of youth; *mādhurya-bhara* — with all the sweetness; *ullasat* — shining; *śrī* — beautiful; *gātra* — of His body; *abhra*

— like a cloud; *kānti* — by the effulgence; *ujjvalita* — made brilliant; *akhila* — all; *āśaḥ* — the directions; *tatratya* — living in that place (Vraja); *nitya* — eternally; *priya* — dear; *loka* — of the people; *citta* — the hearts; *grāhya* — which captured; *adbhuta* — amazing; *aneka* — countless; *mahattva* — of excellences; *sindhuḥ* — an ocean.

**The effulgence of His cloud-colored body, shining with the full sweetness of youth, lit up all corners of the sky. His beauty, which captured the hearts of the ever-dear devotees of Vraja, was an ocean abounding with countless excellences.**

COMMENTARY: Unable to express much more about the beauty of Kṛṣṇa's body, which glowed like a new rain cloud, Gopakumāra sums up Kṛṣṇa's beauty by describing it as an ocean of excellences. As an ocean is constant and unfathomably deep, so are all of Kṛṣṇa's personal qualities. In Goloka, Kṛṣṇa's beloved devotees know the value of His beauty and other virtues because the hearts of those devotees are completely attracted to Him, as His heart is to them.

## TEXT 60

स्वदीनलोकप्रियतानियन्त्रितो
बलादथोत्प्लुत्य समीपमागतः ।
तदीक्षणप्रेमविमोहितं हि मां
गले गृहीत्वा सहसापतद्भुवि ॥

*sva-dīna-loka-priyatā-niyantrito*
*balād athotplutya samīpam āgataḥ*
*tad-īkṣaṇa-prema-vimohitaṁ hi māṁ*
*gale gṛhītvā sahasāpatad bhuvi*

*sva* — His own; *dīna* — helpless; *loka* — of the devotee; *priyatā* — by the affection; *niyantritaḥ* — compelled; *balāt* — forcefully; *atha* — there; *utplutya* — jumping; *samīpam* — close by; *āgataḥ* — coming; *tat* — Him; *īkṣaṇa* — from seeing; *prema* — by love; *vimohitam* — bewildered; *hi* — indeed; *mām* — me; *gale* — by the neck; *gṛhītvā* — seizing; *sahasā* — suddenly; *apatat* — He fell; *bhuvi* — on the ground.

**He leaped forward and came close to me, compelled by the affection of His helpless devotee. I fainted in love at seeing Him. He caught hold of me by the neck. And suddenly He too fell to the ground.**

COMMENTARY: Gopa-kumāra was already aware, at least theoretically, that Kṛṣṇa is very affectionate to His helpless devotees, but now he learned that Kṛṣṇa had affection specifically for him. Merely seeing Kṛṣṇa was enough to utterly enchant Gopa-kumāra, but this new discovery pushed him toward the limit of ecstasy.

## TEXT 61

क्षणेन संज्ञामहमेत्य तस्माद्
विमोच्य यत्नाद्गलमुत्थितः सन् ।
पश्यामि भूमौ पतितो विमुह्य
वर्त्मार्द्रयन्नस्ति रजोमयं सः ॥

*kṣaṇena saṁjñām aham etya tasmād*
*vimocya yatnād galam utthitaḥ san*
*paśyāmi bhūmau patito vimuhya*
*vartmārdrayann asti rajo-mayaṁ saḥ*

*kṣaṇena* — after a moment; *saṁjñām* — to consciousness; *aham* — I; *etya* — returning; *tasmāt* — from Him; *vimocya* — freeing; *yatnāt* — with endeavor; *galam* — my neck; *utthitaḥ san* — standing up; *paśyāmi* — I saw; *bhūmau* — on the ground; *patitaḥ* — fallen; *vimuhya* — having fainted; *vartma* — the path; *ārdrayan* — making wet; *asti* — was; *rajaḥ-mayam* — covered with dust; *saḥ* — He.

**A moment later I reawoke and carefully freed my neck from His grasp. I stood up and saw Him on the ground, in a faint, moistening the dust-covered path with His tears.**

COMMENTARY: Even though Kṛṣṇa was unconscious, He was crying so profusely that His tears were turning the dust on the road into mud.

TEXT 62

गोप्यः समेत्याहुरहो बतायं
कोऽत्रागतो वा किमिदं चकार ।
एतां दशां नोऽसुगतिं निनाय
हा हा हताः स्मो व्रजवासिलोकाः ॥

*gopyaḥ sametyāhur aho batāyaṁ*
*ko 'trāgato vā kim idaṁ cakāra*
*etāṁ daśāṁ no 'su-gatiṁ nināya*
*hā hā hatāḥ smo vraja-vāsi-lokāḥ*

*gopyaḥ* — *gopīs; sametya* — coming; *āhuḥ* — said; *aho bata* — alas; *ayam* — this; *kaḥ* — who; *atra* — here; *āgataḥ* — come; *vā* — and; *kim* — what; *idam* — this; *cakāra* — has done; *etām* — to this; *daśām* — condition; *naḥ* — our; *asu* — of the lives; *gatim* — the goal; *nināya* — has brought; *hā hā* — oh, oh; *hatāḥ* — killed; *smaḥ* — we are; *vraja-vāsi* — residing in Vraja; *lokāḥ* — the people.

**Some gopīs came and said, "Look! Who has come here? What has he done? He has put our life and soul into such a state! Alas! Alas! Just see, people of Vraja — now we are all dead!**

COMMENTARY: The *gopīs* didn't know who Gopa-kumāra was, other than some stranger dressed as a cowherd boy.

TEXT 63

कंसस्य मायाविवरस्य भृत्यः
कश्चिद्भविष्यत्ययमत्र नूनम् ।
एवं विलापं विविधं चरन्त्यस्
तमुद्रुदत्यः परिवव्रुरार्ताः ॥

*kaṁsasya māyāvi-varasya bhṛtyaḥ*
*kaścid bhaviṣyaty ayam atra nūnam*
*evaṁ vilāpaṁ vividhaṁ carantyas*
*tam udrudatyaḥ parivavrur ārtāḥ*

*kaṁsasya* — of Kaṁsa; *māyāvi* — the wizard; *varasya* — best; *bhṛtyaḥ* — servant; *kaścit* — some; *bhaviṣyati* — must be; *ayam* — this; *atra* — here; *nūnam* — indeed; *evam* — thus; *vilāpam* — lamentation; *vividham* — various; *carantyaḥ* — carrying on; *tam* — Him (Kṛṣṇa); *udrudatyaḥ* — crying loudly; *parivavruḥ* — they surrounded; *ārtāḥ* — distressed.

**"This must be some servant of that great wizard Kaṁsa." Lamenting like this in many ways, the gopīs cried loudly in distress as they surrounded Kṛṣṇa.**

TEXT 64

अथास्य पृष्ठतो वेगाद् गोपसङ्घाः समागताः ।
दृष्ट्वा तादृगवस्थं तं रुरुदुः करुणस्वरैः ॥

*athāsya pṛṣṭhato vegād*
*gopa-saṅghāḥ samāgatāḥ*
*dṛṣṭvā tādṛg-avasthaṁ taṁ*
*ruruduḥ karuṇa-svaraiḥ*

*atha* — then; *asya* — Him; *pṛṣṭhataḥ* — from behind; *vegāt* — quickly; *gopa-saṅghāḥ* — groups of cowherds; *samāgatāḥ* — approached; *dṛṣṭvā* — seeing; *tādṛk* — such; *avastham* — in a condition; *tam* — Him; *ruruduḥ* — they cried; *karuṇa* — pitiful; *svaraiḥ* — in tones.

**Then, from behind Kṛṣṇa, several groups of cowherds quickly approached. Seeing Him in such a state, they cried with pitiful voices.**

## TEXTS 65–66

तमाक्रन्दध्वनिं घोरं दूराच्छ्रुत्वा व्रजस्थिताः ।
वृद्धा नन्दादयो गोपा यशोदा पुत्रवत्सला ॥

जरत्योऽन्यास्तथा दास्यः सर्वे तत्र समागताः ।
धावन्तः प्रस्खलत्पादा मुग्धा हा हेति वादिनः ॥

*tam ākranda-dhvaniṁ ghoraṁ*
*dūrāc chrutvā vraja-sthitāḥ*
*vṛddhā nandādayo gopā*
*yaśodā putra-vatsalā*

*jaratyo 'nyās tathā dāsyaḥ*
*sarve tatra samāgatāḥ*
*dhāvantaḥ praskhalat-pādā*
*mugdhā hā heti vādinaḥ*

*tam* — that; *ākranda* — of crying; *dhvanim* — the sound; *ghoram* — terrible; *dūrāt* — from afar; *śrutvā* — hearing; *vraja-sthitāḥ* — present in Vraja; *vṛddhāḥ* — elder; *nanda-ādayaḥ* — Nanda and others; *gopāḥ* — cowherds; *yaśodā* — Yaśodā; *putra-vatsalā* — very affectionate to her son; *jaratyaḥ* — elderly ladies; *anyāḥ* — other; *tathā* — also; *dāsyaḥ* — maidservants; *sarve* — all; *tatra* — there; *samāgatāḥ* — assembled; *dhāvantaḥ* — running; *praskhalat* — stumbling; *pādāḥ* — whose feet; *mugdhāḥ* — bewildered; *hā hā* — alas, alas; *iti* — thus; *vādinaḥ* — saying.

**From far away in the village, Nanda and the other elder cowherds heard this terrible sound of crying. So too did Yaśodā, ever affectionate to her son, and so did the other elder ladies and the maidservants. Together they all ran to that place, their feet stumbling on the path. Bewildered, they too cried "Alas! Alas!"**

## TEXT 67

ततो गावो वृषा वत्साः कृष्णसारादयो मृगाः ।
आगतास्तां दशां तस्य दृष्ट्वा रोदनकातराः ॥

*tato gāvo vṛṣā vatsāḥ*
*kṛṣṇasārādayo mṛgāḥ*
*āgatās tāṁ daśāṁ tasya*
*dṛṣṭvā rodana-kātarāḥ*

*tataḥ* — then; *gāvaḥ* — cows; *vṛṣāḥ* — bulls; *vatsāḥ* — calves; *kṛṣṇa-sāra* — black deer; *ādayaḥ* — and others; *mṛgāḥ* — animals; *āgatāḥ* — coming; *tām* — that; *daśām* — condition; *tasya* — His; *dṛṣṭvā* — seeing; *rodana* — with crying; *kātarāḥ* — agonized.

**Then the cows and bulls and calves came there, and the black deer and other animals. Seeing Kṛṣṇa in that state, they wept in agony.**

## TEXT 68

अश्रुधाराभिर्धौतास्या नदन्तः स्नेहतो मृदु ।
आगत्यागत्य जिघ्रन्तो लिहन्त्येतं मुहुर्मुहुः ॥

*aśru-dhārābhir dhautāsyā*
*nadantaḥ snehato mṛdu*
*āgatyāgatya jighranto*
*lihanty etaṁ muhur muhuḥ*

*aśru* — of tears; *dhārābhiḥ* — with floods; *dhauta* — drenched; *āsyāḥ* — their faces; *nadantaḥ* — crying out; *snehataḥ* — out of love; *mṛdu* — gently; *āgatya āgatya* — approaching one by one; *jighrantaḥ* — smelling; *lihanti* — they licked; *etam* — Him; *muhuḥ muhuḥ* — repeatedly.

**The animals, all crying out in love, their faces drenched with floods of tears, approached Kṛṣṇa one by one and gently smelled and licked Him again and again.**

COMMENTARY: The men, women, and animals all spontaneously reacted so desperately because Kṛṣṇa was the exclusive center of their existence.

## TEXT 69

खगास्तस्योपरिष्टाच्च भ्रमन्तो व्योम्नि दुःखिताः ।
रुदन्त इव कुर्वन्ति कोलाहलमनेकशः ॥

*khagās tasyopariṣṭāc ca*
*bhramanto vyomni duḥkhitāḥ*
*rudanta iva kurvanti*
*kolāhalam anekaśaḥ*

*khagāḥ* — birds; *tasya upariṣṭāt* — above Him; *ca* — and; *bhramantaḥ* — flying; *vyomni* — in the sky; *duḥkhitāḥ* — miserable; *rudantaḥ* — crying; *iva* — as if; *kurvanti* — they made; *kolāhalam* — a tumultuous noise; *anekaśaḥ* — in great numbers.

**Great numbers of birds, flying overhead, told also of their misery by making a tumultuous noise that sounded like people crying.**

COMMENTARY: The birds roaming in the sky could not discern exactly what was going on below, but they responded sympathetically nonetheless.

## TEXT 70

स्थावराश्चान्तरुत्तप्ताः सद्यः शुष्का इवाभवन् ।
बहुनोक्तेन किं सर्वे मृता इव चराचराः ॥

*sthāvarāś cāntar uttaptāḥ*
*sadyaḥ śuṣkā ivābhavan*
*bahunoktena kiṁ sarve*
*mṛtā iva carācarāḥ*

*sthāvarāḥ* — the nonmoving creatures; *ca* — also; *antaḥ* — within themselves; *uttaptāḥ* — greatly pained; *sadyaḥ* — suddenly; *śuṣkāḥ* — dried up; *iva* — as if; *abhavan* — became; *bahunā* — much more; *uktena* — with speaking; *kim* — what is the use; *sarve* — all; *mṛtāḥ* — dead; *iva* — almost; *cara-acarāḥ* — moving and nonmoving beings.

**And the immobile creatures, in great pain within, seemed suddenly to dry up. What more is there to say? All beings, moving and nonmoving, were on the verge of death.**

## TEXT 71

अहं महाशोकसमुद्रमग्नः
स्वकृत्यमूढः परमार्तिमाप्तः ।
निधाय तत्पादयुगं स्वमस्ते
रुदन्प्रवृत्तो बहुधा विलापे ॥

*ahaṁ mahā-śoka-samudra-magnaḥ*
*sva-kṛtya-mūḍhaḥ paramārtim āptaḥ*
*nidhāya tat-pāda-yugaṁ sva-maste*
*rudan pravṛtto bahudhā vilāpe*

*aham* — I; *mahā* — vast; *śoka* — of sorrow; *samudra* — in an ocean; *magnaḥ* — drowning; *sva* — by me; *kṛtya* — about what should be done; *mūḍhaḥ* — bewildered; *parama* — most severe; *ārtim* — torment; *āptaḥ* — experiencing; *nidhāya* — placing; *tat* — His; *pāda-yugam* — two feet; *sva-maste* — on my head; *rudan* — sobbing; *pravṛttaḥ* — began; *bahudhā* — in various ways; *vilāpe* — lamenting.

**As for me, I was drowning in a vast ocean of sorrow. Confused about what to do, severely tormented, I put Kṛṣṇa's feet on my head and began profusely sobbing and lamenting.**

COMMENTARY: When he put Kṛṣṇa's feet on his head, he could see how beautiful, soft, and attractive they were.

## TEXT 72

विदूरवर्ती बलभद्रदेवो
ऽनुजोपमाकल्पवयोऽभिरामः ।
नीलाम्बरालंकृतगौरकान्तिस्
ततः समायात्सभयं सवेगम् ॥

*vidūra-vartī balabhadra-devo*
*'nujopamākalpa-vayo-'bhirāmaḥ*
*nīlāmbarālaṅkṛta-gaura-kāntis*
*tataḥ samāyāt sa-bhayaṁ sa-vegam*

*vidūra* — far away; *vartī* — located; *balabhadra-devaḥ* — Lord Balabhadra; *anuja* — His younger brother; *upama* — like; *ākalpa* — by whose dress; *vayaḥ* — and age; *abhirāmaḥ* — charming; *nīla* — blue; *ambara* — with a garment; *alaṅkṛta* — adorned; *gaura-kāntiḥ* — white-complexioned; *tataḥ* — then; *samāyāt* — approached; *sa-bhayam* — fearful; *sa-vegam* — quickly.

**Then Lord Balabhadra, Kṛṣṇa's older brother, quickly arrived from some distance away, full of fear. White-**

**complexioned and arrayed in blue garments, He appeared charming, for He was the same age as Kṛṣṇa and as nicely dressed.**

COMMENTARY: Unable to keep up with Kṛṣṇa when Kṛṣṇa had run to meet Gopa-kumāra, Balarāma had fallen behind with the other cowherd boys. But now He anxiously hurried forward, concerned for Kṛṣṇa's safety. Gopa-kumāra saw that Balarāma was of the same *kiśora* age as Nanda-nandana, but differed from Him in being white like the fibers in a lotus stem and being dressed in blue.

## TEXT 73

विशारदेन्द्रः परितो विलोक्य
रुदन्क्षणाद्धैर्यमिवावलम्ब्य ।
मदीयदोर्भ्यामनुजस्य कण्ठं
सङ्ग्राहयामास निजप्रयत्नात् ॥

*viśāradendraḥ parito vilokya*
*rudan kṣaṇād dhairyam ivāvalambya*
*madīya-dorbhyām anujasya kaṇṭhaṁ*
*saṅgrāhayām āsa nija-prayatnāt*

*viśārada-indraḥ* — the most skillful of persons (Balarāma); *paritaḥ* — on all sides; *vilokya* — looking; *rudan* — and crying; *kṣaṇāt* — after a moment; *dhairyam* — His composure; *iva* — as if; *avalambya* — regaining; *madīya* — my; *dorbhyām* — with the arms; *anujasya* — of His younger brother; *kaṇṭham* — the neck; *saṅgrāhayām āsa* — made hold; *nija-prayatnāt* — with all His might.

**Lord Balabhadra, that most skillful of persons, cried for a moment but then seemed to regain His composure and looked all around. With great care and attention, He made me hold His younger brother by the neck with my arms.**

Dec 20



COMMENTARY: At first Balarāma cried in distress to see Kṛṣṇa in such a condition. But He quickly gathered His wits and looked all around to find out what had made Kṛṣṇa faint.

## TEXT 74

सम्मार्जयामास मदीयपाणिना
श्रीमत्तदङ्गानि तथा तमुच्चकैः ।
आह्वाययामास विचित्रकाकुभिः
प्रोत्थापयामास मयैव भूतलात् ॥

*sammārjayām āsa madīya-pāṇinā*
*śrīmat-tad-aṅgāni tathā tam uccakaiḥ*
*āhvāyayām āsa vicitra-kākubhiḥ*
*protthāpayām āsa mayaiva bhū-talāt*

*sammārjayām āsa* — He caused to be wiped; *madīya* — my; *pāṇinā* — with the hand; *śrīmat* — beautiful; *tat* — His (Kṛṣṇa's); *aṅgāni* — limbs; *tathā* — and; *tam* — to Him; *uccakaiḥ* — in a loud voice; *āhvāyayām āsa* — made me call; *vicitra* — various; *kākubhiḥ* — with plaintive cries; *protthāpayām āsa* — He caused to be lifted; *mayā* — by me; *eva* — only; *bhū-talāt* — from the ground.

**He wiped Kṛṣṇa's beautiful limbs clean with my hand and made me loudly call out to Him with many plaintive cries. Then He made me lift Kṛṣṇa up from the ground.**

## TEXT 75

सद्योऽश्रुधारापरिमुद्रिते ते
श्रीनेत्रपद्मे उदमीलयत्सः ।
मां वीक्ष्य हर्षात्परिरभ्य चुम्बन्
लज्जामगच्छत्परितोऽवलोक्य ॥

*sadyo 'śru-dhārā-parimudrite te*
*śrī-netra-padme udamīlayat saḥ*
*māṁ vīkṣya harṣāt parirabhya cumban*
*lajjām agacchat parito 'valokya*

*sadyaḥ* — suddenly; *aśru-dhārā* — by a flood of tears; *parimudrite* — which were sealed; *te* — the two; *śrī* — beautiful; *netra-padme* — lotus eyes; *udamīlayat* — opened; *saḥ* — He (Kṛṣṇa); *mām* — me; *vīkṣya* — seeing; *harṣāt* — joyfully; *parirabhya* — He embraced; *cumban* — kissing; *lajjām* — embarrassment; *agacchat* — He obtained; *paritaḥ* — all around; *avalokya* — looking.

**Suddenly Kṛṣṇa opened His eyes, sealed till then by a flood of tears. Seeing me, He joyfully embraced and kissed me. But then He looked around and became embarrassed.**

COMMENTARY: Kṛṣṇa had become helplessly bewildered by love for His friend, and He was embarrassed by the thought that from His tearful reaction to Gopa-kumāra's arrival everyone could see this.

## TEXT 76

चिरादृष्टप्राणप्रियसखमिवावाप्य स तु मां
करे धृत्वा वामस्वकरकमलेन प्रभुवरः ।
विचित्रं सम्प्रश्नं विदधदखिलांस्तान्व्रजजनान्
समानन्द्य श्रीमानविशदिभगामी व्रजवरम् ॥

*cirādṛṣṭa-prāṇa-priya-sakham ivāvāpya sa tu māṁ*
*kare dhṛtvā vāma-sva-kara-kamalena prabhu-varaḥ*
*vicitraṁ sampraśnaṁ vidadhad akhilāṁs tān vraja-janān*
*samānandya śrīmān aviśad ibha-gāmī vraja-varam*

*cira* — for a long time; *adṛṣṭa* — not seen; *prāṇa-priya* — as dear as His own life; *sakham* — a friend; *iva* — as if; *avāpya* —

obtaining; *saḥ* — He; *tu* — and; *mām* — me; *kare* — by the hand; *dhṛtvā* — taking; *vāma* — left side; *sva-kara-kamalena* — by His lotus hand; *prabhu-varaḥ* — the best of Lords; *vicitram* — various; *sampraśnam* — questions; *vidadhat* — presenting; *akhilān* — all; *tān* — them; *vraja-janān* — the people of Vraja; *samānandya* — greeting; *śrīmān* — the blessed Lord; *aviśat* — entered; *ibha-gāmī* — with the gait of an elephant; *vraja* — the cowherd village; *varam* — best.

**That best of Lords took my hand in His own — His own left lotus hand — and received me as a long-lost bosom friend. He asked me various questions. Then He greeted all the people of Vraja and entered the best of cowherd villages with the gait of an elephant.**

COMMENTARY: Kṛṣṇa's closest friends are as dear to Him as life itself. Holding Gopa-kumāra's hand, Kṛṣṇa welcomed him with such questions as "Dear friend, are you healthy and happy?"

## TEXT 77

वन्या मृगास्तस्य वियोगदीना
गन्तुं विना तं हि कुतोऽप्यशक्ताः ।
प्रातर्भविष्यत्प्रभुदर्शनाशास्
तस्थुर्व्रजद्वारि निशां नयन्तः ॥

*vanyā mṛgās tasya viyoga-dīnā*
*gantuṁ vinā taṁ hi kuto 'py aśaktāḥ*
*prātar-bhaviṣyat-prabhu-darśanāśās*
*tasthur vraja-dvāri niśāṁ nayantaḥ*

*vanyāḥ* — of the forest; *mṛgāḥ* — the animals; *tasya* — from Him; *viyoga* — because of separation; *dīnāḥ* — miserable; *gantum* — to go; *vinā* — without; *tam* — Him; *hi* — indeed; *kutaḥ api* — anywhere; *aśaktāḥ* — unable; *prātaḥ* — in the morning; *bhaviṣyat* — upcoming; *prabhu* — of the Lord; *darśana*

— for the seeing; *āśāḥ* — whose hope; *tasthuḥ* — they stood; *vraja* — of the cowherd village; *dvāri* — at the entrance; *niśām* — the night; *nayantaḥ* — spending.

**The forest animals were miserable because now they had to part from Him. Unable to go anywhere without Him, they simply stood at the entrance of the village, ready to spend the entire night there in the hope of seeing their Lord again the next morning.**

## TEXT 78

उड्डीयोड्डीय पश्यन्तो विहगास्तं व्रजान्तरे ।
रात्रावदृष्ट्वा क्रोशन्तो रुदन्त इव निर्ययुः ॥

*uḍḍīyoḍḍīya paśyanto*
*vihagās taṁ vrajāntare*
*rātrāv adṛṣṭvā krośanto*
*rudanta iva niryayuḥ*

*uḍḍīya uḍḍīya* — flying high in various directions; *paśyantaḥ* — watching; *vihagāḥ* — the birds; *tam* — Him; *vraja-antare* — in the cowherd village; *rātrau* — at night; *adṛṣṭvā* — not seeing; *krośantaḥ* — making loud noises; *rudantaḥ* — crying; *iva* — like; *niryayuḥ* — they flew away.

**The birds flew here and there high over the village to watch Him, but when night came and they could no longer see Him they cried out as if weeping and flew away.**

COMMENTARY: All the creatures in Goloka, including the jungle beasts and the birds, are fixed in unalloyed devotion to Kṛṣṇa.

## TEXT 79

गोदोहनानन्तरमाग्रहेण
नन्दस्य पुत्रप्रणयाकुलस्य ।

सम्भालनं साधु गवामकृत्वा
तौ भ्रातरौ जग्मतुरात्मगेहम् ॥

*go-dohanānantaram āgraheṇa*
*nandasya putra-praṇayākulasya*
*sambhālanaṁ sādhu gavām akṛtvā*
*tau bhrātarau jagmatur ātma-geham*

*go* — of the cows; *dohana* — the milking; *anantaram* — after; *āgraheṇa* — on the insistence; *nandasya* — of Nanda; *putra* — for his sons; *praṇaya* — with affection; *ākulasya* — who was feeling anxious; *sambhālanam* — attention; *sādhu* — properly; *gavām* — to the cows; *akṛtvā* — without giving; *tau* — the two; *bhrātarau* — brothers; *jagmatuḥ* — went; *ātma* — Their; *geham* — to the home.

**At the insistence of Nanda Mahārāja, who was anxious with love for his sons, just after milking the cows the two brothers went to Their home. They went home at once, not even giving the cows proper attention.**

COMMENTARY: Nanda Mahārāja anxiously told Kṛṣṇa, "My boy, You must be tired from so much wandering in the forest. Go home with Your elder brother and take Your bath. I will look after the cows. Please don't delay any longer or Your mother will be unhappy and scold me. Please cooperate and go right now."

TEXT 80

स्नेहस्नुवत्स्तन्यदृगश्रुधारया
धौताम्बराङ्ग्या त्वरया यशोदया ।
भूत्वा पुरोऽकारि सरोहिणीकया
प्रत्यङ्गनीराजनमेतयोर्मुहुः ॥

*sneha-snuvat-stanya-dṛg-aśru-dhārayā*
*dhautāmbarāṅgyā tvarayā yaśodayā*

*bhūtvā puro 'kāri sa-rohiṇīkayā*
*praty-aṅga-nīrājanam etayor muhuḥ*

*sneha* — due to love; *snuvat* — flowing; *stanya* — milk; *dṛk* — from her eyes; *aśru* — of tears; *dhārayā* — with a flood; *dhauta* — washed; *ambara* — her clothing; *aṅgyā* — and body; *tvarayā* — quickly; *yaśodayā* — Yaśodā; *bhūtvā* — coming; *puraḥ* — in front; *akāri* — did; *sa-rohiṇīkayā* — along with Rohiṇī; *prati-aṅga* — of all the limbs; *nīrājanam* — worship by offering of lamps; *etayoḥ* — of the two of Them; *muhuḥ* — repeatedly.

**Mother Yaśodā quickly came to meet the boys, her clothing and body wet with the milk flowing from her breasts and the tears that flooded from her eyes in love. Together with Rohiṇī, she worshiped each limb of both brothers again and again.**

COMMENTARY: The mothers of the two boys worshiped Them by offering *ārati* to all the parts of Their bodies.

## TEXT 81

नीराजयन्त्यात्मशिरोरुहैः सुतं
सालिङ्गति स्नेहभरेण चुम्बति ।
नो वेत्ति रक्षिष्यति शीर्ष्णि किं निजे
वक्षोऽन्तरे वा जठरान्तरे वा ॥

*nīrājayanty ātma-śiroruhaiḥ sutaṁ*
*sāliṅgati sneha-bhareṇa cumbati*
*no vetti rakṣiṣyati śīrṣṇi kiṁ nije*
*vakṣo-'ntare vā jaṭharāntare vā*

*nīrājayantī* — performing the *ārati* ceremony; *ātma* — her own; *śiroruhaiḥ* — with the hair; *sutam* — her son; *sā* — she (Yaśodā); *āliṅgati* — embraced; *sneha-bhareṇa* — full of love; *cumbati* — kissed; *na* — not; *u* — indeed; *vetti* — she could decide; *rakṣiṣyati* — will keep; *śīrṣṇi* — on her head; *kim* — or; *nije* — her own; *vakṣaḥ-antare* — on the breast; *vā* — or; *jaṭhara-antare* — in the womb; *vā* — or.

**Yaśodā performed ārati to her son Kṛṣṇa by caressing Him with her own hair, and affectionately embraced and kissed Him. She couldn't decide whether she ought to keep Him on her head, at her breast, or within her womb to protect Him.**

TEXT 82

तत्रैव नीतं प्रणयाकुलेन मां
तेन स्वयं कारितमातृवन्दनम् ।
सा लालयामास मुदा स्वपुत्रवद्
दृष्ट्वा मयि प्रेमभरं सुतस्य तम् ॥

*tatraiva nītaṁ praṇayākulena māṁ*
*tena svayaṁ kārita-mātṛ-vandanam*
*sā lālayām āsa mudā sva-putra-vad*
*dṛṣṭvā mayi prema-bharaṁ sutasya tam*

*tatra* — there; *eva* — just; *nītam* — brought; *praṇaya* — by love; *ākulena* — who was anxious; *mām* — me; *tena svayam* — by Himself; *kārita* — made to do; *mātṛ* — to His mother; *vandanam* — offering of respects; *sā* — she; *lālayām āsa* — caressed; *mudā* — happily; *sva* — own; *putra-vat* — just like a son; *dṛṣṭvā* — seeing; *mayi* — for me; *prema* — of love; *bharam* — the abundance; *sutasya* — of her son; *tam* — that.

**Kṛṣṇa, anxious with love for me, brought me there outside His home and had me offer respects to her. And Mother Yaśodā, seeing the great love Kṛṣṇa had for me, happily caressed me as though I were her own son.**

COMMENTARY: Inspired by Kṛṣṇa's obvious love for Gopa-kumāra, Yaśodā also took Gopa-kumāra on her lap and embraced him. She had seen how enthusiastically Kṛṣṇa had greeted him when he and Kṛṣṇa had first met on the road.

## TEXT 83

तावदागत्य मिलिता युगपत्तत्र गोपिकाः ।
काश्चिद्व्याजेन केनापि काश्चित्सर्वानपेक्षया ॥

*tāvad āgatya militā*
*yugapat tatra gopikāḥ*
*kāścid vyājena kenāpi*
*kāścit sarvānapekṣayā*

*tāvat* — then; *āgatya* — coming; *militāḥ* — met; *yugapat* — all at once; *tatra* — there; *gopikāḥ* — the *gopīs;* *kāścit* — some; *vyājena* — by an excuse; *kena api* — some; *kāścit* — some; *sarva* — everyone; *anapekṣayā* — disregarding.

**Then the gopīs all arrived there at once. Some had made excuses for coming, and others had paid no regard to what anyone thought.**

COMMENTARY: The *gopīs* were beyond concern for public opinion and ordinary religious principles.

## TEXTS 84–85

मातृभ्यां स्नापनारम्भं द्वाभ्यां भ्रात्रोर्द्वयोः कृतम् ।
आलक्ष्य भगवानाह बलुवीररतिलम्पटः ॥

मातरौ भ्रातरावावां क्षुधार्तौ स्वस्तदोदनम् ।
निष्पाद्य भोजयेथां नौ तातमानाय्य सत्वरम् ॥

*mātṛbhyāṁ snāpanārambhaṁ*
*dvābhyāṁ bhrātror dvayoḥ kṛtam*

*ālakṣya bhagavān āha*
*ballavī-rati-lampaṭaḥ*

*mātarau bhrātarāv āvāṁ*
*kṣudhārtau svas tad odanam*
*niṣpādya bhojayethāṁ nau*
*tātam ānāyya satvaram*

*mātṛbhyām* — by the mothers; *snāpana* — of bathing; *ārambham* — the commencement; *dvābhyām* — by the two; *bhrātroḥ* — of the brothers; *dvayoḥ* — two; *kṛtam* — done; *ālakṣya* — seeing; *bhagavān* — the Lord; *āha* — said; *ballavī* — with the cowherd girls; *rati* — for intimate enjoyment; *lampaṭaḥ* — eager; *mātarau* — O mothers; *bhrātarau* — the two brothers; *āvām* — We; *kṣudhā* — by hunger; *ārtau* — distressed; *svaḥ* — are; *tat* — therefore; *odanam* — rice; *niṣpādya* — preparing; *bhojayethām* — please feed; *nau* — Us; *tātam* — father; *ānāyya* — bringing; *satvaram* — quickly.

**Mother Yaśodā and Mother Rohiṇī got ready to bathe Kṛṣṇa and His brother. But when Lord Kṛṣṇa saw this, being eager to enjoy with the cowherd girls, He said, "Dear mothers, We brothers are very hungry. So please make some rice, send for Our father, and feed Us right away."**

## TEXT 86

तच्छ्रुत्वाहुः प्रियं गोप्यः श्रीयशोदे व्रजेश्वरि ।
देवि रोहिणि कर्तव्यादस्माद्विरमतां युवाम् ॥

*tac chrutvāhuḥ priyaṁ gopyaḥ*
*śrī-yaśode vrajeśvari*
*devi rohiṇi kartavyād*
*asmād viramatāṁ yuvām*

*tat* — that; *śrutvā* — hearing; *āhuḥ* — said; *priyam* — affectionately; *gopyaḥ* — the *gopīs; śrī-yaśode* — O Śrī Yaśodā; *vraja-*

*īśvari* — Queen of Vraja; *devi* — divine; *rohiṇi* — O Rohiṇī; *kartavyāt* — from the work; *asmāt* — this; *viramatām* — please desist; *yuvām* — you.

**Upon hearing those words, the gopīs said affectionately: Śrī Yaśodā, Queen of Vraja, and dear Rohiṇī-devī, please set this work of bathing aside.**

COMMENTARY: The *gopīs* were happy to hear Kṛṣṇa's request because it gave them an excuse for sending away Mother Yaśodā, Rohiṇī, and Balarāma.

## TEXT 87

शीघ्रं भोजनसामग्रीं सम्पादयतमेतयोः ।
वयमेव सुखं सम्यक्स्नापयेमाचिरादिमौ ॥

*śīghraṁ bhojana-sāmagrīṁ*
*sampādayatam etayoḥ*
*vayam eva sukhaṁ samyak*
*snāpayemācirād imau*

*śīghram* — quickly; *bhojana* — for feeding; *sāmagrīm* — the items; *sampādayatam* — please prepare; *etayoḥ* — of these two; *vayam* — we; *eva* — only; *sukham* — happily; *samyak* — properly; *snāpayema* — will bathe; *acirāt* — without delay; *imau* — Them.

**Please quickly prepare everything to feed these two boys. We shall gladly give Them a proper bath without delay.**

## TEXT 88

श्रीयशोदोवाच
प्रथमं त्वरया ज्येष्ठः स्नापयित्वा प्रहीयताम् ।
नन्दस्यानयनायात्र भोजनार्थाय बालिकाः ॥

*śrī-yaśodovāca*
*prathamaṁ tvarayā jyeṣṭhaḥ*
*snāpayitvā prahīyatām*
*nandasyānayanāyātra*
*bhojanārthāya bālikāḥ*

*śrī-yaśodā uvāca* — Śrī Yaśodā said; *prathamam* — first; *tvarayā* — quickly; *jyeṣṭhaḥ* — the elder boy; *snāpayitvā* — having bathed; *prahīyatām* — send Him; *nandasya* — of Nanda; *ānayanāya* — for bringing; *atra* — here; *bhojana-arthāya* — for the meal; *bālikāḥ* — O girls.

**Śrī Yaśodā said: Dear girls, first quickly bathe the older boy. Then send Him to fetch Nanda for the meal.**

COMMENTARY: Unsuspecting, Yaśodā addressed the *gopīs* as *bālikāḥ,* innocent girls.

## TEXT 89

श्रीसरूप उवाच
प्रशस्य तद्वचो हृद्यं रामं ताः कतिचिद् द्रुतम् ।
आप्लाव्य प्रेषयामासुस्तयोर्गेहं प्रविष्टयोः ॥

*śrī-sarūpa uvāca*
*praśasya tad-vaco hṛdyaṁ*
*rāmaṁ tāḥ katicid drutam*
*āplāvya preṣayām āsus*
*tayor gehaṁ praviṣṭayoḥ*

*śrī-sarūpaḥ uvāca* — Śrī Sarūpa said; *praśasya* — praising; *tat-vacaḥ* — her words; *hṛdyam* — welcome; *rāmam* — Balarāma; *tāḥ* — they; *katicit* — some; *drutam* — quickly; *āplāvya* — bathing; *preṣayām āsuḥ* — dispatched; *tayoḥ* — the two of them (Yaśodā and Rohiṇī); *geham* — the house; *praviṣṭayoḥ* — while they entered.

**Śrī Sarūpa said: Welcoming and praising Yaśodā's words, several of the gopīs quickly bathed Balarāma and sent Him off. Meanwhile, the two mothers went into the house.**

COMMENTARY: Gopa-kumāra has now assumed his original identity as Kṛṣṇa's friend Sarūpa. From now on he will be referred to by that name.

In the presence of Kṛṣṇa's elder brother, the *gopīs* were shy. They were not able to relax and enjoy His company as they did Kṛṣṇa's. Therefore they were glad to see Balarāma and the two mothers go as soon as possible.

## TEXT 90

श्रीकृष्णस्य विचित्राणि भूषणानि विभागशः ।
क्रमेणोत्तार्य ताः स्वीयैर्वस्त्रैर्गात्राण्यमार्जयन् ॥

*śrī-kṛṣṇasya vicitrāṇi*
*bhūṣaṇāni vibhāgaśaḥ*
*krameṇottārya tāḥ svīyair*
*vastrair gātrāṇy amārjayan*

*śrī-kṛṣṇasya* — of Śrī Kṛṣṇa; *vicitrāṇi* — various; *bhūṣaṇāni* — the ornaments; *vibhāgaśaḥ* — dividing up the services; *krameṇa* — gradually; *uttārya* — removing; *tāḥ* — they (the *gopīs*); *svīyaiḥ* — their own; *vastraiḥ* — with the garments; *gātrāṇi* — His limbs; *amārjayan* — they wiped.

**The gopīs divided up the service among themselves. They removed Kṛṣṇa's various ornaments one by one and wiped His limbs with their own garments.**

COMMENTARY: There were many *gopīs* who wanted to serve Kṛṣṇa, too many for all of them to do the same thing at once, so they divided the tasks. One *gopī* took off one of Kṛṣṇa's ornaments, a different *gopī* another, and so on. They did the preliminary wiping either with cloths they had brought from their homes or with their own shawls.

## TEXT 91

वंशीं सपत्नीमिव याच्यमानां
ताभिः कराब्जाच्च जिघृक्ष्यमाणाम् ।
सङ्केतभंग्या स तु मां प्रबोध्य
चिक्षेप दूरान्मम मुक्तहस्ते ॥

*vaṁśīṁ sapatnīm iva yācyamānāṁ*
*tābhiḥ karābjāc ca jighṛkṣyamāṇām*
*saṅketa-bhaṅgyā sa tu māṁ prabodhya*
*cikṣepa dūrān mama mukta-haste*

*vaṁśīm* — the flute; *sapatnīm* — a rival consort; *iva* — as if; *yācyamānām* — being asked for; *tābhiḥ* — by them; *kara-abjāt* — from the lotus hand; *ca* — and; *jighṛkṣyamāṇām* — which they wanted to take; *saṅketa-bhaṅgyā* — with the sign of a gesture; *saḥ* — He; *tu* — and; *mām* — to me; *prabodhya* — alerting; *cikṣepa* — threw; *dūrāt* — at a distance; *mama* — my; *mukta* — open; *haste* — into the hand.

**But when they asked for His flute, who was like their rival consort, and tried to snatch it from His lotus hand, Kṛṣṇa made a sign to alert me and threw it from a distance into my open palm.**

COMMENTARY: The *gopīs* were removing Kṛṣṇa's ornaments one after another, but He didn't want the girls to take His flute. The girls, seeing the flute as a competitor for the nectar of His lips, had some ill feelings toward it and might dispose of it. As it was, several of the girls were greedily demanding, "Give it to me! No, give it to me!" and were threatening to rip it away by force. Therefore Kṛṣṇa raised His eyebrows to signal Sarūpa, who was standing some distance behind Him, and swiftly threw it into Sarūpa's outstretched hand.

## TEXT 92

अभ्यज्योत्तमतैलैस्ताः कर्तुमुद्वर्तनं शनैः ।
आरेभिरे स्वहस्ताब्जकोमलस्पर्शपाटवैः ॥

*abhyajyottama-tailais tāḥ*
*kartum udvartanaṁ śanaiḥ*
*ārebhire sva-hastābja-*
*komala-sparśa-pāṭavaiḥ*

*abhyajya* — smearing; *uttama* — fine; *tailaiḥ* — with oils; *tāḥ* — they (the *gopīs*); *kartum* — to do; *udvartanam* — removal of the excess oil; *śanaiḥ* — slowly; *ārebhire* — began; *sva* — their own; *hasta-abja* — with the lotus hands; *komala* — soft; *sparśa* — in touching; *pāṭavaiḥ* — which were expert.

**The gopīs smeared fine oils on Kṛṣṇa and slowly removed the excess with their soft lotus hands, expert in touch.**

## TEXT 93

तथापि सौकुमार्याद्वा लीलाकौतुकतोऽपि वा ।
स करोत्यार्तिसीत्कारं समं श्रीमुखभङ्गिभिः ॥

*tathāpi saukumāryād vā*
*līlā-kautukato 'pi vā*
*sa karoty ārti-sītkāraṁ*
*samaṁ śrī-mukha-bhaṅgibhiḥ*

*tathā api* — nonetheless; *saukumāryāt* — because of His tenderness; *vā* — or; *līlā* — playful; *kautukataḥ* — out of naughtiness; *api vā* — or else; *saḥ* — He; *karoti* — made; *ārti* — of pain; *sīt-kāram* — a sound made by suddenly drawing in one's breath; *samam* — along with; *śrī* — beautiful; *mukha* — of His face; *bhaṅgibhiḥ* — with distortions.

**Yet Kṛṣṇa, either because His body was so tender or else simply out of playful naughtiness, suddenly drew in His breath, making a sound of pain, and distorted His beautiful face.**

## TEXT 94

पुत्रैकप्राणयाकर्ण्य तं तदार्तिस्वरं तया ।
बहिर्भूयाशु किं वृत्तं किं वृत्तमिति पृच्छ्यते ॥

*putraika-prāṇayākarṇya*
*taṁ tad-ārti-svaraṁ tayā*
*bahir-bhūyāśu kiṁ vṛttaṁ*
*kiṁ vṛttam iti pṛcchyate*

*putra* — for her son; *eka* — only; *prāṇayā* — whose life; *ākarṇya* — hearing; *tam* — that; *tat* — His; *ārti* — of pain; *svaram* — sound; *tayā* — by her (Yaśodā); *bahiḥ* — outside; *bhūya* — coming; *āśu* — quickly; *kim vṛttam* — what has happened; *kim vṛttam* — what has happened; *iti* — thus; *pṛcchyate* — was asked.

**His mother, her life dedicated only to His welfare, heard that sound and quickly came outside and asked, "What has happened? What has happened?"**

## TEXT 95

सुतस्य सस्मितं वक्त्रं वीक्ष्याथो विश्यते गृहम् ।
ताभिस्तु सस्मितत्रासं गीतैर्निष्पाद्यतेऽस्य तत् ॥

*sutasya sa-smitaṁ vaktraṁ*
*vīkṣyātho viśyate gṛham*

*tābhis tu sa-smita-trāsaṁ*
*gītair niṣpādyate 'sya tat*

*sutasya* — of the son; *sa-smitam* — smiling; *vaktram* — face; *vīkṣya* — seeing; *atha u* — then; *viśyate* — was entered; *gṛham* — the house; *tābhiḥ* — by them; *tu* — but; *sa-smita* — with laughter; *trāsam* — and fear; *gītaiḥ* — with singing; *niṣpādyate* — was finished; *asya* — His; *tat* — that.

**But when she saw her son's smiling face she went back into the house. And the gopīs, laughing yet afraid, started to sing as they finished Kṛṣṇa's massage.**

COMMENTARY: The *gopīs* were amused by Kṛṣṇa's false show of pain and frightened by Mother Yaśodā's rebuke. They started singing not only because He was very fond of songs but also because they wanted to prevent Mother Yaśodā from hearing any further outcries.

## TEXT 96

अथ कोष्णैः सुवासैस्तं यामुनैर्निर्मलैर्जलैः ।
सलीलं स्नापयामासू रत्नकुम्भघटीभृतैः ॥

*atha koṣṇaiḥ su-vāsais taṁ*
*yāmunair nirmalair jalaiḥ*
*sa-līlaṁ snāpayām āsū*
*ratna-kumbha-ghaṭī-bhṛtaiḥ*

*atha* — next; *ka-uṣṇaiḥ* — warm; *su-vāsaiḥ* — fragrant; *tam* — Him; *yāmunaiḥ* — of the Yamunā; *nirmalaiḥ* — clear; *jalaiḥ* — with water; *sa-līlam* — playfully; *snāpayām āsuḥ* — they bathed; *ratna-kumbha* — in jewel-studded vessels; *ghaṭī* — and small clay pots; *bhṛtaiḥ* — which was carried.

**Next they playfully bathed Him with warm, clear, fragrant**

**water, carried from the Yamunā in jewel-studded vessels and small clay pots.**

COMMENTARY: Careful to make Kṛṣṇa's bath water just slightly warm, not hot, the *gopīs* used the freshest, most fragrant water they could find, namely water from the river Yamunā.

## TEXT 97

नीतैः स्वस्वगृहान्मालालेपनाम्बरभूषणैः ।
विचित्रैर्नटवेषेणाभूषयंस्तं यथारुचि ॥

*nītaiḥ sva-sva-gṛhān mālā-*
*lepanāmbara-bhūṣaṇaiḥ*
*vicitrair naṭa-veṣeṇā-*
*bhūṣayaṁs taṁ yathā-ruci*

*nītaiḥ* — brought; *sva-sva* — each from her own; *gṛhāt* — house; *mālā* — with garlands; *lepana* — perfumed pastes; *ambara* — clothes; *bhūṣaṇaiḥ* — and ornaments; *vicitraiḥ* — various; *naṭa-veṣeṇa* — with the dress of a dramatic performer; *abhūṣayan* — they decorated; *tam* — Him; *yathā-ruci* — according to His taste.

**They dressed Him like an actor and decorated Him the way He liked, with clothes, jewelry, wonderful garlands, and perfumed pastes, all brought from their homes.**

COMMENTARY: *Yathā-ruci* can be understood to mean either "according to His taste" or "according to their taste." In any event, His taste and theirs were the same.

## TEXT 98

भोग्यं च निभृतं किञ्चिद्भोजयित्वोक्तवस्तुभिः ।
मुहुर्नीराजनं कृत्वा दधुस्तानि स्वमूर्धसु ॥

*bhogyaṁ ca nibhṛtaṁ kiñcid*
*bhojayitvokta-vastubhiḥ*
*muhur nīrājanaṁ kṛtvā*
*dadhus tāni sva-mūrdhasu*

*bhogyam* — food; *ca* — and; *nibhṛtam* — secretly; *kiñcit* — some; *bhojayitvā* — feeding; *ukta* — prescribed; *vastubhiḥ* — with items; *muhuḥ* — again and again; *nīrājanam* — worship; *kṛtvā* — doing; *dadhuḥ* — they placed; *tāni* — those items; *sva-mūrdhasu* — on their own heads.

**They stealthily fed Him something, worshiped Him again and again with prescribed items, and then placed those items on their heads.**

COMMENTARY: The *gopīs* stealthily fed Kṛṣṇa butter and other nice food. They wanted to keep these dealings confidential, and they specifically wanted to keep Yaśodā from finding out and becoming angry that Kṛṣṇa was being fed between meals and might therefore get indigestion. After feeding Him, the *gopīs* worshiped Him with standard paraphernalia, such as camphor lamps and mustard seeds.

## TEXT 99

दिव्यचन्दनकाश्मीरकस्तुरीपङ्कमुद्रया ।
गलभालकपोलादौ चित्रयामासुरद्भुतम् ॥

*divya-candana-kāśmīra-*
*kasturī-paṅka-mudrayā*
*gala-bhāla-kapolādau*
*citrayām āsur adbhutam*

*divya* — first-class; *candana* — of sandal paste; *kāśmīra* — saffron; *kasturī* — musk; *paṅka* — and clay; *mudrayā* — with marks; *gala* — His throat; *bhāla* — forehead; *kapola* — cheeks; *ādau* — and so on; *citrayām āsuḥ* — they decorated; *adbhutam* — wonderfully.

**They decorated His throat, His forehead, His cheeks, and so on with wonderful designs made with first-class pastes of sandal, saffron, and musk.**

TEXT 100

सभावं वीक्ष्यमाणास्ता हस्तं संस्तभ्य यत्नतः ।
प्रवृत्ता नेत्रकमले तस्योज्ज्वलयितुं मुदा ॥

*sa-bhāvaṁ vīkṣyamāṇās tā*
*hastaṁ saṁstabhya yatnataḥ*
*pravṛttā netra-kamale*
*tasyojjvalayituṁ mudā*

*sa-bhāvam* — with love; *vīkṣyamāṇāḥ* — being looked at; *tāḥ* — they; *hastam* — their hands; *saṁstabhya* — keeping steady; *yatnataḥ* — with endeavor; *pravṛttāḥ* — they became engaged; *netra-kamale* — the lotus eyes; *tasya* — His; *ujjvalayitum* — to make brilliant; *mudā* — with pleasure.

**While He lovingly gazed at the gopīs, they tried hard to keep their hands steady, as with pleasure they set about daubing collyrium on His lotus eyes to make them shine.**

COMMENTARY: Because Kṛṣṇa's loving glance made the *gopīs* ecstatic, their hands began to tremble, and they had difficulty applying Kṛṣṇa's *kajjala* neatly.

TEXT 101

वन्यक्रीडासुखं कृष्णो भूरिशस्तासु भाषते ।
विचित्राणि च नर्माणि काञ्चिच्च तनुते रतिम् ॥

*vanya-krīḍā-sukhaṁ kṛṣṇo*
*bhūriśas tāsu bhāṣate*
*vicitrāṇi ca narmāṇi*
*kāñcic ca tanute ratim*

*vanya* — in the forest; *krīḍā* — of sporting; *sukham* — about the pleasure; *kṛṣṇaḥ* — Kṛṣṇa; *bhūriśaḥ* — freely; *tāsu* — with them; *bhāṣate* — spoke; *vicitrāṇi* — various; *ca* — and; *narmāṇi* — jokes; *kāñcit* — a certain; *ca* — and; *tanute* — expanded; *ratim* — conjugal attraction.

**Kṛṣṇa spoke freely with them about how He enjoyed sporting in the forest. And by joking with them in various charming ways, He inspired their special conjugal love.**

COMMENTARY: In this situation Kṛṣṇa took the liberty to touch some of the *gopīs* on their breasts.

TEXT 102

एवमन्योन्यसौहार्दभरप्रकटनेन हि ।
वेशः समाप्तिं नायाति लोप्यमानस्तथा मुहुः ॥

*evam anyonya-sauhārda-*
*bhara-prakaṭanena hi*
*veśaḥ samāptiṁ nāyāti*
*lopyamānas tathā muhuḥ*

*evam* — thus; *anyonya* — mutual; *sauhārda* — of loving exchanges; *bhara* — of the multitude; *prakaṭanena* — while manifesting; *hi* — indeed; *veśaḥ* — the decoration; *samāptim* — to completion; *na āyāti* — did not reach; *lopyamānaḥ* — being erased; *tathā* — also; *muhuḥ* — again.

**In the midst of all these loving exchanges, the decoration never quite got finished. The gopīs had to keep erasing their attempts and trying again and again.**

COMMENTARY: These distractions made it difficult for the *gopīs* to finish the final touches of putting *tilaka* on Kṛṣṇa's forehead, painting His hands, and so on. Several times they decided, "This hasn't been done right. Erase it and do it again."

## TEXT 103

भूयो भूयो यशोदा च पुत्रस्नेहातुरान्तरा ।
बहिर्निर्गत्य पश्यन्ती वदत्येवं रुषेव ताः ॥

*bhūyo bhūyo yaśodā ca*
*putra-snehāturāntarā*
*bahir nirgatya paśyantī*
*vadaty evaṁ ruṣeva tāḥ*

*bhūyaḥ bhūyaḥ* — several times; *yaśodā* — Yaśodā; *ca* — and; *putra* — for her son; *sneha* — by affection; *ātura* — disturbed; *antarā* — her heart; *bahiḥ* — outside; *nirgatya* — coming; *paśyantī* — seeing; *vadati* — spoke; *evam* — thus; *ruṣā* — in anger; *iva* — as if; *tāḥ* — to them.

**Mother Yaśodā, her heart perturbed by affection for her son, came outside several times to see what was going on and spoke to the girls as if angry.**

COMMENTARY: Mother Yaśodā was only apparently angry (*ruṣā iva*). She could never actually harbor any ill feelings towards the young *gopīs*.

## TEXT 104

श्रीयशोदोवाच
लोलप्रकृतयो बाल्यादहो गोपकुमारिकाः ।
स्नानालङ्करणं नास्याधुनापि समपद्यत ॥

*śrī-yaśodovāca*
*lola-prakṛtayo bālyād*
*aho gopa-kumārikāḥ*
*snānālaṅkaraṇaṁ nāsyā-*
*dhunāpi samapadyata*

*śrī-yaśodā uvāca* — Śrī Yaśodā said; *lola* — unsteady; *prakṛtayaḥ* — you girls whose nature; *bālyāt* — due to being children;

*aho* — O; *gopa* — of the cowherds; *kumārikāḥ* — young daughters; *snāna* — the bathing; *alaṅkaraṇam* — and decorating; *na* — not; *asya* — His; *adhunā* — now; *api* — even; *samapadyata* — has been finished.

**Śrī Yaśodā said: O daughters of the cowherds, you are just unreliable children. Haven't you finished bathing and decorating Him yet?**

COMMENTARY: Having known these girls from the beginning of their lives, Yaśodā was very familiar with their behavior. They couldn't carry out such a simple task in a reasonable time, and this proved her judgment of them.

### TEXT 105

श्रीसरूप उवाच
तासां निरीक्षमाणानां परितः स्वप्रियं मुहुः ।
परिहासोत्सुकं चित्तं वृद्धाभिप्रेत्य साब्रवीत् ॥

*śrī-sarūpa uvāca*
*tāsāṁ nirīkṣamāṇānāṁ*
*paritaḥ sva-priyaṁ muhuḥ*
*parihāsotsukaṁ cittaṁ*
*vṛddhābhipretya sābravīt*

*śrī-sarūpaḥ uvāca* — Śrī Sarūpa said; *tāsām* — as they (the *gopīs*); *nirīkṣamāṇānām* — looked on; *paritaḥ* — on all sides; *sva-priyam* — at their beloved; *muhuḥ* — continuously; *parihāsa* — for humorous conversation; *utsukam* — eager; *cittam* — His mind; *vṛddhā* — an elderly lady; *abhipretya* — noticing; *sā* — she; *abravīt* — spoke.

**Śrī Sarūpa said: As the gopīs stood around their beloved Kṛṣṇa, glancing at Him again and again, one elderly lady noticed that Kṛṣṇa seemed eager for some joking words. She therefore spoke up.**

## TEXT 106

अरे पुत्रि यशोदेऽत्र हर्षादेत्य निरीक्ष्यताम् ।
भवत्याः श्यामलं पुत्रं निन्युः सुन्दरतामिमाः ॥

*are putri yaśode 'tra*
*harṣād etya nirīkṣyatām*
*bhavatyāḥ śyāmalaṁ putraṁ*
*ninyuḥ sundaratām imāḥ*

*are putri* — O daughter; *yaśode* — Yaśodā; *atra* — here; *harṣāt* — happily; *etya* — coming; *nirīkṣyatām* — should be seen; *bhavatyāḥ* — your; *śyāmalam* — dark-blue; *putram* — son; *ninyuḥ* — they have brought; *sundaratām* — to a beautiful state; *imāḥ* — these girls.

**"My goodness, come here, my daughter Yaśodā! You will be happy to see this! These girls have made your dark-blue son very handsome."**

## TEXT 107

स्वधात्र्या वाक्यमाकर्ण्य मुखरायाः पुनर्बहिः ।
भूत्वाभिप्रेत्य तन्नर्म सरोषमिव साब्रवीत् ॥

*sva-dhātryā vākyam ākarṇya*
*mukharāyāḥ punar bahiḥ*
*bhūtvābhipretya tan-narma*
*sa-roṣam iva sābravīt*

*sva-dhātryāḥ* — of her nurse; *vākyam* — the words; *ākarṇya* — hearing; *mukharāyāḥ* — of Mukharā; *punaḥ* — again; *bahiḥ* — outside; *bhūtvā* — coming; *abhipretya* — understanding; *tat* — her; *narma* — joking; *sa-roṣam* — angrily; *iva* — as if; *sā* — she (Yaśodā); *abravīt* — said.

**Hearing these joking words from the elderly lady (her**

**nurse Mukharā), Yaśodā again came outside. And when she understood the joke, she spoke out as if angry.**

TEXT 108

श्रीयशोदोवाच
सहजाशेषसौन्दर्यनीराजितपदाम्बुजः ।
जगन्मूर्ध्नि नरीनर्ति मदीयश्यामसुन्दरः ॥

*śrī-yaśodovāca*
*sahajāśeṣa-saundarya-*
*nīrājita-padāmbujaḥ*
*jagan-mūrdhni narīnarti*
*madīya-śyāmasundaraḥ*

*śrī-yaśodā uvāca* — Śrī Yaśodā said; *sahaja* — natural; *aśeṣa* — by all; *saundarya* — beauty; *nīrājita-pada-ambujaḥ* — He whose lotus feet are worshiped; *jagat* — of the universe; *mūrdhni* — on the head; *narīnarti* — dances with abandon; *madīya* — my; *śyāma-sundaraḥ* — dark and beautiful Kṛṣṇa.

**Śrī Yaśodā declared: All kinds of natural beauty worship the lotus feet of my Śyāmasundara, who dances with abandon on the head of the universe.**

COMMENTARY: There may be many beautiful boys in the world, but in the eyes of Mother Yaśodā her son excels all of them. After all, He is not only *sundara* but also *śyāma;* in other words, His dark complexion makes His beauty unique.

TEXT 109

एतत्पादनखाग्रैकसौन्दर्यस्यापि नार्हति ।
सौन्दर्यभारः सर्वासामासां नीराजनं ध्रुवम् ॥

*etat-pāda-nakhāgraika-*
*saundaryasyāpi nārhati*

*saundarya-bhāraḥ sarvāsām*
*āsāṁ nīrājanaṁ dhruvam*

*etat* — His; *pāda-nakha* — of a toenail; *agra* — of an end; *eka* — one; *saundaryasya* — of the beauty; *api* — even; *na arhati* — does not deserve; *saundarya-bhāraḥ* — the combined beauty; *sarvāsām* — of all; *āsām* — of them; *nīrājanam* — worship; *dhruvam* — certainly.

**For sure, the beauty of all these gopīs combined deserves not even a show of respect from the beauty of even the tip of one of His toenails.**

COMMENTARY: Someone might argue with Yaśodā that although no one's beauty approaches Kṛṣṇa's, Śrī Rādhā and Her *gopī* companions are exceptions; after all, they are the most beautiful beings in creation. But Yaśodā says no, not even their beauty dares stand in comparison with His. Whatever little beauty they may have is of no use, since they are not meant to become His wives.

## TEXT 110

श्रीसरूप उवाच
तत्सौन्दर्यं सा च लावण्यलक्ष्मीस्
तन्माधुर्यं तस्य किं वर्णितं स्यात् ।
द्रव्यैर्योग्या लौकिकैर्नोपमा स्यात्
किं वान्येन द्वारकेन्द्रेण नापि ॥

*śrī-sarūpa uvāca*
*tat saundaryaṁ sā ca lāvaṇya-lakṣmīs*
*tan mādhuryaṁ tasya kiṁ varṇitaṁ syāt*
*dravyair yogyā laukikair nopamā syāt*
*kiṁ vānyena dvārakendreṇa nāpi*

*śrī-sarūpaḥ uvāca* — Śrī Sarūpa said; *tat* — that; *saundaryam* — beauty; *sā* — it; *ca* — and; *lāvaṇya* — of His effulgent complexion; *lakṣmīḥ* — the splendor; *tat* — that; *mādhuryam* — sweetness; *tasya* — His; *kim* — whether; *varṇitam syāt* — can be described; *dravyaiḥ* — with things; *yogyā* — suitable; *laukikaiḥ* — belonging to this world; *na* — not; *upamā* — comparison; *syāt* — there can be; *kim vā* — or else; *anyena* — with anyone else; *dvārakā-indreṇa* — with the Lord of Dvārakā; *na* — not; *api* — even.

**Śrī Sarūpa said: Is it possible to describe His beauty, the splendor of His effulgent complexion, or His charming sweetness? With that sweetness no things in this world can compare, nor can even the sweetness of God Himself in other forms, not even as the Lord of Dvārakā.**

COMMENTARY: In His unique bodily luster, in the sublime proportion and symmetry of all His limbs, and in the overall splendor and charm of His form, Kṛṣṇa's beauty is amazing. Attempts to compare His eyes and other features to beautiful things such as lotuses do little justice to His beauty. In fact, it is useless to compare Kṛṣṇa's beauty even to that of Śrī Viṣṇu and other forms of Godhead, who imitate the ways of the material world, or even to that of Śrī Nārāyaṇa, or the Lord of Ayodhyā, or Śrī Yadunātha Kṛṣṇa of Dvārakā.

## TEXT 111

कृष्णो यथा नागरशेखराग्र्यो
राधा तथा नागरिकावराग्र्या ।
राधा यथा नागरिकावराग्र्या
कृष्णस्तथा नागरशेखराग्र्यः ॥

*kṛṣṇo yathā nāgara-śekharāgryo*
*rādhā tathā nāgarikā-varāgryā*
*rādhā yathā nāgarikā-varāgryā*
*kṛṣṇas tathā nāgara-śekharāgryaḥ*

*kṛṣṇaḥ* — Kṛṣṇa; *yathā* — as; *nāgara* — of romantic heroes; *śekhara-agryaḥ* — the most superb; *rādhā* — Rādhā; *tathā* — so; *nāgarikā* — of heroines; *vara-agryā* — the most superb; *rādhā* — Radhā; *yathā* — as; *nāgarikā* — of heroines; *vara-agryā* — the most superb; *kṛṣṇaḥ* — Kṛṣṇa; *tathā* — so; *nāgara* — of heroes; *śekhara-agryaḥ* — the most superb.

**As Kṛṣṇa of all romantic heroes is the most superb, so Rādhā of all romantic heroines. And as Rādhā of all heroines is the most superb, so Kṛṣṇa of all heroes.**

COMMENTARY: The only beauty than can truly compare with Kṛṣṇa's is the equal beauty of Śrīmatī Rādhārāṇī. The two lovers are comparable only with one another.

TEXT 112

स्नात्वागतं गोपराजं बलरामेण संयुतम् ।
संलक्ष्य लीनास्ताः सर्वा द्रुतं कृष्णोऽग्रतोऽभवत् ॥

*snātvāgataṁ gopa-rājaṁ*
*balarāmeṇa saṁyutam*
*saṁlakṣya līnās tāḥ sarvā*
*drutaṁ kṛṣṇo 'grato 'bhavat*

*snātvā* — having taken his bath; *āgatam* — come; *gopa-rājam* — the king of cowherds; *balarāmeṇa* — with Balarāma; *saṁyutam* — together; *saṁlakṣya* — seeing; *līnāḥ* — disappeared; *tāḥ* — they; *sarvāḥ* — all; *drutam* — quickly; *kṛṣṇaḥ* — Kṛṣṇa; *agrataḥ* — forward; *abhavat* — came.

**When the gopīs saw that Nanda, king of the cowherds, had taken his bath and had arrived with Balarāma, they all speedily disappeared, and Kṛṣṇa came forward.**

COMMENTARY: As Nanda Mahārāja approached, the *gopīs* recognized his voice. Without waiting for him to see them, they hid themselves nearby.

## TEXT 113

नन्दो भोजनशालायामासीनः कनकासने ।
भोजनं कर्तुमारेभे तथा तौ तस्य पार्श्वयोः ॥

*nando bhojana-śālāyām*
*āsīnaḥ kanakāsane*
*bhojanaṁ kartum ārebhe*
*tathā tau tasya pārśvayoḥ*

*nandaḥ* — Nanda Mahārāja; *bhojana-śālāyām* — in the dining hall; *āsīnaḥ* — seated; *kanaka* — golden; *āsane* — on his seat; *bhojanam* — the meal; *kartum* — to take; *ārebhe* — started; *tathā* — also; *tau* — the two (Kṛṣṇa and Balarāma); *tasya* — his; *pārśvayoḥ* — at the sides.

**Nanda sat down on his golden seat in the dining hall and began to have his meal, with the two brothers at his sides.**

COMMENTARY: Kṛṣṇa and Balarāma also had golden seats.

## TEXT 114

यशोदानन्दनो वामे दक्षिणे रोहिणीसुतः ।
तेषामहं तु महताग्रहेणाभिमुखे पृथक् ॥

*yaśodā-nandano vāme*
*dakṣiṇe rohiṇī-sutaḥ*
*teṣām ahaṁ tu mahatā-*
*graheṇābhimukhe pṛthak*

*yaśodā-nandanaḥ* — the darling son of Yaśodā; *vāme* — on the left; *dakṣiṇe* — on the right; *rohiṇī-sutaḥ* — the son of Rohiṇī; *teṣām* — Their; *aham* — I; *tu* — but; *mahatā* — strong; *āgraheṇa* — on the insistence; *abhimukhe* — opposite; *pṛthak* — separately.

**Yaśodā's darling child sat on his left, the son of Rohiṇī on his right. And at the strong insistence of these brothers, I sat directly opposite, in my own place.**

COMMENTARY: For the oldest son to sit on his father's right is standard etiquette. And this also made it easier for Nanda Mahārāja to feed Kṛṣṇa with his own hand. The two brothers asked for Sarūpa to sit just opposite them and Nanda. Though Sarūpa was served separately, Nanda shared his own food with his two sons. This was acceptable for him to do with two boys who had not yet received the sacred-thread initiation.

## TEXTS 115–116

श्रीरोहिण्या परिष्कृत्य रात्नसौवर्णराजतैः ।
विविधैर्भाजनैर्दिव्यैः प्रहितं गृहमध्यतः ॥

परिवेष्यमाणं स्नेहेन मात्रा भोगपुरन्दरम् ।
सर्वसद्गुणसम्पन्नमन्नं भुङ्क्ते चतुर्विधम् ॥

*śrī-rohiṇyā pariṣkṛtya*
*rātna-sauvarṇa-rājataiḥ*
*vividhair bhājanair divyaiḥ*
*prahitaṁ gṛha-madhyataḥ*

*pariveṣyamāṇaṁ snehena*
*mātrā bhoga-purandaram*
*sarva-sad-guṇa-sampannam*
*annaṁ bhuṅkte catur-vidham*

*śrī-rohiṇyā* — by Śrī Rohiṇī; *pariṣkṛtya* — being arranged; *rātna* — jeweled; *sauvarṇa* — of gold; *rājataiḥ* — and silver; *vividhaiḥ* — various; *bhājanaiḥ* — in vessels; *divyaiḥ* — of superior quality; *prahitam* — sent; *gṛha-madhyataḥ* — from inside the house; *pariveṣyamāṇam* — being served; *snehena* — with affection; *mātrā* — by the mother; *bhoga* — of meals;

*purandaram* — the emperor; *sarva* — all; *sat-guṇa* — with good qualities; *sampannam* — endowed; *annam* — food; *bhuṅkte* — (Kṛṣṇa) ate; *catuḥ-vidham* — of four kinds (to be chewed, licked, sucked, and drunk).

**From inside the house Śrī Rohiṇī sent the emperor of meals, arranged in many jewel-bedecked vessels of gold and silver. Mother Yaśodā with great affection served the food, of all four kinds and endowed with all good qualities, and Kṛṣṇa began to eat.**

COMMENTARY: Since Śrī Kṛṣṇa was the star attraction at dinner, Sarūpa gives particular attention to how Kṛṣṇa was fed. Mother Rohiṇī arranged the meal artistically on excellent serving dishes and sent it out to the dining hall. The food displayed all admirable qualities — good fragrance, good color, good taste, and so on.

## TEXT 117

पृथक् पृथक् कचोलासु विचित्रासु प्रपूरितम् ।
विस्तीर्णकनकस्थल्यां नीत्वा कवलयन्भृशम् ॥

*pṛthak pṛthak kacolāsu*
*vicitrāsu prapūritam*
*vistīrṇa-kanaka-sthalyāṁ*
*nītvā kavalayan bhṛśam*

*pṛthak pṛthak* — separately; *kacolāsu* — in bowls; *vicitrāsu* — various; *prapūritam* — filled; *vistīrṇa* — large; *kanaka* — gold; *sthalyām* — on a platter; *nītvā* — being brought; *kavalayan* — devouring; *bhṛśam* — heartily.

**He heartily devoured the various delicacies, which filled many separate bowls, brought in on a large gold platter.**

COMMENTARY: Literally, *kavalayan* means "rolling the food into morsels to be chewed and swallowed."

## TEXT 118

मात्रा कदाचित्पित्रा च भ्रात्रापि क्रमशो मुखे ।
समर्प्यमाणं यत्नेन कवलं लीलयाददत् ॥

*mātrā kadācit pitrā ca*
*bhrātrāpi kramaśo mukhe*
*samarpyamāṇaṁ yatnena*
*kavalaṁ līlayādadat*

*mātrā* — by His mother; *kadācit* — at one time; *pitrā* — by His father; *ca* — and; *bhrātrā* — by His brother; *api* — also; *kramaśaḥ* — in turns; *mukhe* — in His mouth; *samarpyamāṇam* — being offered; *yatnena* — carefully; *kavalam* — a morsel; *līlayā* — playfully; *ādadat* — He accepted.

**At one point His mother, His father, and His brother took turns carefully putting morsels into His mouth, morsels He playfully accepted.**

## TEXT 119

तथा पानकजातं च कचोलाभृतमुत्तमम् ।
भृङ्गारिकाभृताश्चापो मध्ये मध्ये पिबञ्शिवाः ॥

*tathā pānaka-jātaṁ ca*
*kacolā-bhṛtam uttamam*
*bhṛṅgārikā-bhṛtāś cāpo*
*madhye madhye pibañ śivāḥ*

*tathā* — then; *pānaka-jātam* — various beverages; *ca* — and; *kacolā* — in bowls; *bhṛtam* — carried; *uttamam* — first-class; *bhṛṅgārikā* — in pitchers; *bhṛtāḥ* — carried; *ca* — and; *āpaḥ* — water; *madhye madhye* — at intervals; *piban* — drinking; *śivāḥ* — pure.

**Now and then He also drank all sorts of splendid bev-**

**erages, carried in large bowls, and pure water carried in pitchers.**

### TEXT 120

आदौ सुमृष्टमुत्कृष्टं कोष्णं सघृतशर्करम् ।
पायसं नाडिकापूपफेणिकारोटिकायुतम् ॥

*ādau su-mṛṣṭam utkṛṣṭaṁ*
*koṣṇaṁ sa-ghṛta-śarkaram*
*pāyasaṁ nāḍikāpūpa-*
*pheṇikā-roṭikā-yutam*

*ādau* — in the beginning; *su-mṛṣṭam* — very sweet; *utkṛṣṭam* — excellent; *koṣṇam* — warm; *sa-ghṛta* — with ghee; *śarkaram* — and sugar; *pāyasam* — sweet rice; *nāḍikā* — by *jalebīs; apūpa* — cakes; *pheṇikā* — pies; *roṭikā* — and flatbreads; *yutam* — joined.

**At the start of the meal He ate warm sweet rice with ghee and sugar — very tasty — together with cakes, pies, jalebīs, and flatbreads.**

### TEXT 121

अन्यानि घृतपक्वानि रसालासहितानि च ।
दधिदुग्धविकारोत्थमिष्टान्नान्यपराण्यपि ॥

*anyāni ghṛta-pakvāni*
*rasālā-sahitāni ca*
*dadhi-dugdha-vikārottha-*
*miṣṭānnāny aparāṇy api*

*anyāni* — other; *ghṛta* — in ghee; *pakvāni* — cooked; *rasālā* — yogurt mixed with sugar and spices; *sahitāni* — together with; *ca* — and; *dadhi* — of yogurt; *dugdha* — and milk; *vikāra* — as transformations; *uttha* — produced; *miṣṭa-annāni* — sweets; *aparāṇi* — different; *api* — and.

**He ate other items fried in ghee, and He also had sweetened yogurt and various things made from transformations of yogurt and milk.**

## TEXT 122

मध्ये सूक्ष्मं सितं भक्तं कोष्णं सुरभि कोमलम् ।
वटकैः पर्पटैः शाकैः सूपैश्च व्यञ्जनैः परैः ॥

*madhye sūkṣmaṁ sitaṁ bhaktaṁ*
*koṣṇaṁ surabhi komalam*
*vaṭakaiḥ parpaṭaiḥ śākaiḥ*
*sūpaiś ca vyañjanaiḥ paraiḥ*

*madhye* — in the middle; *sūkṣmam* — fine; *sitam* — white; *bhaktam* — rice; *koṣṇam* — warm; *surabhi* — fragrant; *komalam* — soft; *vaṭakaiḥ* — with fried *dāl* balls; *parpaṭaiḥ* — *papadams* (*dāl* wafers); *śākaiḥ* — leafy greens; *sūpaiḥ* — soups; *ca* — and; *vyañjanaiḥ* — vegetable dishes; *paraiḥ* — other.

**In the middle of the meal He ate fine white rice, warm, fragrant, and tender, with fried dāl balls, and dāl wafers, and leafy greens, and soups, and other vegetable dishes.**

## TEXT 123

मधुराम्लरसप्रायैः प्रायो गोरससाधितैः ।
कटुचूर्णान्वितैरम्लद्रव्यैः सलवणैर्युतम् ॥

*madhurāmla-rasa-prāyaiḥ*
*prāyo go-rasa-sādhitaiḥ*
*kaṭu-cūrṇānvitair amla-*
*dravyaiḥ sa-lavaṇair yutam*

*madhura* — sweet; *amla* — and sour; *rasa* — of tastes; *prāyaiḥ* — mostly; *prāyaḥ* — mostly; *go-rasa* — of cow products; *sādhitaiḥ* — made; *kaṭu* — pungent; *cūrṇa* — with spice powders; *anvitaiḥ* — mixed; *amla-dravyaiḥ* — with sour things; *sa-lavaṇaiḥ* — salty things; *yutam* — together with.

**He ate other items made mostly of milk products and mainly sweet and sour in taste, plus sour things mixed with salt and pungent spices.**

COMMENTARY: Among the spices used were hot pepper and a mixture of salt and roasted cumin seeds.

## TEXT 124

अन्ते पुनः शिखरिणीं विकारान्दधिसम्भवान् ।
हिंग्वादिसंस्कृतं तक्रं बुभुजे मां च भोजयन् ॥

*ante punaḥ śikhariṇīṁ*
*vikārān dadhi-sambhavān*
*hiṅgv-ādi-saṁskṛtaṁ takraṁ*
*bubhuje māṁ ca bhojayan*

*ante* — at the end; *punaḥ* — again; *śikhariṇīm* — a kind of sweetened yogurt; *vikārān* — transformations; *dadhi* — from yogurt; *sambhavān* — produced; *hiṅgu-ādi* — with asafetida and other spices; *saṁskṛtam* — garnished; *takram* — buttermilk; *bubhuje* — He partook; *mām* — me; *ca* — and; *bhojayan* — feeding.

**Toward the end He once again ate sweetened yogurt, various other items made from yogurt, and buttermilk garnished with asafetida and other spices. And while He Himself ate, He also fed me.**

COMMENTARY: The *Rāja-nighaṇṭu* dictionary gives a recipe for the sweetened yogurt preparation known as *śikhariṇī*. To yogurt are added cinnamon, rock sugar, ground black pepper, and ground green cardamom, as well as honey and ghee. Then the mixture is kept for some time in a vessel packed in ice.

## TEXT 125

सा चर्वणोद्यदरुणाधरचारुजिह्वा
गण्डस्थलाननसरोजविलासभङ्गी ।
भ्रूचापलोचनसरोरुहनर्तनश्री-
विद्योतिता न वचसा मनसापि गम्या ॥

*sā carvaṇodyad-aruṇādhara-cāru-jihvā*
*gaṇḍa-sthalānana-saroja-vilāsa-bhaṅgī*
*bhrū-cāpa-locana-saroruha-nartana-śrī-*
*vidyotitā na vacasā manasāpi gamyā*

*sā* — it; *carvaṇa* — while chewing; *udyat* — rising; *aruṇa* — dawn pink; *adhara* — to His lip; *cāru* — lovely; *jihvā* — His tongue; *gaṇḍa-sthala* — the place of His cheeks; *ānana-saroja* — in His lotus face; *vilāsa-bhaṅgī* — sportive; *bhrū* — His eyebrows; *cāpa* — bowlike; *locana-saroruha* — and lotus eyes; *nartana* — dancing; *śrī* — lovely; *vidyotitā* — resplendent; *na* — not; *vacasā* — by words; *manasā* — by the mind; *api* — and; *gamyā* — accessible.

**Neither words nor the mind can form a picture of how Kṛṣṇa's lovely tongue, rising to His dawn-pink upper lip while He chewed, sported within the cheeks of His lotus face, a face resplendent with the beautiful dancing of His lotus eyes and bowlike eyebrows.**

COMMENTARY: Even how Kṛṣṇa chews on *jalebīs* and other foods is a wonder to behold. Everything the Supreme Lord does is attractive, and so too is everything done by His fully surrendered devotees.

## TEXT 126

गोपिकाभिश्च मिष्टान्नमानीय स्वस्वगेहतः ।
क्षीराज्यशर्करापक्वं यशोदाग्रे धृतं तदा ॥

*gopikābhiś ca miṣṭānnam*
*ānīya sva-sva-gehataḥ*
*kṣīrājya-śarkarā-pakvaṁ*
*yaśodāgre dhṛtaṁ tadā*

*gopikābhiḥ* — by the *gopīs; ca* — and; *miṣṭa-annam* — sweetmeats; *ānīya* — being brought; *sva-sva-gehataḥ* — each from her home; *kṣīra* — in milk; *ājya* — ghee; *śarkarā* — and sugar; *pakvam* — cooked; *yaśodā-agre* — before Yaśodā; *dhṛtam* — placed; *tadā* — then.

**The gopīs brought from their homes many sweets cooked in milk, ghee, and sugar and placed them before Mother Yaśodā.**

## TEXT 127

विचित्रलीलया तत्तत्सश्लाघं बुभुजेऽसकृत् ।
ताः सर्वाः रञ्जयन्किञ्चिद्भोजयन्स्वकरेण माम् ॥

*vicitra-līlayā tat tat*
*sa-ślāghaṁ bubhuje 'sakṛt*
*tāḥ sarvāḥ rañjayan kiñcid*
*bhojayan sva-kareṇa mām*

*vicitra* — wonderful; *līlayā* — with playful gestures; *tat tat* — each preparation; *sa-ślāgham* — with praise; *bubhuje* — He ate; *asakṛt* — more than once; *tāḥ* — they (the *gopīs*); *sarvāḥ* — all; *rañjayan* — making happy; *kiñcit* — some; *bhojayan* — feeding; *sva-kareṇa* — with His own hand; *mām* — to me.

**With wonderful playful gestures, Kṛṣṇa ate from all the dishes the gopīs had brought, praising every item and eating from each dish more than once. He thus made all the gopīs happy. And He also fed some of those items to me, with His own hand.**

### TEXT 128

अथ श्रीराधिकानीय सा मनोहरलड्डुकम् ।
कृष्णस्य वामतो दध्रे गुटिकापूरिकान्वितम् ॥

*atha śrī-rādhikānīya*
*sā manohara-laḍḍukam*
*kṛṣṇasya vāmato dadhre*
*guṭikā-pūrikānvitam*

*atha* — then; *śrī-rādhikā* — Śrī Rādhikā; *ānīya* — bringing; *sā* — She; *manohara-laḍḍukam* — manohara-laḍḍus; *kṛṣṇasya* — of Kṛṣṇa; *vāmataḥ* — on the left side; *dadhre* — placed; *guṭikā* — round ones; *pūrikā* — large flat ones; *anvitam* — together with.

**Next Śrī Rādhikā brought manohara-laḍḍus, both small round ones and large flat ones, and set them down on Kṛṣṇa's left.**

COMMENTARY: The *manohara-laḍḍu* is aptly named the sweetball that "steals the heart." Śrī Rādhā placed these *laḍḍus* on Kṛṣṇa's left, where He could easily reach them.

### TEXT 129

निष्कृष्य तन्नखाग्रेण तर्जन्यङ्गुष्ठयोः कियत् ।
जिह्वाग्रे न्यस्य चक्रेऽसौ निम्बवन्मुखविक्रियाम् ॥

*niṣkṛṣya tan nakhāgreṇa*
*tarjany-aṅguṣṭhayoḥ kiyat*

*jihvāgre nyasya cakre 'sau*
*nimba-van mukha-vikriyām*

*niṣkṛṣya* — picking up; *tat* — that; *nakha* — of His fingernails; *agreṇa* — with the ends; *tarjanī* — the index finger; *aṅguṣṭhayoḥ* — and thumb; *kiyat* — some; *jihvā* — of His tongue; *agre* — on the front; *nyasya* — placing; *cakre* — made; *asau* — He; *nimba-vat* — as if from bitter neem; *mukha* — of His mouth; *vikriyām* — a contortion.

**Kṛṣṇa picked up a few of those sweets with the nails of His thumb and forefinger and put them on the tip of His tongue. He then made a face as if they tasted like bitter neem.**

## TEXT 130

भ्रातुः स्मितं रुषं मातुस्तस्यां तातस्य विस्मयम् ।
तन्वन्सखीनां मुग्धानामाधिं तस्या द्विषां मुदम् ॥

*bhrātuḥ smitaṁ ruṣaṁ mātus*
*tasyāṁ tātasya vismayam*
*tanvan sakhīnāṁ mugdhānām*
*ādhiṁ tasyā dviṣāṁ mudam*

*bhrātuḥ* — of His brother; *smitam* — smiles; *ruṣam* — anger; *mātuḥ* — of His mother; *tasyām* — at Her (Śrī Rādhikā); *tātasya* — of His father; *vismayam* — surprise; *tanvan* — producing; *sakhīnām* — of Her girlfriends; *mugdhānām* — innocent; *ādhim* — mental pain; *tasyāḥ* — Her; *dviṣām* — of the antagonists; *mudam* — joy.

**Kṛṣṇa's brother smiled, His mother was angry at Śrī Radhikā, and His father was surprised. Rādhā's innocent girlfriends were pained, and Her antagonists were delighted.**

COMMENTARY: Mother Yaśodā was angry at the girls for bringing Kṛṣṇa bitter sweets. Nanda was surprised, doubting how the girls could possibly have done this. Though the *gopīs* in rival parties were enlivened by the mistake, Śrī Rādhikā's innocent-minded *sakhīs* were upset by the thought that something bitter must have been put in the *laḍḍus*. Among the *sakhīs,* however, the more clever could see a joke being played that would further highlight Śrī Rādhikā's good fortune.

## TEXT 131

तद्भ्रातृवंशजातस्य मम चिक्षेप भाजने ।
तत्सर्वं परमस्वादु भुक्त्वाहं विस्मितोऽभवम् ॥

*tad-bhrātṛ-vaṁśa-jātasya*
*mama cikṣepa bhājane*
*tat sarvaṁ parama-svādu*
*bhuktvāhaṁ vismito 'bhavam*

*tat* — Her; *bhrātṛ* — of the brother; *vaṁśa* — in the family; *jātasya* — who was born; *mama* — my; *cikṣepa* — He threw; *bhājane* — in the plate; *tat* — that; *sarvam* — all; *parama* — extremely; *svādu* — tasty; *bhuktvā* — eating; *aham* — I; *vismitaḥ* — surprised; *abhavam* — became.

**Since I was born in the family of Rādhārāṇī's brother, Kṛṣṇa threw all the laḍḍus onto my plate. Surprised to find them extremely tasty, I ate them all.**

COMMENTARY: Śrīdāmā is the brother of Śrīmatī Rādhārāṇī, and Sarūpa is also a member of their family. So Kṛṣṇa thought it fit to dump the *laḍḍus* onto his plate. "These bitter *laḍḍus* are not fit for Me. Her relatives deserve to eat them." In truth, however, Kṛṣṇa knew that the *laḍḍus* were most perfectly prepared, and He gave them to Sarūpa out of great love.

TEXT 132

राधया निभृतं कृष्णः सभ्रूभङ्गं निरीक्षितः ।
मृदुस्मितानतास्यस्तां कटाक्षेणान्वरञ्जयत् ॥

*rādhayā nibhṛtaṁ kṛṣṇaḥ*
*sa-bhrū-bhaṅgaṁ nirīkṣitaḥ*
*mṛdu-smitānatāsyas tāṁ*
*kaṭākṣeṇānvarañjayat*

*rādhayā* — by Rādhā; *nibhṛtam* — secretly; *kṛṣṇaḥ* — Kṛṣṇa; *sa-bhrū-bhaṅgam* — with arching of the eyebrows; *nirīkṣitaḥ* — looked at; *mṛdu* — gentle; *smita* — with a smile; *ānata* — nodding; *āsyaḥ* — His head; *tām* — Her; *kaṭa-akṣeṇa* — with a sidelong glance; *anvarañjayat* — He gratified.

**Rādhā secretly looked at Kṛṣṇa and arched Her eyebrows, and Kṛṣṇa, nodding His head, gratified Her with a gentle smile and a sidelong glance.**

COMMENTARY: To make sure that Śrī Rādhā was not ashamed and unhappy because Mother Yaśodā was angry at Her, Kṛṣṇa divulged His true feelings.

TEXT 133

सद्यो बुद्धा मया लीला सा विदग्धशिरोमणेः ।
निजप्रेमभरार्तानां परमप्रीणनात्मिका ॥

*sadyo buddhā mayā līlā*
*sā vidagdha-śiromaṇeḥ*
*nija-prema-bharārtānāṁ*
*parama-prīṇanātmikā*

*sadyaḥ* — suddenly; *buddhā* — was understood; *mayā* — by me; *līlā* — pastime; *sā* — that; *vidagdha* — of skillful actors; *śiromaṇeḥ* — by the crest jewel; *nija* — for Him; *prema* — of their love; *bhara* — by the weight; *ārtānāṁ* — of those who are tormented; *parama* — absolutely; *prīṇana* — of pleasing; *ātmikā* — for the purpose.

**Suddenly I understood — this was a pastime by the crest jewel of skillful actors to thoroughly please the devotees tormented by the weight of their love for Him.**

### TEXT 134

अथाचम्य यथान्यायं ताम्बूलं लीलयोत्तमम् ।
चर्वन्स राधिकां पश्यञ्चर्वितं मन्मुखे न्यधात् ॥

*athācamya yathā-nyāyaṁ*
*tāmbūlaṁ līlayottamam*
*carvan sa rādhikāṁ paśyañ*
*carvitaṁ man-mukhe nyadhāt*

*atha* — then; *ācamya* — washing His mouth; *yathā-nyāyam* — as is the custom; *tāmbūlam* — *pān; līlayā* — playfully; *uttamam* — excellent; *carvan* — chewing; *saḥ* — He; *rādhikām* — at Rādhikā; *paśyan* — looking; *carvitam* — chewed; *mat* — my; *mukhe* — in the mouth; *nyadhāt* — He put.

**Then Kṛṣṇa properly washed His mouth and playfully chewed some excellent pān. Glancing at Rādhikā, He put the chewed pān into my mouth.**

COMMENTARY: Without arousing suspicion in the other *gopīs,* Kṛṣṇa, the most expert romantic hero, pleased Rādhikā by placing this desirable remnant into the mouth of Her family member.

### TEXT 135

माता स्नेहातुरा मन्त्रान्पठन्ती भुक्तजारकान् ।
वामपाणितलेनास्योदरं मुहुरमार्जयत् ॥

*mātā snehāturā mantrān*
*paṭhantī bhukta-jārakān*
*vāma-pāṇi-talenāsyo-*
*daraṁ muhur amārjayat*

*mātā* — His mother; *sneha* — because of her love; *āturā* — filled with anxiety; *mantrān* — *mantras; paṭhantī* — chanting; *bhukta* — of what was eaten; *jārakān* — assuring the digestion; *vāma* — left; *pāṇi-talena* — with the palm of her hand; *asya* — His; *udaram* — belly; *muhuḥ* — repeatedly; *amārjayat* — she rubbed.

**Kṛṣṇa's mother, anxious with affection, chanted mantras and rubbed His belly with her left palm again and again to make sure He would digest what He had eaten.**

COMMENTARY: There was no real danger that such a lovingly prepared meal would cause indigestion, but Mother Yaśodā was obsessed with keeping her son happy and comfortable. Such was her unique love for Him.

## TEXT 136

गोव्रजान्तर्गतो नन्दो रामः सुप्तो विचक्षणः ।
चङ्क्रम्यते स्म गीतानि गायन्कृष्णो व्रजाङ्गने ॥

*go-vrajāntar-gato nando*
*rāmaḥ supto vicakṣaṇaḥ*
*caṅkramyate sma gītāni*
*gāyan kṛṣṇo vrajāṅgane*

*go-vraja* — the cow pastures; *antaḥ* — into; *gataḥ* — went; *nandaḥ* — Nanda Mahārāja; *rāmaḥ* — Balarāma; *suptaḥ* — went to sleep; *vicakṣaṇaḥ* — intelligent; *caṅkramyate sma* — wandered; *gītāni* — songs; *gāyan* — singing; *kṛṣṇaḥ* — Kṛṣṇa; *vraja-aṅgane* — in the village courtyard.

**Nanda Mahārāja went out into the cow pastures, intelligent Balarāma went to sleep, and Kṛṣṇa, singing songs, wandered about the village courtyard.**

COMMENTARY: Perceptive Balarāma could understand that this was a good chance for Kṛṣṇa to enjoy some of His more private pastimes. He therefore rested inside the house. Yaśodā was also inside, busy with housework.

## TEXT 137

क्षणं विहृत्य व्रजसुन्दरीरतः
स मातुराकारणगौरवादरात् ।
सुखं स्म शेते शयनालयं गतस्
तल्पे पयःफेणमनोज्ञतूलिके ॥

*kṣaṇaṁ vihṛtya vraja-sundarī-rataḥ*
*sa mātur ākāraṇa-gauravād arāt*
*sukhaṁ sma śete śayanālayaṁ gatas*
*talpe payaḥ-pheṇa-manojña-tūlike*

*kṣaṇam* — for a short time; *vihṛtya* — having played; *vraja-sundarī* — to the beautiful girls of Vraja; *rataḥ* — fondly attached; *saḥ* — He; *mātuḥ* — of His mother; *ākāraṇa* — for the calling; *gauravāt* — out of respect; *arāt* — from a distance; *sukham* — comfortably; *sma śete* — He lay down; *śayana-ālayam* — into His bedroom; *gataḥ* — going; *talpe* — on His bed; *payaḥ* — of milk; *pheṇa* — like the foam; *manojña* — attractive; *tūlike* — on the cotton sheets.

**Eager to enjoy with the beautiful girls of Vraja, Kṛṣṇa played for a short time outside. Then, out of respect for His mother, He responded to her distant call and came home and went straight to His bedroom and lay down comfortably on the bed, its cotton sheets as soft and white as the foam of milk.**

COMMENTARY: *Gaurava* means "great respect." Although Kṛṣṇa is always eager to consort with the *gopīs,* He is also attracted by the special love of His mother. He is *akhila-rasāmṛta-mūrti,* the embodiment of all relationships, not just the *mādhurya-rasa.*

## TEXT 138

निरङ्कपूर्णेन्दुसमैस्तथापरैर्
मृदूपधानैर्युतमस्ति यत्ततम् ।
अनर्घ्यरत्नाचितकाञ्चनोल्लसल्-
ललामपल्यङ्कवरे महाप्रभे ॥

*niraṅka-pūrṇendu-samais tathāparair*
*mṛdūpadhānair yutam asti yat tatam*
*anarghya-ratnācita-kāñcanollasal-*
*lalāma-palyaṅka-vare mahā-prabhe*

*niraṅka* — without spots; *pūrṇa* — full; *indu* — moons; *samaiḥ* — like; *tathā* — and; *aparaiḥ* — with other; *mṛdu* — soft; *upadhānaiḥ* — pillows; *yutam* — equipped; *asti* — it was; *yat* — which; *tatam* — spacious; *anarghya* — priceless; *ratna* — with gems; *ācita* — bedecked; *kāñcana* — golden; *ullasat* — shining; *lalāma* — ornamented; *palyaṅka* — on a bedstead; *vare* — best; *mahā* — greatly; *prabhe* — effulgent.

**That spacious bed had soft pillows, some like spotless full moons, others of various kinds. And it lay on an effulgent bedstead beautifully ornamented with shining gold bedecked with priceless gems.**

COMMENTARY: Some of Kṛṣṇa's pillows in Nanda Mahārāja's home resemble the full moon in shape and color, but they aren't marred by spots. Kṛṣṇa's bed also has other, long pillows. Especially soft are the ones He uses to rest His head.

## TEXT 139

यः शोभते मौक्तिकमालिकावृतैश्
चित्रैर्वितानैरुपशोभिते धृतः ।
प्रासादसिंहेऽगुरुधूपवासिते
रम्यप्रकोष्ठे बहुरत्ननिर्मिते ॥

*yaḥ śobhate mauktika-mālikāvṛtaiś*
*citrair vitānair upaśobhite dhṛtaḥ*
*prāsāda-siṁhe 'guru-dhūpa-vāsite*
*ramya-prakoṣṭhe bahu-ratna-nirmite*

*yaḥ* — which; *śobhate* — is made more beautiful; *mauktika* — of pearls; *mālikā* — with strings; *āvṛtaiḥ* — hanging; *citraiḥ* — splendid; *vitānaiḥ* — by a canopy; *upaśobhite* — adorned; *dhṛtaḥ* — held; *prāsāda* — in the palatial room; *siṁhe* — (regal) like a lion; *aguru-dhūpa* — with *aguru* incense; *vāsite* — fragrant; *ramya* — attractive; *prakoṣṭhe* — with closets; *bahu* — many; *ratna* — with gems; *nirmite* — constructed.

**A splendid canopy draped with strings of pearls further enhanced the beauty of that bed, which stood in a room fragrant with aguru incense, a room whose beautiful closets were built with many valuable gems, a palatial room that excelled all others as the lion excels all other animals.**

COMMENTARY: The canopies above the bed were not only decorative; they also served the practical purpose of shading Kṛṣṇa on nights when the moon was bright. All four corners of the room were decorated with curiously constructed closets.

## TEXT 140

राधार्पयत्यस्य मुखान्तरे सा
संस्कृत्य ताम्बूलपुटं विदग्धा ।

चन्द्रावली श्रीललितापि पाद-
पद्मे तु संवाहयतः सलीलम् ॥

*rādhārpayaty asya mukhāntare sā*
*saṁskṛtya tāmbūla-puṭaṁ vidagdhā*
*candrāvalī śrī-lalitāpi pāda-*
*padme tu saṁvāhayataḥ sa-līlam*

*rādhā* — Śrī Rādhā; *arpayati* — offered; *asya* — His; *mukha-antare* — into the mouth; *sā* — She; *saṁskṛtya* — preparing; *tāmbūla* — of *pān; puṭam* — wrapped packets; *vidagdhā* — skillful; *candrāvalī* — Candrāvalī; *śrī-lalitā* — Śrī Lalitā; *api* — also; *pāda-padme* — His lotus feet; *tu* — and; *saṁvāhayataḥ* — massaged; *sa-līlam* — playfully.

**Skillful Rādhā had made pān and wrapped it into packets and now offered them to Kṛṣṇa by placing them into His mouth. And Candrāvalī and Śrī Lalitā playfully massaged His lotus feet.**

## TEXT 141

काश्चिच्च बालव्यजनान्युपाददुः
काश्चिच्च ताम्बूलसमुद्गकावलिम् ।
काश्चित्पतद्ग्राहचयं विभागशो
भृङ्गारिकाः काश्चन सज्जलैर्भृताः ॥

*kāścic ca bāla-vyajanāny upādaduḥ*
*kāścic ca tāmbūla-samudgakāvalim*
*kāścit patad-grāha-cayaṁ vibhāgaśo*
*bhṛṅgārikāḥ kāścana saj-jalair bhṛtāḥ*

*kāścit* — some (*gopīs*); *ca* — and; *bāla* — of (yak-tail) hair; *vyajanāni* — fans; *upādaduḥ* — took up; *kāścit* — some; *ca* — and; *tāmbūla* — of *pān; samudgaka* — of boxes; *āvalim* — a number; *kāścit* — some; *patat* — falling; *grāha-cayam* —

vessels for collecting the remnants; *vibhāgaśaḥ* — in various groups; *bhṛṅgārikāḥ* — large pots; *kāścana* — some; *sat-jalaiḥ* — with fresh water; *bhṛtāḥ* — carried.

**The gopīs divided the various services among themselves. Some took up yak-tail whisks, others held boxes in a row with more pān, others had several vessels for catching the falling remnants of pān, and others carried large pots of fresh water.**

### TEXT 142

अन्याश्च तच्छ्रोत्रमनोहराणि
गायन्ति गीतानि सकीर्तनानि ।
वाद्यानि काश्चिद्बहु वादयन्ति
तन्वन्ति नर्माण्यमुना सहान्याः ॥

*anyāś ca tac-chrotra-manoharāṇi*
*gāyanti gītāni sa-kīrtanāni*
*vādyāni kāścid bahu vādayanti*
*tanvanti narmāṇy amunā sahānyāḥ*

*anyāḥ* — others; *ca* — and; *tat* — His; *śrotra* — to the ears; *manoharāṇi* — pleasant; *gāyanti* — sang; *gītāni* — songs; *sa-kīrtanāni* — along with recitation of prayers; *vādyāni* — instrumental music; *kāścit* — some; *bahu* — of various kinds; *vādayanti* — played; *tanvanti* — engaged in; *narmāṇi* — joking conversation; *amunā saha* — with Him; *anyāḥ* — others.

**Other gopīs sang songs and recited prayers that were pleasing to His ears, some played various musical instruments, and yet others exchanged joking words with Him.**

COMMENTARY: The *gopīs* are always fully dedicated to satisfying Kṛṣṇa. They sang His names and offered Him prayers because such *saṅkīrtana* pleases Him very much.

TEXT 143

सर्वाभिरेवं परिषेव्यमाणस्
ताभिः स सौहार्दभरार्द्रिताभिः ।
ताम्बूलिकं चर्वितमत्यभीष्टं
ताभ्यो ददेऽन्योन्यमलक्ष्यमाणम् ॥

*sarvābhir evaṁ pariṣevyamāṇas*
*tābhiḥ sa sauhārda-bharārdritābhiḥ*
*tāmbūlikaṁ carvitam aty-abhīṣṭaṁ*
*tābhyo dade 'nyonyam alakṣyamāṇam*

*sarvābhiḥ* — by all; *evam* — thus; *pariṣevyamāṇaḥ* — being served; *tābhiḥ* — by them; *saḥ* — He; *sauhārda-bhara* — out of great affection; *ārdritābhiḥ* — whose hearts were melting; *tāmbūlikam* — *pān; carvitam* — chewed; *ati-abhīṣṭam* — very much desired; *tābhyaḥ* — to them; *dade* — He gave; *anyonyam* — by one other; *alakṣyamāṇam* — not noticed.

**Kṛṣṇa, served by all those gopīs, their hearts melting in great affection for Him, responded by giving to each one, unseen by the others, the prized remnants of His chewed pān.**

COMMENTARY: Kṛṣṇa is more eager to fulfill the desires of His devotees than to receive their service. On this occasion He gave the *prasāda* of His *pān* to all the *gopīs*. This does not mean, however, that Kṛṣṇa treated all the *gopīs* exactly the same way; He reciprocated with each of them individually, unseen by the others.

TEXT 144

एवं महाधूर्तसदःशिरोमणिः
सर्वाः प्रियास्ता रमयन्स्वचेष्टितैः ।
श्रीराधिकाप्रेमकथासु निर्वृतः
प्रस्वापलीलामभजत्क्षणादयम् ॥

*evaṁ mahā-dhūrta-sadaḥ-śiromaṇiḥ*
*sarvāḥ priyās tā ramayan sva-ceṣṭitaiḥ*
*śrī-rādhikā-prema-kathāsu nirvṛtaḥ*
*prasvāpa-līlām abhajat kṣaṇād ayam*

*evam* — thus; *mahā-dhūrta* — of great rogues; *sadaḥ* — of the assembly; *śiromaṇiḥ* — the crest jewel; *sarvāḥ* — all the girls; *priyāḥ* — beloved; *tāḥ* — them; *ramayan* — gratifying; *sva-ceṣṭitaiḥ* — with His behavior; *śrī-rādhikā* — of Śrī Rādhikā; *prema-kathāsu* — by the loving talks; *nirvṛtaḥ* — pleased; *prasvāpa* — of sleeping; *līlām* — of the pastime; *abhajat* — partook; *kṣaṇāt* — for a short time; *ayam* — He.

**In this way the most eminent member of the assembly of great rogues gratified all His beloved girlfriends with His behavior. Then, pleased by the loving talks of Śrī Rādhikā, as a pastime He took a short nap.**

COMMENTARY: Even while exchanging affection with all the *gopīs,* Kṛṣṇa showed special favor to the chief of them, Śrīmatī Rādhārāṇī. He took special pleasure in talking with Her.

## TEXT 145

कयापि संज्ञया तास्तु तेन सङ्केतिताः किल ।
सर्वाः स्वस्वगृहं जग्मुर्हर्षपूरपरिप्लुताः ॥

*kayāpi saṁjñayā tās tu*
*tena saṅketitāḥ kila*
*sarvāḥ sva-sva-gṛhaṁ jagmur*
*harṣa-pūra-pariplutāḥ*

*kayā api* — by a certain; *saṁjñayā* — gesture; *tāḥ* — they; *tu* — and; *tena* — by Him; *saṅketitāḥ* — signaled; *kila* — indeed; *sarvāḥ* — all; *sva-sva* — each their own; *gṛham* — home; *jagmuḥ* — went; *harṣa* — of happiness; *pūra* — with a flood; *pariplutāḥ* — filled.

**Signaled by a gesture from Kṛṣṇa, the gopīs, overflowing with happiness, all left for their own homes.**

COMMENTARY: Even when Kṛṣṇa sent the *gopīs* home they were happy because as they were leaving He secretly asked each of them to meet Him later.

## TEXT 146

श्रीदाम्नागत्य गेहं स्वमहं नीतः प्रयत्नतः ।
अन्यत्तस्य निशाक्रीडावृत्तं नार्हामि भाषितुम् ॥

*śrīdāmnāgatya gehaṁ svam*
*ahaṁ nītaḥ prayatnataḥ*
*anyat tasya niśā-krīḍā-*
*vṛttaṁ nārhāmi bhāṣitum*

*śrīdāmnā* — by Śrīdāmā; *āgatya* — who came; *geham* — to the home; *svam* — his; *aham* — I; *nītaḥ* — brought; *prayatnataḥ* — with effort; *anyat* — other; *tasya* — His; *niśā* — in the night; *krīḍā* — of the pastimes; *vṛttam* — description; *na arhāmi* — I cannot; *bhāṣitum* — speak.

**Śrīdāmā came and with some effort brought me away to his house. And about Kṛṣṇa's pastimes during the night there is nothing I can say.**

COMMENTARY: Sarūpa's disciple might be curious about the pastimes Kṛṣṇa hinted at to the *gopīs* by moving His eyebrows, but, as Sarūpa tells him, that topic is not theirs to discuss.

## TEXT 147

नीत्वा महार्त्या तां रात्रिं प्रातर्नन्दगृहे गतः ।
अपश्यं स हि सुप्तोऽस्ति पर्यङ्के रतिचिह्नभाक् ॥

*nītvā mahārtyā tāṁ rātriṁ*
*prātar nanda-gṛhe gataḥ*
*apaśyaṁ sa hi supto 'sti*
*paryaṅke rati-cihna-bhāk*

*nītvā* — spending; *mahā-ārtyā* — in great distress; *tām* — that; *rātrim* — night; *prātaḥ* — early in the morning; *nanda-gṛhe* — to the residence of Nanda Mahārāja; *gataḥ* — gone; *apaśyam* — I saw; *saḥ* — He; *hi* — indeed; *suptaḥ* — sleeping; *asti* — was; *paryaṅke* — on His bed; *rati* — of conjugal enjoyment; *cihna* — signs; *bhāk* — showing.

**I spent that night in great distress. And early next morning I went to the house of Nanda Mahārāja and saw Kṛṣṇa asleep in bed, His body showing signs of conjugal enjoyment.**

COMMENTARY: Sarūpa stayed awake all night, so there is no mention of his waking up. At dawn he went to Kṛṣṇa and saw fingernail scratches all over Kṛṣṇa's body.

## TEXT 148

सरलप्रकृतिर्माता निविष्टा तस्य पार्श्वतः ।
बहुधा लालयन्ती तं किञ्चिदात्मन्यभाषत ॥

*sarala-prakṛtir mātā*
*niviṣṭā tasya pārśvataḥ*
*bahudhā lālayantī taṁ*
*kiñcid ātmany abhāṣata*

*sarala* — simple; *prakṛtiḥ* — whose nature; *mātā* — His mother; *niviṣṭā* — entered; *tasya* — His; *pārśvataḥ* — by the side; *bahudhā* — in various ways; *lālayantī* — attending to; *tam* — Him; *kiñcit* — something; *ātmani* — to herself; *abhāṣata* — she said.

**Kṛṣṇa's simple-hearted mother came in and sat down at His side. While attending to Him in various ways, she said something under her breath.**

COMMENTARY: Mother Yaśodā saw the same marks as Sarūpa but was not capable of wondering what had caused them. Her mind worked in a simple, straightforward way. She busied herself in bathing Kṛṣṇa and getting Him ready for the day.

## TEXT 149

श्रीयशोदोवाच
हन्त बालो ममावित्वा गा वनेष्वखिलं दिनम् ।
श्रान्तो निद्रासुखं प्राप्तो न जागर्त्यधुनाप्ययम् ॥

*śrī-yaśodovāca*
*hanta bālo mamāvitvā*
*gā vaneṣv akhilaṁ dinam*
*śrānto nidrā-sukhaṁ prāpto*
*na jāgarty adhunāpy ayam*

*śrī-yaśodā uvāca* — Śrī Yaśodā said; *hanta* — oh; *bālaḥ* — boy; *mama* — my; *avitvā* — tending; *gāḥ* — the cows; *vaneṣu* — in the forests; *akhilam* — the entire; *dinam* — day; *śrāntaḥ* — fatigued; *nidrā* — of sleep; *sukham* — the happiness; *prāptaḥ* — obtaining; *na jāgarti* — has not woken up; *adhunā* — now; *api* — even; *ayam* — He.

**Śrī Yaśodā said: Dear me! All day my little boy tended the cows in the forests. Fatigued, He was happy to go to sleep, and now He is still not awake.**

COMMENTARY: Yaśodā could hardly think that Kṛṣṇa was not yet up because He had been awake all night dancing with the *gopīs*. Instead she thought He was still asleep because He was just a little boy.

## TEXT 150

अरण्यकण्टकैर्दुष्टैः क्षतानीमानि सर्वतः ।
आक्रियन्तास्य गात्रेषु परितो धावतो मुहुः ॥

*araṇya-kaṇṭakair duṣṭaiḥ*
*kṣatānīmāni sarvataḥ*
*ākriyantāsya gātreṣu*
*parito dhāvato muhuḥ*

*araṇya* — of the forest; *kaṇṭakaiḥ* — by the thorns; *duṣṭaiḥ* — nasty; *kṣatāni* — cuts; *imāni* — those; *sarvataḥ* — everywhere; *ākriyanta* — were made; *asya* — His; *gātreṣu* — on the limbs; *paritaḥ* — on all sides; *dhāvataḥ* — who was running; *muhuḥ* — continuously.

**As He ran about the forest, nasty thorns made cuts all over His body.**

COMMENTARY: This was Yaśodā's explanation for the scratches made by the fingernails of the amorous *gopīs*. But as she carefully examined and gently touched the marks with her hand, she wondered, How could thorns in the forest have cut His lips? Well, running all over and playing wildly with the boys, He must have fallen, face first, into a bush.

## TEXT 151

अहो कष्टं न जानाति किञ्चिन्निद्रावशं गतः ।
म्रक्षयामास गात्रेषु स्वस्येदं नेत्रकज्जलम् ॥

*aho kaṣṭaṁ na jānāti*
*kiñcin nidrā-vaśaṁ gataḥ*
*mrakṣayām āsa gātreṣu*
*svasyedaṁ netra-kajjalam*

*aho* — oh; *kaṣṭam* — how painful; *na jānāti* — He does not know; *kiñcit* — anything; *nidrā* — of sleep; *vaśam* — under the sway; *gataḥ* — gone; *mrakṣayām āsa* — He smeared; *gātreṣu* — on the limbs; *svasya* — His; *idam* — this; *netra* — from His eyes; *kajjalam* — the collyrium.

**Oh, how painful this must be for Him! But now, fast asleep, He is not aware of anything. And He has smeared the kajjala from His eyes all over His body.**

COMMENTARY: This *kajjala* was from the *gopīs'* eyes, which Kṛṣṇa had been kissing.

## TEXT 152

तथात्माधरताम्बूलरागं चेतस्ततोऽविदन् ।
चिच्छेद हारमालादिपरिवृत्तिं मुहुर्भजन् ॥

*tathātmādhara-tāmbūla-*
*rāgaṁ cetas tato 'vidan*
*ciccheda hāra-mālādi-*
*parivṛttiṁ muhur bhajan*

*tathā* — also; *ātma* — His own; *adhara* — from the lips; *tāmbūla* — of *pān; rāgam* — the red juice; *ca* — and; *itaḥ tataḥ* — here and there; *avidan* — unaware; *ciccheda* — He broke; *hāra* — His necklaces; *mālā-ādi* — garlands and so on; *parivṛttim* — turning; *muhuḥ* — repeatedly; *bhajan* — doing.

**He doesn't even know that He has spilled red pān juice from His lips all over Himself, and that by turning over and over in bed He has broken His necklaces and garlands and other ornaments.**

COMMENTARY: The red stains on Kṛṣṇa's cheeks were actually from the *pān* chewed by the *gopīs,* and His garlands and necklaces had broken while He was embracing them. Kṛṣṇa's clothing and the protective thread on His neck were also in disarray. But Mother Yaśodā ascribed all this to His rolling about in His sleep.

## TEXT 153

नूनं काश्मीरवर्णेयं यमुनातीरमृत्तिका ।
न परित्याजिता हन्त स्नानेनापि वपुःसखी ॥

*nūnaṁ kāśmīra-varṇeyaṁ*
*yamunā-tīra-mṛttikā*
*na parityājitā hanta*
*snānenāpi vapuḥ-sakhī*

*nūnam* — indeed; *kāśmīra* — like saffron; *varṇā* — colored; *iyam* — this; *yamunā-tīra* — from the Yamunā's shore; *mṛttikā* — clay; *na* — not; *parityājitā* — removed; *hanta* — oh; *snānena* — by bathing; *api* — even; *vapuḥ* — of His body; *sakhī* — a constant companion.

**My goodness! This saffron-colored clay from the shore of the Yamunā — it seems that even His bath couldn't wash it off. It has become like an inseparable friend to His body.**

COMMENTARY: This "red clay" was actually *kuṅkuma* from the *gopīs'* breasts.

## TEXT 154

बालाभिश्चपलाभिर्ह्यः सन्ध्यायामवधानतः ।
स्नानं न कारितं सम्यङ् नाभ्यङ्गोद्वर्तने तथा ॥

*bālābhiś capalābhir hyaḥ*
*sandhyāyām avadhānataḥ*
*snānaṁ na kāritaṁ samyaṅ*
*nābhyaṅgodvartane tathā*

*bālābhiḥ* — by the girls; *capalābhiḥ* — thoughtless; *hyaḥ* — yesterday; *sandhyāyām* — in the evening; *avadhānataḥ* — attentively; *snānam* — the bath; *na* — not; *kāritam* — given;

*samyak* — properly; *na* — nor; *abhyaṅga* — application of oil; *udvartane* — and removing the excess oil; *tathā* — either.

**Yesterday evening, those fickle girls didn't bathe Him with proper attention. They didn't nicely apply the oil and wipe off what was left.**

COMMENTARY: If those silly girls had bathed Kṛṣṇa more carefully, she thought, the dirt would have come off.

TEXT 155

श्रीसरूप उवाच
माता यशोदा मुहुरेवमाह
तासां समक्षं व्रजकन्यकानाम् ।
तत्रागतानां भयहासलज्जा-
विर्भावमुद्राविलसन्मुखीनाम् ॥

*śrī-sarūpa uvāca*
*mātā yaśodā muhur evam āha*
*tāsāṁ samakṣaṁ vraja-kanyakānām*
*tatrāgatānāṁ bhaya-hāsa-lajjā-*
*virbhāva-mudrā-vilasan-mukhīnām*

*śrī-sarūpaḥ uvāca* — Śrī Sarūpa said; *mātā yaśodā* — Mother Yaśodā; *muhuḥ* — again and again; *evam* — thus; *āha* — spoke; *tāsām* — of them; *samakṣam* — in the presence; *vraja-kanyakānām* — the young girls of Vraja; *tatra* — there; *āgatānām* — who had arrived; *bhaya* — of fear; *hāsa* — laughter; *lajjā* — and embarrassment; *āvirbhāva* — of the manifesting; *mudrā* — gestures; *vilasat* — playing; *mukhīnām* — on their faces.

**Śrī Sarūpa said: Mother Yaśodā spoke like that again and again, right in front of the young girls of Vraja, who had just arrived and who now had signs of fear, laughter, and embarrassment playfully shining on their faces.**

COMMENTARY: Mother Yaśodā's name implies that she added to Kṛṣṇa's fame (*yaśo dadau*). The *gopīs* arrived at Nanda Mahārāja's house just as she was complaining about Kṛṣṇa's disheveled state. Listening to her, they became afraid that she might begin to understand what Kṛṣṇa had actually been doing at night. Still, they couldn't help but laugh at her naive statements and shrink in embarrassment at seeing the obvious signs of their dalliance with Kṛṣṇa.

## TEXT 156

ततोऽसौ स्वापलीलाया विरतः स्नापितस्तया ।
भूषणैर्भूषितः साकं बलरामेण भोजितः ॥

*tato 'sau svāpa-līlāyā*
*virataḥ snāpitas tayā*
*bhūṣaṇair bhūṣitaḥ sākaṁ*
*balarāmeṇa bhojitaḥ*

*tataḥ* — then; *asau* — He; *svāpa* — of sleeping; *līlāyāḥ* — the pastime; *virataḥ* — having finished; *snāpitaḥ* — bathed; *tayā* — by her; *bhūṣaṇaiḥ* — with ornaments; *bhūṣitaḥ* — decorated; *sākam* — along with; *balarāmeṇa* — Balarāma; *bhojitaḥ* — fed.

**Kṛṣṇa then finished His pastime of sleep, and His mother bathed Him, adorned Him with ornaments, and fed both Him and Balarāma.**

## TEXT 157

विश्रमय्य क्षणं तं च गोपीनां सुखवार्तया ।
वने शुभप्रयाणाय तस्य कृत्यानि साकरोत् ॥

*viśramayya kṣaṇaṁ taṁ ca*
*gopīnāṁ sukha-vārtayā*
*vane śubha-prayāṇāya*
*tasya kṛtyāni sākarot*

*viśramayya* — making relax; *kṣaṇam* — for a short time; *tam* — Him; *ca* — and; *gopīnām* — with the *gopīs; sukha* — enjoyable; *vārtayā* — with talk; *vane* — in the forest; *śubha* — auspicious; *prayāṇāya* — for the departure; *tasya* — His; *kṛtyāni* — preparations; *sā* — she; *akarot* — made.

**She made Kṛṣṇa relax a short while, and He enjoyed talking with the gopīs. Then she got things ready for His auspicious departure to the forest.**

## TEXT 158

तासामप्यन्तरार्तानां भाविविच्छेदचिन्तया ।
दिव्यमङ्गलगीतेन पूर्णकुम्भादिकं न्यधात् ॥

*tāsām apy antar-ārtānāṁ*
*bhāvi-viccheda-cintayā*
*divya-maṅgala-gītena*
*pūrṇa-kumbhādikaṁ nyadhāt*

*tāsām* — of them, the *gopīs; api* — although; *antaḥ* — within themselves; *ārtānām* — who were pained; *bhāvi* — imminent; *viccheda* — of the separation; *cintayā* — from thinking; *divya* — transcendental; *maṅgala* — auspicious; *gītena* — with songs; *pūrṇa-kumbha* — full pots; *ādikam* — and other items; *nyadhāt* — she provided.

**Though the young gopīs were pained at heart at the thought of soon being separated from Kṛṣṇa, Mother Yaśodā had them sing transcendental songs for His good fortune and ceremoniously carry full pots and other auspicious items.**

COMMENTARY: No matter what ecstasy impeded them, the *gopīs* had to do their service. After all, they had to sing and carry *pūrṇa-kumbhas* — full pots of water with yogurt, flowers, unhusked barley, parched rice, and other pure substances — or else Kṛṣṇa's departure for the forest would not be auspicious.

## TEXT 159

निवेश्य साग्रजं पुत्रं पीठेऽरण्योचितानि सा ।
पर्यधापयदङ्गेषु भूषणान्यौषधानि च ॥

*niveśya sāgrajaṁ putraṁ*
*pīṭhe 'raṇyocitāni sā*
*paryadhāpayad aṅgeṣu*
*bhūṣaṇāny auṣadhāni ca*

*niveśya* — seating; *sa-agrajam* — along with His elder brother; *putram* — Her son; *pīṭhe* — on a chair; *araṇya* — for the forest; *ucitāni* — suitable; *sā* — she; *paryadhāpayat* — placed; *aṅgeṣu* — on the limbs; *bhūṣaṇāni* — ornaments; *auṣadhāni* — medicinal herbs; *ca* — and.

**She sat Kṛṣṇa on a chair with His elder brother and adorned Their limbs with ornaments and medicinal herbs suitable for the forest.**

COMMENTARY: Besides decorative ornaments, Yaśodā placed various items on Their bodies to assure Their safety, such as tiger nails, enchanted talismans, protective threads, herbs meant for healing wounds, and *gāruḍa-maṇi* (emeralds for guarding against poison).

## TEXT 160

प्रयोज्य वृद्धविप्राभिरन्याभिश्च शुभाशिषः ।
बलाद्यात्राविधिं तेन सर्वं सा समपादयत् ॥

*prayojya vṛddha-viprābhir*
*anyābhiś ca śubhāśiṣaḥ*

*balād yātrā-vidhiṁ tena*
*sarvaṁ sā samapādayat*

*prayojya* — invoking; *vṛddha* — elderly; *viprābhiḥ* — by *brāhmaṇa* ladies; *anyābhiḥ* — others; *ca* — and; *śubha-āśiṣaḥ* — blessings; *balāt* — by force; *yātrā* — for the journey; *vidhim* — prescribed rituals; *tena* — by Him; *sarvam* — all; *sā* — she; *samapādayat* — caused to be carried out.

**She engaged elderly brāhmaṇa ladies and other ladies in offering blessings, and she made Kṛṣṇa do all the prescribed rituals to prepare for His outing.**

COMMENTARY: Elderly *brāhmaṇīs* blessed Kṛṣṇa, as did the older *gopīs*. Kṛṣṇa was more eager to get going than to touch His nose with His fingers and carry out other protective rituals, but His mother gave Him no choice.

## TEXT 161

भोग्यं माध्याह्निकं मात्रार्पितमादाय किञ्चन ।
उत्थाप्य गाः पुरः कुर्वन्प्रस्थितो वेणुमीरयन् ॥

*bhogyaṁ mādhyāhnikaṁ mātrā-*
*rpitam ādāya kiñcana*
*utthāpya gāḥ puraḥ kurvan*
*prasthito veṇum īrayan*

*bhogyam* — food; *mādhya-ahnikam* — for the midday; *mātrā* — by His mother; *arpitam* — given; *ādāya* — taking; *kiñcana* — some; *utthāpya* — raising; *gāḥ* — the cows; *puraḥ* — in front; *kurvan* — putting; *prasthitaḥ* — set off; *veṇum* — His flute; *īrayan* — playing.

**Kṛṣṇa took the lunch His mother gave Him for noontime, stirred the cows from their rest and got them in front of Him, and set off, playing His flute.**

COMMENTARY: Mother Yaśodā had prepared lunch for Kṛṣṇa to take with Him, and He packed as much of it as He could in a bag tied to a stick. Then He roused the cows, who were lying down, and drove them forward, urging them on with the music of His flute.

## TEXT 162

तावत्सहचराः सर्वे तस्याभ्यर्णे समागताः ।
निर्गत्य वर्गशो घोषात्तत्सख्योचिततां गताः ॥

*tāvat sahacarāḥ sarve*
*tasyābhyarṇe samāgatāḥ*
*nirgatya vargaśo ghoṣāt*
*tat-sakhyocitatāṁ gatāḥ*

*tāvat* — just then; *saha-carāḥ* — His companions; *sarve* — all; *tasya* — to Him; *abhyarṇe* — close; *samāgatāḥ* — assembled; *nirgatya* — came out; *vargaśaḥ* — in groups; *ghoṣāt* — from the cowherd village; *tat* — with Him; *sakhya* — for friendship; *ucitatām* — competence; *gatāḥ* — having attained.

**Just then His companions came out in groups from the cowherd village and gathered around Him. The boys were all fit to be His intimate friends.**

COMMENTARY: Because the attention of the cowherd boys was never diverted to anything other than pleasing Kṛṣṇa, the boys needed only to hear Kṛṣṇa's flute to know that it was time to leave. It hardly mattered whether they had finished having breakfast or preparing themselves; if Kṛṣṇa was going to the forest they had to follow right behind. There were a great number of these companions of Kṛṣṇa, and they naturally divided themselves into groups, led by prominent boys. All the boys, however, were completely fit to be with the Supreme Lord in close friendship.

## TEXT 163

कदाचित्तैः समं वंशीः शृङ्गाणि च कदापि सः ।
कदाचित्पत्रवाद्यानि बहुधा वादयन्बभौ ॥

*kadācit taiḥ samaṁ vaṁśīḥ*
*śṛṅgāṇi ca kadāpi saḥ*
*kadācit patra-vādyāni*
*bahudhā vādayan babhau*

*kadācit* — at one moment; *taiḥ samam* — together with them; *vaṁśīḥ* — flutes; *śṛṅgāṇi* — buffalo horns; *ca* — and; *kadā api* — at one moment; *saḥ* — He; *kadācit* — at another moment; *patra* — made of leaves; *vādyāni* — musical instruments; *bahudhā* — in various ways; *vādayan* — playing; *babhau* — He showed off.

**At one moment He and the boys played their flutes, at another their buffalo horns, at still another some instruments fashioned from leaves. Thus He and the boys showed off by playing various kinds of music.**

COMMENTARY: The boys made noisemakers out of leaves and blades of *darbha* grass they picked up from the side of the path.

## TEXT 164

समं भ्रात्रावतस्थेऽसावात्तक्रीडापरिच्छदैः ।
गायद्भिस्तैश्च नृत्यद्भिः स्तुवद्भिस्तं प्रहर्षतः ॥

*samaṁ bhrātrāvatasthe 'sāv*
*ātta-krīḍā-paricchadaiḥ*
*gāyadbhis taiś ca nṛtyadbhiḥ*
*stuvadbhis taṁ praharṣataḥ*

*samam* — together; *bhrātrā* — with His brother; *avatasthe* — stood; *asau* — He; *ātta* — holding; *krīḍā-paricchadaiḥ* — their playthings; *gāyadbhiḥ* — who were singing; *taiḥ* — by them; *ca* — and; *nṛtyadbhiḥ* — dancing; *stuvadbhiḥ* — and praising; *tam* — Him (Kṛṣṇa); *praharṣataḥ* — joyfully.

**As His friends, playthings in hand, joyfully sang, danced, and glorified Him, Kṛṣṇa stood with His brother.**

COMMENTARY: Among the various things the boys carried were balls, drums, fans, flags, seats, umbrellas, *cāmara* fans, hand cymbals, wooden shoes, and food and drink. This was the paraphernalia for their games in the forest. The boys were very happy to be away from their homes and on the way to the forest, where they could play however they liked.

## TEXT 165

अग्रे ज्यायानहं पृष्ठे ताश्चानुव्रजनच्छलात् ।
आकृष्टाः प्रेमपाशेन प्रस्थिता विरहासहाः ॥

*agre jyāyān ahaṁ pṛṣṭhe*
*tāś cānuvrajana-cchalāt*
*ākṛṣṭāḥ prema-pāśena*
*prasthitā virahāsahāḥ*

*agre* — in front; *jyāyān* — His elder brother; *aham* — I; *pṛṣṭhe* — in the rear; *tāḥ* — the girls; *ca* — and; *anuvrajana* — of following; *chalāt* — on some excuse; *ākṛṣṭāḥ* — pulled; *prema* — of love; *pāśena* — by the ropes; *prasthitāḥ* — setting off; *viraha* — separation; *asahāḥ* — not able to tolerate.

**Kṛṣṇa's elder brother walked in front and I walked behind. And the girls, unable to tolerate being separated from Kṛṣṇa, found excuses to follow and came out from the village, helplessly pulled by ropes of love.**

COMMENTARY: Here Sarūpa gives the *gopīs* only a slight mention, referring to them simply as *tāḥ* ("those girls"), because anything he says about them might stir his memories of the special relations between the *gopīs* and Kṛṣṇa and disturb the mood he is trying to set. Even though his relationship with Kṛṣṇa was in *sakhya-rasa,* if he were to remember the *gopīs'* love for Kṛṣṇa he would be unable to control his ecstasy.

The *gopīs* could hardly justify walking out of the village in broad daylight and in front of everyone, but because they were helplessly attracted to Kṛṣṇa they were unable to tolerate His absence.

## TEXT 166

भावेन केनचित्स्विन्नं पुत्रस्योद्वीक्ष्य सा मुखम् ।
सम्मार्ज्य प्रस्नुवत्स्तन्या बहिर्द्वारान्तमन्वगात् ॥

*bhāvena kenacit svinnaṁ*
*putrasyodvīkṣya sā mukham*
*sammārjya prasnuvat-stanyā*
*bahir-dvārāntam anvagāt*

*bhāvena* — due to an esctatic mood; *kenacit* — some; *svinnam* — perspiring; *putrasya* — of her son; *udvīkṣya* — noticing; *sā* — she (Yaśodā); *mukham* — the face; *sammārjya* — wiping; *prasnuvat* — dripping; *stanyā* — milk from her breasts; *bahiḥ* — outer; *dvāra* — the gates; *antam* — up to; *anvagāt* — she followed.

**Mother Yaśodā saw Kṛṣṇa perspiring from a mood of ecstasy and came to wipe His face and went with Him as far as the outer gates of the village, her breasts wet with milk.**

COMMENTARY: Kṛṣṇa's face may have been perspiring because of the longing to be with the *gopīs* that arose in Him when He saw them following behind. Mother Yaśodā, however, was concerned only with wiping His face. First she wiped with her hand, and when that didn't work she used the edge of her garment.

## TEXT 167

तेनोक्तापि गृहं यान्ती ग्रीवामुद्वर्तयन्त्यहो ।
पदान्यतीत्य द्वित्राणि पुनर्व्यग्रा ययौ सुतम् ॥

*tenoktāpi gṛhaṁ yāntī*
*grīvām udvartayanty aho*
*padāny atītya dvi-trāṇi*
*punar vyagrā yayau sutam*

*tena* — by Him; *uktā* — told; *api* — and; *gṛham* — to the house; *yāntī* — going; *grīvām* — her neck; *udvartayantī* — raising; *aho* — oh; *padāni* — steps; *atītya* — taking; *dvi-trāṇi* — two or three; *punaḥ* — again; *vyagrā* — anxious; *yayau* — she went; *sutam* — to her son.

**At His request she then turned back toward the house. But — oh! — after two or three steps she craned her neck and anxiously went back to her son.**

## TEXT 168

उपस्कृत्यास्य ताम्बूलं मुखे हस्ते समर्प्य च ।
पुनर्निवृत्य प्राग्वत्सा तं वेगैराययौ पुनः ॥

*upaskṛtyāsya tāmbūlaṁ*
*mukhe haste samarpya ca*
*punar nivṛtya prāg-vat sā*
*taṁ vegair āyayau punaḥ*

*upaskṛtya* — preparing; *asya* — for Him; *tāmbūlam* — *pān;* *mukhe* — in His mouth; *haste* — in His hand; *samarpya* — placing; *ca* — and; *punaḥ* — again; *nivṛtya* — going back; *prāk-vat* — as before; *sā* — she; *tam* — to Him; *vegaiḥ* — quickly; *āyayau* — came; *punaḥ* — once more.

**She made pān for Him and put some in His mouth and some in His hand and then again turned toward the house. But once again she quickly came back to Him.**

COMMENTARY: Just like the first time, Yaśodā again nervously turned around, craned her neck to see Him, and came back to Him.

### TEXT 169

मिष्टं फलादिकं किञ्चिद्भोजयित्वा सुतं पथि ।
पाययित्वा च गेहाय यान्ती प्राग्वन् न्यवर्तत ॥

*miṣṭaṁ phalādikaṁ kiñcid*
*bhojayitvā sutaṁ pathi*
*pāyayitvā ca gehāya*
*yāntī prāg-van nyavartata*

*miṣṭam* — sweet; *phala-ādikam* — fruits and so on; *kiñcit* — some; *bhojayitvā* — feeding; *sutam* — to her son; *pathi* — on the path; *pāyayitvā* — giving something to drink; *ca* — and; *gehāya* — toward home; *yāntī* — going; *prāk-van* — as before; *nyavartata* — she turned around.

**Right on the path she fed Him some fruits and some other sweet things and gave Him something to drink. Then she again started going back to the house, and then again turned around.**

### TEXT 170

मुहुर्निरीक्ष्य वस्त्रादि सन्निवेश्य सुतस्य सा ।
पुनर्निवृत्याथागत्य दीना पुत्रमशिक्षयत् ॥

*muhur nirīkṣya vastrādi*
*sanniveśya sutasya sā*

*punar nivṛtyāthāgatya*
*dīnā putram aśikṣayat*

*muhuḥ* — again; *nirīkṣya* — scrutinizing; *vastra-ādi* — the clothing and so on; *sanniveśya* — adjusting; *sutasya* — of her son; *sā* — she; *punaḥ* — again; *nivṛtya* — turning back; *atha* — then; *āgatya* — coming; *dīnā* — plaintive; *putram* — to her son; *aśikṣayat* — she gave instructions.

**She gave Him a thorough looking over and adjusted His clothes and the other things He had on, and then she once more turned back. But then she again returned, and plaintively gave Him some instructions.**

COMMENTARY: Yaśodā spoke to Kṛṣṇa anxiously because she knew He was naughty and would likely ignore her advice.

## TEXT 171

भो वत्स दुर्गमेऽरण्ये न गन्तव्यं विदूरतः ।
सकण्टकवनान्तश्च प्रवेष्टव्यं कदापि न ॥

*bho vatsa durgame 'raṇye*
*na gantavyaṁ vidūrataḥ*
*sa-kaṇṭaka-vanāntaś ca*
*praveṣṭavyaṁ kadāpi na*

*bhoḥ* — oh; *vatsa* — dear child; *durgame* — impenetrable; *araṇye* — in the forest; *na gantavyam* — you should not go; *vidūrataḥ* — very far; *sa-kaṇṭaka* — full of thorns; *vana-antaḥ* — in the forest; *ca* — and; *praveṣṭavyam* — to be entered; *kadā api* — ever; *na* — not.

**"My dear child, don't go too far into the impenetrable woods. And never enter deep into the forest where there are thorns!"**

## TEXT 172

तदर्थं चात्मशपथं माता विस्तार्य काकुभिः ।
पुनर्निवृत्य कतिचित्पदानि पुनराययौ ॥

*tad-arthaṁ cātma-śapathaṁ*
*mātā vistārya kākubhiḥ*
*punar nivṛtya katicit*
*padāni punar āyayau*

*tat-artham* — for the sake of this; *ca* — and; *ātma* — her; *śapatham* — solemn advice; *mātā* — His mother; *vistārya* — expounding; *kākubhiḥ* — in sorrowful tones; *punaḥ* — again; *nivṛtya* — turning back; *katicit* — some; *padāni* — steps; *punaḥ* — again; *āyayau* — she came back.

**After speaking this way at length, beseeching Him to take care, she once again turned home and took a few steps, and yet again came back.**

## TEXT 173

भोस्तात राम स्थातव्यं भवताग्रेऽनुजस्य हि ।
त्वया च सख्युः श्रीदामन्ससरूपेण पृष्ठतः ॥

*bhos tāta rāma sthātavyaṁ*
*bhavatāgre 'nujasya hi*
*tvayā ca sakhyuḥ śrīdāman*
*sa-sarūpeṇa pṛṣṭhataḥ*

*bhoḥ* — O; *tāta* — my dear boy; *rāma* — Balarāma; *sthātavyam* — should stay; *bhavatā* — You; *agre* — in front; *anujasya* — of Your younger brother; *hi* — indeed; *tvayā* — you; *ca* — and; *sakhyuḥ* — of your friend; *śrīdāman* — O Śrīdāmā; *sa-sarūpeṇa* — along with Sarūpa; *pṛṣṭhataḥ* — in the rear.

**"My dear boy Rāma," she said, "You stay in front of Your younger brother. And you, Śrīdāmā, stay behind your friend Kṛṣṇa with Sarūpa.**

### TEXT 174

अंशोऽस्य दक्षिणे स्थेयं वामे च सुबल त्वया ।
इत्यादिकमसौ प्रार्थ्य सतृणं पुत्रमैक्षत ॥

*aṁśo 'sya dakṣiṇe stheyaṁ*
*vāme ca subala tvayā*
*ity-ādikam asau prārthya*
*sa-tṛṇaṁ putram aikṣata*

*aṁśo* — O Aṁśu; *asya* — His; *dakṣiṇe* — on the right side; *stheyam* — you should stay; *vāme* — on the left; *ca* — and; *subala* — O Subala; *tvayā* — you; *iti* — in this way; *ādikam* — and so on; *asau* — she; *prārthya* — imploring; *sa-tṛṇam* — with straw between her teeth; *putram* — at her son; *aikṣata* — she looked.

**"You, Aṁśu, should stay on Kṛṣṇa's right, and you, Subala, on His left." Straw between her teeth, she implored the boys with such requests. Then she looked intently at her son.**

COMMENTARY: Balarāma, the most competent of the boys, should walk in front of Kṛṣṇa. Though the others would spontaneously take up their proper places, she directed them anyway, just to make sure. The phrase *ity-ādikam* indicates other requests: The boys should not let Kṛṣṇa go into thorny and dangerous places, they should provide Him shade if the sun became too intense, and they should be sure He ate nicely at lunch. Coming to the end of her list of requests, Mother Yaśodā looked intently at Kṛṣṇa's face to evoke promises from Kṛṣṇa and the other boys that they would do what she had asked.

## TEXT 175

एवं व्यग्रधिया यातायातं सा कुर्वती मुहुः ।
नवप्रसूतामजयत्सुरभिं वरवत्सलाम् ॥

*evaṁ vyagra-dhiyā yātā-*
*yātaṁ sā kurvatī muhuḥ*
*nava-prasūtām ajayat*
*surabhiṁ vara-vatsalām*

*evam* — thus; *vyagra* — anxious; *dhiyā* — her mind; *yāta-āyātam* — going back and forth; *sā* — she; *kurvatī* — doing; *muhuḥ* — repeatedly; *nava-prasūtām* — who has just given birth; *ajayat* — she exceeded; *surabhim* — a cow; *vara* — very; *vatsalām* — affectionate.

**In this way Mother Yaśodā, anxiously going back and forth again and again, showed more love than a cow who has just given birth to a calf.**

COMMENTARY: This exchange between Yaśodā and Kṛṣṇa went on for some time, but Sarūpa wanted to avoid prolonging his description.

## TEXT 176

तां सपादग्रहं नत्वाश्लिष्य पुत्रः प्रयत्नतः ।
विविधच्छलतः स्वीयशपथैश्च न्यवर्तयत् ॥

*tāṁ sa-pāda-grahaṁ natvā-*
*śliṣya putraḥ prayatnataḥ*
*vividha-cchalataḥ svīya-*
*śapathaiś ca nyavartayat*

*tām* — her; *sa-pāda-graham* — with taking hold of the feet; *natvā* — bowing down to; *āśliṣya* — embracing; *putraḥ* — her son; *prayatnataḥ* — with endeavor; *vividha* — various; *chalataḥ*

— on pretexts; *svīya* — His own; *śapathaiḥ* — with strong statements; *ca* — and; *nyavartayat* — He turned her back.

**Her son then bowed down to her, took hold of her feet, and embraced her. And with various rationales, and finally with words of insistence of His own, with great effort He made her turn back.**

COMMENTARY: Kṛṣṇa hoped that by showing this elaborate display of respect and affection He could convince His mother of how seriously He took her words. He reminded her that she also had to eat breakfast and attend to various household chores. But when all His reasons failed to convince her, He finally simply insisted very strongly that she go back. All this He had to do several times before she finally relented.

## TEXT 177

तस्थौ तत्रैव सा दूरात्पश्यन्ती तं वनान्तिके ।
चित्रितेव स्नुतस्तन्या सास्रोत्तुङ्गस्थलोपरि ॥

*tasthau tatraiva sā dūrāt*
*paśyantī taṁ vanāntike*
*citriteva snuta-stanyā*
*sāsrottuṅga-sthalopari*

*tasthau* — stood; *tatra eva* — right there; *sā* — she; *dūrāt* — from a distance; *paśyantī* — watching; *tam* — Him; *vana-antike* — near the forest; *citritā* — painted; *iva* — as if; *snuta* — dripping; *stanyā* — milk from her breasts; *sa-asrā* — tearful; *uttuṅga* — high; *sthala* — a place; *upari* — on.

**And she, crying, milk dripping from her breasts, stood right there, motionless like a painted picture, and distantly watched from that high place near the forest.**

## TEXTS 178–179

श्रीगोप्यस्त्वनुगच्छन्त्यो बाष्पसंरुद्धकण्ठिकाः ।
गानाशक्ताः स्खलत्पादा अश्रुधारास्तदृष्टयः ॥

कर्तुं वक्तुं च ताः किञ्चिदशक्ता लज्जया भिया ।
महाशोकार्णवे मग्नास्तत्प्रतीकरणेऽक्षमाः ॥

*śrī-gopyas tv anugacchantyo*
*bāṣpa-saṁruddha-kaṇṭhikāḥ*
*gānāśaktāḥ skhalat-pādā*
*aśru-dhārāsta-dṛṣṭayaḥ*

*kartuṁ vaktuṁ ca tāḥ kiñcid*
*aśaktā lajjayā bhiyā*
*mahā-śokārṇave magnās*
*tat-pratīkaraṇe 'kṣamāḥ*

*śrī-gopyaḥ* — the lovely *gopīs; tu* — however; *anugacchantyaḥ* — following; *bāṣpa* — with tears; *saṁruddha* — choked; *kaṇṭhikāḥ* — their throats; *gāna* — to sing; *aśaktāḥ* — unable; *skhalat* — stumbling; *pādāḥ* — their feet; *aśru* — of tears; *dhārā* — by a downpour; *asta* — blocked; *dṛṣṭayaḥ* — their vision; *kartum* — to do; *vaktum* — to say; *ca* — and; *tāḥ* — they; *kiñcit* — anything; *aśaktāḥ* — incapable; *lajjayā* — due to shyness; *bhiyā* — and fear; *mahā* — great; *śoka* — of sorrow; *arṇave* — in an ocean; *magnāḥ* — immersed; *tat* — that; *pratīkaraṇe* — to counteract; *akṣamāḥ* — unable.

**But the lovely gopīs kept following Him. Their throats choked with weeping, they could no longer sing, nor see through their streams of tears, and their feet stumbled. In their shyness and fear, they had nothing they could do or say. Drowning in a great ocean of sorrow, they had no way to hold back their feelings.**

COMMENTARY: As expressed by the word *tu* ("however"), the mood of the *gopīs* is even more exalted than that of Mother Yaśodā. The *gopīs,* the Lord's most beloved devotees, are endowed with all excellent qualities. And now the *gopīs* were overwhelmed by various emotions, such as their natural shyness, which decorated their personalities most of the time, and their fear of what their elders must be thinking and what the consequences might be of having left the village without permission. In the village, moreover, the *gopīs* could counteract the pain of separation from Kṛṣṇa by embracing and kissing Him, but now that He was leaving for the day there was nothing they could do. They lacked the strength even to ask, "How can we live like this?" According to a well-known psychological principle, *nivedya duḥkhaṁ sukhino bhavanti:* "Unhappy people can regain their peace of mind by revealing the cause of their distress." But here the *gopīs* couldn't even express themselves, so they remained adrift in the vast ocean of their misery.

## TEXT 180

व्रजाद्बहिर्दूरतरं गतानां
तदङ्गनानां हृदयेक्षणानि ।
जहार यत्नेन निवर्तयंस्ता
मुहुः परावृत्य निरीक्षमाणाः ॥

*vrajād bahir dūra-taraṁ gatānāṁ*
*tad-aṅganānāṁ hṛdayekṣaṇāni*
*jahāra yatnena nivartayaṁs tā*
*muhuḥ parāvṛtya nirīkṣamāṇāḥ*

*vrajāt* — from the village; *bahiḥ* — outside; *dūra-taram* — quite far; *gatānām* — who had gone; *tat* — of those; *aṅganānām* — young girls; *hṛdaya* — the hearts; *īkṣaṇāni* — and eyes; *jahāra* — He took away; *yatnena* — with endeavor; *nivartayan* — making stop; *tāḥ* — them; *muhuḥ* — repeatedly; *parāvṛtya* — making turn back; *nirīkṣamāṇāḥ* — who were looking at Him.

**Kṛṣṇa had stolen the hearts and eyes of these young girls. The girls had come so far from the cowherd village, and now with some endeavor He stopped them. And as they looked at Him, He repeatedly tried to send them home.**

## TEXTS 181–182

व्यग्रात्मनाथ तेनेष्टदूतेन स्वयमेव च ।
ग्रीवामुद्वर्त्य सप्रेमदृष्ट्याश्वासयता मुहुः ॥

भ्रूसङ्केतादिना लज्जाभये जनयता बलात् ।
संस्तम्भितास्तास्तन्मातुरग्रे तद्वदवस्थिताः ॥

*vyagrātmanātha teneṣṭa-*
*dūtena svayam eva ca*
*grīvām udvartya sa-prema-*
*dṛṣṭyāśvāsayatā muhuḥ*

*bhrū-saṅketādinā lajjā-*
*bhaye janayatā balāt*
*saṁstambhitās tās tan-mātur*
*agre tadvad avasthitāḥ*

*vyagra* — anxious; *ātmanā* — whose mind; *atha* — then; *tena* — by Him; *iṣṭa* — trusted; *dūtena* — through a messenger; *svayam* — Himself; *eva* — indeed; *ca* — also; *grīvām* — His neck; *udvartya* — by raising; *sa-prema* — lovingly; *dṛṣṭyā* — by glancing; *āśvāsayatā* — encouraging; *muhuḥ* — repeatedly; *bhrū* — from His eyebrows; *saṅketa* — by signals; *ādinā* — and by other means; *lajjā* — shyness; *bhaye* — and fear; *janayatā* — creating; *balāt* — by force; *saṁstambhitāḥ* — rendered motionless; *tāḥ* — they; *tat* — His; *mātuḥ* — of the mother; *agre* — in front; *tadvat* — like her; *avasthitāḥ* — stationed.

**He anxiously reassured them again and again, through a trusted messenger and by His own gestures. He stretched His neck to glance at the girls with love, signaled with His**

**eyebrows, and did what He could to make the girls shy and even afraid. In this way He forced them to stop, and they stood in front of His mother, motionless just like her.**

COMMENTARY: The boys were now approaching the dense forest, an unsafe place for young girls, so Kṛṣṇa had to send them back. By sending a boy as His go-between and by making His own gestures, like knitting His eyebrows, shaking His head, and biting the tip of His tongue, He managed to convince them not to go any further. The *gopīs* then joined Mother Yaśodā on the same hill, where the *gopīs* stood still like pictures and cried profusely, just like her.

## TEXT 183

बल्लवेन्द्रश्च सुस्निग्धः स्वत एव विशेषतः ।
पत्नीवात्सल्यदृष्ट्या च स्नेहोद्रेकेण यन्त्रितः ॥

*ballavendraś ca su-snigdhaḥ*
*svata eva viśeṣataḥ*
*patnī-vātsalya-dṛṣṭyā ca*
*snehodrekeṇa yantritaḥ*

*ballava-indraḥ* — the king of the cowherds (Nanda); *ca* — and; *su-snigdhaḥ* — very affectionate; *svataḥ* — naturally; *eva* — indeed; *viśeṣataḥ* — especially; *patnī* — of his wife; *vātsalya* — the loving concern; *dṛṣṭyā* — by seeing; *ca* — and; *sneha* — of affection; *udrekeṇa* — by an excess; *yantritaḥ* — driven.

**Nanda, the king of the cowherds, naturally loved Kṛṣṇa ever so much, but upon seeing his wife's loving concern he was enslaved by overwhelming affection.**

## TEXT 184

सर्वव्रजजनस्नेहभरं पुत्रे विलोक्य तम् ।
वृद्धैः सहानुयातोऽपि दूरं त्यक्तुं न चाशकत् ॥

*sarva-vraja-jana-sneha-*
*bharaṁ putre vilokya tam*
*vṛddhaiḥ sahānuyāto 'pi*
*dūraṁ tyaktuṁ na cāśakat*

*sarva* — all; *vraja-jana* — of the people of Vraja; *sneha* — of love; *bharam* — the heavy burden; *putre* — for his son; *vilokya* — seeing; *tam* — that; *vṛddhaiḥ* — elder people; *saha* — accompanied by; *anuyātaḥ* — following; *api* — even though; *dūram* — for a long distance; *tyaktum* — to give up; *na* — not; *ca* — and; *aśakat* — was able.

**Though Nanda Mahārāja had gone with Kṛṣṇa a great distance, and the elder cowherds with him, when Nanda saw the great burden of love all the people of Vraja bore for his son he was unable to turn back.**

COMMENTARY: As the king of the cowherd community, Nanda would normally be surrounded by priests, advisers, and other Vraja-vāsīs. So along with Nanda other leaders of the community, including his elder brother Upananda, were also following Kṛṣṇa. But even out of regard for their comfort Nanda couldn't bring himself to turn back.

## TEXT 185

शुभानि शकुनान्युच्चैः पश्वादीनां च हृष्टताम् ।
संलक्ष्यान्तः प्रहृष्टोऽपि पुत्रविच्छेदकातरः ॥

*śubhāni śakunāny uccaiḥ*
*paśv-ādīnāṁ ca hṛṣṭatām*
*saṁlakṣyāntaḥ prahṛṣṭo 'pi*
*putra-viccheda-kātaraḥ*

*śubhāni* — auspicious; *śakunāni* — signs; *uccaiḥ* — prominent; *paśu-ādīnām* — of the animals and others; *ca* — and; *hṛṣṭatām* — the happiness; *saṁlakṣya* — noting; *antaḥ* — within himself;

*prahṛṣṭaḥ* — rejoicing; *api* — even though; *putra* — from his son; *viccheda* — because of separation; *kātaraḥ* — distraught.

**Nanda was delighted to see many aupicious omens and see the animals and other creatures all very happy. Yet he was distraught at having to be parted from his son Kṛṣṇa.**

COMMENTARY: The animals showed auspicious symptoms: They had full faces and bodies and were circling Nanda clockwise. The deer, birds, and other forest creatures were happy because their time for being separated from Kṛṣṇa was night and now it was time for Kṛṣṇa to join them in the forest.

TEXT 186

साग्रजं पृथगालिंग्य युगपच्चात्मजं मुहुः ।
शिरस्याघ्राय च स्नेहभरार्तोऽश्रूण्यवासृजत् ॥

*sāgrajaṁ pṛthag āliṅgya*
*yugapac cātmajaṁ muhuḥ*
*śirasy āghrāya ca sneha-*
*bharārto 'śrūṇy avāsṛjat*

*sa-agrajam* — with His elder brother; *pṛthak* — separately; *āliṅgya* — embracing; *yugapat* — together; *ca* — and; *ātmajam* — his son; *muhuḥ* — repeatedly; *śirasi* — on the head; *āghrāya* — smelling; *ca* — and; *sneha* — of love; *bhara* — by the burden; *ārtaḥ* — pained; *aśrūṇi* — tears; *avāsṛjat* — he shed.

**Again and again he embraced Kṛṣṇa, and Kṛṣṇa's elder brother, both separately and together. He smelled Their heads and shed tears in the pain of great love for Them.**

TEXT 187

अथ प्रणम्य पुत्रेण कृत्यं दर्शयता बहु ।
प्रस्थापितः परावृत्य तमेवालोकयन्स्थितः ॥

*atha praṇamya putreṇa*
*kṛtyaṁ darśayatā bahu*
*prasthāpitaḥ parāvṛtya*
*tam evālokayan sthitaḥ*

*atha* — then; *praṇamya* — being bowed down to; *putreṇa* — by his son; *kṛtyam* — duties; *darśayatā* — who showed; *bahu* — many; *prasthāpitaḥ* — sent; *parāvṛtya* — being turned back; *tam* — at Him; *eva* — only; *ālokayan* — looking; *sthitaḥ* — standing.

**Then Kṛṣṇa bowed down to Nanda, reminded him of the many duties Nanda had to perform, and sent him home. Turned back, Nanda stood motionless, looking at Kṛṣṇa and nothing else.**

COMMENTARY: Kṛṣṇa convinced Nanda, "You are needed at home to save the villagers from becoming too wretched over My absence." Also, in the afternoon Nanda would have to organize the decorating of the village for Kṛṣṇa's return.

## TEXT 188

अरण्यान्तरितो दूरे गतौ पुत्रावलोकयन् ।
शब्दं कञ्चिदशृण्वंश्च निववर्त व्रजं प्रति ॥

*araṇyāntarito dūre*
*gatau putrāv alokayan*
*śabdaṁ kañcid aśṛṇvaṁś ca*
*nivavarta vrajaṁ prati*

*araṇya* — the forest; *antaritaḥ* — into; *dūre* — far; *gatau* — gone; *putrau* — his two sons; *alokayan* — not seeing; *śabdam* — sound; *kañcit* — any; *aśṛṇvan* — not hearing; *ca* — and; *nivavarta* — he turned back; *vrajam* — the cowherd village; *prati* — toward.

**When Nanda's two sons had gone so deep into the forest he could no longer see Them or hear any sound, he finally turned back toward the cowherd village.**

COMMENTARY: For a while, even after the boys and their animals were too far away to be seen, some sounds could still be heard, like cows mooing and horns being blown. But when even those sounds were inaudible, Nanda finally went home.

## TEXT 189

नियुज्य जाङ्घिकान्भृत्यान्तद्वार्ताहरणाय सः ।
गोपीभिरन्वितां पत्नीं सान्त्वयित्वानयद् गृहान् ॥

*niyujya jāṅghikān bhṛtyān*
*tad-vārtā-haraṇāya saḥ*
*gopībhir anvitāṁ patnīṁ*
*sāntvayitvānayad gṛhān*

*niyujya* — engaging; *jāṅghikān* — who were acting as couriers; *bhṛtyān* — servants; *tat* — of Him (Kṛṣṇa); *vārtā* — news; *haraṇāya* — for carrying; *saḥ* — he (Nanda); *gopībhiḥ* — with the *gopīs;* *anvitām* — accompanied; *patnīm* — his wife; *sāntvayitvā* — consoling; *anayat* — he brought; *gṛhān* — to their homes.

**He deputed some servants as messengers to bring news of what Kṛṣṇa was doing. Then he consoled his wife and the gopīs and took them back to their homes.**

## TEXT 190

तास्तु तस्य विलासांस्तान् गायन्त्यो विविशुर्व्रजम् ।
दिनमारेभिरे नेतुं ध्यायन्त्यस्तस्य सङ्गमम् ॥

*tās tu tasya vilāsāṁs tān*
*gāyantyo viviśur vrajam*

*dinam ārebhire netuṁ*
*dhyāyantyas tasya saṅgamam*

*tāḥ* — they (the *gopīs*); *tu* — but; *tasya* — His; *vilāsān* — pastimes; *tān* — them; *gāyantyaḥ* — singing; *viviśuḥ* — entered; *vrajam* — the cowherd village; *dinam* — the day; *ārebhire* — began; *netum* — to pass; *dhyāyantyaḥ* — meditating; *tasya* — His; *saṅgamam* — on the association.

**The gopīs, singing Kṛṣṇa's pastimes, entered the village, where they began the day absorbed in thoughts of His company.**

COMMENTARY: The *gopīs* are Kṛṣṇa's greatest devotees, dedicated to Him even more intensely than Śrī Nanda and the other elder cowherd men and women. The *gopīs* spent the entire day fully absorbed in the *saṅkīrtana* of singing about the *rāsa* dance and other pastimes they had shared with Kṛṣṇa. They remembered how they had enjoyed these pastimes, and they looked forward to having more pastimes with Him soon.

Some of the songs the *gopīs* sang are recorded in the Tenth Canto, Thirty-Fifth Chapter, of *Śrīmad-Bhāgavatam:*

*vāma-bāhu-kṛta-vāma-kapolo*
*valgita-bhrur adharārpita-veṇum*
*komalāṅgulibhir āśrita-mārgaṁ*
*gopya īrayati yatra mukundaḥ*

*vyoma-yāna-vanitāḥ saha siddhair*
*vismitās tad upadhārya sa-lajjāḥ*
*kāma-mārgaṇa-samarpita-cittāḥ*
*kaśmalaṁ yayur apasmṛta-nīvyaḥ*

"When Mukunda vibrates the flute He has placed to His lips, stopping its holes with His tender fingers, He rests His left cheek on His left arm and makes His eyebrows dance. At that time the demigoddesses traveling in the sky with their husbands, the

Siddhas, become amazed. As those ladies listen, they are embarrassed to find their minds yielding to the pursuit of lusty desires, and in their distress they are unaware that the belts of their garments are loosening." (*Bhāgavatam* 10.35.2–3)

## TEXT 191

तत्तद्विशेषो निर्वाच्योऽनन्तशक्त्यापि नापरः ।
महार्तिजनके तस्मिन्को वा धीमान्प्रवर्तते ॥

*tat-tad-viśeṣo nirvācyo*
*'nanta-śaktyāpi nāparaḥ*
*mahārti-janake tasmin*
*ko vā dhīmān pravartate*

*tat-tat* — of all those dealings; *viśeṣaḥ* — details; *nirvācyaḥ* — can be described; *ananta-śaktyā* — with infinite power; *api* — even; *na* — not; *aparaḥ* — further; *mahā-ārti* — great distress; *janake* — which produces; *tasmin* — in that; *kaḥ* — who; *vā* — or; *dhīmān* — being intelligent; *pravartate* — would proceed.

**Even a person with unlimited power could not describe those dealings in further detail. But why would someone intelligent even try? It would only create abysmal distress.**

COMMENTARY: The Mathurā *brāhmaṇa* might be eager to hear everything about Kṛṣṇa's day — from the moment His mother wakes Him till the time He returns home in the evening — but Sarūpa says that only someone equal to Ananta Śeṣa could satisfy the demand to tell all this. But the Lord, the *brāhmaṇa* might counter, has been addressed with the words *māyā-balena bhavatāpi nigūhyamānaṁ paśyanti kecit:* "Some people can see what by Your own power of illusion You keep hidden." (*Stotra-ratna* 13) And the *brāhmaṇa* might insist that Śrī Sarūpa is indeed a great devotee of the Lord and therefore able to do anything.

"But I cannot do this," Sarūpa might then say, "because those pastimes are infinite."

"Then please describe at least some part of them in detail," the *brāhmaṇa* might persist.

"No," Sarūpa would finally answer, "an intelligent person should not speak what will create unhappiness for the entire world. If one does so, he is not intelligent." Indeed, even the son of Badarāyaṇa Vyāsa did not speak elaborately in *Śrīmad-Bhāgavatam* on these topics of the Vraja-vāsīs' daily separation from Kṛṣṇa.

## TEXT 192

स तु प्रस्थाप्य ताः स्वान्तरार्तोऽपि सखिभिर्बलात् ।
नीतोऽग्रे प्राविशत्तूर्णं श्रीमद्वृन्दावनान्तरम् ॥

*sa tu prasthāpya tāḥ svāntar-*
*ārto 'pi sakhibhir balāt*
*nīto 'gre prāviśat tūrṇaṁ*
*śrīmad-vṛndāvanāntaram*

*saḥ* — He; *tu* — but; *prasthāpya* — sending home; *tāḥ* — them (the *gopīs*); *sva-antaḥ* — within Himself; *ārtaḥ* — distressed; *api* — although; *sakhibhiḥ* — by His friends; *balāt* — by force; *nītaḥ* — brought; *agre* — forward; *prāviśat* — He entered; *tūrṇam* — quickly; *śrīmat* — beautiful; *vṛndāvana* — of the Vṛndāvana forest; *antaram* — the interior.

**Kṛṣṇa felt heavy at heart from sending the gopīs back. But His friends quickly pulled Him forward and made Him enter the beautiful Vṛndāvana forest.**

## TEXT 193

सन्दर्श्यमानः सखिभिः स तु वृन्दावनश्रियम् ।
स्वयं च वर्णयन्युक्त्या निर्गताधिरिवाभवत् ॥

*sandarśyamānaḥ sakhibhiḥ*
*sa tu vṛndāvana-śriyam*

*svayaṁ ca varṇayan yuktyā*
*nirgatādhir ivābhavat*

*sandarśyamānaḥ* — being shown; *sakhibhiḥ* — by His companions; *saḥ* — He; *tu* — but; *vṛndāvana-śriyam* — the splendors of Vṛndāvana; *svayam* — Himself; *ca* — and; *varṇayan* — describing; *yuktyā* — with logical reasons; *nirgata-ādhiḥ* — freed from mental pain; *iva* — more or less; *abhavat* — He became.

**And as His companions pointed out the splendors of Vṛndāvana and as He described them Himself and supported His praise with logic, He was more or less freed of distress.**

COMMENTARY: Texts 192 and 193 describe how Kṛṣṇa was able to tolerate the pain He felt from having to separate from the *gopīs*. As indicated in the first of these verses by the word *tu* ("but"), the pain Kṛṣṇa felt was even greater than that of the *gopīs*. The cowherd boys had to drag Kṛṣṇa away by force because otherwise He and the *gopīs* would never have stopped gazing at one another. The boys took Him into the deep forest, where the girls couldn't go. Of course, Kṛṣṇa also sent home His parents and the others, but the *gopīs* are especially mentioned here because their heartfelt pain was the greatest. And the word *iva* indicates that despite entering the forest with His friends, Kṛṣṇa was not completely relieved of His anxiety about the *gopīs*.

Once inside the Vṛndāvana forest, Kṛṣṇa praised its beauty on the pretext of glorifying His brother, as we hear from Śrī Śukadeva Gosvāmī. Kṛṣṇa said:

*aho amī deva-varāmarārcitaṁ*
*pādāmbujaṁ te sumanaḥ-phalārhaṇam*
*namanty upādāya śikhābhir ātmanas*
*tamo-'pahatyai taru-janma yat-kṛtam*

"O greatest of Lords, just see how these trees are bowing their heads at Your lotus feet, which are worshiped by the immortal demigods. The trees are offering You their fruits and flowers to eradicate the dark ignorance that has caused their birth as trees." (*Bhāgavatam* 10.15.5)

## TEXT 194

ततोऽतनोद्यान्स तु गोपविभ्रमान्
अतोऽभजन्यादृशतां चराचराः ।
हृदा न तद्वृत्तमुपासितं भवेत्
कथं परस्मिन् रसना निरूपयेत् ॥

*tato 'tanod yān sa tu gopa-vibhramān*
*ato 'bhajan yādṛśatāṁ carācarāḥ*
*hṛdā na tad-vṛttam upāsitaṁ bhavet*
*kathaṁ parasmin rasanā nirūpayet*

*tataḥ* — then; *atanot* — expanded; *yān* — which; *saḥ* — He; *tu* — and; *gopa* — of the cowherds; *vibhramān* — the wanderings; *ataḥ* — thus; *abhajan* — assumed; *yādṛśatām* — such a condition; *cara-acarāḥ* — the moving and nonmoving beings; *hṛdā* — by exercise of the heart; *na* — not; *tat* — that; *vṛttam* — activity; *upāsitam* — worshiped; *bhavet* — would be; *katham* — how; *parasmin* — to someone else; *rasanā* — the tongue; *nirūpayet* — can describe.

**His wanderings then with the cowherd boys, and the state of ecstasy all creatures thereby achieved, the moving and the nonmoving — one cannot conceive of this even by meditation in the heart. How then can the tongue describe this to anyone else?**

## TEXT 195

गोवर्धनाद्रिनिकटेषु स चारयन् गा
रेमे कलिन्दतनयाम्बु निपाययंस्ताः ।

सायं तथैव पुनरेत्य निजं व्रजं तं
विक्रीडति व्रजवधूभिरसौ व्रजेशः ॥

*govardhanādri-nikaṭeṣu sa cārayan gā*
*reme kalinda-tanayāmbu nipāyayaṁs tāḥ*
*sāyaṁ tathaiva punar etya nijaṁ vrajaṁ taṁ*
*vikrīḍati vraja-vadhūbhir asau vrajeśaḥ*

*govardhana-adri* — of Govardhana Hill; *nikaṭeṣu* — in the places in the vicinity; *saḥ* — He; *cārayan* — tending; *gāḥ* — the cows; *reme* — enjoyed; *kalinda-tanayā* — of Yamunā, the daughter of Kalinda; *ambu* — water; *nipāyayan* — making drink; *tāḥ* — them (the cows); *sāyam* — in the evening; *tathā eva* — and so; *punaḥ* — again; *etya* — coming; *nijam* — His own; *vrajam* — to the cowherd village; *tam* — that; *vikrīḍati* — played; *vraja-vadhūbhiḥ* — with the young women of Vraja; *asau* — He; *vraja-īśaḥ* — the Lord of Vraja.

**In the places around Govardhana Hill, He enjoyed tending the cows and making them drink water from the Yamunā. And as evening approached, the Lord of Vraja returned to His cowherd village and later played with Vraja's young girls.**

COMMENTARY: This verse gives a short summary of Kṛṣṇa's activities throughout the day and night. The *gopīs* and everyone and everything else in Vraja exist only for Kṛṣṇa's enjoyment.

## TEXT 196

श्रीगोपराजस्य यदप्यसौ पुरी
नन्दीश्वराख्ये विषये विराजते ।
ते तस्य कृष्णस्य मतानुवर्तिनः
कुञ्जादिरासं बहु मन्यते सदा ॥

*śrī-gopa-rājasya yad apy asau purī*
*nandīśvarākhye viṣaye virājate*
*te tasya kṛṣṇasya matānuvartinaḥ*
*kuñjādi-rāsaṁ bahu manyate sadā*

*śrī* — opulent; *gopa-rājasya* — of the king of the cowherds; *yat api* — although; *asau* — that; *purī* — city; *nandīśvara-ākhye* — named Nandīśvara; *viṣaye* — in the precinct; *virājate* — is resplendent; *te* — they (the Vraja-vāsīs); *tasya* — of Him; *kṛṣṇasya* — Kṛṣṇa; *mata* — the opinions; *anuvartinaḥ* — following; *kuñja-ādi* — in the groves and other locations; *rāsam* — the pleasure pastimes; *bahu* — highly; *manyate* — regard; *sadā* — always.

**Though the capital of the opulent king of the cowherds shines forth in the region called Nandīśvara, the Vraja-vāsīs, in tune with Kṛṣṇa's liking, always think more highly of His pleasure pastimes in the groves and other places in the forests.**

COMMENTARY: For all its sweetness, Nanda Mahārāja's town is more magnificent than Vaikuṇṭha. Even so, the residents of Vraja think mostly about Kṛṣṇa playing among the trees and creepers of the forests, because that is where He enjoys the most.

## TEXT 197

तत्रैव वसता ब्रह्मन्नानन्दो योऽनुभूयते ।
सुखं यच्च स वा तद्वा कीदृगित्युच्यतां कथम् ॥

*tatraiva vasatā brahmann*
*ānando yo 'nubhūyate*
*sukhaṁ yac ca sa vā tad vā*
*kīdṛg ity ucyatāṁ katham*

*tatra* — there (in Goloka Vṛndāvana); *eva* — only; *vasatā* — by one who is living; *brahman* — O brāhmaṇa; *ānandaḥ* — the bliss; *yaḥ* — which; *anubhūyate* — is perceived; *sukham* — the satisfaction; *yat* — which; *ca* — and; *saḥ* — that (bliss); *vā* — or; *tat* — that (satisfaction); *vā* — or else; *kīdṛk* — of what kind; *iti* — thus; *ucyatām* — can be described; *katham* — how.

**O brāhmaṇa, the satisfaction and ecstasy one tastes from living in Goloka Vṛndāvana are beyond describing. To what can they be compared?**

COMMENTARY: According to the laws of spiritual nature, *sukha* ("satisfaction") is the cause of *ānanda* ("bliss"). In other words, *sukha* can be said to be the external aspect of spiritual happiness and *ānanda* the internal. And both are beyond the scope of material understanding.

## TEXT 198

मुक्तानां सुखतोऽत्यन्तं महद्वैकुण्ठवासिनाम् ।
भगवद्भक्तिमाहात्म्यादुक्तं तद्वेदिभिः सुखम् ॥

*muktānāṁ sukhato 'tyantaṁ*
*mahad vaikuṇṭha-vāsinām*
*bhagavad-bhakti-māhātmyād*
*uktaṁ tad-vedibhiḥ sukham*

*muktānām* — of liberated persons; *sukhataḥ* — than the happiness; *atyantam* — very much; *mahat* — greater; *vaikuṇṭha-vāsinām* — of the residents of Vaikuṇṭha; *bhagavat-bhakti* — of devotional service to the Supreme Lord; *māhātmyāt* — due to the greatness; *uktam* — is said; *tat* — that; *vedibhiḥ* — by those who know; *sukham* — happiness.

**Because devotional service to the Supreme Lord is so wondrous, those who truly know say that the residents of Vaikuṇṭha taste a happiness much greater than that of mere liberated souls.**

## TEXT 199

अयोध्याद्वारवत्यादिवासिनां च ततोऽपि तत् ।
उक्तं रसविशेषेण केनचित्केनचिन्महत् ॥

*ayodhyā-dvāravaty-ādi-*
*vāsināṁ ca tato 'pi tat*
*uktaṁ rasa-viśeṣeṇa*
*kenacit kenacin mahat*

*ayodhyā* — of Ayodhyā; *dvāravatī* — Dvārakā; *ādi* — and so on; *vāsinām* — of the residents; *ca* — and; *tataḥ* — than that; *api* — even; *tat* — that; *uktam* — is said; *rasa-viśeṣeṇa* — due to special tastes; *kenacit kenacit* — certain various; *mahat* — greater.

**And the happiness of souls who reside in places like Ayodhyā and Dvārakā is said to be even greater because of certain various special tastes.**

COMMENTARY: We have already heard that in Ayodhyā and Dvārakā the Supreme Lord's devotees serve Him with special intimacy. The eternal servants of Śrī Raghunātha's lotus feet are happier than the associates of Śrī Nārāyaṇa in Vaikuṇṭha; and happier still are the eternal relatives of Śrī Yādavendra in Dvārakā. The devotees of Ayodhyā enjoy the privilege of eternal personal service to the Lord, but the devotees of Dvārakā, being entitled to taste the *rasa* of friendship with Kṛṣṇa, are even more privileged.

## TEXT 200

गोलोकवासिनां यत्तत्सर्वतोऽप्यधिकाधिकम् ।
सुखं तद्युक्तयतिक्रान्तं दध्याद्वाचि कथं पदम् ॥

*goloka-vāsināṁ yat tat*
*sarvato 'py adhikādhikam*

*sukhaṁ tad yukty-atikrāntaṁ*
*dadhyād vāci kathaṁ padam*

*goloka-vāsinām* — of the residents of Goloka; *yat* — which; *tat* — that; *sarvataḥ* — than all; *api* — even; *adhika-adhikam* — superior by far; *sukham* — happiness; *tat* — that; *yukti* — reason; *atikrāntam* — transcending; *dadhyāt* — can allow; *vāci* — in speech; *katham* — how; *padam* — scope.

**But the happiness of the residents of Goloka far exceeds any other. It transcends reason, so how can it give room for words?**

## TEXT 201

तस्यानुभविनो नित्यं तत्रत्या एव ते विदुः ।
तत्त्वं ये हि प्रभोस्तस्य तादृक्सौहार्दगोचराः ॥

*tasyānubhavino nityaṁ*
*tatratyā eva te viduḥ*
*tattvaṁ ye hi prabhos tasya*
*tādṛk-sauhārda-gocarāḥ*

*tasya* — it; *anubhavinaḥ* — who experience; *nityam* — constantly; *tatratyāḥ* — who live there; *eva* — only; *te* — they; *viduḥ* — know; *tattvam* — the true nature; *ye* — who; *hi* — indeed; *prabhoḥ* — of the Lord; *tasya* — Him; *tādṛk* — such; *sauhārda* — of the friendly affection; *gocarāḥ* — objects.

**Only those who live in Goloka and always perceive that happiness know its true nature, because the Lord has such friendly feelings toward them.**

## TEXTS 202–203

एषामेवावतारास्ते नित्या वैकुण्ठपार्षदाः ।
प्रपञ्चान्तर्गतास्तेषां प्रतिरूपाः सुरा यथा ॥

यथा च तेषां देवानामवतारा धरातले ।
क्रीडां चिकीर्षतो विष्णोर्भवन्ति प्रीतये मुहुः ॥

*eṣām evāvatārās te*
*nityā vaikuṇṭha-pārṣadāḥ*
*prapañcāntar-gatās teṣāṁ*
*pratirūpāḥ surā yathā*

*yathā ca teṣāṁ devānām*
*avatārā dharā-tale*
*krīḍāṁ cikīrṣato viṣṇor*
*bhavanti prītaye muhuḥ*

*eṣām* — of them (the Goloka devotees); *eva* — indeed; *avatārāḥ* — incarnations; *te* — they; *nityāḥ* — eternal; *vaikuṇṭha* — of the Lord of Vaikuṇṭha; *pārṣadāḥ* — the associates; *prapañca* — the material creation; *antaḥ-gatāḥ* — who have entered within; *teṣām* — their; *pratirūpāḥ* — counterparts; *surāḥ* — the demigods; *yathā* — as; *yathā* — as; *ca* — and; *teṣām* — of them; *devānām* — the demigods; *avatārāḥ* — incarnations; *dharā-tale* — on the earth; *krīḍām* — pastimes; *cikīrṣataḥ* — who desires; *viṣṇoḥ* — of Lord Viṣṇu; *bhavanti* — they (the incarnations) are present; *prītaye* — for the pleasure; *muhuḥ* — from time to time.

**Just as the demigods who have entered the material creation are counterparts of the Lord's Vaikuṇṭha associates, those eternal associates from Vaikuṇṭha are incarnations of the Goloka devotees. Yet like the demigods themselves, those very devotees appear on earth now and again for the pleasure of Lord Viṣṇu when He wants to enjoy various pastimes.**

COMMENTARY: Some say that many of the Vraja-vāsīs who appeared on earth during Kṛṣṇa's pastimes five thousand years ago were incarnations of demigods. Nanda Mahārāja, for example, is said to be an *avatāra* of the Vasu named Droṇa. If taken literally, this idea would rule out the possibility that the earthly Vraja-vāsīs are eternal associates of the Supreme Lord. But the truth is just the opposite: As confirmed in scriptures such as the *Padma Purāṇa* (*Uttara-khaṇḍa*), demigods like Droṇa are partial expansions of the original Vraja-vāsīs, and those original Vraja-vāsīs accompany Kṛṣṇa when He descends to earth.

Goparāja Nanda and other devotees in Goloka expand as *avatāras* in Vaikuṇṭha to become Śrī Nanda and other associates of Lord Nārāyaṇa. The same devotees thus enjoy pastimes in two worlds simultaneously, Goloka and Vaikuṇṭha. And so it would be incorrect to assert that because the Vaikuṇṭha associates of Nārāyaṇa are *avatāras* they are not eternal.

The same associates of Lord Nārāyaṇa expand again into the material world to become demigods. This verse calls those demigods *pratirūpāḥ* ("counterparts"), rather than *avatāras,* because the demigods are materially conditioned living beings. Still, those demigods are empowered representatives of the Supreme Lord's personal associates.

In the next few verses, Śrī Sarūpa will describe the incarnations of the Goloka-vāsīs as parallel to Kṛṣṇa's incarnations; that is, just as Kṛṣṇa's *avatāras* are nondifferent from Him, the earthly associates of Kṛṣṇa are nondifferent from the original Goloka-vāsīs.

Alternatively, the word *pratirūpa* ("counterpart" or "representative") can be taken as synonymous with the word *avatāra*. Then the idea implied is that the associates of the Lord in Vaikuṇṭha who expand from the original Goloka-vāsīs are like direct reflections (*pratibimba*) of those Goloka-vāsīs, and the further expansions as demigods are like shadows (*pratichāyā*). Both a reflection and a shadow follow a person as expansions, but the shadow represents him less fully than does his mirror image. Thus if Nanda Mahārāja on earth is called an *avatāra* of Droṇa, it is only because both of them are *avatāras* of Nanda Mahārāja in Goloka. In fact, Nanda on earth is identical with Nanda in Goloka, and Droṇa is only a partial expansion; but by worldly calculations demigods are considered relatively superior to humans, so Nanda on earth is considered Droṇa's incarnation. Thus it is said that demigods like Vasu Droṇa descend to earth to assist Lord Viṣṇu, the younger brother of Indra, in His enjoyment.

Just as Lord Viṣṇu's incarnations appear only briefly in the material world but periodically reappear, the Lord's associates who manifest themselves as demigods also incarnate as earthly *avatāras* whenever there is a need. For example, Śrī Nanda Goparāja, the eternal beloved father of Kṛṣṇa in Goloka, appears in Vaikuṇṭha as the eternal associate of Nārāyaṇa called Nanda, and he also occasionally descends to earth in his original identity. So too, Śrī Balarāma, who originally resides in Goloka, manifests Himself in Vaikuṇṭha as the eternal associate named Śeṣa. Yet He appears among the demigods as the bearer of the earth in the seventh Pātāla region, and He sometimes comes to earth as the selfsame Balarāma. Kṛṣṇa's friend Śrīdāmā in Goloka appears as Garuḍa in two different forms, one an eternal associate of the Lord in Vaikuṇṭha and the other a son of Vinatā among the demigods; and occasionally he appears on earth as the original Śrīdāmā. Kṛṣṇa's parents in Goloka, Śrī Vasudeva and Devakī, appear as Sutapā and Pṛśni in Vaikuṇṭha, Kaśyapa and Aditi in Svarga, and sometimes in their original forms as Vasudeva and Devakī on earth. The *avatāras* of other devotees follow the same pattern.

## TEXT 204

यथावताराः कृष्णस्याभिन्नास्तेनावतारिणा ।
तथैषामवतारास्ते न स्युरेतैः समं पृथक् ॥

*yathāvatārāḥ kṛṣṇasyā-*
*bhinnās tenāvatāriṇā*
*tathaiṣām avatārās te*
*na syur etaiḥ samaṁ pṛthak*

*yathā* — as; *avatārāḥ* — the incarnations; *kṛṣṇasya* — of Kṛṣṇa; *abhinnāḥ* — nondifferent; *tena* — from Him; *avatāriṇā* — the source of all incarnations; *tathā* — so; *eṣām* — of them (the residents of Goloka); *avatārāḥ* — the incarnations; *te* — these; *na syuḥ* — are not; *etaiḥ samam* — from them; *pṛthak* — different.

**And just as the incarnations of Kṛṣṇa, the source of all incarnations, are nondifferent from Him, the incarnations of the Goloka-vāsīs, the residents of Goloka, are nondifferent from them.**

COMMENTARY: The devotees from Goloka may change their names and appearance when they descend, but still they are the same persons. As the expanded forms of Godhead are all nondifferent from the original Kṛṣṇa, the single fountainhead of existence, so when devotees like Nanda and Yaśodā appear in expanded forms in Vaikuṇṭha, those forms are in essence nondifferent from the original forms in Goloka. Kaśyapa and Aditi in heaven, however, being incomplete portions of Vasudeva and his wife Devakī, are partially different from the Vasudeva and Devakī on earth and partially the same.

## TEXT 205

कदाप्यंशेन जायन्ते पूर्णत्वेन कदाचन ।
यथाकालं यथाकार्यं यथास्थानं च कृष्णवत् ॥

*kadāpy aṁśena jāyante*
*pūrṇatvena kadācana*
*yathā-kālaṁ yathā-kāryaṁ*
*yathā-sthānaṁ ca kṛṣṇa-vat*

*kadā api* — sometimes; *aṁśena* — in partial expansions; *jāyante* — are born; *pūrṇatvena* — in their full selves; *kadācana* — sometimes; *yathā-kālam* — according to time; *yathā-kāryam* — according to necessity; *yathā-sthānam* — according to place; *ca* — and; *kṛṣṇa-vat* — like Kṛṣṇa.

**The Goloka-vāsīs are born sometimes as partial expan-**

**sions and sometimes as their full selves. Like Kṛṣṇa, they vary their appearance for the time, place, and need.**

COMMENTARY: In this verse the verb *jāyante* ("they are born") is equivalent to *prādurbhavanti* ("they become visible") and *avataranti* ("they descend"). Whenever and wherever there is a need for a full or partial incarnation of a particular devotee, that same devotee reveals either his whole self or a partial expansion of himself. The example of Kṛṣṇa and His expansions is cited to clarify this point. In previous ages Kṛṣṇa manifested various partial forms of Himself in this world. In Satya-yuga, for example, Lord Varāha descended from the Śaukara-purī of Vaikuṇṭha for such purposes as lifting the earth from the lower regions. And at the end of Dvāpara-yuga the same Kṛṣṇa descended to Śrī Mathurā-maṇḍala in His full form to display special blissful pastimes that would broadcast His loving devotional service all over the universe.

## TEXT 206

एवं कदाचित्केनापि समाकृष्टा रसेन ते ।
निजनाथेन सहिताः कुत्राप्यतितितीर्षवः ॥

*evaṁ kadācit kenāpi*
*samākṛṣṭā rasena te*
*nija-nāthena sahitāḥ*
*kutrāpy atititīrṣavaḥ*

*evam* — thus; *kadācit* — at times; *kena api* — by some; *samākṛṣṭāḥ* — attracted; *rasena* — mood; *te* — they; *nija* — their own; *nāthena* — with the Lord; *sahitāḥ* — together; *kutra api* — somewhere; *atititīrṣavaḥ* — desiring to descend.

**Thus Kṛṣṇa's companions, impelled by their own moods of loving exchange, from time to time want to descend somewhere with their Lord.**

## TEXTS 207–208

अवतारैर्निजैः सर्वैः परमेश्वरवद्यदा ।
ऐक्यं व्याजेन केनापि गताः प्रादुर्भवन्ति हि ॥

तदैषामवतारास्ते गच्छन्त्येतेषु वै लयम् ।
अतोऽभवंस्त एवैत इति ते मुनयोऽवदन् ॥

*avatārair nijaiḥ sarvaiḥ*
*parameśvara-vad yadā*
*aikyaṁ vyājena kenāpi*
*gatāḥ prādurbhavanti hi*

*tadaiṣām avatārās te*
*gacchanty eteṣu vai layam*
*ato 'bhavaṁs ta evaita*
*iti te munayo 'vadan*

*avatāraiḥ* — with the incarnations; *nijaiḥ* — their own; *sarvaiḥ* — all; *parama-īśvara-vat* — like the Supreme Lord; *yadā* — when; *aikyam* — oneness; *vyājena* — on a pretext; *kena api* — some; *gatāḥ* — gone; *prādurbhavanti* — they incarnate; *hi* — indeed; *tadā* — then; *eṣām* — of them; *avatārāḥ* — the incarnations; *te* — these; *gacchanti* — go; *eteṣu* — into them; *vai* — indeed; *layam* — the merging; *ataḥ* — thus; *abhavan* — become; *te* — these; *eva* — just; *ete* — they; *iti* — thus; *te* — they; *munayaḥ* — the sages; *avadan* — have said.

**When devotees who live with Kṛṣṇa in Goloka appear to merge, on some pretext, into their own expanded incarnations, this is just like the merging of Kṛṣṇa's expansions with Him. When sages tell us, therefore, that expansions of Kṛṣṇa's associates descend to become the original associates, what they mean is that the expansions merge into the originals.**

COMMENTARY: In Goloka, Nanda Mahārāja eternally serves Kṛṣṇa in the role of father. So when Kṛṣṇa plans to descend to earth to display childhood pastimes, Nanda is naturally attracted to come with Him. By Kṛṣṇa's arrangement Lord Brahmā then blesses Nanda's partial expansion Vasu Droṇa to attain perfect devotion for Viṣṇu. Of course, this blessing is only a pretext because Droṇa is already an expansion of Kṛṣṇa's eternal associate. Yet on the strength of that blessing, Droṇa merges into the original Nanda Mahārāja and joins the entourage of Kṛṣṇa's *avatāra*. It is in this sense that the *Purāṇas* tell us "Droṇa became Nanda." This explanation also reconciles the account in the *Padma Purāṇa* (*Kārtika-māhātmya*) of Śrī Rādhā's previous lives. Attracted to descend from Goloka for the service of Her worshipable Lord, who is more attractive than millions of Cupids, She incarnated in those various births, in various forms and places.

## TEXT 209

कृत्स्नमेतत्परं चेत्थं तत्रत्यं विद्ध्यसंशयम् ।
पूर्वोक्तनारदोद्दिष्टसिद्धान्ताद्यनुसारतः ॥

*kṛtsnam etat paraṁ cetthaṁ*
*tatratyaṁ viddhy asaṁśayam*
*pūrvokta-nāradoddiṣṭa-*
*siddhāntādy-anusārataḥ*

*kṛtsnam* — all; *etat* — this; *param* — other things; *ca* — and; *ittham* — in this way; *tatratyam* — existing there; *viddhi* — please understand; *asaṁśayam* — without doubt; *pūrva* — previously; *ukta* — spoken; *nārada* — by Nārada; *uddiṣṭa* — taught; *siddhānta* — the philosophical conclusions; *ādi* — and so on; *anusārataḥ* — according to.

**All this and everything else about Goloka please try to understand in this way, without doubt or confusion. Comprehend it according to the philosophical conclusions taught by Nārada, as spoken of before.**

COMMENTARY: Śrī Sarūpa's disciple may still have doubts about Goloka. He may question, for example, how demons can be present in a place superior to Vaikuṇṭha or how the Goloka-vāsīs could even have an impression of having seen demons there before. Moreover, if Goloka is purely spiritual, *sac-cid-ānanda,* how can inanimate things like logs, stones, carts, and dust from cows' hooves exist there? And Goloka is not generally accepted to be greater and higher than Vaikuṇṭha. So how can the dear associates of Kṛṣṇa descend from Goloka to become Vaikuṇṭha *pārṣadas?*

Sarūpa already answered these doubts in his description of the glories of Goloka. He briefly recounted the teachings Nārada had given him earlier, in Vaikuṇṭha, about Goloka's unique stature and elucidated those teachings with his own comments. If the Mathurā *brāhmaṇa* wants more scriptural support, he can refer to various statements of the *Padma Purāṇa* (*Uttara-khaṇḍa*) and the *Pañcarātras.*

In upcoming verses of *Śrī Bṛhad-bhāgavatāmṛta,* Śrī Sarūpa will tell more about the pastimes the transcendental Personality of Godhead enjoys with His personal associates and paraphernalia in Goloka. The *brāhmaṇa* will then be informed how it is that Kaṁsa and other demons reside in Kṛṣṇa's abode. In brief, Kaṁsa and the other enemies of Kṛṣṇa join Kṛṣṇa's eternal pastimes for the same reason Kṛṣṇa's Vaikuṇṭha associates join Him in their spiritual identities, namely to enhance Kṛṣṇa's enjoyment. The carts and other apparently lifeless objects in Kṛṣṇa's abode are all in fact alive and completely spiritual *sac-cid-ānanda* beings. According to the descriptions of *Śrī Bṛhad-bhāgavatāmṛta,* everything in Kṛṣṇa's abode Goloka is transcendental the same way as in Vaikuṇṭha. Scriptural evidence to support this conclusion will be cited later on.

## TEXT 210

माथुरोत्तम तत्रत्यं महाश्चर्यमिदं शृणु ।
कथ्यमानं मया किञ्चित् श्रीकृष्णस्य प्रभावतः ॥

*māthurottama tatratyaṁ*
*mahāścaryam idaṁ śṛṇu*
*kathyamānaṁ mayā kiñcit*
*śrī-kṛṣṇasya prabhāvataḥ*

*māthura* — of Mathurā *brāhmaṇas; uttama* — O best; *tatratyam* — about that place; *mahā-aścaryam* — great wonder; *idam* — this; *śṛṇu* — please hear; *kathyamānam* — being told; *mayā* — by me; *kiñcit* — something; *śrī-kṛṣṇasya* — of Śrī Kṛṣṇa; *prabhāvataḥ* — by powerful influence.

**O best of Mathurā brāhmaṇas, listen and by the powerful influence of Kṛṣṇa I will tell you more about the great wonders of that place.**

COMMENTARY: The glories of Goloka and the ecstasies of its devotees are beyond the power of words and thought, but a devotee empowered by Kṛṣṇa's special grace can describe them to some extent. To encourage the disciple to listen with careful attention, Sarūpa calls him "best of the *brāhmaṇas* from Mathurā."

## TEXT 211

बालकास्तरुणा वृद्धा गोपास्ते कोटिकोटिशः ।
सर्वे विदुर्महाप्रेयानहं कृष्णस्य नेतरः ॥

*bālakās taruṇā vṛddhā*
*gopās te koṭi-koṭiśaḥ*
*sarve vidur mahā-preyān*
*ahaṁ kṛṣṇasya netaraḥ*

*bālakāḥ* — who are children; *taruṇāḥ* — who are young people; *vṛddhāḥ* — and who are elders; *gopāḥ* — the cowherds; *te* — they; *koṭi-koṭiśaḥ* — millions upon millions; *sarve* — all; *viduḥ* — think; *mahā-preyān* — most dear; *aham* — I; *kṛṣṇasya* — of Kṛṣṇa; *na* — not; *itaraḥ* — anyone else.

**Every one of the millions and millions of cowherds — the children, young people, and elders — thinks, "I alone am most dear to Kṛṣṇa."**

COMMENTARY: Texts 211 through 213 reveal the ecstatic attitude of the cowherd boys and men of Goloka.

TEXT 212

तथैव व्यवहारोऽपि तेषां कृष्णे सदेक्ष्यते ।
प्रत्येकं तेषु तस्यापि विशुद्धस्तादृगेव सः ॥

*tathaiva vyavahāro 'pi*
*teṣāṁ kṛṣṇe sadekṣyate*
*praty-ekaṁ teṣu tasyāpi*
*viśuddhas tādṛg eva saḥ*

*tathā eva* — just so; *vyavahāraḥ* — the behavior; *api* — also; *teṣām* — of them; *kṛṣṇe* — toward Kṛṣṇa; *sadā* — always; *īkṣyate* — is seen; *prati-ekam* — toward each one; *teṣu* — of them; *tasya* — His; *api* — also; *viśuddhaḥ* — pure; *tādṛk* — similar; *eva* — only; *saḥ* — that (behavior).

**Just as the pure way they behave toward Kṛṣṇa always confirms this ecstatic mentality, so does the way He behaves toward every one of them.**

COMMENTARY: This Goloka ecstasy is not just an idle meditation. It manifests itself actively in the way the devotees deal with Kṛṣṇa. The cowherds express their intimate love for Him in everything they do, including their eating and ordinary household chores. And Kṛṣṇa also shows by His behavior that He considers Himself their property. There is never even a trace of duplicity in the loving exchanges between Kṛṣṇa and His devotees in Goloka; their dealings are *viśuddha,* absolutely pure. It is not that Kṛṣṇa truly loves only one of His devotees and with everyone else only pretends.

## TEXT 213

तथापि तृप्तिः कस्यापि नैवोदेति कदाचन ।
प्रेमतृष्णा च विविधा दैन्यमाता विवर्धते ॥

*tathāpi tṛptiḥ kasyāpi*
*naivodeti kadācana*
*prema-tṛṣṇā ca vividhā*
*dainya-mātā vivardhate*

*tathā api* — nonetheless; *tṛptiḥ* — satisfaction; *kasya api* — of anyone; *na* — does not; *eva* — even; *udeti* — arise; *kadācana* — ever; *prema* — of love; *tṛṣṇā* — the thirst; *ca* — and; *vividhā* — various; *dainya* — of utter humility; *mātā* — the mother; *vivardhate* — grows stronger.

**Yet not one of them ever becomes satiated. Their love shows a thirst that is the mother of sheer humility and that simply grows stronger and stronger.**

COMMENTARY: The devotees' thirst for having more and more of Kṛṣṇa is unquenchable and ever increasing, without limit. The phrase *prema-tṛṣṇā,* the "thirst of pure love," means *lobha* ("greed"). This thirst is the mother of perfect humility because the highest love of God naturally evolves into the sorrow of separation, even while devotees are directly enjoying Kṛṣṇa's company.

## TEXT 214

गोपीषु च सदा तासु प्रत्येकं कोटिकोटिषु ।
परा प्रीतिः कृपासक्तिरपि सा तस्य वीक्ष्यते ॥

*gopīṣu ca sadā tāsu*
*praty-ekaṁ koṭi-koṭiṣu*
*parā prītiḥ kṛpāsaktir*
*api sā tasya vīkṣyate*

*gopīṣu* — for the *gopīs; ca* — and; *sadā* — always; *tāsu* — for them; *prati-ekam* — each one; *koṭi-koṭiṣu* — by the millions upon millions; *parā* — supreme; *prītiḥ* — love; *kṛpā* — compassion; *āsaktiḥ* — attachment; *api* — also; *sā* — that; *tasya* — on His part; *vīkṣyate* — is seen.

**Still, it is towards each of the gopīs — in the millions and millions — that Krsna always clearly shows the greatest attachment, compassion, and love.**

COMMENTARY: In this context, *prīti* ("affection") means "pure ecstatic love," *kṛpā* ("mercy") means "the signs that display this love," and *āsakti* ("attachment") means "exclusive dedication."

TEXT 215

यया युक्तिशतैर्व्यक्तं मादृशैरनुमन्यते ।
आभिः समो न कोऽप्यन्यत्रत्योऽप्यस्य प्रियो जनः ॥

*yayā yukti-śatair vyaktaṁ*
*mādṛśair anumanyate*
*ābhiḥ samo na ko 'py anya-*
*tratyo 'py asya priyo janaḥ*

*yayā* — by which; *yukti* — of logical arguments; *śataiḥ* — by hundreds; *vyaktam* — made apparent; *mādṛśaiḥ* — by persons like me; *anumanyate* — it is deduced; *ābhiḥ* — to them (the *gopīs*); *samaḥ* — equally; *na kaḥ api* — no one; *anyatratyaḥ* — found anywhere else; *api* — even; *asya* — to Him; *priyaḥ* — dear; *janaḥ* — a person.

**This serves as evidence for hundreds of logical arguments by which persons like me can understand that no one, in that abode or elsewhere, is as dear to Him as the gopīs.**

COMMENTARY: Kṛṣṇa's love, compassion, and attachment for the *gopīs* are proof enough to convince Sarūpa that no one, not even any other resident of Goloka, is as dear to Kṛṣṇa as the *gopīs*. These three signs have led Sarūpa to discover hundreds of arguments in favor of this conclusion.

## TEXT 216

तत्रापि यां प्रति प्रेमविशेषोऽस्य यदेक्ष्यते ।
तदा प्रतीयते कृष्णस्यैषैव नितरां प्रिया ॥

*tatrāpi yāṁ prati prema-*
*viśeṣo 'sya yadekṣyate*
*tadā pratīyate kṛṣṇa-*
*syaiṣaiva nitarāṁ priyā*

*tatra* — among them; *api* — however; *yām* — which (*gopī*); *prati* — towards; *prema* — love; *viśeṣaḥ* — special; *asya* — His; *yadā* — when; *īkṣyate* — is seen; *tadā* — then; *pratīyate* — it is apparent; *kṛṣṇasya* — of Kṛṣṇa; *eṣā* — she; *eva* — only; *nitarām* — most; *priyā* — dear.

**Yet when Kṛṣṇa shows special love for one of the gopīs, it then becomes apparent that she is the most dear to Him.**

## TEXT 217

सर्वास्तदुचितां तास्तु क्रीडासुखपरम्पराम् ।
सर्वदानुभवन्त्योऽपि मन्यन्ते प्रेम न प्रभोः ॥

*sarvās tad-ucitāṁ tās tu*
*krīḍā-sukha-paramparām*
*sarvadānubhavantyo 'pi*
*manyante prema na prabhoḥ*

*sarvāḥ* — all; *tat* — for that (supreme love); *ucitām* — suitable; *tāḥ* — they; *tu* — but; *krīḍā-sukha* — of pleasure pastimes; *paramparām* — the sequence; *sarvadā* — constantly; *anubha-*

*vantyaḥ* — experiencing; *api* — although; *manyante* — imagine; *prema* — love; *na* — not; *prabhoḥ* — of the Lord.

**All the gopīs partake of that exalted and most perfect love, and they all constantly know the pleasure of Kṛṣṇa's never-ending chain of pastimes. Yet none of the gopīs even imagines that Kṛṣṇa has special love for her.**

COMMENTARY: Even though there are so many *gopīs* eager to have Kṛṣṇa's mercy, none of them lacks opportunities to satisfy Him by her service. This is proof that all the *gopīs* have attained the highest perfection of pure devotional service. Yet none of them thinks herself Kṛṣṇa's only beloved. Caring nothing for their own happiness, they want only to do whatever pleases Him.

TEXT 218

प्रत्येकं चिन्तयन्त्येवमहो किं भविता कियत् ।
सौभाग्यं मम येन स्यां कृष्णस्याधमदास्यपि ॥

*praty-ekaṁ cintayanty evam*
*aho kiṁ bhavitā kiyat*
*saubhāgyaṁ mama yena syāṁ*
*kṛṣṇasyādhama-dāsy api*

*prati-ekam* — each of them; *cintayanti* — thinks; *evam* — thus; *aho* — oh; *kim* — whether; *bhavitā* — there will be; *kiyat* — to whatever extent; *saubhāgyam* — good fortune; *mama* — my; *yena* — by which; *syām* — I can become; *kṛṣṇasya* — of Kṛṣṇa; *adhama* — the lowliest; *dāsī* — maidservant; *api* — even.

**Each of them thinks, "Oh, when will I be fortunate enough to become even the lowliest maidservant of Kṛṣṇa?"**

COMMENTARY: The ambition of every young *gopī* in Goloka is to someday gain the good fortune to be allowed to enter Kṛṣṇa's service, even in the lowest position. Such utter humility distinguishes them from the young *gopas,* the male cowherds, who tend to consider themselves Kṛṣṇa's favorites and presume themselves very fortunate. The *gopas* often feel dissatisfied with themselves for various reasons due to the nature of their exalted love for Kṛṣṇa. They then become anxious to be better servants of Kṛṣṇa. The *gopīs'* love, however, is on the highest level of perfection. They are never satisfied with themselves, for their humility is absolute. Each of them considers herself Kṛṣṇa's worst maidservant, her only hope being to somehow be permitted to continue serving Him despite her disqualifications. In this way the moods of the *gopas* and *gopīs* are different.

The devotees of Nārāyaṇa in Śrī Vaikuṇṭha also never feel they have had enough of the ecstasy of worshiping the Lord's lotus feet. But every one of them assumes that the all-powerful Personality of Godhead is completely merciful to all of them, without discrimination. The Goloka-vāsīs cannot think like that.

## TEXT 219

अहो स्वामिन् गभीरोऽयं दुस्तर्को महतामपि ।
गाढप्रेमरसावेशस्वभावमहिमाद्भुतः ॥

*aho svāmin gabhīro 'yaṁ*
*dustarko mahatām api*
*gāḍha-prema-rasāveśa-*
*svabhāva-mahimādbhutaḥ*

*aho* — indeed; *svāmin* — O Lord; *gabhīraḥ* — grave; *ayam* — this; *dustarkaḥ* — incomprehensible; *mahatām* — to great sages; *api* — even; *gāḍha* — deep; *prema* — of love; *rasa* — in the ecstatic mood; *āveśa* — of the absorption; *svabhāva* — of the nature; *mahimā* — the greatness; *adbhutaḥ* — amazing.

**O my Lord! It is amazing how intently these devotees are absorbed in the fathomless rasa of pure love. The exalted nature of their mood is incomprehensible even to great sages.**

TEXT 220

एकदा यमुनातीरे विहरन्नन्दनन्दनः ।
शुश्रावात्मह्रदे तस्मिन्कालियं पुनरागतम् ॥

*ekadā yamunā-tīre*
*viharan nanda-nandanaḥ*
*śuśrāvātma-hrade tasmin*
*kāliyaṁ punar āgatam*

*ekadā* — one day; *yamunā* — of the Yamunā; *tīre* — on the shore; *viharan* — playing; *nanda-nandanaḥ* — the darling son of Nanda Mahārāja; *śuśrāva* — heard; *ātma* — his; *hrade* — to the lake; *tasmin* — that; *kāliyam* — the Kāliya serpent; *punaḥ* — again; *āgatam* — come.

**One day, while playing on the shore of the Yamunā, Lord Kṛṣṇa, Nanda-nandana, heard that Kāliya had come back to his lake.**

COMMENTARY: The lake in which Kāliya once stayed continued to be known as Kāliya-hrada ("Kāliya's lake") even after his expulsion from Vraja.

TEXT 221

एकाकी तत्र गत्वाशु नीपमारुह्य वेगतः ।
कूर्दित्वा निपपातास्मिन्ह्रदे निःसारयन्नपः ॥

*ekākī tatra gatvāśu*
*nīpam āruhya vegataḥ*
*kūrditvā nipapātāsmin*
*hrade niḥsārayann apaḥ*

*ekākī* — alone; *tatra* — there; *gatvā* — going; *āśu* — quickly; *nīpam* — a *kadamba* tree; *āruhya* — climbing; *vegataḥ* — rapidly; *kūrditvā* — jumping; *nipapāta* — He threw Himself; *asmin* — this; *hrade* — into the lake; *niḥsārayan* — pushing out; *apaḥ* — water.

**Kṛṣṇa rushed there alone, swiftly climbed a nīpa tree, and dived into the lake, splashing water onto the shore.**

COMMENTARY: Kṛṣṇa thought it wise not to bring His companions with Him to Kāliya's lake, which had become poisoned again. He was also concerned that they might try to stop Him from jumping into the lake. The vigorous way Kṛṣṇa dived is described in *Śrīmad-Bhāgavatam* (10.16.7):

*sarpa-hradaḥ puruṣa-sāra-nipāta-vega-*
*saṅkṣobhitoraga-viṣocchvasitāmbu-rāśiḥ*
*paryak pluto viṣa-kaṣāya-bibhīṣaṇormir*
*dhāvan dhanuḥ-śatam ananta-balasya kiṁ tat*

"When the Supreme Personality of Godhead landed in the serpent's lake, the snakes there became extremely agitated and began breathing heavily, further polluting it with volumes of poison. The force of the Lord's entrance into the lake made it overflow on all sides, and poisonous, fearsome waves flooded the surrounding lands up to a distance of one hundred bow-lengths. This is not at all amazing, however, for the Supreme Lord possesses infinite strength."

TEXT 222

विचित्रसन्तारवितारलीलया
जले लसंस्तद्बहुधा निनादयन् ।
खलेन भोगैरमुनैत्य वेष्टितः
स कौतुकी काञ्चिददर्शयद्दशाम् ॥

*vicitra-santāra-vitāra-līlayā*
*jale lasaṁs tad bahudhā ninādayan*

*khalena bhogair amunaitya veṣṭitaḥ*
*sa kautukī kāñcid adarśayad daśām*

*vicitra* — varied; *santāra* — of swimming across; *vitāra* — and swimming back; *līlayā* — with the sport; *jale* — in the water; *lasan* — playing; *tat* — thus; *bahudhā* — in various ways; *ninādayan* — making loud sounds; *khalena* — by the cruel being; *bhogaiḥ* — with his coils; *amunā* — by him; *etya* — coming; *veṣṭitaḥ* — enveloped; *saḥ* — He (Kṛṣṇa); *kautukī* — curious; *kāñcit* — a certain; *adarśayat* — displayed; *daśām* — condition.

**Kṛṣṇa frolicked in the water, enjoying the sport of swimming back and forth and making all sorts of loud noises. But then He drew near the cruel Kāliya and out of curiosity allowed Himself to be enveloped in the serpent's coils.**

COMMENTARY: When Kṛṣṇa played in the water, the noise He created was not ordinary; it sounded like very pleasing music.

## TEXT 223

तत्सङ्गिनस्तं सहसा प्रयातं
गोपास्त्वनालोक्य मृता इवाभवन् ।
सर्वे तदन्वेषणकातरा ययुस्
तत्पादचिह्नैर्ह्रदमीक्षितैरमुम् ॥

*tat-saṅginas taṁ sahasā prayātaṁ*
*gopās tv anālokya mṛtā ivābhavan*
*sarve tad-anveṣaṇa-kātarā yayus*
*tat-pāda-cihnair hradam īkṣitair amum*

*tat* — His (Kṛṣṇa's); *saṅginaḥ* — companions; *tam* — Him; *sahasā* — unexpectedly; *prayātam* — gone somewhere; *gopāḥ* — the cowherd boys; *tu* — but; *anālokya* — not seeing; *mṛtāḥ* — dead; *iva* — as if; *abhavan* — became; *sarve* — all of them;

*tat* — for Him; *anveṣaṇa* — for seeking; *kātarāḥ* — anxious; *yayuḥ* — they went; *tat* — His; *pāda* — of the feet; *cihnaiḥ* — by the marks; *hradam* — to the lake; *īkṣitaiḥ* — which were seen; *amum* — that.

**When Kṛṣṇa's companions, the cowherd boys, saw that for no good reason He was gone, they all became as if struck down by death. In great anxiety to find Him they followed His footprints to the lake.**

COMMENTARY: At first the cowherd boys had no idea where Kṛṣṇa might have gone, and they didn't know what to do. But soon they noticed footprints leading out of the village. Those footprints could not have been those of anyone but Kṛṣṇa because they had special marks, such as a flag and an elephant goad.

## TEXT 224

दृष्ट्वैव कृष्णं तमदृष्टचेष्टं
मोहं गतास्तेऽस्य वयस्यसङ्घाः ।
आच्छादितं यं वनवीथिभिर्ये
ऽनालोकयन्तो न जिजीविषन्ति ॥

*dṛṣṭvaiva kṛṣṇaṁ tam adṛṣṭa-ceṣṭaṁ*
*mohaṁ gatās te 'sya vayasya-saṅghāḥ*
*ācchāditaṁ yaṁ vana-vīthibhir ye*
*'nālokayanto na jijīviṣanti*

*dṛṣṭvā* — seeing; *eva* — indeed; *kṛṣṇam* — Kṛṣṇa; *tam* — Him; *adṛṣṭa-ceṣṭam* — in whom no activity was visible; *moham gatāḥ* — fainted; *te* — they; *asya* — His; *vayasya* — of young companions; *saṅghāḥ* — the throng; *ācchāditam* — hidden; *yam* — whom; *vana* — of the forest; *vīthibhiḥ* — on the paths; *ye* — who; *anālokayantaḥ* — not seeing; *na jijīviṣanti* — did not want to continue living.

**These many young friends were the same boys who, losing sight of Krsna on the forest paths for but a moment, would lose their will to live. And now when they saw Him motionless they all fainted.**

COMMENTARY: The footprints led the boys to the lake, but there they saw Kṛṣṇa immobilized, enwrapped in the serpent's coils. When Kṛṣṇa and the boys had been on excursions in the forest and Kṛṣṇa had passed for even a moment behind a tree and the boys couldn't see Him, the boys would lose all enthusiasm for living. And now to see Kāliya about to kill Kṛṣṇa filled them with dread.

## TEXT 225

गावो वृषा वत्सतरास्तथान्ये
ग्राम्याः समग्राः पशवोऽथ वन्याः ।
तीरे स्थितास्तत्र महार्तनादैः
क्रन्दन्ति कृष्णाननदत्तनेत्राः ॥

*gāvo vṛṣā vatsatarās tathānye*
*grāmyāḥ samagrāḥ paśavo 'tha vanyāḥ*
*tīre sthitās tatra mahārta-nādaiḥ*
*krandanti kṛṣṇānana-datta-netrāḥ*

*gāvaḥ* — the cows; *vṛṣāḥ* — bulls; *vatsatarāḥ* — calves; *tathā* — and; *anye* — others; *grāmyāḥ* — of the village; *samagrāḥ* — all; *paśavaḥ* — animals; *atha* — also; *vanyāḥ* — of the forest; *tīre* — on the shore; *sthitāḥ* — standing; *tatra* — there; *mahā-ārta* — of great distress; *nādaiḥ* — with sounds; *krandanti* — were crying; *kṛṣṇa* — of Kṛṣṇa; *ānana* — on the face; *datta* — fixed; *netrāḥ* — their eyes.

**All the village animals — the cows, the bulls, the calves — and also the animals of the forest stood on the shore, eyes fixed on Kṛṣṇa's face, and their cries made a great roar of suffering.**

## TEXT 226

आक्रन्ददीना विहगा ह्रदस्य
तस्यान्तरुड्डीय पतन्ति वेगात् ।
वृक्षादयस्तत्क्षणमेव शोषं
प्राप्ता महोत्पातचयाश्च जाताः ॥

*ākranda-dīnā vihagā hradasya*
*tasyāntar uḍḍīya patanti vegāt*
*vṛkṣādayas tat-kṣaṇam eva śoṣaṁ*
*prāptā mahotpāta-cayāś ca jātāḥ*

*ākranda* — from crying; *dīnāḥ* — exhausted; *vihagāḥ* — birds; *hradasya* — the lake; *tasya* — that; *antaḥ* — within; *uḍḍīya* — flying; *patanti* — fell; *vegāt* — with speed; *vṛkṣa-ādayaḥ* — trees and so on; *tat-kṣaṇam* — at once; *eva* — indeed; *śoṣam* — dryness; *prāptāḥ* — obtained; *mahā* — prominent; *utpāta-cayāḥ* — many omens; *ca* — and; *jātāḥ* — occurred.

**Birds exhausted from loudly crying flew precipitously into the lake. Trees and plants suddenly dried up. And many terribly inauspicious omens appeared.**

COMMENTARY: All creatures, including the birds and plants, agonized over Kṛṣṇa's predicament. They were all on the verge of death. The earth trembled, amidst other portentous omens:

*atha vraje mahotpātās*
*tri-vidhā hy ati-dāruṇāḥ*
*utpetur bhuvi divy ātmany*
*āsanna-bhaya-śaṁsinaḥ*

"In the Vṛndāvana area there then arose all three types of fearful omens — those on the earth, those in the sky, and those in the bodies of living creatures — which announced imminent danger." (*Bhāgavatam* 10.16.12)

### TEXT 227

सम्प्रेरितोऽन्तः प्रभुणैव तेन
धावञ्जगाम व्रजमेकवृद्धः ।
हाहामहारावगणैः सुघोरैः
क्रन्दन्नुदन्तं तमथाचचक्षे ॥

*samprerito 'ntaḥ prabhuṇaiva tena*
*dhāvañ jagāma vrajam eka-vṛddhaḥ*
*hā-hā-mahā-rāva-gaṇaiḥ su-ghoraiḥ*
*krandann udantaṁ tam athācacakṣe*

*sampreritaḥ* — dispatched; *antaḥ* — from within; *prabhuṇā* — by the Lord; *eva* — only; *tena* — by Him; *dhāvan* — running; *jagāma* — went; *vrajam* — to the cowherd village; *eka* — one; *vṛddhaḥ* — old man; *hā hā* — alas, alas; *mahā* — great; *rāva-gaṇaiḥ* — with many exclamations; *su-ghoraiḥ* — fearful; *krandan* — crying; *udantam* — news; *tam* — that; *atha* — then; *ācacakṣe* — he announced.

**Inspired by Lord Kṛṣṇa from within, one old man went running to the cowherd village. He wept and made dreadful cries of "Alas! Alas!" and told the cowherds what was happening.**

COMMENTARY: Śrī Nanda and the other cowherds, having seen the bad omens and received no news about Kṛṣṇa, were about to die from anxiety. To relieve their suffering, Kṛṣṇa telepathically inspired an old cowherd to go tell them of the situation. Had Kṛṣṇa not ordered him in that way, the old man would not have had the strength to run back to Vraja. Kṛṣṇa is *prabhu,* the Lord, so He can empower anyone to do anything. He made an old person His messenger because an elder's words are less likely to interfere with anyone's intimate *rasa* and more likely to be trusted.

Actually the desperation the Vraja-vāsīs felt over seeing evil omens and having no news about Kṛṣṇa was designed to increase their special love for Him. Surely they would come quickly to Kāliya's lake when they learned He was there.

## TEXT 228

प्रागेव दृष्ट्वा महतो भयङ्करान्
उत्पातवारान्बहुसम्भ्रमाकुलाः ।
अन्वेषणार्थं व्रजमङ्गलस्य ते
घोषस्थिताः सन्ति बहिर्विनिःसृताः ॥

*prāg eva dṛṣṭvā mahato bhayaṅ-karān*
*utpāta-vārān bahu-sambhramākulāḥ*
*anveṣaṇārthaṁ vraja-maṅgalasya te*
*ghoṣa-sthitāḥ santi bahir viniḥsṛtāḥ*

*prāk eva* — already; *dṛṣṭvā* — noticing; *mahataḥ* — very; *bhayam-karān* — frightening; *utpāta* — phenomena; *vārān* — many; *bahu* — very much; *sambhrama* — with concern; *ākulāḥ* — disturbed; *anveṣaṇa-artham* — for searching; *vraja* — of Vraja; *maṅgalasya* — for the source of the good fortune; *te* — they; *ghoṣa* — in the cowherd village; *sthitāḥ* — present; *santi* — were; *bahiḥ* — outside; *viniḥsṛtāḥ* — gone.

**The people of the cowherd village had already noticed many frightening omens. Kṛṣṇa was the source of Vraja's good fortune, and the cowherds, frantic with concern for Him, had already started out to seek Him.**

COMMENTARY: The Vraja-vāsīs knew that as long as Kṛṣṇa was safe nothing bad would ever happen. The evil portents might therefore indicate that Kṛṣṇa was in great danger. With this terrible thought in mind, they all went at once to look for Him. They were already outside the village when the old messenger met them.

TEXT 229

पुनः प्रवयसस्तस्य भग्नकण्ठस्वरस्य तु ।
तद्वाक्यं तेषु सहसा वज्रपात इवाभवत् ॥

*punaḥ pravayasas tasya*
*bhagna-kaṇṭha-svarasya tu*
*tad-vākyaṁ teṣu sahasā*
*vajra-pāta ivābhavat*

*punaḥ* — again; *pravayasaḥ* — of the old man; *tasya* — him; *bhagna* — choked; *kaṇṭha* — in his throat; *svarasya* — whose voice; *tu* — and; *tat* — his; *vākyam* — words; *teṣu* — upon them; *sahasā* — suddenly; *vajra-pātaḥ* — a lightning bolt; *iva* — as if; *abhavat* — was.

**The added force of the old man's report, spoken with a voice choking in his throat, struck them suddenly like a bolt of lightning.**

COMMENTARY: The shock of hearing that Kāliya had returned and was again holding Kṛṣṇa in his coils was unbearable.

TEXT 230

स गृहेऽवस्थितो रामो मिथ्या मिथ्येति घोषयन् ।
सान्त्वयन्व्रजलोकांस्तान्मृतप्रायान्प्रधावतः ॥

*sa gṛhe 'vasthito rāmo*
*mithyā mithyeti ghoṣayan*
*sāntvayan vraja-lokāṁs tān*
*mṛta-prāyān pradhāvataḥ*

*saḥ* — He; *gṛhe* — in His house; *avasthitaḥ* — sitting; *rāmaḥ* — Balarāma; *mithyā mithyā* — untrue, untrue; *iti* — thus; *ghoṣayan* — exclaiming; *sāntvayan* — consoling; *vraja-lokān* — the people of Vraja; *tān* — them; *mṛta* — dead; *prāyān* — almost; *pradhāvataḥ* — who were running forward.

**Balarāma, who was sitting in His house, tried to console the people of Vraja, who were running forward like living corpses. "This can't be true!" He cried out. "This can't be true!"**

TEXT 231

मातरं रोहिणीं यत्नात्प्रबोध्य गृहरक्षणे ।
नियुज्य पुरतो यातैर्धावित्वा तैः सहामिलत् ॥

*mātaraṁ rohiṇīṁ yatnāt*
*prabodhya gṛha-rakṣaṇe*
*niyujya purato yātair*
*dhāvitvā taiḥ sahāmilat*

*mātaram* — His mother; *rohiṇīm* — Rohiṇī; *yatnāt* — with effort; *prabodhya* — informing; *gṛha* — the house; *rakṣaṇe* — in watching; *niyujya* — engaging; *purataḥ* — ahead; *yātaiḥ* — who had gone; *dhāvitvā* — running; *taiḥ saha* — with them; *amilat* — He met up.

**Balarāma somehow told His mother Rohiṇī of the news, got her to stay back to watch the house, and ran to catch up with those who had left.**

COMMENTARY: Knowing the power of His younger brother Kṛṣṇa, Balarāma couldn't believe that Kāliya had defeated Him. Balarāma came out of the house and ran into the street spontaneously shouting, "This can't be true!" Seeing the Vraja-vāsīs hurrying on their way to join the search for Kṛṣṇa, Balarāma tried to calm them. And He had to speak to His mother before He left. So He was one of the last to arrive on the scene.

TEXT 232

अचिरात्तं ह्रदं प्राप्तः सोऽनुजं वीक्ष्य तादृशम् ।
नाशक्नोद्रक्षितुं धैर्यं रुरोद प्रेमकातरः ॥

*acirāt taṁ hradaṁ prāptaḥ*
*so 'nujaṁ vīkṣya tādṛśam*
*nāśaknod rakṣituṁ dhairyaṁ*
*ruroda prema-kātaraḥ*

*acirāt* — soon; *tam* — that; *hradam* — the lake; *prāptaḥ* — reaching; *saḥ* — He; *anujam* — His younger brother; *vīkṣya* — seeing; *tādṛśam* — in such a condition; *na aśaknot* — He could not; *rakṣitum* — keep; *dhairyam* — His gravity; *ruroda* — He cried; *prema* — by love; *kātaraḥ* — distressed.

**He soon reached the lake. Seeing His younger brother in such a state, He couldn't keep His gravity and wept in the distress of love.**

TEXT 233

विलापं विविधं चक्रे काष्ठपाषाणभेदकम् ।
क्षणान्मूर्छामनुप्राप्तो यशोदानन्दवत्स तु ॥

*vilāpaṁ vividhaṁ cakre*
*kāṣṭha-pāṣāṇa-bhedakam*
*kṣaṇān mūrchām anuprāpto*
*yaśodā-nanda-vat sa tu*

*vilāpam* — lamentation; *vividham* — various; *cakre* — He did; *kāṣṭha* — logs; *pāṣāṇa* — and rocks; *bhedakam* — shattering; *kṣaṇāt* — suddenly; *mūrchām* — unconsciousness; *anuprāptaḥ* — He experienced; *yaśodā-nanda-vat* — like Yaśodā and Nanda; *saḥ* — He; *tu* — and.

**As He lamented in ways that would shatter logs and stones, suddenly He fainted, just like Yaśodā and Nanda.**

COMMENTARY: In the bewildering commotion, Yaśodā and Nanda had already fainted and fallen to the ground.

## TEXT 234

ततस्तेषां च सर्वेषां प्राणिनामार्तिपूरिताः ।
महाक्रन्दवरा घोरा बभूवुर्विश्वरोदकाः ॥

*tatas teṣāṁ ca sarveṣāṁ*
*prāṇinām ārti-pūritāḥ*
*mahā-kranda-varā ghorā*
*babhūvur viśva-rodakāḥ*

*tataḥ* — then; *teṣām* — of them; *ca* — and; *sarveṣām* — all; *prāṇinām* — living beings; *ārti* — with agony; *pūritāḥ* — filled; *mahā* — vast; *kranda* — crying; *varāḥ* — great; *ghorāḥ* — frightful roar; *babhūvuḥ* — arose; *viśva* — the whole universe; *rodakāḥ* — causing to cry.

**Then all living beings there made a great and fearful cry, full of agony, that made the whole universe cry in pain.**

## TEXT 235

तेन नादेन महता बलरामः स चेतितः ।
आत्मानं स्तम्भयामास यत्नाद्धीरशिरोमणिः ॥

*tena nādena mahatā*
*balarāmaḥ sa cetitaḥ*
*ātmānaṁ stambhayām āsa*
*yatnād dhīra-śiromaṇiḥ*

*tena* — by that; *nādena* — noise; *mahatā* — great; *balarāmaḥ* — Balarāma; *saḥ* — He; *cetitaḥ* — awoken; *ātmānam* — Himself; *stambhayām āsa* — steadied; *yatnāt* — with difficulty; *dhīra* — of sober heroes; *śiromaṇiḥ* — the crown jewel.

**Awakened by that tumult, Balarāma, the most determined of heroes, with great effort steadied Himself.**

## TEXT 236

क्षणेन संज्ञां पितरौ गतौ तौ
दृष्ट्वा सुतं तादृशमुद्रुदन्तौ ।
वेगात्तमेव ह्रदमाविशन्तौ
रुद्धौ बलाच्छ्रीबलिना कराभ्याम् ॥

*kṣaṇena saṁjñāṁ pitarau gatau tau*
*dṛṣṭvā sutaṁ tādṛśam udrudantau*
*vegāt tam eva hradam āviśantau*
*ruddhau balāc chrī-balinā karābhyām*

*kṣaṇena* — after a moment; *saṁjñām* — consciousness; *pitarau* — parents; *gatau* — regaining; *tau* — the two; *dṛṣṭvā* — seeing; *sutam* — the son; *tādṛśam* — such; *udrudantau* — crying loudly; *vegāt* — quickly; *tam* — that; *eva* — indeed; *hradam* — lake; *āviśantau* — in the process of entering; *ruddhau* — stopped; *balāt* — by strength; *śrī* — divine; *balinā* — by the powerful (Balarāma); *karābhyām* — with His two arms.

**A moment later, Kṛṣṇa's parents again became conscious. Seeing their son in such a plight, they cried loudly and rushed to enter the lake. But powerful Śrī Balarāma held them back with the strength of His arms.**

COMMENTARY: It had taken all of Lord Balarāma's mental strength to convince His mother to stay home, and now it took all His physical strength to restrain Nanda and Yaśodā.

## TEXT 237

मूर्छितान्मृततुल्यांस्तान्सर्वान्दृष्ट्वार्तियन्त्रितः ।
सुगद्गदस्वरेणोच्चैः कृष्णं सम्बोध्य सोऽब्रवीत् ॥

*mūrchitān mṛta-tulyāṁs tān*
*sarvān dṛṣṭvārti-yantritaḥ*

*su-gadgada-svareṇoccaiḥ*
*kṛṣṇaṁ sambodhya so 'bravīt*

*mūrchitān* — unconscious; *mṛta* — corpses; *tulyān* — just like; *tān* — them; *sarvān* — all; *dṛṣṭvā* — seeing; *ārti* — by distress; *yantritaḥ* — impelled; *su* — very much; *gadgada* — choking; *svareṇa* — in a voice; *uccaiḥ* — loudly; *kṛṣṇam* — Kṛṣṇa; *sambodhya* — addressing; *saḥ* — He; *abravīt* — spoke.

**Seeing everyone unconscious on the ground as if dead, Balarāma was overcome with sorrow. In a voice choked with emotion, He called out to Kṛṣṇa.**

## TEXT 238

श्रीबलदेव उवाच
एते न वैकुण्ठनिवासिपार्षदा
नो वानरास्ते न च यादवा अपि ।
गोलोकलोका भवदेकजीवना
नश्यन्त्यशक्या भगवन्मयावितुम् ॥

*śrī-baladeva uvāca*
*ete na vaikuṇṭha-nivāsi-pārṣadā*
*no vānarās te na ca yādavā api*
*goloka-lokā bhavad-eka-jīvanā*
*naśyanty aśakyā bhagavan mayāvitum*

*śrī-baladevaḥ uvāca* — Śrī Baladeva said; *ete* — these; *na* — not; *vaikuṇṭha* — in Vaikuṇṭha; *nivāsi* — residing; *pārṣadāḥ* — associates; *na u* — nor; *vānarāḥ* — forest monkeys; *te* — they; *na* — not; *ca* — and; *yādavāḥ* — members of the Yadu dynasty; *api* — also; *goloka-lokāḥ* — residents of Goloka; *bhavat* — You; *eka* — only; *jīvanāḥ* — whose life; *naśyanti* — are being destroyed; *aśakyāḥ* — not able; *bhagavan* — My Lord; *mayā* — by Me; *avitum* — to be saved.

**Śrī Baladeva said: These are not the attendants who live with You in Vaikuṇṭha. They are not the forest monkeys. They are not the Yādavas. These are Your devotees of Goloka, who have no life other than You. They are dying, My Lord, and there is nothing I can do to save them.**

COMMENTARY: Here Balarāma reminds Kṛṣṇa that the Goloka devotees are different from Kṛṣṇa's other eternal associates — His Vaikuṇṭha *pārṣadas,* His monkey soldiers of Ayodhyā like Hanumān, and the Yadus of Dvārakā like Uddhava. More than all these other devotees, the Goloka-vāsīs are exclusively dependent on Kṛṣṇa. The Lord's devotees in Vaikuṇṭha, Ayodhyā, and Dvārakā, being always aware of Kṛṣṇa's omnipotence, manage to tolerate separation from Him, and so they could have responded favorably to Balarāma's consoling words. But the hearts of these Goloka-vāsīs, under the intolerable weight of their *prema,* have lost all equilibrium. The Goloka-vāsīs cannot accurately estimate Kṛṣṇa's power, so they are convinced that Kāliya is about to finish Him. If Kṛṣṇa Himself does not act soon to relieve them, surely they will die.

## TEXT 239

प्राणैर्वियुक्ता न भवन्ति यावत्
तावद्विनोदं करुण त्यजैतम् ।
कृष्णान्यथा गोष्ठजनैकबन्धो
गन्तासि शोकं मृदुलस्वभावः ॥

*prāṇair viyuktā na bhavanti yāvat*
*tāvad vinodaṁ karuṇa tyajaitam*
*kṛṣṇānyathā goṣṭha-janaika-bandho*
*gantāsi śokaṁ mṛdula-svabhāvaḥ*

*prāṇaiḥ* — from their life airs; *viyuktāḥ* — separated; *na bhavanti yāvat* — before they become; *tāvat* — before then; *vinodam* — game; *karuṇa* — O merciful one; *tyaja* — abandon; *etam* —

this; *kṛṣṇa* — O Kṛṣṇa; *anyathā* — otherwise; *goṣṭha-jana* — of the cowherd community; *eka* — only; *bandho* — O friend; *gantā asi* — You will experience; *śokam* — sorrow; *mṛdula* — gentle; *svabhāvaḥ* — whose nature.

**O merciful Kṛṣṇa, please give up this game before these devotees die! Otherwise, O Kṛṣṇa, sole friend of the cowherds, Your gentle heart will come to grief.**

COMMENTARY: Kṛṣṇa is the reservoir of all *rasas,* and so He feels pathos (*karuṇa-rasa*). But although He enjoys the sport of pretending to be lifeless, His devotees are driven to desperation by it. If He doesn't stop this sport, He will be the last one to lament — when all His devotees have died. Lord Balarāma is playing on Kṛṣṇa's emotions because He knows that Kṛṣṇa cannot tolerate seeing His devotees suffer.

## TEXT 240

श्रीसरूप उवाच
गोप्यो विलापैर्विविधै रुदन्त्यो
मोमुह्यमानाः परमार्तगात्र्यः ।
पार्श्वे प्रभोर्गन्तुमिव प्रविष्टास्
तास्तं ह्रदं शोकविनष्टचित्ताः ॥

*śrī-sarūpa uvāca*
*gopyo vilāpair vividhai rudantyo*
*momuhyamānāḥ paramārta-gātryaḥ*
*pārśve prabhor gantum iva praviṣṭās*
*tās taṁ hradaṁ śoka-vinaṣṭa-cittāḥ*

*śrī-sarūpaḥ uvāca* — Śrī Sarūpa said; *gopyaḥ* — the *gopīs;* *vilāpaiḥ* — with laments; *vividhaiḥ* — various; *rudantyaḥ* — crying; *momuhyamānāḥ* — fainting repeatedly; *parama* — terribly; *ārta* — pained; *gātryaḥ* — the limbs of their bodies; *pārśve* — at the side; *prabhoḥ* — of the Lord; *gantum* — to go; *iva* — as if; *praviṣṭāḥ* — entered; *tāḥ* — they; *tam* — that; *hradam* — lake; *śoka* — by sorrow; *vinaṣṭa* — shattered; *cittāḥ* — their hearts.

**Śrī Sarūpa said: The gopīs cried and lamented in so many ways, their limbs in terrible pain, their hearts shattered by sorrow. They fainted and fainted. And as if to go to the side of their Lord, they tried to enter the lake.**

COMMENTARY: On the way to the lake, the *gopīs* repeatedly fainted at the mere thought of Kṛṣṇa's distress, and so they arrived last. Their hair was scattered, and their broken bangles and other ornaments scratched their arms. They tried to enter the lake "as if" to join Kṛṣṇa, but their real purpose was to drown themselves.

Someone might question, "How could these *gopīs,* who are worshiped by the wisest scholars in creation, be so ignorant of the Supreme Lord's power?" The answer is that their minds were distracted by sorrow. It is unreasonable to think that the exalted *gopīs* cannot suffer sorrow; in fact, they simply cannot bear to be apart from Kṛṣṇa, even for a moment.

## TEXT 241

तावद्विहाय प्रभुरात्मकौतुकं
निर्गत्य तत्कालियभोगबन्धनात् ।
उत्तुङ्गविस्तीर्णसहस्रतत्फणेष्व्
आरुह्य हस्ताब्जयुगं व्यसारयत् ॥

*tāvad vihāya prabhur ātma-kautukaṁ*
*nirgatya tat-kāliya-bhoga-bandhanāt*
*uttuṅga-vistīrṇa-sahasra-tat-phaṇeṣv*
*āruhya hastābja-yugaṁ vyasārayat*

*tāvat* — just then; *vihāya* — giving up; *prabhuḥ* — the Lord; *ātma* — His; *kautukam* — sport; *nirgatya* — coming out; *tat* — that; *kāliya* — of Kāliya; *bhoga* — of the coils; *bandhanāt* — from the bondage; *uttuṅga* — upraised; *vistīrṇa* — expanded wide; *sahasra* — thousands; *tat* — his; *phaṇeṣu* — on the hoods; *āruhya* — climbing; *hasta-abja* — of His lotus arms; *yugam* — the pair; *vyasārayat* — He extended.

**Suddenly the Lord stopped His self-invented sport and freed Himself from the grip of Kāliya's coils. He climbed up on the serpent's thousands of upraised, outspread hoods and extended His lotus arms.**

COMMENTARY: To save the *gopīs* from despair, Kṛṣṇa extracted Himself from the clutches of Kāliya's embrace before the girls could reach the water. He jumped up onto Kāliya's uncountable hoods and spread His arms to lift the *gopīs* up to be with Him, even though the *gopīs* were out of arm's reach. He is *prabhu* and so can do anything He wants. He is never restricted by the laws of nature.

## TEXT 242

तेष्वेव नीत्वा युगपन्निजप्रियास्
ता गोपिकाः सत्वरमध्यरोहयत् ।
रत्नस्थलीपङ्क्तिसमेषु सर्वतश्
चित्रातिचित्रभ्रमणाभिरामिषु ॥

*teṣv eva nītvā yugapan nija-priyās*
*tā gopikāḥ satvaram adhyarohayat*
*ratna-sthalī-paṅkti-sameṣu sarvataś*
*citrāticitra-bhramaṇābhirāmiṣu*

*teṣu* — onto those (hoods); *eva* — indeed; *nītvā* — leading; *yugapat* — all at once; *nija* — His own; *priyāḥ* — beloved ones; *tāḥ* — those; *gopikāḥ* — young *gopīs;* *satvaram* — briskly; *adhyarohayat* — He raised up; *ratna* — jeweled; *sthalī* — of platforms; *paṅkti* — rows; *sameṣu* — equal to; *sarvataḥ* — on all sides; *citra-ati-citra* — most wonderful; *bhramaṇa* — with swaying; *abhirāmiṣu* — which were attractive.

**Taking hold of all His beloved gopīs at once, Kṛṣṇa briskly raised them onto the hoods of the snake. Those hoods, delightfully swaying back and forth, appeared like rows of jeweled platforms, creating a most impressive sight.**

TEXT 243

ताभिः समं तेषु महाद्भुतेषु
रङ्गेषु दिव्यैर्बहुगीतवादनैः ।
नृत्यन्विचित्रं स तु कौतुकार्णवो
लेभे सुखं रासविलाससम्भवम् ॥

*tābhiḥ samaṁ teṣu mahādbhuteṣu*
*raṅgeṣu divyair bahu-gīta-vādanaiḥ*
*nṛtyan vicitraṁ sa tu kautukārṇavo*
*lebhe sukhaṁ rāsa-vilāsa-sambhavam*

*tābhiḥ* — with them (the *gopīs*); *samam* — together; *teṣu* — on those; *mahā-adbhuteṣu* — most wonderful; *raṅgeṣu* — dramatic stages; *divyaiḥ* — celestial; *bahu* — many; *gīta* — with songs; *vādanaiḥ* — and instrumental performances; *nṛtyan* — dancing; *vicitram* — variously; *saḥ* — He; *tu* — and; *kautuka* — of amusement; *arṇavaḥ* — the ocean; *lebhe* — obtained; *sukham* — pleasure; *rāsa-vilāsa* — the *rāsa* dance; *sambhavam* — whose source.

**Kṛṣṇa artfully danced with the gopīs on those most amazing stages, accompanied by many celestial singers and musicians. Thus Lord Kṛṣṇa, the source of all amusement, enjoyed His rāsa dance pastime.**

COMMENTARY: Never before had anyone seen such stages for dancing as these. To complement the festivities, many demigods appeared in the sky overhead, singing and playing musical instruments. In this atmosphere Kṛṣṇa and the *gopīs* fully enjoyed their dancing. The entire spectacle was created by the energies of Kṛṣṇa, who is *kautukārṇava* ("the source of all entertainment"). Śrī Nanda and the other older cowherds, slow to recover from their deep shock, did not witness this *rāsa* dance.

## TEXT 244

रामेण प्रापितैर्बोधं वर्तमानैस्तटोपरि ।
कृष्णं नन्दादिभिर्दृष्ट्वा प्राप्तौ तैर्हर्षविस्मयौ ॥

*rāmeṇa prāpitair bodhaṁ*
*vartamānais taṭopari*
*kṛṣṇaṁ nandādibhir dṛṣṭvā*
*prāptau tair harṣa-vismayau*

*rāmeṇa* — by Balarāma; *prāpitaiḥ* — restored; *bodham* — whose consciousness; *vartamānaiḥ* — present; *taṭa* — the shore; *upari* — upon; *kṛṣṇam* — Kṛṣṇa; *nanda-ādibhiḥ* — by Nanda and others; *dṛṣṭvā* — being seen; *prāptau* — attained; *taiḥ* — by them; *harṣa* — delight; *vismayau* — and surprise.

**Nanda and the others on the shore, brought back to consciousness by Balarāma, gazed at Kṛṣṇa with delight and surprise.**

COMMENTARY: Even though Kṛṣṇa was saved, the older cowherds were still wary of what else Kāliya might do.

## TEXT 245

दमयित्वाहिराजं स स्तुवतीनां समाच्छिनत् ।
वस्त्राणि नागपत्नीनामुत्तरीयाणि सस्मितम् ॥

*damayitvāhi-rājaṁ sa*
*stuvatīnāṁ samācchinat*
*vastrāṇi nāga-patnīnām*
*uttarīyāṇi sa-smitam*

*damayitvā* — subduing; *ahi* — of snakes; *rājam* — the king; *saḥ* — He; *stuvatīnām* — who were offering prayers; *samācchinat* — seized; *vastrāṇi* — the garments; *nāga-patnīnām* — of the serpent's wives; *uttarīyāṇi* — upper; *sa-smitam* — with a smile.

**Having thus subdued the king of snakes, Kṛṣṇa, grinning, seized the shawls of the serpent's wives, the Nāga-patnīs, who were offering Him prayers.**

TEXT 246

तैरेकं प्रग्रहं दीर्घं विरचय्यास्य नासिकाम् ।
विध्वा प्रवेश्य वामेन पाणिनाधात्स कौतुकी ॥

*tair ekaṁ pragrahaṁ dīrghaṁ*
*viracayyāsya nāsikām*
*vidhvā praveśya vāmena*
*pāṇinādhāt sa kautukī*

*taiḥ* — with them; *ekam* — one; *pragraham* — rein; *dīrgham* — long; *viracayya* — fashioning; *asya* — his (Kāliya's); *nāsikām* — nose; *vidhvā* — piercing; *praveśya* — making it go through; *vāmena* — left; *pāṇinā* — with His hand; *adhāt* — He placed; *saḥ* — He; *kautukī* — playful.

**From these garments He made a long rein and with His left hand playfully pierced and threaded Kāliya's nose.**

TEXT 247

नागमश्वमिवारूढश्चोदयामास तं हठात् ।
धृतां दक्षिणहस्तेन मुरलीं वादयन्मुदा ॥

*nāgam aśvam ivārūḍhaś*
*codayām āsa taṁ haṭhāt*

*dhṛtāṁ dakṣiṇa-hastena*
*muralīṁ vādayan mudā*

*nāgam* — the serpent; *aśvam* — a horse; *iva* — like; *ārūḍhaḥ* — mounting; *codayām āsa* — He drove forward; *tam* — him; *haṭhāt* — with force; *dhṛtām* — held; *dakṣiṇa* — right; *hastena* — with His hand; *muralīm* — His flute; *vādayan* — playing; *mudā* — happily.

**Mounting the serpent like a horse, Kṛṣṇa toughly drove him forward, all the while, with His right hand, happily playing the flute.**

TEXT 248

कशयेव कदाचित्तं तया सञ्चालयन्बलात् ।
निजवाहनतां निन्ये प्रसादभरमाचरन् ॥

*kaśayeva kadācit taṁ*
*tayā sañcālayan balāt*
*nija-vāhanatāṁ ninye*
*prasāda-bharam ācaran*

*kaśayā* — with a whip; *iva* — as if; *kadācit* — occasionally; *tam* — him (Kāliya); *tayā* — with it (His flute); *sañcālayan* — urging on; *balāt* — forcefully; *nija* — His own; *vāhanatām* — the role of carrier; *ninye* — bestowed; *prasāda* — of His favor; *bharam* — the full extent; *ācaran* — manifesting.

**From time to time Kṛṣṇa forcefully urged Kāliya on with the flute, as if it were a whip. Thus He showered great mercy on Kāliya by making that serpent His carrier.**

COMMENTARY: Having to carry Kṛṣṇa like a horse is hardly a degrading punishment. Only rare souls like Garuḍa can have the honor of being the Supreme Lord's carriers. As the Nāga-patnīs stated in their prayers to Kṛṣṇa in the Tenth Canto (10.16.34):

*anugraho 'yaṁ bhavataḥ kṛto hi no*
*daṇḍo 'satāṁ te khalu kalmaṣāpahaḥ*
*yad dandaśūkatvam amuṣya dehinaḥ*
*krodho 'pi te 'nugraha eva sammataḥ*

"What You have done here is actually mercy for us, since the punishment You give to the wicked certainly drives away all their contamination. Indeed, because this conditioned soul, our husband, is so sinful that he has assumed the body of a serpent, Your anger toward him is obviously to be understood as Your mercy."

## TEXT 249

तत्पत्नीभिरुपानीतमनर्घ्यं रत्नभूषणम् ।
वस्त्रमाल्यानुलेपं च तत्फणेष्वेव सोऽदधात् ॥

*tat-patnībhir upānītam*
*anarghyaṁ ratna-bhūṣaṇam*
*vastra-mālyānulepaṁ ca*
*tat-phaṇeṣv eva so 'dadhāt*

*tat* — of him (Kāliya); *patnībhiḥ* — by the wives; *upānītam* — presented; *anarghyam* — priceless; *ratna* — jeweled; *bhūṣaṇam* — ornaments; *vastra* — clothing; *mālya* — flower garlands; *anulepam* — fragrant paste; *ca* — and; *tat* — his; *phaṇeṣu* — on the hoods; *eva* — indeed; *saḥ* — Kṛṣṇa; *adadhāt* — placed.

**The Nāga-patnīs offered Kṛṣṇa clothing, fragrant paste, flower garlands, and priceless jeweled ornaments, and Kṛṣṇa placed these on the serpent's hoods.**

## TEXT 250

पद्मोत्पलादिभिः पुष्पैर्यामुनैस्ताभिराहृतैः ।
भूषणैस्तैश्च ता गोपीरात्मानं च व्यभूषयत् ॥

*padmotpalādibhiḥ puṣpair*
*yāmunais tābhir āhṛtaiḥ*
*bhūṣaṇais taiś ca tā gopīr*
*ātmānaṁ ca vyabhūṣayat*

*padma-utpala-ādibhiḥ* — *padma, utpala,* and others; *puṣpaiḥ* — with flowers; *yāmunaiḥ* — from the Yamunā; *tābhiḥ* — by them (the Nāga-patnīs); *āhṛtaiḥ* — brought; *bhūṣaṇaiḥ* — with the ornaments; *taiḥ* — by them; *ca* — and; *tāḥ* — those; *gopīḥ* — *gopīs; ātmānam* — Himself; *ca* — and; *vyabhūṣayat* — He decorated.

**Then, with the padma, utpala, and other lotus flowers those wives had brought to offer Him from the Yamunā — and with the same ornaments He had already put on Kāliya — Kṛṣṇa decorated the gopīs and Himself.**

COMMENTARY: When the Nāga-patnīs presented ornaments to Kṛṣṇa, He did not immediately put them on His own body. First He placed them on Kāliya's hoods, and then, while He and the *gopīs* were all still standing on the hoods, He decorated the *gopīs* and Himself.

## TEXT 251

स्तूयमानः फणीन्द्रेण तेनासंख्यमुखेन सः ।
निःससार ह्रदात्सर्वान्स्वीयान् हर्षेण नर्तयन् ॥

*stūyamānaḥ phaṇīndreṇa*
*tenāsaṅkhya-mukhena saḥ*
*niḥsasāra hradāt sarvān*
*svīyān harṣeṇa nartayan*

*stūyamānaḥ* — being praised; *phaṇī* — of serpents; *indreṇa* — by the king; *tena* — him; *asaṅkhya* — countless; *mukhena* — with his mouths; *saḥ* — He (Kṛṣṇa); *niḥsasāra* — came out; *hradāt* — from the lake; *sarvān* — all; *svīyān* — His relatives; *harṣeṇa* — with joy; *nartayan* — making dance.

**While the king of serpents with his countless mouths recited prayers to Kṛṣṇa, Kṛṣṇa emerged from the lake, making all His friends and family dance with joy.**

COMMENTARY: With so many mouths, Kāliya could nicely offer prayers. In this way he was blessed by Kṛṣṇa to become like Ananta Śeṣa.

## TEXT 252

सुपर्णदुष्प्रापमहाप्रसाद-
वरावलीलाभमहाप्रहृष्टात् ।
स कालियाद्गोपवधूसमूहैः
समं महाश्चर्यतरोऽवरूढः ॥

*suparṇa-duṣprāpa-mahā-prasāda-*
*varāvalī-lābha-mahā-prahṛṣṭāt*
*sa kāliyād gopa-vadhū-samūhaiḥ*
*samaṁ mahāścarya-taro 'varūḍhaḥ*

*suparṇa* — by Garuḍa; *duṣprāpa* — difficult to obtain; *mahā-prasāda* — of great favor; *vara* — most excellent; *āvalī* — an abundance; *lābha* — by attaining; *mahā* — greatly; *prahṛṣṭāt* — who was enlivened; *saḥ* — He (Kṛṣṇa); *kāliyāt* — from Kāliya; *gopa-vadhū* — of young cowherd girls; *samūhaiḥ* — with the multitude; *samam* — together; *mahā-āścarya-taraḥ* — most amazing; *avarūḍhaḥ* — dismounted.

**Together with the troupe of young cowherd girls, most amazing Kṛṣṇa dismounted Kāliya. The serpent was filled with happiness, for he had obtained great favors and benedictions difficult for even Garuḍa to achieve.**

COMMENTARY: Kāliya had good reason to be satisfied, for his heads had been graced by the presence of Kṛṣṇa and the *gopīs*. And Kṛṣṇa offered him other benedictions, including the boon that Kāliya's hoods would always bear the auspicious marks of

Kṛṣṇa's feet. Kṛṣṇa is the most amazing person because He shows such kindness even to wicked creatures like Kāliya.

## TEXT 253

नीराजनालिङ्गनराजिकापरैर्
नन्दादिभिर्हर्षदृगश्रुधारया ।
आप्लावितोऽसौ कृपयानुशिष्य तं
किञ्चित्फणीन्द्रं निरसारयद् ध्रदात् ॥

*nīrājanāliṅgana-rājikā-parair*
*nandādibhir harṣa-dṛg-aśru-dhārayā*
*āplāvito 'sau kṛpayānuśiṣya taṁ*
*kiñcit phaṇīndraṁ nirasārayad dhradāt*

*nīrājana* — of worship; *āliṅgana* — and embraces; *rājikā* — in a series; *paraiḥ* — busily absorbed; *nanda-ādibhiḥ* — by Nanda and the others; *harṣa* — of joy; *dṛk* — from the eyes; *aśru* — of tears; *dhārayā* — by a downpour; *āplāvitaḥ* — drenched; *asau* — He; *kṛpayā* — mercifully; *anuśiṣya* — giving instructions; *tam* — to him; *kiñcit* — some; *phaṇī-indram* — the king of serpents; *nirasārayat* — expelled; *hradāt* — from the lake.

**Kṛṣṇa was drenched by a flood of joyful tears from the eyes of Nanda and the others, who absorbed themselves in worshiping and embracing Him again and again. Kṛṣṇa then mercifully gave the king of the serpents some instructions and exiled him from the lake.**

COMMENTARY: Kṛṣṇa's command is recorded in *Śrīmad-Bhāgavatam* (10.16.60–61):

*nātra stheyaṁ tvayā sarpa*
*samudraṁ yāhi mā ciram*
*sva-jñāty-apatya-dārāḍhyo*
*go-nṛbhir bhujyate nadī*

"O serpent, you may not remain here any longer. Go back to the ocean immediately, accompanied by your retinue of children, wives, other relatives, and friends. Let this river be enjoyed by the cows and humans.

*ya etat saṁsmaren martyas*
*tubhyaṁ mad-anuśāsanam*
*kīrtayann ubhayoḥ sandhyor*
*na yuṣmad bhayam āpnuyāt*

"If a mortal being attentively remembers My command to you — to leave Vṛndāvana and go to the ocean — and narrates this account at sunrise and sunset, he will never be afraid of you."

## TEXT 254

तैर्गोपगोपीनिवहैः प्रहृष्टैर्
विस्तार्यमाणेन मनोहरेण ।
वादित्रगीतादिमहोत्सवेन
सन्तोषितोऽगाद्भगवान्स्वघोषम् ॥

*tair gopa-gopī-nivahaiḥ prahṛṣṭair*
*vistāryamāṇena manohareṇa*
*vāditra-gītādi-mahotsavena*
*santoṣito 'gād bhagavān sva-ghoṣam*

*taiḥ* — by them; *gopa* — of cowherd men; *gopī* — and cowherd ladies; *nivahaiḥ* — the multitude; *prahṛṣṭaiḥ* — who were delighted; *vistāryamāṇena* — being raised; *manohareṇa* — charming; *vāditra-gīta-ādi* — of music, song, and so on; *mahā-utsavena* — by the festival; *santoṣitaḥ* — satisfied; *agāt* — went; *bhagavān* — the Lord; *sva* — to His own; *ghoṣam* — cowherd village.

**Out of sheer spontaneous joy, the throng of cowherd men and women celebrated a charming festival of music, song,**

**and other expressions of gaiety. Completely satisfied, Kṛṣṇa returned to His village.**

TEXT 255

कदाचित्तस्य दुष्टस्य कंसस्यानुचरौ प्रियौ ।
बहिश्चरासुरूपौ तौ केश्यरिष्टौ महासुरौ ॥

*kadācit tasya duṣṭasya*
*kaṁsasyānucarau priyau*
*bahiś-carāsu-rūpau tau*
*keśy-ariṣṭau mahāsurau*

*kadācit* — once; *tasya* — of him; *duṣṭasya* — wicked; *kaṁsasya* — Kaṁsa; *anucarau* — two followers; *priyau* — favorite; *bahiḥ-cara* — externally manifest; *asu* — of his life air; *rūpau* — the embodiments; *tau* — the two; *keśī-ariṣṭau* — Keśī and Ariṣṭa; *mahā-asurau* — great demons.

**Once the two great demons Keśī and Ariṣṭa came to Vraja. They were favorite servants of wicked Kaṁsa, visible manifestations of his life air.**

TEXT 256

आद्यो महाहयाकारो द्वितीयस्तु वृषाकृतिः ।
गोपान्भीषयमाणौ तान्मर्दयन्तौ च गोकुलम् ॥

*ādyo mahā-hayākāro*
*dvitīyas tu vṛṣākṛtiḥ*
*gopān bhīṣayamāṇau tān*
*mardayantau ca gokulam*

*ādyaḥ* — the first; *mahā-haya* — of a huge horse; *ākāraḥ* — in the form; *dvitīyaḥ* — the other; *tu* — and; *vṛṣa* — of a bull; *ākṛtiḥ* — in the form; *gopān* — the cowherds; *bhīṣayamāṇau* —

terrifying; *tān* — them; *mardayantau* — trampling; *ca* — and; *gokulam* — Gokula.

**The first of these two assumed the form of a huge horse, and the other a bull. They terrified the cowherds, trampling the land of Gokula.**

## TEXT 257

गगनस्पृङ्महाकायौ नादेन प्राणिनोऽखिलान् ।
निपातयन्तौ भूपृष्ठे युगपद्व्रजमागतौ ॥

*gagana-spṛṅ-mahā-kāyau*
*nādena prāṇino 'khilān*
*nipātayantau bhū-pṛṣṭhe*
*yugapad vrajam āgatau*

*gagana* — the sky; *spṛk* — touching; *mahā* — vast; *kāyau* — their bodies; *nādena* — by roaring; *prāṇinaḥ* — living beings; *akhilān* — all; *nipātayantau* — making fall; *bhū-pṛṣṭhe* — to the ground; *yugapat* — simultaneously; *vrajam* — the cowherd village; *āgatau* — entered.

**Both at once, they entered the cowherd village, their vast bodies touching the sky, their roars throwing everyone to the ground.**

COMMENTARY: The pastime of subduing Kāliya involved the combined *rasas* of pathos and heroism, but the next pastime recounted is one of pure heroism (*vīra-rasa*). In this instance the two famous demons Keśī and Ariṣṭa, friends of Kaṁsa, arrived in Vraja at the same time. Assuming animal bodies, abnormally large, they terrified the cowherd village and harassed the cows, trampling them with heavy feet. Śrīla Sanātana Gosvāmī says the demons harassed *gokula*. He uses this word to mean both "the cowherd village" and "the herds of cows."

## TEXT 258

तयोर्भियाकृष्य बलेन कृष्णो
निवार्यमाणोऽपि निजेष्टलोकैः ।
आश्वास्य तान्दर्शितवीरदर्पः
स्वपाणिनास्फोट्य भुजं पुरोऽभूत् ॥

*tayor bhiyākṛṣya balena kṛṣṇo*
*nivāryamāṇo 'pi nijeṣṭa-lokaiḥ*
*āśvāsya tān darśita-vīra-darpaḥ*
*sva-pāṇināsphoṭya bhujaṁ puro 'bhūt*

*tayoḥ* — of the two; *bhiyā* — out of fear; *ākṛṣya* — being pulled back; *balena* — with all strength; *kṛṣṇaḥ* — Kṛṣṇa; *nivāryamāṇaḥ* — being restrained; *api* — although; *nija* — His own; *iṣṭa-lokaiḥ* — by the beloved people; *āśvāsya* — assuring; *tān* — them; *darśita* — showing; *vīra* — of a hero; *darpaḥ* — the courage; *sva-pāṇinā* — with His hand; *āsphoṭya* — slapping; *bhujam* — His arm; *puraḥ* — forward; *abhūt* — He went.

**Though Kṛṣṇa's frightened loved ones tried to stop Kṛṣṇa, pulling Him back with all their might, Kṛṣṇa reassured them. Showing the courage of a hero, He slapped His arm with His hand and went forward to confront the demons.**

COMMENTARY: Frightened by this monstrous horse and bull, the men and women of the cowherd community wanted to prevent Kṛṣṇa from going near the demons.

## TEXT 259

प्रागागतं वेगभरेण केशिनं
पादप्रहारेण निरस्य दूरतः ।
पश्चाद्वृषं प्राप्य विभिद्य नासिकां
बद्ध्वाशु गोपीश्वरसम्मुखे न्यधात् ॥

*prāg āgataṁ vega-bhareṇa keśinaṁ*
*pāda-prahāreṇa nirasya dūrataḥ*
*paścād vṛṣaṁ prāpya vibhidya nāsikāṁ*
*baddhvāśu gopīśvara-sammukhe nyadhāt*

*prāk* — first; *āgatam* — who had come; *vega-bhareṇa* — very swiftly; *keśinam* — Keṣī; *pāda* — of His foot; *prahāreṇa* — with a kick; *nirasya* — casting; *dūrataḥ* — far away; *paścāt* — then; *vṛṣam* — the bull; *prāpya* — finding; *vibhidya* — piercing; *nāsikām* — his nose; *baddhvā* — binding; *āśu* — quickly; *gopīśvara* — of Lord Gopīśvara; *sammukhe* — before; *nyadhāt* — He placed him.

**Keśī, running very fast, appeared before Kṛṣṇa first, and Kṛṣṇa, with a kick, tossed him far away. Kṛṣṇa next found Ariṣṭa the bull, pierced a hole in his nose, tied him up, and brought him before Lord Śiva, Gopīśvara.**

COMMENTARY: Since horses generally travel faster than bulls, Kṛṣṇa first encountered Keśī. Kṛṣṇa kicked the horse demon so far away that he was unlikely ever to come back. Kṛṣṇa then subdued Ariṣṭa and offered him to Śrī Gopīśvara, the famous *śiva-liṅga* of the Vṛndāvana forest, to remain sitting before Gopīśvara Mahādeva, tied up for safekeeping as Lord Gopīśvara's carrier, so that Ariṣṭa would not be free to wander about and cause more trouble.

## TEXT 260

पुनस्तमायातममन्दविक्रमो
हयं समुत्प्लुत्य महापराक्रमः ।
बलात्समारुह्य गतीरनेकशो
ऽनुशिक्षयन्निर्दमयन्व्यराजत ॥

*punas tam āyātam amanda-vikramo*
*hayaṁ samutplutya mahā-parākramaḥ*

*balāt samāruhya gatīr anekaśo*
*'nuśikṣayan nirdamayan vyarājata*

*punaḥ* — again; *tam* — him (Keśī); *āyātam* — come back; *amanda* — never hesitant; *vikramaḥ* — whose valor; *hayam* — the horse; *samutplutya* — jumping up; *mahā* — great; *parākramaḥ* — whose prowess; *balāt* — forcefully; *samāruhya* — mounting; *gatīḥ* — movements; *anekaśaḥ* — numerous; *anuśikṣayan* — teaching; *nirdamayan* — taming; *vyarājata* — He appeared splendid.

**Then Keśī the horse returned, but powerful Kṛṣṇa, whose valor never falters, jumped up and forcibly mounted him. Training him to move here and there, Kṛṣṇa splendidly displayed His own prowess by taming Keśī completely.**

COMMENTARY: How could Kṛṣṇa have brought Ariṣṭa to Gopīśvara and then returned so quickly to meet Keśī? Kṛṣṇa is *amanda-vikrama,* anything but slow. His abilities have no limit.

## TEXT 261

हयं तमारुह्य निजान्वयस्यान्
सुशीघ्रहस्तेन सहस्रशस्तान् ।
विचित्रतत्कूर्दनकौतुकेन
भ्रमन्भुवि व्योम्नि च सोऽभिरेमे ॥

*hayaṁ tam āruhya nijān vayasyān*
*su-śīghra-hastena sahasraśas tān*
*vicitra-tat-kūrdana-kautukena*
*bhraman bhuvi vyomni ca so 'bhireme*

*hayam* — the horse; *tam* — him; *āruhya* — having mounted; *nijān* — His; *vayasyān* — young friends; *su-śīghra* — very swift; *hastena* — with His hand; *sahasraśaḥ* — by the thousands; *tān* — them (the cowherd boys); *vicitra* — in various ways; *tat* — of him (Keśī); *kūrdana* — of jumping; *kautukena* — with the sport; *bhraman* — roaming; *bhuvi* — on the earth; *vyomni* — in the sky; *ca* — and; *saḥ* — Kṛṣṇa; *abhireme* — enjoyed.

**Kṛṣṇa had thousands of His friends also mount the horse and with His swift hand made the horse jump in many ways, allowing these friends to roam both the earth and the sky. Thus He took His pleasure.**

TEXT 262

क्षणान्नियम्य स्ववशे विधाय
निबध्य पाशैस्तमपि व्रजान्तः ।
अरक्षदारोहणकेलयेऽमुं
वृषं तथानोगणवाहनाय ॥

*kṣaṇān niyamya sva-vaśe vidhāya*
*nibadhya pāśais tam api vrajāntaḥ*
*arakṣad ārohaṇa-kelaye 'muṁ*
*vṛṣaṁ tathāno-gaṇa-vāhanāya*

*kṣaṇāt* — in a short time; *niyamya* — restraining; *sva-vaśe* — under His control; *vidhāya* — bringing; *nibadhya* — tying; *pāśaiḥ* — with ropes; *tam* — him (Keśī); *api* — also; *vraja-antaḥ* — within the cowherd village; *arakṣat* — He kept; *ārohaṇa* — of riding; *kelaye* — for the entertainment; *amum* — him; *vṛṣam* — the bull; *tathā* — and; *anaḥ-gaṇa* — carts; *vāhanāya* — for pulling.

**Having brought the horse under His control in no time, Kṛṣṇa tied him up with ropes and kept him within the cowherd village for the entertainment of riding. And for pulling carts, He also kept the bull.**

COMMENTARY: Kṛṣṇa took Ariṣṭa, whom He had placed before Śrī Gopīśvara, and kept him in the cow pasture for pulling carts.

## TEXT 263

नन्दीश्वरपुरे तत्र वसन्तं कृष्णमेकदा ।
कंसाज्ञयागतोऽक्रूरो नेतुं मधुपुरीं व्रजात् ॥

*nandīśvara-pure tatra*
*vasantaṁ kṛṣṇam ekadā*
*kaṁsājñayāgato 'krūro*
*netuṁ madhu-purīṁ vrajāt*

*nandīśvara-pure* — in the town of Nandīśvara; *tatra* — there; *vasantam* — living; *kṛṣṇam* — Kṛṣṇa; *ekadā* — one day; *kaṁsa* — of Kaṁsa; *ājñayā* — on the order; *āgataḥ* — came; *akrūraḥ* — Akrūra; *netum* — to take; *madhu-purīm* — to Mathurā; *vrajāt* — from Vraja.

**One day while Kṛṣṇa was living in the town of Nandīśvara, Akrūra came, on Kaṁsa's order, to take Kṛṣṇa from Vraja to Madhupurī.**

COMMENTARY: The next pastime, described in texts 263 through 344, is one of pure extreme pathos (*karuṇa-rasa*). Both in Goloka and in the earthly Gokula, Nandīśvara Hill is the site of Nanda Mahārāja's residence. The Vṛndāvana pastimes thus far related by Śrī Sarūpa happened mostly in the forests, but on this occasion Kṛṣṇa was at home in Nanda-grāma.

## TEXT 264

तस्मिंस्तदानीं यद्वृत्तं तच्छ्रुत्वान्यत्रिका अपि ।
शिलाकाष्ठादयो नूनं रुदन्ति विदलन्ति च ॥

*tasmiṁs tadānīṁ yad vṛttaṁ*
*tac chrutvānyatrikā api*
*śilā-kāṣṭhādayo nūnaṁ*
*rudanti vidalanti ca*

...ja; *tadānīm* — at that time; *yat* — what; *vṛttam* ... *tat* — that; *śrutvā* — hearing; *anyatrikāḥ* — in ...; *api* — even; *śilā* — stones; *kāṣṭha* — logs; *ādayaḥ* ... on; *nūnam* — indeed; *rudanti* — cry; *vidalanti* — ... *ca* — and.

**...tones, logs, and other inert objects, even from other ...laces, hear what happened then in Vraja, they cry and shatter to pieces.**

COMMENTARY: We have already been told about the exceptional ecstatic symptoms of the trees and rocks of Vṛndāvana, but now we are informed that such objects even outside Kṛṣṇa's abode are devastated when they hear the pastime of Akrūra's taking Kṛṣṇa away from Vraja.

TEXT 265

रात्रावाकर्ण्य तां वार्तां लोका गोकुलवासिनः ।
व्यलपन्बहुधा सर्वे रुदन्तो मुमुहुर्भृशम् ॥

*rātrāv ākarṇya tāṁ vārtāṁ*
*lokā gokula-vāsinaḥ*
*vyalapan bahudhā sarve*
*rudanto mumuhur bhṛśam*

*rātrau* — at night; *ākarṇya* — hearing; *tām* — that; *vārtām* — news; *lokāḥ* — the people; *gokula-vāsinaḥ* — residing in Gokula; *vyalapan* — lamented; *bahudhā* — in many ways; *sarve* — all; *rudantaḥ* — crying; *mumuhuḥ* — they fainted; *bhṛśam* — repeatedly.

**The night the residents of Gokula heard the news that Akrūra had arrived, they all lamented profusely in various ways. They cried and fainted again and again.**

COMMENTARY: The Vraja-vāsīs all knew who Akrūra was and why he had come.

"O Nārada, best of the Lord's associates in the guise of an exalted sage, I see you just everywhere — in the heavenly planets, in Vaikuṇṭha, and now here — looking just the same. How fascinated I am to see this!" (5.50)

Kṛṣṇa was dressed for the forest. His garments, earrings, and peacock-feather crown all swayed to and fro, and so did His garland of *kadamba* flowers. His fragrance perfumed all directions, and His beautiful lotus face blossomed with a playful smile. His lotus eyes beamed with a merciful glance, and the varied assets of beauty decorated Him in a singular way. (6.56–57)

He leaped forward and came close to me, compelled by the affection of His helpless devotee. I fainted in love at seeing Him. He caught hold of me by the neck. And suddenly He too fell to the ground. (6.60)

Nanda sat down on his golden seat in the dining hall and began to have his meal, with the two brothers at his sides. Yaśodā's darling child sat on his left, the son of Rohiṇī on his right. And at the strong insistence of these brothers, I sat directly opposite, in my own place. (6.113–114)

She gave Him a thorough looking over and adjusted His clothes and the other things He had on. (6.170)

Then Keśī the horse returned, but powerful Kṛṣṇa, whose valor never falters, jumped up and forcibly mounted him. Training him to move here and there, Kṛṣṇa splendidly displayed His own prowess by taming Keśī completely. (6.260)

Early this morning Śrī Rādhikā-devī Herself came and ordered me: "Sarūpa, a *brāhmaṇa* from Mathurā who is My devotee is coming to My grove. Go there alone, the first thing today. Enlighten him with good instructions, console him, and help him quickly attain Kṛṣṇa's grace." (7.9–10)

Kṛṣṇa's friends examined all the preparations, picked out those they found especially tasty, and with their own hands reverentially placed them into His divine mouth. (7.58)

## TEXT 266

पुत्रप्राणा यशोदा च बिभ्यती दुष्टकंसतः ।
जुगोप कृष्णमेकान्ते निह्नुत्य शपथैर्निजैः ॥

*putra-prāṇā yaśodā ca*
*bibhyatī duṣṭa-kaṁsataḥ*
*jugopa kṛṣṇam ekānte*
*nihnutya śapathair nijaiḥ*

*putra* — her son; *prāṇā* — whose very life; *yaśodā* — Yaśodā; *ca* — and; *bibhyatī* — afraid; *duṣṭa* — wicked; *kaṁsataḥ* — of Kaṁsa; *jugopa* — she hid; *kṛṣṇam* — Kṛṣṇa; *ekānte* — in a solitary place; *nihnutya* — covering Him; *śapathaiḥ* — with oaths; *nijaiḥ* — her own.

**Yaśodā, her son her very life, was terrified of wicked Kaṁsa. Hiding herself and hiding Kṛṣṇa by keeping Him covered with her cloth, she uttered special vows for His protection.**

COMMENTARY: Mother Yaśodā was aware of how difficult it would be to keep Kṛṣṇa hidden. Her only hope was to recite magic incantations.

## TEXT 267

प्रातः प्रबोधितो नन्दोऽक्रूरेण बहुयुक्तिभिः ।
प्रबोध्य रुदतीं पत्नीं स्वपुत्रं बहिरानयत् ॥

*prātaḥ prabodhito nando*
*'krūreṇa bahu-yuktibhiḥ*
*prabodhya rudatīṁ patnīṁ*
*sva-putraṁ bahir ānayat*

*prātaḥ* — in the morning; *prabodhitaḥ* — waking up; *nandaḥ* — Nanda Mahāraja; *akrūreṇa* — by Akrūra; *bahu-yuktibhiḥ* —

with numerous arguments; *prabodhya* — convinced; *rudatīm* — sobbing; *patnīm* — his wife; *sva* — his; *putram* — son; *bahiḥ* — outside; *ānayat* — brought.

**When Nanda woke up in the morning, Akrūra explained things and presented numerous arguments to convince him. Nanda in turn convinced his sobbing wife and then brought Kṛṣṇa outside.**

COMMENTARY: Akrūra reminded Nanda how wicked Kaṁsa was, yet assured Nanda that Kṛṣṇa was fully capable of dealing with the evil king. Nanda had no choice but to let Kṛṣṇa go to the aid of their friends in Mathurā.

## TEXT 268

हा हेत्यार्तस्वरैरुच्चै रुदतीनामलज्जितम ।
गोपीनां वीक्षमाणानां प्राणानिव समाच्छिनत् ॥

*hā hety ārta-svarair uccai*
*rudatīnām alajjitam*
*gopīnāṁ vīkṣamāṇānāṁ*
*prāṇān iva samācchinat*

*hā hā* — alas, alas; *iti* — thus; *ārta* — agonized; *svaraiḥ* — with voices; *uccaiḥ* — loudly; *rudatīnām* — who were crying; *alajjitam* — without shame; *gopīnām* — of the *gopīs; vīkṣamāṇānām* — who were watching; *prāṇān* — the life airs; *iva* — as if; *samācchinat* — he took away.

**The gopīs watched helplessly, as if Nanda were depriving them of their life airs, and without shame cried out in agonized voices, "Alas! Alas!"**

COMMENTARY: By sending Kṛṣṇa away, Nanda Mahārāja was taking away the *gopīs'* very life. But when Nanda personally escorted Kṛṣṇa out of the house to the waiting Akrūra, there was nothing the *gopīs* could do but stare incredulously.

## TEXT 269

तदा यशोदा बहिरेत्य दीना
निजाश्रुधाराः परिमार्जयन्ती ।
धृत्वा करे न्यासमिवात्मपुत्रं
श्वफल्कपुत्रस्य करे न्यधत्त ॥

*tadā yaśodā bahir etya dīnā*
*nijāśru-dhārāḥ parimārjayantī*
*dhṛtvā kare nyāsam ivātma-putraṁ*
*śvaphalka-putrasya kare nyadhatta*

*tadā* — then; *yaśodā* — Yaśodā; *bahiḥ* — outside; *etya* — coming; *dīnā* — miserable; *nija* — her; *aśru* — of tears; *dhārāḥ* — the torrents; *parimārjayantī* — wiping away; *dhṛtvā* — taking; *kare* — in her hand; *nyāsam* — a deposit for safekeeping; *iva* — as if; *ātma* — her own; *putram* — son; *śvaphalka-putrasya* — of the son of Śvaphalka; *kare* — in the hand; *nyadhatta* — she placed.

**Then Yaśodā came outside. Miserable, wiping the torrents of tears from her eyes, she took her son's hand and placed it in the hand of Akrūra, the son of Śvaphalka, as if giving Kṛṣṇa to him for safekeeping.**

COMMENTARY: In the civil law discussed in the *Manu-saṁhitā* and other *Dharma-śāstras, nyāsa* or *nikṣepa* is a major topic. When a person deposits property with someone for safekeeping, the person holding the property is held gravely responsible. Anyone found guilty of betraying this trust — for example, by failing to return the property to its legitimate owner — the government should punish severely.

## TEXT 270

प्रोवाच नन्दं च तवापि हस्ते
न्यस्तो मया प्राणधनाधिकोऽयम् ।

कुत्राप्यविश्वस्य निधाय पार्श्वे
ऽत्रानीय देयो भवता करे मे ॥

*provāca nandaṁ ca tavāpi haste*
*nyasto mayā prāṇa-dhanādhiko 'yam*
*kutrāpy aviśvasya nidhāya pārśve*
*'trānīya deyo bhavatā kare me*

*provāca* — she told; *nandam* — Nanda; *ca* — and; *tava* — your; *api* — and; *haste* — in the hand; *nyastaḥ* — given; *mayā* — by me; *prāṇa* — than life; *dhana* — and wealth; *adhikaḥ* — greater; *ayam* — Him; *kutra api* — in anyone; *aviśvasya* — without believing; *nidhāya* — delivering; *pārśve* — to my side; *atra* — here; *ānīya* — bringing; *deyaḥ* — He should be given; *bhavatā* — by your good self; *kare* — in the hand; *me* — my.

**She then told Nanda, "I place in your hand this son, more dear to me than life and wealth. Don't trust anyone. Just bring Him back here to my side and return Him to my hand."**

COMMENTARY: In her own oblique way, Yaśodā advises her husband not to place too much trust in Akrūra.

## TEXT 271

एवं सुतस्नेहभरातुरा सती
मोमुह्यमाना समयं विधाय सा ।
कृष्णं विनैकात्मगृहं यदा गता
क्रन्दस्तदासीद्व्रजयोषितां महान् ॥

*evaṁ suta-sneha-bharāturā satī*
*momuhyamānā samayaṁ vidhāya sā*
*kṛṣṇaṁ vinaikātma-gṛhaṁ yadā gatā-*
*krandas tadāsīd vraja-yoṣitāṁ mahān*

*evam* — thus; *suta* — for her son; *sneha* — of her love; *bhara* — by the burden; *āturā* — pained; *satī* — the faithful wife; *momuhyamānā* — repeatedly losing consciousness; *samayam* — the agreement; *vidhāya* — making; *sā* — she (Yaśodā); *kṛṣṇam vinā* — without Kṛṣṇa; *eka-ātma* — lonely; *gṛham* — to her home; *yadā* — when; *gatā* — gone; *ākrandaḥ* — moaning; *tadā* — then; *āsīt* — there was; *vraja-yoṣitām* — among the women of Vraja; *mahān* — great.

**Having made that agreement, the faithful wife Yaśodā, so pained by the weight of love for her son that she fainted again and again, returned without Kṛṣṇa to her lonely home. A great lament then arose from the women of Vraja.**

COMMENTARY: Seeing Kṛṣṇa about to leave, the women of Vraja now lost all hope.

## TEXT 272

यस्मिन्स्मृतेऽद्यापि शिलापि रोदिति
स्रवत्यपो दारु पविश्च दीर्यते ।
नूनं जगन्मज्जति शोकसागरे
प्राणैर्वियुक्तं न भवेद्यदि क्षणात् ॥

*yasmin smṛte 'dyāpi śilāpi roditi*
*sravaty apo dāru paviś ca dīryate*
*nūnaṁ jagan majjati śoka-sāgare*
*prāṇair viyuktaṁ na bhaved yadi kṣaṇāt*

*yasmin* — which; *smṛte* — being remembered; *adya* — today; *api* — even; *śilā* — a stone; *api* — even; *roditi* — cries; *sravati* — sheds; *apaḥ* — watery tears; *dāru* — a tree; *paviḥ* — a lightning bolt; *ca* — and; *dīryate* — is shattered; *nūnam* — whole; *jagat* — the universe; *majjati* — submerges; *śoka* — of sorrow; *sāgare* — in an ocean; *prāṇaiḥ* — from their life airs; *viyuktam* — separated; *na bhavet* — might not be; *yadi* — if; *kṣaṇāt* — at once.

**Even today, remembrance of that scene makes stones cry, trees shed tears, and lightning bolts shatter. All living beings are submerged in an ocean of grief, if they don't at once give up their lives.**

## TEXT 273

यशोदया ता बहुधानुसान्त्विताः
प्रबोध्यमानाः सरलस्वभावया ।
महार्तिशोकार्णवमग्नमानसाः
सकोपमूचुर्बत तां व्रजस्त्रियः ॥

*yaśodayā tā bahudhānusāntvitāḥ*
*prabodhyamānāḥ sarala-svabhāvayā*
*mahārti-śokārṇava-magna-mānasāḥ*
*sa-kopam ūcur bata tāṁ vraja-striyaḥ*

*yaśodayā* — by Yaśodā; *tāḥ* — they; *bahudhā* — in various ways; *anusāntvitāḥ* — being consoled; *prabodhyamānāḥ* — being informed; *sarala* — simple-hearted; *svabhāvayā* — whose (Yaśodā's) nature; *mahā* — vast; *ārti* — of pain; *śoka* — and sorrow; *arṇava* — in an ocean; *magna* — immersed; *mānasāḥ* — whose minds; *sa-kopam* — angrily; *ūcuḥ* — said; *bata* — alas; *tām* — to her; *vraja-striyaḥ* — the ladies of Vraja.

**Simple-hearted Yaśodā told the ladies of Vraja all sorts of things, trying to console them. But their minds were immersed in a vast ocean of pain and sorrow, and so they answered her with anger:**

COMMENTARY: Yaśodā suggested to the ladies that because she had turned her son Kṛṣṇa over to Akrūra, the son of a *muni,* and to Nanda Mahārāja, there was no reason to worry about Him. One can assume that anything left on deposit with a saintly person is safe. "I am sure that Akrūra will come back soon with my husband to return Kṛṣṇa to me." She was too simple-hearted to question Akrūra's promise, even though she knew he could be duplicitous.

### TEXT 274

रे निर्दयेऽरे धिषणाविहीने
वत्सं निजं व्याघ्रकरे समर्प्य ।
शक्तासि दाहार्हमिदं प्रवेष्टुं
रिक्तं गृहं तेन कथं त्वमेका ॥

*re nirdaye 're dhiṣaṇā-vihīne*
*vatsaṁ nijaṁ vyāghra-kare samarpya*
*śaktāsi dāhārham idaṁ praveṣṭuṁ*
*riktaṁ gṛhaṁ tena kathaṁ tvam ekā*

*re* — O; *nirdaye* — merciless woman; *are* — just see; *dhiṣaṇā* — of sense; *vihīne* — devoid; *vatsam* — calf; *nijam* — your own; *vyāghra* — of a tiger; *kare* — into the hands; *samarpya* — having offered; *śaktā* — able; *asi* — you are; *dāha-arham* — deserving to be burned; *idam* — this; *praveṣṭum* — to be entered; *riktam* — empty; *gṛham* — house; *tena* — by you; *katham* — how; *tvam* — you; *ekā* — alone.

**"O merciless woman, devoid of sense! Just see — you have offered your own calf into the hands of a tiger. This empty house is fit to burn down. How can you enter it alone?"**

COMMENTARY: Even a less intelligent animal like a cow would never willingly allow a tiger to take away her calf. How then could Yaśodā have offered her son to Kaṁsa's servant? And after doing so, how could she have returned alone to a home devoid of Kṛṣṇa's presence?

### TEXT 275

तामेवमन्यांश्च विगर्हयन्त्यो
ऽक्रूरं शपन्त्योऽधिकशोकवेगात् ।

निर्गत्य गेहात्प्रभुमाह्वयन्त्यो
ऽधावन्सवेगं करुणं रुदत्यः ॥

*tām evam anyāṁś ca vigarhayantyo*
*'krūraṁ śapantyo 'dhika-śoka-vegāt*
*nirgatya gehāt prabhum āhvayantyo*
*'dhāvan sa-vegaṁ karuṇaṁ rudatyaḥ*

*tām* — her (Yaśodā); *evam* — thus; *anyān* — the others; *ca* — and; *vigarhayantyaḥ* — reviling; *akrūram* — Akrūra; *śapantyaḥ* — cursing; *adhika* — extreme; *śoka* — of misery; *vegāt* — by the force; *nirgatya* — coming out; *gehāt* — from their homes; *prabhum* — to Lord Kṛṣṇa; *āhvayantyaḥ* — calling out; *adhāvan* — they ran; *sa-vegam* — quickly; *karuṇam* — pitifully; *rudatyaḥ* — crying.

**Reviling Yaśodā and the others and cursing Akrūra, the ladies burst out of their homes, frenzied by misery, and rushed after Lord Kṛṣṇa, calling out to Him and crying pitifully.**

COMMENTARY: After Yaśodā, Nanda Mahārāja was next to receive the ladies' censure. They also blamed the other responsible cowherds for not objecting.

## TEXT 276

तैस्तैर्महाशोकदृढार्तिरोदनैर्
अक्रूरनन्दौ बलबल्लवान्वितौ ।
यानाधिरूढं प्रियमप्यरोदयन्
व्यामोहयन्त व्रजवासिनोऽखिलान् ॥

*tais tair mahā-śoka-dṛḍhārti-rodanair*
*akrūra-nandau bala-ballavānvitau*
*yānādhirūḍhaṁ priyam apy arodayan*
*vyāmohayanta vraja-vāsino 'khilān*

*taiḥ taiḥ* — by the various; *mahā-śoka* — in extreme sorrow; *dṛḍha* — severe; *ārti* — pain; *rodanaiḥ* — and crying; *akrūra* — Akrūra; *nandau* — and Nanda; *bala* — by Balarāma; *ballava* — and the cowherds; *anvitau* — joined; *yāna* — the chariot; *adhirūḍham* — who had mounted; *priyam* — their beloved (Kṛṣṇa); *api* — also; *arodayan* — making cry; *vyāmohayanta* — (these displays) bewildered; *vraja-vāsinaḥ* — the residents of Vraja; *akhilān* — all.

**This crying, this extreme sorrow, this insufferable pain made everyone else cry as well — Akrūra and Nanda, Balarāma and the cowherds, and even beloved Kṛṣṇa, who had mounted Akrūra's chariot. All the residents of Vraja were bewildered.**

## TEXT 277

स्वास्थ्यं क्षणात्प्राप्य स गोपिकागतिस्
ता वीक्ष्य लब्धान्त्यदशा इव स्वयम् ।
सञ्जीवयन्यानवरादवाप्लुतस्
ताभिर्वृतः कुञ्जमगादलक्षितम् ॥

*svāsthyaṁ kṣaṇāt prāpya sa gopikā-gatis*
*tā vīkṣya labdhāntya-daśā iva svayam*
*sañjīvayan yāna-varād avāplutas*
*tābhir vṛtaḥ kuñjam agād alakṣitam*

*svāsthyam* — normal consciousness; *kṣaṇāt* — after a moment; *prāpya* — gaining; *saḥ* — He (Kṛṣṇa); *gopikā* — of the young *gopīs; gatiḥ* — the life and soul; *tāḥ* — them (the *gopīs*); *vīkṣya* — seeing; *labdha* — who had reached; *antya-daśāḥ* — the final stage of life (death); *iva* — as if; *svayam* — Himself; *sañjīvayan* — reviving them; *yāna* — from the chariot; *varāt* — most excellent; *avāplutaḥ* — getting down; *tābhiḥ* — by them; *vṛtaḥ* — surrounded; *kuñjam* — to a forest grove; *agāt* — went; *alakṣitam* — unnoticed.

**After a moment, Kṛṣṇa, the life and soul of the young gopīs, came to His senses. He saw the gopīs apparently on the verge of death, and He got down from the fine chariot to revive them. Surrounded by them, and unseen by others, He went into a forest grove.**

## TEXT 278

कंसदूतस्ततः स्वस्थोऽपश्यन्कृष्णं रथोपरि ।
अनुतप्य बलं वाक्यपाटवैरनुनीतवान् ॥

*kaṁsa-dūtas tataḥ svastho*
*'paśyan kṛṣṇaṁ rathopari*
*anutapya balaṁ vākya-*
*pāṭavair anunītavān*

*kaṁsa-dūtaḥ* — Kaṁsa's messenger; *tataḥ* — then; *svasthaḥ* — coming back to his senses; *apaśyan* — not seeing; *kṛṣṇam* — Kṛṣṇa; *ratha-upari* — on the chariot; *anutapya* — feeling remorse; *balam* — Balarāma; *vākya* — of words; *pāṭavaiḥ* — with clever use; *anunītavān* — tried to convince.

**When Kaṁsa's messenger Akrūra came back to himself and saw that Kṛṣṇa was not on the chariot, he felt remorse for having allowed this to happen. With clever words he then tried to win the confidence of Balarāma.**

## TEXT 279

दुःखं च कथयामास देवकीवसुदेवयोः ।
यादवानां च सर्वेषां तच्च कृष्णैकहेतुकम् ॥

*duḥkhaṁ ca kathayām āsa*
*devakī-vasudevayoḥ*
*yādavānāṁ ca sarveṣāṁ*
*tac ca kṛṣṇaika-hetukam*

*duḥkham* — the misery; *ca* — and; *kathayām āsa* — he described; *devakī* — of Devakī; *vasudevayoḥ* — and Vasudeva; *yādavānām* — of the Yādavas; *ca* — and; *sarveṣām* — all of them; *tat* — that; *ca* — and; *kṛṣna* — Kṛṣṇa; *eka* — only; *hetukam* — having as its cause.

**He described how agonized were Devakī, Vasudeva, and all the Yādavas, only on account of Kṛṣṇa.**

## TEXT 280

ततः श्रीरौहिणेयोऽसौ वासुदेवोऽमुना सह ।
पितृव्येणानुजं मृग्यन्कुञ्जं तत्प्राप लक्षणैः ॥

*tataḥ śrī-rauhiṇeyo 'sau*
*vāsudevo 'munā saha*
*pitṛvyeṇānujaṁ mṛgyan*
*kuñjaṁ tat prāpa lakṣaṇaiḥ*

*tataḥ* — then; *śrī* — divine; *rauhiṇeyaḥ* — the son of Rohiṇī; *asau* — He (Balarāma); *vāsudevaḥ* — the son of Vasudeva; *amunā* — with him (Akrūra); *saha* — together; *pitṛvyeṇa* — His paternal uncle; *anujam* — for His younger brother; *mṛgyan* — searching; *kuñjam* — grove; *tat* — that; *prāpa* — He located; *lakṣaṇaiḥ* — by signs.

**Lord Balarāma, Kṛṣṇa's older brother, the divine son of Rohiṇī and Vasudeva, then went with His uncle Akrūra to search for Kṛṣṇa. By certain signs He was able to locate the grove.**

COMMENTARY: Like Kṛṣṇa, Balarāma is also called Vāsudeva, because He is a son of Vasudeva by another wife. Akrūra used Lord Balarāma's inability to tolerate Vasudeva's suffering as leverage to secure Balarāma's help in finding Kṛṣṇa. Once Balarāma agreed to bring Kṛṣṇa back, it was easy to spot Kṛṣṇa's footprints and follow them to the place where Kṛṣṇa and the *gopīs* had gone.

## TEXT 281

गोपीभिरावृतं कृष्णमालक्ष्यारात्स्थितोऽग्रजः ।
अक्रूरस्त्वब्रवीत्कृष्णं श्रावयन्निदमुद्रुदन् ॥

*gopībhir āvṛtaṁ kṛṣṇam*
*ālakṣyārāt sthito 'grajaḥ*
*akrūras tv abravīt kṛṣṇaṁ*
*śrāvayann idam udrudan*

*gopībhiḥ* — by the *gopīs; āvṛtam* — surrounded; *kṛṣṇam* — Kṛṣṇa; *ālakṣya* — finding; *ārāt* — at a distance; *sthitaḥ* — standing; *agrajaḥ* — His elder brother; *akrūraḥ* — Akrūra; *tu* — but; *abravīt* — spoke; *kṛṣṇam* — Kṛṣṇa; *śrāvayan* — addressing; *idam* — this; *udrudan* — while crying.

**Finding Kṛṣṇa surrounded by the gopīs, Balarāma stood at a distance; but Akrūra, in a tearful voice, spoke out so that Kṛṣṇa would hear these words.**

## TEXT 282

श्रीमदक्रूर उवाच
निर्भर्त्स्येते दुष्टकंसेन नित्यं
दीनौ वृद्धौ खड्गमुद्यम्य हन्तुम् ।
इष्येते च त्रासशोकार्तिमग्नौ
भक्तौ युक्तौ जातु नोपेक्षितुं तौ ॥

*śrīmad-akrūra uvāca*
*nirbhartsyete duṣṭa-kaṁsena nityaṁ*
*dīnau vṛddhau khaḍgam udyamya hantum*
*iṣyete ca trāsa-śokārti-magnau*
*bhaktau yuktau jātu nopekṣituṁ tau*

*śrīmat-akrūraḥ uvāca* — blessed Akrūra said; *nirbhartsyete* — are threatened; *duṣṭa* — evil; *kaṁsena* — by Kaṁsa; *nityam* — constantly; *dīnau* — poor; *vṛddhau* — Your old parents; *khaḍgam* — his sword; *udyamya* — holding high; *hantum* — to be killed; *iṣyete* — are intended; *ca* — and; *trāsa* — in fear; *śoka* — sorrow; *ārti* — and pain; *magnau* — drowning; *bhaktau* — Your devotees; *yuktau* — deserving; *jātu* — certainly; *na* — not; *upekṣitum* — to be neglected; *tau* — they.

**Śrīmān Akrūra said: Evil Kaṁsa unceasingly harasses Your old parents. Sword held high, he is ready to kill them. Surely You should not neglect them, Your devotees, so burdened by fear, by sorrow, by pain.**

COMMENTARY: Akrūra is trying to impress upon Kṛṣṇa that Kṛṣṇa should not neglect the plight of His helpless elderly parents. There is every chance that Kaṁsa will kill them. They are terrified of Kaṁsa, and sorrowful because they cannot see their son, and pained by Kaṁsa's slander of Kṛṣṇa. And there is no time to delay; even if Kaṁsa does not murder them, their own distress could kill them.

## TEXT 283

सर्वेऽनन्यालम्बना यादवास्ते
मद्वर्त्मान्तर्दत्तनेत्रा महार्ताः ।
शोकोत्तप्ता मा हताशा भवन्तु
त्रस्ताः कंसाद्देवविप्रादयश्च ॥

*sarve 'nanyālambanā yādavās te*
*mad-vartmāntar-datta-netrā mahārtāḥ*
*śokottaptā mā hatāśā bhavantu*
*trastāḥ kaṁsād deva-viprādayaś ca*

*sarve* — all; *ananya* — no other; *alambanāḥ* — having shelter; *yādavāḥ* — the Yādavas; *te* — they; *mat* — my; *vartma* — path;

*antaḥ* — upon; *datta* — fixed; *netrāḥ* — their eyes; *mahā-ārtāḥ* — greatly distressed; *śoka* — in lamentation; *uttaptāḥ* — burning; *mā* — do not; *hata-āśāḥ* — deprived of their hopes; *bhavantu* — let them become; *trastāḥ* — living in terror; *kaṁsāt* — of Kaṁsa; *deva* — the demigods; *vipra* — the *brāhmaṇas; ādayaḥ* — and others; *ca* — also.

**The Yādavas have no shelter but You. All in great distress, their eyes fixed upon the path for my return, they are burning in a fire of lamentation. They all live in terror of Kaṁsa, and so also do the demigods, brāhmaṇas, and other exalted persons. Don't deprive them of hope.**

COMMENTARY: Vasudeva and Devakī are not the only ones suffering with no hope of relief but Kṛṣṇa. So too are all the members of the Yadu clan. Related to Him both by family ties and by devotion, they look only to Him for their salvation. They are already in great anxiety because Akrūra has not yet returned to Mathurā with Kṛṣṇa, and if Akrūra returns without Him they will be devastated. By the very nature of the Yadus' pure love for Kṛṣṇa they are *mahārtāḥ,* greatly distressed, and *śokottaptāḥ,* burned by sorrow; now, on top of that, they should not be *hatāśāḥ,* deprived of their last hope. And besides the Yādava princes, yet others depending on Kṛṣṇa to save them from Kaṁsa's terror include demigods like Indra, learned *brāhmaṇas* like Garga, and all the cows and Vaiṣṇavas.

## TEXT 284

स श्लाघते बाहुबलं सदात्मनो
नो मन्यते कञ्चन देवमर्दनः ।
आत्मानुरूपैरसुरैर्बलाबलैः
कंसस्तथा राजकुलैः सदार्चितः ॥

*sa ślāghate bāhu-balaṁ sadātmano*
*no manyate kañcana deva-mardanaḥ*

*ātmānurūpair asurair balābalaiḥ*
*kaṁsas tathā rāja-kulaiḥ sadārcitaḥ*

*saḥ* — he; *ślāghate* — brags; *bāhu* — of his arms; *balam* — about the strength; *sadā* — always; *ātmanaḥ* — his own; *na u* — not at all; *manyate* — respects; *kañcana* — anyone; *deva* — of the demigods; *mardanaḥ* — subduer; *ātma-anurūpaiḥ* — like himself; *asuraiḥ* — by demons; *bala* — powerful; *abalaiḥ* — and impotent; *kaṁsaḥ* — Kaṁsa; *tathā* — and; *rāja-kulaiḥ* — by the royal order; *sadā* — constantly; *arcitaḥ* — worshiped.

**Kaṁsa, the subduer of demigods, always brags about the strength of his own arms. He has no regard for anyone. He is constantly worshiped by demons like himself — some impotent, some very powerful — and by the rulers of men.**

COMMENTARY: When Kṛṣṇa fails to respond, Akrūra tries to change Kṛṣṇa's mood from compassion to anger. In the beginning of Akrūra's statement, he refers to Kaṁsa merely as "he" (*saḥ*); in other words, so numerous and abominable are Kaṁsa's bad qualities that his name is not to be mentioned. His many demon friends in Mathurā help increase his influence, and they share his arrogance and other bad qualities. Powerful demonic rulers of other kingdoms like Bāṇa and Bhauma also support him.

## TEXT 285

श्रीसरूप उवाच
एवं ब्रुवाणः स तृणानि धृत्वा
दन्तैर्महाकाकुकुलं चकार ।
एकैकशस्ताः प्रणमन्व्रजस्त्रीर्
अक्रूरनामा परमोग्रकर्मा ॥

*śrī-sarūpa uvāca*
*evaṁ bruvāṇaḥ sa tṛṇāni dhṛtvā*
*dantair mahā-kāku-kulaṁ cakāra*

*ekaikaśas tāḥ praṇaman vraja-strīr*
*akrūra-nāmā paramogra-karmā*

*śrī-sarūpaḥ uvāca* — Śrī Sarūpa said; *evam* — thus; *bruvāṇaḥ* — speaking; *saḥ* — he; *tṛṇāni* — blades of grass; *dhṛtvā* — taking up; *dantaiḥ* — with his teeth; *mahā* — great; *kāku* — of plaintive cries; *kulam* — a series; *cakāra* — made; *eka-ekaśaḥ* — to each and every one; *tāḥ* — of them; *praṇaman* — bowing down; *vraja-strīḥ* — to the women of Vraja; *akrūra-nāmā* — the person named Akrūra; *parama* — most; *ugra* — cruel; *karmā* — whose duty.

**Śrī Sarūpa said: Akrūra, having said this, took blades of grass between his teeth and cried plaintively again and again. Then that person named "Uncruel," who had a most brutal duty to perform, offered his obeisances to all the women of Vraja, one by one.**

COMMENTARY: When Kṛṣṇa still didn't leave the grove, Akrūra, knowing Kṛṣṇa to be controlled by His dearest devotees, appealed to the *gopīs*. He approached them with all the humility he could muster. This wasn't easy because, despite Akrūra's name, taking Kṛṣṇa to Mathurā was the cruelest thing anyone could do to them.

## TEXT 286

श्रीमदक्रूर उवाच
मा घातयध्वं यदुवंशजातान्
लोकांश्च कृत्स्नान्कृपयध्वमेतान् ।
कृष्णस्य दीनौ पितरौ च देव्यः
कंसेन रुद्धौ परिरक्षताम् ॥

*śrīmad-akrūra uvāca*
*mā ghātayadhvaṁ yadu-vaṁśa-jātān*
*lokāṁś ca kṛtsnān kṛpayadhvam etān*

*kṛṣṇasya dīnau pitarau ca devyaḥ*
*kaṁsena ruddhau parirakṣatām ū*

*śrīmat-akrūraḥ uvāca* — Śrīmān Akrūra said; *mā ghātaya-dhvam* — please do not cause to be killed; *yadu-vaṁśa* — in the dynasty of Yadu; *jātān* — those who are born; *lokān* — for people; *ca* — and; *kṛtsnān* — all; *kṛpayadhvam* — please have mercy; *etān* — these; *kṛṣṇasya* — of Kṛṣṇa; *dīnau* — poor; *pitarau* — the parents; *ca* — and; *devyaḥ* — dear goddesses; *kaṁsena* — by Kaṁsa; *ruddhau* — imprisoned; *parirakṣatām* — should be protected; *ū* — oh.

**Śrīmān Akrūra said: Don't be death for the descendants of the Yadu dynasty, and for all the people of the world. Please have mercy on them. Dear goddesses, Kṛṣṇa's wretched parents are imprisoned by Kaṁsa. Please help rescue them.**

COMMENTARY: Everyone was afraid of Kaṁsa, including the cowherds of Vraja. Were Kṛṣṇa not to come soon to Mathurā, the lives of many innocent persons would be at risk, and the first to be killed might well be Vasudeva and Devakī. Therefore the *gopīs* should be merciful by consenting to Kṛṣṇa's departure and giving their blessings for an auspicious journey.

## TEXT 287

श्रीगोपिका ऊचुः
हे हे महाधूर्त मृषाप्रलापक
कंसानुवर्तिन्पितरौ कुतोऽस्य ।
पुत्रस्य वै नन्दयशोदयोस्तौ
मा गोकुलं मारय मा जहि स्त्रीः ॥

*śrī-gopikā ūcuḥ*
*he he mahā-dhūrta mṛṣā-pralāpaka*
*kaṁsānuvartin pitarau kuto 'sya*
*putrasya vai nanda-yaśodayos tau*
*mā gokulaṁ māraya mā jahi strīḥ*

*śrī-gopikāḥ ūcuḥ* — the divine *gopīs* said; *he* — O; *he* — O; *mahā-dhūrta* — great cheat; *mṛṣā* — untruths; *pralāpaka* — you who speak loosely; *kaṁsa* — of Kaṁsa; *anuvartin* — O follower; *pitarau* — the parents; *kutaḥ* — how; *asya* — of Him; *putrasya* — of the son; *vai* — indeed; *nanda* — of Nanda; *yaśodayoḥ* — and Yaśodā; *tau* — the two of Them; *mā* — do not; *gokulam* — Gokula; *māraya* — kill; *mā jahi* — do not do violence; *strīḥ* — to women.

**The divine gopīs said: You great cheat, you speaker of falsehoods, you follower of Kaṁsa! How can those you speak of be Kṛṣṇa's parents? These two boys are the sons of Nanda and Yaśodā! Don't murder Gokula. Do not become a killer of women.**

COMMENTARY: Why do the *gopīs* call the son of Śvaphalka Muni a great cheat and liar? Because he is a follower of Kaṁsa. The *gopīs'* statement that Vasudeva and Devakī cannot be Kṛṣṇa's parents is correct in the sense that Vasudeva and Devakī are really His unalloyed devotees acting as His parents, roles they accept only for His service.

By telling Akrūra not to kill the people of Gokula, and especially not to become a killer of women, the *gopīs* mean to say that his immediate concern should not be over Vasudeva and Devakī. The threat of their being killed lies in the future, and enough time remains for measures to prevent such a tragedy. The threat, however, that Akrūra will become the direct cause of the deaths of the inhabitants of Gokula, including the cows and women, is imminent. Akrūra should therefore think twice before committing these terrible sins.

## TEXT 288

श्रीसरूप उवाच
दुष्टस्य कंसस्य निशम्य चेष्टितं
दुःखं निजानां च तदात्महेतुकम् ।

आश्वास्य गोपीर्निरगाद्रुषा शुचा
कुञ्जाद्बलस्यानुमतिं विलक्ष्य च ॥

*śrī-sarūpa uvāca*
*duṣṭasya kaṁsasya niśamya ceṣṭitaṁ*
*duḥkhaṁ nijānāṁ ca tad ātma-hetukam*
*āśvāsya gopīr niragād ruṣā śucā*
*kuñjād balasyānumatiṁ vilakṣya ca*

*śrī-sarūpaḥ uvāca* — Śrī Sarūpa said; *duṣṭasya* — wicked; *kaṁsasya* — of Kaṁsa; *niśamya* — hearing; *ceṣṭitam* — about the activity; *duḥkham* — about the misery; *nijānām* — of His family members; *ca* — and; *tat* — that; *ātma-hetukam* — whose cause was Himself; *āśvāsya* — apologizing; *gopīḥ* — to the *gopīs; niragāt* — He came out; *ruṣā* — with anger; *śucā* — and with sadness; *kuñjāt* — from the grove; *balasya* — of Balarāma; *anumatim* — the agreement; *vilakṣya* — seeing; *ca* — and.

**Śrī Sarūpa said: When Kṛṣṇa heard of wicked Kaṁsa's deeds, when He heard of the misery He Himself had caused His own relatives, and when He saw that Balarāma agreed with Akrūra, He apologized to the gopīs, and showing anger and sadness He left the grove.**

COMMENTARY: The anger Kṛṣṇa felt was directed solely at Kaṁsa, and the sorrow He felt was for His faultless devotees. He interpreted His elder brother's silence as a sign that Lord Balarāma accepted Akrūra's proposal to take Them to Madhupurī.

TEXT 289

ततः प्रमुदितोऽक्रूरो बलरामानुमोदितः ।
तत्रैव रथमानेतुं धावन्वेगाद्बहिर्गतः ॥

*tataḥ pramudito 'krūro*
*balarāmānumoditaḥ*

*tatraiva ratham ānetuṁ*
*dhāvan vegād bahir gataḥ*

*tataḥ* — at that; *pramuditaḥ* — overjoyed; *akrūraḥ* — Akrūra; *balarāma* — by Balarāma; *anumoditaḥ* — permitted; *tatra* — there; *eva* — just; *ratham* — the chariot; *ānetum* — to bring; *dhāvan* — running; *vegāt* — quickly; *bahiḥ* — outside; *gataḥ* — went.

**Akrūra was overjoyed. With Balarāma's permission, He quickly left the grove and ran to bring the chariot.**

TEXT 290

निर्णीय कृष्णस्य पुरे प्रयाणं
तस्याननाब्जं मुहुरीक्षमाणाः ।
भीता वियोगानलतो रुदत्यो
गोप्यः पदाब्जे पतितास्तमाहुः ॥

*nirṇīya kṛṣṇasya pure prayāṇaṁ*
*tasyānanābjaṁ muhur īkṣamāṇāḥ*
*bhītā viyogānalato rudatyo*
*gopyaḥ padābje patitās tam āhuḥ*

*nirṇīya* — ascertaining; *kṛṣṇasya* — of Kṛṣṇa; *pure* — for the city; *prayāṇam* — the departure; *tasya* — His; *ānana-abjam* — lotus face; *muhuḥ* — constantly; *īkṣamāṇāḥ* — looking at; *bhītāḥ* — frightened; *viyoga* — of separation; *analataḥ* — of the fire; *rudatyaḥ* — crying; *gopyaḥ* — the *gopīs; pada-abje* — at his lotus feet; *patitāḥ* — falling; *tam* — to Kṛṣṇa; *āhuḥ* — said.

**When the gopīs understood that Kṛṣṇa was about to leave for the city, they fixed their eyes on His lotus face. In dread of the imminent fire of separation, they cried and spoke to Kṛṣṇa, falling at His lotus feet.**

COMMENTARY: For the *gopīs* to address Kṛṣṇa so boldly in public might have appeared audacious, but they were afraid of burning up in the fire of separation. And besides, the *gopīs* are not the only devotees who sometimes frankly express their agony to Kṛṣṇa in the presence of others. For example, in *Śrīmad-Bhāgavatam* (10.23.29) we hear from the wives of the Vedic *brāhmaṇas:*

*maivaṁ vibho 'rhati bhavān gadituṁ nṛ-śaṁsaṁ*
*satyaṁ kuruṣva nigamaṁ tava pāda-mūlam*
*prāptā vayaṁ tulasi-dāma padāvasṛṣṭaṁ*
*keśair nivoḍhum atilaṅghya samasta-bandhūn*

"O almighty one, please do not speak such cruel words. Rather, You should fulfill Your promise that You always reciprocate with Your devotees in kind. Now that we have attained Your lotus feet, we simply wish to remain here in the forest so we may carry upon our heads the garlands of *tulasī* leaves You may neglectfully kick away with Your lotus feet. We are ready to give up all material relationships."

## TEXT 291

श्रीगोप्य ऊचुः
न शक्नुमो नाथ कदापि जीवितुं
विना भवन्तं लवमप्यनाश्रयाः ।
न मुञ्च दासीस्तदिमा निजाः प्रभो
नयस्व तत्रैव यतो गमिष्यसि ॥

*śrī-gopya ūcuḥ*
*na śaknumo nātha kadāpi jīvituṁ*
*vinā bhavantaṁ lavam apy anāśrayāḥ*
*na muñca dāsīs tad imā nijāḥ prabho*
*nayasva tatraiva yato gamiṣyasi*

*śrī-gopyaḥ ūcuḥ* — the divine *gopīs* said; *na śaknumaḥ* — we are not able; *nātha* — O master; *kadā api* — at any time; *jīvitum* — to live; *vinā* — without; *bhavantam* — You; *lavam*

— a fraction of a second; *api* — even; *anāśrayāḥ* — having no shelter; *na muñca* — please do not abandon; *dāsīḥ* — Your maidservants; *tat* — therefore; *imāḥ* — these; *nijāḥ* — Your own; *prabho* — O Lord; *nayasva* — please take; *tatra* — there; *eva* — just; *yataḥ* — wherever; *gamiṣyasi* — You will go.

**The divine gopīs said: O master, we cannot live even a moment without You. We have no other shelter. Do not abandon us, Your maidservants. O Lord, take us with You wherever You go!**

## TEXT 292

वनं गृहं नोऽभवदालयो वनं
द्विषत्सुहृद्बन्धुगणाश्च वैरिणः ।
विषं च पीयूषमुतामृतं विषं
यदर्थमस्मात्त्वदृते म्रियामहे ॥

*vanaṁ gṛhaṁ no 'bhavad ālayo vanaṁ*
*dviṣat suhṛd bandhu-gaṇāś ca vairiṇaḥ*
*viṣaṁ ca pīyūṣam utāmṛtaṁ viṣaṁ*
*yad-artham asmāt tvad ṛte mriyāmahe*

*vanam* — the forest; *gṛham* — home; *naḥ* — our; *abhavat* — has become; *ālayaḥ* — home; *vanam* — a forest; *dviṣat* — an enemy; *suhṛt* — our friend; *bandhu-gaṇāḥ* — friends; *ca* — and; *vairiṇaḥ* — enemies; *viṣam* — poison; *ca* — and; *pīyūṣam* — nectar; *uta* — moreover; *amṛtam* — nectar; *viṣam* — poison; *yat* — of whom; *artham* — for the sake; *asmāt* — Him; *tvat* — You; *ṛte* — without; *mriyāmahe* — we will die.

**For the sake of You, the forests have become our homes and our homes forests, our enemies our friends and our friends enemies, poison sweet nectar and nectar poison. Without You we will die.**

COMMENTARY: The *gopīs* are sure that if Kṛṣṇa refuses to accept their prayer they will very soon die. After all, didn't Kṛṣṇa turn their lives upside down? The forests were their homes because in the forests they enjoyed Kṛṣṇa's company. And their homes were like an empty wilderness because Kṛṣṇa wasn't there. Their rivals for Kṛṣṇa's affection were actually friends because with the help of those friends they were able to meet Kṛṣṇa. And by preventing the *gopīs* from going to Kṛṣṇa, their husbands and children acted as enemies. In fact the *gopīs'* love for Kṛṣṇa was so potent that it even transformed poisonous substances into the most palatable nectar. And for *gopīs* eager to die in the torment of separation, poison became attractive. Nectarean things like moonlight, sandalwood paste, and nice food were like poison for the *gopīs* because the gratification afforded by such things impeded their association with Kṛṣṇa, and when they were suffering separation from Him their so-called pleasures became unbearable. Śrī Nārada has already explained to Gopa-kumāra why pure love for Kṛṣṇa affected the *gopīs* in these strange ways.

## TEXT 293

कथं तवेदं स्मितसुन्दराननं
मनोहरं पादसरोरुहद्वयम् ।
उरःस्थलं चाखिलशोभयार्चितं
कुतोऽप्यनालोक्य चिरं म्रियेमहि ॥

*katham̐ tavedam̐ smita-sundarānanam̐*
*manoharam̐ pāda-saroruha-dvayam*
*uraḥ-sthalam̐ cākhila-śobhayārcitam̐*
*kuto 'py anālokya ciram̐ mriyemahi*

*katham* — how; *tava* — Your; *idam* — this; *smita* — smiling; *sundara* — beautiful; *ānanam* — face; *manoharam* — all-attractive; *pāda-saroruha* — lotus feet; *dvayam* — two; *uraḥ-sthalam* — chest; *ca* — and; *akhila* — all; *śobhayā* — by auspiciousness; *arcitam* — adorned; *kutaḥ api* — anywhere; *anālokya* — not seeing; *ciram* — after long; *mriyemahi* — we will die.

**How could we not die a slow death if we could no longer see anywhere Your beautiful smiling face, Your all-attractive lotus feet, and Your chest, adorned by all splendor?**

COMMENTARY: When Kṛṣṇa was getting ready to leave for Mathurā, He suggested to the *gopīs,* "I am going to Mathurā to satisfy My well-wishers there, who have no goal in life but Me. Until I return, you can keep yourselves happy by hearing, chanting, and remembering My glories." This is the *gopis'* answer. If for any length of time the *gopīs* cannot see Kṛṣṇa's face anywhere (*kuto 'pi*) — either in His home or in the forest — they will surely die. Kṛṣṇa might also try to excuse Himself by saying that if because of Him His friends in Mathurā remain unhappy His reputation will be ruined. But (with *kuto 'pi* construed as "for whatever reason") the *gopīs* would respond, "We do not care what reason You have. If You leave us we will die a slow death."

## TEXT 294

वृन्दावनं गोपविलासलोभात्
त्वयि प्रयाते सह मित्रवृन्दैः ।
सायं समायास्यसि खल्ववश्यम्
इत्याशयाहर्गमयेम कृच्छ्रात् ॥

*vṛndāvanaṁ gopa-vilāsa-lobhāt*
*tvayi prayāte saha mitra-vṛndaiḥ*
*sāyaṁ samāyāsyasi khalv avaśyam*
*ity āśayāhar gamayema kṛcchrāt*

*vṛndāvanam* — to the Vṛndāvan forest; *gopa* — of cowherds; *vilāsa* — for the pastimes; *lobhāt* — due to eagerness; *tvayi* — when You; *prayāte* — go off; *saha* — together; *mitra-vṛndaiḥ* — with Your many friends; *sāyam* — in the evening;

*samāyāsyasi* — You will return; *khalu* — indeed; *avaśyam* — certainly; *iti* — thus; *āśayā* — by the hope; *ahaḥ* — the daytime; *gamayema* — we manage to pass; *kṛcchrāt* — with difficulty.

**When you go off to the Vṛndāvana forest with Your friends, eager to enjoy Your cowherd pastimes, we manage to pass our days — only with difficulty — by holding on to the hope that in the evening You will certainly return.**

COMMENTARY: Only for at best a few hours can the *gopīs* tolerate the pain they feel from Kṛṣṇa's absence. If ever an evening were to pass without His coming home from the forest, their lives would be finished.

## TEXT 295

दूरं गते तत्पुरमाज्ञया पुनः
कंसस्य दुष्टस्य तदिष्टसङ्गतः ।
जीवेम नानाविधशङ्कयाकुलाः
कथं प्रवासार्तिविचिन्तनेन च ॥

*dūraṁ gate tat-puram ājñayā punaḥ*
*kaṁsasya duṣṭasya tad-iṣṭa-saṅgataḥ*
*jīvema nānā-vidha-śaṅkayākulāḥ*
*kathaṁ pravāsārti-vicintanena ca*

*dūram* — away; *gate* — having gone; *tat* — that; *puram* — to the city; *ājñayā* — on the order; *punaḥ* — furthermore; *kaṁsasya* — of Kaṁsa; *duṣṭasya* — wicked; *tat* — his; *iṣṭa* — of friends; *saṅgataḥ* — in the association; *jīvema* — we can live; *nānā-vidha* — of various kinds; *śaṅkayā* — by worry; *ākulāḥ* — distraught; *katham* — how; *pravāsa* — of absence from home; *ārti* — of Your suffering; *vicintanena* — with thought; *ca* — and.

**But if You go so far away, on the order of wicked Kaṁsa, to**

**the city and the company of his friends, how shall we be able to live? Thinking of the pain You will suffer away from home and of what might happen to You, we'll be distraught with all sorts of worries.**

COMMENTARY: Kṛṣṇa might assert that in the big city He will be able to take care of Himself with the same power He showed when He subdued Kāliya — but still He is bound to feel homesick. The *gopīs* cannot bear to think of Kṛṣṇa suffering in any way.

TEXT 296

न ज्ञायते सानुचरस्य तस्य
कंसस्य घातेन कियाञ्श्रमः स्यात् ।
कालश्च तत्रत्यजनार्तिहत्या
स्याद्वा न वा तत्र बत स्मृतिर्नः ॥

*na jñāyate sānucarasya tasya*
*kaṁsasya ghātena kiyāñ śramaḥ syāt*
*kālaś ca tatratya-janārti-hatyā*
*syād vā na vā tatra bata smṛtir naḥ*

*na jñāyate* — it is not known; *sa-anucarasya* — along with his followers; *tasya* — of him; *kaṁsasya* — Kaṁsa; *ghātena* — in the killing; *kiyān* — how much; *śramaḥ* — trouble; *syāt* — there will be; *kālaḥ* — time; *ca* — and; *tatratya* — residing in that place (Mathurā); *jana* — of the people; *ārti* — the distress; *hatyā* — in eradicating; *syāt* — there will be; *vā* — whether; *na vā* — or not; *tatra* — there; *bata* — alas; *smṛtiḥ* — remembrance; *naḥ* — of us.

**We cannot imagine how much trouble You will have to endure to kill Kaṁsa and his followers, nor how long it will take to wipe out the misery of the people of Mathurā. Nor can we be sure You will remember us.**

COMMENTARY: Kṛṣṇa might argue that because His dear cows, His young friends, and His father will accompany Him to Mathurā He will not become too homesick. So here the *gopīs* give other reasons for their distress. Conceding that to kill Kaṁsa and many other demons would be mere play for Kṛṣṇa, the desires of all His devotees in Mathurā will take a long time to satisfy. And if Kṛṣṇa were to insist that because of remembering His dear girlfriends He could not stay away very long, the *gopīs* would answer: "No, we are not so confident You will even remember us."

## TEXT 297

श्रीसरूप उवाच
इत्येवमादिकं काकुकुलं ता विदधुस्तथा ।
येन तत्रत्यमखिलं रुरोद च मुमोह च ॥

*śrī-sarūpa uvāca*
*ity evam-ādikaṁ kāku-*
*kulaṁ tā vidadhus tathā*
*yena tatratyam akhilaṁ*
*ruroda ca mumoha ca*

*śrī-sarūpaḥ uvāca* — Śrī Sarūpa said; *iti* — thus speaking; *evam* — these; *ādikam* — and other; *kāku-kulam* — many pitiful laments; *tāḥ* — they (the *gopīs*); *vidadhuḥ* — expressed; *tathā* — also; *yena* — by which; *tatratyam* — present there; *akhilam* — everyone; *ruroda* — cried; *ca* — and; *mumoha* — became bewildered; *ca* — and.

**Śrī Sarūpa said: Thus the gopīs uttered many pitiful laments, which made all who were present cry till their minds were lost.**

COMMENTARY: All living beings reacted in this way to the *gopīs'* complaints.

## TEXT 298

कथञ्चिद्भगवान्धैर्यमालम्ब्याश्रूणि मार्जयन् ।
स्वस्य तासां च नेत्रेभ्योऽब्रवीदेतत्सगद्गदम् ॥

*kathañcid bhagavān dhairyam*
*ālambyāśrūṇi mārjayan*
*svasya tāsāṁ ca netrebhyo*
*'bravīd etat sa-gadgadam*

*kathañcit* — somehow; *bhagavān* — the Supreme Lord; *dhairyam* — to calmness; *ālambya* — bringing Himself; *aśrūṇi* — the tears; *mārjayan* — wiping away; *svasya* — His own; *tāsām* — of the *gopīs; ca* — and; *netrebhyaḥ* — from their eyes; *abravīt* — spoke; *etat* — this; *sa-gadgadam* — with a choking voice.

**The Supreme Lord somehow steadied Himself. Wiping the tears from His own eyes and from the eyes of the gopīs, He spoke with a voice choked with feeling.**

## TEXT 299

श्रीभगवानुवाच
सत्यं ममापि द्विषतोऽल्पशक्तेर्
विधाय कंसस्य शमं सहेलम् ।
मामागतप्रायमिदं प्रतीत
सख्यो रुदित्वा कुरुताशिवं मा ॥

*śrī-bhagavān uvāca*
*satyaṁ mamāpi dviṣato 'lpa-śakter*
*vidhāya kaṁsasya śamaṁ sa-helam*
*mām āgata-prāyam idaṁ pratīta*
*sakhyo ruditvā kurutāśivaṁ mā*

*śrī-bhagavān uvāca* — the blessed Personality of Godhead said; *satyam* — truly; *mama* — My; *api* — indeed; *dviṣataḥ* — of the enemy; *alpa* — little; *śakteḥ* — whose strength; *vidhāya* — carrying out; *kaṁsasya* — of Kaṁsa; *śamam* — the quieting; *sahelam* — without effort; *mām* — Me; *āgata* — returned; *prāyam* — practically; *idam* — this person; *pratīta* — you should be convinced; *sakhyaḥ* — My dear companions; *ruditvā* — by crying; *kuruta* — create; *aśivam* — inauspiciousness; *mā* — do not.

**The Personality of Godhead said: My enemy Kaṁsa is certainly weak. With no effort I shall dispose of Him. Consider Me practically returned to you already. My dear friends, please don't create misfortune by crying.**

TEXT 300

श्रीसरूप उवाच
अथ तत्रैव नन्दाद्या गोपाः सर्वे गता जवात् ।
रोहिणी श्रीयशोदा च परेऽपि पशवस्तथा ॥

*śrī-sarūpa uvāca*
*atha tatraiva nandādyā*
*gopāḥ sarve gatā javāt*
*rohiṇī śrī-yaśodā ca*
*pare 'pi paśavas tathā*

*śrī-sarūpaḥ uvāca* — Śrī Sarūpa said; *atha* — there; *tatra* — there; *eva* — indeed; *nanda-ādyāḥ* — Nanda and the others; *gopāḥ* — the cowherds; *sarve* — all; *gatāḥ* — went; *javāt* — with haste; *rohiṇī* — Rohiṇī; *śrī-yaśodā* — Yaśodā; *ca* — and; *pare* — others; *api* — also; *paśavaḥ* — the animals; *tathā* — also.

**Śrī Sarūpa said: Then everyone hurried to that spot — Nanda and the other cowherds, and Rohiṇī and Yaśodā, and all the others, even the animals.**

COMMENTARY: Everyone came to where Kṛṣṇa had been hiding with the *gopīs,* including all the members of Nanda Mahārāja's household — his priests, his servants, his maidservants — and the cows, buffaloes, and other village animals.

## TEXT 301

अक्रूरेण द्रुतानीतमारुरोह रथं हरिः ।
साग्रजो गोपिकालग्नां दृष्टिं यत्नान्निवर्तयन् ॥

*akrūreṇa drutānītam*
*āruroha rathaṁ hariḥ*
*sāgrajo gopikā-lagnāṁ*
*dṛṣṭiṁ yatnān nivartayan*

*akrūreṇa* — by Akrūra; *druta* — quickly; *ānītam* — brought; *āruroha* — mounted; *ratham* — the chariot; *hariḥ* — Lord Hari; *sa-agrajaḥ* — together with His elder brother; *gopikā* — on the *gopīs; lagnām* — fixed; *dṛṣṭim* — His gaze; *yatnāt* — with effort; *nivartayan* — withdrawing.

**Lord Hari and His elder brother mounted the chariot, which Akrūra had quickly brought. With great effort Kṛṣṇa withdrew His gaze from the gopīs.**

## TEXT 302

यशोदा रुदतीर्दृष्ट्वा पतिता धूलिपङ्किलाः ।
मुह्यतीर्विह्वला गोपीः प्रारुदत्करुणस्वरम् ॥

*yaśodā rudatīr dṛṣṭvā*
*patitā dhūli-paṅkilāḥ*
*muhyatīr vihvalā gopīḥ*
*prārudat karuṇa-svaram*

*yaśodā* — Yaśodā; *rudatīḥ* — who were sobbing; *dṛṣṭvā* — seeing; *patitāḥ* — fallen; *dhūli-paṅkilāḥ* — covered with dust; *muhyatīḥ* — fainting; *vihvalāḥ* — overwhelmed; *gopīḥ* — the *gopīs; prārudat* — began to cry; *karuṇa* — pitiful; *svaram* — with a voice.

**Seeing the gopīs sobbing, fainting, falling to the ground overwhelmed, and covered with dust, Yaśodā also cried pitifully.**

TEXT 303

यत्नात्तां सान्त्वयन्नाह नन्दोऽन्तर्दुःखितोऽपि सन् ।
प्रस्तुतार्थसमाधाननैपुण्यं दर्शयन्निव ॥

*yatnāt tāṁ sāntvayann āha*
*nando 'ntar-duḥkhito 'pi san*
*prastutārtha-samādhāna-*
*naipuṇyaṁ darśayann iva*

*yatnāt* — with great effort; *tām* — her (Yaśodā); *sāntvayan* — consoling; *āha* — spoke; *nandaḥ* — Nanda Mahārāja; *antaḥ* — within; *duḥkhitaḥ* — unhappy; *api* — although; *san* — being; *prastuta* — at hand; *artha* — of the business; *samādhāna* — in taking care; *naipuṇyam* — expertise; *darśayan* — showing; *iva* — as if.

**Though Nanda Mahārāja was also miserable within, with great effort he consoled Yaśodā, showing seeming expertise in taking care of the business at hand.**

COMMENTARY: Here the word *iva* ("as if") indicates that even though Nanda seemed to be consoling his wife very competently, he couldn't actually get very far.

TEXT 304

श्रीनन्द उवाच
मा विद्धि हर्षेण पुरीं प्रयामि तां
कृष्णं कदाप्यन्यसुतं च वेद्म्यहम् ।

हित्वेममायानि कथञ्चन व्रजं
तस्यां विधास्ये च विलम्बमुन्मनाः ॥

*śrī-nanda uvāca*
*mā viddhi harṣeṇa purīṁ prayāmi tāṁ*
*kṛṣṇaṁ kadāpy anya-sutaṁ ca vedmy aham*
*hitvemam āyāni kathañcana vrajaṁ*
*tasyāṁ vidhāsye ca vilambam unmanāḥ*

*śrī-nandaḥ uvāca* — Śrī Nanda Mahārāja said; *mā viddhi* — do not think; *harṣeṇa* — happily; *purīm* — city; *prayāmi* — I am going; *tām* — to that; *kṛṣṇam* — Kṛṣṇa; *kadā api* — at any time; *anya* — another's; *sutam* — son; *ca* — and; *vedmi* — consider; *aham* — I; *hitvā* — leaving; *imam* — Him; *āyāni* — I might come back; *kathañcana* — somehow; *vrajam* — to Vraja; *tasyām* — there; *vidhāsye* — I will allow; *ca* — and; *vilambam* — a delay; *unmanāḥ* — having lost my intelligence.

**Śrī Nanda said: Don't think that I'm going to that city happily, or could ever accept Kṛṣṇa to be someone else's son, or leave Him there for any reason and come home alone, or lose my wits and allow Him to stay there very long.**

COMMENTARY: It is hardly for sightseeing that Nanda is eager to take Kṛṣṇa to Mathurā. Though Mathurā is the home of intimate friends like Vasudeva and may be a great city, the real reason Nanda is going is that Kaṁsa ordered him. And this is hardly a cause for delight. Mathurā may be the home of the Yadus, but as long as it is ruled by Kaṁsa it will be a disagreeable place to visit.

Akrūra's assertion that Kṛṣṇa is the son of Vasudeva is a lie. As far as Nanda is concerned, Kṛṣṇa could never transfer His affection to anyone else. Even if Vasudeva and the Yadus were to try to keep Kṛṣṇa in Mathurā by force, Nanda would never return to Vṛndāvana without Him. And even if Kṛṣṇa, after killing Kaṁsa, were to be crowned king and want to stay in Mathurā to enjoy the kingdom, Nanda would never allow that to happen.

TEXT 305

जाने न किं ते तनयं विना क्षणं
जीवेम नेमे व्रजवासिनो वयम् ।
तद्विद्धि मामाशु सपुत्रमागतं
श्रीदेवकीशूरसुतौ विमोच्य तौ ॥

*jāne na kiṁ te tanayaṁ vinā kṣaṇaṁ*
*jīvema neme vraja-vāsino vayam*
*tad viddhi mām āśu sa-putram āgataṁ*
*śrī-devakī-śūra-sutau vimocya tau*

*jāne na* — I do not know; *kim* — whether; *te* — your; *tanayam* — son; *vinā* — without; *kṣaṇam* — for a moment; *jīvema na* — would not live; *ime* — these; *vraja-vāsinaḥ* — residents of Vraja; *vayam* — we; *tat* — therefore; *viddhi* — know; *mām* — me; *āśu* — quickly; *sa-putram* — with the son; *āgatam* — returned; *śrī-devakī* — Śrī Devakī; *śūra-sutau* — and the son of Śūra; *vimocya* — having freed; *tau* — the two.

**I doubt whether we or any of the Vraja-vāsīs could live for a moment without your son. So you can take it for granted that as soon as we free Śrī Devakī and Vasudeva, I will very quickly come back with Kṛṣṇa.**

TEXT 306

श्रीसरूप उवाच
इत्थं सशपथं तेन यशोदाश्वासिता मुहुः ।
चित्ते शान्तिमिवाधाय गोपीराश्वासयद्बहु ॥

*śrī-sarūpa uvāca*
*itthaṁ sa-śapathaṁ tena*
*yaśodāśvāsitā muhuḥ*
*citte śāntim ivādhāya*
*gopīr āśvāsayad bahu*

*śrī-sarūpaḥ uvāca* — Śrī Sarūpa said; *ittham* — thus; *sa-śapatham* — with vows; *tena* — by Nanda; *yaśodā* — Mother Yaśodā; *āśvāsitā* — assured; *muhuḥ* — thoroughly; *citte* — in her mind; *śāntim* — peace; *iva* — as if; *ādhāya* — placing; *gopīḥ* — the *gopīs; āśvāsayat* — she consoled; *bahu* — much.

**Śrī Sarūpa said: Thus assured again and again by Nanda's solemn vows, Mother Yaśodā became peaceful, more or less. She then made a great effort to console the gopīs.**

## TEXT 307

यत्नात्सन्तर्प्य बहुधा ताः समुत्थापितास्तया ।
अनांस्यारुरुहुर्गोपाः सोऽक्रूरोऽचालयद्रथम् ॥

*yatnāt santarpya bahudhā*
*tāḥ samutthāpitās tayā*
*anāṁsy āruruhur gopāḥ*
*so 'krūro 'cālayad ratham*

*yatnāt* — with endeavor; *santarpya* — pacifying; *bahudhā* — in various ways; *tāḥ* — them; *samutthāpitāḥ* — lifted from the ground; *tayā* — by her; *anāṁsi* — their carts; *āruruhuḥ* — climbed; *gopāḥ* — the cowherd men; *saḥ* — he; *akrūraḥ* — Akrūra; *acālayat* — started; *ratham* — the chariot.

**She tried hard to calm them in various ways and induced them to get up off the ground. Then the cowherd men mounted their carts, and Akrūra started driving the chariot.**

COMMENTARY: Yaśodā sprinkled water on the *gopīs* and somehow brought them to their senses. Akrūra was anxious to go.

## TEXTS 308–309

प्रयान्तं कृष्णमालोक्य किञ्चित्तद्धिरहासहाः ।
हा हेत्याक्रोशशुष्कास्याः प्रस्खलत्पादविक्रमाः ॥

भग्नकण्ठस्वरैर्दीर्घैर्महार्त्या काकुरोदनैः ।
पूरयन्त्यो दिशः सर्वा अन्वधावन्व्रजस्त्रियः ॥

*prayāntaṁ kṛṣṇam ālokya*
*kiñcit-tad-virahāsahāḥ*
*hā hety ākrośa-śuṣkāsyāḥ*
*praskhalat-pāda-vikramāḥ*

*bhagna-kaṇṭha-svarair dīrghair*
*mahārtyā kāku-rodanaiḥ*
*pūrayantyo diśaḥ sarvā*
*anvadhāvan vraja-striyaḥ*

*prayāntam* — departed; *kṛṣṇam* — Kṛṣṇa; *ālokya* — seeing; *kiñcit* — at all; *tat* — from; *viraha* — separation; *asahāḥ* — incapable of tolerating; *hā hā* — alas, alas; *iti* — thus; *ākrośa* — with cries; *śuṣka* — dried up; *āsyāḥ* — their faces; *praskhalat* — faltering; *pāda* — of their feet; *vikramāḥ* — steps; *bhagna* — choking; *kaṇṭha* — with throats; *svaraiḥ* — with voices; *dīrghaiḥ* — drawn-out; *mahā-ārtyā* — in great pain; *kāku* — pitiful; *rodanaiḥ* — with cries; *pūrayantyaḥ* — filling; *diśaḥ* — the directions; *sarvāḥ* — all; *anvadhāvan* — ran behind; *vraja-striyaḥ* — the women of Vraja.

**The women of Vraja couldn't tolerate, even slightly, being separated from Kṛṣṇa. As they watched Him depart they cried "Alas! Alas!" Their faces dried up, their steps faltered, and they sobbed pitifully in great anguish, with long drawn-out cries, their voices choking in their throats. They ran behind the chariot, their laments filling all directions.**

TEXT 310

काश्चिद्रथं दधुः काश्चिच्चक्राधो न्यपतञ्जवात् ।
काश्चिन्मोहं गताः काश्चिन्नाशकन् गन्तुमग्रतः ॥

*kāścid rathaṁ dadhuḥ kāścic*
*cakrādho nyapatañ javāt*
*kāścin mohaṁ gatāḥ kāścin*
*nāśakan gantum agrataḥ*

*kāścit* — some of them; *ratham* — the chariot; *dadhuḥ* — held on to; *kāścit* — some; *cakra* — the wheels; *adhaḥ* — beneath; *nyapatan* — fell; *javāt* — with force; *kāścit* — some; *moham gatāḥ* — fainted; *kāścit* — some; *na aśakan* — could not; *gantum* — move; *agrataḥ* — forward.

**Some of them held on to the chariot, others forcefully fell beneath its wheels, some fainted, and still others couldn't even go forward.**

COMMENTARY: Some *gopīs* threw themselves in front of the chariot to try to stop it, or else to kill themselves.

## TEXT 311

ततो गावो वृषा वत्सा मृगाश्चान्येऽपि जन्तवः ।
आक्रोशन्तोऽश्रुधौतास्यास्तस्थुरावृत्य तं रथम् ॥

*tato gāvo vṛṣā vatsā*
*mṛgāś cānye 'pi jantavaḥ*
*ākrośanto 'śru-dhautāsyās*
*tasthur āvṛtya taṁ ratham*

*tataḥ* — at that time; *gāvaḥ* — the cows; *vṛṣāḥ* — bulls; *vatsāḥ* — calves; *mṛgāḥ* — deer; *ca* — and; *anye* — other; *api* — also; *jantavaḥ* — animals; *ākrośantaḥ* — bellowing; *aśru* — with tears; *dhauta* — drenched with tears; *āsyāḥ* — their faces; *tasthuḥ* — stood; *āvṛtya* — surrounding; *tam* — that; *ratham* — chariot.

**The cows, bulls, calves, deer — all the animals — stood around the chariot, bellowing, their faces drenched with tears.**

COMMENTARY: Even wolves and jackals approached the chariot to join the chorus of lamenting animals.

## TEXT 312

खगाश्च बभ्रमुस्तस्योपरि कोलाहलाकुलाः ।
सपद्युद्भिज्जजातीनामशुष्यन्पत्रसञ्चयाः ॥

*khagāś ca babhramus tasyo-*
*pari kolāhalākulāḥ*
*sapady udbhijja-jātīnām*
*aśuṣyan patra-sañcayāḥ*

*khagāḥ* — the birds; *ca* — and; *babhramuḥ* — wandered; *tasya* — Him (Kṛṣṇa); *upari* — above; *kolāhala* — with a commotion; *ākulāḥ* — frantic; *sapadi* — suddenly; *udbhijja-jātīnām* — of the plant species; *aśuṣyan* — dried up; *patra* — of leaves; *sañcayāḥ* — the groups.

**Frantic birds flew here and there above Kṛṣṇa, making a commotion, and suddenly the leaves of the plants dried up.**

## TEXT 313

स्खलन्ति स्म महाद्रीणां सवनस्पतिकाः शिलाः ।
नद्यश्च शुष्कजलजाः क्षीणाः सस्रुः प्रतिस्रवम् ॥

*skhalanti sma mahādrīṇāṁ*
*sa-vanaspatikāḥ śilāḥ*
*nadyaś ca śuṣka-jalajāḥ*
*kṣīṇāḥ sasruḥ pratisravam*

*skhalanti sma* — tumbled down; *mahā* — great; *adrīṇām* — of the mountains; *sa-vanaspatikāḥ* — along with mighty trees; *śilāḥ* — stones; *nadyaḥ* — the rivers; *ca* — and; *śuṣka* — left dry;

*jalajāḥ* — whose aquatic creatures; *kṣīṇāḥ* — shrunk; *sasruḥ* — flowed; *pratisravam* — in reverse direction.

**Stones and mighty trees fell from the tall mountains. The rivers shrank and flowed upstream, leaving their creatures high and dry.**

COMMENTARY: Govardhana and other mountains threw down large stones and trees. In some places the rivers dried up, stranding their flowers and vegetation on the land, and in other places the rivers began to flow upstream.

## TEXT 314

तेषां दशां तां परमप्रियाणां
वीक्ष्यार्तिशोकाकुलमानसोऽसौ ।
उद्रोदनं रोद्धुमभूदशक्तो
व्यग्रोऽश्रुधारापरिमार्जनैश्च ॥

*teṣāṁ daśāṁ tāṁ parama-priyāṇāṁ*
*vīkṣyārti-śokākula-mānaso 'sau*
*udrodanaṁ roddhum abhūd aśakto*
*vyagro 'śru-dhārā-parimārjanaiś ca*

*teṣām* — of them; *daśām* — condition; *tām* — that; *parama* — supreme; *priyāṇām* — His beloved devotees; *vīkṣya* — seeing; *ārti* — by pain; *śoka* — and sorrow; *ākula* — disturbed; *mānasaḥ* — His heart; *asau* — He (Kṛṣṇa); *udrodanam* — the wild crying; *roddhum* — to stop; *abhūt* — was; *aśaktaḥ* — unable; *vyagraḥ* — busy; *aśru* — of tears; *dhārā* — the flood; *parimārjanaiḥ* — with wiping; *ca* — and.

**Seeing His most beloved devotees in such a state churned Kṛṣṇa's heart with pain and sorrow. Nothing He could do could stop their wailing, and from His own eyes He had to wipe a flood of tears.**

TEXT 315

रथादवप्लुत्य पुनः प्रयाणं
प्रभोरथाशंक्य स वृष्णिवृद्धः ।
दधार पृष्ठे प्रणयादिवामुं
कदापि मोहेन पतेत्किलेति ॥

*rathād avaplutya punaḥ prayāṇaṁ*
*prabhor athāśaṅkya sa vṛṣṇi-vṛddhaḥ*
*dadhāra pṛṣṭhe praṇayād ivāmuṁ*
*kadāpi mohena patet kileti*

*rathāt* — from the chariot; *avaplutya* — jumping off; *punaḥ* — again; *prayāṇam* — going off; *prabhoḥ* — by the Lord; *atha* — so; *āśaṅkya* — fearing; *saḥ* — he; *vṛṣṇi-vṛddhaḥ* — the elder Vṛṣṇi (Akrūra); *dadhāra* — supported; *pṛṣṭhe* — from the back; *praṇayāt* — due to affectionate concern; *iva* — as if; *amum* — this; *kadā api* — sometime; *mohena* — due to fainting; *patet* — He might fall; *kila* — indeed; *iti* — thus.

**The elder Vṛṣṇi Akrūra, fearing that Kṛṣṇa might jump down from the chariot and go off again somewhere, supported the Lord from behind, as if affectionately concerned that the Lord might faint and fall down.**

COMMENTARY: Akrūra had practical intelligence acquired from many years of service to the Vṛṣṇi rulers. Now that he was finally on the way to Mathurā with Kṛṣṇa, he did everything in his power to assure that nothing would go wrong. He made a show of holding Kṛṣṇa to protect Him from falling, but the fact was that he wanted to prevent Kṛṣṇa from again running off.

TEXT 316

कृष्णं मुग्धमिवालक्ष्य कशाघातैः प्रचोदिताः ।
रामनन्दादिसम्मत्या रथाश्वास्तेन वेगतः ॥

*kṛṣṇaṁ mugdham ivālakṣya*
*kaśā-ghātaiḥ pracoditāḥ*
*rāma-nandādi-sammatyā*
*rathāśvās tena vegataḥ*

*kṛṣṇam* — Kṛṣṇa; *mugdham* — fainting; *iva* — as if; *ālakṣya* — noticing; *kaśā* — of his whip; *ghātaiḥ* — with strikes; *pracoditāḥ* — made to start; *rāma* — of Balarāma; *nanda* — Nanda; *ādi* — and others; *sammatyā* — with the permission; *ratha* — of the chariot; *aśvāḥ* — the horses; *tena* — by him (Akrūra); *vegataḥ* — vigorously.

**Noticing that Kṛṣṇa was indeed about to faint, Akrūra took permission from Balarāma, Nanda, and the others, cracked his whip, and vigorously made the chariot's horses set out.**

## TEXT 317

इतस्ततो निपतिता गोपनारीः पशूंश्च सः ।
वर्जयन्वक्रगत्याशु रथं तं निरसारयत् ॥

*itas tato nipatitā*
*gopa-nārīḥ paśūṁś ca saḥ*
*varjayan vakra-gatyāśu*
*rathaṁ taṁ nirasārayat*

*itaḥ tataḥ* — here and there; *nipatitāḥ* — fallen; *gopa-nārīḥ* — the cowherd women; *paśūn* — the animals; *ca* — and; *saḥ* — he (Akrūra); *varjayan* — avoiding; *vakra* — skewed; *gatyā* — by movements; *āśu* — quickly; *ratham* — chariot; *tam* — that; *nirasārayat* — drove away.

**He quickly drove the chariot away, swerving to avoid the animals and the cowherd women who had fallen here and there.**

## TEXT 318

क्रोशन्तीनां च गोपीनां कुररीणामिवोल्बणम् ।
पश्यन्तीनां प्रभुं जह्रेऽक्रूरः श्येन इवामिषम् ॥

*krośantīnāṁ ca gopīnāṁ*
*kurarīṇām ivolbaṇam*
*paśyantīnāṁ prabhuṁ jahre*
*'krūraḥ śyena ivāmiṣam*

*krośantīnām* — as they were crying; *ca* — and; *gopīnām* — the *gopīs; kurarīṇām* — *kurarī* birds; *iva* — like; *ulbaṇam* — woefully; *paśyantīnām* — and as they were looking; *prabhum* — the Lord; *jahre* — took away; *akrūraḥ* — Akrūra; *śyena* — by an eagle; *iva* — like; *amiṣam* — meat.

**As the gopīs looked on, crying woefully like kurarī birds, Akrūra drove off with Kṛṣṇa like an eagle carrying a piece of flesh.**

COMMENTARY: Akrūra seemed to carry Kṛṣṇa off as swiftly as an eagle flies off with its prey, and just as cruelly.

## TEXT 319

तथा सञ्चोदितास्तेन हयास्ते वेगवत्तराः ।
क्वासौ गतो न केनापि शक्तो लक्षयितुं यथा ॥

*tathā sañcoditās tena*
*hayās te vegavat-tarāḥ*
*kvāsau gato na kenāpi*
*śakto lakṣayituṁ yathā*

*tathā* — so; *sañcoditāḥ* — driven; *tena* — by Akrūra; *hayāḥ* — the horses; *te* — they; *vega-vat-tarāḥ* — with the most extreme speed; *kva* — where; *asau* — he; *gataḥ* — went; *na* — not; *kena api* — by anyone; *śaktaḥ* — possible; *lakṣayitum* — to be ascertained; *yathā* — as.

**He drove the horses so swiftly that no one could tell where he went.**

COMMENTARY: The horses were well-trained, faithful followers of Kaṁsa.

TEXT 320

स्वं स्वं शकटमारूढा महावृषभयोजितम् ।
सवेगमनुजग्मुस्तं गोपा नन्दादयोऽखिलाः ॥

*svaṁ svaṁ śakaṭam ārūḍhā*
*mahā-vṛṣabha-yojitam*
*sa-vegam anujagmus taṁ*
*gopā nandādayo 'khilāḥ*

*svam svam* — each his own; *śakaṭam* — cart; *ārūḍhāḥ* — mounting; *mahā* — large; *vṛṣabha* — bulls; *yojitam* — yoked to; *sa-vegam* — swiftly; *anujagmuḥ* — followed; *tam* — him (Akrūra); *gopāḥ* — the cowherd men; *nanda-ādayaḥ* — Nanda and the others; *akhilāḥ* — all.

**All the cowherd men, headed by Nanda, mounted their own carts, yoked to large bulls, and quickly followed Akrūra.**

TEXT 321

नीत्वा ब्रह्महृदेऽक्रूरः स्तुत्वा बहुविधैः स्तवैः ।
प्रबोध्य न्यायसन्तानैः कृष्णं स्वास्थ्यमिवानयत् ॥

*nītvā brahma-hrade 'krūraḥ*
*stutvā bahu-vidhaiḥ stavaiḥ*
*prabodhya nyāya-santānaiḥ*
*kṛṣṇaṁ svāsthyam ivānayat*

*nītvā* — leading; *brahma-hrade* — to Brahmā's lake; *akrūraḥ* — Akrūra; *stutvā* — praising; *bahu-vidhaiḥ* — of various kinds; *stavaiḥ* — with prayers; *prabodhya* — counseling; *nyāya* — of logical arguments; *santānaiḥ* — with a series; *kṛṣṇam* — Kṛṣṇa; *svāsthyam* — to a normal state; *iva* — as if; *ānayat* — brought.

**Akrūra brought Kṛṣṇa to Lord Brahmā's lake, offered Him many kinds of prayers, and counseled Him with a continuous flow of logical arguments, in this way restoring Him to an almost normal state.**

COMMENTARY: Akrūra hoped that being at Brahma-hrada, better known as Akrūra-tīrtha, would remind Kṛṣṇa of how Kṛṣṇa had given the cowherds a vision of Vaikuṇṭha. And that memory might further remind Kṛṣṇa of one of the purposes for which He had descended to the earth — to kill Kaṁsa.

## TEXT 322

तेषां व्रजजनानां तु या दशाजनि दुःश्रवा ।
दलन्ति कथया तस्या हा हा वज्रादयोऽप्यलम् ॥

*teṣāṁ vraja-janānāṁ tu*
*yā daśājani duḥśravā*
*dalanti kathayā tasyā*
*hā hā vajrādayo 'py alam*

*teṣām* — of them; *vraja-janānām* — the people of Vraja; *tu* — but; *yā* — which; *daśā* — condition; *ajani* — happened; *duḥśravā* — painful to hear; *dalanti* — shatter; *kathayā* — with the narrating; *tasyāḥ* — of this; *hā hā* — alas, alas; *vajra-ādayaḥ* — lightning bolts and so on; *api* — even; *alam* — enough.

**How the people of Vraja then suffered is too painful to hear. Alas, alas! Telling of this topic shatters even lightning bolts. I have said enough.**

COMMENTARY: Those who hear about the misery the Vraja-vāsīs underwent after Kṛṣṇa left them will endure the same misery. Therefore in the company of those unprepared to suffer, this topic is best left undiscussed.

## TEXT 323

श्रीपरीक्षिदुवाच
एवं वदन्नये मातः सरूपः करुणस्वरैः ।
रुदन्नुच्चैः सकातर्यं मुमोह प्रेमविह्वलः ॥

*śrī-parīkṣid uvāca*
*evaṁ vadann aye mātaḥ*
*sarūpaḥ karuṇa-svaraiḥ*
*rudann uccaiḥ sa-kātaryaṁ*
*mumoha prema-vihvalaḥ*

*śrī-parīkṣit uvāca* — Śrī Parīkṣit said; *evam* — thus; *vadan* — saying; *aye mātaḥ* — O mother; *sarūpaḥ* — Sarūpa; *karuṇa* — plaintive; *svaraiḥ* — in tones; *rudan* — crying; *uccaiḥ* — loudly; *sa-kātaryam* — with anxiety; *mumoha* — fainted; *prema* — by pure love; *vihvalaḥ* — overwhelmed.

**Śrī Parīkṣit said: Sarūpa, having said this, his voice full of grief, loudly wept, dear mother. And overwhelmed by the ecstasy of pure love, he fainted.**

## TEXT 324

तेन माथुरवर्येण व्यग्रेण रुदता क्षणात् ।
प्रयासैर्विविधैः स्वास्थ्यं नीतोऽसौ पुनरब्रवीत् ॥

*tena māthura-varyeṇa*
*vyagreṇa rudatā kṣaṇāt*
*prayāsair vividhaiḥ svāsthyaṁ*
*nīto 'sau punar abravīt*

*tena* — by that; *māthura* — the *brāhmaṇa* from Mathurā; *varyeṇa* — excellent; *vyagreṇa* — who was disturbed; *rudatā* — and who was crying; *kṣaṇāt* — after a moment; *prayāsaiḥ* — by endeavors; *vividhaiḥ* — various; *svāsthyam* — to a normal state; *nītaḥ* — brought; *asau* — he (Sarūpa); *punaḥ* — again; *abravīt* — spoke.

**The excellent but shaken brāhmaṇa of Mathurā cried for a moment, and then, by trying this way and that, he brought Sarūpa back to normal. Sarūpa then continued to speak.**

TEXT 325

श्रीसरूप उवाच
कृष्णो मधुपुरीं गत्वा तत्रत्यान्परितोष्य तान् ।
कंसं सानुचरं हत्वा पितरौ तौ व्यमोचयत् ॥

*śrī-sarūpa uvāca*
*kṛṣṇo madhu-purīṁ gatvā*
*tatratyān paritoṣya tān*
*kaṁsaṁ sānucaraṁ hatvā*
*pitarau tau vyamocayat*

*śrī-sarūpaḥ uvāca* — Śrī Sarūpa said; *kṛṣṇaḥ* — Kṛṣṇa; *madhu-purīm* — to Mathurā; *gatvā* — going; *tatratyān* — the residents there; *paritoṣya* — pleasing; *tān* — them; *kaṁsam* — Kaṁsa; *sa-anucaram* — along with his followers; *hatvā* — killing; *pitarau* — His parents; *tau* — two; *vyamocayat* — delivered.

**Śrī Sarūpa said: Kṛṣṇa went to Madhupurī, where He pleased all its residents. He killed Kaṁsa and his followers and delivered His own parents.**

COMMENTARY: To avoid the risk of again losing control of himself, Śrī Sarūpa changed the subject. When Kṛṣṇa first entered Mathurā He blessed many of its residents, including a tailor and a garland-maker.

## TEXT 326

उग्रसेनं च कंसस्य तातं राज्येऽभ्यषेचयत् ।
आनिन्ये यादवान्दिग्भ्यः पौरांश्चाश्वासयज्जनान् ॥

*ugrasenaṁ ca kaṁsasya*
*tātaṁ rājye 'bhyaṣecayat*
*āninye yādavān digbhyaḥ*
*paurāṁś cāśvāsayaj janān*

*ugrasenam* — Ugrasena; *ca* — and; *kaṁsasya* — of Kaṁsa; *tātam* — the father; *rājye* — as ruler of the kingdom; *abhyaṣecayat* — He anointed; *āninye* — He brought; *yādavān* — the Yādavas; *digbhyaḥ* — from the various directions; *paurān* — who resided in the city; *ca* — and; *āśvāsayat* — He consoled; *janān* — the people.

**He installed Ugrasena, Kaṁsa's father, as king, brought the Yādavas back from all directions, and consoled the people of the city.**

## TEXTS 327–328

यदूनां परमार्तानां तदेकगतिजीविनाम् ।
कंसेष्टनृपभीतानामाग्रहाद्भक्तवत्सलः ॥

तत्रावात्सीत्सुखं कर्तुं साग्रजो गोकुले च तान् ।
नन्दादीन्प्रेषयामास तत्रत्याश्वासनाय सः ॥

*yadūnāṁ paramārtānāṁ*
*tad-eka-gati-jīvinām*
*kaṁseṣṭa-nṛpa-bhītānām*
*āgrahād bhakta-vatsalaḥ*

*tatrāvātsīt sukhaṁ kartuṁ*
*sāgrajo gokule ca tān*

*nandādīn preṣayām āsa*
*tatratyāśvāsanāya saḥ*

*yadūnām* — for the Yadus; *parama* — greatly; *ārtānām* — who had suffered; *tat* — Him; *eka* — only; *gati* — having as the goal; *jīvinām* — whose lives; *kaṁsa* — by Kaṁsa; *iṣṭa* — favored; *nṛpa* — of the kings; *bhītānām* — who were terrified; *āgrahāt* — out of concern; *bhakta* — to His devotees; *vatsalaḥ* — compassionate; *tatra* — there; *avātsīt* — He lived; *sukham* — happy; *kartum* — to make; *sa-agrajaḥ* — along with His elder brother; *gokule* — to Gokula; *ca* — and; *tān* — them; *nanda-ādīn* — Nanda and the others; *preṣayām āsa* — sent; *tatratya* — of the residents of that place; *āśvāsanāya* — for pacifying; *saḥ* — He.

**The Yadus, who had no goal in life but Kṛṣṇa, had suffered greatly and were terrified of the kings favored by Kaṁsa. Out of concern for those Yadus, the Lord, always compassionate to His devotees, stayed with them with His elder brother. And to comfort His devotees in Gokula, He sent back Nanda and the other cowherd men.**

COMMENTARY: Kṛṣṇa is *bhakta-vatsala*. He feels obliged to take care of anyone who takes exclusive shelter of Him. Because Kaṁsa hated the Yadus, they suffered terrible persecution under his rule. Now Kaṁsa was dead, but Jarāsandha and other powerful friends of Kaṁsa were still alive and could attack Mathurā at any moment.

## TEXT 329

पितरादौ भवान्यातु गोपवर्गैः सह द्रुतम् ।
यावन्न म्रियते कोऽपि तत्रत्योऽस्मान्विना जनः ॥

*pitar ādau bhavān yātu*
*gopa-vargaiḥ saha drutam*
*yāvan na mriyate ko 'pi*
*tatratyo 'smān vinā janaḥ*

*pitaḥ* — dear father; *ādau* — first; *bhavān* — your good self; *yātu* — should go; *gopa-vargaiḥ* — the cowherd men; *saha* — with; *drutam* — quickly; *yāvat na* — before; *mriyate* — dies; *kaḥ api* — any; *tatratyaḥ* — residing there; *asmān* — Us; *vinā* — without; *janaḥ* — person.

**"Father," the Lord said, "first you should quickly go home with the cowherds, before any of Gokula's residents die in our absence.**

COMMENTARY: Kṛṣṇa cleverly argued that if Nanda Mahārāja were to return home, the Vraja-vāsīs might be pacified enough to at least stay alive.

## TEXT 330

अहं च तव मित्राणामेषामुद्विग्नचेतसाम् ।
अचिरात्सुखमाधाय तमेषोऽस्म्याव्रजन्व्रजम् ॥

*ahaṁ ca tava mitrāṇām*
*eṣām udvigna-cetasām*
*acirāt sukham ādhāya*
*tam eṣo 'smy āvrajan vrajam*

*aham* — I; *ca* — and; *tava* — your; *mitrāṇām* — of the well-wishers; *eṣām* — these; *udvigna* — disturbed; *cetasām* — whose hearts; *acirāt* — soon; *sukham* — the happiness; *ādhāya* — arranging for; *tam* — there; *eṣaḥ* — this person, I; *asmi* — am; *āvrajan* — coming; *vrajam* — to Vraja.

**"I will soon arrange for the happiness of these well-wishers of yours in Mathurā, whose hearts are so distressed. Then I will come back to Vraja."**

COMMENTARY: Nanda should have no doubt that Kṛṣṇa will return home as soon as possible, because Kṛṣṇa's heart always stays in Vraja.

## TEXT 331

श्रीनन्द उवाच
त्वमन्यदीयोऽसि विहाय यादृशान्
कुतोऽपि वस्तुं च परत्र शक्नुयाः ।
इति प्रतीतिर्न भवेत्कदापि मे
ततः प्रतिज्ञाय तथा मयागतम् ॥

*śrī-nanda uvāca*
*tvam anyadīyo 'si vihāya yādṛśān*
*kuto 'pi vastuṁ ca paratra śaknuyāḥ*
*iti pratītir na bhavet kadāpi me*
*tataḥ pratijñāya tathā mayāgatam*

*śrī-nandaḥ uvāca* — Śrī Nanda said; *tvam* — You; *anyadīyaḥ* — another's; *asi* — are; *vihāya* — abandoning; *yādṛśān* — such persons; *kutaḥ api* — for any reason; *vastum* — to live; *ca* — and; *paratra* — elsewhere; *śaknuyāḥ* — You could be able; *iti* — thus; *pratītiḥ* — this belief; *na bhavet* — cannot be; *kadā api* — ever; *me* — my; *tataḥ* — therefore; *pratijñāya* — declaring; *tathā* — thus; *mayā* — by me; *āgatam* — came.

**Śrī Nanda said: Before I came here, I declared to the Vrajavāsīs that I could never believe that You are someone else's son nor ever believe that You could abandon such friends as them and live elsewhere.**

## TEXT 332

तद्रक्ष रक्षात्मसमीपतोऽस्मान्
मा मुञ्च मा मुञ्च निजान्कथञ्चन ।
आत्मेच्छया तत्र यदा प्रयास्यसि
त्वत्सङ्गतो याम तदैव हा वयम् ॥

*tad rakṣa rakṣātma-samīpato 'smān*
*mā muñca mā muñca nijān kathañcana*
*ātmecchayā tatra yadā prayāsyasi*
*tvat-saṅgato yāma tadaiva hā vayam*

*tat* — therefore; *rakṣa* — please protect; *rakṣa* — please protect; *ātma-samīpataḥ* — next to You; *asmān* — us; *mā muñca* — do not let us go; *mā muñca* — do not let us go; *nijān* — Your own; *kathañcana* — for any reason; *ātma* — Your; *icchayā* — by the sweet will; *tatra* — there; *yadā* — when; *prayāsyasi* — You will go; *tvat* — Your; *saṅgataḥ* — in the company; *yāma* — may we go; *tadā* — then; *eva* — just; *hā* — oh; *vayam* — we.

**Therefore please save us. Save us! Don't ever, ever — for any reason — send us away from You! Wherever You might go by Your sweet will — oh, there may we also go with You.**

## TEXT 333

मदाशया ते व्रजवासिनो जना
भवज्जनन्या सह सन्ति सासवः ।
गते विना त्वां मयि दारुणान्तरे
ध्रुवं विनंक्ष्यन्ति सपद्यमी पितः ॥

*mad-āśayā te vraja-vāsino janā*
*bhavaj-jananyā saha santi sāsavaḥ*
*gate vinā tvāṁ mayi dāruṇāntare*
*dhruvaṁ vinaṅkṣyanti sapady amī pitaḥ*

*mat* — given by me; *āśayā* — by the hope; *te* — they; *vraja-vāsinaḥ* — residing in Vraja; *janāḥ* — the people; *bhavat* — Your; *jananyāḥ* — with the mother; *saha* — together; *santi* — are; *sa-asavaḥ* — alive and breathing; *gate* — in case of going; *vinā* — without; *tvām* — You; *mayi* — I; *dāruṇa* — hard like wood; *antare* — whose heart; *dhruvam* — certainly; *vinaṅkṣyanti* — they will die; *sapadi* — at once; *amī* — they; *pitaḥ* — O father.

**The Vraja-vāsīs and Your mother still live and breathe only because I gave them hope. If I were to turn so hardhearted as to go back without You, O father, surely they would die on the spot.**

COMMENTARY: All the people of Vraja trusted Nanda when he gave his word that he would not come back without Kṛṣṇa. To violate that word would be to sentence them all to death. Desperate to change Kṛṣṇa's mind, Nanda tries to reawaken Kṛṣṇa's family sentiments and the memory of His poor mother and curiously reverses roles with Kṛṣṇa by calling Him father.

## TEXT 334

श्रीदामोवाच
गोचारणेन लसति त्वयि गोष्ठभूम्याम्
आच्छादिते तरुलतादिभिरेव यस्मिन् ।
जीवेम ये न वयमीश तमन्तरा ते
स्थातुं चिरं कथममुत्र भवेम शक्ताः ॥

*śrīdāmovāca*
*go-cāraṇena lasati tvayi goṣṭha-bhūmyām*
*ācchādite taru-latādibhir eva yasmin*
*jīvema ye na vayam īśa tam antarā te*
*sthātuṁ ciraṁ katham amutra bhavema śaktāḥ*

*śrīdāmā uvāca* — Śrīdāmā said; *go-cāraṇena* — with grazing of the cows; *lasati* — when exhibiting the glories; *tvayi* — You; *goṣṭha* — of the cowherd pastures; *bhūmyām* — in the land; *ācchādite* — being hidden; *taru* — by trees; *latā* — creepers; *ādibhiḥ* — and so on; *eva* — only; *yasmin* — who (You); *jīvema* — can live; *ye* — who; *na* — not; *vayam* — we; *īśa* — O Lord; *tam* — Him (You); *antarā* — without; *te* — they; *sthātum* — to remain; *ciram* — for a long time; *katham* — how; *amutra* — in that condition; *bhavema* — we can be; *śaktāḥ* — able.

**Śrīdāmā said: When You display Your glories by grazing the cows in the pastures, dear Lord, and You are hidden behind trees or creepers for but a moment, we cannot bear to live. How then can we possibly stay without You for a long time?**

TEXT 335

श्रीसरूप उवाच
एवं विक्लवितं तेषां श्रुत्वा तूष्णीं स्थिते प्रभौ ।
व्रजं जिगमिषां तस्याशंक्य शूरसुतोऽब्रवीत् ॥

*śrī-sarūpa uvāca*
*evaṁ viklavitaṁ teṣāṁ*
*śrutvā tūṣṇīṁ sthite prabhau*
*vrajaṁ jigamiṣāṁ tasyā-*
*śaṅkya śūra-suto 'bravīt*

*śrī-sarūpaḥ uvāca* — Śrī Sarūpa said; *evam* — thus; *viklavitam* — the complaints; *teṣām* — their; *śrutvā* — hearing; *tūṣṇīm* — silently; *sthite* — standing; *prabhau* — the Lord; *vrajam* — to Vraja; *jigamiṣām* — desire to go; *tasya* — His; *āśaṅkya* — fearing; *śūra-sutaḥ* — the son of Śūrasena (Vasudeva); *abravīt* — spoke.

**Śrī Sarūpa said: As the Lord heard these complaints from His devotees, He stood in silence. Then Vasudeva, the son of Śūrasena, spoke up, afraid that the Lord might decide to go to Vraja.**

TEXT 336

श्रीवसुदेव उवाच
भ्रातर्नन्द भवत्सूनोः साग्रजस्यास्य निर्वृतिः ।
भवेत्तत्रैव वसतः सर्वथान्यत्र तु व्यथा ॥

*śrī-vasudeva uvāca*
*bhrātar nanda bhavat-sūnoḥ*
*sāgrajasyāsya nirvṛtiḥ*
*bhavet tatraiva vasataḥ*
*sarvathānyatra tu vyathā*

*śrī-vasudevaḥ uvāca* — Śrī Vasudeva said; *bhrātaḥ* — O brother; *nanda* — Nanda; *bhavat* — your; *sūnoḥ* — of the son; *sa-agrajasya* — along with the elder brother; *asya* — His; *nirvṛtiḥ* — complete happiness; *bhavet* — can be; *tatra* — there; *eva* — only; *vasataḥ* — living; *sarvathā* — by all means; *anyatra* — elsewhere; *tu* — but; *vyathā* — distress.

**Śrī Vasudeva said: Brother Nanda, surely your son and His elder brother can be happy in all respects only by living there in Vraja. They will suffer nothing but distress anywhere else.**

## TEXT 337

किन्तूपनयनस्यायं कालस्तद् ब्रह्मचारिणौ ।
भूत्वा स्थानान्तरे गत्वाधीत्येमौ व्रजमेष्यतः ॥

*kintūpanayanasyāyaṁ*
*kālas tad brahma-cāriṇau*
*bhūtvā sthānāntare gatvā-*
*dhītyemau vrajam eṣyataḥ*

*kintu* — however; *upanayanasya* — for initiation; *ayam* — this; *kālaḥ* — time; *tat* — therefore; *brahma-cāriṇau* — celibate students; *bhūtvā* — becoming; *sthāna-antare* — to another place; *gatvā* — going; *adhītya* — having studied; *imau* — They; *vrajam* — to Vraja; *eṣyataḥ* — will return.

**But now is the time for Them to be initiated. They should go as brahmacārīs to another place to study. And afterwards They can return to Vraja.**

COMMENTARY: As the *dharma-śāstras* prescribe, sons of *vaiśyas* at the age of eleven should undergo the *upanayana-saṁskāra* (acceptance of the sacred thread by initiation). Balarāma and Kṛṣṇa, Vasudeva suggests, are not exceptions. They too should be sent to the *gurukula* of a learned *brāhmaṇa* to study the *Vedas*. They should stay neither in Mathurā nor at home in Vṛndāvana with their parents. But until the *upanayana* ceremony is arranged, Balarāma and Kṛṣṇa can safely stay with Vasudeva while They finish Their business in Mathurā.

## TEXT 338

श्रीसरूप उवाच
सम्मतिं वसुदेवस्य वाक्ये स्वस्य त्वसम्मतिम् ।
कृष्णस्य नन्दः संलक्ष्य प्रतस्थे रोदनाकुलः ॥

*śrī-sarūpa uvāca*
*sammatiṁ vasudevasya*
*vākye svasya tv asammatim*
*kṛṣṇasya nandaḥ saṁlakṣya*
*pratasthe rodanākulaḥ*

*śrī-sarūpaḥ uvāca* — Śrī Sarūpa said; *sammatim* — the agreement; *vasudevasya* — of Vasudeva; *vākye* — with the words; *svasya* — of himself; *tu* — but; *asammatim* — disagreement; *kṛṣṇasya* — on the part of Kṛṣṇa; *nandaḥ* — Nanda; *saṁlakṣya* — noticing; *pratasthe* — departed; *rodana* — with crying; *ākulaḥ* — distressed.

**Śrī Sarūpa said: When Nanda saw that Kṛṣṇa disagreed with his words and agreed with those of Vasudeva, Nanda departed, crying in distress.**

COMMENTARY: Only because Nanda was confident that Kṛṣṇa couldn't stay away from home without His father was Nanda willing to leave; surely Kṛṣṇa would decide at the last minute to come back with him to Vraja.

## TEXT 339

स यादवकुलैर्देवो गोपराजमनुव्रजन् ।
रुदद्भिः क्रमशो गोपैर्धृतः कण्ठेऽरुदत्तराम् ॥

*sa yādava-kulair devo*
*gopa-rājam anuvrajan*
*rudadbhiḥ kramaśo gopair*
*dhṛtaḥ kaṇṭhe 'rudat-tarām*

*saḥ* — He (Kṛṣṇa); *yādava-kulaiḥ* — with the members of the Yadu dynasty; *devaḥ* — the Lord; *gopa-rājam* — the king of the cowherds (Nanda); *anuvrajan* — following; *rudadbhiḥ* — who were crying; *kramaśaḥ* — one after another; *gopaiḥ* — by the cowherd men; *dhṛtaḥ* — held; *kaṇṭhe* — by the neck; *arudat* — He cried; *tarām* — very much.

**Lord Kṛṣṇa, along with the princes of the Yādava dynasty, followed Nanda, the king of the cowherds. The cowherd men, one after another, embraced Kṛṣṇa by the neck, and Kṛṣṇa cried profusely, and so did they.**

## TEXT 340

व्याकुलं कृष्णमालक्ष्य यियासुं सन्न्यवर्तयन् ।
वसुदेवादयो धीरा यादवा युक्तिपङ्क्तिभिः ॥

*vyākulaṁ kṛṣṇam ālakṣya*
*yiyāsuṁ sannyavartayan*
*vasudevādayo dhīrā*
*yādavā yukti-paṅktibhiḥ*

*vyākulam* — upset; *kṛṣṇam* — Kṛṣṇa; *ālakṣya* — seeing; *yiyāsum* — desiring to go; *sannyavartayan* — turned Him back; *vasudeva-ādayaḥ* — Vasudeva and the others; *dhīrāḥ* — intelligent; *yādavāḥ* — Yādavas; *yukti* — of arguments; *paṅktibhiḥ* — by several series.

**Vasudeva and the other Yādavas, all astute, saw that Kṛṣṇa was overwrought, wanting to go, and with many arguments they coaxed Him back.**

COMMENTARY: It seemed that Nanda was right; Kṛṣṇa wanted to go home with him. But the Yādavas implored Kṛṣṇa not to go, arguing that He was needed in Mathurā to save them from great catastrophes, not least of which was the threat of invasion by Jarāsandha. And they persisted in putting forward their reasons until Kṛṣṇa agreed to stay.

## TEXT 341

कृष्णेच्छयैव ते सर्वे नन्दाद्याः प्रापिता व्रजम् ।
श्रुत्वायान्तं च नन्दं ते मुदाभीयुर्व्रजस्थिताः ॥

*kṛṣṇecchayaiva te sarve*
*nandādyāḥ prāpitā vrajam*
*śrutvāyāntaṁ ca nandaṁ te*
*mudābhīyur vraja-sthitāḥ*

*kṛṣṇa-icchayā* — according to Kṛṣṇa's desire; *eva* — only; *te* — they (the cowherd men); *sarve* — all; *nanda-ādyāḥ* — Nanda and the others; *prāpitāḥ* — reached; *vrajam* — Vraja; *śrutvā* — hearing; *āyāntam* — come; *ca* — and; *nandam* — Nanda; *te* — they; *mudā* — happily; *abhīyuḥ* — came out; *vraja-sthitāḥ* — those who lived in Vraja.

**Obeying Kṛṣṇa's desire, Nanda and the other cowherd men went back to Vraja. And when the Vraja-vāsīs heard that he had arrived, they all came out to greet him, full of joy.**

COMMENTARY: Only because Kṛṣṇa asked the cowherds to return did they take the unimaginable step of going home without Him. Kṛṣṇa's desire was the only force that could move them to do such a thing. Even the carts went down the road by their own force, without being driven, by Kṛṣṇa's desire. The devotees that had stayed in Vraja also lived only according to Kṛṣṇa's desire; naturally, then, they assumed that Kṛṣṇa was with Nanda, and they greeted Nanda joyfully.

## TEXT 342

नन्दस्तु शोकलज्जाभ्यां मुखमाच्छाद्य वाससा ।
रुदन् गेहं गतोऽशेत भूमौ परमदुःखितः ॥

*nandas tu śoka-lajjābhyāṁ*
*mukham ācchādya vāsasā*
*rudan gehaṁ gato 'śeta*
*bhūmau parama-duḥkhitaḥ*

*nandaḥ* — Nanda; *tu* — however; *śoka* — with sorrow; *lajjā-bhyām* — and shame; *mukham* — his face; *ācchādya* — covering; *vāsasā* — with his cloth; *rudan* — crying; *geham* — to his home; *gataḥ* — going; *aśeta* — lay down; *bhūmau* — on the ground; *parama* — supremely; *duḥkhitaḥ* — unhappy.

**Nanda, however, overcome with sorrow and shame, covered his face with his cloth and went home. There he lay on the ground and cried, supremely miserable.**

COMMENTARY: Bereft of Kṛṣṇa, Nanda had good reason to feel sorrowful and, having broken his promise not to return without Kṛṣṇa, good reason to feel ashamed.

## TEXT 343

ते चाविलोक्य प्रभुमार्तिकातराः
कर्तव्यमूढा बहुशङ्कयातुराः ।
शुष्काननाः प्रष्टुमनीश्वराः प्रभोर्
वार्तामशृण्वन्बत वृद्धगोपतः ॥

*te cāvilokya prabhum ārti-kātarāḥ*
*kartavya-mūḍhā bahu-śaṅkayāturāḥ*

*śuṣkānanāḥ praṣṭum anīśvarāḥ prabhor*
*vārtām aśṛṇvan bata vṛddha-gopataḥ*

*te* — they (the Vraja-vāsīs); *ca* — and; *avilokya* — not seeing; *prabhum* — the Lord; *ārti* — with distress; *kātarāḥ* — beside themselves; *kartavya* — about what was to be done; *mūḍhāḥ* — confused; *bahu* — many; *śaṅkayā* — by anxieties for what was going to happen; *āturāḥ* — disturbed; *śuṣka* — dried up; *ānanāḥ* — their faces; *praṣṭum* — to inquire; *anīśvarāḥ* — incapable; *prabhoḥ* — about the Lord; *vārtām* — news; *aśṛṇvan* — not hearing; *bata* — alas; *vṛddha* — elder; *gopataḥ* — from the cowherds.

**The Vraja-vāsīs, not seeing their Lord, were beside themselves with distress, confused about what to do, and sick with forebodings and apprehensions. Their faces withered. They heard no news from the elder cowherds about their Lord, and they couldn't bring themselves to ask.**

COMMENTARY: Since no one told the Vraja-vāsīs that Kaṁsa was dead, they were still afraid of what he might do to Kṛṣṇa. Nanda was silent about what had happened to Kṛṣṇa in Mathurā, and they feared what they might be told if they were to ask.

## TEXT 344

हा हेति हा हेति महार्तिनादैर्
उच्चै रुदत्यः सह कृष्णमात्रा ।
प्रापुर्दशां यां पुनरङ्गनास्ता
हा हन्त हा हन्त कथं ब्रुवेताम् ॥

*hā heti hā heti mahārti-nādair*
*uccai rudatyaḥ saha kṛṣṇa-mātrā*
*prāpur daśāṁ yāṁ punar aṅganās tā*
*hā hanta hā hanta kathaṁ bruvetām*

*hā hā* — alas, alas; *iti* — thus; *hā hā* — alas, alas; *iti* — thus; *mahā-ārti* — most painful; *nādaiḥ* — with sounds; *uccaiḥ* —

loudly; *rudatyaḥ* — crying out; *saha* — along with; *kṛṣṇa-mātrā* — Kṛṣṇa's mother; *prāpuḥ* — attained; *daśām* — the condition; *yām* — which; *punaḥ* — also; *aṅganāḥ* — women; *tāḥ* — those; *hā* — oh; *hanta* — alas; *hā* — oh; *hanta* — alas; *katham* — how; *bruvetām* — it can be spoken.

**Kṛṣṇa's mother cried, "Alas! Alas! Alas! Alas!" And the other women cried out too, all in great pain. How can one speak about the state they were in? Oh, alas! Oh, alas!**

## TEXT 345

श्रीपरीक्षिदुवाच
एवं मनस्यागततत्प्रवृत्ति-
प्रादुष्कृतात्यन्तशुगग्निदग्धः ।
मुग्धोऽभवद्गोपकुमारवर्यो
मातः सरूपो नितरां पुनः सः ॥

*śrī-parīkṣid uvāca*
*evaṁ manasy āgata-tat-pravṛtti-*
*prāduṣkṛtātyanta-śug-agni-dagdhaḥ*
*mugdho 'bhavad gopa-kumāra-varyo*
*mātaḥ sarūpo nitarāṁ punaḥ saḥ*

*śrī-parīkṣit uvāca* — Śrī Parīkṣit said; *evam* — thus; *manasi* — in his heart; *āgata* — come; *tat* — that; *pravṛtti* — by the news of what had occurred; *prāduṣkṛta* — manifest; *atyanta* — extreme; *śuk* — of sorrow; *agni* — in a fire; *dagdhaḥ* — burning; *mugdhaḥ* — confused; *abhavat* — became; *gopa-kumāra* — of young cowherds; *varyaḥ* — the best; *mātaḥ* — dear mother; *sarūpaḥ* — Sarūpa; *nitarām* — completely; *punaḥ* — again; *saḥ* — he.

**Śrī Parīkṣit said: Dear mother, that best of young cowherds, Sarūpa, then again grew utterly confused. As he contemplated what had happened in Vraja, his heart burned in a fire of sorrow.**

TEXT 346

तेनैव विप्रप्रवरेण यत्नतो
नीतो मनाक्स्वास्थ्यमिव स्वयुक्तिभिः ।
आशंक्य मोहं पुनरात्मनोऽधिकं
वार्तां विशेषेण न तामवर्णयत् ॥

*tenaiva vipra-pravareṇa yatnato*
*nīto manāk svāsthyam iva sva-yuktibhiḥ*
*āśaṅkya mohaṁ punar ātmano 'dhikaṁ*
*vārtāṁ viśeṣeṇa na tām avarṇayat*

*tena* — by him; *eva* — indeed; *vipra* — of *brāhmaṇas; pravareṇa* — the most excellent; *yatnataḥ* — carefully; *nītaḥ* — brought; *manāk* — somewhat; *svāsthyam* — to a normal condition; *iva* — as if; *sva* — his own; *yuktibhiḥ* — by devices; *āśaṅkya* — fearing; *moham* — bewilderment; *punaḥ* — again; *ātmanaḥ* — himself; *adhikam* — further; *vārtām* — the topic; *viśeṣeṇa* — with details; *na* — not; *tām* — that; *avarṇayat* — he described.

**The most excellent brāhmaṇa carefully brought Sarūpa somewhat back to normal. And Sarūpa, fearful of becoming confused again, spoke no further details on that topic.**

COMMENTARY: The Mathurā *brāhmaṇa,* just to bring his *guru* back to external consciousness, called out to him, touched his feet, and sprinkled him with water.

TEXT 347

तत्कथाशेषशुश्रूषाव्यग्रं तं वीक्ष्य माथुरम् ।
यत्नात्सोऽन्तरवष्टभ्य पुनराह महाशयः ॥

*tat-kathā-śeṣa-śuśrūṣā-*
*vyagraṁ taṁ vīkṣya māthuram*

*yatnāt so 'ntar avaṣṭabhya*
*punar āha mahāśayaḥ*

*tat* — of that; *kathā* — narration; *śeṣa* — the remainder; *śuśrūṣā* — with eagerness to hear; *vyagram* — intent; *tam* — him; *vīkṣya* — seeing; *māthuram* — the Mathurā *brāhmaṇa; yatnāt* — with endeavor; *saḥ* — he (Sarūpa); *antaḥ* — his inner self (mind); *avaṣṭabhya* — placing under control; *punaḥ* — again; *āha* — spoke; *mahā-āśayaḥ* — the generous person.

**But when kind-hearted Sarūpa saw that the Mathurā brāhmaṇa was eager to hear the rest of the story, he controlled his mind and continued to speak.**

COMMENTARY: Because Sarūpa's disciple the *brāhmaṇa* had a strong desire to hear, Sarūpa, even at the cost of his own well-being, felt the compassionate duty to help him spiritually advance.

## TEXT 348

श्रीसरूप उवाच
तेषां तु शोकार्तिभरं कदापि तं
परैः प्रकारैरनिवर्त्यमाप्ततः ।
जनात्स विख्याप्य जनेषु सर्वतो
व्रजं प्रियप्रेमवशोऽचिराद्गतः ॥

*śrī-sarūpa uvāca*
*teṣāṁ tu śokārti-bharaṁ kadāpi taṁ*
*paraiḥ prakārair anivartyam āptataḥ*
*janāt sa vikhyāpya janeṣu sarvato*
*vrajaṁ priya-prema-vaśo 'cirād gataḥ*

*śrī-sarūpaḥ uvāca* — Śrī Sarūpa said; *teṣām* — of them (the Vraja-vāsīs); *tu* — but; *śoka* — of sorrow; *ārti* — and pain; *bharam* — the burden; *kadā api* — at any time; *tam* — that;

*paraiḥ* — by other; *prakāraiḥ* — means; *anivartyam* — impossible to counteract; *āptataḥ* — reliable; *janāt* — from a person; *saḥ* — He (Kṛṣṇa); *vikhyāpya* — being informed; *janeṣu* — the people; *sarvataḥ* — fully; *vrajam* — to Vraja; *priya* — of His dear devotees; *prema* — of the love; *vaśaḥ* — under the control; *acirāt* — soon; *gataḥ* — went.

**Śrī Sarūpa said: When Kṛṣṇa heard from a reliable person that the heavy sorrow the Vraja-vāsīs felt could never be removed by any other means, He fully explained this state of affairs to the people of Mathurā, and controlled by the love of His dearest devotees, He soon went back to Vraja.**

COMMENTARY: According to the advice of Uddhava and other dependable counselors, only Kṛṣṇa's return would calm the Vraja-vāsīs. Kṛṣṇa and Balarāma therefore exchanged Their royal garments for Their old cowherd dress and went home.

## TEXT 349

विदग्धमूर्धन्यमणिः कृपाकुलो
व्रजस्थितानां स ददत्सपद्यसून् ।
तथा समं तैर्विजहार ते यथा
विसस्मरुर्दुःखमदः समूलकम् ॥

*vidagdha-mūrdhanya-maṇiḥ kṛpākulo*
*vraja-sthitānāṁ sa dadat sapady asūn*
*tathā samaṁ tair vijahāra te yathā*
*visasmarur duḥkham adaḥ sa-mūlakam*

*vidagdha* — of expert heroes; *mūrdhanya-maṇiḥ* — the crest-jewel; *kṛpā* — by compassion; *ākulaḥ* — agitated; *vraja-sthitānām* — to the residents of Vraja; *saḥ* — He (Kṛṣṇa); *dadat* — giving back; *sapadi* — at once; *asūn* — their lives; *tathā* — and; *samam* — together; *taiḥ* — with them; *vijahāra* — He enjoyed; *te* — they; *yathā* — so; *visasmaruḥ* — forgot; *duḥkham* — misery; *adaḥ* — that; *sa-mūlakam* — with its root causes.

**Impelled by compassion for the residents of Vraja, Kṛṣṇa, that crest jewel of artful heroes, quickly gave them back their lives. He enjoyed with them until they forgot their misery, and what had caused it.**

COMMENTARY: Kṛṣṇa made sure that the Vraja-vāsīs forgot every last thought that had caused them anguish, including Akrūra's having come to Vraja and taken Him away to Mathurā. Kṛṣṇa took this trouble for two reasons: because He is *vidagdha-mūrdhanya-maṇiḥ,* the most gracious performer of valorous deeds, and because He is *kṛpākula,* driven by compassion for His suffering devotees.

## TEXT 350

यदि च कोऽपि कदाचिदनुस्मरेद्
वदति तर्हि मया स्वपता बत ।
किमपि दुष्टमनन्वयमीक्षितं
सरुदितं च भयाद्बहु शोचति ॥

*yadi ca ko 'pi kadācid anusmared*
*vadati tarhi mayā svapatā bata*
*kim api duṣṭam ananvayam īkṣitaṁ*
*sa-ruditaṁ ca bhayād bahu śocati*

*yadi* — if; *ca* — and; *kaḥ api* — someone; *kadācit* — at any time; *anusmaret* — would remember; *vadati* — speaks; *tarhi* — then; *mayā* — by me; *svapatā* — while sleeping; *bata* — alas; *kim* — what; *api* — even; *duṣṭam* — horrible; *ananvayam* — unprecedented; *īkṣitam* — seeing; *sa-ruditam* — with crying; *ca* — and; *bhayāt* — out of fear; *bahu* — much; *śocati* — he laments.

**And if any Vraja-vāsīs ever remembered that suffering, they would bitterly lament and cry out in fear, "What a horrible, unheard-of thing I saw in my dream!"**

COMMENTARY: Even in their dreams, the Vraja-vāsīs couldn't

imagine Kṛṣṇa leaving them to go elsewhere. Their panic at the mere thought of it was but another aspect of their ecstatic love for Kṛṣṇa.

## TEXT 351

चिरेण गोपालविहारमाधुरी-
भरैः समाकृष्टविमोहितेन्द्रियाः ।
न सस्मरुः किञ्चिदतीतमेष्यदप्य्
अमी विदुर्न व्रजवासिनो जनाः ॥

*cireṇa gopāla-vihāra-mādhurī-*
*bharaiḥ samākṛṣṭa-vimohitendriyāḥ*
*na sasmaruḥ kiñcid atītam eṣyad apy*
*amī vidur na vraja-vāsino janāḥ*

*cireṇa* — for a long time; *gopāla* — of a cowherd; *vihāra* — of the pastimes; *mādhurī-bharaiḥ* — with the full sweetness; *samākṛṣṭa* — totally attracted; *vimohita* — and enchanted; *indriyāḥ* — their senses; *na sasmaruḥ* — they could not remember; *kiñcit* — anything; *atītam* — past; *eṣyat* — future; *api* — also; *amī* — they; *viduḥ na* — they were not aware of; *vraja-vāsinaḥ* — residing in Vraja; *janāḥ* — the people.

**The fullness of Kṛṣṇa's sweet cowherd pastimes so utterly attracted and enchanted the Vraja-vāsīs' senses that after a time they forgot everything, even that there was a past or a future.**

## TEXT 352

स हि कालान्तरेऽक्रूरोऽपूर्वागत इवागतः ।
तथैव रथमादाय पुनस्तस्मिन्व्रजे सखे ॥

*sa hi kālāntare 'krūro*
*'pūrvāgata ivāgataḥ*

*tathaiva ratham ādāya*
*punas tasmin vraje sakhe*

*saḥ* — he; *hi* — indeed; *kāla-antare* — at a different time; *akrūraḥ* — Akrūra; *apūrva* — never before; *āgataḥ* — come; *iva* — as if; *āgataḥ* — came; *tathā eva* — and also; *ratham* — his chariot; *ādāya* — bringing; *punaḥ* — again; *tasmin* — to this; *vraje* — Vraja; *sakhe* — O friend.

**O friend, on another occasion that same Akrūra came to Vraja on his chariot, as if he had never come before.**

COMMENTARY: On the order of Kaṁsa, the same Akrūra came again to bring Kṛṣṇa to Mathurā. Because everyone, including Akrūra, was bewildered by the influence of the Goloka atmosphere, no one could remember that this was not the first time Akrūra had arrived in Vṛndāvana.

## TEXT 353

नीयमाने पुनस्तेन तथैव व्रजजीवने ।
तत्रत्यानां दशा कापि पूर्ववत्समजायत ॥

*nīyamāne punas tena*
*tathaiva vraja-jīvane*
*tatratyānāṁ daśā kāpi*
*pūrva-vat samajāyata*

*nīyamāne* — being taken away; *punaḥ* — again; *tena* — by him; *tathā* — so; *eva* — just; *vraja* — of Vraja; *jīvane* — the life; *tatratyānām* — of the residents there; *daśā* — a state; *kā api* — certain; *pūrva-vat* — as before; *samajāyata* — arose.

**He once again took away the life of Vraja, and its residents went again into the same state.**

## TEXT 354

मधुपुर्यां पुनर्गत्वा कंसं हत्वा पुनर्व्रजम् ।
आगतः पूर्ववत्तत्र तथैव विहरत्यसौ ॥

*madhu-puryāṁ punar gatvā*
*kaṁsaṁ hatvā punar vrajam*
*āgataḥ pūrva-vat tatra*
*tathaiva viharaty asau*

*madhu-puryām* — to Mathurā; *punaḥ* — again; *gatvā* — going; *kaṁsam* — Kāṁsa; *hatvā* — killing; *punaḥ* — again; *vrajam* — to Vraja; *āgataḥ* — came; *pūrva-vat* — as before; *tatra* — there; *tathā* — so; *eva* — just; *viharati* — enjoyed; *asau* — He.

**Again Kṛṣṇa went to Madhupurī, again killed Kaṁsa, and again returned to Vraja, where He continued, as before, to enjoy His pastimes.**

## TEXT 355

एवं पुनः पुनर्याति तत्पुरे पूर्वपूर्ववत् ।
पुनः पुनः समायाति व्रजे क्रीडेत्तथैव सः ॥

*evaṁ punaḥ punar yāti*
*tat-pure pūrva-pūrva-vat*
*punaḥ punaḥ samāyāti*
*vraje krīḍet tathaiva saḥ*

*evam* — thus; *punaḥ punaḥ* — again and again; *yāti* — goes; *tat* — that; *pure* — to the city; *pūrva-pūrva-vat* — as each time before; *punaḥ punaḥ* — again and again; *samāyāti* — returns; *vraje* — to Vraja; *krīḍet* — plays; *tathā* — so; *eva* — just; *saḥ* — He.

**Thus Kṛṣṇa again and again goes to Kaṁsa's city, as He many times did before, and again and again returns to sport in Vraja.**

## TEXT 356

तथैव कालीयदमः पुनः पुनस्
तथैव गोवर्धनधारणं मुहुः ।
परापि लीला विविधाद्भुतासकृत्
प्रवर्तते भक्तमनोहरा प्रभोः ॥

*tathaiva kālīya-damaḥ punaḥ punas*
*tathaiva govardhana-dhāraṇaṁ muhuḥ*
*parāpi līlā vividhādbhutāsakṛt*
*pravartate bhakta-manoharā prabhoḥ*

*tathā eva* — similarly; *kālīya* — of Kāliya; *damaḥ* — the subduing; *punaḥ punaḥ* — again and again; *tathā eva* — and similarly; *govardhana* — of Govardhana Hill; *dhāraṇam* — the lifting; *muhuḥ* — repeatedly; *parā* — other; *api* — also; *līlā* — pastimes; *vividha* — various; *adbhutā* — wonderful; *asakṛt* — repeatedly; *pravartate* — occur; *bhakta* — to the devotees; *manoharā* — all-attractive; *prabhoḥ* — of the Lord.

**Kṛṣṇa subdues Kāliya time and again, in the same way, and time and again lifts Govardhana Hill. And again and yet again He performs His many other wonderful pastimes. Thus the Lord enchants the hearts of His devotees.**

COMMENTARY: Since all of Kṛṣṇa's pastimes, beginning with the killing of Pūtanā, are eternal, Kṛṣṇa enjoys them with His devotees in Goloka as often as they like. Yet each time a pastime is repeated, it seems completely new, as if never seen or heard of before. This description may confuse us. How can Kṛṣṇa replay pastimes He has already performed, and how can demons like Pūtanā repeatedly be killed? But Kṛṣṇa's pastimes are transcendental. They are unlimitedly attractive to all His devotees, whether eternal companions or new converts to pure devotional service. Even newly elevated devotees feel extraordinary love for the Supreme Person whenever they hear and remember His pastimes. Those pastimes generate such a force of loving attraction as to fix the memories of them in the hearts of the devotees. Meditation on those pastimes then gives rise to a very special happiness. In this way Kṛṣṇa's pastimes steal the hearts of even neophyte devotees, and Kṛṣṇa's eternal devotees taste a sweetness and wonder unknown to anyone else.

## TEXT 357

तत्रत्यास्ते तु तां सर्वामपूर्वां मन्यन्ते सदा ।
श्रीकृष्णपरमप्रेमकालकूटविमोहिताः ॥

*tatratyās te tu tāṁ sarvām*
*apūrvāṁ manyante sadā*
*śrī-kṛṣṇa-parama-prema-*
*kālakūṭa-vimohitāḥ*

*tatratyāḥ* — the residents of that place; *te* — they; *tu* — however; *tām* — those (pastimes); *sarvām* — all; *apūrvām* — never occurred before; *manyante* — consider; *sadā* — always; *śrī-kṛṣṇa* — for Śrī Kṛṣṇa; *parama* — supreme; *prema* — of their love; *kālakūṭa* — by the *kālakūṭa* poison; *vimohitāḥ* — bewildered.

**But the residents of Vraja, completely bewildered by the kālakūṭa poison of their supreme love for Śrī Kṛṣṇa, never think that any of these events has ever occurred before.**

COMMENTARY: Because the Vraja-vāsīs are never aware that Kṛṣṇa's pastimes are repeat performances, the attraction they feel for those pastimes is never impeded. The highest states of *kṛṣṇa-prema* have the power to create such bewilderment.

## TEXT 358

अतस्तेषां हि नितरां स वरीवृध्यते महान् ।
वियोगयोगयोः प्रेमावेशावेगो निरन्तरम् ॥

*atas teṣāṁ hi nitarāṁ*
*sa varīvṛdhyate mahān*
*viyoga-yogayoḥ premā-*
*veśāvego nirantaram*

*ataḥ* — consequently; *teṣām* — of them; *hi* — indeed; *nitarām* — extremely; *saḥ* — it; *varīvṛdhyate* — increases continuously; *mahān* — great; *viyoga* — in separation; *yogayoḥ* — and association; *prema* — in pure love; *āveśa* — of their obsession; *vegaḥ* — the force; *nirantaram* — always.

**Thus the powerful force of their obsessive love ever-increasingly grows, both in union and in separation.**

TEXT 359

दूरेऽस्तु तावद्वार्तेयं तत्र नित्यनिवासिनाम् ।
न तिष्ठेदनुसन्धानं नूत्नानां मादृशामपि ॥

*dūre 'stu tāvad vārteyaṁ*
*tatra nitya-nivāsinām*
*na tiṣṭhed anusandhānaṁ*
*nūtnānāṁ mādṛśām api*

*dūre* — left far aside; *astu* — let it be; *tāvat* — even; *vārtā* — topic; *iyam* — this; *tatra* — there (in Vraja); *nitya* — eternal; *nivāsinām* — of the residents; *na tiṣṭhet* — there cannot be present; *anusandhānam* — remembrance; *nūtnānām* — of the newcomers; *mādṛśām* — like me; *api* — even.

**As true as this is for the eternal residents of Vraja, even newcomers like me can hardly remember those past events.**

COMMENTARY: In pure devotional life everyone is fully absorbed in transcendence. Some devotees, however, can be distinguished as *nūtna* ("new") because they were conditioned souls and have recently been reinstated in their original position by devotional practice and the Supreme Lord's personal grace.

## TEXT 360

तादृङ्महामोहनमाधुरीसरिद्-
धारासमुद्रे सततं निमज्जनात् ।
तादृक्प्रियप्रेममहाधनावली-
लाभोन्मदात्के हि न विस्मरन्ति किम् ॥

*tādṛṅ-mahā-mohana-mādhurī-sarid-*
*dhārā-samudre satataṁ nimajjanāt*
*tādṛk-priya-prema-mahā-dhanāvalī-*
*lābhonmadāt ke hi na vismaranti kim*

*tādṛk* — such; *mahā-mohana* — most enchanting; *mādhurī* — of sweetness; *sarit* — of the rivers; *dhārā* — created by the currents; *samudre* — in the ocean; *satatam* — constantly; *nimajjanāt* — because of being immersed; *tādṛk* — such; *priya* — most desirable; *prema* — of pure love; *mahā-dhana* — of vast treasures; *āvalī* — the series; *lābha* — by attaining; *unmadāt* — due to being maddened; *ke* — who; *hi* — indeed; *na vismaranti* — do not forget; *kim* — how.

**How can any resident of Vraja not forget in this way? The Vraja-vāsīs, after all, are ever immersed in the ocean made by these river currents of most enchanting sweetness. And by gaining the vast, most desirable treasure of pure love, the Vraja-vāsīs become maddened.**

## TEXT 361

अहो महैश्वर्यमसावपि प्रभुर्
निजप्रियप्रेमसमुद्रसम्प्लुतः ।
कृतं च कार्यं च न किञ्चिदीश्वरः
सदानुसन्धातुमभिज्ञशेखरः ॥

*aho mahaiśvaryam asāv api prabhur*
*nija-priya-prema-samudra-samplutaḥ*
*kṛtaṁ ca kāryaṁ ca na kiñcid īśvaraḥ*
*sadānusandhātum abhijña-śekharaḥ*

*aho* — oh; *mahā* — the greatest; *aiśvaryam* — glory; *asau* — He; *api* — even; *prabhuḥ* — the Lord; *nija* — His own; *priya* — for the dear devotees; *prema* — of the love; *samudra* — in the ocean; *samplutaḥ* — drowning; *kṛtam* — done; *ca* — and; *kāryam* — to be done; *ca* — and; *na kiñcit* — not at all; *īśvaraḥ* — capable; *sadā* — always; *anusandhātum* — of remembering; *abhijña* — of enlightened persons; *śekharaḥ* — the foremost.

**And, oh, the most glorious thing is that the foremost of enlightened persons, the Lord Himself, while drowning in an ocean of love for His dear devotees, cannot always remember what He has done and what He is going to do.**

COMMENTARY: Isn't perfect knowledge an automatic by-product of love of God? Why then are the pure devotees of Goloka so forgetful? Yes, to one who has *prema* omniscience comes naturally, but *prema,* being all-powerful, can redefine what is knowledge and what is ignorance. The Personality of Godhead Himself, by the influence of His Yogamāyā, also forgets what He did before. But though He often forgets, He sometimes remembers, if it serves the purpose of His pastimes.

## TEXT 362

लीलैव नित्या प्रभुपादपद्मयोः
सा सच्चिदानन्दमयी किल स्वयम् ।
आकृष्यमाणेव तदीयसेवया
तत्तत्परीवारयुता प्रवर्तते ॥

*līlaiva nityā prabhu-pāda-padmayoḥ*
*sā sac-cid-ānanda-mayī kila svayam*

*ākṛṣyamāṇeva tadīya-sevayā*
*tat-tat-parīvāra-yutā pravartate*

*līlā* — the pastimes; *eva* — indeed; *nityā* — eternal; *prabhu* — of the Lord; *pāda-padmayoḥ* — of the lotus feet; *sā* — they; *sat* — eternity; *cit* — knowledge; *ānanda* — and bliss; *mayī* —composed of; *kila* — indeed; *svayam* — themselves; *ākṛṣyamāṇā* — being attracted; *iva* — as if; *tadīya* — His; *sevayā* — by the service; *tat-tat* — various; *parīvāra* — entourage and paraphernalia; *yutā* — joined with; *pravartate* — they go on.

**The pastimes of the Lord are ever existing and purely spiritual, formed of eternity, knowledge, and bliss. Of their own accord, those pastimes, attracted to the Lord's lotus feet to engage in service, follow Him everywhere, supplying the entourage and paraphernalia for each occasion.**

COMMENTARY: Kṛṣṇa's pastimes are *sac-cid-ānanda-mayī,* composed of *sat* ("eternal existence"), *cit* ("full awareness"), and *ānanda* ("pure ecstasy"). In this context the suffix *-mayī* could mean either "identity" or "transformation." In other words, since Kṛṣṇa's *līlās* are a display of Kṛṣṇa's internal energy, they are nondifferent from Him, and they are also a manifestation of transcendental variety.

There are never any defects in Kṛṣṇa's *līlās,* even when Kṛṣṇa seems to behave like an ordinary person:

*evaṁ dhārṣṭyāny uśati kurute mehanādīni vāstau*
*steyopāyair viracita-kṛtiḥ su-pratīko yathāste*
*itthaṁ strībhiḥ sa-bhaya-nayana-śrī-mukhālokinībhir*
*vyākhyātārthā prahasita-mukhī na hy upālabdhum aicchat*

"[The ladies of the neighborhood complained to Yaśodā:] 'When Kṛṣṇa is caught in His naughty activities, the master of the house will say to Him, "Oh, You are a thief!" and artificially express anger at Kṛṣṇa. Kṛṣṇa will then reply, "I am not a thief. You are a thief!" Sometimes, being angry, Kṛṣṇa passes urine and stool in a neat, clean place in our houses. But now, our dear friend Yaśodā, this expert thief is sitting before you like a very good boy.' Sometimes all the *gopīs* would look at Kṛṣṇa sitting there, His eyes fearful so that His mother would not chastise Him, and when they saw Kṛṣṇa's beautiful face, instead of continuing to complain about Him they would simply look upon His face and enjoy transcendental bliss. Mother Yaśodā would mildly smile at all this fun, and she would not want to chastise her blessed transcendental child." (*Bhāgavatam* 10.8.31)

To Kṛṣṇa's feet His pastimes are attracted by their own desire to serve Him, and they are attracted by the service attitude of His devotees. In the words of *Śrī Viṣṇu Purāṇa* (5.22.18):

*manuṣya-dehināṁ ceṣṭām*
*ity evam anuvartataḥ*
*līlā jagat-pates tasya*
*chandataḥ sampravartate*

"The pastimes of the Lord of the universe unfold by their sweet will, as He imitates the activities of living beings embodied as humans."

## TEXT 363

इयं ते कथिता ब्रह्मन् गोलोकस्य विलक्षणा ।
माहात्म्यमाधुरीधाराप्रान्तकाष्ठा हि सर्वतः ॥

*iyaṁ te kathitā brahman*
*golokasya vilakṣaṇā*
*māhātmya-mādhurī-dhārā-*
*prānta-kāṣṭhā hi sarvataḥ*

*iyam* — this; *te* — to you; *kathitā* — told; *brahman* — O *brāhmaṇa; golokasya* — of Goloka; *vilakṣaṇā* — unique; *māhātmya* — of the greatness; *mādhurī* — and sweetness; *dhārā* — of a constant flood; *prānta* — extreme; *kāṣṭhā* — the limit; *hi* — indeed; *sarvataḥ* — entirely.

**O brāhmaṇa, thus I have told you about Goloka's unique, most extreme greatness and sweetness, which flow everywhere like a flooding river.**

## TEXT 364

श्रीमाथुर उवाच
कृष्णे मधुपुरीं याते वसेत्कुत्र भवान्कथम् ।
यश्चिरात्तत्पदं प्राप्तः प्रयत्नैस्तत्तदाशया ॥

*śrī-māthura uvāca*
*kṛṣṇe madhu-purīṁ yāte*
*vaset kutra bhavān katham*
*yaś cirāt tat-padaṁ prāptaḥ*
*prayatnais tat-tad-āśayā*

*śrī-māthuraḥ uvāca* — the Mathurā *brāhmaṇa* said; *kṛṣṇe* — Kṛṣṇa; *madhu-purīm* — to Madhupurī; *yāte* — having gone; *vaset* — will reside; *kutra* — where; *bhavān* — your good self; *katham* — how; *yaḥ* — who; *cirāt* — for a long time; *tat* — His; *padam* — abode; *prāptaḥ* — achieved; *prayatnaiḥ* — with great efforts; *tat-tat* — various; *āśayā* — with desires.

**The Mathurā brāhmaṇa said: After striving for so long, in so many ways and with so many desires in your heart, you achieved Kṛṣṇa's abode. Now that He has gone to Madhupurī, where will you reside, and how will you live?**

COMMENTARY: For a very long time, Gopa-kumāra had harbored the desire to see Śrī Gopāladeva and join Him in His pastimes. Now Gopa-kumāra has finally reached his destination, Goloka Vṛndāvana, but Kṛṣṇa has left Vṛndāvana to go to Mathurā. Under the circumstances, how can Gopa-kumāra tolerate living in Vraja? And since he is attached to the countryside where Kṛṣṇa performed His childhood pastimes, how can he consider living in Mathurā?

## TEXT 365

श्रीसरूप उवाच
आदेशेन प्रभोस्तस्य व्रजे नन्दादिभिः सह ।
वसन्ति मादृशाः सर्वे तत्र स्वसदृशैस्तदा ॥

*śrī-sarūpa uvāca*
*ādeśena prabhos tasya*
*vraje nandādibhiḥ saha*
*vasanti mādṛśāḥ sarve*
*tatra sva-sadṛśais tadā*

*śrī-sarūpaḥ uvāca* — Śrī Sarūpa said; *ādeśena* — on the order; *prabhoḥ* — of the Lord; *tasya* — His; *vraje* — in Vraja; *nanda-ādibhiḥ* — with Nanda and the others; *saha* — together; *vasanti* — live; *mādṛśāḥ* — persons like me; *sarve* — all; *tatra* — there; *sva* — to ourselves; *sadṛśaiḥ* — who are similar; *tadā* — then.

**Śrī Sarūpa said: By the order of the Lord, I and all devotees like me continue to live in Vraja in the company of Nanda and the others whose moods resemble ours.**

COMMENTARY: When Kṛṣṇa left Vraja, He gave special instructions to the new devotees who had come to His abode on the strength of His mercy and their spontaneous (*rāgānuga*) *sādhana*. He told them to remain in Vraja and continue to associate with great devotees like Nanda, whose ways of devotion were similar to their own. Otherwise, if the new devotees were to go to Mathurā, the incompatible local mood would disturb them, and their spiritual development would be impeded. With such considerations in mind, *Śrī Hari-bhakti-sudhodaya* (8.51) states:

*sva-kulardhyai tato dhīmān*
*sva-yūthān eva saṁśrayet*

"If an intelligent person wants to see his family prosper, he should stay with his own kind."

## TEXT 366

तल्लोकस्य स्वभावोऽयं कृष्णसङ्गं विनापि यत् ।
भवेत्तत्रैव तिष्ठासा न चिकीर्षा च कस्यचित् ॥

*tal-lokasya svabhāvo 'yaṁ*
*kṛṣṇa-saṅgaṁ vināpi yat*
*bhavet tatraiva tiṣṭhāsā*
*na cikīrṣā ca kasyacit*

*tat* — of His; *lokasya* — world; *svabhāvaḥ* — the nature; *ayam* — this; *kṛṣṇa* — of Kṛṣṇa; *saṅgam* — the association; *vinā* — without; *api* — indeed; *yat* — that; *bhavet* — there would be; *tatra* — in that place; *eva* — only; *tiṣṭhāsā* — desire to remain; *na* — not; *cikīrṣā* — desire to do anything else; *ca* — and; *kasyacit* — of anyone.

**This is the nature of Goloka, Kṛṣṇa's world. Even in His absence the residents want to stay. None want to go anywhere else.**

## TEXT 367

तत्रत्यं यच्च तद् दुःखं तत्सर्वसुखमूर्धसु ।
स नरीनर्ति शोकश्च कृत्स्नानन्दभरोपरि ॥

*tatratyaṁ yac ca tad duḥkhaṁ*
*tat sarva-sukha-mūrdhasu*
*sa narīnarti śokaś ca*
*kṛtsnānanda-bharopari*

*tatratyam* — belonging to that place; *yat* — which; *ca* — and; *tat* — that; *duḥkham* — misery; *tat* — that; *sarva* — of all varieties; *sukha* — of happiness; *mūrdhasu* — on the heads; *saḥ* — it; *narīnarti* — dances vigorously; *śokaḥ* — the mental distress; *ca* — and; *kṛtsna* — all; *ānanda* — of bliss; *bhara* — the intensity; *upari* — above.

**There, sorrow dances vigorously on the head of every kind of happiness, and anguish gives a joy more intense than any bliss.**

COMMENTARY: In Goloka the apparent misery of separation from Kṛṣṇa is in fact the greatest happiness, and the anxiety felt by the Goloka-vāsīs is more ecstatic than any other pleasure. As already explained, both these contrary effects are due to the unique nature of the special love for Kṛṣṇa found only in Goloka.

## TEXT 368

इत्थं वसंस्तत्र चिरेण वाञ्छितं
वाञ्छाधिकं चाविरतं परं फलम् ।
चित्तानुपूर्त्यानुभवन्नपि ध्रुवं
वस्तुस्वभावेन न तृप्तिमाप्नुयाम् ॥

*ittham vasaṁs tatra cireṇa vāñchitaṁ*
*vāñchādhikaṁ cāviratam paraṁ phalam*
*cittānupūrtyānubhavann api dhruvaṁ*
*vastu-svabhāvena na tṛptim āpnuyām*

*ittham* — thus; *vasan* — residing; *tatra* — there; *cireṇa* — after a long time; *vāñchitam* — what I desired; *vāñchā* — my desire; *adhikam* — beyond; *ca* — and; *aviratam* — endlessly; *param* — the highest; *phalam* — fruit; *citta* — of my heart; *anupūrtyā* — with complete fulfillment; *anubhavan* — experiencing; *api* — although; *dhruvam* — certainly; *vastu* — of the reality; *svabhāvena* — due to the nature; *na* — not; *tṛptim* — satisfaction; *āpnuyām* — I can attain.

**After so long, having attained my desires, there I reside, beyond all desires, and to my heart's content I relish the supreme and endless perfection of life. Yet the nature of that reality is such that I never feel satiated.**

## TEXT 369

अतो व्रजस्त्रीकुचकुंकुमाचितं
मनोरमं तत्पदपङ्कजद्वयम् ।
कदापि केनापि निजेन्द्रियादिना
न हातुमीशे लवलेशमप्यहम् ॥

*ato vraja-strī-kuca-kuṅkumācitaṁ*
*manoramaṁ tat-pada-paṅkaja-dvayam*
*kadāpi kenāpi nijendriyādinā*
*na hātum īśe lava-leśam apy aham*

*ataḥ* — therefore; *vraja-strī* — of the women of Vraja; *kuca* — from the breasts; *kuṅkuma-ācitam* — smeared with the *kuṅkuma; manoramam* — enchanting; *tat* — His; *pada-paṅkaja* — of the lotus feet; *dvayam* — the pair; *kadā api* — ever; *kena api* — for any reason; *nija* — one's own; *indriya* — by the senses; *ādinā* — and so on; *na* — not; *hātum* — to abandon; *īśe* — am able; *lava* — of a fraction of a second; *leśam* — for a small part; *api* — even; *aham* — I.

**Never, then, for any reason, can I give up Kṛṣṇa's all-attractive lotus feet, smeared with kuṅkuma from the breasts of the women of Vraja. Never can I stop serving those feet with my senses, body, and mind, not even for a fraction of a second.**

## TEXT 370

तस्यापि यो दीनतरे जनेऽस्मिन्
माधुर्यनिष्ठाप्तकृपाप्रसादः ।
अन्यैरसम्भाव्यतया न वक्तुं
कुत्रापि युज्येत तथाप्यनूक्तः ॥

*tasyāpi yo dīna-tare jane 'smin*
*mādhurya-niṣṭhāpta-kṛpā-prasādaḥ*

*anyair asambhāvyatayā na vaktuṁ*
*kutrāpi yujyeta tathāpy anūktaḥ*

*tasya* — His; *api* — and; *yaḥ* — which; *dīna-tare* — the most wretched; *jane* — on the person; *asmin* — this (myself); *mādhurya* — for the sweetness; *niṣṭhā* — with strong attachment; *āpta* — endowed; *kṛpā* — of His mercy; *prasādaḥ* — the favor; *anyaiḥ* — by others; *asambhāvyatayā* — never to be hoped for; *na* — not; *vaktum* — to be spoken; *kutra api* — anywhere; *yujyeta* — is appropriate; *tathā api* — nonetheless; *anūktaḥ* — recounted.

**Kṛṣṇa showed this most wretched person the favor of His mercy — mercy others can never hope for — enhanced with the taste of His divine sweetness. To no one should this be disclosed. Yet I have recounted my story to you.**

COMMENTARY: As Śrīla Sanātana Gosvāmī has revealed earlier in his commentary, Śrīmatī Rādhārāṇī personally ordered Śrī Sarūpa to enlighten the Mathurā *brāhmaṇa.*

## TEXT 371

एवं तत्र चिरं तिष्ठन्मर्त्यलोकस्थितं त्विदम् ।
मथुरामण्डलं श्रीमदपश्यं खलु तादृशम् ॥

*evaṁ tatra ciraṁ tiṣṭhan*
*martya-loka-sthitaṁ tv idam*
*mathurā-maṇḍalaṁ śrīmad*
*apaśyaṁ khalu tādṛśam*

*evam* — thus; *tatra* — there; *ciram* — for a long time; *tiṣṭhan* — remaining; *martya-loka* — in the mortal world; *sthitam* — situated; *tu* — and; *idam* — this; *mathurā-maṇḍalam* — Mathurā-maṇḍala; *śrīmat* — splendid; *apaśyam* — I realized; *khalu* — indeed; *tādṛśam* — just like it.

**After staying some time in Goloka, I realized: This splendid Mathurā-maṇḍala, here in the mortal world, is not different.**

COMMENTARY: Knowledge of Goloka applies equally to Gokula, and vice versa, because these two places are identical. Just as a *jñānī's* realization of impersonal Brahman includes realization of the individual spirit soul, realization of either Goloka or Gokula includes realization of the other. Were impersonal realization to disallow the *brahma-vādīs* from perceiving their own selves, they would have no impetus to follow their own discipline, because knowledge of Brahman, in the beginning of its development, is too subtle to perceive. Impersonal Brahman cannot be known by the untrained mind, and so for the benefit of neophyte *jñānīs* the *Upaniṣads* refer to Brahman merely as *tat* ("that"), as in the famous aphorism of the *Chāndogya Upaniṣad* (6.8.7) *tat tvam asi* ("you are that").

## TEXT 372

तत्तच्छ्रीगोपगोपीभिस्ताभिर्गोभिश्च तादृशैः ।
पशुपक्षिकृमिक्ष्माभृत्सरित्तर्वादिभिर्वृतम् ॥

*tat-tac-chrī-gopa-gopībhis*
*tābhir gobhiś ca tādṛśaiḥ*
*paśu-pakṣi-kṛmi-kṣmābhṛt-*
*sarit-tarv-ādibhir vṛtam*

*tat-tat* — the various; *śrī* — divine; *gopa* — with the cowherd men; *gopībhiḥ* — and cowherd women; *tābhiḥ* — these; *gobhiḥ* — with the cows; *ca* — and; *tādṛśaiḥ* — exactly similar; *paśu* — with the animals; *pakṣi* — birds; *kṛmi* — insects; *kṣmā-bhṛt* — mountains; *sarit* — rivers; *taru* — trees; *ādibhiḥ* — and so on; *vṛtam* — abounding.

**Divine gopas, gopīs, and cows abound in variety in Gokula, just as in Goloka. And so do the other animals, and the**

**birds, and the insects, and the mountains, rivers, trees, and other beings.**

COMMENTARY: Goloka and Gokula resemble one another down to the details of individual living beings. The individual persons playing the roles in one place may be distinct from those in the other, but the functions they serve in the pleasure pastimes of the Personality of Godhead are exactly the same. Gokula's cowherd men and women and all its creatures, down to the creepers and bushes, closely resemble their counterparts in the spiritual world.

## TEXT 373

तथैवाविरतं श्रीमत्कृष्णचन्द्रेण तेन हि ।
विस्तार्यमाणया तादृक्क्रीडाश्रेण्यापि मण्डितम् ॥

*tathaivāviratam̐ śrīmat-*
*kṛṣṇa-candreṇa tena hi*
*vistāryamāṇayā tādṛk-*
*krīḍā-śreṇyāpi maṇḍitam*

*tathā eva* — and also; *aviratam* — constantly; *śrīmat* — glorious; *kṛṣṇa-candreṇa* — by Kṛṣṇacandra; *tena* — Him; *hi* — indeed; *vistāryamāṇayā* — expanded; *tādṛk* — similar; *krīḍā* — of pastimes; *śreṇyā* — by a series; *api* — indeed; *maṇḍitam* — adorned.

**And this place is adorned with a never-ending stream of similar pastimes, expanded by the glorious Kṛṣṇacandra.**

## TEXT 374

तत्कदाचिदितस्तत्र कदापि विदधे स्थितिम् ।
भेदं नोपलभे कश्चित्पदयोरधुनैतयोः ॥

*tat kadācid itas tatra*
*kadāpi vidadhe sthitim*
*bhedaṁ nopalabhe kañcit*
*padayor adhunaitayoḥ*

*tat* — therefore; *kadācit* — sometimes; *itaḥ* — here; *tatra* — there; *kadā api* — and sometimes; *vidadhe* — I make; *sthitim* — my residence; *bhedam* — difference; *na upalabhe* — I do not perceive; *kañcit* — any; *padayoḥ* — between the two abodes; *adhunā* — now; *etayoḥ* — these.

**I reside, therefore, sometimes here and sometimes there. No longer do I perceive any difference between these two abodes.**

COMMENTARY: Śrī Sarūpa and his disciple are in Vraja-bhūmi on earth. Now Śrī Sarūpa sees no difference between the two abodes, but before he attained this realization he had to make a great endeavor to transfer himself from Gokula to Goloka.

## TEXT 375

गमनागमनैर्भेदो यः प्रसज्जेत केवलम् ।
तं चाहं तत्तदासक्त्या न जानीयामिव स्फुटम् ॥

*gamanāgamanair bhedo*
*yaḥ prasajjeta kevalam*
*taṁ cāhaṁ tat-tad-āsaktyā*
*na jānīyām iva sphuṭam*

*gamana-āgamanaiḥ* — because of traveling back and forth; *bhedaḥ* — difference; *yaḥ* — which; *prasajjeta* — is found; *kevalam* — only; *tam* — that; *ca* — and; *aham* — I; *tat-tat* — to each of them; *āsaktyā* — because of my attachment; *na jānīyām* — I do not notice; *iva* — as if; *sphuṭam* — apparent.

**Traveling from one to the other, back and forth, may make**

**it seem that there is some distinction, but I am so attached to both places that I hardly notice any difference.**

COMMENTARY: Śrī Sarūpa perceives a distance as he moves from the middle of the material universe to the topmost limit of the spiritual sky, but to him this distraction is insignificant. The journey is no more troublesome than the walk a farmer has to take to a field near his home.

## TEXT 376

अस्मात्स्थानद्वयादन्यत्पदं किञ्चित्कथञ्चन ।
नैव स्पृशति मे दृष्टिः श्रवणं वा मनोऽपि वा ॥

*asmāt sthāna-dvayād anyat*
*padaṁ kiñcit kathañcana*
*naiva spṛśati me dṛṣṭiḥ*
*śravaṇaṁ vā mano 'pi vā*

*asmāt* — than these; *sthāna* — places; *dvayāt* — two; *anyat* — other; *padam* — location; *kiñcit* — any; *kathañcana* — in any way; *na* — not; *eva* — even; *spṛśati* — touches; *me* — my; *dṛṣṭiḥ* — sight; *śravaṇam* — hearing; *vā* — or; *manaḥ* — mind; *api* — even; *vā* — or.

**Neither my sight, nor my hearing, nor even my mind ever touches any other abode than these two.**

COMMENTARY: Being exclusively attached to Kṛṣṇa and His abodes, Śrī Sarūpa is oblivious to everything else.

## TEXT 377

अन्यत्र वर्तते क्वापि श्रीकृष्णो भगवान्स्वयम् ।
तादृशास्तस्य भक्ता वा सन्तीति मनुते न हृत् ॥

*anyatra vartate kvāpi*
*śrī-kṛṣṇo bhagavān svayam*
*tādṛśās tasya bhaktā vā*
*santīti manute na hṛt*

*anyatra* — elsewhere; *vartate* — resides; *kva api* — in some place; *śrī-kṛṣṇaḥ* — Śrī Kṛṣṇa; *bhagavān* — the Supreme Lord; *svayam* — Himself; *tādṛśāḥ* — like this; *tasya* — His; *bhaktāḥ* — devotees; *vā* — or; *santi* — are present; *iti* — thus; *manute na* — does not consider; *hṛt* — my heart.

**My heart never thinks that the original Supreme Lord Śrī Kṛṣṇa, or His devotees like those present here, could ever reside anywhere else.**

COMMENTARY: Here Sarūpa is talking only about *svayaṁ bhagavān,* the original Personality of Godhead, and His Vraja devotees, not about the Lord's expansions, like Vāsudeva in Dvārakā, and Their devotees like Vasudeva.

## TEXT 378

कदाचिद्दर्शनं वा स्याद्वैकुण्ठादिनिवासिनाम् ।
श्रीकृष्णविरहेणार्तानिव पश्यामि तानपि ॥

*kadācid darśanaṁ vā syād*
*vaikuṇṭhādi-nivāsinām*
*śrī-kṛṣṇa-viraheṇārtān*
*iva paśyāmi tān api*

*kadācit* — sometimes; *darśanam* — sight; *vā* — or; *syāt* — there may be; *vaikuṇṭha-ādi* — of Vaikuṇṭha and other places; *nivāsinām* — of residents; *śrī-kṛṣṇa* — from Śrī Kṛṣṇa; *viraheṇa* — by separation; *ārtān* — tormented; *iva* — as if; *paśyāmi* — I see; *tān* — them; *api* — indeed.

**From time to time I may see residents of Vaikuṇṭha or**

**some other place, but to my eyes they appear tormented by separation from Śrī Kṛṣṇa.**

COMMENTARY: Śrī Sarūpa's vision is that of a *paramahaṁsa* situated in *vraja-bhāva,* the mood of Vraja. He sees everyone, even outsiders, as if they were also in that mood. When he meets devotees from Dvārakā, Ayodhyā, and Vaikuṇṭha, he projects his own feelings onto them and presumes that they are anguished by not being with Kṛṣṇa in Vraja. In this way, nothing distracts Sarūpa from his meditation on the glories of Goloka, and he remains satisfied in all circumstances.

TEXT 379

कदापि तेषु व्रजवासिलोक-
सादृश्यभावानवलोकनान्मे ।
जातानुतापेन भवेत्ततोऽपि
प्रेमप्रकाशात्परमं सुखं तत् ॥

*kadāpi teṣu vraja-vāsi-loka-*
*sādṛśya-bhāvānavalokanān me*
*jātānutāpena bhavet tato 'pi*
*prema-prakāśāt paramaṁ sukhaṁ tat*

*kadā api* — sometimes; *teṣu* — in them; *vraja-vāsi* — residing in Vraja; *loka* — of the people; *sādṛśya* — similar; *bhāva* — a mood; *anavalokanāt* — because of not seeing; *me* — my; *jāta* — born; *anutāpena* — by the painful disappointment; *bhavet* — there is; *tataḥ* — from that; *api* — nonetheless; *prema* — of pure love; *prakāśāt* — due to the manifestation; *paramam* — utmost; *sukham* — happiness; *tat* — that.

**By not seeing in those other devotees a mood like that of the residents of Vraja, I may occasionally be disappointed. Yet that only makes my love for Kṛṣṇa shine forth more brightly. And so my disappointment becomes a cause of supreme joy.**

COMMENTARY: Because the devotees of all the expansions of Godhead are eternally blissful, Sarūpa sometimes notices that even outside Vraja, even without Kṛṣṇa's direct company, such devotees are happy. That anyone could think himself happy without being in the mood of Vraja disturbs Sarūpa occasionally, but that very agitation impels his love for Kṛṣṇa in Goloka to increase. He can thus remain happy even while passing through Vaikuṇṭha or the material world.

## TEXT 380

अहो गोलोकीयैर्निखिलभुवनावासिमहितैः
सदा तैस्तैर्लोकैः समनुभवनीयस्य महतः ।
पदार्थस्याख्यातुं कति विवरणानि प्रभुरहं
तदास्तां तल्लोकाखिलपरिकरेभ्यो मम नमः ॥

*aho golokīyair nikhila-bhuvanāvāsi-mahitaiḥ*
*sadā tais tair lokaiḥ samanubhavanīyasya mahataḥ*
*padārthasyākhyātuṁ kati vivaraṇāni prabhur ahaṁ*
*tad āstāṁ tal-lokākhila-parikarebhyo mama namaḥ*

*aho* — oh; *golokīyaiḥ* — of Goloka; *nikhila* — all; *bhuvana* — of the worlds; *āvāsi* — by the residents; *mahitaiḥ* — who are glorified; *sadā* — always; *taiḥ taiḥ* — by the various; *lokaiḥ* — residents; *samanubhavanīyasya* — which can be perceived; *mahataḥ* — of the greatness; *pada-arthasya* — the reality; *ākhyātum* — to describe; *kati* — how many; *vivaraṇāni* — descriptions; *prabhuḥ* — capable; *aham* — I; *tat āstām* — so be it; *tat* — of that; *loka* — world; *akhila* — to all; *parikarebhyaḥ* — the Lord's associates; *mama* — my; *namaḥ* — obeisances.

**How much can I say about that supreme reality — oh, the world of Goloka! Its multitude of residents, honored by all the worlds, always perceive its greatness. So now I have said enough. To all who live with the Lord in that abode, I offer my obeisances.**

COMMENTARY: Goloka is the ultimate reality, and the essence of that reality is pure love for the lotus feet of Śrī Nanda-nandana. Hearing about and describing the wonderful sports of Kṛṣṇa in Goloka and in Mathurā Gokula on earth are the most worthwhile engagements for anyone. Ultimately, however, one can only say so much, and one must finish by simply offering one's respects to the most fortunate inhabitants of Lord Kṛṣṇa's abode. By honoring them one honors their pure love for Kṛṣṇa, a love which is the highest goal of all endeavors.

*Thus ends the sixth chapter of Part Two of Śrīla Sanātana Gosvāmī's Bṛhad-bhāgavatāmṛta, entitled "Abhīṣṭa-lābha: The Attainment of All Desires."*

SEVEN

# *Jagad-ānanda: The Bliss of the Worlds*

## TEXT 1

श्रीसरूप उवाच
एवं यत्परमं साध्यं परमं साधनं च यत् ।
तद्विचार्याधुना ब्रह्मन्स्वयं निश्चीयतां त्वया ॥

*śrī-sarūpa uvāca*
*evaṁ yat paramaṁ sādhyaṁ*
*paramaṁ sādhanaṁ ca yat*
*tad vicāryādhunā brahman*
*svayaṁ niścīyatāṁ tvayā*

*śrī-sarūpaḥ uvāca* — Śrī Sarūpa said; *evam* — thus; *yat* — what; *paramam* — the highest; *sādhyam* — goal; *paramam* — the highest; *sādhanam* — means for achievement; *ca* — and; *yat* — what; *tad* — this; *vicārya* — considering; *adhunā* — now; *brahman* — O *brāhmaṇa*; *svayam* — on your own; *niścīyatām* — should be decided; *tvayā* — by you.

**Śrī Sarūpa said: My dear brāhmaṇa, now think carefully and decide for yourself what is the highest goal of life and what is the best way to achieve it.**

COMMENTARY: This seventh chapter describes how the Mathurā *brāhmaṇa,* by the mercy of Śrī Sarūpa, achieved pure love for Kṛṣṇa and on the strength of that love received Kṛṣṇa's special favor.

Sarūpa has depicted the most important aspects of the glories of Goloka. Now all that remains is for him to give an explicit answer to the *brāhmaṇa's* earlier query:

*śrutvā bahu-vidhaṁ sādhyaṁ*
*sādhanaṁ ca tatas tataḥ*
*prāpyaṁ kṛtyaṁ ca nirṇetuṁ*
*na kiñcic chakyate mayā*

"From various sources I have heard of various goals and various methods to achieve them, but still I cannot definitely decide what goal I should strive for and what I should do to reach it." (*Bṛhad-bhāgavatāmṛta* 2.1.98) To test whether the *brāhmaṇa* disciple has now correctly understood what he has been taught, Sarūpa asks him to give his own opinion about what should be his *sādhya* and *sādhana* — his goal and his means to achieve it.

## TEXT 2

माथुरब्राह्मणश्रेष्ठ मद्वत्प्राप्यं त्वयापि तत् ।
सर्वं देव्याः प्रसादेन प्राप्तमेवेति मन्यताम् ॥

*māthura-brāhmaṇa-śreṣṭha*
*mad-vat prāpyaṁ tvayāpi tat*
*sarvaṁ devyāḥ prasādena*
*prāptam eveti manyatām*

*māthura* — of Mathurā; *brāhmaṇa-śreṣṭha* — O best of *brāhmaṇas; mat-vat* — as I have; *prāpyam* — the goal; *tvayā* — by you; *api* — already; *tat* — that; *sarvam* — completely; *devyāḥ* — of the divine goddess; *prasādena* — by the mercy; *prāptam* — achieved; *eva* — indeed; *iti* — thus; *manyatām* — please understand.

**Please understand, O best of Mathurā brāhmaṇas: Just like me you have already fully achieved your goal, by the mercy of the divine goddess.**

COMMENTARY: Sarūpa's disciple, on the verge of perfection, has yet to realize the glories of Goloka directly, but soon he will. Instead of trying to explain more about those glories, his *guru* advises that he merely be patient and soon he will see everything with his own eyes.

## TEXT 3

वर्तते चावशिष्टं यद् भूतप्रायं च विद्धि तत् ।
वीक्षे कृपाभरं तस्य व्यक्तं भगवतस्त्वयि ॥

*vartate cāvaśiṣṭaṁ yad*
*bhūta-prāyaṁ ca viddhi tat*
*vīkṣe kṛpā-bharaṁ tasya*
*vyaktaṁ bhagavatas tvayi*

*vartate* — there is; *ca* — and; *avaśiṣṭam* — the remainder; *yat* — which; *bhūta-prāyam* — nearly manifest; *ca* — and; *viddhi* — know; *tat* — that; *vīkṣe* — I see; *kṛpā-bharam* — the complete mercy; *tasya* — of Him; *vyaktam* — visible; *bhagavataḥ* — of the Supreme Lord; *tvayi* — on you.

**Whatever is left for you to achieve, you have already nearly attained. Please know this. I can see that the Supreme Lord has bestowed upon you His full mercy.**

COMMENTARY: "But visible signs of perfection have not yet appeared in me," the *brāhmaṇa* might humbly assert. Here Sarūpa disagrees. Śrī Golokanātha has already singled the *brāhmaṇa* out as a recipient of His full mercy.

## TEXT 4

पश्य यच्चात्मनस्तस्य तदीयानामपि ध्रुवम् ।
वृत्तं परमगोप्यं तत्सर्वं ते कथितं मया ॥

*paśya yac cātmanas tasya*
*tadīyānām api dhruvam*
*vṛttaṁ parama-gopyaṁ tat*
*sarvaṁ te kathitaṁ mayā*

*paśya* — please see; *yat* — what; *ca* — and; *ātmanaḥ* — to myself; *tasya* — to Him; *tadīyānām* — to His devotees; *api* — and; *dhruvam* — indeed; *vṛttam* — occurred; *parama* — extremely; *gopyam* — confidential; *tat* — that; *sarvam* — all; *te* — to you; *kathitam* — told; *mayā* — by me.

**Just see! I have indeed told you everything that happened to me, and to the Lord, and to His devotees, even though these topics are most confidential.**

## TEXTS 5–7

निजभावविशेषश्च भगवच्चरणाश्रयः ।
न प्रकाशयितुं योग्यो ह्रिया स्वमनसेऽपि यः ॥

जाते दशाविशेषे च वृत्तं स्वपरविस्मृतेः ।
विशेषज्ञानराहित्यान्नानुभूतं यदात्मना ॥

तत्तत्सर्वमिदं तेन कृष्णेनाविश्य मे हृदि ।
निःसारितमिवायातं बलाद्वक्त्रे त्वदग्रतः ॥

*nija-bhāva-viśeṣaś ca*
*bhagavac-caraṇāśrayaḥ*
*na prakāśayituṁ yogyo*
*hriyā sva-manase 'pi yaḥ*

*jāte daśā-viśeṣe ca*
*vṛttaṁ sva-para-vismṛteḥ*
*viśeṣa-jñāna-rāhityān*
*nānubhūtaṁ yad ātmanā*

*tat tat sarvam idaṁ tena*
*kṛṣṇenāviśya me hṛdi*
*niḥsāritam ivāyātaṁ*
*balād vaktre tvad-agrataḥ*

*nija* — one's own; *bhāva* — mood; *viśeṣaḥ* — special; *ca* — and; *bhagavat* — of the Supreme Lord; *caraṇa* — of the lotus feet; *āśrayaḥ* — the shelter; *na* — not; *prakāśayitum* — to reveal; *yogyaḥ* — proper; *hriyā* — out of shyness; *sva-manase* — to one's own mind; *api* — even; *yaḥ* — which; *jāte* — when it has developed; *daśā* — a condition; *viśeṣe* — special; *ca* — and; *vṛttam* — what occurred; *sva* — of myself; *para* — and of others; *vismṛteḥ* — because of forgetting; *viśeṣa* — particular; *jñāna* — of awareness; *rāhityāt* — because of the absence; *na* — not; *anubhūtam* — experienced; *yat* — what; *ātmanā* — by myself; *tat* — that; *tat* — that; *sarvam* — all; *idam* — this; *tena* — by Him; *kṛṣṇena* — Kṛṣṇa; *āviśya* — entering; *me* — my; *hṛdi* — heart; *niḥsāritam* — made to come out; *iva* — as if; *āyātam* — come; *balāt* — by force; *vaktre* — into the mouth; *tvat* — your; *agrataḥ* — in the presence.

**The special ecstasies one relishes in the shelter of the Personality of Godhead's lotus feet are private. One should feel shy to reveal them, even to one's own mind. And sometimes I entered special states of consciousness in which I could no longer recognize myself or others, nor distinguish one thing from the next, and so there were events I didn't see. Yet Kṛṣṇa, in your presence, has entered my heart and brought all these topics out, forcing them to come from my mouth.**

COMMENTARY: A spiritual master can certainly reveal even the most secret knowledge to a faithful, deserving disciple. The Mathurā *brāhmaṇa,* before hearing his *guru's* personal history, was a raw neophyte, and Sarūpa was at different times too distracted by ecstasy to perceive clearly what was going on and so had difficulty recounting some of the events of his spiritual journey.

But despite all this and despite Sarūpa's reluctance, Kṛṣṇa forced the whole story from Sarūpa's mouth.

TEXT 8

भवतश्चात्र विश्वासो नितरां समपद्यत ।
लक्षणैर्लक्षितश्चायं मया शीघ्रफलप्रदः ॥

*bhavataś cātra viśvāso*
*nitarāṁ samapadyata*
*lakṣaṇair lakṣitaś cāyaṁ*
*mayā śīghra-phala-pradaḥ*

*bhavataḥ* — of your good self; *ca* — and; *atra* — here; *viśvāsaḥ* — faith; *nitarām* — especially; *samapadyata* — has arisen; *lakṣaṇaiḥ* — from signs; *lakṣitaḥ* — noticed; *ca* — and; *ayam* — this (faith); *mayā* — by me; *śīghra* — soon; *phala-pradaḥ* — bestowing the benefits.

**I have noted clear signs that you have gained strong faith in these topics, a faith that will soon bestow upon you all its rewards.**

COMMENTARY: The disposition of another's heart is difficult to read, but an elevated person with clear intelligence can discern from one's gestures where one's faith lies. From the satisfied expressions on the *brāhmaṇa's* face, Sarūpa knew, "This disciple has developed confidence in the truth of my story." In other words, Sarūpa's mission had achieved success. Once strong faith in the transcendental reality is established, one's spiritual practice very quickly bears fruit.

TEXT 9

स्वयं श्रीराधिका देवी प्रातरद्यादिदेश माम् ।
सरूपायाति मत्कुञ्जे मद्भक्तो माथुरो द्विजः ॥

*svayaṁ śrī-rādhikā devī*
*prātar adyādideśa mām*
*sarūpāyāti mat-kuñje*
*mad-bhakto māthuro dvijaḥ*

*svayam* — Herself; *śrī-rādhikā devī* — Śrī Rādhikā-devī; *prātaḥ* — early in the morning; *adya* — today; *ādideśa* — ordered; *mām* — me; *sarūpa* — O Sarūpa; *āyāti* — is coming; *mat* — My; *kuñje* — to the grove; *mat* — My; *bhaktaḥ* — devotee; *māthuraḥ* — of Mathurā; *dvijaḥ* — a *brāhmaṇa.*

**Early this morning Śrī Rādhikā-devī Herself came and ordered me: "Sarūpa, a brāhmaṇa from Mathurā who is My devotee is coming to My grove.**

COMMENTARY: The Mathurā *brāhmaṇa* considered himself a devotee of Durgā, but she is a partial expansion of Śrī Rādhikā, Lord Madana-gopāla's eternal consort.

TEXT 10

तत्रैकाकी त्वमद्यादौ गत्वा सदुपदेशतः ।
प्रबोध्याश्वास्य तं कृष्णप्रसादं प्रापय द्रुतम् ॥

*tatraikākī tvam adyādau*
*gatvā sad-upadeśataḥ*
*prabodhyāśvāsya taṁ kṛṣṇa-*
*prasādaṁ prāpaya drutam*

*tatra* — there; *ekaikī* — alone; *tvam* — you; *adya* — today; *ādau* — first of all; *gatvā* — going; *sat* — good; *upadeśataḥ* — by instructions; *prabodhya* — enlightening; *āśvāsya* — consoling; *tam* — him; *kṛṣṇa* — of Kṛṣṇa; *prasādam* — the grace; *prāpaya* — cause him to attain; *drutam* — quickly.

**"Go there alone, the first thing today. Enlighten him with good instructions, console him, and help him quickly attain Kṛṣṇa's grace."**

COMMENTARY: Had Sarūpa not awakened the *brāhmaṇa's* higher intelligence, the *brāhmaṇa* would not have obtained Śrī Kṛṣṇa's favor.

## TEXT 11

अस्मात्तस्याः समादेशाच्छीघ्रमत्राहमागतः ।
न प्रहर्षादपेक्षे स्म कृष्णसङ्गसुखं च तत् ॥

*asmāt tasyāḥ samādeśāc*
*chīghram atrāham āgataḥ*
*na praharṣād apekṣe sma*
*kṛṣṇa-saṅga-sukhaṁ ca tat*

*asmāt* — on the basis of this; *tasyāḥ* — Her; *samādeśāt* — instruction; *śīghram* — swiftly; *atra* — here; *aham* — I; *āgataḥ* — came; *na* — not; *praharṣāt* — due to joy; *apekṣe sma* — I thought of; *kṛṣṇa-saṅga* — of Kṛṣṇa's company; *sukham* — enjoyment; *ca* — and; *tat* — that.

**On Her instruction I swiftly came here, overjoyed, without even a thought about missing the enjoyment of Kṛṣṇa's company.**

COMMENTARY: To carry out his assignment, Sarūpa left home early in the morning, before Kṛṣṇa went out to the forest with His friends. Sarūpa did not mind missing Kṛṣṇa's company for one day, because he knew that carrying out Śrī Rādhā's order would endear him to Kṛṣṇa — and this would surely increase the happiness he enjoyed with Kṛṣṇa.

## TEXT 12

श्रीपरीक्षिदुवाच
एवमुक्तेऽपि विप्रस्य तस्य हि प्रेमसम्पदः ।
उदयादर्शनान्मूर्ध्नि सरूपः करमर्पयत् ॥

*śrī-parīkṣid uvāca*
*evam ukte 'pi viprasya*
*tasya hi prema-sampadaḥ*
*udayādarśanān mūrdhni*
*sarūpaḥ karam arpayat*

*śrī-parīkṣit uvāca* — Śrī Parīkṣit said; *evam* — thus; *ukte* — spoken to; *api* — even; *viprasya* — of the *brāhmaṇa; tasya* — his; *hi* — indeed; *prema-sampadaḥ* — of the treasure of pure love; *udaya* — the awakening; *adarśanāt* — because of not seeing; *mūrdhni* — on his head; *sarūpaḥ* — Sarūpa; *karam* — his hand; *arpayat* — placed.

**Śrī Parīkṣit said: When Sarūpa saw that the brāhmaṇa, even after spoken to in this way, had not awakened to the treasure of pure love, Sarūpa put his hand on the brāhmaṇa's head.**

TEXT 13

सद्यस्तस्यास्फुरच्चित्ते स्वानुभूतमिवाखिलम् ।
श्रीसरूपानुभूतं यत्कृपया तन्महात्मनः ॥

*sadyas tasyāsphurac citte*
*svānubhūtam ivākhilam*
*śrī-sarūpānubhūtaṁ yat*
*kṛpayā tan mahātmanaḥ*

*sadyaḥ* — immediately; *tasya* — his; *asphurat* — became manifest; *citte* — in the heart; *sva-anubhūtam* — experienced for himself; *iva* — as if; *akhilam* — all; *śrī-sarūpa* — of Śrī Sarūpa; *anubhūtam* — the experience; *yat* — which; *kṛpayā* — by the mercy; *tat* — that; *mahā-ātmanaḥ* — of the great soul.

**By the mercy of the great soul Sarūpa, everything Sarūpa had experienced became manifest at once in the brāhmaṇa's heart, as if the brāhmaṇa had experienced it himself.**

## TEXT 14

महत्सङ्गममाहात्म्यमेवैतत्परमाद्भुतम् ।
कृतार्थो येन विप्रोऽसौ सद्योऽभूत्तत्स्वरूपवत् ॥

*mahat-saṅgama-māhātmyam*
*evaitat paramādbhutam*
*kṛtārtho yena vipro 'sau*
*sadyo 'bhūt tat-svarūpa-vat*

*mahat* — with a great soul; *saṅgama* — of association; *māhātmyam* — the greatness; *eva* — indeed; *etat* — this; *parama-adbhutam* — supremely amazing; *kṛta-arthaḥ* — successful; *yena* — by which; *vipraḥ* — the *brāhmaṇa; asau* — he; *sadyaḥ* — suddenly; *abhūt* — became; *tat* — his; *svarūpa-vat* — realizing the true identity.

**Such are the most amazing glories of contact with a great saint. By that contact, this brāhmaṇa suddenly achieved perfection, realizing his eternal identity.**

COMMENTARY: Usually, only the Lord's most qualified devotees attain pure love of God, after long endeavor for the Lord's special mercy. How then could this *brāhmaṇa* have achieved *prema* so quickly? Only by coming into contact with a powerful saint. The *brāhmaṇa's* own efforts alone would have been of no avail. His success was possible by the unique glories of Vaiṣṇava association, incomprehensible to material minds.

In *Śrīmad-Bhāgavatam* (3.23.55) Śrī Devahūti remarks:

*saṅgo yaḥ saṁsṛter hetur*
*asatsu vihito 'dhiyā*
*sa eva sādhuṣu kṛto*
*niḥsaṅgatvāya kalpate*

"Association to gratify the senses is certainly the path of bondage. But the same type of association, performed with a saintly person, leads to the path of liberation, even if performed without knowledge."

When an ignorant person mixes with other degraded persons, the result is entanglement in material existence, in the enjoyment of food, drink, sex, and so on. But the company of pure souls, even if entered into with the same ignorance, enables one to become *niḥsaṅga,* free in two ways: detached from matter and uplifted to pure love of God. *Prema* is a form of detachment because it shuns all pursuits other than the attempt to please the Personality of Godhead. Therefore, as stated in the *Yoga-vāsiṣṭha-rāmāyaṇa:*

*sadā santo 'bhigantavyā*
*yady apy upadiśanti na*
*yā hi svaira-kathās teṣāṁ*
*upadeśā bhavanti te*

*śūnyam āpūrṇatām eti*
*mṛtir apy amṛtāyate*
*āpat sampad ivābhāti*
*vidvaj-jana-samāgamāt*

"In all circumstances, one should approach saintly persons. Even if one receives no teachings, spontaneous dialogue with them imparts valuable lessons. When one approaches persons who have real knowledge, emptiness overflows with fullness, death becomes immortal nectar, and disasters can seem like good fortune."

In *Śrīmad-Bhāgavatam* (3.7.19) Śrī Vidura says:

*yat-sevayā bhagavataḥ*
*kūṭa-sthasya madhu-dviṣaḥ*
*rati-rāso bhavet tīvraḥ*
*pādayor vyasanārdanaḥ*

"By serving the feet of the spiritual master, one develops transcendental ecstasy in the service of the Personality of Godhead, who is the unchangeable enemy of the Madhu demon and whose service vanquishes one's material distresses."

Vidura here speaks to his *śikṣā-guru,* Maitreya Muni. By serving Maitreya, Vidura expects to obtain the service of the Supreme Lord, who is difficult to understand but whom one can approach by serving His pure devotees. The Supreme Person is *kūṭa-stha,* which means both "unchanging" and "inconceivable." He is also *kūṭa-stha* in the sense that He is famous for being offered *anna-kūṭa,* a mountain of food, while standing on a special peak — that of Govardhana. At the lotus feet of Kṛṣṇa, the enemy of the demon Madhu, a sincere servant of the Vaiṣṇavas can obtain *rati-rāsa,* a never-ending festival of *prema,* from which comes an enjoyment so intense (*tīvra*) that nothing can impede or interrupt it. Material existence is full of various miseries, but devotional service at Lord Kṛṣṇa's lotus feet (*pādayoḥ*) eradicates them all (*vyasanārdanaḥ*). Or if we take *pādayoḥ* to modify *vyasanārdanaḥ,* the meaning of the two words together is "that which destroys the pain felt by the feet." Kṛṣṇa's *rāsa-līlā* is mostly a festival of dancing, and dancing means moving the feet. By entering the *rāsa* dance one's feet will be relieved of the distress they feel from doing other things.

As Śrī Kapiladeva tells His mother:

*satāṁ prasaṅgān mama vīrya-saṁvido*
*bhavanti hṛt-karṇa-rasāyanāḥ kathāḥ*
*taj-joṣaṇād āśv apavarga-vartmani*
*śraddhā ratir bhaktir anukramiṣyati*

"In the association of pure devotees, discussion of the pastimes of the Supreme Personality of Godhead is very pleasing and satisfying to the ear and the heart. By cultivating knowledge of the Lord's activities one gradually becomes advanced on the path of liberation, and thereafter one is freed, and one's attraction becomes fixed. Then real devotion and devotional service begin." (*Bhāgavatam* 3.25.25)

Here Lord Kapiladeva mentions three symptoms of the gradual development of *prema:* firm conviction (*śraddhā*), love for the Lord (*rati*), and unswerving dedication to His service (*bhakti*). In the course of devotional advancement, each of these symptoms becomes manifest naturally, without separate endeavor. Lord Kapiladeva does not intend to say that the sequence of development is literally *śraddhā,* then *rati,* and then *bhakti.* Rather, we should understand that first a new devotee acquires faith (*śraddhā*), then takes up the process of *bhakti* by hearing, chanting, and serving, and later achieves *rati.* Because *bhakti* means both the practice of devotional service and the mature stage of spontaneous love, to say that *rati* (*prema*) is the fruit of *bhakti* is correct.

With this same concept of *bhakti* in mind, Śrī Dhruva prays to Lord Viṣṇu:

*bhaktiṁ muhuḥ pravahatāṁ tvayi me prasaṅgo*
*bhūyād ananta mahatām amalāśayānām*
*yenāñjasolbaṇam uru-vyasanaṁ bhavābdhiṁ*
*neṣye bhavad-guṇa-kathāmṛta-pāna-mattaḥ*

"O unlimited Lord, kindly bless me so that I may associate with great devotees who engage in Your transcendental loving service constantly, as the waves of a river constantly flow. Such transcendental devotees are completely situated in an uncontaminated state of life. By the process of devotional service, surely I will be able to cross the nescient ocean of material existence, which is filled with the waves of blazing, firelike dangers. It will be very easy for me, for I am becoming mad to hear about Your transcendental qualities and pastimes, which are eternally existent." (*Bhāgavatam* 4.9.11)

Because the devotees of Viṣṇu serve Him constantly (*bhaktiṁ muhuḥ pravahatām*), their hearts are completely pure (*amalāśayānām*), and for that reason they are exalted souls (*mahatām*). The association of such Vaiṣṇavas is extremely desirable. One who achieves it need not bother aspiring for the fourth goal of life, liberation, for liberation comes automatically as a by-product of pure devotion. Dhruva anticipates that in the company of Vaiṣṇavas he will drink the nectar of topics about the Supreme Lord, which will intoxicate him and empower him to cross effortlessly the dangerous ocean of *saṁsāra*. Drunkards are mainly interested in the taste of their liquor; they have only a superficial interest in the secondary effects of alcohol, such as its ability to ease the discomfort of cold weather. In the same way, devotees who have a taste for drinking the nectar of *bhagavad-bhakti* consider relishing that elixir forever their principal goal. They accept liberation and other secondary benefits only when such boons do not obstruct that eternal delight.

In *Śrīmad-Bhāgavatam* (4.24.57–58) Lord Śiva gives this opinion:

*kṣaṇārdhenāpi tulaye*
*na svargaṁ nāpunar-bhavam*
*bhagavat-saṅgi-saṅgasya*
*martyānāṁ kim utāśiṣaḥ*

*athānaghāṅghres tava kīrti-tīrthayor*
*antar-bahiḥ-snāna-vidhūta-pāpmanām*
*bhūteṣv anukrośa-susattva-śīlināṁ*
*syāt saṅgamo 'nugraha eṣa nas tava*

"If one by chance associates with a devotee, even for a fraction of a moment, one is no longer subject to attraction by the results of *karma* or *jñāna*. What interest then can he have in the benedictions of the demigods, who are subject to the laws of birth and death? My dear Lord, Your lotus feet are the cause of all auspicious things and the destroyer of all the contamination of sin. I therefore beg Your Lordship to bless me with the association of Your devotees, who are completely purified by worshiping Your lotus feet and who are so merciful upon the conditioned souls. I think that Your real benediction will be to allow me to associate with such devotees."

Rather than liberation, what to speak of royal power and the other kinds of success that ordinary people value, Lord Śiva would prefer even a moment's association with those who keep company with the Personality of Godhead. In other words, the company of the Supreme Lord's devotees dances on the heads of all other goals of life. The lotus feet of the Supreme Lord, who killed the demon named Agha, remove all sin. The Lord's fame is the source of all holy *tīrthas,* including the river Gaṅgā and also the river Yamunā, whose bathing *ghāṭas* the *gopīs* approach to fetch water. Lord Śiva takes two purifying baths — one externally in the Gaṅgā and the other internally in the Yamunā. Similarly, a bath in the Supreme Lord's fame purifies His devotees in two ways, externally by absolving them from hellish punishment and internally by cleansing their hearts of desires for material enjoyment. Persons dedicated to the fame of the Supreme Lord, and to His lotus feet, are merciful to all creatures. Such devotees always live purely, devoid of lust and other contaminations of the heart, and they have simplicity and all other exemplary qualities. Lord Śiva prays that Lord Viṣṇu's greatest mercy on him would be simply to let him come in touch with the Supreme Lord's devotees.

In the Fifth Canto (5.12.12–13) Śrī Jaḍa Bharata speaks likewise:

*rahūgaṇaitat tapasā na yāti*
*na cejyayā nirvapaṇād gṛhād vā*
*na cchandasā naiva jalāgni-sūryair*
*vinā mahat-pāda-rajo-'bhiṣekam*

"My dear King Rahūgaṇa, unless one has the opportunity to smear his entire body with the dust of the lotus feet of great devotees, one cannot realize the Absolute Truth. One cannot realize the Absolute Truth simply by observing celibacy [*brahmacarya*], by strictly following the rules and regulations of householder life, by leaving home as a *vānaprastha,* by accepting *sannyāsa,* or by undergoing severe penances in winter by keeping oneself submerged in water or in summer by surrounding oneself by fire and the scorching heat of the sun. There are many other processes to understand the Absolute Truth, but the Absolute Truth is revealed only to one who has attained the mercy of a great devotee.

*yatrottamaḥ-śloka-guṇānuvādaḥ*
*prastūyate grāmya-kathā-vighātaḥ*
*niṣevyamāṇo 'nu-dinaṁ mumukṣor*
*matiṁ satīṁ yacchati vāsudeve*

"Who are the pure devotees mentioned here? In an assembly of pure devotees, there is no question of discussing material subjects like politics and sociology. In an assembly of pure devotees, there is discussion only of the qualities, forms, and pastimes of the Supreme Personality of Godhead, who is praised and worshiped with full attention. In the association of pure devotees, by constantly hearing such topics respectfully, even a person who wants to merge into the existence of the Absolute Truth abandons this idea and gradually becomes attached to the service of Vāsudeva."

In the verse just before the two quoted here, Jaḍa Bharata identified the Absolute Truth as Bhagavān, the Personality of Godhead, and as Vāsudeva, the darling son of Vasudeva. Now he tells King Rahūgaṇa that this Supreme Person is impossible to achieve by any of the usual methods of spiritual advancement unless, along with those methods, one bathes in dust from the feet of pure Vaiṣṇavas. It is not enough to follow the prescribed duties of one's *varṇa* and *āśrama,* concentrate one's mind in one-pointed *tapas,* execute Vedic sacrifices, distribute food and other charity, work piously as a householder, study the *Vedas,* or worship water, fire, the other elements of nature, and their presiding deities — Varuṇa, Agni, and so on. These efforts may help one achieve the favor of Lord Vāsudeva only when the *sādhaka* has also pleased the Lord's devotees. And by satisfying the devotees one can win the mercy of the Supreme Lord even if one has not performed any of these purifying acts.

Lord Kṛṣṇa is known as Uttama-śloka, He whose spotless fame drives away all ignorance. When one has bathed in the dust of the feet of His devotees, one can enter the company of those devotees and hear from them about Kṛṣṇa's transcendental qualities, beginning with His incessant kindness toward His devotees. Hearing day after day this pure *kṛṣṇa-kathā* raises a materialist to the level of an aspirant for liberation, and such an aspirant to the level of sincere interest in devotional service to Kṛṣṇa.

In the same narration, Rahūgaṇa replies to Jaḍa Bharata:

*aho nṛ-janmākhila-janma-śobhanaṁ*
*kiṁ janmabhis tv aparair apy amuṣmin*
*na yad dhṛṣīkeśa-yaśaḥ-kṛtātmanāṁ*
*mahātmanāṁ vaḥ pracuraḥ samāgamaḥ*

"This birth as a human being on earth is the best of all. Even birth among the demigods in the heavenly planets is not as glorious. What is the use of the exalted position of a demigod? In the heavenly planets, due to profuse material comforts, there is no possibility of associating with devotees." (*Bhāgavatam* 5.13.21)

Human life is the most congenial situation for becoming attracted to *bhagavad-bhakti*. Demigod life may be desirable to foolish people, but great saints like Jaḍa Bharata rarely even visit the heavenly planets. The demigods, being too much absorbed in sense gratification, generally do not deserve the company of such pure Vaiṣṇavas. Rather than travel to heaven, saintly Vaiṣṇavas who keep their hearts cleansed by contemplating the glories of Lord Hṛṣīkeśa usually prefer to wander among the holy places on earth.

In the opinion of Śrī Prahlāda Mahārāja:

*naiṣāṁ matis tāvad urukramāṅghriṁ*
*spṛśaty anarthāpagamo yad-arthaḥ*
*mahīyasāṁ pāda-rajo-'bhiṣekaṁ*
*niṣkiñcanānāṁ na vṛṇīta yāvat*

"Unless persons very much inclined toward materialistic life smear upon their bodies the dust of the lotus feet of a Vaiṣṇava completely freed from material contamination, such persons cannot be attached to the lotus feet of the Lord, who is glorified for His uncommon activities. Only by becoming Kṛṣṇa conscious and taking shelter at the lotus feet of the Lord in this way can one be freed from material contamination." (*Bhāgavatam* 7.5.32)

Just before Prahlāda made this statement, he expressed concern for the ignorant materialists of this world, who cannot recognize that the best goal for their own self-interest is Lord Viṣṇu. Such gross materialists must bathe in the foot-dust of pure Vaiṣṇavas who reject all forms of selfish enjoyment and care about nothing but *bhagavad-bhakti,* for otherwise the minds of such gross materialists can never shift toward devotional service to the Lord. Without the mercy of great devotees, foolish materialists cannot ascertain spiritual truth even theoretically, what to speak of reap its tangible fruits.

In the words of King Mucukunda:

*bhavāpavargo bhramato yadā bhavej*
*janasya tarhy acyuta sat-samāgamaḥ*
*sat-saṅgamo yarhi tadaiva sad-gatau*
*parāvareśe tvayi jāyate ratiḥ*

"When the material life of a wandering soul has come to an end, O Acyuta, he may attain the association of Your devotees. And when he associates with them, there awakens within him devotion unto You, who are the goal of the devotees and the Lord of all causes and effects." (*Bhāgavatam* 10.51.53)

Conditioned souls wander aimlessly in the cycle of birth and death, and only after they have become fed up with this wandering are they allowed to come in touch with pure Vaiṣṇavas. Then, by the company of saintly Vaiṣṇavas, a few of those fortunate souls are not only released from the cycle of birth and death (*saṁsāra*) but also given something much more precious — pure love for the supreme controller of all causes and effects. And if they are not fortunate enough to achieve intimate love for the Supreme Lord, at least they learn how to reverentially serve Him, the ruler of all great demigods and ordinary creatures.

These opinions are confirmed by Lord Kṛṣṇa Himself in the Eleventh Canto of *Śrīmad-Bhāgavatam* (11.26.31–34):

*yathopaśrayamāṇasya*
*bhagavantaṁ vibhāvasum*

*śītaṁ bhayaṁ tamo 'pyeti*
*sādhūn saṁsevatas tathā*

"Just as cold, fear, and darkness are eradicated for one who has approached the sacrificial fire, so dullness, fear, and ignorance are destroyed for one engaged in serving the devotees of the Lord.

*nimajjyonmajjatāṁ ghore*
*bhavābdhau paramāyaṇam*
*santo brahma-vidaḥ śāntā*
*naur dṛḍhevāpsu majjatām*

"The devotees of the Lord, peacefully fixed in absolute knowledge, are the ultimate shelter for those who are repeatedly rising and falling within the fearful ocean of material life. The devotees are just like a strong boat that comes to rescue persons at the point of drowning.

*annaṁ hi prāṇināṁ prāṇa*
*ārtānāṁ śaraṇaṁ tv aham*
*dharmo vittaṁ nṛṇāṁ pretya*
*santo 'rvāg bibhyato 'raṇam*

"Just as food is the life of all creatures, just as I am the ultimate shelter for the distressed, and just as religion is the wealth of those who are passing away from this world, My devotees are the only refuge of persons fearful of falling into a miserable condition of life.

*santo diśanti cakṣūṁsi*
*bahir arkaḥ samutthitaḥ*
*devatā bāndhavāḥ santaḥ*
*santa ātmāham eva ca*

"My devotees bestow divine eyes, whereas the sun allows only external sight, and that only when risen in the sky. My devotees are one's real worshipable deities and real family; they are one's own self, and ultimately they are nondifferent from Me."

Just as by approaching fire one can get relief from darkness and fear of snakes and wild animals, by approaching pure Vaiṣṇavas one can be freed from the darkness of materialistic life, from fear of what will happen in the future, and from forgetfulness of blissful service to the Lord, a forgetfulness that underlies all material ignorance and fear.

The prefix *upa-* in the verse beginning *yathopa-śrayamāṇasya* (that is, *yathā upa-śrayamāṇasya*) indicates the idea of approaching from a distance. This implies that one can gain the blessings of Vaiṣṇavas by serving them even in separation. Saintly Vaiṣṇavas who understand the Absolute Truth as He appears in Vraja-dhāma can deliver persons entrapped in the cycle of higher and lower births. The Vaiṣṇavas are qualified to give such a priceless gift because they have realized the glories of Kṛṣṇa's devotional service, which is the confidential essence of the Vedic teachings. Such devotees, peaceful and unagitated even by the prospect of being liberated, bestow upon fortunate souls various types of spiritual vision — realization of the impersonal and personal features of the Absolute Truth and discernment of the many different modes of *bhagavad-bhakti*. The external sun, in contrast, gives light, but only in a limited way.

Rather than attempt to enumerate all the glories of Vaiṣṇavas — an impossible task — we should know that a single saintly devotee equals all the demigods combined. Pure devotees are our real friends and our own dear soul, the source of our life. In fact, in Kṛṣṇa's opinion the Vaiṣṇavas are nondifferent from Himself.

Earlier in *Śrīmad-Bhāgavatam* (11.11.49) Kṛṣṇa said to Uddhava, "Now I will tell you something especially confidential because you are My servant, well-wisher, and companion." Kṛṣṇa then said:

*na rodhayati māṁ yogo*
*na sāṅkhyaṁ dharma eva ca*
*na svādhyāyas tapas tyāgo*
*neṣṭā-pūrtaṁ na dakṣiṇā*

*vratāni yajñaś chandāṁsi*
*tīrthāni niyamā yamāḥ*
*yathāvarundhe sat-saṅgaḥ*
*sarva-saṅgāpaho hi mām*

"My dear Uddhava, by associating with My pure devotees one can destroy one's attachment for all objects of material sense gratification. Such purifying association brings Me under one's control. One may perform the *aṣṭāṅga-yoga* system, engage in philosophical analysis of the elements of material nature, practice nonviolence and other ordinary principles of piety, or chant the *Vedas*. One may perform penances, take to the renounced order of life, execute sacrificial performances, and dig wells, plant trees, and perform other public-welfare activities. One may give charity, carry out severe vows, worship the demigods, chant confidential *mantras,* visit holy places, or accept major and minor disciplinary injunctions. But even by performing such activities one does not bring Me under one's control." (*Bhāgavatam* 11.12.1–2)

The first and second steps of Patañjali Ṛṣi's *aṣṭāṅga-yoga* method are the twelve *niyamas* ("minor regulations") and twelve *yamas* ("major regulations"). Śrī Kṛṣṇa lists these for Uddhava:

*ahiṁsā satyam asteyam*
*asaṅgo hrīr asañcayaḥ*
*āstikyaṁ brahmacaryaṁ ca*
*maunaṁ sthairyaṁ kṣamābhayam*

*śaucaṁ japas tapo homaḥ*
*śraddhātithyaṁ mad-arcanam*
*tīrthāṭanaṁ parārthehā*
*tuṣṭir ācārya-sevanam*

*ete yamāḥ sa-niyamā*
*ubhayor dvādaśa smṛtāḥ*
*puṁsām upāsitās tāta*
*yathā-kāmaṁ duhanti hi*

"Nonviolence; truthfulness; unwillingness to covet or steal the property of others; detachment; humility; freedom from possessiveness; trust in the principles of religion; celibacy; silence; steadiness; forgiveness; and fearlessness are the twelve primary disciplinary principles. Internal cleanliness; external cleanliness; chanting the holy names of the Lord; austerity; sacrifice; faith; hospitality; worship of Me; visiting holy places; acting for and desiring only the supreme interest; satisfaction; and service to the spiritual master are the twelve elements of regular prescribed duties. These twenty-four elements bestow all desired benedictions upon those persons who devotedly cultivate them." (*Bhāgavatam* 11.19.33–35)

The company of exalted Vaiṣṇavas counteracts not only material attachment but also attachment to the Supreme Lord's pastimes in Vaikuṇṭha and abodes other than Goloka. What to speak of the power of direct contact with Vaiṣṇavas, even hearing descriptions of their greatness leads to the highest success, as Śrī Vidura states in the Third Canto of *Śrīmad-Bhāgavatam* (3.13.4):

*śrutasya puṁsāṁ sucira-śramasya*
*nanv añjasā sūribhir īḍito 'rthaḥ*
*tat-tad-guṇānuśravaṇaṁ mukunda-*
*pādāravindaṁ hṛdayeṣu yeṣām*

"Persons who hear from a spiritual master with great labor and for a long time must hear from his mouth about the character and activities of pure devotees, who always think within their hearts of the lotus feet of Mukunda, the Personality of Godhead, He who awards them liberation."

In the Fourth Canto (4.9.10) Dhruva Mahārāja makes a similar statement:

*yā nirvṛtis tanu-bhṛtāṁ tava pāda-padma-*
*dhyānād bhavaj-jana-kathā-śravaṇena vā syāt*
*sā brahmaṇi sva-mahimany api nātha mā bhūt*
*kiṁ v antakāsi-lulitāt patatāṁ vimānāt*

"My Lord, the transcendental bliss derived from meditating upon Your lotus feet or hearing about the glories of Your pure devotees is so unlimited that it is far beyond the stage of *brahmānanda,* wherein one thinks himself merged in the impersonal Brahman as one with the Supreme. Since *brahmānanda* is also defeated by the transcendental bliss derived from devotional service, then what to speak of the temporary bliss of elevating oneself to the heavenly planets, which is ended by the separating sword of time? Although one may be elevated to the heavenly planets, he falls down in due course of time."

And not only is complete success in life guaranteed by any contact with the Supreme Lord's devotees, but even the company of the devotee of His devotees is enough to assure perfection. Thus Dhruva Mahārāja says:

*te na smaranty atitarāṁ priyam īśa martyaṁ*
*ye cānv adaḥ suta-suhṛd-gṛha-vitta-dārāḥ*
*ye tv abja-nābha bhavadīya-padāravinda-*
*saugandhya-lubdha-hṛdayeṣu kṛta-prasaṅgāḥ*

"O Lord who have a lotus navel, if a person happens to associate with someone whose heart hankers after the lotus feet of Your devotees — whose heart always seeks the fragrance of those lotus feet — he is never attached to the material body or, in a bodily relationship, to offspring, friends, home, wealth, and wife, which are very, very dear to materialistic persons. Indeed, he does not care for them." (*Bhāgavatam* 4.9.12)

Unlike anyone else, including the impersonalist *yogī,* the advanced devotees who have pure love for the Supreme Lord's lotus feet are completely free from the falsity of identifying themselves with the body. In the words of Lord Viṣṇu's Haṁsa incarnation (*Bhāgavatam* 11.13.36):

*dehaṁ ca naśvaram avasthitam utthitaṁ vā*
*siddho na paśyati yato 'dhyagamat svarūpam*
*daivād apetam atha daiva-vaśād upetaṁ*
*vāso yathā parihitaṁ madirā-madāndhaḥ*

"Just as a drunken man doesn't notice whether or not he is wearing his coat or shirt, one who is perfect in self-realization and has thus achieved his eternal identity doesn't notice whether the temporary body is sitting or standing. Indeed, if by God's will the body is finished or by God's will he obtains a new body, a self-realized soul doesn't notice, just as a drunken man doesn't notice the situation of his outward dress."

Lord Ṛṣabhadeva describes the characteristics of great devotees:

*mahāntas te sama-cittāḥ praśāntā*
*vimanyavaḥ suhṛdaḥ sādhavo ye*

"The *mahātmās* are equipoised. They see no difference between one living entity and another. They are very peaceful, fully engaged in devotional service, and devoid of anger, and they work for the benefit of all. They do not behave in any abominable way.

*ye vā mayīśe kṛta-sauhṛdārthā*
*janeṣu deham-bhara-vārtikeṣu*
*gṛheṣu jāyātmaja-rātimatsu*
*na prīti-yuktā yāvad-arthāś ca loke*

"Those who are interested in reviving Kṛṣṇa consciousness and increasing their love of Godhead do not like to do anything that is not related to Kṛṣṇa. They are not interested in mingling with people who are busy maintaining their bodies — eating, sleeping, mating, and defending. They are not attached to their homes, although they may be householders. Nor are they attached to wives, children, friends, or wealth. At the same time, they are not indifferent to the execution of their duties. Such people are interested in collecting only enough money to keep the body and soul together." (*Bhāgavatam* 5.5.2–3)

Because *mahātmās* are free from the material agitations of love and hate, they maintain an equal disposition toward friends, enemies, and neutral parties. In other words, the great souls are peaceful. This peacefulness is due to their being free from anger, this freedom is due to their being causeless benefactors of everyone, and this benefaction is due to their being firmly committed to saintly behavior. Their aim in life is to become trustworthy friends of the Personality of Godhead. Concentrating exclusively on that goal, they take no pleasure in being with persons who, instead of pursuing the higher interests of spiritual life, are interested only in maintaining their bodies. The *mahātmās,* rather, expend as little energy as possible working to sustain their material bodies.

Lord Kṛṣṇa gives His own appraisal of the *mahātmā* Vaiṣṇavas to Uddhava in the Eleventh Canto of *Śrīmad-Bhāgavatam* (11.14.17):

*niṣkiñcanā mayy anurakta-cetasaḥ*
*śāntā mahānto 'khila-jīva-vatsalāḥ*
*kāmair anālabdha-dhiyo juṣanti te*
*yan nairapekṣyaṁ na viduḥ sukhaṁ mama*

"Those who are without any desire for personal gratification, whose minds are always attached to Me, who are peaceful, free from false ego, and merciful to all living entities, and whose consciousness is never affected by opportunities for sense gratification — such persons enjoy in Me a happiness that cannot be known or achieved by those lacking such detachment from the material world."

Devotees whose hearts are fully dedicated to the Supreme Person are the only real *mahātmās.* There are certain external symptoms by which such great souls can be known: they avoid acquisitiveness, they are beyond attraction and repulsion, they are affectionately concerned for all living beings, and they are pure in heart, untouched by the spirit of selfish enjoyment. Their internal characteristic is the happiness they taste from a relationship with the Personality of Godhead, a happiness no one but the pure Vaiṣṇavas can know.

The Lord's own happiness is also nothing like the *brahmānanda* of self-satisfied impersonalists. Because Kṛṣṇa is the servant of His own servants, He is always eager to share with His devotees the ecstatic tastes of *bhakti-rasa:*

*ahaṁ bhakta-parādhīno*
*hy asvatantra iva dvija*
*sādhubhir grasta-hṛdayo*
*bhaktair bhakta-jana-priyaḥ*

"I am completely under the control of My devotees. Indeed, I am not at all independent. Because My devotees are completely devoid of material desires, I sit only within the cores of their hearts. What to speak of My devotees, even the devotees of My devotee are very dear to Me." (*Bhāgavatam* 9.4.63)

A devotee with strong faith engages sincerely in worshiping the Lord. And when, by that worship, he develops transcendental attraction, he becomes a true *mahātmā*. Thus faith that leads to attachment is the principal inner symptom of an advanced Vaiṣṇava. Śrī Havis, one of the nine Yogendras, has described this most essential characteristic of pure devotees:

*visṛjati hṛdayaṁ na yasya sākṣād*
*dharir avaśābhihito 'py aghaugha-nāśaḥ*
*praṇaya-rasanayā dhṛtāṅghri-padmaḥ*
*sa bhavati bhāgavata-pradhāna uktaḥ*

"The Supreme Personality of Godhead is so kind to the conditioned souls that if they call upon Him by speaking His holy name, even unintentionally or unwillingly, the Lord is inclined to destroy innumerable sinful reactions in their hearts. Therefore, when a devotee who has taken shelter of the Lord's lotus feet chants the holy name of Kṛṣṇa with genuine love, the Lord can never give up the heart of such a devotee. One who has thus bound the Supreme Lord within his heart with ropes of love is to be known as *bhāgavata-pradhāna,* the most exalted devotee of the Lord." (*Bhāgavatam* 11.2.55)

The most elevated Vaiṣṇavas worship Lord Hari in His original form of Kṛṣṇa, *kṛṣṇas tu bhagavān svayam.* (*Bhāgavatam* 1.3.28) The holy names of Kṛṣṇa, being nondifferent from Him (*sākṣād dhariḥ*), are so potent that even when uttered unintentionally they destroy heaps of sins. Kṛṣṇa, in His inconceivably wonderful Vṛndāvana pastimes, nullifies the threat of many demons, such as Aghāsura, by killing them and awarding them liberation. In Vṛndāvana, Kṛṣṇa's loving devotees have bound Him within their hearts so that He can never escape. The statement above describes these most intimate devotees by using the word *bhāgavata-pradhānaḥ,* a word grammatically singular in form, because they are relatively few in number.

*evaṁ sal-lakṣaṇā loke*
*durlabhā mānavāḥ kalau*
*na hi siṁha-samūhā vai*
*dṛśyante yatra kutracit*

"During Kali-yuga, human beings with such saintly qualities are rarely found in this world. Certainly we never see many lions together in one place." Or as the goddess Earth says in *Śrī Hari-bhakti-sudhodaya* (13.2), *su-durlabhā bhāgavatā hi loke:* "Pure devotees are very rare in this world." And in the words of Mahārāja Nimi:

*durlabho mānuṣo deho*
*dehināṁ kṣaṇa-bhaṅguraḥ*
*tatrāpi durlabhaṁ manye*
*vaikuṇṭha-priya-darśanam*

"For the conditioned souls, the human body is most difficult to achieve, and it can be lost at any moment. But I think that even those who have achieved human life can rarely gain the association of pure devotees, who are dear to the Lord of Vaikuṇṭha." (*Bhāgavatam* 11.2.29)

Pure Vaiṣṇavas are rarely found in the material world because devotion for Śrī Kṛṣṇa arises only in a person who has been relieved of all traces of sinful reactions and has properly carried out all pious duties.

*yeṣāṁ tv anta-gataṁ pāpaṁ*
*janānāṁ puṇya-karmaṇām*

*te dvandva-moha-nirmuktā*
*bhajante māṁ dṛḍha-vratāḥ*

"Persons who have acted piously in previous lives and in this life and whose sinful actions are completely eradicated are freed from the dualities of delusion, and they engage themselves in My service with determination." (*Bhagavad-gītā* 7.28)

*dāna-vrata-tapo-homa-*
*japa-svādhyāya-saṁyamaiḥ*
*śreyobhir vividhaiś cānyaiḥ*
*kṛṣṇe bhaktir hi sādhyate*

"To attain devotional service unto Lord Kṛṣṇa one must perform charity, follow strict vows, perform austerities and fire sacrifices, chant *japa*, study Vedic texts, observe regulative principles, and follow many other auspicious practices." (*Bhāgavatam* 10.47.24)

*janmāntara-sahasreṣu*
*tapo-jñāna-samādhibhiḥ*
*narāṇāṁ kṣīṇa-pāpānāṁ*
*kṛṣṇe bhaktiḥ prajāyate*

"Human beings whose sins have been completely eradicated—by thousands of lifetimes cultivating austerities, knowledge, and meditative trance—can develop devotion for Kṛṣṇa." (*Yoga-vāsiṣṭha-rāmāyaṇa*)

From these statements we can infer that a person with no devotion for the Supreme Lord must be sinful. Nor can the knowledge gained by seekers of impersonal liberation be called *bhakti,* because even texts like the *Yoga-vāsiṣṭha,* which are tinged with impersonalism, indicate that *tapas, jñāna,* and *samādhi* are means toward the end of *bhagavad-bhakti*. As Śrīla Śrīdhara Svāmī writes at the end of his commentary on the *Bhagavad-gītā, jñānasya bhakty-avāntara-vyāpāratvam eva:* "*Jñāna* is but a secondary activity, subordinate to *bhakti*." And in the *Bhagavad-gītā* itself (10.10, 18.54–55) Kṛṣṇa clearly describes knowledge (*buddhi-yoga*) as but a means to achieve the ultimate goal, pure devotion to Him:

*teṣāṁ satata-yuktānāṁ*
*bhajatāṁ prīti-pūrvakam*
*dadāmi buddhi-yogaṁ taṁ*
*yena mām upayānti te*

"To those who are constantly devoted to serving Me with love, I give the understanding by which they can come to Me."

*brahma-bhūtaḥ prasannātmā*
*na śocati na kāṅkṣati*
*samaḥ sarveṣu bhūteṣu*
*mad-bhaktiṁ labhate parām*

"One who is transcendentally situated at once realizes the Supreme Brahman and becomes fully joyful. He never laments or desires to have anything. He is equally disposed toward every living entity. In that state he attains pure devotional service unto Me.

*bhaktyā mām abhijānāti*
*yāvān yaś cāsmi tattvataḥ*
*tato māṁ tattvato jñātvā*
*viśate tad-anantaram*

"One can understand Me as I am, as the Supreme Personality of Godhead, only by devotional service. And when one is in full consciousness of Me by such devotion, he can enter into the kingdom of God."

Thus Kṛṣṇa always makes a distinction between *jñāna* and *bhakti,* and so do His faithful devotees. This means, of course, that the impersonal worshipers of the Absolute are not as spiritually advanced as the devotees of the Supreme Person. In the Fourth Canto of *Śrīmad-Bhāgavatam* (4.22.69) Sanat-kumāra tells Mahārāja Pṛthu:

*yat-pāda-paṅkaja-palāśa-vilāsa-bhaktyā*
*karmāśayaṁ grathitam udgrathayanti santaḥ*
*tadvan na rikta-matayo yatayo 'pi ruddha-*
*sroto-gaṇās tam araṇaṁ bhaja vāsudevam*

"The devotees, who are always engaged in the service of the toes of the lotus feet of the Lord, can very easily overcome hard-knotted desires for fruitive activities. Because this is very difficult, the nondevotees — the *jñānīs* and *yogīs* — although trying to stop the waves of sense gratification, cannot do so. Therefore you are advised to engage in the devotional service of Kṛṣṇa, the son of Vasudeva."

The unlimited ways the Supreme Lord employs His energies are all His *vilāsa* ("expansions for play"). But pure Vaiṣṇavas are especially attracted to serving Him by hearing and chanting about His *vilāsa* in Śrī Vṛndāvana and His other spiritual abodes. Thus Lord Kapiladeva, after instructing His mother at length about several varieties of progressive discipline, advised her that, of all *sādhanas,* recitation of the pastimes of the Lord of Vaikuṇṭha is the most important.

Devotional service itself is also *vilāsa,* an expression of pure joy. By taking part in the *bhakti-vilāsa* of honoring the Supreme Lord's *mahā-prasāda* and dancing, singing, and performing other services for His pleasure, saintly devotees untie the knots of material bondage — the materialistic attitudes born from false ego — within their hearts. Impersonalist *sannyāsīs* may subdue the senses, but they are unable to untie the knots of *karma* binding their hearts. Or even if able to begin to unravel those knots, they cannot undo them completely. The impulses of the senses are compared to the current of a mighty river like the Gaṅgā, which can never be stopped; without the special protection of the Supreme Lord's internal energy in pure devotional service, no one can stop the incessant flow of sensory agitation. Nondevotee *sannyāsīs* fall from their elevated status, therefore, whereas fully surrendered devotees never fall. While Kṛṣṇa was in the womb of Devakī the demigods prayed:

*tathā na te mādhava tāvakāḥ kvacid*
*bhraśyanti mārgāt tvayi baddha-sauhṛdāḥ*

"O Mādhava, Supreme Personality of Godhead, Lord of the goddess of fortune, if devotees completely in love with You sometimes fall from the path of devotion, they do not fall like nondevotees." (*Bhāgavatam* 10.2.33)

Though this statement concedes that pure devotees may in theory fall down, saintly authorities never accept that possibility. *Paramahaṁsa* Vaiṣṇavas are solidly established in intimate friendship with the Supreme Lord; therefore they never fall into illusion under any circumstances.

Impersonalists conceive of the Supreme Self as formless, or as a void. To reciprocate with them in kind, the Supreme Lord presents Himself to suit their taste, as the personified *Vedas* describe in their prayers. *Viyata ivāpadasya tava śūnya-tulāṁ dadhataḥ:* "Just as the ethereal sky has no connection with perceptible qualities, so also You resemble a void." (*Bhāgavatam* 10.87.29) The impersonal conception of the Supreme is deficient, however, because it ignores the essence of self-realization — pure devotion for the Supreme Lord's lotus feet. Thus only the faithful Vaiṣṇavas are true saints, *sat,* and everyone else is *asat.* Following the example of such saints, one who desires to succeed should take shelter of the son of Vasudeva and worship Him.

Persons who spurn the protection of the Personality of Godhead are not Vaiṣṇavas. Without shelter they are in effect spiritual orphans. But the Vaiṣṇavas, under the Lord's protection, free from fear, free to use all the activities of their senses in the Lord's service, easily gain liberation from the bondage of material existence. And beyond that, at every moment they enjoy an abundance of fresher and fresher ecstasy that those who are merely liberated can never know. Impersonalist *sannyāsīs* can obtain deliverance from the vast ocean of *saṁsāra* only after long, severe endeavor, but the Supreme Lord's devotees cross that ocean happily, effortlessly. As the presiding demigods of the causal elements prayed to Lord Viṣṇu at the beginning of creation:

*namāma te deva padāravindaṁ*
*prapanna-tāpopaśamātapatram*
*yan-mūla-ketā yatayo 'ñjasoru-*
*saṁsāra-duḥkhaṁ bahir utkṣipanti*

"O Lord, Your lotus feet are like an umbrella for the surrendered souls, protecting them from all the miseries of material existence. All the sages under that shelter easily throw off all material miseries. We therefore offer our respectful obeisances unto Your lotus feet." (*Bhāgavatam* 3.5.39)

Devotees who take full shelter of Lord Viṣṇu's lotus feet are much more elevated than ordinary sages or *sannyāsīs*. Such devotees abandon reliance on anything else and depend solely on the Lord. In contrast, impersonalist *sannyāsīs,* by leaving their families and changing their dress, only seem to renounce materialism. In reality, however, when they subscribe to the Advaita idea of pure consciousness, they imagine themselves to be the Supreme Lord, Nārāyaṇa. Such a state of mind forces them to presume that everything they see or hear about, other than themselves, is an illusory product of their own Māyā. These adherents of the Advaita Vedānta philosophy call themselves *yatis* or *sannyāsīs,* but they must be distinguished from the Vaiṣṇavas, whom the *Bhāgavatam* designates as real saints.

In fact the Advaita-vādī *yatis* are not free from the reactions of their past and present sins, nor are their hearts cleansed of the taste for sense gratification. Though ignorant of the truth, they consider themselves learned, and their personal character is just like that of the demonic enemies of Viṣṇu and His devotees. As the demigods prayed to Kṛṣṇa while He was in the womb:

*ye 'nye 'ravindākṣa vimukta-māninas*
*tvayy asta-bhāvād aviśuddha-buddhayaḥ*
*āruhya kṛcchreṇa paraṁ padaṁ tataḥ*
*patanty adho 'nādṛta-yuṣmad-aṅghrayaḥ*

"O lotus-eyed Lord, although nondevotees who accept severe austerities and penances to achieve the highest position may think themselves liberated, their intelligence is impure. They fall down from their position of imagined superiority because they have no regard for Your lotus feet." (*Bhāgavatam* 10.2.32)

The personified *Vedas* similarly prayed:

*yadi na samuddharanti yatayo hṛdi kāma-jaṭā*
*duradhigamo 'satāṁ hṛdi gato 'smṛta-kaṇṭha-maṇiḥ*
*asu-tṛpa-yoginām ubhayato 'py asukhaṁ bhagavann*
*anapagatāntakād anadhirūḍha-padād bhavataḥ*

"Members of the renounced order who fail to uproot the last traces of material desire in their hearts remain impure, and thus You do not allow them to understand You. Although You are present within their hearts, for them You are like a jewel worn around the neck of a man who has totally forgotten that the jewel is there. O Lord, those who practice *yoga* only for sense gratification must suffer punishment both in this life and in the next: from death, who will not release them, and from You, whose kingdom they cannot reach." (*Bhāgavatam* 10.87.39)

According to the *Yoga-vāsiṣṭha-rāmāyaṇa:*

*ajñasyārdha-prabuddhasya*
*sarvaṁ brahmeti yo vadet*
*mahā-naraka-jāleṣu*
*tenaiva viniyojitaḥ*

"When an ignorant, half-conscious person declares 'Everything is Brahman,' the result is that He becomes entangled in a network of most hellish existence."

The *Brahma-vaivarta Purāṇa* also states:

*viṣaya-sneha-saṁyukto*
*brahmāham iti yo vadet*
*kalpa-koṭi-sahasrāṇi*
*narake sa tu pacyate*

"A person absorbed in enjoyment of sense objects who says 'I am Brahman' will burn in hell for ten billion days of Brahmā."

And in another *Purāṇa* we read:

*saṁsāra-sukha-saṁyuktaṁ*
*brahmāham iti vādinam*
*karma-brahma-paribhraṣṭaṁ*
*taṁ tyajed antyajaṁ yathā*

"If a person absorbed in the pleasures of material life says 'I am Brahman,' he is fallen both from Vedic duties and from transcendental engagements. He should be rejected like an outcaste."

Before meeting Sarūpa, the *brāhmaṇa* from Mathurā was ignorant of the glories of the Supreme Lord's devotional service. But by the company of Sarūpa, his saintly spiritual master, he at once became as successful as those who realize their spiritual identities after long disciplined efforts. Such is the power of association with pure Vaiṣṇavas. Earlier in this book, all kinds of spiritual practices were explained, but this special glory of Vaiṣṇava association was not. Vaiṣṇava association is the most sublime secret. It is the very best means of spiritual attainment and is in fact an essential aspect of the ultimate goal.

## TEXT 15

तद्वन्महाप्रेमरसार्णवाप्लुतस्
तत्तद्विकारोर्मिभिराचितो भृशम् ।
हा कृष्ण कृष्णेति किशोरशेखरं
तं दर्शयस्वेति रुराव स द्विजः ॥

*tadvan mahā-prema-rasārṇavāplutas*
*tat-tad-vikārormibhir ācito bhṛśam*
*hā kṛṣṇa kṛṣṇeti kiśora-śekharaṁ*
*taṁ darśayasveti rurāva sa dvijaḥ*

*tadvat*—just like him; *mahā-prema*—of pure love; *rasa-arṇava*—in an ocean of spiritual tastes; *āplutaḥ*—submerged; *tat-tat*—various; *vikāra*—of symptoms; *ūrmibhiḥ*—with waves; *ācitaḥ*—marked; *bhṛśam*—thoroughly; *hā*—alas;

*kṛṣṇa kṛṣṇa* — O Kṛṣṇa, Kṛṣṇa; *iti* — thus; *kiśora* — of youths; *śekharam* — the foremost; *tam* — to Him; *darśayasva* — please show; *iti* — thus; *rurāva* — cried; *saḥ* — he; *dvijaḥ* — the *brāhmaṇa.*

**The brāhmaṇa was submerged, just like Sarūpa, in an ocean of the tastes of pure exalted love. And his whole body, just like Sarūpa's, was filled with many symptoms of that love. He cried out to Kṛṣṇa, the foremost of youths, "O Kṛṣṇa, Kṛṣṇa! Please show Yourself!"**

## TEXT 16

तृणं गृहीत्वा दशनैः सकाकु
नमन्नपृच्छत्स सरूपमेव ।
चरस्थिरप्राणिगणांश्च कृष्णः
कुतोऽस्ति दृष्टोऽत्र किमु त्वयेति ॥

*tṛṇaṁ gṛhītvā daśanaiḥ sa-kāku*
*namann apṛcchat sa sarūpam eva*
*cara-sthira-prāṇi-gaṇāṁś ca kṛṣṇaḥ*
*kuto 'sti dṛṣṭo 'tra kim u tvayeti*

*tṛṇam* — a blade of grass; *gṛhītvā* — taking; *daśanaiḥ* — with his teeth; *sa-kāku* — with plaintive cries; *naman* — bowing down; *apṛcchat* — asked; *saḥ* — he; *sarūpam* — of Sarūpa; *eva* — indeed; *cara* — moving; *sthira* — and nonmoving; *prāṇi-gaṇān* — of the living entities; *ca* — and; *kṛṣṇaḥ* — Kṛṣṇa; *kutaḥ* — where; *asti* — is; *dṛṣṭaḥ* — seen; *atra* — here; *kim u* — whether; *tvayā* — by you; *iti* — thus.

**He placed a blade of grass between his teeth, bowed down, and with plaintive cries asked of Sarūpa — and of all moving and nonmoving living beings — "Where is Kṛṣṇa? Have you seen Him here?"**

COMMENTARY: The *brāhmaṇa's* voice expressed fear and sorrow.

## TEXT 17

नामानि कृष्णस्य मनोरमाणि
सङ्कीर्तयंस्तस्य पदौ गृहीत्वा ।
प्रेमाब्धिमग्नस्य गुरो रुरोद
तत्प्रेमदृष्ट्या विवशस्य विप्रः ॥

*nāmāni kṛṣṇasya mano-ramāṇi*
*saṅkīrtayaṁs tasya padau gṛhītvā*
*premābdhi-magnasya guro ruroda*
*tat-prema-dṛṣṭyā vivaśasya vipraḥ*

*nāmāni* — the names; *kṛṣṇasya* — of Kṛṣṇa; *manaḥ-ramāṇi* — enchanting; *saṅkīrtayan* — chanting loudly; *tasya* — his (Sarūpa's); *padau* — two feet; *gṛhītvā* — taking hold of; *prema* — of pure love; *abdhi* — in an ocean; *magnasya* — who was drowning; *guroḥ* — of his *guru;* *ruroda* — cried; *tat* — his; *prema* — love; *dṛṣṭyā* — by seeing; *vivaśasya* — beside himself; *vipraḥ* — the *brāhmaṇa.*

**Loudly chanting the all-attractive names of Kṛṣṇa, the brāhmaṇa clutched Sarūpa's feet. The brāhmaṇa saw that Sarūpa, his guru, was drowning in an ocean of love and had lost control of himself by witnessing the love in him, and so the brāhmaṇa wept.**

COMMENTARY: Śrī Sarūpa was already constantly submerged in an ocean of *kṛṣṇa-prema,* but seeing his disciple transformed plunged him into even deeper ecstasy. Now both *guru* and disciple were utterly immersed in happiness.

## TEXT 18

क्षणान्महाप्रेमजवेन यन्त्रितो
वने महोन्मत्तवदुत्थितो भ्रमन् ।

विमूर्छितस्तत्र स कण्टकाचिते
करीरकुञ्जे निपपात माथुरः ॥

*kṣaṇān mahā-prema-javena yantrito*
*vane mahonmatta-vad utthito bhraman*
*vimūrchitas tatra sa kaṇṭakācite*
*karīra-kuñje nipapāta māthuraḥ*

*kṣaṇāt* — after a moment; *mahā-prema* — of exalted pure love; *javena* — by an upswell; *yantritaḥ* — impelled; *vane* — in the forest; *mahā-unmatta-vat* — like a completely insane person; *utthitaḥ* — getting up; *bhraman* — wandering; *vimūrchitaḥ* — fainting; *tatra* — there; *sa-kaṇṭaka-ācite* — full of thorns; *karīra* — of *karīra* trees; *kuñje* — in a grove; *nipapāta* — fell down; *māthuraḥ* — the Mathurā *brāhmaṇa.*

**A moment later, compelled by a great upsurge of love, the Mathurā brāhmaṇa got up and began to wander in the forest. There he fainted and fell into a thorny grove of karīra trees.**

TEXT 19

मातः सपद्येव विमिश्रिता गवां
हम्बारवैर्वेणुविषाणनिक्कणाः ।
तौम्बेयवीणादलवाद्यचर्चिता
जाता गभीरा मधुरा विदूरतः ॥

*mātaḥ sapady eva vimiśritā gavāṁ*
*hambā-ravair veṇu-viṣāṇa-nikkaṇāḥ*
*taumbeya-vīṇā-dala-vādya-carcitā*
*jātā gabhīrā madhurā vidūrataḥ*

*mātaḥ* — dear mother; *sapadi* — at that moment; *eva* — just; *vimiśritāḥ* — which were mixed; *gavām* — of the cows; *hambā-ravaiḥ* — with the mooing; *veṇu* — of flutes; *viṣāṇa* — of horns; *nikkaṇāḥ* — the sounds; *taumbeya* — made of gourds; *vīṇā* —

by *vīṇās; dala* — made of leaves; *vādya* — and by horns; *carcitāḥ* — joined; *jātāḥ* — appearing; *gabhīrāḥ* — rich; *madhurāḥ* — and sweet; *vidūrataḥ* — from a distance.

**Dear mother, all of a sudden from a distance came rich and sweet sounds of flutes and horns, mixed with the mooing of cows and the sounds of vīṇās made from gourds, and whistles made from leaves.**

TEXT 20

तौ प्रापितौ बोधममीभिरुत्थितौ
तद्दीर्घनादाभिमुखेऽभ्यधावताम् ।
गोपालदेवं तमपश्यतामथो
सुश्यामगात्रद्युतिमण्डलोज्ज्वलम् ॥

*tau prāpitau bodham amībhir utthitau*
*tad-dīrgha-nādābhimukhe 'bhyadhāvatām*
*gopāla-devaṁ tam apaśyatām atho*
*su-śyāma-gātra-dyuti-maṇḍalojjvalam*

*tau* — they two; *prāpitau bodham* — restored to consciousness; *amībhiḥ* — by these (sounds); *utthitau* — rising; *tat* — of that; *dīrgha* — persistent; *nāda* — sound; *abhimukhe* — in the direction; *abhyadhāvatām* — ran; *gopāla-devam* — Gopāladeva; *tam* — Him; *apaśyatām* — they saw; *atha u* — then; *su-śyāma* — which was beautifully dark; *gātra* — from His body; *dyuti-maṇḍala* — with a ring of effulgence; *ujjvalam* — who was brilliant.

**Awakened by the persistent sounds, Sarūpa and the brāhmaṇa ran in its direction. Then they saw Gopāladeva, His body beautifully dark, encircled by a brilliant effulgence.**

TEXT 21

पशून्पयः पाययितुं वयस्यैः
समं विहर्तुं तरणेः सुतायाम् ।

गजेन्द्रलीलार्चितनृत्यगत्या-
न्तिके समायान्तमनन्तलीलम् ॥

*paśūn payaḥ pāyayituṁ vayasyaiḥ*
*samaṁ vihartuṁ taraṇeḥ sutāyām*
*gajendra-līlārcita-nṛtya-gatyā-*
*ntike samāyāntam ananta-līlam*

*paśūn* — the animals; *payaḥ* — water; *pāyayitum* — to have drink; *vayasyaiḥ* — with His friends; *samam* — together; *vihartum* — to play; *taraṇeḥ* — of the sun; *sutāyām* — within the daughter (the Yamunā); *gaja-indra* — of the elephant king; *līla* — by the sporting; *arcita* — honored; *nṛtya* — dancing; *gatyā* — with a gait; *antike* — near; *samāyāntam* — who was coming; *ananta* — unlimited; *līlam* — whose pastimes.

**The Lord, unlimited in pastimes, was coming nearby to water His animals and play with His friends in the Yamunā, daughter of the sun. As He approached, He danced with a gait worthy of honor from the playful walk of the king of elephants.**

COMMENTARY: There is no limit to Kṛṣṇa's enjoyment. As both *guru* and disciple looked on, Kṛṣṇa approached the Yamunā, with more than one purpose in mind: He wanted to let His cows and other animals drink from the Yamunā, He wanted to play with the cowherd boys in the water, and He also wanted to meet the *gopīs,* who would later take Him across the river in a boat. Kṛṣṇa and His friends, while coming near, were throwing balls and imitating the forest creatures and playing in various other ways.

## TEXT 22

स्वकीयकैशोरमहाविभूषणं
विचित्रलावण्यतरङ्गसागरम् ।
जगन्मनोनेत्रमुदां विवर्धनं
मुहुर्मुहुर्नूतनमाधुरीभृतम् ॥

*svakīya-kaiśora-mahā-vibhūṣaṇaṁ*
*vicitra-lāvaṇya-taraṅga-sāgaram*
*jagan-mano-netra-mudāṁ vivardhanaṁ*
*muhur muhur nūtana-mādhurī-bhṛtam*

*svakīya* — His own; *kaiśora* — youth; *mahā* — principal; *vibhūṣaṇam* — whose ornament; *vicitra* — wonderful; *lāvaṇya* — of beauty; *taraṅga* — with waves; *sāgaram* — an ocean; *jagat* — of the world; *manaḥ* — the mind; *netra* — the eyes; *mudām* — the joy; *vivardhanam* — increasing; *muhuḥ muhuḥ* — again and again; *nūtana* — new; *mādhurī* — sweetness; *bhṛtam* — assuming.

**His chief ornament was His own unique youth. He was an ocean filled with wonderful waves of beauty. Ever adorned with newer and newer charms, He redoubled the joy of everyone's mind and eyes.**

## TEXT 23

निःशेषसल्लक्षणसुन्दराङ्गं
नीपावतंसं शिखिपिच्छचूडम् ।
मुक्तावलीमण्डितकम्बुकण्ठं
कौशेयपीताम्बरयुग्मदीप्तम् ॥

*niḥśeṣa-sal-lakṣaṇa-sundarāṅgaṁ*
*nīpāvataṁsaṁ śikhi-piccha-cūḍam*
*muktāvalī-maṇḍita-kambu-kaṇṭhaṁ*
*kauśeya-pītāmbara-yugma-dīptam*

*niḥśeṣa* — all; *sat-lakṣaṇa* — with auspicious signs; *sundara* — beautiful; *aṅgam* — whose body; *nīpa* — of *nīpa* garlands; *avataṁsam* — whose ornament of the ears; *śikhi-piccha* — of a peacock feather; *cūḍam* — whose head ornament; *mukta-āvalī* — by a string of pearls; *maṇḍita* — decorated; *kambu* — like a conch; *kaṇṭham* — whose neck; *kauśeya* — of silk; *pīta* —

yellow; *ambara* — of garments; *yugma* — by the pair; *dīptam* — brilliant.

**All auspicious signs marked His beautiful body. Garlands of nīpa flowers adorned His ears, and a peacock feather His hair. A string of pearls decorated His conchlike neck. And His yellow silken garments, upper and lower, shone brilliantly.**

COMMENTARY: As described in such texts as the *Sāmudrika* (3), these are the bodily signs of a *mahā-puruṣa,* or great person:

*pañca-sūkṣmaḥ pañca-dīrghaḥ*
*sapta-raktaḥ ṣaḍ-unnataḥ*
*tri-hrasva-pṛthu-gambhīro*
*dvā-triṁśal-lakṣaṇo mahān*

"A great person is marked in thirty-two ways: Five parts of his body are tender, five long, seven red, six high, three short, three broad, and three deep." The five tender parts of a *mahā-puruṣa's* body are the skin, teeth, and finger joints, the hair on the head, and the hair on the body. The five long parts are the nose, chin, eyes, arms, and knees. The seven red parts are the nails, the palate, the upper and lower lips, the edges of the eyes, and the surface of the feet and hands. The six high parts are the nose, mouth, nails, chest, waist, and shoulders. The three short parts are the neck, ankles, and genitals. The three broad parts are the waist, chest, and forehead. And the three deep parts are the voice, navel, and intelligence.

## TEXT 24

गुञ्जामहाहारविलम्बभूषित-
श्रीवत्सलक्ष्म्यालयपीनवक्षसम् ।
सिंहेन्द्रमध्यं शतसिंहविक्रमं
सौभाग्यसारार्चितपादपङ्कजम् ॥

*guñjā-mahā-hāra-vilamba-bhūṣita-*
*śrīvatsa-lakṣmy-ālaya-pīna-vakṣasam*
*siṁhendra-madhyaṁ śata-siṁha-vikramaṁ*
*saubhāgya-sārārcita-pāda-paṅkajam*

*guñjā* — made of *guñjā* berries; *mahā-hāra* — by a long garland; *vilamba* — hanging; *bhūṣita* — adorned; *śrīvatsa* — the Śrīvatsa mark; *lakṣmī* — and of the goddess of fortune; *ālaya* — the home; *pīna* — broad; *vakṣasam* — whose chest; *siṁha-indra* — of a kingly lion; *madhyam* — the middle part; *śata* — one hundred; *siṁha* — of lions; *vikramam* — whose prowess; *saubhāgya* — of good fortune; *sāra* — by the essence; *arcita* — worshiped; *pāda* — whose feet; *paṅkajam* — lotuslike.

**On His broad chest, home to the Śrīvatsa mark and Lakṣmī, hung a long garland of guñjā berries. His waist was like a kingly lion's, His prowess like that of hundreds of lions. The essence of all good fortune worshiped His lotus feet.**

COMMENTARY: Kṛṣṇa is lionlike not only in external appearance but also in His strength and courage, which cannot be equaled by hundreds of lions together.

TEXT 25

कदम्बगुञ्जातुलसीशिखण्ड-
प्रवालमालावलिचारुवेशम् ।
कटीतटीराजितचित्रपुष्प-
काञ्चीविलम्बाढ्यनितम्बदेशम् ॥

*kadamba-guñjā-tulasī-śikhaṇḍa-*
*pravāla-mālāvali-cāru-veśam*
*kaṭī-taṭī-rājita-citra-puṣpa-*
*kāñcī-vilambāḍhya-nitamba-deśam*

*kadamba* — of *kadamba* flowers; *guñjā* — *guñjā* berries; *tulasī*

— *tulasī* leaves; *śikhaṇḍa* — from the *śikhaṇḍa* plant; *pravāla* — and sprouts; *māla-avali* — with many garlands; *cāru* — attractive; *veśam* — whose dress; *kaṭī-taṭī* — whose waistline; *rājita* — adorned; *citra* — various, colorful; *puṣpa* — with flowers; *kāñcī* — of His belt; *vilamba* — by the way of hanging; *āḍhya* — beautified; *nitamba-deśam* — whose hips.

**Enhancing His dress were many garlands of kadamba flowers, guñjā berries, tulasī leaves, and sprouts of śikhaṇḍa. Variously colored flowers adorned His waist, and His belt hung in a way that beautified His hips.**

## TEXT 26

सौवर्णदिव्याङ्गदकङ्कणोल्लसद्-
वृत्तायतस्थूलभुजाभिरामम् ।
बिम्बाधरन्यस्तमनोज्ञवेणु-
वाद्योल्लसत्पद्मकराङ्गुलीकम् ॥

*sauvarṇa-divyāṅgada-kaṅkaṇollasad-*
*vṛttāyata-sthūla-bhujābhirāmam*
*bimbādhara-nyasta-manojña-veṇu-*
*vādyollasat-padma-karāṅgulīkam*

*sauvarṇa* — gold; *divya* — splendid; *aṅgada* — with armlets; *kaṅkaṇa* — and bangles; *ullasat* — shining; *vṛtta* — round; *āyata* — broad; *sthūla* — stout; *bhuja* — whose arms; *abhirāmam* — pleasing to see; *bimba-adhara* — on His lips, red like *bimba* fruit; *nyasta* — held; *manojña* — charming; *veṇu* — on His flute; *vādya* — playing; *ullasat* — shining; *padma-kara* — of whose lotus hands; *aṅgulīkam* — the fingers.

**His arms — round, broad, and stout and pleasing to the eyes — shone with splendid golden armlets and bracelets. The fingers of His lotus hands happily played on His charming flute as He held it to His bimba-red lips.**

## TEXT 27

स्वोत्प्रेक्षितापौर्विकवेणुगीत-
भङ्गीसुधामोहितविश्वलोकम् ।
तिर्यग्मनाग्लोलविलोकलीला-
लङ्कारसंलालितलोचनाब्जम् ॥

*svotprekṣitāpaurvika-veṇu-gīta-*
*bhaṅgī-sudhā-mohita-viśva-lokam*
*tiryag-manāg-lola-viloka-līlā-*
*laṅkāra-saṁlālita-locanābjam*

*sva-utprekṣita* — anticipated only by Him; *apaurvika* — unprecedented; *veṇu-gīta* — of the flute's song; *bhaṅgī* — of the embellishments; *sudhā* — by the nectar; *mohita* — bewildered; *viśva-lokam* — the entire universe; *tiryak* — sideways; *manāk* — slight; *lola* — unsteady; *viloka* — of the glances; *līlā* — of the play; *alaṅkāra* — by the decoration; *saṁlālita* — complemented; *locana-abjam* — whose lotus eyes.

**The unprecedented embellishments of His flute song, anticipated by Him alone, bewildered all the universe like an intoxicating nectar. And the restless play of His glances, sidelong and slight, gently decorated His lotus eyes.**

## TEXT 28

चापोपमभ्रूयुगनर्तनश्री-
संवर्धितप्रेष्यजनानुरागम् ।
श्रीमत्सदास्मेरमुखारविन्द-
शोभासमाकृष्टमुनीन्द्रचित्तम् ॥

*cāpopama-bhrū-yuga-nartana-śrī-*
*saṁvardhita-preṣya-janānurāgam*
*śrīmat-sadā-smera-mukhāravinda-*
*śobhā-samākṛṣṭa-munīndra-cittam*

*cāpa* — to bows; *upama* — comparable; *bhrū-yuga* — of whose two eyebrows; *nartana* — of the dancing; *śrī* — by the splendor; *saṁvardhita* — nourished; *preṣya-jana* — of His servants; *anurāgam* — the loving attraction; *śrīmat* — beautiful; *sadā* — always; *smera* — smiling; *mukha-aravinda* — of whose lotus face; *śobhā* — by the beauty; *samākṛṣṭa* — attracted; *muni-indra* — of the best of sages; *cittam* — the hearts.

**The splendid dance of His eyebrows, a pair of archer's bows, nourished His servants' loving feelings. And His beautiful ever-smiling lotus face attracted the hearts of the best of sages.**

COMMENTARY: Kṛṣṇa is the transcendental Cupid. As Cupid carries a bow from which he shoots flower arrows of desire into the hearts of conditioned souls, so Kṛṣṇa arches His eyebrows into a shape like Cupid's bow, and when He equips this weapon with His invincible smile, the gravity of self-satisfied mystics is soundly defeated.

## TEXT 29

तिलप्रसूनोत्तमनासिकाग्रतो
विराजमानैकगजेन्द्रमौक्तिकम् ।
कदापि गोधूलिविभूषितालक-
द्विरेफसम्भालनतो लसत्करम् ॥

*tila-prasūnottama-nāsikāgrato*
*virājamānaika-gajendra-mauktikam*
*kadāpi go-dhūli-vibhūṣitālaka-*
*dvirepha-sambhālanato lasat-karam*

*tila* — sesame; *prasūna* — like a flower; *uttama* — exquisite; *nāsikā* — of whose nose; *agrataḥ* — on the tip; *virājamāna* — shining; *eka* — a single; *gaja-indra* — from a lordly elephant; *mauktikam* — pearl; *kadā api* — sometimes; *go-dhūli* — with dust raised by the cows; *vibhūṣita* — adorned; *alaka* — whose locks of hair; *dvirepha* — the bees; *sambhālanataḥ* — by warding off; *lasat* — charming; *karam* — whose hand.

**On the tip of His nose — a nose exquisite like a sesame flower — shone a single pearl, born from the forehead of a lordly elephant. Now and then His hand would gracefully brush aside the bees of His locks of hair, which were adorned with dust raised by the cows.**

COMMENTARY: The *āgama* scripture confirms that on the tip of His nose Lord Gopāla wears a rare pearl taken from an elephant's brow: *nāsāgre gaja-mauktikam*.

## TEXT 30

सूर्यात्मजामृद्रचितोर्ध्वपुण्ड्र-
स्फीतार्धचन्द्राकृतिभालपट्टम् ।
नानाद्रिधातुप्रतिचित्रिताङ्गं
नानामहारङ्गतरङ्गसिन्धुम् ॥

*sūryātmajā-mṛd-racitordhva-puṇḍra-*
*sphītārdha-candrākṛti-bhāla-paṭṭam*
*nānādri-dhātu-praticitritāṅgaṁ*
*nānā-mahā-raṅga-taraṅga-sindhum*

*sūrya* — of the sun; *ātma-jā* — of the daughter (Śrī Yamunā); *mṛt* — with clay; *racita* — fashioned; *ūrdhva-puṇḍra* — with vertical *tilaka; sphīta* — splendorous; *ardha-candra* — of a half moon; *ākṛti* — in the shape; *bhāla* — of whose forehead; *paṭṭam* — the surface; *nānā* — various; *adri* — from mountains; *dhātu* — with minerals; *praticitrita* — painted; *aṅgam* — the limbs of whose body; *nānā* — various; *mahā* — huge; *raṅga* — of pleasure; *taraṅga* — with waves; *sindhum* — ocean.

**His broad forehead, shaped like a half moon, glowed with**

**the splendor of His straight-up tilaka, formed with clay from the Yamunā. His limbs were painted with designs made with various mountain minerals. He was an ocean full of huge waves of sportive pastimes.**

COMMENTARY: Śrī Yamunā took birth as the daughter of Vivasvān, the sun-god, and assumed the form of the most sacred of rivers, flowing through the land of Kṛṣṇa's favorite pastimes. To further expand her glories, Kṛṣṇa wears clay from her banks as His auspicious *tilaka*. He also paints designs on His body with local minerals like red *gairika* and yellow *haritāla*.

## TEXT 31

स्थित्वा त्रिभङ्गीललितं कदाचिन्
नर्माणि वंश्या बहु वादयन्तम् ।
तैर्हासयन्तं निजमित्रवर्गान्
भूमिं पदैः स्वैः परिभूषयन्तम् ॥

*sthitvā tri-bhaṅgī-lalitaṁ kadācin*
*narmāṇi vaṁśyā bahu vādayantam*
*tair hāsayantaṁ nija-mitra-vargān*
*bhūmiṁ padaiḥ svaiḥ paribhūṣayantam*

*sthitvā* — by standing; *tri-bhaṅgī* — in a threefold-bending posture; *lalitam* — charming; *kadācit* — sometimes; *narmāṇi* — entertainment; *vaṁśyā* — with His flute; *bahu* — variously; *vādayantam* — playing; *taiḥ* — by these; *hāsayantam* — making laugh; *nija* — His own; *mitra-vargān* — many friends; *bhūmim* — the earth; *padaiḥ* — with the feet; *svaiḥ* — His; *paribhūṣayantam* — decorating everywhere.

**Standing in His charming threefold-bending pose, sometimes He played various entertaining melodies on His flute, making His dear friends laugh. His feet decorated the earth in all directions.**

COMMENTARY: As Kṛṣṇa wanders to every corner of Vraja, He leaves the ground marked with His footprints.

### TEXT 32

तादृग्वयोवेशवताग्रजन्मना
नीलांशुकालंकृतगौरकान्तिना ।
रामेण युक्तं रमणीयमूर्तिना
तैश्चात्मतुल्यैः सखिभिः प्रियैर्वृतम् ॥

*tādṛg-vayo-veśavatāgrajanmanā*
*nīlāṁśukālaṅkṛta-gaura-kāntinā*
*rāmeṇa yuktaṁ ramaṇīya-mūrtinā*
*taiś cātma-tulyaiḥ sakhibhiḥ priyair vṛtam*

*tādṛk* — similar; *vayaḥ* — in age; *veśa-vatā* — and dress; *agra-janmanā* — with His elder brother; *nīla* — blue; *aṁśuka* — with fine garments; *alaṅkṛta* — bedecked; *gaura* — white; *kāntinā* — whose complexion; *rāmeṇa* — with Balarāma; *yuktam* — together; *ramaṇīya* — most attractive; *mūrtinā* — whose body; *taiḥ* — those; *ca* — and; *ātma-tulyaiḥ* — similar to Himself; *sakhibhiḥ* — by friends; *priyaiḥ* — dear; *vṛtam* — surrounded.

**Surrounding Him on all sides were dear friends, whose appearance resembled His. And He stood with His elder brother Rāma, whose complexion was white, who was bedecked with blue silk garments, whose body was most attractive, and whose age and dress were just like His own.**

### TEXT 33

तद्दर्शनोद्भूतमहामुदावली-
भारेण गाढेन निपातितौ हि तौ ।
दण्डप्रणामार्थमिवाशु पेततुः
सम्भ्रान्तिविध्वंसितसर्वनैपुणौ ॥

*tad-darśanodbhūta-mahā-mudāvalī-*
*bhāreṇa gāḍhena nipātitau hi tau*
*daṇḍa-praṇāmārtham ivāśu petatuḥ*
*sambhrānti-vidhvaṁsita-sarva-naipuṇau*

*tat* — Him; *darśana* — from seeing; *udbhūta* — arisen; *mahā-mudā* — of great joy; *āvalī* — of the series; *bhāreṇa* — by the burden; *gāḍhena* — persistent; *nipātitau* — made to fall down; *hi* — indeed; *tau* — those two; *daṇḍa-praṇāma* — of offering prostrate obeisances; *artham* — for the sake; *iva* — as if; *āśu* — suddenly; *petatuḥ* — they dropped; *sambhrānti* — in their excitement; *vidhvaṁsita* — lost; *sarva* — all; *naipuṇau* — competence.

**The weight of the persistent heavy joy of seeing Kṛṣṇa made the two devotees fall. Indeed, they suddenly threw themselves to the ground as if to offer prostrate obeisances, all their competence lost in the excitement of the moment.**

COMMENTARY: In this situation, both *guru* and disciple forgot themselves. In no condition to carry out their social roles, they simply threw themselves helplessly at the feet of Śrī Gopāladeva, unable even to coherently offer prayers.

## TEXT 34

स च प्रियप्रेमवशः प्रधावन्
समागतो हर्षभरेण मुग्धः ।
तयोरुपर्येव पपात दीर्घ-
महाभुजाभ्यां परिरभ्य तौ द्वौ ॥

*sa ca priya-prema-vaśaḥ pradhāvan*
*samāgato harṣa-bhareṇa mugdhaḥ*
*tayor upary eva papāta dīrgha-*
*mahā-bhujābhyāṁ parirabhya tau dvau*

*saḥ* — He (Lord Gopāla); *ca* — and; *priya* — for His dear devotees; *prema* — of love; *vaśaḥ* — under the control; *pradhāvan* — running; *samāgataḥ* — reaching; *harṣa-bhareṇa* — because of the burden of joy; *mugdhaḥ* — fainting; *tayoḥ* — of them; *upari* — on top; *eva* — even; *papāta* — fell; *dīrgha* — long; *mahā* — mighty; *bhujābhyām* — with His two arms; *parirabhya* — embracing; *tau* — them; *dvau* — the two.

**The Lord, compelled by His love for His dear devotees, ran toward them. And when He reached them He fainted and fell on top of them, embracing them both with His long, mighty arms.**

TEXT 35

प्रेमाश्रुधाराभिरहो महाप्रभुः
स स्नापयामास कृपार्द्रमानसः ।
क्षणात्समुत्थाय करद्वयेन ताव्
उत्थापयामास चकार च स्थिरौ ॥

*premāśru-dhārābhir aho mahā-prabhuḥ*
*sa snāpayām āsa kṛpārdra-mānasaḥ*
*kṣaṇāt samutthāya kara-dvayena tāv*
*utthāpayām āsa cakāra ca sthirau*

*prema-aśru* — of tears of love; *dhārābhiḥ* — with a shower; *aho* — oh; *mahā-prabhuḥ* — the supreme master; *saḥ* — He; *snāpayām āsa* — bathed; *kṛpā* — with compassion; *ārdra* — melting; *mānasaḥ* — His heart; *kṣaṇāt* — after a moment; *samutthāya* — standing up; *kara-dvayena* — with both hands; *tau* — the two of them; *utthāpayām āsa* — picked up; *cakāra* — made them; *ca* — and; *sthirau* — steady.

**Imagine! That supreme master, His heart melting with compassion, bathed them with a shower of tears of love! In a moment He stood up, lifted the two devotees from the ground with both hands, and steadied them.**

## TEXT 36

सम्मार्जयन्नश्रु रजश्च गात्रे
लग्नं दयालुर्मुहुरालिलिङ्ग ।
तत्रैव ताभ्यामुपविश्य भूमौ
वाक्यामृतैर्विप्रमतोषयच्च ॥

*sammārjayann aśru rajaś ca gātre*
*lagnaṁ dayālur muhur āliliṅga*
*tatraiva tābhyām upaviśya bhūmau*
*vākyāmṛtair vipram atoṣayac ca*

*sammārjayan* — wiping off; *aśru* — the tears; *rajaḥ* — dust; *ca* — and; *gātre* — on their bodies; *lagnam* — smeared; *dayāluḥ* — merciful; *muhuḥ* — repeatedly; *āliliṅga* — He embraced; *tatra* — there; *eva* — just; *tābhyām* — with them; *upaviśya* — sitting; *bhūmau* — on the ground; *vākya* — with words; *amṛtaiḥ* — which were like nectar; *vipram* — the *brāhmaṇa; atoṣayat* — He satisfied; *ca* — and.

**Wiping off the tears and dust smeared on the bodies of these devotees, the merciful Lord embraced them over and over again. And right at that spot, He sat on the ground with them and spoke nectarean words to please the brāhmaṇa.**

## TEXT 37

श्रीभगवानुवाच
माथुरानुगृहीतार्य विप्रवंशाब्धिचन्द्रमः ।
क्षेमं श्रीजनशर्मंस्ते कच्चिद्राजति सर्वतः ॥

*śrī-bhagavān uvāca*
*māthurānugṛhītārya*
*vipra-vaṁśābdhi-candramaḥ*
*kṣemaṁ śrī-janaśarmaṁs te*
*kaccid rājati sarvataḥ*

*śrī-bhagavān uvāca* — the Personality of Godhead said; *māthura* — hailing from Mathurā; *anugṛhīta* — O blessed; *ārya* — and noble one; *vipra* — of *brāhmaṇas; vaṁśa* — of the dynasty; *abdhi* — from the ocean; *candramaḥ* — O moon; *kṣemam* — welfare; *śrī-jana-śarman* — O Śrī Janaśarmā; *te* — your; *kaccit* — whether; *rājati* — is splendid; *sarvataḥ* — in all respects.

**The Supreme Lord said: Blessed and noble Mathurā brāhmaṇa, Śrī Janaśarmā! You are the moon born from the ocean of the dynasty of brāhmaṇas! Are your peace and well-being resplendent in every way?**

COMMENTARY: As the moon by its gravitational force swells the ocean with high tides, so a *brāhmaṇa* by his noble qualities exalts his family. From Śrī Kṛṣṇa's mouth we now hear for the first time the name of the Mathurā *brāhmaṇa*.

## TEXT 38

क्षेमं सपरिवारस्य मम त्वदनुभावतः ।
त्वत्कृपाकृष्टचित्तोऽस्मि नित्यं त्वद्वर्त्मवीक्षकः ॥

*kṣemaṁ sa-parivārasya*
*mama tvad-anubhāvataḥ*
*tvat-kṛpākṛṣṭa-citto 'smi*
*nityaṁ tvad-vartma-vīkṣakaḥ*

*kṣemam* — the welfare; *sa-parivārasya* — with My family; *mama* — of Me; *tvat* — your; *anubhāvataḥ* — by the influence; *tvat* — your; *kṛpā* — by mercy; *ākṛṣṭa* — attracted; *cittaḥ* — whose heart; *asmi* — I am; *nityam* — always; *tvat* — your; *vartma* — to the path; *vīkṣakaḥ* — looking.

**Only by your influence are My family and I well. By your mercy, My heart is attracted to you. I have always looked toward the path by which you would come.**

COMMENTARY: Kṛṣṇa wants very much to please Janaśarmā with a warm welcome. He honestly feels that the *brāhmaṇa's* arrival is auspicious for Him. He has been awaiting Janaśarmā's arrival for a long time.

## TEXT 39

दिष्ट्या स्मृतोऽस्मि भवता दिष्ट्या दृष्टश्चिरादसि ।
स्वाधीनोऽस्मि तव ब्रह्मन्रमस्वात्र यदृच्छया ॥

*diṣṭyā smṛto 'smi bhavatā*
*diṣṭyā dṛṣṭaś cirād asi*
*svādhīno 'smi tava brahman*
*ramasvātra yadṛcchayā*

*diṣṭyā* — by good fortune; *smṛtaḥ* — remembered; *asmi* — I am; *bhavatā* — by you; *diṣṭyā* — by good fortune; *dṛṣṭaḥ* — seen; *cirāt* — after a long time; *asi* — you are; *sva-adhīnaḥ* — under control; *asmi* — I am; *tava* — your; *brahman* — dear *brāhmaṇa; ramasva* — please enjoy; *atra* — here; *yadṛcchayā* — as you like.

**By good fortune you have remembered Me, and by good fortune I have seen you again after so long. Dear brāhmaṇa, I am totally under your control. Please feel free to enjoy here as you like.**

## TEXT 40

श्रीपरीक्षिदुवाच
समग्रसम्भ्रमप्रेमानन्दभारेण यन्त्रितः ।
नाशकत्प्रतिवक्तुं तं जनशर्मापि वीक्षितुम् ॥

*śrī-parīkṣid uvāca*
*samagra-sambhrama-premā-*
*nanda-bhāreṇa yantritaḥ*
*nāśakat prativaktuṁ taṁ*
*janaśarmāpi vīkṣitum*

*śrī-parīkṣit uvāca* — Śrī Parīkṣit said; *samagra* — total; *sambhrama* — of reverence; *prema-ānanda* — and of the ecstasy of love; *bhāreṇa* — by a flood; *yantritaḥ* — carried away; *na aśakat* — was unable; *prativaktum* — to reply; *tam* — to Him; *janaśarmā* — Janaśarmā; *api* — even; *vīkṣitum* — to look.

**Śrī Parīkṣit said: Swept away by a great flood of loving ecstasy, Janaśarmā, completely awed, was unable to reply to Kṛṣṇa or even look at Him directly.**

TEXT 41

बाष्पसंरुद्धकण्ठः सन्नस्रोपहतलोचनः ।
परं तच्चरणाम्भोजे मूर्ध्नि धृत्वारुदत्तराम् ॥

*bāṣpa-saṁruddha-kaṇṭhaḥ sann*
*asropahata-locanaḥ*
*paraṁ tac-caraṇāmbhoje*
*mūrdhni dhṛtvārudat-tarām*

*bāṣpa* — with sobs; *saṁruddha* — choking; *kaṇṭhaḥ* — his throat; *san* — being; *asra* — by tears; *upahata* — blocked; *locanaḥ* — his eyes; *param* — only; *tat* — His (Kṛṣṇa's); *caraṇa-ambhoje* — on the lotus feet; *mūrdhni* — his head; *dhṛtvā* — putting; *arudat-tarām* — he cried profusely.

**His throat choking with sobs, his eyes burning with tears, all he could do was place his head on Kṛṣṇa's lotus feet and cry profusely.**

TEXT 42

वदान्यचूडामणिरात्मनोऽधिकं
किमप्यपश्यन्प्रतिदेयमाकुलः ।
स्वभूषणानि व्यपकृष्य गात्रतो
विभूष्य तैस्तं विदधे सरूपवत् ॥

*vadānya-cūḍāmaṇir ātmano 'dhikaṁ*
*kim apy apaśyan pratideyam ākulaḥ*
*sva-bhūṣaṇāni vyapakṛṣya gātrato*
*vibhūṣya tais taṁ vidadhe sarūpa-vat*

*vadānya* — of munificent persons; *cūḍāmaṇiḥ* — the crest jewel; *ātmanaḥ* — than Himself; *adhikam* — better; *kim api* — anything; *apaśyan* — not seeing; *pratideyam* — to be offered as a gift; *ākulaḥ* — feeling distressed; *sva* — His own; *bhūṣaṇāni* — ornaments; *vyapakṛṣya* — removing; *gātrataḥ* — from His body; *vibhūṣya* — decorating; *taiḥ* — with them; *tam* — him (Janaśarmā); *vidadhe* — He made; *sarūpa-vat* — similar to Sarūpa.

**Lord Kṛṣṇa, that crest jewel of munificent persons, was distressed because He couldn't find anything better than Himself to offer as a gift. So He removed the ornaments from His own body and decorated the brāhmaṇa with them, making him look like Sarūpa.**

COMMENTARY: "This learned *brāhmaṇa* has offered Me his very self," Kṛṣṇa thought, "but in return I must give him something more valuable than My self; otherwise I won't be showing any more generosity than I normally do. But I can't find anything more precious than My self. What can I give him?" Thinking like this made Kṛṣṇa anxious. He then decided to give Janaśarmā something He had never before given to anyone — His own ornaments. But Kṛṣṇa had to consider seriously before He made that decision, because to give such a gift would verify that He considers His devotees more important than Himself. Along with His ornaments, Kṛṣṇa also gave Janaśarmā a cowherd's form similar to Sarūpa's.

TEXT 43

इत्थमात्मानुरूपां स व्यतनोत्परमां कृपाम् ।
जनशर्मापि तेनैव परिपूर्णार्थतां गतः ॥

*ittham ātmānurūpāṁ sa*
*vyatanot paramāṁ kṛpām*
*janaśarmāpi tenaiva*
*paripūrṇārthatāṁ gataḥ*

*ittham* — in this way; *ātma* — for Himself only; *anurūpām* — suitable; *saḥ* — He (Kṛṣṇa); *vyatanot* — bestowed; *paramām* — the highest; *kṛpām* — mercy; *janaśarmā* — Janaśarmā; *api* — and; *tena* — by that; *eva* — indeed; *paripūrṇa* — complete; *arthatām* — a feeling of success; *gataḥ* — achieved.

**In this way Kṛṣṇa bestowed on Janaśarmā a supreme mercy that only He could give. And Janaśarmā felt completely fulfilled.**

COMMENTARY: By converting the dry *brāhmaṇa* Janaśarmā into a young cowherd fit to join the assembly of intimate cowherd friends, Kṛṣṇa proved that in giving mercy He is unsurpassed. And Janaśarmā, having attained a form like his own *guru's,* was fully satisfied; like all pure devotees, he aspired only to advance in devotional service to the Lord.

As Kṛṣṇa Himself told Uddhava:

*na pārameṣṭhyaṁ na mahendra-dhiṣṇyaṁ*
*na sārvabhaumaṁ na rasādhipatyam*
*na yoga-siddhīr apunar-bhavaṁ vā*
*mayy arpitātmecchati mad vinānyat*

"One who has fixed his consciousness on Me does not desire the position or abode of Lord Brahmā or Lord Indra, nor an empire on earth, nor sovereignty in the lower planetary systems, nor the eightfold perfection of *yoga,* nor liberation from birth and death. Such a person desires Me alone." (*Bhāgavatam* 11.14.14)

*na kiñcit sādhavo dhīrā*
*bhaktā hy ekāntino mama*
*vāñchanty api mayā dattaṁ*
*kaivalyam apunar-bhavam*

"Because My devotees are possessed of saintly behavior and deep intelligence, they completely dedicate themselves to Me and desire nothing besides Me, even if I offer them liberation from birth and death." (*Bhāgavatam* 11.20.34)

Lord Kapiladeva similarly tells His mother:

*sālokya-sārṣṭi-sāmīpya-*
*sārūpyaikatvam apy uta*
*dīyamānaṁ na gṛhṇanti*
*vinā mat-sevanaṁ janāḥ*

"Even if I offer My devotees any kind of liberation — *sālokya, sārṣṭi, sāmīpya, sārūpya,* or *ekatva* — they do not accept it, if it means giving up My service." (*Bhāgavatam* 3.29.13) In the liberated state, five kinds of perfection are available — residence on the same planet as the Supreme Lord (*sālokya*), opulence equal to His (*sārṣṭi*), access to His personal presence (*sāmīpya*), a form similar in appearance to His (*sārūpya*), and oneness with Him (*ekatva*). But absent devotional service, the Lord's pure devotees refuse these perfections even when offered by the Lord Himself. Certainly, then, pure devotees harbor no hidden desires to achieve such rewards.

Lord Kapila also says:

*naikātmatāṁ me spṛhayanti kecin*
*mat-pāda-sevābhiratā mad-īhāḥ*
*ye 'nyonyato bhāgavatāḥ prasajya*
*sabhājayante mama pauruṣāṇi*

"Pure devotees, attached to the activities of devotional service and always engaging in the service of My lotus feet, never desire to become one with Me. Such devotees unflinchingly engage in My service and always join together to glorify My pastimes and activities." (*Bhāgavatam* 3.25.34)

As Lord Nārāyaṇa tells Durvāsā Muni:

*mat-sevayā pratītaṁ te*
*sālokyādi-catuṣṭayam*

*necchanti sevayā pūrṇāḥ*
*kuto 'nyat kāla-viplutam*

"My devotees, always satisfied to be engaged in My loving service, are not interested even in the four principles of liberation [*sālokya, sārūpya, sāmīpya,* and *sārṣṭi*], though these are automatically achieved by their service. What then is to be said of such perishable happiness as elevation to the higher planetary systems?" (*Bhāgavatam* 9.4.67)

The wives of the serpent Kāliya pray:

*na nāka-pṛṣṭhaṁ na ca sārva-bhaumaṁ*
*na pārameṣṭhyaṁ na rasādhipatyam*
*na yoga-siddhīr apunar-bhavaṁ vā*
*vāñchanti yat-pāda-rajaḥ-prapannāḥ*

"Those who have attained the dust of Your lotus feet never hanker for the kingship of heaven, nor limitless sovereignty, nor the position of Brahmā, nor rulership over the earth. They are not interested even in the perfections of *yoga* or in liberation itself." (*Bhāgavatam* 10.16.37)

And the queens of Kṛṣṇa confide to Śrī Draupadī:

*na vayaṁ sādhvi sāmrājyaṁ*
*svārājyaṁ bhaujyam apy uta*
*vairājyaṁ pārameṣṭhyaṁ vā*
*ānantyaṁ vā hareḥ padam*

*kāmayāmaha etasya*
*śrīmat-pāda-rajaḥ śriyaḥ*
*kuca-kuṅkuma-gandhāḍhyaṁ*
*mūrdhnā voḍhuṁ gadā-bhṛtaḥ*

"O saintly lady, we do not desire dominion over the earth, nor the sovereignty of the king of heaven, nor unlimited means for enjoyment. Nor do we desire mystic power, or the position of Lord Brahmā, or immortality, or even attainment of the kingdom of God. We simply desire to carry on our heads the glorious dust of Lord Kṛṣṇa's feet, dust enriched by the fragrance of *kuṅkuma* from His consort's bosom." (*Bhāgavatam* 10.83.41–42) The words *sāmrājyam* and *svārājyam* mean, respectively, rulership over the earth and rulership over heaven. *Bhaujyam* refers to the means for enjoyment that both kinds of sovereignty make available, and *vairājyam* refers to the powers (*siddhis*) of mystic *yogīs*.

The *Bahvṛca Brāhmaṇa* gives alternative meanings to these words, referring to them in the same order to describe lordship over each of the four cardinal directions, beginning with the east. Kṛṣṇa's queens have no interest in such lordship. Nor have they any interest in the opulences called *pārameṣṭhyam* (the position of Brahmā), *ānantyam* (liberation), or residence in Vaikuṇṭha, the abode of Śrī Hari. They want only the dust of Kṛṣṇa's feet. Why? Because it is mixed with the aroma of goddess Lakṣmī's *kuṅkuma*. This is another way of saying that Mahā-lakṣmī aspires to serve Kṛṣṇa even though Brahmā and all the demigods serve her.

Mahā-lakṣmī is also one of Kṛṣṇa's wives, and the dust from His feet mixes with her *kuṅkuma*. Therefore the queens of Dvārakā are eager to have that dust. The queens will accept dust only from the feet of the darling son of Devakī, not from the feet of any other form of God, because only in Śrī Devakī-nandana can they find an unlimited ocean of sweetness. The supreme goddess of fortune who associates with that original form of Godhead is Śrīmatī Rukmiṇī, His first queen.

As the queens reveal in the next verse they speak, the women of Vraja also hanker to obtain that same dust:

*vraja-striyo yad vāñchanti*
*pulindyas tṛṇa-vīrudhaḥ*
*gāvaś cārayato gopāḥ*
*pada-sparśaṁ mahātmanaḥ*

"We desire the same contact with the Supreme Lord's feet that the young women of Vraja desire, and the cowherd boys, and even the aborigine Pulinda women — the touch of the dust He leaves on the plants and grass as He tends His cows." (*Bhāgavatam* 10.83.43) That the *gopīs* of Vraja aspire for the dust of Kṛṣṇa's feet proves beyond any doubt that His feet are the repository of ultimate sweetness. As difficult as it is to obtain that dust, it is easy for devotees like the Vraja-vāsīs, who are fully dedicated to Kṛṣṇa.

The queens want the mercy of Kṛṣṇa with His supreme consort, not His alone. Kṛṣṇa may sometimes remain satisfied within Himself, but pure Vaiṣṇavas like the queens of Dvārakā are not interested in that aspect of His personality. They want to serve Him in the company of His pleasure potency. They want to know Him as the topmost enjoyer of intimate loving exchanges. Gopa-kumāra had a similar attitude. He always wanted to find Śrī Madana-gopāla in His original form. Gopa-kumāra had opportunities to see and associate with the Supreme Lord in many different places, but he became satisfied only when he finally met Kṛṣṇa in Vraja-bhūmi.

To achieve ultimate perfection, devotees should first gain the *darśana,* the divine vision, of Śrī Kṛṣṇa. Kṛṣṇa's *darśana* arises from the playful impulses of devotional service and stimulates extreme happiness in Kṛṣṇa's fortunate devotees. It is the prime means for achieving Him completely.

## TEXT 44

अथापोऽपाययद्वेणुसङ्केतध्वनिना पशून् ।
समाहूय विचित्रेण मुखशब्देन केनचित् ॥

*athāpo 'pāyayad veṇu-*
*saṅketa-dhvaninā paśūn*
*samāhūya vicitreṇa*
*mukha-śabdena kenacit*

*atha* — then; *apaḥ* — water; *apāyayat* — He made drink; *veṇu* — from His flute; *saṅketa* — of a signal; *dhvaninā* — with a sound; *paśūn* — the animals; *samāhūya* — calling; *vicitreṇa* —

special; *mukha* — from the mouth; *śabdena* — by a sound; *kenacit* — certain.

**Then Kṛṣṇa, with a signal from His flute and a special sound from His mouth, called the cows and made them drink water.**

COMMENTARY: Immediately after giving the *brāhmaṇa* mercy, Kṛṣṇa turned His attention to watering His cows, buffaloes, and other animals.

TEXT 45

तेनैव सुखदेशेषु तान्निरुध्योपवेश्य च ।
ताभ्यामन्यैश्च सखिभिर्विजहाराप्सु साग्रजः ॥

*tenaiva sukha-deśeṣu*
*tān nirudhyopaveśya ca*
*tābhyām anyaiś ca sakhibhir*
*vijahārāpsu sāgrajaḥ*

*tena* — with that (sound); *eva* — only; *sukha* — comfortable; *deśeṣu* — in places; *tān* — them (the animals); *nirudhya* — stopping; *upaveśya* — making sit; *ca* — and; *tābhyām* — with them (Sarūpa and Janaśarmā); *anyaiḥ* — with other; *ca* — and; *sakhibhiḥ* — friends; *vijahāra* — He played; *apsu* — in the water; *sa-agra-jaḥ* — with His elder brother.

**And just by that same peculiar sound, He made the animals stop and lie down in comfortable places. Then with the two devotees and His elder brother and His other friends, He played in the water.**

TEXT 46

परस्परं वार्यभिषिञ्चतः सखीन्
कदाचिदुत्क्षिप्य जलानि भञ्जयेत् ।

कदापि तैरेव विनोदकोविदो
विलम्भितो भङ्गभरं जहर्ष सः ॥

*parasparaṁ vāry abhiṣiñcataḥ sakhīn*
*kadācid utkṣipya jalāni bhañjayet*
*kadāpi tair eva vinoda-kovido*
*vilambhito bhaṅga-bharaṁ jaharṣa saḥ*

*parasparam* — one another; *vāri* — with water; *abhiṣiñcataḥ* — who were splashing; *sakhīn* — His friends; *kadācit* — sometimes; *utkṣipya* — splashing; *jalāni* — water; *bhañjayet* — He would shower them with waves; *kadāpi* — sometimes; *taiḥ* — by them (the boys); *eva* — indeed; *vinoda-kovidaḥ* — the expert in sports; *vilambhitaḥ* — subjected; *bhaṅga-bharam* — to a torrent of waves; *jaharṣa* — delighted; *saḥ* — He.

**Now and then Kṛṣṇa would come near His friends who were splashing one another and drench them with waves. And sometimes the boys would come up to Him, the most expert in all sports, and subject Him to a torrent of waves. In all this the Lord took delight.**

COMMENTARY: When His devotees would sneak up on Him from behind and splash water on Him, the Supreme Lord would take no offense; rather, He would very much appreciate being treated to this indignity. As *vinoda-kovida,* the most expert knower of sports, He values the "attacks" of His friends more than the worship offered Him by others.

## TEXT 47

कीलालवाद्यानि शुभानि साकं
तैर्वादयञ्छ्रीयमुनाप्रवाहे ।
स्रोतोऽनुलोमप्रतिलोमतोऽसौ
सन्तारलीलामकरोद्विचित्राम् ॥

*kīlāla-vādyāni śubhāni sākaṁ*
*tair vādayañ chrī-yamunā-pravāhe*
*sroto-'nuloma-pratilomato 'sau*
*santāra-līlām akarod vicitrām*

*kīlāla* — in the water; *vādyāni* — various kinds of music; *śubhāni* — auspicious; *sākam* — along; *taiḥ* — with them; *vādayan* — playing musically; *śrī-yamunā* — of Śrī Yamunā; *pravāhe* — in the current; *srotaḥ-anuloma* — with the current; *pratilomataḥ* — against the current; *asau* — He; *santāra* — of crossing; *līlām* — the pastime; *akarot* — did; *vicitrām* — in various ways.

**Using Śrī Yamunā's flowing water as an instrument, He and His friends played all kinds of auspicious music. And He sported by crossing the river in various ways, both with the current and against it.**

## TEXT 48

कदापि कृष्णाजलमध्यतो निजं
वपुः स निह्नुत्य सरोजकानने ।
मुखं च विन्यस्य कुतूहली स्थितो
यथा न केनापि भवेत्स लक्षितः ॥

*kadāpi kṛṣṇā-jala-madhyato nijaṁ*
*vapuḥ sa nihnutya saroja-kānane*
*mukhaṁ ca vinyasya kutūhalī sthito*
*yathā na kenāpi bhavet sa lakṣitaḥ*

*kadā api* — sometimes; *kṛṣṇā* — of the Yamunā; *jala* — of the water; *madhyataḥ* — in the middle; *nijam* — His own; *vapuḥ* — body; *saḥ* — Kṛṣṇa; *nihnutya* — concealing; *saroja* — of lotuses; *kānane* — in a grove; *mukham* — His face; *ca* — and; *vinyasya* — placing; *kutūhalī-sthitaḥ* — playful; *yathā* — as; *na* — not; *kena api* — by anyone; *bhavet* — would be; *saḥ* — He; *lakṣitaḥ* — noticed.

**Sometimes Kṛṣṇa playfully hid His body in the Yamunā's water and His face in a cluster of lotuses so that no one could find Him.**

COMMENTARY: The river Yamunā is called Kṛṣṇā because the hue of her water closely resembles Kṛṣṇa's complexion. And when Kṛṣṇa hid Himself among lotus flowers that closely resembled His face, it would be difficult for anyone to search Him out.

## TEXT 49

ततस्तदेकेक्षणजीवनास्ते
न तं समन्विष्य यदालभन्त ।
तदा महार्ताः सुहृदो रुदन्तो
विचुक्रुशुर्व्यग्रधियः सुघोरम् ॥

*tatas tad-ekekṣaṇa-jīvanās te*
*na taṁ samanviṣya yadālabhanta*
*tadā mahārtāḥ suhṛdo rudanto*
*vicukruśur vyagra-dhiyaḥ su-ghoram*

*tataḥ* — then; *tat* — Him; *eka* — only; *īkṣaṇa* — seeing; *jīvanāḥ* — whose life; *te* — they; *na* — not; *tam* — Him; *samanviṣya* — looking for; *yadā* — when; *alabhanta* — found; *tadā* — then; *mahā-ārtāḥ* — greatly distressed; *suhṛdaḥ* — His friends; *rudantaḥ* — crying; *vicukruśuḥ* — called out; *vyagra* — completely agitated; *dhiyaḥ* — whose minds; *su-ghoram* — ardently.

**When His friends, who had no purpose in life but to see Him, looked for Him but failed, they wept in terrible distress, their minds bewildered, and called out to Him in ardent voices.**

## TEXT 50

ततो हसन्पद्मवनाद्विनिःसृतः
प्रहर्षपूरेण विकासितेक्षणैः ।

सकूर्दनं तैः पुरतोऽभिसारिभिः
सङ्गम्यमानो विजहार कौतुकी ॥

*tato hasan padma-vanād viniḥsṛtaḥ*
*praharṣa-pūreṇa vikāsitekṣaṇaiḥ*
*sa-kūrdanaṁ taiḥ purato 'bhisāribhiḥ*
*saṅgamyamāno vijahāra kautukī*

*tataḥ* — then; *hasan* — laughing; *padma* — of lotuses; *vanāt* — from the cluster; *viniḥsṛtaḥ* — He came out; *praharṣa* — of joy; *pūreṇa* — with a flood; *vikāsita* — opened wide; *īkṣaṇaiḥ* — their eyes; *sa-kūrdanam* — jumping; *taiḥ* — by them; *purataḥ* — forward; *abhisāribhiḥ* — who were coming forward to meet; *saṅgamyamānaḥ* — being met; *vijahāra* — He enjoyed; *kautukī* — crafty.

**Just then, wily Kṛṣṇa emerged, laughing, from the cluster of lotuses. The boys, their wide-open eyes flooded with joy, rushed forward and jumped into the water to be with Him, and in this way He sported.**

TEXT 51

मृणालजालेन मनोरमेण
विरच्य हाराञ्जलपुष्पजातैः ।
सखीनलंकृत्य समुत्ततार
जलात्समं तैः स च भूषितस्तैः ॥

*mṛṇāla-jālena mano-rameṇa*
*viracya hārāñ jala-puṣpa-jātaiḥ*
*sakhīn alaṅkṛtya samuttatāra*
*jalāt samaṁ taiḥ sa ca bhūṣitas taiḥ*

*mṛṇāla* — of filaments; *jālena* — with a mesh; *manaḥ-rameṇa* — charming; *viracya* — making; *hārān* — garlands; *jala* — of the water; *puṣpa-jātaiḥ* — made from flowers; *sakhīn* — His friends; *alaṅkṛtya* — decorating; *samuttatāra* — He came out; *jalāt* — from the water; *samam* — together; *taiḥ* — with them; *saḥ* — He; *ca* — and; *bhūṣitaḥ* — was decorated; *taiḥ* — by them.

**He decorated His friends with charming garlands made from various water flowers strung together with fibers of lotus stems. Then He and His friends came out of the water, and in the same way they decorated Him.**

TEXT 52

माध्याह्निकं भोजनमत्र कर्तुं
विस्तीर्णकृष्णापुलिने मनोज्ञे ।
गोपैः समं मण्डलशो निविष्टैर्
न्यवेशयत्सोऽग्रजमेव मध्ये ॥

*mādhyāhnikaṁ bhojanam atra kartuṁ*
*vistīrṇa-kṛṣṇā-puline mano-jñe*
*gopaiḥ samaṁ maṇḍalaśo niviṣṭair*
*nyaveśayat so 'grajam eva madhye*

*mādhya-ahnikam* — of midday; *bhojanam* — the meal; *atra* — here; *kartum* — to take; *vistīrṇa* — broad; *kṛṣṇā* — of the Yamunā; *puline* — on the shore; *manaḥ-jñe* — attractive; *gopaiḥ* — with the cowherd boys; *samam* — together; *maṇḍalaśaḥ* — in circles; *niviṣṭaiḥ* — sitting; *nyaveśayat* — seated; *saḥ* — Kṛṣṇa; *agra-jam* — His elder brother; *eva* — indeed; *madhye* — in the middle.

**To have lunch there on the broad, attractive bank of the Yamunā, Kṛṣṇa seated His elder brother in the middle of the cowherd boys, who sat down around Them in concentric circles.**

COMMENTARY: Earlier the boys had all had breakfast, but now it was time for lunch. We can understand from descriptions in the

Tenth Canto that they ate breakfast sometimes in the forest and sometimes at home:

*tau vatsa-pālakau bhūtvā*
*sarva-lokaika-pālakau*
*saprātar-āśau go-vatsāṁś*
*cārayantau viceratuḥ*

"After Kṛṣṇa and Balarāma finished Their breakfast in the morning, They went to take care of the calves and wandered here and there. Kṛṣṇa and Balarāma, the Supreme Personalities of Godhead, who maintain the entire creation, now took charge of the calves as if cowherd boys." (*Bhāgavatam* 10.11.45)

*kvacid vanāśāya mano dadhad vrajāt*
*prātaḥ samutthāya vayasya-vatsapān*
*prabodhayañ chṛṅga-raveṇa cāruṇā*
*vinirgato vatsa-puraḥsaro hariḥ*

"O King, one day Kṛṣṇa decided to take His breakfast as a picnic in the forest. Having risen early in the morning, He blew His bugle made of horn and woke all the cowherd boys and calves with its beautiful sound. Then Kṛṣṇa and the boys, keeping their respective groups of calves before them, proceeded from Vrajabhūmi to the forest." (*Bhāgavatam* 10.12.1)

## TEXT 53

स्वयं च लीलाञ्चितनृत्यगत्या
भ्रमन्विचित्रं परितः पुरैव ।
नीतानि तत्रालयतोऽद्भुतानि
भोज्यानि रेमे परिवेशयन्सः ॥

*svayaṁ ca līlāñcita-nṛtya-gatyā*
*bhraman vicitraṁ paritaḥ puraiva*
*nītāni tatrālayato 'dbhutāni*
*bhojyāni reme pariveśayan saḥ*

*svayam* — Himself; *ca* — and; *līlā-añcita* — playful; *nṛtya* — dancing; *gatyā* — with a gait; *bhraman* — walking; *vicitram* — in various ways; *paritaḥ* — on all sides; *purā* — previously; *eva* — even; *nītāni* — brought; *tatra* — there; *ālayataḥ* — from their homes; *adbhutāni* — wonderful; *bhojyāni* — foods; *reme* — enjoyed; *pariveśayan* — serving; *saḥ* — He (Kṛṣṇa).

**Kṛṣṇa enjoyed serving the boys the wonderful delicacies they had brought from their homes. As He served, He moved back and forth in front of the boys with a playful dancing gait.**

## TEXT 54

सर्वर्तुशश्वत्फलपुष्पशालिनां
वृन्दाटवीदिव्यविचित्रशाखिनाम् ।
तैराहृतान्येव फलानि लीलया
स्वादूनि तेभ्यो विभजन्यथारुचि ॥

*sarvartu-śaśvat-phala-puṣpa-śālināṁ*
*vṛndāṭavī-divya-vicitra-śākhinām*
*tair āhṛtāny eva phalāni līlayā*
*svādūni tebhyo vibhajan yathā-ruci*

*sarva-ṛtu* — belonging to all seasons; *śaśvat* — always fresh; *phala* — fruits; *puṣpa* — flowers; *śālinām* — and grains; *vṛndā-aṭavī* — of the Vṛndāvana forest; *divya* — divine; *vicitra* — various; *śākhinām* — from the trees; *taiḥ* — by them; *āhṛtāni* — taken; *eva* — indeed; *phalāni* — fruits; *līlayā* — playfully; *svādūni* — delicious; *tebhyaḥ* — to the boys; *vibhajan* — serving; *yathā-ruci* — according to the taste.

**The boys also had delicious fruits, flowers, and grains, all provided fresh in every season by the many kinds of divine trees in the Vṛndāvana forest. Kṛṣṇa enjoyed serving to all the boys the fruits that pleased each of them most.**

COMMENTARY: The boys ate not only what their mothers had packed for them but also what they collected from the forest.

## TEXTS 55–56

रसालतालबिल्वानि बदरामलकानि च ।
नारिकेलानि पनसद्राक्षाकदलकानि च ॥

नागरङ्गानि पीलूनि करीराण्यपराण्यपि ।
खर्जूरदाडिमादीनि पक्वानि रसवन्ति च ॥

*rasāla-tāla-bilvāni*
*badarāmalakāni ca*
*nārikelāni panasa-*
*drākṣā-kadalakāni ca*

*nāgaraṅgāni pīlūni*
*karīrāṇy aparāṇy api*
*kharjūra-dāḍimādīni*
*pakvāni rasavanti ca*

*rasāla* — *rasālas; tāla* — palm fruits; *bilvāni* — *bel* fruits; *badara* — *badara* berries; *āmalakāni* — *āmalaka* fruits; *ca* — and; *nārikelāni* — coconuts; *panasa* — jackfruits; *drākṣā* — grapes; *kadalakāni* — bananas; *ca* — and; *nāgaraṅgāni* — oranges; *pīlūni* — *pīlū* fruits; *karīrāṇi* — *karīra* fruits; *aparāṇi* — others; *api* — and; *kharjūra* — dates; *dāḍima* — pomegranates; *ādīni* — and so on; *pakvāni* — ripe; *rasavanti* — tasty; *ca* — and.

**He served rasālas, palm fruits, and bilva fruits, and badaras and āmalakas, and coconuts, jackfruit, grapes, and bananas. He served oranges, pīlus, karīras, and other ripe, tasty fruits, like dates and pomegranates.**

COMMENTARY: Only in the Vṛndāvana forest can one find all these fruits ripe at the same time, and only there can one find blooming simultaneously the flowers described in texts 63 through 66. Words from another source portray the beauty of Vṛndāvana by saying *sarvasminn eva ṛtau śaśvat punaḥ punaḥ phala-śālinām:* "There the trees repeatedly bring forth all sorts of fruits in every season."

## TEXT 57

हर्षाय तेषामादाय प्रत्येकं किञ्चिदच्युतः ।
तिष्ठंस्तत्तत्समीपेऽसौ भुङ्क्ते तानपि भोजयेत् ॥

*harṣāya teṣām ādāya*
*praty-ekaṁ kiñcid acyutaḥ*
*tiṣṭhaṁs tat-tat-samīpe 'sau*
*bhuṅkte tān api bhojayet*

*harṣāya* — for their pleasure; *teṣām* — from them; *ādāya* — taking; *prati-ekam* — each one; *kiñcit* — a little; *acyutaḥ* — Kṛṣṇa; *tiṣṭhan* — standing; *tat-tat* — of each; *samīpe* — in front; *asau* — He; *bhuṅkte* — ate; *tān* — them; *api* — and; *bhojayet* — fed.

**The infallible Lord Kṛṣṇa stood in front of each boy, one after another, and took a morsel from each plate and consumed it, and fed the boy as well. In this way He pleased them all.**

COMMENTARY: Kṛṣṇa stood in front of each boy and ate from that boy's plate. But though He did this with one boy after another, every boy thought that Kṛṣṇa was with him alone.

## TEXTS 58–59

परीक्ष्य मिष्टमिष्टानि श्रीमुखान्तः स्वपाणिभिः ।
उत्थायोत्थाय सखिभिरर्प्यमाणानि सादरम् ॥

सश्लाघं नर्महासार्द्रं विचित्रमुखभङ्गिभिः ।
मधुरं परिचर्वंस्तान् हासयित्वा व्यमोहयत् ॥

*parīkṣya miṣṭa-miṣṭāni*
*śrī-mukhāntaḥ sva-pāṇibhiḥ*
*utthāyotthāya sakhibhir*
*arpyamāṇāni sādaram*

*sa-ślāghaṁ narma-hāsārdraṁ*
*vicitra-mukha-bhaṅgibhiḥ*
*madhuraṁ paricarvaṁs tān*
*hāsayitvā vyamohayat*

*parīkṣya* — examining; *miṣṭa-miṣṭāni* — especially palatable; *śrī* — divine; *mukha-antaḥ* — in His mouth; *sva-pāṇibhiḥ* — with their own hands; *utthāya utthāya* — picking up, one after another; *sakhibhiḥ* — by His friends; *arpyamāṇāni* — being offered; *sa-ādaram* — reverentially; *sa-ślāgham* — with praise; *narma-hāsa* — with humor; *ārdram* — melting; *vicitra* — various; *mukha-bhaṅgibhiḥ* — with grimaces; *madhuram* — in a charming manner; *paricarvan* — devouring; *tān* — them; *hāsayitvā* — making laugh; *vyamohayat* — He enchanted.

**Kṛṣṇa's friends examined all the preparations, picked out those they found especially tasty, and with their own hands reverentially placed them into His divine mouth. And Kṛṣṇa, bubbling with humor, heartily ate each offering, praised its qualities, and made wry faces. In this way He made His friends laugh and completely enchanted them.**

COMMENTARY: To determine which items were most suitable for Kṛṣṇa to eat, the boys first ate a little of each. Then they presented to Kṛṣṇa the delicacies they deemed most suitable by offering them with a great flourish directly into His mouth.

## TEXTS 60–61

आम्लिकं पानकं मिष्टं परं च विविधं बहु ।
तक्रं च तुम्बीपात्रादिभृतं वार्यपि यामुनम् ॥

पिबन्निपाययन्सर्वान्रमयामास बल्लवान् ।
नानाविधसुखक्रीडाकुतूहलविशारदः ॥

*āmlikaṁ pānakaṁ miṣṭaṁ*
*paraṁ ca vividhaṁ bahu*
*takraṁ ca tumbī-pātrādi-*
*bhṛtaṁ vāry api yāmunam*

*piban nipāyayan sarvān*
*ramayām āsa ballavān*
*nānā-vidha-sukha-krīḍā-*
*kutūhala-viśāradaḥ*

*āmlikam* — of tamarind; *pānakam* — a drink; *miṣṭam* — savory; *param* — others; *ca* — and; *vividham* — various; *bahu* — of many varieties; *takram* — buttermilk; *ca* — and; *tumbī* — of *tumbī* gourd; *pātra* — in vessels; *ādi* — and so on; *bhṛtam* — carried; *vāri* — water; *api* — also; *yāmunam* — from the Yamunā; *piban* — drinking; *nipāyayan* — making them drink; *sarvān* — all; *ramayām āsa* — He delighted; *ballavān* — the cowherd boys; *nānā-vidha* — of all sorts; *sukha-krīḍā* — of happy games; *kutūhala* — in pleasure; *viśāradaḥ* — expert.

**That most expert enjoyer of all kinds of amusing sports drank a savory tamarind nectar, many other beverages, and buttermilk and Yamunā water, carried in tumbī gourds and other sorts of vessels, and He made the boys drink too. In this way He delighted all the cowherd boys.**

COMMENTARY: Among the various vessels from which Kṛṣṇa drank Yamunā water were cups made of bamboo and of folded leaves.

TEXT 62

आचम्य ताम्बूलमथो सुगन्धं
कर्पूरपूर्णं स्वगृहोपनीतम् ।

वन्यं च भुङ्क्ते स्म विभज्य नूत्नं
सनागवल्लीदलपूगमार्द्रम् ॥

*ācamya tāmbūlam atho su-gandhaṁ*
*karpūra-pūrṇaṁ sva-gṛhopanītam*
*vanyaṁ ca bhuṅkte sma vibhajya nūtnaṁ*
*sa-nāga-vallī-dala-pūgam ārdram*

*ācamya* — after sipping water; *tāmbūlam* — betel nut; *atha u* — then; *su-gandham* — fragrant; *karpūra* — with camphor; *pūrṇam* — rich; *sva-gṛha* — from each boy's house; *upanītam* — brought; *vanyam* — from the forest; *ca* — and; *bhuṅkte sma* — He enjoyed; *vibhajya* — distributing; *nūtnam* — fresh; *sa* — along with; *nāga-vallī* — of *nāga* creepers; *dala* — of small leaves; *pūgam* — with an abundance; *ārdram* — soaked.

**Kṛṣṇa did ācamana and then chewed fragrant, camphor-rich betel nut that each boy had brought from his home, and also fresh forest betel nut, soaked and wrapped in many leaves of nāga creepers. He enjoyed the betel nut and also gave it out.**

COMMENTARY: When Kṛṣṇa finished eating, He washed His hands and mouth and performed the ritual sipping of water. All the boys had brought betel nut from their homes, and now they offered it all to Kṛṣṇa, who ate some Himself and distributed the rest among them.

## TEXTS 63–66

तुलसीमालतीजातीमल्लिकाकुन्दकुब्जकैः ।
लवङ्गकेतकीझिण्टीमाधवीयूथिकाद्वयैः ॥

काञ्चनैः करवीराभ्यां शतपत्रीयुगेन च ।
पलाशैर्नवमल्लीभिरोड्रैर्दमनकादिभिः ॥

कदम्बनीपबकुलैर्नागपुन्नागचम्पकैः ।
कूटजाशोकमन्दारैः कर्णिकारासनार्जुनैः ॥

पाटलैः प्रियकैरन्यैरपि पुष्पैः सपल्लवैः ।
विचित्रा निर्मिता मित्रैर्मालाश्चाधाद्विभज्य सः ॥

*tulasī-mālatī-jātī-*
*mallikā-kunda-kubjakaiḥ*
*lavaṅga-ketakī-jhiṇṭī-*
*mādhavī-yūthikā-dvayaiḥ*

*kāñcanaiḥ karavīrābhyāṁ*
*śatapatrī-yugena ca*
*palāśair navamallībhir*
*oḍrair damanakādibhiḥ*

*kadamba-nīpa-bakulair*
*nāga-punnāga-campakaiḥ*
*kūṭajāśoka-mandāraiḥ*
*karṇikārāsanārjunaiḥ*

*pāṭalaiḥ priyakair anyair*
*api puṣpaiḥ sa-pallavaiḥ*
*vicitrā nirmitā mitrair*
*mālāś cādhād vibhajya saḥ*

*tulasī-mālatī-jātī-mallikā-kunda-kubjakaiḥ* — with *tulasī, mālatī, jātī, mallikā, kunda,* and *kubjaka; lavaṅga-ketakī-jhiṇṭī-mādhavī-yūthikā-dvayaiḥ* — with clove, *ketakī, jhiṇṭī, mādhavī,* and two kinds of *yūthikā; kāñcanaiḥ* — with *kāñcana* flowers; *karavīrābhyām* — with two kinds of *karavīrā; śatapatrī-yugena* — with two kinds of *śatapatrī; ca* — and; *palāśaiḥ* — with *palāśa; navamallībhiḥ* — with *navamallī; oḍraiḥ* — with *oḍra; damanaka-ādibhiḥ* — with *damanaka* and so on; *kadamba-nīpa-bakulaiḥ* — with *kadamba, nīpa,* and *bakula; nāga-punnāga-campakaiḥ* — with *nāga, punnāga,* and *campaka;*

*kūṭaja-aśoka-mandāraiḥ* — with *kūṭaja, aśoka,* and *mandāra; karṇikāra-āsana-arjunaiḥ* — with *karṇikāra, āsana,* and *arjuna; pāṭalaiḥ* — with *pāṭala; priyakaiḥ* — with *priyaka; anyaiḥ* — others; *api* — also; *puṣpaiḥ* — with flowers; *sa-pallavaiḥ* — and leaves; *vicitrāḥ* — various; *nirmitāḥ* — made; *mitraiḥ* — by His friends; *mālāḥ* — garlands; *ca* — and; *adhāt* — gave; *vibhajya* — distributing; *saḥ* — He.

**His friends made for Him various garlands from flowers and leaves. There were flowers and leaves of tulasī, mālatī, and jātī, of mallikā, kunda jasmine, and kubjaka, of clove, ketakī, and jhiṇṭī, of mādhavī and two kinds of yūthikā. The garlands had kāñcana and karavīra and śatapatrī (two kinds each), and flowers and leaves of palāśa and nava-mallī, and oḍra and damanaka and others. There were flowers and leaves of kadamba, and of nīpa and bakula, and nāga, punnāga, and campaka. The garlands had kūṭaja and aśoka and mandara. They had karṇikāra, āsana, arjuna, pāṭala, priyaka — and still other flowers and leaves. Kṛṣṇa put these garlands on Himself and passed them out among His friends.**

COMMENTARY: The boys made many kinds of flower garlands for Kṛṣṇa, including the famous *vaijayantī. Mālatī* and *jātī* are subtypes of white night-blooming jasmine. *Nīpa* and *kadamba* are also two varieties of one species. The two kinds of *yūthikā* are the golden (*svarṇa-yūthikā*) and white (*śubhra-yūthikā*). The *karavīra* and *śatrapatrī* both have white and red varieties. *Palāśa* is also known as *kiṁśuka.*

The second of these verses ends with the word *damanakādibhiḥ,* which implies that there were other flowers with petals like the *damanaka,* such as the *maruvaka.* In the fourth verse the "others" indicated at the end of the first line include the *śṛṅgāra-hāra, sthala-kamala,* and *bhūmi-campaka.* Many flowers that grow in water are not mentioned here, because they play more of a part in Kṛṣṇa's water sports; nonetheless, the many water flowers used in these forest garlands are also referred to indirectly by the phrase "and others." The garlands also included new leaves and flower buds from trees such as the *kadamba*. And on His head Kṛṣṇa always wore peacock feathers and berries of *guñjā*.

## TEXT 67

चन्दनागुरुकस्तुरीकुंकुमैराहृतैर्वनात् ।
द्रव्यैः सुगन्धिभिश्चान्यैः पिष्टैरङ्गान्यलेपयत् ॥

*candanāguru-kasturī-*
*kuṅkumair āhṛtair vanāt*
*dravyaiḥ su-gandhibhiś cānyaiḥ*
*piṣṭair aṅgāny alepayat*

*candana* — with sandalwood; *aguru* — *aguru; kasturī* — musk; *kuṅkumaiḥ* — and *kuṅkuma; āhṛtaiḥ* — brought; *vanāt* — from the forest; *dravyaiḥ* — substances; *su-gandhibhiḥ* — fragrant; *ca* — and; *anyaiḥ* — with other substances; *piṣṭaiḥ* — made into paste; *aṅgāni* — His limbs; *alepayat* — He smeared.

**He smeared His limbs with a paste of sandalwood, aguru, kuṅkuma, musk, and other fragrant substances brought from the forest.**

COMMENTARY: Kṛṣṇa's friends brought these fragrant substances from the Vṛndāvana forest for His pleasure and made them into a paste by adding water and grinding them on rocks. Kṛṣṇa smeared this paste on His body and once again shared it with His friends. All enjoyable things are available in the Vṛndāvana forest.

## TEXTS 68–69

निकुञ्जवर्ये सुरभिप्रसून-
सुवासिते गुञ्जदलिप्रघुष्टे ।

विनिर्मिते तल्पवरे नवीन-
मृदुप्रवालच्छदपुष्पजातैः ॥

श्रीदामनामदयिताङ्गसुखोपधानः
सुस्वाप मित्रनिकरैः परिचर्यमाणः ।
केशप्रसाधनसुगीतकराङ्घ्रिपद्म-
संवाहनस्तवनवीजनचातुरीभिः ॥

*nikuñja-varye surabhi-prasūna-*
*suvāsite guñjad-ali-praghuṣṭe*
*vinirmite talpa-vare navīna-*
*mṛdu-pravāla-cchada-puṣpa-jātaiḥ*

*śrīdāma-nāma-dayitāṅga-sukhopadhānaḥ*
*susvāpa mitra-nikaraiḥ paricaryamāṇaḥ*
*keśa-prasādhana-sugīta-karāṅghri-padma-*
*saṁvāhana-stavana-vījana-cāturībhiḥ*

*nikuñja-varye* — in a choice grove; *surabhi* — fragrant; *prasūna* — with flowers; *su-vāsite* — well scented; *guñjat* — humming; *ali* — with bees; *praghuṣṭe* — resounding; *vinirmite* — fashioned; *talpa-vare* — on an excellent bed; *navīna* — new; *mṛdu* — soft; *pravāla* — young shoots; *chada* — leaves; *puṣpa* — and flowers; *jātaiḥ* — with many; *śrīdāma-nāma* — named Śrīdāmā; *dayita* — of His dear friend; *aṅga* — the body; *sukha* — comfortable; *upadhānaḥ* — whose pillow; *susvāpa* — He rested; *mitra-nikaraiḥ* — by His many friends; *paricaryamāṇaḥ* — being attended; *keśa-prasādhana* — in hairdressing; *sugīta* — sweet singing; *kara* — of His hands; *aṅghri* — and feet; *padma* — lotuslike; *saṁvāhana* — massaging; *stavana* — reciting prayers; *vījana* — and fanning; *cāturībhiḥ* — who were expert.

**Then, in a choice grove, fragrant with sweet-smelling flowers and resonant with humming bees, Kṛṣṇa rested a while on an excellent bed made of many new soft leaves, sprouts, and flowers. The body of His dear friend Śrīdāmā**

**provided a comfortable pillow. And countless friends served Kṛṣṇa by expertly reciting prayers, singing sweetly, fanning Him, dressing His hair, and massaging His lotus feet and hands.**

COMMENTARY: Kṛṣṇa's flower bed was so fragrant that many bees were attracted to it. Kṛṣṇa pleasantly rested on this very comfortable bed while His friends attended to Him. Śrī Bādarāyaṇi has described this scene in *Śrīmad-Bhāgavatam* (10.15.16–18):

*kvacit pallava-talpeṣu*
*niyuddha-śrama-karśitaḥ*
*vṛkṣa-mūlāśrayaḥ śete*
*gopotsaṅgopabarhaṇaḥ*

"Sometimes Lord Kṛṣṇa grew tired from fighting and lay down at the base of a tree, resting upon a bed made of soft twigs and buds and using the lap of a cowherd friend as His pillow.

*pāda-saṁvāhanaṁ cakruḥ*
*kecit tasya mahātmanaḥ*
*apare hata-pāpmāno*
*vyajanaiḥ samavījayan*

"Some of the cowherd boys, who were all great souls, would then massage His lotus feet, and others, qualified by being free of all sin, would expertly fan Him.

*anye tad-anurūpāṇi*
*mano-jñāni mahātmanaḥ*
*gāyanti sma mahā-rāja*
*sneha-klinna-dhiyaḥ śanaiḥ*

"My dear King, other boys would sing enchanting songs appropriate to the occasion, and their hearts would melt out of love for the Lord."

TEXT 70

नानानुकारमुखपद्मविकारनर्म-
भङ्गीशतैर्हसितरोधनकेलिदक्षान् ।
निर्जित्य तानसुखयत्सुहृदो मुदैवं
विश्रामकेलिमतनोद्विविधं सरामः ॥

*nānānukāra-mukha-padma-vikāra-narma-*
*bhaṅgī-śatair hasita-rodhana-keli-dakṣān*
*nirjitya tān asukhayat suhṛdo mudaivaṁ*
*viśrāma-kelim atanod vividhaṁ sa-rāmaḥ*

*nānā-anukāra* — various; *mukha-padma* — lotus face; *vikāra* — defeated; *narma* — jokes; *bhaṅgī* — distortions; *śataiḥ* — hundreds; *hasita* — from laughing; *rodhana* — of restraining; *keli-dakṣān* — competent in the sport; *nirjitya* — defeated; *tān* — them; *asukhayat* — gave pleasure; *suhṛdaḥ* — to the friends; *mudā* — with delight; *evam* — thus; *viśrāma-kelim* — the pastime of resting; *atanot* — spread; *vividham* — in various ways; *sa-rāmaḥ* — along with Balarāma.

**Kṛṣṇa enjoyed pleasing His friends and in various ways, along with Balarāma, indulged in His pastime of relaxing. Though Kṛṣṇa's friends were very competent in the sport of keeping themselves from laughing, Kṛṣṇa defeated them by imitating various characters, distorting His face, and cutting hundreds of jokes.**

COMMENTARY: The boys served Kṛṣṇa, and He reciprocated by entertaining them.

TEXT 71

अथ सङ्केतितैर्वेणुशृङ्गनादैः पशून्पुनः ।
उत्थाप्य चारयन्रेमे गोवर्धनसमीपतः ॥

*atha saṅketitair veṇu-*
*śṛṅga-nādaiḥ paśūn punaḥ*
*utthāpya cārayan reme*
*govardhana-samīpataḥ*

*atha* — then; *saṅketitaiḥ* — with signals; *veṇu* — of His flute; *śṛṅga* — and buffalo horn; *nādaiḥ* — by the sounds; *paśūn* — His animals; *punaḥ* — again; *utthāpya* — making rise; *cārayan* — grazing; *reme* — He enjoyed; *govardhana-samīpataḥ* — near Govardhana Hill.

**Then, making the animals rise by sounding signals from His flute and buffalo horn, He enjoyed grazing them near Govardhana Hill.**

TEXT 72

भूषणेन विचित्रेण वन्येन सखिभिः पुनः ।
अहंपूर्विकया सर्वैर्भूषितोऽसौ यथारुचि ॥

*bhūṣaṇena vicitreṇa*
*vanyena sakhibhiḥ punaḥ*
*ahaṁ-pūrvikayā sarvair*
*bhūṣito 'sau yathā-ruci*

*bhūṣaṇena* — with ornaments; *vicitreṇa* — various; *vanyena* — made of forest items; *sakhibhiḥ* — by His friends; *punaḥ* — again; *aham-pūrvikayā* — with the idea "I am best"; *sarvaiḥ* — by all; *bhūṣitaḥ* — decorated; *asau* — He; *yathā-ruci* — according to their individual tastes.

**And again all His friends, each according to his own taste, tried to outdo the others in decorating Kṛṣṇa with an assortment of wonderful items from the forest.**

COMMENTARY: Some boys applied *tilaka* made from *haritāla* to Kṛṣṇa's forehead, others arranged flower garlands in His hair, and still others decorated His head with *guñjā* berries.

## TEXT 73

सरूपपाणौ जनशर्मसंज्ञं
समर्प्य तं विप्रमपूर्वयातम् ।
सायं यथापूर्वमयं प्रविश्य
घोषेऽभिरेमे व्रजहर्षकारी ॥

*sarūpa-pāṇau janaśarma-saṁjñaṁ*
*samarpya taṁ vipram apūrva-yātam*
*sāyaṁ yathā-pūrvam ayaṁ praviśya*
*ghoṣe 'bhireme vraja-harṣa-kārī*

*sarūpa* — of Sarūpa; *pāṇau* — into the hand; *janaśarma-saṁjñam* — named Janaśarmā; *samarpya* — turned over; *tam* — him; *vipram* — the *brāhmaṇa; apūrva* — never before; *yātam* — come there; *sāyam* — in the evening; *yathā* — as; *pūrvam* — previously; *ayam* — He; *praviśya* — entering; *ghoṣe* — the cowherd village; *abhireme* — took pleasure; *vraja* — to Vraja; *harṣa-kārī* — the giver of joy.

**In the evening Kṛṣṇa, the giver of joy to all of Vraja, left the newcomer brāhmaṇa Janaśarmā in the hands of Sarūpa and as before took pleasure in entering the cowherd village.**

COMMENTARY: Kṛṣṇa's return to His father's village in the evening has already been described. So that Janaśarmā would not be confused about what to do back in the village, Kṛṣṇa asked Sarūpa to guide him.

## TEXT 74

गोपीनाथप्रसादाप्तमहासाधुमतिस्थिते ।
विचार्य स्वयमादत्स्व स्वप्रश्नस्याधुनोत्तरम् ॥

*gopīnātha-prasādāpta-*
*mahā-sādhu-mati-sthite*

*vicārya svayam ādatsva*
*sva-praśnasyādhunottaram*

*gopīnātha* — of Lord Gopīnātha; *prasāda* — by the mercy; *āpta* — obtained; *mahā-sādhu* — superexcellent; *mati* — in understanding; *sthite* — fixed; *vicārya* — thinking over; *svayam* — yourself; *ādatsva* — give; *sva* — your own; *praśnasya* — to the question; *adhunā* — now; *uttaram* — the answer.

**O mother, you are fixed in the superexcellent intelligence attained only by the mercy of Lord Gopīnātha. Now, reflecting on all you have heard, you can answer your own questions.**

COMMENTARY: Having reached the end of his narration, Śrī Parīkṣit now suggests to his mother that he has told her everything she needs to know to answer the questions with which she had approached him. She should not doubt her ability to think of the correct answers, because she is fully graced with Kṛṣṇa's mercy.

At the beginning of *Śrī Bṛhad-bhāgavatāmṛta* (1.1.18) Śrī Uttarā asked Parīkṣit:

*yac chukenopadiṣṭaṁ te*
*vatsa niṣkṛṣya tasya me*
*sāraṁ prakāśaya kṣipraṁ*
*kṣīrāmbhodher ivāmṛtam*

"My dear son, please extract the essence of what Śukadeva has taught you and quickly reveal it to me, as if churning the nectar of immortality from the Ocean of Milk."

And at the beginning of Part Two (2.1.24) Uttarā inquired further whether higher than Vaikuṇṭha there is a realm where the Supreme Lord's most intimate devotees can associate with Him freely:

*tad-artham ucitaṁ sthānam*
*ekaṁ vaikuṇṭhataḥ param*

*apekṣitam avaśyaṁ syāt*
*tat prakāśyoddharasva mām*

"A suitable place must surely exist for them, beyond Vaikuṇṭha. Please reveal it to me and rescue me."

### TEXT 75

श्रीगोलोके निखिलपरमानन्दपूरान्त्यसीम-
गम्भीराब्धौ जननि गमनं साधय स्वप्रयासैः ।
यस्मिंस्तास्ता विविधरतयस्तेन नाथेन साकं
यात्रामात्रान्मधुरमधुराः सन्ततं सङ्घटन्ते ॥

*śrī-goloke nikhila-paramānanda-pūrāntya-sīma-*
*gambhīrābdhau janani gamanaṁ sādhaya sva-prayāsaiḥ*
*yasmiṁs tās tā vividha-ratayas tena nāthena sākaṁ*
*yātrā-mātrān madhura-madhurāḥ santataṁ saṅghaṭante*

*śrī-goloke* — in Śrī Goloka; *nikhila* — all; *parama-ānanda* — of transcendental bliss; *pūra* — of the flood; *antya-sīma* — of the ultimate extreme; *gambhīra* — deep; *abdhau* — to the ocean; *janani* — O mother; *gamanam* — the going; *sādhaya* — please attempt; *sva* — your own; *prayāsaiḥ* — by the endeavors; *yasmin* — where; *tāḥ tāḥ* — all those; *vividha* — various; *ratayaḥ* — loving exchanges; *tena* — with that; *nāthena* — Lord; *sākam* — together; *yātrā-mātrāt* — just by going there; *madhura-madhurāḥ* — most sweet; *santatam* — eternally; *saṅghaṭante* — occur.

**By your own endeavors, dear mother, please try to reach Śrī Goloka, the deep ocean where the flood of all transcendental bliss finds its ultimate limit. Just by going there you will eternally relish all sorts of most sweet loving exchanges with that same Supreme Lord.**

COMMENTARY: Out of love for his mother, Parīkṣit is eager to help her find the answer to her questions. This he does in four verses (texts 75 through 78) by reminding her of the ultimate perfection she can achieve. He advises her to try by all means to achieve Goloka, Kṛṣṇa's abode. Goloka can be reached only by the special mercy of the Personality of Godhead; still, devotees are recommended to make their own efforts to achieve that goal with enthusiasm and confidence in their regulative practices, for devotees who become indifferent to everything will fail to attract the Supreme Lord's favor.

## TEXT 76

भौमे चास्मिन्सपदि मथुरामण्डले यानमात्रात्
सिध्येयुस्ताः सकलसमये यस्य कस्यापि नैव ।
किन्त्वेतस्य प्रियजनकृपापूरतः कस्यचित्स्युस्
तद्भो मातश्चिनु पदरजस्तत्पदैकप्रियाणाम् ॥

*bhaume cāsmin sapadi mathurā-maṇḍale yāna-mātrāt*
*sidhyeyus tāḥ sakala-samaye yasya kasyāpi naiva*
*kintv etasya priya-jana-kṛpā-pūrataḥ kasyacit syus*
*tad bho mātaś cinu pada-rajas tat-padaika-priyāṇām*

*bhaume* — on the earth; *ca* — and; *asmin* — to this; *sapadi* — immediately; *mathurā-maṇḍale* — to the district of Mathurā; *yāna-mātrāt* — simply by going; *sidhyeyuḥ* — would be attained; *tāḥ* — those; *sakala-samaye* — at all times; *yasya kasya api* — by just anyone; *na eva* — not at all; *kintu* — rather; *etasya* — of Him (the Supreme Lord); *priya-jana* — of the dear devotees; *kṛpā* — of the mercy; *pūrataḥ* — by a full dose; *kasyacit* — by someone; *syuḥ* — they may happen; *tat* — therefore; *bhoḥ mātaḥ* — O mother; *cinu* — please gather; *pada* — from the feet; *rajaḥ* — the dust; *tat* — His; *pada* — for the feet; *eka* — exclusive; *priyāṇām* — of those who have love.

**It's not that just anyone at any time can achieve those perfections at once just by traveling to the district of Mathurā**

**on earth. Rather, only a rare person achieves them, when he has obtained full mercy from the Lord's dear devotees. O mother, please, therefore, gather dust from the feet of devotees who have exclusive love for the lotus feet of the Lord.**

COMMENTARY: Mother Uttarā might propose that according to what she has heard from Parīkṣit she could achieve perfection simply by traveling to the nearby Vraja-bhūmi of the Mathurā district, which is nondifferent from Goloka in the spiritual sky. But Parīkṣit answers that to realize the boundless variety of loving exchanges with Śrī Golokanātha is not so easy. Only during the short time of Kṛṣṇa's *avatāra* — when He makes Himself visible on earth, at the end of but one Dvāpara-yuga in each day of Brahmā — can anyone who simply visits Vraja become perfect. At that time, Kṛṣṇa descends to earth to bestow causeless good fortune to all the *jīvas*. At other times, one can achieve the full realization of Kṛṣṇa consciousness only by receiving a flood of mercy from a dear devotee of Śrī Gopīnātha. This, indeed, was how the *brāhmaṇa* Janaśarmā became fortunate — by the mercy of Sarūpa. Parīkṣit therefore begs his mother that, rather than associate with persons interested in liberation or anything else, she search out the dust from the feet of Vaiṣṇavas who want only love for Kṛṣṇa. With great care she should collect that dust and place it on her head. Then her visit to Vraja-bhūmi will result in complete perfection.

## TEXT 77

स्थानं गोपीगणकुचतटीकुंकुमश्रीभरार्द्र-
श्रीमत्पादाम्बुजयुगसदाप्रीतिसङ्गप्रदायि ।
जिज्ञासोस्ते जननि कथितोऽशेषसन्देहघाती
गोलोकोऽयं मधुरगहनप्रश्नभावानुसारात् ॥

*sthānaṁ gopī-gaṇa-kuca-taṭī-kuṅkuma-śrī-bharārdra-*
*śrīmat-pādāmbuja-yuga-sadā-prīti-saṅga-pradāyi*

*jijñāsos te janani kathito 'śeṣa-sandeha-ghātī*
*goloko 'yaṁ madhura-gahana-praśna-bhāvānusārāt*

*sthānam* — the place; *gopī-gaṇa* — of the *gopīs; kuca* — of the breasts; *taṭī* — from the slopes; *kuṅkuma* — of the *kuṅkuma* powder; *śrī* — with the opulence; *bhara-ārdra* — heavily covered; *śrīmat* — beautiful; *pāda-ambuja* — of lotus feet; *yuga* — of the pair; *sadā* — perpetual; *prīti* — loving; *saṅga* — the association; *pradāyi* — giving; *jijñāsoḥ* — who are eager to know; *te* — to you; *janani* — O mother; *kathitaḥ* — described; *aśeṣa* — all; *sandeha* — doubts; *ghātī* — destroying; *golokaḥ* — Goloka; *ayam* — that; *madhura* — affectionate; *gahana* — deeply thoughtful; *praśna* — of the inquiry; *bhāva* — the spirit; *anusārāt* — according to.

**That place Goloka bestows eternal loving contact with Kṛṣṇa's beautiful lotus feet, which are thickly smeared with the kuṅkuma from the slopes of the gopīs' breasts. Dear mother, I have thus replied according to the spirit of your affectionate and deeply thoughtful questions, and all your doubts should now have been destroyed.**

COMMENTARY: Now that Parīkṣit has told his mother what she ought to do, he wants to remind her that Goloka is the final goal and that meditation on Goloka will greatly foster her progress. Uttarā's original request was "Please deliver me," and in this verse Parīkṣit responds directly. Considering Uttarā's plea altogether praiseworthy, he has gladly satisfied her. Simply by hearing in detail the glories of Goloka, all doubts are vanquished.

## TEXT 78

वैकुण्ठस्याप्युपरि नितरां राजते यो नितान्त-
श्रीमद्गोपीरमणचरणप्रेमपूरैकलभ्यः ।
वाञ्छावाञ्छोपरिगुरुफलप्राप्तिर्भूमिर्यदीया
लोका ध्याता दधति परमां प्रेमसम्पत्तिनिष्ठाम् ॥

*vaikuṇṭhasyāpy upari nitarāṁ rājate yo nitānta-*
*śrīmad-gopī-ramaṇa-caraṇa-prema-pūraika-labhyaḥ*
*vāñchā-vāñchopari-guru-phala-prāptir bhūmir yadīyā*
*lokā dhyātā dadhati paramāṁ prema-sampatti-niṣṭhām*

*vaikuṇṭhasya* — than Vaikuṇṭha; *api* — even; *upari* — higher; *nitarām* — especially; *rājate* — shines; *yaḥ* — which; *nitānta* — perfectly; *śrīmat* — blessed; *gopī* — of the *gopīs; ramaṇa* — of the lover; *caraṇa* — for the feet; *prema* — of love; *pūra* — by an abundance; *eka* — only; *labhyaḥ* — achievable; *vāñchā-vāñchā-upari* — beyond all desires; *guru* — the most significant; *phala* — of the benefits; *prāptiḥ* — where there is the attainment; *bhūmiḥ* — the land; *yadīyāḥ* — of which; *lokāḥ* — the people; *dhyātāḥ* — meditated on; *dadhati* — grant; *paramām* — the highest; *prema* — of *prema; sampatti* — in the treasure; *niṣṭhām* — establishment.

**That world Goloka, shining even above Vaikuṇṭha, can be achieved only by firm, boundless love for the blessed feet of the lover of the gopīs. In that land one reaps the most valuable rewards, far beyond one's desires. When one meditates on the residents of that world, they grant the highest fortune of firm standing in prema.**

COMMENTARY: The only effective *sādhana* for reaching the highest world Goloka is the special kind of love that holds fast to the lotus feet of Śrī Gopīnātha. And since that love reposes in the residents of Goloka, remembering the exalted Vaiṣṇavas of Goloka is the key to all success.

## TEXT 79

अधुनात्राभियुक्तानि मुनीनां महतां शृणु ।
इमानि वचनान्यात्मचित्तसन्तोषणानि हि ॥

*adhunātrābhiyuktāni*
*munīnāṁ mahatāṁ śṛṇu*

*imāni vacanāny ātma-*
*citta-santoṣaṇāni hi*

*adhunā* — now; *atra* — in this regard; *abhiyuktāni* — relevant; *munīnām* — of sages; *mahatām* — great; *śṛṇu* — please hear; *imāni* — these; *vacanāni* — statements; *ātma* — your; *citta* — mind; *santoṣaṇāni* — able to fully satisfy; *hi* — indeed.

**Now please hear some relevant statements of great sages, statements that will fully satisfy your mind.**

COMMENTARY: Parīkṣit has answered his mother's inquiries by narrating two histories, one about Nārada and the other about Gopa-kumāra. Earlier in this second half of *Bṛhad-bhāgavatāmṛta* (2.1.33) he told his mother:

*śruti-smṛtīnāṁ vākyāni*
*sākṣāt tātparyato 'py aham*
*vyākhyāya bodhayitvaitat*
*tvāṁ santoṣayituṁ kṣamaḥ*

"I could satisfy your request by explaining to you the statements of the *śrutis* and *smṛtis,* both in their literal meaning and in their implications." To conclude, he will now cite the supporting opinions of reputable authorities about the glories of Goloka.

## TEXT 80

स्वर्गादूर्ध्वं ब्रह्मलोको ब्रह्मर्षिगणसेवितः ।
तत्र सोमगतिश्चैव ज्योतिषां च महात्मनाम् ॥

*svargād ūrdhvaṁ brahma-loko*
*brahmarṣi-gaṇa-sevitaḥ*
*tatra soma-gatiś caiva*
*jyotiṣāṁ ca mahātmanām*

*svargāt ūrdhvam* — above heaven; *brahma-lokaḥ* — Brahmaloka; *brahma-ṛṣi-gaṇa* — by many *brahmarṣis; sevitaḥ* — served; *tatra* — there; *sa-uma* — of Lord Śiva and Umā; *gatiḥ* — the goal; *ca* — and; *eva* — indeed; *jyotiṣām* — who are luminous; *ca* — and; *mahā-ātmanām* — of great souls.

**"Above heaven is Brahmaloka, which is served by many brahmarṣis. It is the goal of Lord Śiva and his wife, Umā, and of great luminous souls who are liberated in the Supreme.**

COMMENTARY: Texts 80 through 85, cited from *Śrī Hari-vaṁśa* (2.19.29–30, 32–35), are part of the prayers offered to Kṛṣṇa by Lord Indra after Kṛṣṇa lifted Govardhana Hill. Here the term *svarga* is used in the same sense as in the following verse from *Śrīmad-Bhāgavatam* (2.5.42):

*bhūr-lokaḥ kalpitaḥ padbhyāṁ*
*bhuvar-loko 'sya nābhitaḥ*
*svar-lokaḥ kalpito mūrdhnā*
*iti vā loka-kalpanā*

"Others may divide the whole planetary system into three divisions, namely the lower planetary systems on the legs of the Supreme Person, the middle planetary systems on the navel, and the upper planetary systems [Svarloka] from the chest to the head."

In other words, *svarga* can be taken to mean the five upper planetary systems from Indra's world up to Brahmā's. Above those planets is found the end of the material universe, and above that is Brahmaloka (Vaikuṇṭha), the transcendental realm. Vaikuṇṭha is also called Brahmaloka because it is the abode of *brahma,* pure spirit, and because it is the world presided over by the Personality of Godhead, the Supreme Brahman, Śrī Kṛṣṇa.

Of course, beyond the five higher *lokas,* or worlds, mentioned here are the seven coverings of the universe, beyond them is the abode of liberation (*mukti-pada*), then comes Śrī

Śivaloka, and then the spiritual world. The verse quoted above, however, mentions only Svargaloka and Vaikuṇṭha because the universal coverings are not normally understood to be "worlds" and because Svarga is well known as the heavenly destination of pious workers. To give some idea of the greatness of Vaikuṇṭha, therefore, a description that conceives of the spiritual world as simply lying beyond Svarga is sufficient.

Rather than refer to the Supreme Personality of Godhead merely as Brahman, it is more correct to refer to Him as Para-brahman, the Supreme Brahman. Kṛṣṇa is called *paraṁ brahma narākṛti,* "the Supreme Absolute Truth appearing in human form." Thus in *Bhagavad-gītā* (10.12) Arjuna says to Kṛṣṇa:

*paraṁ brahma paraṁ dhāma*
*pavitraṁ paramaṁ bhavān*

"You are the Supreme Personality of Godhead, the ultimate abode, the purest, the Absolute Truth." Ātmā and Brahman, therefore, may also be accepted as secondary names of Kṛṣṇa because they identify His expansions, namely the Supersoul and the impersonal Supreme. Therefore in a later verse of the Tenth Chapter of *Bhagavad-gītā* (10.20) Kṛṣṇa begins to describe His opulent material expansions (*vibhūtis*) by saying:

*aham ātmā guḍākeśa*
*sarva-bhūtāśaya-sthitaḥ*

"I am the Supersoul, O Arjuna, seated in the hearts of all living entities." The *Bṛhat-sahasra-nāma-stotra,* when referring to the Supreme Person's *vibhūtis* in its list of secondary names, also calls Him Ātmā: *ātmā tattvādhipaḥ* ("He is the Supreme Soul and the ruler of the elements of creation"). The words of saintly Vaiṣṇavas also identify impersonal Brahman as one of the Supreme Lord's *vibhūtis: parāt paraṁ brahma ca te vibhūtayaḥ* ("These — including the Supreme Brahman, which is beyond everything else — are Your opulent expansions"). Therefore, since the *Bṛhat-sahasra-nāma-stotra* includes among its one thousand names of the Personality of Godhead the names of His *vibhūtis,* these are factually His names, and Śrī Kṛṣṇa can properly be called Brahman.

Consequently, Śrī Śukadeva has said:

*mūrdhabhiḥ satya-lokas tu*
*brahma-lokaḥ sanātanaḥ*

"Satyaloka, the topmost planetary system, is situated on the head of the universal form. Brahmaloka, however, is eternal." (*Bhāgavatam* 2.5.39) Śrīla Śrīdhara Svāmī paraphrases this idea in his commentary: "The world of Brahman, known as Vaikuṇṭha, is perpetual, eternal. It is not contained within the material creation." In other words, Brahmaloka means Vaikuṇṭha.

The verse from *Śrī Hari-vaṁśa* cited here in the *Bṛhad-bhāgavatāmṛta* by Mahārāja Parīkṣit says that *brahmarṣis* — either those absorbed in Brahman or great devotees like Nārada dedicated to Para-brahman, Bhagavān — always serve Brahmaloka. That spiritual realm is aspired for by the most exalted persons, including Lord Śiva and his consort as well as liberated sages who have realized oneness with the self-luminous Supreme. In truth such candidates for entrance into Brahmaloka are not impersonalists but great devotees of the Personality of Godhead's lotus feet, like Sanaka-kumāra and his brothers, who know from their direct experience the insignificance of impersonal liberation. Nārada and other associates of Lord Nārāyaṇa are also on this level of spiritual competence, but because they are considered eternal residents, not candidates for entrance into Vaikuṇṭha, the second sentence of this verse from *Śrī Hari-vaṁśa* does not mention them among persons who make Vaikuṇṭha their goal.

If the word *jyotiṣām* in the last line of this verse were taken literally to mean the sun, moon, and stars, the statement being made would be weak. To say that the spiritual world is beyond the sun and moon is not to say much, since even Maharloka lies beyond the solar and lunar orbits. The sun and moon cannot approach Satyaloka, what to speak of Vaikuṇṭha. The word *jyotiṣām,* therefore, is better understood to refer to the spiritually effulgent sages who worship the Supreme Person.

## TEXT 81

तस्योपरि गवां लोकः साध्यास्तं पालयन्ति हि ।
स हि सर्वगतः कृष्ण महाकाशगतो महान् ॥

*tasyopari gavāṁ lokaḥ*
*sādhyās taṁ pālayanti hi*
*sa hi sarva-gataḥ kṛṣṇa*
*mahākāśa-gato mahān*

*tasya upari* — above it; *gavām* — of the cows; *lokaḥ* — the planet; *sādhyāḥ* — the Sādhyas; *tam* — it; *pālayanti* — protect; *hi* — indeed; *saḥ* — it; *hi* — indeed; *sarva-gataḥ* — all-pervading; *kṛṣṇa* — O Kṛṣṇa; *mahā-akāśa* — the total ether; *gataḥ* — pervading; *mahān* — infinitely expansive.

**"Above Brahmaloka is the planet of the cows, which is protected by the Sādhyas. O Kṛṣṇa, that great planet is infinitely expansive, pervading the unlimited spiritual sky.**

## TEXT 82

उपर्युपरि तत्रापि गतिस्तव तपोमयी ।
यां न विद्मो वयं सर्वे पृच्छन्तोऽपि पितामहम् ॥

*upary upari tatrāpi*
*gatis tava tapo-mayī*
*yāṁ na vidmo vayaṁ sarve*
*pṛcchanto 'pi pitāmaham*

*upari upari* — further above; *tatra* — there; *api* — also; *gatiḥ* — goal; *tava* — Your; *tapaḥ-mayī* — gained by intense concentration; *yām* — which; *na vidmaḥ* — cannot understand; *vayam* —

we; *sarve* — all; *pṛcchantaḥ* — inquiring; *api* — although; *pitāmaham* — from our grandfather.

**"That planet is above all others, and there You are to be achieved by intense concentration of the heart. None of us can understand that world, though we have inquired about it from our grandfather.**

COMMENTARY: Since Vaikuṇṭha is unlimited, nothing can be beyond it in ordinary time and space. Yet there is a transcendental sense in which Goloka, the planet of the cows, lies above Vaikuṇṭha. Just as Śrī Śivaloka, due to its comparative excellences, is considered "above" the infinite abode of liberation, and just as Vaikuṇṭha is understood to be "above" the boundless Śivaloka, so Śrī Goloka is above Vaikuṇṭha. To assert that Goloka lies beyond even Vaikuṇṭha is valid because only on Goloka do the pastime energies of the Personality of Godhead display reality in its most perfect state.

Goloka is presided over by the Sādhyas, meaning "those who are worshiped by great saints." These Sādhyas are Kṛṣṇa's dearmost devotees — Śrī Nanda and others — whom Brahmā, Sanaka, Śiva, and Nārada try to emulate by all the means of spiritual discipline at their command. Another way to understand the word *sādhya* — as derived from the verb meaning "to accomplish" — is that all the cowherd men and women of Goloka manage to bring Kṛṣṇa under their control by the unique ecstatic sentiments they have for Him. Or else these Sādhyas are the *gopīs,* headed by Śrī Rādhā, Kṛṣṇa's dearest devotees and therefore the most important residents of Goloka, who perpetually manage to maintain the glories of that abode by their wonderful pastimes with Kṛṣṇa.

The term *sādhyas* normally refers to a class of ordinary demigods. But the notion that texts 81 and 82 refer to these demigods is no more reasonable than the idea that the luminaries mentioned in Text 80 refer to the sun, moon, and stars. The ordinary Sādhyas, like the celestial bodies of the material world, cannot travel even to Satyaloka, what to speak of Vaikuṇṭha.

Certainly, therefore, these Sādhyas cannot reach Goloka, and their being its protectors is out of the question.

Goloka pervades the spiritual sky, exceeds all limiting conditions of material existence, and most fully manifests pure eternity, cognizance, and bliss. In contrast to the tiny sky of the material world, the spiritual sky is infinite. Goloka has its place in that infinite sky. The Absolute Truth is called *ākāśa* ("the sky") because as the sky, or the material ether, pervades the created universe and remains unchanged as long as the universe exists, Brahman is all-pervading and eternal. The greatest sky, *mahākāśa,* is Para-brahman, the Supreme Person Śrī Kṛṣṇa with His dense, dark-blue effulgence. Vaikuṇṭha, the complete manifestation of *sac-cid-ānanda,* is present within Kṛṣṇa, and thus in essence nondifferent from Him. And within that spiritual existence, Goloka is the supreme abode. It is above Śrī Vaikuṇṭha, which is above all other worlds.

As difficult as it is for conditioned souls to comprehend Vaikuṇṭha, Goloka is even more mysterious. Goloka can be understood only by the *tapas* of complete concentration of the heart. Mundane reason fails even to begin to approach it. And it remains unknown even to the great sages, who for information about it approach the grandfather of the universe, Brahmā.

## TEXT 83

गतिः शमदमाद्यानां स्वर्गः सुकृतकर्मणाम् ।
ब्राह्म्ये तपसि युक्तानां ब्रह्मलोकः परा गतिः ॥

*gatiḥ śama-damādyānāṁ*
*svargaḥ sukṛta-karmaṇām*
*brāhmye tapasi yuktānāṁ*
*brahma-lokaḥ parā gatiḥ*

*gatiḥ* — the goal; *śama* — of mind control; *dama* — sense control; *ādyānām* — and so on; *svargaḥ* — Svarga; *sukṛta* — pious; *karmaṇām* — of those whose activities; *brāhmye* — spiritual;

*tapasi* — in discipline; *yuktānām* — who are engaged; *brahma-lokaḥ* — Brahmaloka; *parā* — the highest; *gatiḥ* — destination.

**"Svarga is the goal achieved by such pious practices as control of the mind and senses, and Brahmaloka is the highest destination, achieved by those who engage in intense spiritual discipline.**

TEXTS 84–85

गवामेव तु गोलोको दुरारोहा हि सा गतिः ।
स तु लोकस्त्वया कृष्ण सीदमानः कृतात्मना ॥

धृता धृतिमता धीर निघ्नतोपद्रवान् गवाम् ॥
इति ।

*gavām eva tu goloko*
*durārohā hi sā gatiḥ*
*sa tu lokas tvayā kṛṣṇa*
*sīdamānaḥ kṛtātmanā*

*dhṛtā dhṛtimatā dhīra*
*nighnatopadravān gavām*
*iti.*

*gavām* — of the cows; *eva* — indeed; *tu* — but; *golokaḥ* — Goloka; *durārohā* — difficult to ascend to; *hi* — indeed; *sā* — it; *gatiḥ* — goal; *saḥ* — that; *tu* — but; *lokaḥ* — world; *tvayā* — by You; *kṛṣṇa* — O Kṛṣṇa; *sīdamānaḥ* — under siege; *kṛta-ātmanā* — who are competent; *dhṛtā* — sustained; *dhṛti-matā* — and wise; *dhīra* — O steadfast one; *nighnatā* — who destroy; *upadravān* — disturbances; *gavām* — to the cows; *iti* — thus.

**"But to rise to Goloka, the planet of the cows, is most difficult. That world was under attack — but You, O Kṛṣṇa, competent, steadfast, and wise, saved it by putting an end to all outrages against the cows."**

COMMENTARY: Here the name Goloka is explained. Goloka is the residence mostly of cows and their herders. Hardly anyone can gain the privilege to go there. Svargaloka and the higher planets of the sages are comparatively easy to enter, being open to pious fruitive workers who can keep their minds and senses under control. *Karmīs* with less self-control can still reach the lower heavenly regions, known as Bila-svarga and Bhauma-svarga. In contrast, the world of the Supreme, Vaikuṇṭha, is attained only by those who perfect the Vaiṣṇava discipline of concentrating the mind on the Personality of Godhead, who always engage in spiritual activity, and who have pure love of God. Yet compared to either the higher planets of the material world or the spiritual planets of Vaikuṇṭha, Goloka is in all ways superior. It is the supreme destination, from which one never returns.

Certainly Goloka is not the home only of cows, since the *gopas* and *gopīs* who tend those cows have already been indicated by the words *sādhyās taṁ pālayanti hi* ("The Sādhyas protect it"). Just as Gokula in the Mathurā district on earth, even though named after the cows, is also the residence of cowherds, Goloka in the spiritual world is also populated by devotees in various relationships with Kṛṣṇa.

Reciting these prayers to Kṛṣṇa, Indra confesses that he tried to disturb the peace of Kṛṣṇa's abode. Of course, Goloka is eternal and always fully blissful, and everyone allowed to go there is immune from all troubles. But Indra, not completely aware of the glories of Goloka, wrongly thinks he created a disturbance there. Describing his offenses from his own limited point of view, he imagines that by attacking Gokula on earth he also created anxiety in Goloka, the topmost spiritual kingdom.

## TEXT 86

किं च,
एवं बहुविधै रूपैश्चरामीह वसुन्धराम् ।
ब्रह्मलोकं च कौन्तेय गोलोकं च सनातनम् ॥
इति ।

*kiṁ ca,*
*evaṁ bahu-vidhai rūpaiś*
*carāmīha vasundharām*
*brahma-lokaṁ ca kaunteya*
*golokaṁ ca sanātanam*
*iti.*

*kim ca* — also; *evam* — thus; *bahu-vidhaiḥ* — of many kinds; *rūpaiḥ* — in; *carāmi* — I move; *iha* — here; *vasundharām* — on the earth; *brahma-lokam* — on Brahmaloka; *ca* — and; *kaunteya* — O son of Kuntī; *golokam* — in Goloka; *ca* — and; *sanātanam* — eternal; *iti* — thus.

**Also: "Thus, O son of Kuntī, in many different forms do I move about here on earth, on Brahmaloka, and in the eternal Goloka."**

COMMENTARY: This verse is from a conversation between Śrī Kṛṣṇa and Arjuna found in the *Skanda Purāṇa*. Before making this statement, Kṛṣṇa spoke about several of His incarnations, including Lord Jagannātha in Puruṣottama-kṣetra.

The Goloka in which Kṛṣṇa appears is an eternal spiritual realm, but in the material world there is also another planet of cows. The Surabhi who visited Kṛṣṇa on the earth after Kṛṣṇa lifted Govardhana Hill was the mother of all cows in the material universe. She came from her residence on the material Goloka, in the Satyaloka planetary system, to perform the *abhiṣeka* of Kṛṣṇa. Being very pleased with Him for having saved her descendants in Mathurā Gokula, Surabhi wanted to take part in the ceremony conducted by the demigods to officially recognize Kṛṣṇa as *indro gavām* ("Govinda, the Indra of the cows"). The Goloka where Mother Surabhi lives is the destination of fortunate cows who do not live in Mathurā-maṇḍala and associate with Kṛṣṇa and His *gopas* but who belong to Brahmā and other demigods. Since Kṛṣṇa is always present in Mathurā (*yatra nityaṁ sannihitaḥ*), the cows with whom Śrī Gopāladeva shares His eternal pastimes in Gokula later become eternal residents of the Goloka above Vaikuṇṭha.

## TEXT 87

श्रीजनमेजय उवाच
वैष्णवाग्र्य मया सन्ति वैशम्पायनतः श्रुताः ।
एते श्लोकास्तदानीं च कश्चिदर्थोऽवधारितः ॥

*śrī-janamejaya uvāca*
*vaiṣṇavāgrya mayā santi*
*vaiśampāyanataḥ śrutāḥ*
*ete ślokās tadānīṁ ca*
*kaścid artho 'vadhāritaḥ*

*śrī-janamejayaḥ uvāca* — Śrī Janamejaya said; *vaiṣṇava-agrya* — O foremost of Vaiṣṇavas; *mayā* — by me; *santi* — there are; *vaiśampāyanataḥ* — from Vaiśampāyana; *śrutāḥ* — which were heard; *ete* — these; *ślokāḥ* — verses; *tadānīm* — at that time; *ca* — and; *kaścit* — some; *arthaḥ* — understanding; *avadhāritaḥ* — ascertained.

**Śrī Janamejaya said to the sage Jaimini: O foremost of Vaiṣṇavas, I heard these same verses from Vaiśampāyana, and I derived some understanding from them.**

## TEXT 88

त्वत्तोऽद्य श्रवणादेषां कोऽप्यर्थो भाति मे हृदि ।
अहो भागवतानां हि महिमा परमाद्भुतः ॥

*tvatto 'dya śravaṇād eṣāṁ*
*ko 'py artho bhāti me hṛdi*
*aho bhāgavatānāṁ hi*
*mahimā paramādbhutaḥ*

*tvattaḥ* — from you; *adya* — now; *śravaṇāt* — by hearing; *eṣām* — these; *kaḥ* — what; *api* — also; *arthaḥ* — understanding; *bhāti* — shines; *me* — my; *hṛdi* — in the heart; *aho* — oh;

*bhāgavatānām* — of the devotees of the Lord; *hi* — indeed; *mahimā* — the glories; *parama-adbhutaḥ* — most amazing.

**But now by hearing these verses from you, my heart shines with fresh insight. Oh, just see the most amazing glories of the Supreme Lord's devotees!**

COMMENTARY: The deep meaning of statements such as these from *Śrī Hari-vaṁśa* can be fathomed only by the mercy of exalted devotees of the Supreme Lord. King Janamejaya acknowledges that the great sage Jaimini has kindly blessed him with the ability to understand the purport of these verses. The king praises Jaimini, his spiritual master, hoping to hear more.

## TEXT 89

कथासमाप्तिमाशंक्य मनो मे परितप्यति ।
किञ्चिद्रसायनं देहि तिष्ठेद्येन सुनिर्वृतम् ॥

*kathā-samāptim āśaṅkya*
*mano me paritapyati*
*kiñcid rasāyanaṁ dehi*
*tiṣṭhed yena su-nirvṛtam*

*kathā* — of the narration; *samāptim* — the completion; *āśaṅkya* — anticipating; *manaḥ* — heart; *me* — my; *paritapyati* — burns; *kiñcit* — some; *rasa-āyanam* — medicinal tonic; *dehi* — please give; *tiṣṭhet* — it may remain; *yena* — by which; *su-nirvṛtam* — completely satisfied.

**Fearing that this narration is about to end, my heart burns with sadness. Please dispense some medicinal tonic by which my heart may again be fully satisfied.**

COMMENTARY: Having offered suitable praise, Janamejaya now reveals his heart. Just as a person attacked by fever may dread the approach of death, Janamejaya dreads the end of his conversation with Mahāmuni Jaimini. Janamejaya pleads for something to pacify his heart, as a fever-stricken man might beg medicine from his doctor. Janamejaya wants Jaimini to directly administer a *rasāyana* tonic flavored with the transcendental tastes of the glories of the Supreme Lord and His devotees. That elixir, administered through the ear, will make his heart again feel happy.

## TEXTS 90–91

श्रीजैमिनिरुवाच
युक्तान्युपाख्यानवरद्वयस्य
पद्यानि यान्यस्य जगौ पिता ते ।
गोलोकमाहात्म्यकथाप्रहृष्टो
भो वत्स भावैर्मधुरैर्विचित्रैः ॥

श्रुतिस्मृतीनामखिलार्थसार-
मयानि गायन्रुचिराणि यानि ।
क्षिपन्भवत्तातवियोगदुःखं
सुखी चरामीह वदामि तानि ॥

*śrī-jaiminir uvāca*
*yuktāny upākhyāna-vara-dvayasya*
*padyāni yāny asya jagau pitā te*
*goloka-māhātmya-kathā-prahṛṣṭo*
*bho vatsa bhāvair madhurair vicitraiḥ*

*śruti-smṛtīnām akhilārtha-sāra-*
*mayāni gāyan rucirāṇi yāni*
*kṣipan bhavat-tāta-viyoga-duḥkhaṁ*
*sukhī carāmīha vadāmi tāni*

*śrī-jaiminiḥ uvāca* — Śrī Jaimini said; *yuktāni* — suitable; *upākhyāna* — of narrations; *vara* — the best; *dvayasya* — of the pair; *padyāni* — verses; *yāni* — which; *asya* — this; *jagau* — sang; *pitā* — father; *te* — your; *goloka-māhātmya* — of the glories of Goloka; *kathā* — by the telling; *prahṛṣṭaḥ* — delighted; *bhoḥ vatsa* — my dear child; *bhāvaiḥ* — with ecstasies; *madhuraiḥ* — sweet; *vicitraiḥ* — various; *śruti-smṛtīnām* — of the *śrutis* and *smṛtis; akhila* — all; *artha* — of the meaning; *sāra-mayāni* — containing the essence; *gāyan* — chanting; *rucirāṇi* — charming; *yāni* — which; *kṣipan* — casting aside; *bhavat* — your; *tāta* — from the father; *viyoga* — of separation; *duḥkham* — the sorrow; *sukhī* — happy; *carāmi* — I travel; *iha* — in this world; *vadāmi* — I now tell; *tāni* — them.

**Śrī Jaimini said: My dear child, in the joy of having spoken about the glories of Goloka your father recited several verses that complement these two wonderful histories. Those charming verses express various sweet ecstasies and bear the essential purport of all the śrutis and smṛtis. By chanting them I am able to dispel the sorrow I feel in the absence of your respected father, and thus I travel happily in this world. Now I shall recite those verses to you.**

COMMENTARY: Janamejaya's request reminds Jaimini that Parīkṣit Mahārāja, after finishing the history of Gopa-kumāra, recited a few verses of *Śrī Brahma-saṁhitā* that glorify Goloka and spoke several verses of *Śrīmad-Bhāgavatam's* Tenth Canto that extol Mathurā Vraja-bhūmi and its residents. The verses of the Tenth Canto highlight various special ecstasies of *vraja-bhakti* that will be discussed in the commentaries. Since remembering these verses gives Jaimini relief from the disappointment caused by King Parīkṣit's departure, Janamejaya, Parīkṣit's son, should also feel enlivened to hear them.

## TEXT 92

आनन्दचिन्मयरसप्रतिभाविताभिस्
ताभिर्य एव निजरूपतया कलाभिः ।
गोलोक एव निवसत्यखिलात्मभूतो
गोविन्दमादिपुरुषं तमहं भजामि ॥

*ānanda-cinmaya-rasa-pratibhāvitābhis*
*tābhir ya eva nija-rūpatayā kalābhiḥ*
*goloka eva nivasaty akhilātma-bhūto*
*govindam ādi-puruṣaṁ tam ahaṁ bhajāmi*

*ānanda* — bliss; *cit* — and knowledge; *maya* — consisting of; *rasa* — mellows; *pratibhāvitābhiḥ* — who appear as reflections; *tābhiḥ* — with those; *yaḥ* — who; *eva* — certainly; *nija-rūpatayā* — with His own form; *kalābhiḥ* — who are parts of portions of His pleasure potency; *goloke* — in Goloka Vṛndāvana; *eva* — certainly; *nivasati* — resides; *akhila-ātma* — as the soul of all; *bhūtaḥ* — who exists; *govindam* — Govinda; *ādi-puruṣam* — the original person; *tam* — Him; *aham* — I; *bhajāmi* — worship.

**"I worship Govinda, the primeval Lord. He resides in everyone's heart as the Supersoul and simultaneously in His own realm, Goloka, with Rādhā, who resembles His own spiritual figure and embodies the ecstatic potency [hlādinī]. Their companions are Her confidantes, extensions of Her bodily form who are permeated with everblissful spiritual rasa."**

COMMENTARY: Texts 92 through 95 come from the fifth chapter of *Śrī Brahma-saṁhitā,* in which Lord Brahmā sings the glories of *ādi-puruṣa,* the original Personality of Godhead, Śrī Govinda. Here, in the thirty-seventh verse of that chapter, Lord Brahmā reveals the superexcellence shown by Govinda and His associates and paraphernalia in the supreme abode, Goloka.

In the phrase *nija-rūpatayā kalābhiḥ* ("Kṛṣṇa in Goloka is accompanied by His counterparts") the word *kalābhiḥ* can be understood in different ways. One meaning of *kalā* is "the means of artistic expression," which in this context indicates Kṛṣṇa's skills in the arts of enchantment. By those skills He exploits the wondrous attractions of His beauty and personal qualities. *Kalā* also means "expanded parts," which can be understood to refer either to Śrīmatī Rādhārāṇī and Her principal companions or to all the *gopas* and *gopīs* of Goloka.

The phrase *nija-rūpatayā* means either that the devotee expansions of Kṛṣṇa — the *gopīs* and all the cowherds — are spontaneous in their devotional exchanges with Him or that they are expansions of His personality and similar to Him in form. They are fully endowed with *ānanda-cinmaya-rasa,* direct perception of transcendental ecstasy, which they know in its most intense aspects. In fact the power of *bhakti* eternally manifests these various devotees to serve as prototype emblems of each *rasa.*

Kṛṣṇa is the Supersoul of all beings, the witness and regulator dwelling always in the hearts of everyone, yet He also lives eternally in Goloka to enjoy with His intimate devotees. He is the original Puruṣa, the source of all *avatāras,* greater even than the Lord of Vaikuṇṭha. To indicate greater distance, Brahmā uses the third-person pronoun *tam* to refer to Govinda: *tam ahaṁ bhajāmi* ("I worship that Lord"). In this way Brahmā speaks as if Govinda, who resides in such a far-away place, were impossible for him to see.

## TEXT 93

गोलोकनाम्नि निजधाम्नि तले च तस्य
देवीमहेशहरिधामसु तेषु तेषु ।
ते ते प्रभावनिचया विहिताश्च येन
गोविन्दमादिपुरुषं तमहं भजामि ॥

*goloka-nāmni nija-dhāmni tale ca tasya*
*devī-maheśa-hari-dhāmasu teṣu teṣu*
*te te prabhāva-nicayā vihitāś ca yena*
*govindam ādi-puruṣaṁ tam ahaṁ bhajāmi*

*goloka-nāmni* — in the planet known as Goloka Vṛndāvana; *nija-dhāmni* — the personal abode of the Supreme Personality of Godhead; *tale* — in the part beneath; *ca* — also; *tasya* — of that; *devi* — of the goddess Durgā; *maheśa* — of Lord Śiva; *hari* — and of Nārāyaṇa; *dhāmasu* — in the planets; *teṣu teṣu* — in each of them; *te te* — those respective; *prabhāva-nicayāḥ* —

opulences; *vihitāḥ* — established; *ca* — also; *yena* — by whom; *govindam* — Govinda; *ādi-puruṣam* — the original person; *tam* — Him; *aham* — I; *bhajāmi* — worship.

**"Lowest of all is the mundane world [Devī-dhāma], next above it is the abode of Maheśa [Maheśa-dhāma], above Maheśa-dhāma is the abode of Hari [Hari-dhāma], and above them all is Kṛṣṇa's own realm, named Goloka. I adore the primeval Lord Govinda, who has allotted to the rulers of those graded realms their respective authorities."**

COMMENTARY: This is Verse 43 of the same chapter of *Śrī Brahma-saṁhitā*. Below the abode of the Supreme Personality of Godhead expand countless worlds, presided over by Lord Nārāyaṇa, Lord Śiva, and the goddess Devī. Śrī Nārāyaṇa rules over the Vaikuṇṭha planets and the replicas of Vaikuṇṭha within the material realm, such as Mahākāla-pura, the abode of liberation. Devī rules the entire material universe, and she is the presiding deity of the unmanifested material nature, the eighth layer of the shell that encloses the universe. The infinite variety of wonders displayed in all these worlds is produced by the personal power of Govinda. Thus His energies, nondifferent from Him because they proceed from Him, are the source of endless variety. Govinda's expansions like Nārāyaṇa, Śiva, and Devī are wonderful, and the worlds those expansions create are wonderful. Certainly, then, the original world of Govinda is the most wonderful.

## TEXTS 94–95

श्रियः कान्ताः कान्तः परमपुरुषः कल्पतरवो
द्रुमा भूमिश्चिन्तामणिगणमयी तोयममृतम् ।
कथा गानं नाट्यं गमनमपि वंशी प्रियसखी
चिदानन्दं ज्योतिः परमपि तदास्वाद्यमपि च ॥

स यत्र क्षीराब्धिः सरति सुरभीभ्यश्च सुमहान्
निमेषार्धाख्यो वा व्रजति न हि यत्रापि समयः ।

भजे श्वेतद्वीपं तमहमिह गोलोकमिति यं
विदन्तस्ते सन्तः क्षितिविरलचाराः कतिपये ॥
इति ।

*śriyaḥ kāntāḥ kāntaḥ parama-puruṣaḥ kalpa-taravo*
*drumā bhūmiś cintāmaṇi-gaṇa-mayī toyam amṛtam*
*kathā gānaṁ nāṭyaṁ gamanam api vaṁśī priya-sakhī*
*cid-ānandaṁ jyotiḥ param api tad āsvādyam api ca*

*sa yatra kṣīrābdhiḥ sarati surabhībhyaś ca su-mahān*
*nimeṣārdhākhyo vā vrajati na hi yatrāpi samayaḥ*
*bhaje śvetadvīpaṁ tam aham iha golokam iti yaṁ*
*vidantas te santaḥ kṣiti-virala-cārāḥ katipaye*
*iti.*

*śriyaḥ* — Lakṣmīs, goddesses of fortune; *kāntāḥ* — loving consorts; *kāntaḥ* — the enjoyer, lover; *parama-puruṣaḥ* — the Supreme Personality of Godhead; *kalpa-taravaḥ* — desire trees; *drumāḥ* — all the trees; *bhūmiḥ* — the land; *cintāmaṇi-gaṇa-mayī* — made of the transcendental touchstone jewels; *toyam* — the water; *amṛtam* — nectar; *kathā* — talking; *gānam* — song; *nāṭyam* — dancing; *gamanam* — walking; *api* — also; *vaṁśī* — the flute; *priya-sakhī* — the constant companion; *cit-ānandam* — transcendental bliss; *jyotiḥ* — effulgence; *param* — the supreme; *api* — also; *tat* — that; *āsvādyam* — everywhere perceived; *api ca* — also; *saḥ* — that; *yatra* — where; *kṣīra-abdhiḥ* — an ocean of milk; *sarati* — flows; *surabhībhyaḥ* — from *surabhi* cows; *ca* — and; *su-mahān* — very great; *nimeṣa-ardha* — half a moment; *ākhyaḥ* — called; *vā* — or; *vrajati* — passes; *na* — not; *hi* — certainly; *yatra* — where; *api* — even; *samayaḥ* — time; *bhaje* — I worship; *śveta-dvīpam* — Śveta-dvīpa; *tam* — that; *aham* — I; *iha* — here; *golokam* — Goloka; *iti* — thus; *yam* — which; *vidantaḥ* — know; *te* — they; *santaḥ* — self-realized souls; *kṣiti* — in this world; *virala* — seldom; *cārāḥ* — going; *katipaye* — few; *iti* — thus.

**"I worship that transcendental realm known as Śveta-**

**dvīpa, where as loving consorts the Lakṣmīs in their unalloyed spiritual essence practice the amorous service of the Supreme Lord, Kṛṣṇa, their only lover, where every tree fufills all desires, where the soil is made of purpose gems, and the water is nectar, and every word a song, every step a dance, and the flute is the favorite attendant. Effulgence in that realm is full of transcendental bliss, and the supreme spiritual entities are all to be tasted and enjoyed. There, numberless cows always give transcendental oceans of milk, and transcendental time, ever present, without past or future, eternally exists, not subject to passing away even for the space of half a moment. That realm is known as Goloka only to a very few self-realized souls in this world."**

COMMENTARY: Here *Śrī Brahma-saṁhitā* (5.56) directly speaks of the glories of Śrī Goloka. Brahmā calls Goloka by the esoteric name Śvetadvīpa and portrays it with several short descriptions, tied together by the word *yatra* ("in which place"). All the girlfriends of the Supreme in Goloka are goddesses of fortune, or in other words they are in no way inferior to Mahā-lakṣmī, the consort of Lord Nārāyaṇa. In Goloka, however, the supreme enjoyer is not Nārāyaṇa but the original Godhead, Śrī Govinda. He is the lover of all the Lakṣmīs of Goloka. In some manuscripts of *Brahma-saṁhitā* we find the variant word *parama-puruṣāḥ,* which is in the plural form. With that word the verse can be understood to mean either that the husbands of the *gopīs* in Goloka are all *mahā-puruṣas,* fully surrendered devotees of Govinda, or that Govinda expands Himself into numerous duplicate forms to associate with each *gopī* simultaneously.

All the trees in Goloka can fulfill any desire. All talk is as pleasing as pure music. All movement has the aesthetic grace of dancing. And Kṛṣṇa always holds His flute affectionately in His hands.

In Goloka the *paraṁ jyotiḥ* ("supreme light"), comprising perfect consciousness and bliss, is directly perceivable (*āsvādyam*). This *jyotiḥ* can be identified either with Kṛṣṇa Himself, or with the unique *prema* that pervades Goloka, or even with the lamps and other sources of light in Goloka, all of which radiate absolute light and ecstasy because they emanate from the bodily effulgence of Para-brahman, Śrī Kṛṣṇa. It can also be identified with the nectar of Kṛṣṇa's lips, which in Goloka can be tasted (*āsvādyam*) by His most worthy devotees, the divine *gopīs*.

The cows of Goloka are known as *surabhi* and *kāma-dhenu*. They flood the land with their milk. And absent from Goloka is the passing of time, from the smallest fraction of a second to the ultimate length of Brahmā's life. In the material world, all events are pervaded by the control of time, but in Goloka time has no dominance. Sequences of events may appear for the pleasure of Kṛṣṇa and His devotees in their pastimes, but never manifest are any of the material effects of time — birth, change, fear, destruction.

Goloka is called Śvetadvīpa, but it is a different place from the Śvetadvīpa found within the Ocean of Milk in the material universe. In this universe only a few rare saints know that highest Śvetadvīpa, and they are rarely seen, not only because they are so few but also because they generally prefer to remain in seclusion to avoid materialistic association and to freely relish Kṛṣṇa consciousness. Thus Goloka is a very secret place, unknown to most people.

The Supreme Person also appears in the Śvetadvīpa of the Milk Ocean, but there not all the women are His goddesses of fortune, He is not the only male consort, and His flute is not visible as His constant companion. Śvetadvīpa in the material universe is surrounded by an ocean of milk, but that ocean is not created from cow's milk. All these special features can be seen only in Goloka, the Śvetadvīpa above Vaikuṇṭha. Śrī Goloka is called *śveta* ("white") because it is supremely pure and also because it is flooded by the white milk of Kṛṣṇa's cows. It is a *dvīpa* ("island") not only in the sense of being a place separate from all others but also because it is a secluded place, a shelter, the residence of exalted pure souls such as Nanda Mahārāja. Like Mathurā-maṇḍala on earth, Goloka is shaped like a round island, bordered by the shores of the river Yamunā. And in Goloka milk flows so abundantly that the whole Goloka world seems to be an island floating in the middle of an ocean of milk. Predominated by cows, Śrī Mathurā in the spiritual world is like the Milk Ocean, milk everywhere. And within that region is Śrī Vṛndāvana, the white island Śvetadvīpa, the land where Nanda Mahārāja's cows graze and ever drench the ground with their milk.

## TEXT 96

किं च,
पुण्या बत व्रजभुवो यदयं नृलिङ्ग-
गूढः पुराणपुरुषो वनचित्रमाल्यः ।
गाः पालयन्सहबलः क्वणयंश्च वेणुं
विक्रीडयाञ्चति गिरित्ररमार्चिताङ्घ्रिः ॥

*kiṁ ca,*
*puṇyā bata vraja-bhuvo yad ayaṁ nṛ-liṅga-*
*gūḍhaḥ purāṇa-puruṣo vana-citra-mālyaḥ*
*gāḥ pālayan saha-balaḥ kvaṇayaṁś ca veṇuṁ*
*vikrīḍayāñcati giritra-ramārcitāṅghriḥ*

*kim ca* — and furthermore; *puṇyāḥ* — pious; *bata* — indeed; *vraja-bhuvaḥ* — the various regions of the land of Vraja; *yat* — in which; *ayam* — this; *nṛ* — human; *liṅga* — by characteristics; *gūḍhaḥ* — disguised; *purāṇa-puruṣaḥ* — primeval Personality of Godhead; *vana* — made of flowers and other items of the forest; *citra* — of wonderful variety; *mālyaḥ* — whose garlands; *gāḥ* — the cows; *pālayan* — herding; *saha* — together with; *balaḥ* — Lord Balarāma; *kvaṇayan* — vibrating; *ca* — and; *veṇum* — His flute; *vikrīḍayā* — with various pastimes; *añcati* — He moves about; *giritra* — by Lord Śiva; *ramā* — and the goddess of fortune; *arcita* — worshiped; *aṅghriḥ* — His feet.

**Furthermore: "How pious are the tracts of land in Vraja, for there the primeval Personality of Godhead, disguising**

**Himself with human traits, wanders about, enacting His many pastimes! Adorned with wonderfully variegated forest garlands, Lord Kṛṣṇa, whose feet are worshiped by Lord Śiva and the goddess Ramā, vibrates His flute as He tends the cows in the company of Balarāma."**

COMMENTARY: Starting with this verse, the next fifty-nine verses come from the Tenth Canto of *Śrīmad-Bhāgavatam*. Of these the first eleven (texts 96 through 106) establish in a general way the glories of Vraja-bhūmi and its residents.

The current verse (10.44.13) was spoken by the women of Mathurā City. Kṛṣṇa had just arrived in Mathurā from Nanda-gokula. Early that morning He had killed the elephant Kuvalayāpīḍa, and now as the women watched He was wrestling with Cāṇūra. Shocked to see such an unfair competition between powerful athletes and little boys, some of the women sharply criticized their friends and the other people present:

*mahān ayaṁ batādharma*
*eṣāṁ rāja-sabhā-sadām*
*ye balābalavad yuddha*
*rājño 'nvicchanti paśyataḥ*

"Alas, what a greatly irreligious act the members of this royal assembly are committing! As the king watches this fight between the strong and the weak, these assembly members also want to see it." (*Bhāgavatam* 10.44.7)

Other outraged women spoke the verse under discussion, in which they declared that only Vraja-bhūmi is a pious place, unlike the metropolis of Mathurā. The women referred to *vraja-bhuvaḥ* in the plural to offer Vraja respect, to indicate its large extent, and to include not only the land of Vraja but all its living beings, and even its sticks, stones, and other inert objects.

In Vraja, Śrī Kṛṣṇa is visible to everyone's eyes in all His charm, wandering about to enjoy His many different pastimes. As the speakers of this verse described that scene, they thought, "This assembly, in which Kṛṣṇa is being threatened with defeat, should be condemned. But the land of Vraja, where Kṛṣṇa moves about and plays, is pious. The people of that place are good, but the residents of this city are not." The word *añcati* means "he moves about," but it may also mean "he honors." Taken in that sense, it indicates that Kṛṣṇa honors the people of Vraja by His presence.

While speaking this verse, the women used the pronoun *ayam* ("this"), and one of them pointed her finger towards Kṛṣṇa. The women avoided saying Kṛṣṇa's name because they considered Him like their own husband (a chaste woman does not speak of her husband by name) and because they were afraid that if they pronounced His name out loud they might lose control of themselves in ecstasy.

Someone hearing the women condemn Mathurā might assert that from the authoritative prediction of the venerable *ṛṣi* Garga it was already known that Kṛṣṇa would become the master of Mathurā. That city, then, and all its residents gathered at the assembly were destined to become very fortunate. As unavoidable as this truth might have been, the women of Mathurā still insisted that Vraja-bhūmi is the only truly pious place.

Kṛṣṇa, the primeval Lord of all living beings, is realized by spiritual aspirants in countless ways. He is the Supersoul dwelling in every creature's heart, and His feet are worshiped by Lord Śiva and the goddess Mahā-lakṣmī. Even so, in Vraja He disguises Himself as an ordinary human being. To deceive enemies like Kaṁsa, He hides His prowess, and to enjoy with His devotees He hides in the bushes of Vṛndāvana.

In Vraja Kṛṣṇa wears all sorts of garlands made with forest flowers. He is always accompanied by Bala — His older brother Balarāma — or by forces (*bala*), an army of friends. Kṛṣṇa herds His cows, plays on His flute, and enjoys the *rāsa* dance and other pastimes with His devotees. But the residents of Mathurā think of Kṛṣṇa differently. Mathurā's eminent *kṣatriyas,* steeped in knowledge of the *smṛtis* and *śrutis,* always see Kṛṣṇa as the timeless Personality of Godhead, an attitude that prevents them from having more intimate relationships with Him. They and the other residents of Mathurā, seeing Him as Vāsudeva, the Lord in the heart, feel no urgent need to have Him always present before them outside the heart. Generally, the devotees of Mathurā envision Kṛṣṇa with four arms and all the other opulent features of the Supreme Lord, and they remember how He is worshiped by Lord Śiva and other demigods; consequently, they cannot realize the same fullness of *prema* as the devotees of Vṛndāvana. In Vṛndāvana, all the Vraja-vāsīs are always so eager to see Kṛṣṇa that they cannot tolerate being absent from Him even for a moment. They forever see Him in His most attractive humanlike form, and their love for Him is always fully awakened. Thinking of Him as the darling son of Śrī Nanda and Yaśodā, they feel for Him the sweetest of sentiments. Their relationships with Him are a treasure so precious and confidential, they feel, that their lives depend upon protecting it. Worshiping Him in various intimate ways, they enjoy the extreme limits of happiness. Certainly they are more fortunate than anyone else, and so the land where they live is naturally the most fortunate of places.

Of course, the Yādavas of Mathurā are great Vaiṣṇavas, situated on the transcendental platform of love of God, but Kṛṣṇa never appears among them decorated with wonderful garlands of forest flowers, as He does among the Vraja-vāsīs. And even if by His royal wealth He does sometimes acquire such garlands in the big city of Mathurā, we cannot expect to see Him tending cows there. And even if He owns a royal herd of cows and sometimes plays at taking care of them, how in Mathurā can He always be in the company of Balarāma? Very often one or the other of the two transcendental brothers has to go somewhere else to carry out His duties. And in Mathurā how can Kṛṣṇa play with all the young cowherd boys? The young Yadus may sometimes dress up as cowherd boys in games to imitate Kṛṣṇa's friends in Vraja, but even then in Mathurā Kṛṣṇa doesn't play His flute. Nor does He exhibit the many special pastimes unique to Vraja, like His *rāsa-līlā*. By using the word *krīḍayā* ("with His playful pastimes"), the speakers of this verse hinted at Kṛṣṇa's *rāsa* dance, but due to feminine shyness they avoided mentioning it by name.

The last phrase of this verse states that Kṛṣṇa's feet are

worshiped by *giritra-ramā*—Lord Śiva and Mahā-lakṣmī. But there is another way to understand these words, a way that shows careful regard for the consistency of the verse as glorification of Vraja-bhūmi. While Kṛṣṇa held Govardhana Hill, Śrīmatī Rādhārāṇī freed Him from the danger of dropping the mountain by relieving Him of His fatigue with Her loving glance. Thus She, the original goddess of fortune (*ramā*), saved Him from the mountain (*giri-trā*). Or else Kṛṣṇa Himself, having saved Vraja-bhūmi by means of the mountain, is called Giritra, and because Rādhā gives pleasure to that Govardhana-dhārī, She is called Giritra-ramā. She worships Kṛṣṇa's feet, but only in Vraja, so Vraja alone is pious.

By recounting the glories of Śrī Goloka, Parīkṣit Mahārāja realized such an advanced level of *prema* that he felt the ecstatic mood of the women of Mathurā-purī, and in this frame of mind he sang this verse.

## TEXT 97

अहोऽतिधन्या व्रजगोरमण्यः
स्तन्यामृतं पीतमतीव ते मुदा ।
यासां विभो वत्सतरात्मजात्मना
यत्तृप्तयेऽद्याप्यथ नालमध्वराः ॥

*aho 'ti-dhanyā vraja-go-ramaṇyaḥ*
*stanyāmṛtaṁ pītam atīva te mudā*
*yāsāṁ vibho vatsatarātmajātmanā*
*yat-tṛptaye 'dyāpy atha nālam adhvarāḥ*

*aho*—oh; *ati-dhanyāḥ*—most fortunate; *vraja*—of Vṛndāvana; *go*—the cows; *ramaṇyaḥ*—and the *gopīs; stanya*—the breast milk; *amṛtam*—which is like nectar; *pītam*—has been drunk; *atīva*—fully; *te*—by You; *mudā*—with satisfaction; *yāsām*—of whom; *vibho*—O almighty Lord; *vatsatara-ātmaja-ātmanā*—in the form of the calves and the sons of the cowherd women; *yat*—whose; *tṛptaye*—for the satisfaction;

*adya api* — even until now; *atha* — and; *na* — not; *alam* — sufficient; *adhvarāḥ* — the Vedic sacrifices.

**"O almighty Lord, how greatly fortunate are the cows and ladies of Vṛndāvana! Taking the form of their calves and children, You have happily drunk to Your full satisfaction the nectar of their breast milk. All the Vedic sacrifices performed from time immemorial up to the present day have not given You as much satisfaction.**

COMMENTARY: Texts 97 through 106 form the final part of Lord Brahmā's prayers to Kṛṣṇa in Vṛndāvana (*Bhāgavatam* 10.14.31–40). While in Vṛndāvana, Brahmā witnessed the unlimited mercy of Kṛṣṇa and bathed in the *rasa* of Kṛṣṇa's omnipotence. And after Kṛṣṇa removed the misgivings from Brahmā's heart, Brahmā was also able to taste that *rasa* fully. So Brahmā now understands that the greatest way one can praise the Personality of Godhead is simply to describe the unlimited glories of His devotees and devotional service. From the very beginning of his life, Brahmā had prayed to the Supreme Lord for *bhakti,* the most fortunate of goals, but only now that he has received the special mercy of Kṛṣṇa in Vṛndāvana has the true greatness of the Vraja-vāsīs been revealed to Him. Now that he has some idea of just how much they cherish Kṛṣṇa, he hopes to obtain the same kind of *bhakti* they have, and he acclaims them the Supreme Lord's most fortunate devotees.

First he mentions the greatness of the *gopīs* and cows who serve as Kṛṣṇa's mothers by giving Him their milk. The interjection *aho* expresses great surprise, and the prefix *ati-* in the word *ati-dhanyāḥ* indicates that the good fortune of these mothers is extraordinary. By suckling Kṛṣṇa the ladies and cows of Vraja please Him, and so their glories give pleasure to the entire universe. The motherly *gopīs* are referred to after the cows because the mothers are even more fortunate. Why? Because even though Kṛṣṇa is not fully satisfied by all the Aśvamedha-yajñas and all the other sacrifices performed since the creation of the universe by great demigods and sages like Brahmā himself, He is satisfied at every moment while drinking the milk of these mothers. Exalted *devas* and *ṛṣis* are expert in gratifying anyone they choose to favor, but they cannot so fully satisfy Kṛṣṇa.

Kṛṣṇa assumed the forms of the calves and the sons of all those mothers in Vraja just so He could drink their milk. By using the past tense (*pītam*), Brahmā implies that the time for that special arrangement has come to an end, for the calves and boys he had stolen have now returned to their mothers.

The word *atīva* ("fully") can be understood to be connected either with the preceding word *pītam* ("has been drunk") or the following word *mudā* ("with satisfaction"). Because of the unlimited affection Kṛṣṇa has for His devotees, He drank the milk of all those mothers very much, and He drank with great pleasure.

By addressing Kṛṣṇa with the word *vibho* ("O infinite Lord"), Brahmā establishes that even during the time Kṛṣṇa assumed the forms of calves and calf-herding boys He remained unlimited. The word *vibho* also describes Kṛṣṇa as endowed with supreme mystic power, by which He remains the unlimited Absolute Truth even when He appears in limited sizes to entertain His devotees. Kṛṣṇa can easily do what is ordinarily impossible.

Although it would have been most appropriate to describe first the glories of the best of Kṛṣṇa's beloved devotees — Śrīmatī Rādhārāṇī and Her companions — Brahmā does not do so, because he has not yet realized how extraordinary is the *rasa* of the *gopīs'* love for Kṛṣṇa. Since knowledge of the *gopīs'* supreme devotion has not yet awakened in Brahmā's heart, he does not pray for elevation to their standard of *bhakti*. In Vṛndāvana Brahmā could see Kṛṣṇa only in the form of Bāla-gopāla, so when he begins his prayers he addresses Kṛṣṇa as "the son of a cowherd, with small, tender feet," not as Gopīnātha, the Lord of the *gopīs*. Besides, despite being Kṛṣṇa's oldest servant, Brahmā thinks of himself as Kṛṣṇa's son, so he naturally wants to avoid intruding into Kṛṣṇa's amorous affairs.

As Parīkṣit Mahārāja sang these ten verses, he felt in his own heart the moods of Śrī Brahmā, the spiritual master of all classes of Vaiṣṇavas.

## TEXT 98

अहो भाग्यमहो भाग्यं नन्दगोपव्रजौकसाम् ।
यन्मित्रं परमानन्दं पूर्णं ब्रह्म सनातनम् ॥

*aho bhāgyam aho bhāgyaṁ*
*nanda-gopa-vrajaukasām*
*yan-mitraṁ paramānandaṁ*
*pūrṇaṁ brahma sanātanam*

*aho* — what great; *bhāgyam* — fortune; *aho* — what great; *bhāgyam* — fortune; *nanda* — of Mahārāja Nanda; *gopa* — of the other cowherd men; *vraja-okasām* — of the inhabitants of Vraja-bhūmi; *yat* — of whom; *mitram* — the friend; *parama-ānandam* — the supreme bliss; *pūrṇam* — complete; *brahma* — the Absolute Truth; *sanātanam* — eternal.

**"How greatly fortunate are Nanda Mahārāja, the cowherd men, and all the other inhabitants of Vraja-bhūmi! There is no limit to their good fortune, because the Absolute Truth, the source of transcendental bliss, the eternal Supreme Brahman, has become their friend.**

COMMENTARY: Kṛṣṇa acts for the benefit of the Vraja-vāsīs not just in certain situations but always. And He not only delivers them from fear but also provides for them the highest varieties of ecstasy. Thus He is the source of their intense happiness, and they consider Him their dearmost friend. Were He merely God, their love for Him would be severely restricted. But Kṛṣṇa, at once, is both the Supreme Absolute Truth and the dear friend of the residents of Nanda's cowherd village.

## TEXT 99

एषां तु भाग्यमहिमाच्युत तावदास्ताम्
एकादशैव हि वयं बत भूरिभागाः ।

एतद्धृषीकचषकैरसकृत्पिबामः
शर्वादयोऽङ्घ्र्युदजमध्वमृतासवं ते ॥

*eṣāṁ tu bhāgya-mahimācyuta tāvad āstām*
*ekādaśaiva hi vayaṁ bata bhūri-bhāgāḥ*
*etad-dhṛṣīka-caṣakair asakṛt pibāmaḥ*
*śarvādayo 'ṅghry-udaja-madhv-amṛtāsavaṁ te*

*eṣām* — of these (residents of Vṛndāvana); *tu* — however; *bhāgya* — of the good fortune; *mahimā* — the greatness; *acyuta* — O infallible Supreme Lord; *tāvat* — so much; *āstām* — let it be; *ekādaśa* — the eleven; *eva hi* — indeed; *vayam* — we; *bata* — oh; *bhūri-bhāgāḥ* — are most fortunate; *etat* — of these devotees; *hṛṣīka* — by the senses; *caṣakaiḥ* — (which are like) drinking cups; *asakṛt* — repeatedly; *pibāmaḥ* — we are drinking; *śarva-ādayaḥ* — Lord Śiva and the other chief demigods; *aṅghri-udaja* — of the lotus feet; *madhu* — the honey; *amṛta-āsavam* — which is a nectarean, intoxicating beverage; *te* — of You.

**"Yet even though the extent of the good fortune of these residents of Vṛndāvana is inconceivable, we eleven presiding deities of the various senses, headed by Lord Śiva, are also most fortunate, because the senses of these devotees of Vṛndāvana are the cups through which we repeatedly drink the nectarean, intoxicating beverage of the honey of Your lotus feet.**

COMMENTARY: In the material world, Lord Śiva is the deity who presides over every individual's ego, and Candra and nine other demigods preside over everyone's mind and other senses. These eleven demigods are very fortunate because they perceive — through the ego, intelligence, mind, eyes, ears, skin, tongue, nose, speech, hands, and feet of every Vraja-vāsī — the nectar coming from Kṛṣṇa's lotus feet. These demigods witness how the Vraja-vāsīs use their egos to identify themselves as servants of Kṛṣṇa, their intelligence to make up their minds to act always for

His satisfaction, their eyes to see Him, their tongues to chant, and their ears to hear His glories.

The Vraja-vāsīs experience Kṛṣṇa's lotus feet to be *amṛta,* immortal nectar, and also *āsava,* extremely invigorating to their senses (*asavaḥ*). Or we can understand these words another way: The Vraja-vāsīs perceive His lotus feet to be *āsava,* a beverage extremely intoxicating even for those who are *amṛta,* liberated souls beyond birth and death. This implies that the nectar of Kṛṣṇa's feet provides pleasure even greater than the joy of liberation.

Because the demigods preside over the various senses, each demigod has the opportunity, through the one sense he oversees, to serve Kṛṣṇa by one of the many methods of devotional service. If the demigods attain the success of their lives merely by offering themselves to Kṛṣṇa in this partial way, how can anyone describe the good fortune of the Vraja-vāsīs, who use all the senses to serve Kṛṣṇa in every way possible? The demigods take part in the sensory experience of every living being in the universe, but not even through the senses of other Vaiṣṇavas can the demigods relish the same nectar they receive through the senses of the Vraja-vāsīs. Certainly, therefore, the Vraja-vāsīs are even greater than all other devotees of the Supreme Lord.

Why does Brahmā mention only eleven presiding deities of the senses? Excluding the Supreme Lord Vāsudeva, who rules over the consciousness (*citta*) of the conditioned *jīvas,* there are actually thirteen such deities. One explanation is that because the functions of the anus and genitals cannot be directly engaged in worship of the Personality of Godhead, the presiding demigods of these two senses do not enjoy their share of the nectar of Kṛṣṇa's lotus feet. The *gopīs* may engage their genitals in service to the Lord, but Brahmā wants to avoid being impudent by discussing that subject. Or, alternatively: The demigod Viṣṇu, who presides over the feet, is an empowered incarnation of Lord Vāsudeva, so by not counting him and Mitra, the deity of the anus, we have eleven deities.

Of course, because the residents of Vraja have purely spiritual bodies, their senses are not subject to the control of material demigods. Yet as we have earlier heard from Lord Śiva, the Vraja-vāsīs imitate the behavior of ordinary materially embodied humans. At any rate, the Vaikuṇṭha demigods Candra, Sūrya, and others, who have spiritual bodies, descend to earth to take part in Kṛṣṇa's pastimes in Vraja; therefore Brahmā is not wrong to describe these demigods as being extremely fortunate by association with the Vraja-vāsīs. It is an established fact that Lord Śiva and Lord Brahmā have spiritual bodies, so we can accept that the other demigods Brahmā refers to have spiritual bodies also. Since a connection with the Vraja-vāsīs makes the Vaikuṇṭha demigods especially fortunate, we can deduce that the Vraja-vāsīs are more exalted than anyone else.

## TEXT 100

तद् भूरिभाग्यमिह जन्म किमप्यटव्यां
यद्गोकुलेऽपि कतमाङ्घ्रिरजोऽभिषेकम् ।
यज्जीवितं तु निखिलं भगवान्मुकुन्दस्
त्वद्यापि यत्पदरजः श्रुतिमृग्यमेव ॥

*tad bhūri-bhāgyam iha janma kim apy aṭavyāṁ*
*yad gokule 'pi katamāṅghri-rajo-'bhiṣekam*
*yaj-jīvitaṁ tu nikhilaṁ bhagavān mukundas*
*tv adyāpi yat-pada-rajaḥ śruti-mṛgyam eva*

*tat* — that; *bhūri-bhāgyam* — the greatest good fortune; *iha* — here; *janma* — the birth; *kim api* — any whatsoever; *aṭavyām* — in the forest (of Vṛndāvana); *yat* — which; *gokule* — in Gokula; *api* — even; *katama* — of any (of the devotees); *aṅghri* — of the feet; *rajaḥ* — by the dust; *abhiṣekam* — bathing; *yat* — whose; *jīvitam* — life; *tu* — indeed; *nikhilam* — whole; *bhagavān* — the Supreme Personality of Godhead; *mukundaḥ* — Lord Mukunda; *tu* — but; *adya api* — even until now; *yat* — whose; *pada-rajaḥ* — dust of the feet; *śruti* — by the *Vedas;* *mṛgyam* — sought after; *eva* — certainly.

**"My greatest possible good fortune would be to take any**

**birth whatever in this forest of Gokula and have my head bathed by the dust falling from the lotus feet of any of its residents. Their entire life and soul is the Supreme Personality of Godhead, Mukunda, the dust of whose lotus feet is still being searched for in the Vedic mantras.**

COMMENTARY: In this prayer Brahmā elaborates on the request he has already made:

*tad astu me nātha sa bhūri-bhāgo*
*bhave 'tra vānyatra tu vā tiraścām*
*yenāham eko 'pi bhavaj-janānāṁ*
*bhūtvā niṣeve tava pāda-pallavam*

"My dear Lord, I therefore pray to be so fortunate that in this life as Lord Brahmā or in another life, wherever I take my birth, I may be counted as one of Your devotees. I pray that wherever I may be, even among the animal species, I can engage in devotional service to Your lotus feet." (*Bhāgavatam* 10.14.30)

Lord Brahmā would very gladly take birth again in this world, even as a blade of grass or other lowly being. And that blade of grass could even be in a wild forest. And that forest could even be a residence of cows and cowherds. The only condition Brahmā insists on is that he always be able to serve Kṛṣṇa's lotus feet.

But couldn't Brahmā serve Kṛṣṇa comfortably in liberation or in a high position, such as ruler of a universe? No, Brahmā asserts, he does not aspire for any such advantage. He is willing to neglect the goal of liberation and accept *janma,* another birth. And rather than be born on some glorious planet of his own, he is willing to be born on this earth (*iha*). And rather than in a big city or town, he is willing to be born in a forest. And rather than a *tapo-vana,* a forest where ascetics go for their spiritual advancement, he is willing to belong to a simple cowherd village.

And what would Brahmā gain by trading his Satyaloka for a birth in Gokula? He would get the opportunity to bathe in the foot dust of one or another of Gokula's residents. Such an *abhiṣeka* would be equivalent to a bath in all the sacred waters of the universe because Gokula is the supreme holy *tīrtha.* Such a coronation bath would be equivalent to being exalted to whatever position in this world he might desire.

Why pray to take birth only as a creature who might be touched by the dust of the feet of the Gokula-vāsīs? Why not ask for birth as one of the cowherds in Gokula? To this question Brahmā replies that the *Vedas* have been searching for this dust from the time of their birth yet to this day have not obtained it. What to speak of birth as a cowherd, they are disqualified from achieving even this dust, because they identify themselves with various conceptions of material life and engage people mainly in paths and disciplines leading to material success or impersonal liberation. And since Brahmā is younger than the *Vedas,* who are his teachers, what hope can he have for obtaining dust from the feet of the Vraja-vāsīs? He can only pray for it.

Here Brahmā notes that Kṛṣṇa, being eager to display fully His supreme power, beauty, charm, and compassion in His appearance on earth, is now more than ever Bhagavān, the eternal Personality of Godhead. Thus He is called Mukunda, the giver of the topmost happiness of *prema.* He is the life and soul of the residents of Vraja, for in their lives no time passes, nor does any activity occur, either external or internal, in which He is not present, always submitting Himself to their desires.

Because Brahmā, being much younger than the *Vedas,* considers himself their disciple, he is shy to even imagine becoming a direct associate of Kṛṣṇa in Gokula. He thinks it inappropriate to pray for something that for him is impossible. In his opinion, if he were to submit such a prayer, just like a sickly, poverty-stricken person praying to become a king, people throughout the universe might laugh at him, a prospect that fills him with embarrassment.

## TEXT 101

एषां घोषनिवासिनामुत भवान्किं देव रातेति नश्
चेतो विश्वफलात्फलं त्वदपरं कुत्राप्ययन्मुह्यति ।

सद्वेषादिव पूतनापि सकुला त्वामेव देवापिता
यद्धामार्थसुहृत्प्रियात्मतनयप्राणाशयास्त्वत्कृते ॥

*eṣāṁ ghoṣa-nivāsinām uta bhavān kiṁ deva rāteti naś*
*ceto viśva-phalāt phalaṁ tvad-aparaṁ kutrāpy ayan muhyati*
*sad-veṣād iva pūtanāpi sa-kulā tvām eva devāpitā*
*yad-dhāmārtha-suhṛt-priyātma-tanaya-prāṇāśayās tvat-kṛte*

*eṣām* — to these; *ghoṣa-nivāsinām* — residents of the cowherd community; *uta* — indeed; *bhavān* — Your Lordship; *kim* — what; *deva* — O Supreme Personality of Godhead; *rātā* — will give; *iti* — thinking thus; *naḥ* — our; *cetaḥ* — mind; *viśva-phalāt* — than the supreme source of all benedictions; *phalam* — a reward; *tvat* — than You; *aparam* — other; *kutra api* — anywhere; *ayat* — considering; *muhyati* — becomes bewildered; *sat-veṣāt* — by disguising herself as a devotee; *iva* — indeed; *pūtanā* — the demoness Pūtanā; *api* — even; *sa-kulā* — along with her family members, Bakāsura and Aghāsura; *tvām* — You; *eva* — certainly; *deva* — O Lord; *āpitā* — was made to attain; *yat* — whose; *dhāma* — homes; *artha* — wealth; *suhṛt* — friends; *priya* — dear relatives; *ātma* — bodies; *tanaya* — children; *prāṇa* — life air; *āśayāḥ* — and minds; *tvat-kṛte* — dedicated to You.

**"My mind becomes bewildered just trying to think of what reward other than You could be found anywhere. You are the embodiment of all benedictions, which You bestow upon these residents of the cowherd community of Vṛndāvana. You have already arranged to give Yourself to Pūtanā and her family members in exchange for her disguising herself as a devotee. So what is left for You to give these devotees of Vṛndāvana, whose homes, wealth, friends, dear relations, bodies, children, and very lives and hearts are all dedicated only to You?**

COMMENTARY: Lord Brahmā is amazed at the indescribable perfection of the Vraja-vāsīs, whose unique devotion makes Kṛṣṇa completely indebted to them. But Kṛṣṇa might ask, "How can I ever become insolvent, incapable of clearing a debt?" After all, He is all-powerful. Whatever a person requires from Him, regardless of the situation, He should be able to give. In Brahmā's opinion, however, Kṛṣṇa cannot repay the Vraja-vāsīs properly, not even by giving them His own self. Pūtanā was an envious demon who took pleasure in murdering babies. Disguised as a respectable lady, she entered the company of Kṛṣṇa's devotees just to kill Him. Yet she obtained Kṛṣṇa as her son — in other words, Kṛṣṇa gave Himself to her. Kṛṣṇa, however, might propose that He did more for the Vraja-vāsīs than merely give Himself, because He gave Himself to all their relatives as well. But this too He did for Pūtanā. Baka and Agha were her brothers, and other demons sent to Vraja by Kaṁsa were her close friends. And true as it may be that the main cause of their salvation was their contact with Kṛṣṇa, they achieved even that contact by virtue of being related to Pūtanā. How favored then must Pūtanā have been.

Thus Brahmā considers inadequate Kṛṣṇa's payment of giving the Vraja-vāsīs only Himself, because they have surrendered to His service their homes and everything they have. Kṛṣṇa also gives Himself to demons, so what makes pure devotional service to Him more desirable than demonic behavior? Certainly the Vraja-vāsīs deserve better.

## TEXT 102

तावद्रागादयः स्तेनास्तावत्कारागृहं गृहम् ।
तावन्मोहोऽङ्घ्रिनिगडो यावत्कृष्ण न ते जनाः ॥

*tāvad rāgādayaḥ stenās*
*tāvat kārā-gṛhaṁ gṛham*
*tāvan moho 'ṅghri-nigaḍo*
*yāvat kṛṣṇa na te janāḥ*

*tāvat* — for that long; *rāga-ādayaḥ* — material attachment and so on; *stenāḥ* — thieves; *tāvat* — for that long; *kārā-gṛham* — a prison; *gṛham* — one's home; *tāvat* — for that long; *mohaḥ* — the bewilderment of family affection; *aṅghri* — upon their feet; *nigaḍaḥ* — shackles; *yāvat* — as long as; *kṛṣṇa* — O Lord Kṛṣṇa; *na* — do not become; *te* — Your (devotees); *janāḥ* — any persons.

**"My dear Lord Kṛṣṇa, until people become Your devotees, their material attachments and desires remain plunderers, their homes remain prisons, and their affectionate feelings for their family members remain foot-shackles.**

COMMENTARY: Here Brahmā responds to a question Kṛṣṇa might ask: Why should the Vraja-vāsīs expect any more from Him than do the *sannyāsīs,* who have renounced everything? Renunciants who have freed themselves from all material contamination obtain nothing more than Kṛṣṇa, so why shouldn't the Vraja-vāsīs also be happy by having just Him? Brahmā answers by reminding Kṛṣṇa that material desires, like thieves, rob their victims of discernment, determination, and other assets, and the home in which one lives with spouse and children is a prison that the infatuations of love keep one forever from escaping. Successful *sannyāsīs* deserve credit for somehow avoiding these thieves and securing release from the prison of home life. The Vraja-vāsīs, however, are much more praiseworthy because their homes, attachments, and desires and the love they share among themselves actually free them from bondage. Brahmā argues, therefore, that the Vraja-vāsīs deserve a greater reward for their worship of the Supreme than impersonal *sannyāsīs.*

As we have already heard from the authoritative statements of *Śrīmad-Bhāgavatam* and other scriptures, the spiritual achievements of nondevotee renunciants are similar to those of demons like Kaṁsa. Such demons intensely concentrated on Kṛṣṇa while striving to destroy Him. Being directly killed by Kṛṣṇa elevated them to the status of liberation, oneness with Brahman, which in effect is attainment of the Supreme Lord because Brahman is one of the Personality of Godhead's own opulences. But there is still a great difference between this impersonal liberation and the perfection Vaiṣṇavas achieve when they gain entrance into the spiritual kingdom, Vaikuṇṭha, and reach the lotus feet of the Lord.

Brahmā's apparently simple prayer can be understood in several different ways. One is that Brahmā is answering a potential doubt about why the Vraja-vāsīs, full as they are with attachments and desires, are more praiseworthy than more exemplary Vaiṣṇavas who are renounced both in their external behavior and in the core of their hearts. Here Brahmā argues that although material attachments corrupt anyone who has not developed a personal relationship with Kṛṣṇa, Kṛṣṇa's devotees have learned the value of devotional service to Him, and so they dovetail those same attachments in a spiritually constructive way. Without devotion for Kṛṣṇa, strict *sannyāsīs* practice renunciation in vain, because ultimately none of their disciplines will bear the desired fruit. Most likely the results of their labor will be pride and self-delusion. In contrast, the unlimited desires held by every devotee of Kṛṣṇa can never be satiated, for those desires are all in relationship with Kṛṣṇa. In particular, the Vraja-vāsīs never feel they have had enough of Kṛṣṇa.

Brahmā's statement can also be understood as a response to Kṛṣṇa's suggestion that by sharing with the Vraja-vāsīs the enjoyment of unique loving exchanges Kṛṣṇa can repay them for their devotion. As Brahmā points out, as long as one does not become Kṛṣṇa's devotee one remains in bondage. Thus Kṛṣṇa has a more important reason for coming to this world than just to enjoy with His friends: He displays varieties of captivating attachments and desires because He wants to entice all living beings to enter His devotional service. Therefore, since He performs His pastimes not for the satisfaction of His devotees but for purposes of His own, why should the Vraja-vāsīs consider His debt to them repaid just because He plays with them?

Still another explanation of Brahmā's statement, when one reads its grammar differently, is that Kṛṣṇa will be anxious until everyone in the universe becomes His devotee. Until then Kṛṣṇa's attachments and desires will be like thieves that rob Him of His mental equilibrium and self-satisfaction, and His abodes in Vaikuṇṭha and elsewhere will be like prisons because the company of those who constantly live with Him will restrict His freedom. The special affection He has for Mahā-lakṣmī and others in Vaikuṇṭha will be like foot-shackles that restrict His movement and prevent Him from always enjoying the company of His dearest devotees. He will not feel the ecstasies of intimate reciprocation, therefore, but only the pains of separation. Thus Brahmā predicts that after Kṛṣṇa leaves the Vraja-vāsīs to go to Mathurā He will always feel separation from them and always remain indebted.

## TEXT 103

प्रपञ्चं निष्प्रपञ्चोऽपि विडम्बयसि भूतले ।
प्रपन्नजनतानन्दसन्दोहं प्रथितुं प्रभो ॥

*prapañcaṁ niṣprapañco 'pi*
*viḍambayasi bhū-tale*
*prapanna-janatānanda-*
*sandohaṁ prathituṁ prabho*

*prapañcam* — that which is material; *niṣprapañcaḥ* — completely transcendental to material existence; *api* — although; *viḍambayasi* — You imitate; *bhū-tale* — on the surface of the earth; *prapanna* — who are surrendered; *janatā* — of people; *ānanda-sandoham* — the great variety of different kinds of ecstasies; *prathitum* — in order to spread; *prabho* — O master.

**"My dear master, although You have nothing to do with material existence, You come to this earth and imitate material life just to expand the varieties of ecstatic enjoyment for Your surrendered devotees.**

COMMENTARY: Kṛṣṇa might explain that He comes to Vraja not only to enjoy pastimes with His devotees but also to become their relative. In this way, by imitating the ways of material life, He intends to increase the ecstasy of His devotees. But Brahmā thinks that merely putting on a superficial show of being a son or other family member is not enough to absolve His debt to the

Vraja-vāsīs. Or else Brahmā's statement, if reinterpreted as a rhetorical question, asks whether Kṛṣṇa's becoming the son or other relative of the Vraja-vāsīs on earth isn't in fact an illusion, a false show. The answer, Brahmā implies, is "Of course not." Kṛṣṇa proves the seriousness of His intentions — He shows that He intends to enlighten, not delude — by displaying before Mother Yaśodā His universal form and in other ways revealing to His devotees His identity as the Supreme Lord. And not only the Vraja-vāsīs but anyone who comes in contact with Kṛṣṇa is relieved of material delusion, for Kṛṣṇa cannot hide His true nature from His devotees.

Kṛṣṇa comes to the earth to share with His devotees the highest degrees of ecstasy, whereas on other planets, like Svarga, the corresponding exchanges, such as those between Aditi and her son Vāmanadeva, are hampered by over-awareness of His supremacy. If even in Vraja-bhūmi Kṛṣṇa were known to be God, then how would He ever repay His debt to the Vraja-vāsīs? His attempts to bestow the highest ecstasy on them would be frustrated, just as on Svargaloka.

By Kṛṣṇa's inconceivable potencies, devotees who dedicate themselves fully to Kṛṣṇa, who abandon themselves to the control of *kṛṣṇa-prema,* lose all attachment to material things. They then give up the main causes of delusion — their family entanglements and the affection for relatives and friends. But although Kṛṣṇa's association makes material life dissolve, Brahmā tells Kṛṣṇa, "For certain very special devotees, You create an illusion [*viḍambayasi*] by increasing their attachments and desires. Thus You, O Kṛṣṇa, who are *prabhu,* capable of doing anything, expand the vast ocean of ecstasy for Your devotees on earth, something You never do in Vaikuṇṭha."

Kṛṣṇa's fully surrendered devotees accept all their worldly assets as His *mahā-prasāda* and maintain their attachments only for His sake. Thus their possessions and attachments, which fill them with the variegated sweetness of *bhajanānanda,* the supreme bliss of pure devotional service, do nothing but enhance their spiritual lives. What can Kṛṣṇa do for such exalted devotees? He can only remain in debt to them.

## TEXT 104

जानन्त एव जानन्तु किं बहूक्त्या न मे प्रभो ।
मनसो वपुषो वाचो वैभवं तव गोचरः ॥

*jānanta eva jānantu*
*kiṁ bahūktyā na me prabho*
*manaso vapuṣo vāco*
*vaibhavaṁ tava gocaraḥ*

*jānantaḥ* — persons who think they are aware of Your unlimited potency; *eva* — certainly; *jānantu* — let them think like that; *kim* — what is the use; *bahu-uktyā* — of many words; *na* — are not; *me* — my; *prabho* — O Lord; *manasaḥ* — of the mind; *vapuṣaḥ* — body; *vācaḥ* — and words; *vaibhavam* — opulences; *tava* — Your; *go-caraḥ* — within the range.

**"There are people who say, 'I know everything about Kṛṣṇa.' Let them think that way. As for me, I do not wish to speak very much about this matter. O my Lord, let me say this much: As far as Your opulences are concerned, they are all beyond the reach of my mind, body, and words.**

COMMENTARY: There are three ways to understand the purpose of this statement by Brahmā: First, he is declaring the unimportance of *jñāna* and the superiority of *bhakti*. Second, he began his prayers by focusing on the supreme object of praise, namely the transcendental form of the Personality of Godhead; as his prayers went on he digressed to deal with various doubts; and now, having solidly justified his aim of glorifying Kṛṣṇa's opulences, he is returning to his original topic. Or third, after drinking from the vast nectar ocean of the glories of the Supreme Lord and the Vraja-vāsīs, Brahmā cannot help but laugh at those who think they know those glories.

According to the first of these understandings, Brahmā here addresses the seekers of knowledge. He ironically encourages them to pursue that goal, if that is what they want. He has no desire to argue with them or spend any more time proving *bhakti* more important than *jñāna.* He wants only to state that the unlimited, inconceivable greatness of pure devotion to Kṛṣṇa lies beyond the scope of his body, mind, and words. And, he implies, compared to *bhakti* mere knowledge and whatever is achievable with the help of that knowledge are of limited value.

In the second understanding, we hear Brahmā call Kṛṣṇa *prabhu,* a word derived from the verb *pra-bhū* ("to manifest in an exceptional way"). The idea is that Kṛṣṇa has appeared as the perfection of all beauty and all other attractive qualities, unequaled by anyone else. Thus the physical opulence of Kṛṣṇa's beauty is both incomprehensible to Brahmā's mind and indescribable by his words. Or, reading the grammar another way, the opulences of Kṛṣṇa's body, mind, and words are all unexcelled. And just as the intent of Kṛṣṇa's mind and words are unpredictable, so are His physical activities.

According to the third understanding, because Brahmā's prayers repeatedly refer to the glories of the Vraja-vāsīs, here his statement can be understood to be a glorification of *their* opulences: "O *prabhu,* possessor of unlimited, various energies, the glories of these residents of Vraja are beyond the reach of my body, mind, and words." Even while Brahmā physically composes the words of the Vedic literature, he cannot mentally grasp the extent of the greatness of the Vraja-vāsīs. Brahmā is the Supreme Lord's *guṇa-avatāra;* as such, he has a transcendental body endowed with all potencies. One should expect him, then, to be able to comprehend these glories, somehow or other. But the fact is that he cannot. For this purpose the powers of his body, mind, and words are insufficient.

## TEXT 105

अनुजानीहि मां कृष्ण सर्वं त्वं वेत्सि सर्वदृक् ।
त्वमेव जगतां नाथो जगच्चैतत्तवार्पितम् ॥

*anujānīhi māṁ kṛṣṇa*
*sarvaṁ tvaṁ vetsi sarva-dṛk*

*tvam eva jagatāṁ nātho*
*jagac caitat tavārpitam*

*anujānīhi* — please give leave; *mām* — to me; *kṛṣṇa* — O Lord Kṛṣṇa; *sarvam* — everything; *tvam* — You; *vetsi* — know; *sarva-dṛk* — all-seeing; *tvam* — You; *eva* — alone; *jagatām* — of all the universes; *nāthaḥ* — the master; *jagat* — universe; *ca* — and; *etat* — this; *tava* — to You; *arpitam* — is offered.

**"My dear Kṛṣṇa, I now humbly request permission to leave. Actually, You are the knower and seer of all things. Indeed, You are the Lord of all the universes — and yet I offer this one universe unto You.**

COMMENTARY: Now that Brahmā's prayers have evoked the Lord's mercy, Brahmā's false conception of being lord of the universe has been erased, and he has achieved the priceless treasure of utter humility. Thus he considers himself unfit to stay near the Vraja-vāsīs very long. Fearing he might commit more offenses, he requests permission to return to his own home. Kṛṣṇa knows everything, including His own greatness and the fallen condition of persons like Brahmā. Brahmā, therefore, realizing his inability to offer prayers to Kṛṣṇa properly, asks to be allowed to leave.

This verse can also be understood as Brahmā's reply to a potential request from Kṛṣṇa — that Brahmā further describe the glories of Kṛṣṇa's beauty and other qualities, of devotional service to Him, and of His devotees who reside in Vraja. Anticipating such a request from the Lord, Brahmā asks in astonishment whether Kṛṣṇa actually knows everything about His own glories or not. By asking such a question, Brahmā implies that Kṛṣṇa, though supposedly omniscient, doesn't know His own endless glories in full.

Or, understanding this verse another way: Kṛṣṇa might ask Brahmā why he now wants to leave, just after praying for any birth in Vraja. Why not simply stay here and delight Kṛṣṇa's ears with more descriptions of Vraja's glories? Brahmā answers that

Kṛṣṇa, knowing everything, knows that it will be difficult for Brahmā, in his present four-headed body, to stay in Vraja and very difficult for him to change that body before his destined two-*parārdha* life is finished. Thus Kṛṣṇa knows that Brahmā, in his present life, will not get the opportunity to bathe in the dust of the feet of the residents of Vraja. And Kṛṣṇa knows how embarrassing it would be for Brahmā to try to describe the glories of those great devotees, a task for which Brahmā is altogether unfit. Moreover, Kṛṣṇa Himself is so much in debt to the Vraja-vāsīs that He is totally under their control. Their loving devotion alone attracts Him, and He dislikes spending even a moment doing anything else than indulging them with His pleasure pastimes. Certainly Kṛṣṇa, the only source of happiness for Vraja, knows all this, so why should Brahmā stay just to tell Kṛṣṇa what He already knows?

Or Kṛṣṇa might be asking Brahmā why he submitted prayers without fully considering the complexities of his request. After all, isn't Brahmā the creator of the universe? Shouldn't he know everything? "No," Brahmā answers. "Only You are omniscient; the knowledge of lesser persons like me is limited." Or, taking the word *sarva-dṛk* to mean "one who makes everyone see, who gives all living beings their ability to perceive," Brahmā prayed only as inspired by Kṛṣṇa, the Lord of his heart. Whatever Brahmā said, therefore, is not to his own credit or blame. Any credit deserved for these prayers belongs to the Lord, who inspired them, and if there is anything wrong with the prayers their puppetlike speaker should not be blamed. Kṛṣṇa certainly knows all this very well.

Kṛṣṇa might retort that what Brahmā says is true for a mere servant but Brahmā is much more than a servant — Brahmā is the Lord of the universe. "No," Brahmā replies, "You, Kṛṣṇa, are Jagannātha, the real Lord of the universe." Neither Brahmā nor any other *jīva* should be called the Lord of the universe; everyone is Kṛṣṇa's servant. Still, Kṛṣṇa might ask, "Am I the Lord of the universe? You are the grandsire of the entire visible cosmos, and its rulers are your sons and grandsons and their descendants. How then are you My servant?" Brahmā, using the word *arpita* to mean "placed within," answers this question by saying that since the whole universe is within Kṛṣṇa (*tava arpitam*), all creation is subordinate to Him. Or, taking *tavārpitam* to mean "placed by You," it is only because Kṛṣṇa skillfully placed the universe under Brahmā's authority that the universe seems to be Brahmā's.

And suppose Kṛṣṇa were to admit that He Himself is the Lord of the universe and that everyone in the universe is therefore His servant. Why then did Brahmā condemn nondevotees with such gusto? And why did Brahmā praise devotion to the Lord as something exceptional and beg so enthusiastically to become one of the Lord's servants? Why, in particular, did he pray for any birth in Vraja? What difference should all this make to Brahmā if everyone in the universe is already a servant of the Supreme Lord?

Brahmā answers, "Of course, everyone is naturally Your servant, subordinate to Your control. But a servant with pure love for You in one of *bhakti's* special forms has a superexcellent status. Such a position, rarely achieved, is something everyone should strive for. And because service to You in pure love cannot be achieved without complete surrender, I surrender everything I have unto You." Saying this, Brahmā offers the universe he considers his own and the body he considers himself all to Kṛṣṇa. And he offers his prayers, hoping they will please Kṛṣṇa. Everything that exists belongs to Lord Jagannātha and is known to Him, but that same Lord has directed Brahmā from within. Thus inspired, Brahmā, like an infant bird chewing again what its mother has already chewed, offers this universe, together with his personal realizations, hoping that Kṛṣṇa will accept this offering like a kind parent and excuse him for requesting something impossible.

## TEXT 106

श्रीकृष्ण वृष्णिकुलपुष्करजोषदायिन्
क्ष्मानिर्जरद्विजपशूदधिवृद्धिकारिन् ।
उद्धर्मशार्वरहर क्षितिराक्षसध्रुग्
आकल्पमार्कमर्हन्भगवन्नमस्ते ॥

*śrī-kṛṣṇa vṛṣṇi-kula-puṣkara-joṣa-dāyin*
*kṣmā-nirjara-dvija-paśūdadhi-vṛddhi-kārin*
*uddharma-śārvara-hara kṣiti-rākṣasa-dhrug*
*ā-kalpam ārkam arhan bhagavan namas te*

*śrī-kṛṣṇa* — O Lord Kṛṣṇa; *vṛṣṇi-kula* — of the Yadu dynasty; *puṣkara* — to the lotus; *joṣa* — pleasure; *dāyin* — O You who bestow; *kṣmā* — of the earth; *nirjara* — the demigods; *dvija* — the *brāhmaṇas; paśu* — and of the animals; *udadhi* — of the great oceans; *vṛddhi* — the increase; *kārin* — O You who cause; *uddharma* — of atheistic principles; *śārvara* — of the darkness; *hara* — O dispeller; *kṣiti* — upon the earth; *rākṣasa* — of the demons; *dhruk* — the opponent; *ā-kalpam* — until the end of the universe; *ā-arkam* — as long as the sun shines; *arhan* — O supremely worshipable Deity; *bhagavan* — O Supreme Personality of Godhead; *namaḥ* — I offer my respectful obeisances; *te* — unto You.

**"My dear Śrī Kṛṣṇa, You bestow happiness upon the lotus-like Vṛṣṇi dynasty and expand the great oceans consisting of the earth, the demigods, the brāhmaṇas, and the cows. You dispel the dense darkness of irreligion and oppose the demons who have appeared on this earth. O Supreme Personality of Godhead, as long as this universe exists and as long as the sun shines, I will offer my obeisances unto You."**

COMMENTARY: In this last verse of his prayers, Brahmā begs leave of his master and compares Him to both the sun and the moon. Kṛṣṇa is like the sun because He gives joy to the flowering lotus of the Vṛṣṇi dynasty. He is like the moon because He nourishes the earth, demigods, *brāhmaṇas,* and animals. And He is like both the sun and moon because He counteracts the darkness of irreligion; just by appearing on the earth, Kṛṣṇa checks the power of Rākṣasas like Kaṁsa.

Having said all that, Brahmā reconsiders: Comparing Kṛṣṇa to the sun and moon fails to do Him full justice. Thus Brahmā comments further that Kṛṣṇa deserves the worship of everyone, including the sun (*ā-arkam*). And finally Brahmā offers his obeisances unto Kṛṣṇa and promises to continue bowing down the same way until the end of the millennium (*ā-kalpam*), which lasts the full length of his day. Thus, by chanting Kṛṣṇa's holy names with great devotion and by summarizing the manifold purposes of Kṛṣṇa's descent on earth, Brahmā, in this last prayer, offers the best glorification he can muster.

Kṛṣṇa's birth in the Vṛṣṇi dynasty brought with it all signs of promise for the world's good fortune. Just as the rising sun drives away the darkness of night and awakens the sleeping lotuses, Kṛṣṇa's appearance assured Vasudeva and Kṛṣṇa's other relatives and devotees that the demons who oppressed them would soon be destroyed.

As described by Śrī Śukadeva Gosvāmī in *Śrīmad-Bhāgavatam* (10.2.17):

*sa bibhrat pauruṣaṁ dhāma*
*rājamāno yathā raviḥ*
*durāsado durviṣaho*
*bhūtānāṁ sambabhūva ha*

"While carrying the form of the Supreme Personality of Godhead within the core of his heart, Vasudeva bore the Lord's transcendentally illuminating effulgence, and thus he became as bright as the sun. He was therefore very difficult to see or approach through sensory perception. Indeed, he was unapproachable and unperceivable even for such formidable men as Kaṁsa, and not only Kaṁsa but all living entities."

Similarly, when the demigods come to glorify Mother Devakī, they tell Kṛṣṇa, who is in her womb:

*diṣṭyā hare 'syā bhavataḥ pado bhuvo*
*bhāro 'panītas tava janmaneśituḥ*
*diṣṭyāṅkitāṁ tvat-padakaiḥ su-śobhanair*
*drakṣyāma gāṁ dyāṁ ca tavānukampitām*

"O Lord, we are fortunate because the heavy burden of the demons upon this earth is at once removed by Your appearance. Indeed, we are certainly fortunate, for we shall be able to see upon this earth and in the heavenly planets the marks of lotus, conchshell, club, and disc that adorn Your lotus feet." (*Bhāgavatam* 10.2.38)

The demigods also tell Devakī:

*diṣṭyāmba te kukṣi-gataḥ paraḥ pumān*
*aṁśena sākṣād bhagavān bhavāya naḥ*
*mā bhūd bhayaṁ bhoja-pater mumūrṣor*
*goptā yadūnāṁ bhavitā tavātmajaḥ*

"O Mother Devakī, by your good fortune and ours, the Supreme Personality of Godhead Himself, with all His plenary portions, such as Baladeva, is now within your womb. Therefore you need not fear Kaṁsa, who has decided to be killed by the Lord. Your eternal son, Kṛṣṇa, will be the protector of the entire Yadu dynasty." (*Bhāgavatam* 10.2.41)

And while describing the conditions on the earth when Kṛṣṇa was about to be born, Śukadeva says:

*mahī maṅgala-bhūyiṣṭha-*
*pura-grāma-vrajākarā*

"Decorated with towns, villages, mines, and pasturing grounds, the earth seemed all-auspicious." (*Bhāgavatam* 10.3.2)

Of course when the earth prospers, everyone and everything on the earth automatically prospers, including the Yādavas, the *brāhmaṇas,* and all domestic animals. But Brahmā considers it his duty to highlight the significance of Kṛṣṇa's special compassion for the cows and *brāhmaṇas* in this *avatāra*.

Pure love for Kṛṣṇa was bestowed upon Brahmā by Kṛṣṇa Himself. For this, Brahmā next expresses his gratitude. *Uddharma* can be understood to mean "the higher principles of religion," or in other words, the obligations of individual religious duties. By manifesting the *rāsa-līlā* and other pastimes, Kṛṣṇa removed the *gopīs'* ignorance and fear, along with the dark nighttime of such restrictive *dharma*. When Brahmā offers this prayer, Kṛṣṇa's conjugal pastimes with the *gopīs* have not yet taken place, but Brahmā knows past, present, and future and so speaks of these pastimes as if they have already occurred.

Or we can take the meaning of *uddharma* in another way: The prefix *ud* can mean "away from," so *uddharma* denotes false principles that lead one away from *dharma,* or religion. Real religion is devotional service to Kṛṣṇa. In *Śrīmad-Bhāgavatam* (11.19.27) Kṛṣṇa Himself says, *dharmo mad-bhakti-kṛt proktaḥ:* "True religious principles, it is said, are those that lead one to My devotional service." *Uddharma,* therefore, is whatever deviates one from true *dharma,* pure devotional service to Kṛṣṇa, whether the deviation be by *jñāna, karma,* or anything else. Although the *dharma* of pure *bhakti* is eternal and inviolable, it is sometimes hidden, like a lost treasure sitting deep in a cave, unnoticed even by visitors of the cave because extraneous objects cover it from view. All deviant religious methods, then, are forms of darkness; but Kṛṣṇa's appearance has driven them all away. By descending to earth, Kṛṣṇa has brought back to the light of day the perfect religion of devotion to Him.

Like Rākṣasas, who roam at night and eat men, persons who move about in the darkness of deviant *dharma* try to obstruct the path of *bhakti,* on which every living being depends for his eternal welfare. These deviants — *karmīs* and *jñānīs* — mostly live on the planet earth, also known as *karma-bhūmi,* and so Brahmā refers to Kṛṣṇa as *kṣiti-rākṣasa-dhruk,* the valiant opponent of such Rākṣasas on earth. Also present on earth are other Rākṣasas, namely enemies of the Vṛṣṇis and enemies of other devotees of the Lord — enemies like Kaṁsa and his cohorts, and demons like Śaṅkhacūḍa and Ariṣṭa, who disturbed Kṛṣṇa's *rāsa* dance and other pastimes. Kṛṣṇa displays many wonderful feats in which He destroys all these demons.

As Brahmā indicates by the word *arhan* ("deserving"), only Kṛṣṇa is capable of performing such deeds in the defense of eternal religion. In His expanded forms of Godhead, Kṛṣṇa may possess the same complete potencies, but only Kṛṣṇa Himself reveals the ultimate extent of His supreme powers. Thus He is the right person to perform pastimes for the deliverance of the earth, pastimes never shown even by Lord Nārāyaṇa or any of His incarnations.

By acting as an enemy of relatives like His maternal uncle Kaṁsa, Kṛṣṇa seems to oppose the religious principles and duties prescribed by the *Vedas* for pious men, and this may cause some doubts. Brahmā, however, denies the validity of such doubts by referring to Kṛṣṇa as Bhagavān, the all-merciful Lord. Kṛṣṇa acts as He does solely for the benefit of everyone, even His antagonists. Although persons dedicated to *karma* and *jñāna* harbor within themselves the nature of demons, Kṛṣṇa deals with them in a way that rectifies their miserable asuric mentality. And to the most vicious demons, like Kaṁsa, Kṛṣṇa is even more merciful; to them He gives liberation by killing them with His own hands.

Śrīla Śrīdhara Svāmī, in his commentary on *Śrīmad-Bhāgavatam,* gives another explanation of the words *arhan bhagavan namas te:* "You deserve the worship of everyone because now even those who were dedicated to *karma* and *jñāna,* persons like Akrūra and Bhīṣma, have entered the path of *bhakti.* Avowed demons like Kaṁsa have also resorted to Your devotional service by absorbing themselves in thought of You in moods like fear. While these demons inwardly meditated on You as their enemy, externally they were unable to exercise their natural demonic propensities and so became inactive, like dead men. By killing them, You brought them back to life and gave them liberation." Even while the killing of Kaṁsa and other demons is yet to happen, Brahmā feels free to describe such events as if they have already occurred. Had Kṛṣṇa never performed such feats of delivering the nondevotees, Brahmā implies, Kṛṣṇa would not be worshipable by everyone.

As Brahmā, drowning in a sweet ocean of *prema-rasa,* prepares to leave Vraja, he offers his homage not only to Kṛṣṇa but to all the Vraja-vāsīs. The least important of all species of trees growing in Vraja is the *arka.* Vaiṣṇavas have little regard for that tree because it produces nothing useful for the Supreme Lord's worship. Yet Brahmā's obeisances to everyone in Vraja extend even to the *arka* trees. Brahmā says, "I bow down to You, Kṛṣṇa, and to everyone living in Your abode, whether moving or non-moving." These final words match the mood of his earlier prayer: *tad bhūri-bhāgyam iha janma kim apy aṭavyām,* "I would consider it my greatest fortune to take any birth whatsoever in this forest." (*Bhāgavatam* 10.14.34) In effect Brahmā says, "Because all the residents of this forest, even the *arka* trees, are better devotees of Kṛṣṇa than I, they deserve my homage. I have no right to expect a birth here like any of them. I should pray for less ambitious blessings. O all-wonderful Kṛṣṇa, I can never offer adequate obeisances to You!"

## TEXT 107

धन्येयमद्य धरणी तृणवीरुधस्त्वत्-
पादस्पृशो द्रुमलताः करजाभिमृष्टाः ।
नद्योऽद्रयः खगमृगाः सदयावलोकैर्
गोप्योऽन्तरेण भुजयोरपि यत्स्पृहा श्रीः ॥

*dhanyeyam adya dharaṇī tṛṇa-vīrudhas tvat-*
*pāda-spṛśo druma-latāḥ karajābhimṛṣṭāḥ*
*nadyo 'drayaḥ khaga-mṛgāḥ sadayāvalokair*
*gopyo 'ntareṇa bhujayor api yat-spṛhā śrīḥ*

*dhanyā* — fortunate; *iyam* — this; *adya* — now; *dharaṇī* — earth; *tṛṇa* — her grasses; *vīrudhaḥ* — and bushes; *tvat* — Your; *pāda* — of the feet; *spṛśaḥ* — receiving the touch; *druma* — the trees; *latāḥ* — and creepers; *kara-ja* — by Your fingernails; *abhimṛṣṭāḥ* — touched; *nadyaḥ* — the rivers; *adrayaḥ* — and mountains; *khaga* — the birds; *mṛgāḥ* — and animals; *sa-daya* — merciful; *avalokaiḥ* — by Your glances; *gopyaḥ* — the *gopīs; antareṇa* — between; *bhujayoḥ* — Your two arms; *api* — indeed; *yat* — for which; *spṛhā* — maintains the desire; *śrīḥ* — the goddess of fortune.

**"This earth has now become most fortunate, because You**

**have touched her grass and bushes with Your feet and her trees and creepers with Your fingernails and because You have graced her rivers, mountains, birds, and animals with Your merciful glances. But above all, You have embraced the young cowherd women between Your two arms — a favor hankered after by the goddess of fortune herself."**

COMMENTARY: After reciting for his mother the prayers in which Lord Brahmā glorifies Vraja-bhūmi and its residents in a general way, Mahārāja Parīkṣit now recites this verse (*Bhāgavatam* 10.15.8), spoken by Kṛṣṇa to His elder brother, Balarāma. Here Kṛṣṇa praises Balarāma as the most glorious person and also describes in brief the extreme good fortune of the other Vraja-vāsīs. Kṛṣṇa in His *paugaṇḍa* age wandered all over the area of Vṛndāvana, tending the cows. It gave Him great pleasure to see the exalted qualities of the people, animals, and nonmoving beings. Eager to say something about the excellence of life in Vṛndāvana but reluctant to praise Himself, Kṛṣṇa decided to direct His comments toward Lord Balarāma. By thus showing respect to His elder, He set a good example to follow. And we can understand that everything Kṛṣṇa says about His brother is also applicable to Kṛṣṇa Himself.

The planet earth has been engaged in the service of the Supreme Personality of Godhead since time immemorial. Countless incarnations and empowered representatives of Kṛṣṇa have graced her with their presence. In the distant past, Kṛṣṇa's *līlā-avatāra* Varāhadeva lifted the earth from the darkness of Pātāla-loka and accepted her as His wife. Lord Ananta Śeṣa bears her perpetually upon one of His hoods. But only now, with the appearance of Kṛṣṇa in His original form, has Mother Bhūmi become supremely fortunate.

The word *dhanyā* most obviously means "fortunate," but as the English word *fortunate* is connected with the word *fortune,* the Sanskrit word *dhanyā* is connected with the word *dhana,* meaning "wealth." The greatest possible wealth is religious merit (*dharma*), and the highest *dharma* is *prema-bhakti.* In *Śrīmad-Bhāgavatam* (11.19.39, 27) Lord Kṛṣṇa has said, "*Dharma* is the most desirable wealth of mankind" (*dharma iṣṭaṁ dhanaṁ puṁsām*) and "Actual religious principles are said to be those that lead one to My devotional service" (*dharmo mad-bhakti-kṛt proktaḥ*). In other words, with Kṛṣṇa's appearance the earth has gained the opulence of pure love of God, which relegates the four ordinary goals of human endeavor to insignificance.

Kṛṣṇa describes the prosperity of the earth in detail. Her plants, bushes, and grass are much more fortunate than those of Svarga and the other higher planets because the Supreme Lord, having descended to the earth in Śrī Mathurā in the role of a cowherd boy in the cowherd village of Nanda Mahārāja, is touching those plants, bushes, and grass with His feet. The plant life of the earth previously obtained the touch of Lord Rāmacandra's feet, especially during His exile in the Daṇḍaka forest and elsewhere, but only now that Kṛṣṇa and Balarāma have appeared has the vegetation of the earth become most extremely fortunate.

What Kṛṣṇa is saying may sound like very general praise of the earth, but while speaking He points to the plants, bushes, and grass of Vṛndāvana, to whom His glorification is actually directed. Particularly during His *paugaṇḍa-līlā,* the land of Vṛndāvana has become most fortunate, for He displays His pastimes of tending the cows all over Vṛndāvana and makes known the unique *rasas* of this time of His life.

Even more fortunate than the plants, bushes, and grass are the trees and creepers of Vṛndāvana, for Kṛṣṇa, to pick their fruits and flowers and take their leaves, twigs, and so on for decorating His body, touches them with His hands. And more fortunate still are the rivers like Śrī Yamunā, the mountains like Śrī Govardhana, the birds like the peacocks, and the wild animals like the black deer, for Kṛṣṇa favors all of them by His merciful glances. It is true that Kṛṣṇa casts His glances all over Vṛndāvana, but the good fortune of the rivers, mountains, birds, and forest animals is described here as special because of the special pleasure Kṛṣṇa enjoys from drinking and bathing in the water of the rivers, climbing the mountain peaks and resting in the caves of the mountains, and playing with the birds and animals in wonderful ways.

By associating with the best of rivers, Kṛṣṇa's most beloved Yamunā, and the best of mountains, Giri Govardhana, who is the foremost servant of Lord Hari, the other rivers and mountains in Vṛndāvana obtain Kṛṣṇa's favor. The birds and beasts of Vṛndāvana, who by the nature of their birth have little opportunity to be at the lotus feet of the Supreme Lord, derive their good fortune mostly from His glance. And He also shows His mercy to the birds and animals by calling out to them, by picking up their feathers, by touching them, and by other kinds of gentle dealings.

Kṛṣṇa's feet touch the trees and creepers in Vraja, but it is the surface of the earth that becomes marked with His beautiful and auspicious footprints. Therefore the good fortune of being touched by Kṛṣṇa's feet belongs especially to the earth. The grass, bushes, and low-growing plants also have ample opportunities to be touched by Kṛṣṇa's feet, a privilege seldom given to the trees and higher plants.

But of course the cows and cowherds of Vraja have the greatest opportunities to associate with Kṛṣṇa. Although the cows and the young cowherd boys who tend them with Kṛṣṇa and Balarāma are not explicitly mentioned in this verse, they are by far more fortunate than the plants and other animals. Most fortunate of all, however, are the *gopīs,* whose hearts are always drawn to Kṛṣṇa. Just as Kṛṣṇa, by glorifying the earth, is actually glorifying only the land of Vraja, so by mentioning the *gopīs* He is referring only to the cowherd girls of Vraja, not the *gopīs* of any other place. The goddess Śrī cannot have the good fortune of the *gopīs* of Vraja but can only aspire for it as a distant goal. The *gopīs,* favored by the embrace of Kṛṣṇa's arms, are more fortunate than the birds and animals He glances upon, the trees and creepers He touches with His hands, and the grass, plants, and bushes He touches with His feet. As indicated at the end of the verse by the word *api* ("also"), the *gopīs* also receive the same opportunities as all the others — Kṛṣṇa also touches the *gopīs* with His feet and hands and glances at them very mercifully — but in addition the *gopīs* receive the good fortune of Kṛṣṇa's embrace. In Vṛndāvana, therefore, the *gopīs* are surely Kṛṣṇa's most favored devotees.

## TEXT 108

वृन्दावनं सखि भुवो वितनोति कीर्तिं
यद्देवकीसुतपदाम्बुजलब्धलक्ष्मि ।
गोविन्दवेणुमनु मत्तमयूरनृत्यं
प्रेक्ष्याद्रिसान्ववरतान्यसमस्तसत्त्वम् ॥

*vṛndāvanaṁ sakhi bhuvo vitanoti kīrtiṁ*
*yad devakī-suta-padāmbuja-labdha-lakṣmi*
*govinda-veṇum anu matta-mayūra-nṛtyaṁ*
*prekṣyādri-sānv-avaratānya-samasta-sattvam*

*vṛndāvanam* — Vṛndāvana; *sakhi* — O friend; *bhuvaḥ* — of the earth; *vitanoti* — spreads; *kīrtim* — the glories; *yat* — because; *devakī-suta* — of the son of Devakī; *pada-ambuja* — from the lotus feet; *labdha* — received; *lakṣmi* — the treasure; *govinda-veṇum* — the flute of Govinda; *anu* — upon hearing; *matta* — maddened; *mayūra* — of the peacocks; *nṛtyam* — in which there is the dancing; *prekṣya* — seeing; *adri-sānu* — upon the peaks of the hills; *avarata* — stunned; *anya* — other; *samasta* — all; *sattvam* — creatures.

**"O friend, Vṛndāvana is spreading the glory of the earth, having obtained the treasure of the lotus feet of Kṛṣṇa, the son of Devakī. The peacocks dance madly when they hear Govinda's flute, and upon seeing them from the hilltops other creatures all become stunned."**

COMMENTARY: Simply mentioning the *gopīs'* special love for Kṛṣṇa has put Parīkṣit Mahārāja in their mood. Thus he is inspired to recite some of the prayers the *gopīs* sang in praise of the great personalities of Vraja, beginning with the Vṛndāvana forest itself. When a group of *gopīs* heard the song of Kṛṣṇa's all-enchanting flute as He entered the Vṛndāvana forest, they were immersed in the *rasas* of pure love and shared their thoughts with one another. In this verse (*Bhāgavatam* 10.21.10) one of them says to Śrīmatī Rādhārāṇī that Vṛndāvana has made the earth more glorious than Indra's heaven or, in other words, more glorious than all the other planets in the universe. Kṛṣṇa, by marking Vṛndāvana with His unique auspicious footprints, has bestowed upon every creature in Vṛndāvana the rarely found prize jewel of all goals of life — *bhakti-yoga,* the treasure of blissful devotional service to Him.

Kṛṣṇa marked Vṛndāvana not with His shoes but with His bare feet, which are compared to lotuses because of being very tender. The ground of Vṛndāvana, therefore, is exceedingly lucky to be touched by Kṛṣṇa's lotus feet despite being strewn with pebbles and thorns. Vṛndāvana is most fortunate because of Kṛṣṇa's presence. Though Lord Viṣṇu and other forms of Godhead appear in Svargaloka and other places, they are only *avatāras* of Kṛṣṇa, but Devakī-nandana, who appeared in Vṛndāvana, is the source of all *avatāras.*

Therefore to establish Kṛṣṇa as *avatārī,* the source of all expansions of God, the *gopīs* need only call Him Devakī-suta, the son of Devakī. Saying this is enough to prove that Vṛndāvana has raised the earth to a status higher than that of the heavenly planets, for even when Kṛṣṇa appears as other incarnations on other planets of the universe those planets never become as blessed with opulence (*labdha-lakṣmi*) as the earth does when He appears in Vṛndāvana. In other incarnations Kṛṣṇa behaves like the supreme controller, and this makes it difficult for Him to leave His bare footprints freely here and there.

Although the *gopīs* know everything there is to know, their overwhelming ecstatic love forces them to see the Supreme Lord as the son of Yaśodā, and no one else. They call Him Devakī-suta only because it was Devakī who brought Him, the original *avatārī,* into this world.

Only in Vṛndāvana does the Supreme Person appear as Govinda, the Lord of the cows (*gavām indraḥ*), who delights in playing with the cows and cowherds, wears a peacock feather and *guñjā* berries on His head, decorates Himself with a garland of *kadamba* flowers and other forest ornaments, and holds in His hand His constant friend the flute.

As soon as the peacocks in Vṛndāvana hear the murmuring of Govinda's flute, they conclude that a dark cloud is announcing the approach of rain and begin to dance. And seeing the peacocks dancing, all the other living beings gathered in groups on the peaks of the hills stop whatever they are doing and just stand there, stunned in ecstasy. Thus Vṛndāvana makes the earth more glorious than any other realm, even Vaikuṇṭha.

The words *veṇum anu* ("following the flute") mean that as soon as the peacocks drink with their ears a few drops of the nectar coming from Kṛṣṇa's distant flute they burst into wild dancing. But the words can be split differently. *Veṇu-manu* ("the *mantra* chanted by the flute") indicates that the sound of Kṛṣṇa's flute has the mystic power to enchant the peacocks and make them dance in intoxication. That powerful *mantra* produces various peculiar effects throughout Vṛndāvana. The peacocks are the first to respond to it, but its echoes reach even the peaks of the hills, which are attractive (*prekṣya*) to everyone and are the source of the birth of the bamboo flute. Hearing this *mantra,* all the living beings standing on the peaks cease their activities.

Another possible reading is that the peak of Govardhana Hill is *prekṣya,* most beautiful and always visible to the people of Vraja. At the outset of the Govardhana-pūjā, as the multitude of offerings were being presented to feed Govardhana, the Supreme Personality of Godhead seated Himself on Govardhana's peak and announced, *śailo 'smi:* "I am this hill."

The words *avaratānya-samasta-sattvam* mean that all other creatures become stunned. But these words also apply to Vṛndāvana in the sense that the lower material modes — passion and ignorance — cannot act there and only the perfectly pure mode of *viśuddha-sattva* prevails. As confirmed in *Śrīmad-Bhāgavatam* (10.35.9), even the trees and creepers in Vṛndāvana have attained the status of pure goodness:

*vana-latās tarava ātmani viṣṇuṁ*
*vyañjayantya iva puṣpa-phalāḍhyāḥ*
*praṇata-bhāra-viṭapā madhu-dhārāḥ*
*prema-hṛṣṭa-tanavo vavṛṣuḥ sma*

"The trees and creepers in this forest are so luxuriant with fruits and flowers that they seem to be manifesting Lord Viṣṇu within their hearts. As their branches bend low with the weight, the filaments on their trunks and vines stand erect in the ecstasy of love of God, and both the trees and the creepers pour down a rain of sweet sap."

*Viśuddha-sattva* is the substance of Vaikuṇṭha, as described in the *Bhāgavatam's* Second Canto (2.9.10):

*pravartate yatra rajas tamas tayoḥ*
*sattvaṁ ca miśraṁ na ca kāla-vikramaḥ*
*na yatra māyā kim utāpare harer*
*anuvratā yatra surāsurārcitāḥ*

"In the spiritual world there is neither the mode of passion, nor the mode of ignorance, nor a mixture of both, nor is there adulterated goodness, nor the influence of time or Māyā itself. Only the pure devotees of the Lord, who are worshiped both by demigods and by demons, reside in the spiritual world as the Lord's associates." In other words, the mode of *sattva* in Vaikuṇṭha is never mixed with *rajas* or *tamas;* it is always *viśuddha,* completely pure. Thus in Vaikuṇṭha there is no material goodness, which is a product of Māyā. *Na yatra māyā kim utāpare:* "Māyā and her products have no presence in Vaikuṇṭha." The transcendental nature of Vaikuṇṭha is called *sattva* only because the behavior of Vaikuṇṭha's residents resembles in some ways that of persons influenced by the material *sattva-guṇa;* Vaikuṇṭha has demigods, for example, who resemble their *sāttvika* counterparts in the material world. And since Vṛndāvana on earth equals and surpasses Vaikuṇṭha, Vṛndāvana too is permeated by *viśuddha-sattva.*

And there is yet another way to understand *prekṣyādri-sānv-avaratānya-samasta-sattvam:* When the creatures of Vṛndāvana hear Kṛṣṇa playing His flute, many of them faint from ecstasy and fall on top of one another, and stacked in piles they resemble the peaks (*sānus*) of Govardhana and Vraja's other beautiful hills (*prekṣya-adri*). Others respond to the sound of the flute by standing still and staring into the distance to try to locate Kṛṣṇa. Actually, apart from the peacocks, all living beings at once cease their external activity when they hear Kṛṣṇa's flute, but transcendentally they respond in various ways. When the peacocks dance wildly, the other animals remain motionless to fix their minds on hearing the flute and to look for Kṛṣṇa. Every one of them, however, experiences the greatest limit of ecstasy.

There is also another possible reading: All the living beings of Vraja who were standing in high places (*sānu*) were intently engaged (*avarata*) in offering their services to Kṛṣṇa. The birds, for example, were mildly chirping for Kṛṣṇa's pleasure, and all other beings were happily absorbed in their own personal services. Or else by standing in high places to better view Śrī Kṛṣṇa the various creatures were arranging for their protection (*ava*) from the terrible pain of being separated from Kṛṣṇa, and they were busily absorbed (*ratāni*) in their own services for Kṛṣṇa. Not only the dancing peacocks but all the other animals (*anya-samasta-sattvam*) — the *kokila* birds, for example — were busily engaged in service. And for the mischievous and violent animals the main way to serve Kṛṣṇa was to put aside their natural proclivities.

Alternatively, the logical connection of the phrases in this verse can be understood in a different order: First Kṛṣṇa saw the peacocks dancing, and then responded by playing His flute. When the peacocks first noticed Kṛṣṇa entering the forest, they saw the friend of all peacocks — the one with a peacock feather always decorating His head — pick up their feathers from the ground. They then became mad with joy and began to dance. Seeing the peacocks dance, Kṛṣṇa happily raised His flute to His lips and played. All the living beings on the mountain peaks responded to the sound by stopping all activity other than looking at Kṛṣṇa and listening to His flute. And as implied by the word *samasta* ("all"), the peacocks as well stopped dancing. At first they manifested the ecstasy of dancing, and then after hearing the flute they were stunned, overcome by ecstasy. Such a scene is never observed in Vaikuṇṭha.

## TEXT 109

हन्तायमद्रिरबला हरिदासवर्यो
यद्रामकृष्णचरणस्परशप्रमोदः ।
मानं तनोति सहगोगणयोस्तयोर्यत्
पानीयसूयवसकन्दरकन्दमूलैः ॥

*hantāyam adrir abalā hari-dāsa-varyo*
*yad rāma-kṛṣṇa-caraṇa-sparaśa-pramodaḥ*
*mānaṁ tanoti saha-go-gaṇayos tayor yat*
*pānīya-sūyavasa-kandara-kanda-mūlaiḥ*

*hanta* — oh; *ayam* — this; *adriḥ* — hill; *abalāḥ* — O friends; *hari-dāsa-varyaḥ* — the best among the servants of the Lord; *yat* — because; *rāma-kṛṣṇa-caraṇa* — of the lotus feet of Lord Kṛṣṇa and Balarāma; *sparaśa* — by the touch; *pramodaḥ* — jubilant; *mānam* — respect; *tanoti* — offers; *saha* — with; *go-gaṇayoḥ* — the cows, calves, and cowherd boys; *tayoḥ* — to Them (Śrī Kṛṣṇa and Balarāma); *yat* — because; *pānīya* — with drinking water; *sūyavasa* — very soft grass; *kandara* — caves; *kanda-mūlaiḥ* — and edible roots.

**"Of all the devotees, this Govardhana Hill is the best! O my friends, for Kṛṣṇa and Balarāma, along with Their calves, cows, and cowherd friends, this hill supplies all necessities — caves, fruits, flowers, edible roots, water for drinking, and very soft grass. In this way the hill offers respects to the Lord. Being touched by the lotus feet of Kṛṣṇa and Balarāma, Govardhana Hill appears very jubilant."**

COMMENTARY: Next, Parīkṣit Mahārāja cites a verse in praise of Govardhana (*Bhāgavatam* 10.21.18), spoken by another of the *gopīs*. She addresses her girlfriends with the interjection *hanta,* which expresses both joy and amazement. This hill Govardhana, she says, is certainly the best of all the servants of the Supreme Lord, who is named Hari because He takes away everyone's sins and miseries, and everyone's heart. As evidence that Govardhana is the best of Kṛṣṇa's devotees, she mentions that from the touch of the lotus feet of Kṛṣṇa and Balarāma he displays ecstasy, the grass growing on his body looking just like bodily hair standing on end, the water trickling down his sides looking just like perspiration. Furthermore, Govardhana performs elaborate worship not only of Kṛṣṇa and Balarāma but also of Their cows and cowherd friends. In addition to the cows, the word *go* here indicates the other animals herded by Kṛṣṇa — buffaloes, goats, and others. The *gaṇas* are Kṛṣṇa's companions — Balarāma, Śrīdāmā, and the other cowherd boys. Govardhana worships them all with the things that give them special pleasure, including drinks (*pānīya*) like water, honey, and sugarcane juice. He also offers *sū-yavasa,* excellent grass. Or, taking *sū* to mean various products like fruits and flowers, he offers such things along with fresh grass. In his caves he provides beds and seats made of stones, and lamps and mirrors made of jewels. And he gives various root vegetables for Kṛṣṇa and the boys to eat. Thus he is the best of Kṛṣṇa's devotees because with loving devotion he serves not only Kṛṣṇa but also Kṛṣṇa's brother, His friends, and His cows. By saying this and by calling the other girls *abalāḥ* ("feeble girls"), the *gopī* speaking implies that she and the other *gopīs* are less fortunate than Govardhana; bewildered by their love for Kṛṣṇa, they lack the strength to render such valuable services.

Another way to understand the words *rāma-kṛṣṇa-caraṇa-sparaśa-pramodaḥ* is that Kṛṣṇa's feet give happiness to the entire world and always enjoy many kinds of sports. Govardhana delights those two lotus feet whenever they touch the stones on his surface, which then at once become soft like newly churned butter and very cool, or else slightly warm, as may suit the time. Or, taking yet other meanings of *rāma* and *caraṇa,* Kṛṣṇa's playful behavior (*caraṇa*) is enchanting (*rāma*) for the entire world. Govardhana takes pleasure (*pramoda*) in helping Kṛṣṇa reveal His enchanting pastimes, which bring everyone in the world in contact (*sparaśa*) with His lotus feet.

"Because we *gopīs* cannot do what Govardhana does," the

speaker of this verse seems to say, "we are condemned!" Thus even though the *gopīs* are full in all virtues, they consider themselves inadequate. Such is the natural dissatisfaction of persons on the highest levels of pure love of God.

### TEXT 110

दृष्ट्वातपे व्रजपशून्सहरामगोपैः
सञ्चारयन्तमनु वेणुमुदीरयन्तम् ।
प्रेमप्रवृद्ध उदितः कुसुमावलीभिः
सख्युर्व्यधात्स्ववपुषाम्बुद आतपत्रम् ॥

*dṛṣṭvātape vraja-paśūn saha-rāma-gopaiḥ*
*sañcārayantam anu veṇum udīrayantam*
*prema-pravṛddha uditaḥ kusumāvalībhiḥ*
*sakhyur vyadhāt sva-vapuṣāmbuda ātapatram*

*dṛṣṭvā* — seeing; *ātape* — in the full heat of the sun; *vraja-paśūn* — the domestic animals of Vraja; *saha* — together with; *rāma-gopaiḥ* — Lord Balarāma and the cowherd boys; *sañcārayantam* — herding together; *anu* — repeatedly; *veṇum* — His flute; *udīrayantam* — loudly playing; *prema* — out of love; *pravṛddhaḥ* — expanded; *uditaḥ* — rising high; *kusuma-āvalībhiḥ* — (with droplets of water, which resemble) groups of flowers; *sakhyuḥ* — for his friend; *vyadhāt* — he constructed; *sva-vapuṣā* — out of his own body; *ambudaḥ* — the cloud; *ātapatram* — an umbrella.

**"In the company of Balarāma and the cowherd boys, Lord Kṛṣṇa is continually vibrating His flute as He herds all the animals of Vraja, even under the full heat of the summer sun. Seeing this, the cloud in the sky has expanded himself out of love. He is rising high and constructing from his own body, with its multitude of flowerlike droplets of water, an umbrella for the sake of his friend."**

COMMENTARY: Mahārāja Parīkṣit has glorified Vraja-bhūmi in a general way by praising its principal attractions — the Vṛndāvana forest and Govardhana Hill. Now, in forty-one verses, beginning with this one (*Bhāgavatam* 10.21.16), he will continue to glorify Vraja-bhūmi by praising various forms of life in Vraja. One after another, in order of increasing importance, he selects those living beings that receive Kṛṣṇa's special mercy, each in its own way. We can understand that King Parīkṣit, while reciting each of these verses, felt something of the individual ecstatic moods of the devotees he was describing.

The clouds in the sky above Vraja-bhūmi may not have taken birth inside Vraja and by ordinary judgment may not even be considered living beings, but simply by floating over Vraja and obtaining Kṛṣṇa's mercy these clouds have come to life. Therefore the *gopīs* glorify them.

The *gopīs* single out a particular cloud that went out of his way to serve Kṛṣṇa. That cloud once saw Kṛṣṇa, Balarāma, and Their friends herding their countless cows, buffaloes, and other animals and letting the animals wander, even into the hot summer sun, Kṛṣṇa playing constantly on His flute. The cloud guessed that Kṛṣṇa and His friends might be getting tired, so he placed himself just above the spot where the boys gathered at midday, on the relatively cool ground in the shade of a circle of trees. Listening to Kṛṣṇa play His flute and call out to the cows, the cloud, filled with ecstasy, rumbled with gentle thunder, as if his voice were ecstatically choking in his throat, and sprinkled fine drops of rain, as if to shed ecstatic tears of joy. These offerings of love inspired Kṛṣṇa to encourage the cows even more, in His sweet deep voice, to take advantage of the opportunity to eat plenty of grass.

The cloud's increasing ecstasy as he watched Kṛṣṇa from closer and closer made the cloud grow bigger and bigger. He could presume himself Kṛṣṇa's friend because both he and Kṛṣṇa were fully absorbed in working for the general welfare of the world. So as a person naturally serves a dear friend, the cloud took care to serve Kṛṣṇa. Like a huge umbrella, he shaded Kṛṣṇa, and he poured down a cooling rain. A cloud's raindrops are called its flowers (*megha-puṣpa*), so the drops that fell on the boys were like small flowers. Or else the cloud literally showered them with heavenly flowers.

This cloud gave special pleasure to Kṛṣṇa by trying to serve not only Kṛṣṇa but also His brother Balarāma and all the cowherd boys and cows and the other animals. By describing this situation, the *gopī* speaking means to say, "My dear girls, that cloud is most fortunate, but we are unfortunate. In every respect, our fate is just the opposite of his. When Kṛṣṇa goes out to herd His cows, we hardly ever have a chance to see Him. And even if we do, we become bewildered by hearing His flute. Distressed by love, we become debilitated, unable to act. How then can we do any practical service for Kṛṣṇa, like shading Him from the noontime sun?"

## TEXT 111

नद्यस्तदा तदुपधार्य मुकुन्दगीतम्
आवर्तलक्षितमनोभवभग्नवेगाः ।
आलिङ्गनस्थगितमूर्मिभुजैर्मुरारेर्
गृह्णन्ति पादयुगलं कमलोपहाराः ॥

*nadyas tadā tad upadhārya mukunda-gītam*
*āvarta-lakṣita-manobhava-bhagna-vegāḥ*
*āliṅgana-sthagitam ūrmi-bhujair murārer*
*gṛhṇanti pāda-yugalaṁ kamalopahārāḥ*

*nadyaḥ*—the rivers; *tadā*—then; *tat*—that; *upadhārya*—perceiving; *mukunda*—of Lord Kṛṣṇa; *gītam*—the song of His flute; *āvarta*—by their whirlpools; *lakṣita*—manifest; *manaḥ-bhava*—by their conjugal desire; *bhagna*—broken; *vegāḥ*—their currents; *āliṅgana*—by their embrace; *sthagitam*—held stationary; *ūrmi-bhujaiḥ*—by the arms of their waves; *murāreḥ*—of Lord Murāri; *gṛhṇanti*—they seize; *pāda-yugalam*—the two lotus feet; *kamala-upahārāḥ*—carrying offerings of lotus flowers.

**"When the rivers hear the flute-song of Kṛṣṇa, their minds begin to desire Him, and thus the flow of their currents breaks, and their agitated waters move around in whirlpools. Then with the arms of their waves the rivers embrace Murāri's lotus feet and, holding on to them, present offerings of lotus flowers."**

COMMENTARY: The rivers in Vraja receive even greater mercy than the clouds. To external eyes the rivers of Vraja may seem unconscious, but they are not ordinary bodies of water. Thus another *gopī* sings this verse (*Bhāgavatam* 10.21.15) in praise of all those rivers, headed by Śrī Yamunā and Mānasī-gaṅgā. Or else only one river is being praised, namely the Yamunā, and she is being referred to in the plural out of great respect. In any case, since the other rivers of Vraja are Śrī Yamunā's companions, when she is glorified so are they all.

Kṛṣṇa is called Mukunda because He is the bestower of supreme happiness. The vibration of His flute is the sweetest of all songs. When He plays His flute near the rivers, the sound enters the rivers' ears and captures their hearts, making them feel the intense attraction of Cupid, which brings agitated whirlpools to their surface and stops their flowing currents. Or, understanding the word *lakṣita* differently, the rivers undergo many thousands of ecstatic transformations caused by desire.

If the words *mukunda-gītam āvarta* are split instead as *mukunda-gīta-māvarta,* the luxuriant potency (*mā*) of the song from Śrī Mukunda's flute brings about recurring waves (*āvarta*) of ecstatic symptoms, which disclose that the rivers are feeling agitated by Cupid. The *gopī* speaking, in the depth of her love for Kṛṣṇa, is too confused and fearful to mention His flute explicitly, but obviously enough the words *tat* and *gītam,* which refer back to previous verses, imply the flute.

The waves of the rivers are like arms, with which the rivers take hold of Kṛṣṇa's feet in utter humility, gently covering those lotus feet in their embrace. The rivers do this just to calm the fever of lust in their hearts. If instead of "covered" we take *sthagitam* to mean "unmoving," the rivers embrace Kṛṣṇa's lotus feet with loving enthusiasm even though those feet are unmoved, too proud to reciprocate. Or else, taking *sthagitam* to mean "stopped," Kṛṣṇa's feet are very restless, always moving here and there, yet they become tranquil by the pleasant touch of the rivers' embrace. The rivers express their love for Kṛṣṇa by catching hold of His feet with their waves.

Any river fortunate enough to have Kṛṣṇa standing within her waters would certainly want to offer suitable worship to His divine feet. But the force of Cupid's attraction bewilders the rivers and slows their currents, so despite possessing immense treasures of jewels, pearls, and other riches, the rivers can manage to present only lotus flowers. Or, reading the word *kamalā* as a female name — by convention, a name of the goddess Lakṣmī — the rivers who worship Kṛṣṇa with their embraces are themselves worshiped by Lakṣmī.

When the rivers hear the enchanting song of Kṛṣṇa's flute, they forget their normal tendency to flow toward their husband, the ocean. Instead they turn still and assume humanlike forms. And instead of their own gems and pearls, they offer Kṛṣṇa His favorite Vraja-grown lotuses, presenting them on top of golden necklaces (*upa-hārāḥ*). The rivers would touch the two feet of Śrī Murāri with their many long arms — their waves — and hold His feet firm in their embrace. "Therefore," the *gopī* says, "we are not actually fortunate, but these rivers are. Not only are we unable to listen to the song of Kṛṣṇa's flute, but our desire to be with Kṛṣṇa does not stop the endless flow of service to our husbands, nor our other household duties. We cannot appear before Him in person, nicely dressed and suitably ornamented for His worship. Nor do we have many long, broad arms with which we can stop the restlessness of His lotus feet and place them on our breasts."

## TEXT 112

वनलतास्तरव आत्मनि विष्णुं
व्यञ्जयन्त्य इव पुष्पफलाढ्याः ।

प्रणतभारविटपा मधुधाराः
प्रेमहृष्टतनवो ववृषुः स्म ॥

*vana-latās tarava ātmani viṣṇuṁ*
*vyañjayantya iva puṣpa-phalāḍhyāḥ*
*praṇata-bhāra-viṭapā madhu-dhārāḥ*
*prema-hṛṣṭa-tanavo vavṛṣuḥ sma*

*vana-latāḥ* — the forest creepers; *taravaḥ* — and the trees; *ātmani* — within themselves; *viṣṇum* — the Supreme Lord, Viṣṇu; *vyañjayantyaḥ* — revealing; *iva* — as if; *puṣpa* — with flowers; *phala* — and fruits; *āḍhyāḥ* — richly endowed; *praṇata* — bowed down; *bhāra* — because of the weight; *viṭapāḥ* — whose branches; *madhu* — of sweet sap; *dhārāḥ* — torrents; *prema* — out of ecstatic love; *hṛṣṭa* — hairs standing on end; *tanavaḥ* — on whose bodies (trunks); *vavṛṣuḥ sma* — they have rained down.

**"The trees and creepers in the forest respond to the sound by becoming so luxuriant with fruits and flowers that they seem to be manifesting Lord Viṣṇu within their hearts. As their branches bend low with the weight, the filaments on their trunks and vines stand erect in the ecstasy of love of God, and both the trees and the creepers pour down a rain of sweet sap."**

COMMENTARY: Greater than the clouds and rivers are the forest plants, who are sentient beings. Another of the *gopīs* recites this verse (*Bhāgavatam* 10.35.9) in praise of the trees and creepers of Vṛndāvana, who have the great fortune to associate with Kṛṣṇa during the day. The *gopīs,* by singing these verses to remind themselves of how Kṛṣṇa is enjoying in the forest, achieve some solace from the pain of being separated from Him.

In the previous verse of the *Bhāgavatam* (10.35.8) the *gopīs* sang of Kṛṣṇa's playing His flute to call the cows (*veṇunā āhvayati gāḥ sa yadā hi*). Thus the sound the trees and creepers are responding to is the sound of Kṛṣṇa's flute. The flute song directly addresses the cows, not the trees and creepers, yet the trees and creepers of Vṛndāvana and the other forests of Vraja react in ecstasy, pouring down a continuous flow of sap. It seems that they behold the Supreme Personality of Godhead everywhere, inside their hearts and outside. And though the all-pervasive Supreme Lord Viṣṇu appears in numerous forms, they see Him in the one form who submits Himself to the control of pure devotion — Śrī Nanda-kiśora.

The creepers try to hide that they are seeing Him, as one might try to hide that one is seeing a rare and secret treasure, but their ecstatic love confounds their attempts. Unwittingly, they let everyone see that Kṛṣṇa is manifest in their hearts. The symptoms of Kṛṣṇa's inner presence are obvious: The creepers are outwardly rich with an endless supply of fruits and flowers. And their branches bend low, not only from the weight of those fruits and flowers but also from an inner mood of humbleness, which shows a deep wealth of good qualities derived from piety and spiritual knowledge. Moreover, the gross and subtle bodies of the creepers show signs of transcendental ecstasy, evidence that the creepers possess the deepest inner wealth of pure devotion. The creepers, and also their husbands, the trees, are fully endowed with these symptoms of external and internal wealth. The *gopīs* mention the creepers before the trees because the creepers are women like themselves.

These creepers and trees very much resemble Śrī Kṛṣṇa's devotees, who are rich with the fruits of beauty, aristocracy, wealth, and influence and with the flowers of children and other family members. Kṛṣṇa's devotees are rich with the flowerlike *Vedas* (which offer lush promises of rewards), are richly steeped in study of the *Vedas* and performance of Vedic sacrifices, and are also rich with the fruits of enjoyment in this life and the next. Nonetheless, these devotees remain always bowed down in humility, shyness, and other saintly qualities, and their family members (*viṭapāḥ*) show these qualities as well.

The devotees of the Lord try to keep Śrī Viṣṇu hidden in their hearts, like a housewife who tries to conceal her extramarital affair, but the Lord so thoroughly pervades the inner and outer workings of all the senses that the devotees cannot keep Him from openly shining forth. Especially when they hear the song of Kṛṣṇa's flute, their intensified love expresses itself in their bodies as horripilation on their limbs, and they shed torrents of ecstatic tears and show other signs of joy. As indicated in this verse by the words *vyañjayantya iva* ("as if exhibiting"), Vaiṣṇavas naturally want to respect the sanctity of their *prema* by not showing it to anyone and everyone. *Prema* should not be allowed to degrade into a cheap public spectacle. But when symptoms of increased ecstasy appear in their bodies, Vaiṣṇavas sometimes cannot completely conceal their inner feelings.

The songs, like this one, that the *gopīs* sing in the thirty-fifth chapter of the Tenth Canto differ from their complaints of separation from Kṛṣṇa, cited earlier from previous chapters. Before, the *gopīs* mostly lamented their bad fortune, but now they are seriously trying to raise themselves above the misery of being separated from Kṛṣṇa during the day. By singing these songs, they actually feel great joy. As Śukadeva Gosvāmī states at the end of the chapter (10.35.26):

*evaṁ vraja-striyo rājan*
*kṛṣṇa-līlānugāyatīḥ*
*remire 'haḥsu tac-cittās*
*tan-manaskā mahodayāḥ*

"O King, during the daytime the women of Vṛndāvana thus took pleasure in continuously singing about the pastimes of Kṛṣṇa, and the minds and hearts of those women, absorbed in Him, were filled with great festivity." Although the women intensely felt the pain of separation from Kṛṣṇa, by singing about His pastimes they were able to keep their minds fixed on Him, and so they were happy even during the day.

At the beginning of Chapter Thirty-five (10.35.1) Śrīla Śukadeva also said:

*gopyaḥ kṛṣṇe vanaṁ yāte*
*tam anudruta-cetasaḥ*

*kṛṣṇa-līlāḥ pragāyantyo*
*ninyur duḥkhena vāsarān*

"Whenever Kṛṣṇa went to the forest, the minds of the *gopīs* would run after Him, and thus the young girls, although saddened, spent their days singing of His pastimes." This statement can be understood to mean that even though being apart from Kṛṣṇa made the *gopīs* sad, they managed to pass the days happily (*ninyuḥ*) by singing about His pastimes.

According to the explanation given by Śrīla Śrīdhara Svāmī, the *gopī* praising the creepers and trees of Vṛndāvana means to say, "If even the plant life has such deep love for Kṛṣṇa, how can we be expected to tolerate being separated from Him?" All the same, by singing the glories of Kṛṣṇa, whose transcendental body is the essence of all bliss, the *gopīs* feel great pleasure. Their songs are not pitiful lamentations but the highest revelations of ecstatic love. Or if one prefers to see the negative side of love in separation, the word *mahodaya* ("festivity") can be understood to be used ironically to indicate just the opposite of what it literally means; that is to say, because the hearts of the *gopīs* burn incessantly in the fire of *prema,* they never enjoy a moment's happiness.

## TEXT 113

एतेऽलिनस्तव यशोऽखिललोकतीर्थं
गायन्त आदिपुरुषानुपथं भजन्ते ।
प्रायो अमी मुनिगणा भवदीयमुख्या
गूढं वनेऽपि न जहत्यनघात्मदैवम् ॥

*ete 'linas tava yaśo 'khila-loka-tīrthaṁ*
*gāyanta ādi-puruṣānupathaṁ bhajante*
*prāyo amī muni-gaṇā bhavadīya-mukhyā*
*gūḍhaṁ vane 'pi na jahaty anaghātma-daivam*

*ete* — these; *alinaḥ* — bees; *tava* — Your; *yaśaḥ* — glories;

*akhila-loka* — for the whole world; *tīrtham* — a place of pilgrimage; *gāyantaḥ* — are chanting; *ādi-puruṣa* — O original Personality of Godhead; *anupatham* — following You along the path; *bhajante* — they are worshiping; *prāyaḥ* — for the most part; *amī* — these; *muni-gaṇāḥ* — great sages; *bhavadīya* — among Your devotees; *mukhyāḥ* — the most intimate; *gūḍham* — hidden; *vane* — within the forest; *api* — even though; *na jahati* — they do not abandon; *anagha* — O sinless one; *ātma-daivam* — their own worshipable Deity.

**"O original personality, these bees must all be great sages and most elevated devotees of Yours, for they are worshiping You by following You along the path and chanting Your glories, which are themselves a holy place for the entire world. Though You have disguised Yourself within this forest, O sinless one, they refuse to abandon You, their worshipable Lord."**

COMMENTARY: Better than the nonmoving creatures are those who can move, beginning with the insects, bugs, and worms. Parīkṣit Mahārāja now recounts Lord Kṛṣṇa's praise of the bees who follow His brother Balarāma wherever He goes (*Bhāgavatam* 10.15.6). As mentioned before, Kṛṣṇa is speaking to Balarāma, but whatever He says about Balarāma applies in fact to Himself. The bees, therefore, never stop chanting Kṛṣṇa's glories, which are like holy pilgrimage sites that bestow spiritual upliftment on all living beings. Kṛṣṇa's glories, like a universally magnanimous spiritual master, can deliver any person, whether fit to be saved or not. Those glories bestow upon everyone who comes in contact with them divine knowledge of the greatness of pure devotional service.

The bees that follow Kṛṣṇa are great sages, but not sages like the self-satisfied impersonalists; rather, they are Kṛṣṇa's devotees (*bhavadīya*). And of His devotees they are among the most elevated (*mukhyāḥ*) because although Kṛṣṇa hides Himself in the forest they never stop following Him. He is their all-in-all, the Lord of their life. To join Him in the forest, they disguise themselves as bees and thus take the opportunity to worship Him always with their songs.

Here Lord Kṛṣṇa calls Balarāma *ādi-puruṣa,* the original Supreme Person. This means that the bees who are always with the Lord are among the *ādi-sevakas,* the Lord's original eternal servants. They always worship Him suitably according to the various pastimes He performs. Śrī Kṛṣṇa also calls Balarāma *anagha,* meaning "sinless," "free from all faults," "neglectful of all offenses against Him," and "granting salvation from all miseries." Because the Lord is *anagha* in these ways, the bees can never abandon Him; they worship Him in any circumstance, fearless of reactions for their offenses and confident that devotional service will protect them from all distress. In truth, the bees of Vṛndāvana are better than other sages because the bees never stop singing the glories of Kṛṣṇa whereas other sages sometimes fall silent, absorbed in ecstatic trance.

Those bees are like the great Vaiṣṇava *munis* who never stop seeking Kṛṣṇa even though He is hidden in the forest of the *Vedas.* Though His pastimes are difficult to understand and His service is difficult to achieve, the determined Vaiṣṇavas never abandon Him; they strive to locate His glories even on the paths of *karma* and *jñāna.* They always sing those glories and promote them as the most serviceable spiritual asset, and so they realize Kṛṣṇa directly as the indwelling Supersoul of all *jīvas,* their worshipable Supreme Lord. As Vaiṣṇava sages surrender to Kṛṣṇa, giving up everything to serve Him in pure love, so do the bees in Vṛndāvana.

## TEXT 114

सरसि सारसहंसविहङ्गाश्
चारुगीतहृतचेतस एत्य ।
हरिमुपासत ते यतचित्ता
हन्त मीलितदृशो धृतमौनाः ॥

*sarasi sārasa-haṁsa-vihaṅgāś*
*cāru-gīta-hṛta-cetasa etya*
*harim upāsata te yata-cittā*
*hanta mīlita-dṛśo dhṛta-maunāḥ*

*sarasi* — in the lake; *sārasa* — the cranes; *haṁsa* — swans; *vihaṅgāḥ* — and other birds; *cāru* — charming; *gīta* — by the song (of His flute); *hṛta* — taken away; *cetasaḥ* — whose minds; *etya* — coming forward; *harim* — Lord Kṛṣṇa; *upāsata* — worshiped; *te* — they; *yata* — under control; *cittāḥ* — whose minds; *hanta* — ah; *mīlita* — closed; *dṛśaḥ* — their eyes; *dhṛta* — maintaining; *maunāḥ* — silence.

**"The charming flute song steals away the minds of the cranes, swans, and other lake-dwelling birds. Indeed, they approach Kṛṣṇa, close their eyes and, maintaining strict silence, worship Him by fixing their consciousness upon Him in deep meditation."**

COMMENTARY: This is another verse sung by the *gopīs* who were trying to console one another during the daytime, when Kṛṣṇa was absent. The birds of Vraja are superior to the bugs and insects, but even among the birds there are different levels of Kṛṣṇa consciousness. The waterfowl are a little less fortunate than the others because they have less opportunity to be close to Kṛṣṇa.

The waterfowl described in this verse (*Bhāgavatam* 10.35.11) live in a far-away lake filled with clean water, clusters of lotuses, and various other attractions. Innumerable cranes, swans, and other birds forever sport in that lake. But when they hear the beautiful song of Kṛṣṇa's flute, their minds are captivated. First they become bewildered and fly about madly in all directions. Then they return to the lake and settle down to engage in serious worship of Lord Hari. To fix their attention exclusively on Him, they restrain their minds, bodies, and speech. They subdue their minds, close their eyes, and resort to complete silence, bringing not only mind, sight, and speech but all their senses under strict control. Or, understanding the word *upāsata* to mean "they approached" rather than "they worshiped," the birds leave the lake to come near Kṛṣṇa and sit by His side. Being close to Kṛṣṇa gives them the highest pleasure, as shown by the way they become peaceful, closing their eyes and staying silent.

The word *hanta* in this verse indicates joy and surprise. But it can also be taken to express disappointment, and accordingly the whole statement of the verse can be understood in a different way: The birds approached Kṛṣṇa and apparently calmed down, but were their minds actually peaceful? Not at all. Taking the liberty to add the negative prefix *-a* to the words *mīlita* and *dhṛta-mauna,* we can read *te 'yata-cittā / hantāmīlita-dṛśo 'dhṛta-maunāḥ:* the birds could not control their minds (*ayata-cittāḥ*), could not close their eyes (*amīlita-dṛśaḥ*), and could not be silent (*adhṛta-maunāḥ*). Their meditation on Kṛṣṇa caused such ecstatic mental transformations that they couldn't possibly keep their minds calm. They were in such anxiety from being unable to see Kṛṣṇa that they couldn't close their eyes, which even lost the natural ability to blink. And they took to such loud *saṅkīrtana* of Kṛṣṇa's names that any trace of sobriety was out of the question.

Or, understanding the birds' condition in another way: As a result of worshiping Kṛṣṇa by meditating on Him, they attained the ecstasy of *mūrcchā,* loss of consciousness. Their minds dissolving into oblivion, they simply closed their eyes and fell silent. In other words, the *gopī* speaking implies, though these birds are members of a different species of life, though they live in the sky, though they are males, and though they live in a distant lake, where they are busy enjoying in various ways, the song of Kṛṣṇa's flute has forcibly dragged them into Kṛṣṇa's association. Concentrating their minds on Kṛṣṇa has awakened in the birds a transcendental *prema* that has destroyed their natural peace and thoughtfulness, disturbed their consciousness with all sorts of agitation, and rendered them completely bewildered. What can be said, then, of the constant state of the *gopīs,* who have no other purpose in life than to serve Kṛṣṇa? They too must be suffering, but much more severely.

TEXT 115

प्रायो बताम्ब मुनयो विहगा वनेऽस्मिन्
कृष्णेक्षितं तदुदितं कलवेणुगीतम् ।
आरुह्य ये द्रुमभुजान्रुचिरप्रवालान्
शृण्वन्ति मीलितदृशो विगतान्यवाचः ॥

*prāyo batāmba munayo vihagā vane 'smin*
*kṛṣṇekṣitaṁ tad-uditaṁ kala-veṇu-gītam*
*āruhya ye druma-bhujān rucira-pravālān*
*śṛṇvanti mīlita-dṛśo vigatānya-vācaḥ*

*prāyaḥ* — almost; *bata* — certainly; *amba* — O mother; *munayaḥ* — great sages; *vihagāḥ* — the birds; *vane* — in the forest; *asmin* — this; *kṛṣṇa-īkṣitam* — in order to see Kṛṣṇa; *tat-uditam* — created by Him; *kala* — indistinct yet melodious; *veṇu-gītam* — flute song; *āruhya* — rising; *ye* — who; *druma-bhujān* — to the branches of the trees; *rucira-pravālān* — having beautiful creepers and twigs; *śṛṇvanti* — they hear; *mīlita-dṛśaḥ* — closing their eyes; *vigata-anya-vācaḥ* — stopping all other sounds.

**"O mother, in this forest all the birds have risen onto the beautiful branches of the trees to see Kṛṣṇa. With closed eyes they are simply listening in silence to the sweet vibrations of His flute, and they are not attracted by any other sound. Surely these birds are on the same level as great sages."**

COMMENTARY: Another *gopī,* enchanted by hearing Kṛṣṇa's flute, sings this verse (*Bhāgavatam* 10.21.14) to Mother Yaśodā, or else to a girlfriend. Here even more fortunate birds are glorified, those who live in the same trees that provide shade for Kṛṣṇa as He wanders about the Vṛndāvana forest. All the birds in Vṛndāvana should be recognized as great sages; or, as indicated by the word *prāyaḥ* (taken to mean "many"), sages are not so numerous in Vraja, but there are many birds. These birds are able to hear the mellow song of Kṛṣṇa's flute, which Kṛṣṇa plays for the enjoyment of the cows and the cowherd boys and girls of Śrī Vṛndāvana. When Kṛṣṇa is far away, the birds may not hear the sound distinctly, but still its effect on them is vivid.

That sound bestows upon them the vision of Kṛṣṇa (*kṛṣṇasya īkṣitam*), and by bringing them to the tops of the trees it also becomes the means by which Kṛṣṇa sees them (*kṛṣṇena īkṣitam*). The flute song is also *kṛṣṇekṣitam* ("seen by Kṛṣṇa"), in the sense that only Kṛṣṇa can conceive of such beautiful music. It is produced from Kṛṣṇa (*kṛṣṇasya uditam*), and this suggests also that the sound of the flute creates an opportunity for the birds to perceive Kṛṣṇa by hearing; hearing the sound is another way for them to see Kṛṣṇa, who is not easily visible to them through the abundant foliage.

Though the rich new growth on the branches makes it difficult for the birds to see Kṛṣṇa, it also attracts Kṛṣṇa to the trees to pick the fresh leaves, fruits, and flowers. So the birds put aside their normal business of foraging and fly to the highest branches, where the leaves and twigs don't block the line of sight between them and Kṛṣṇa.

Perched in the treetops, eyes closed in meditation, the birds appear like great sages. Indeed, sages who want to devote themselves to Kṛṣṇa perch themselves on various branches of the tree of the *Vedas,* which bear the attractive, tender twigs of various methods for spiritual advancement. The sages learn from the *Vedas* how to realize Kṛṣṇa, and with enthusiasm they practice the disciplines approved by the *Vedas,* such as offering to Kṛṣṇa the results of all work. But even while seriously studying the *Vedas* and pondering what they mean, the sages become attracted to hearing Kṛṣṇa's all-attractive flute and become eager to see Him. They cease to be attached to their Vedic education and instead become attached to seeing Kṛṣṇa constantly in their hearts. Closing their eyes in great ecstasy, they then dedicate themselves exclusively to His *nāma-saṅkīrtana.*

Or else it may be understood that sages devoted to the Personality of Godhead come to the Vṛndāvana forest to become birds and listen to the song of His flute. According to the commentary of Śrīla Śrīdhara Svāmī, all sages, even if content in their own selves, should become birds in the Vṛndāvana forest. Or, granting that some sages are disqualified from entrance into Vṛndāvana because they are less fortunate and confused by Māyā, at least most of them should (*prāyaḥ*). They should become birds in Vṛndāvana because thus they can easily achieve what they aspire for, and much more.

Because the birds living in the Vṛndāvana forest have the great fortune to be able to hear Kṛṣṇa's flute so often, they should be acknowledged to be greater devotees than the bees. And thinking about the birds makes Kṛṣṇa's girlfriends even more disappointed than before: "How terrible this is! We don't have such unalloyed devotion for Kṛṣṇa. We can't see Kṛṣṇa or hear His flute when He goes to the forest. We can't renounce everything and climb the branches of the trees. And when we don't see Him, we can't simply stop talking and close our eyes like these birds. To hell with us *gopīs*!"

## TEXT 116

धन्याः स्म मूढमतयोऽपि हरिण्य एता
या नन्दनन्दनमुपात्तविचित्रवेषम् ।
आकर्ण्य वेणुरणितं सहकृष्णसाराः
पूजां दधुर्विरचितां प्रणयावलोकैः ॥

*dhanyāḥ sma mūḍha-matayo 'pi hariṇya etā*
*yā nanda-nandanam upātta-vicitra-veṣam*
*ākarṇya veṇu-raṇitaṁ saha-kṛṣṇa-sārāḥ*
*pūjāṁ dadhur viracitāṁ praṇayāvalokaiḥ*

*dhanyāḥ* — fortunate, blessed; *sma* — certainly; *mūḍha-matayaḥ* — ignorant; *api* — although; *hariṇyaḥ* — she-deer; *etāḥ* — these; *yāḥ* — who; *nanda-nandanam* — the son of Mahārāja Nanda; *upātta-vicitra-veṣam* — dressed very attractively; *ākarṇya* — hearing; *veṇu-raṇitam* — the sound of His flute; *saha-kṛṣṇa-sārāḥ* — accompanied by the black deer (their husbands); *pūjām dadhuḥ* — they worshiped; *viracitām* — performed; *praṇaya-avalokaiḥ* — by their affectionate glances.

**"Blessed are all these foolish deer because they have approached Mahārāja Nanda's gorgeously dressed son after hearing Him play on His flute. Indeed, both the doe and the bucks worship the Lord with looks of love and affection."**

COMMENTARY: In this verse (*Bhāgavatam* 10.21.11) another *gopī* glorifies the deer. The deer, being similar in species to the cows and other creatures tended by the Personality of Godhead, are able to accompany them while grazing. *Dhanyāḥ sma* means "they [the deer] are fortunate." Or, considering the grammatical license granted to saintly authors like Vyāsadeva, another way to understand *dhanyāḥ sma* is "we are fortunate." This is possible if we allow Śrīla Vyāsa the liberty of leaving off the final letter of the word *smaḥ* ("we are"), the way it is sometimes left off in the texts of the *Vedas*. In other words, "We consider it our great fortune that these deer have responded to the flute song of our beloved Śrī Nanda-nandana by approaching to worship Him with all respect."

The worship done by the deer was very simple, being performed with nothing more than loving glances. The deer had no paraphernalia at their disposal for worship, and other than those loving glances, nothing would have satisfied Kṛṣṇa. As expressed by the prefix *vi-* in the word *viracitām* ("well arranged"), the deer's method of worship was exceptionally pleasing to Kṛṣṇa.

The deer saw Kṛṣṇa decorated with wonderful forest ornaments like flower garlands and with peacock feathers and *guñjā* berries in His hair. Thus even though the deer had taken birth as unintelligent animals (*mūḍha-mati*), they were supremely fortunate. Or, understanding the meaning of *mūḍha-matayaḥ* differently, just by hearing Kṛṣṇa's flute the deer lost their power to think clearly, and their internal and external senses all became stunned. This is the natural influence of Vraja: even living beings possessed of various skills are deprived of them by the reverberation of Kṛṣṇa's flute and rendered dumb and immobile like inert beings.

The doe normally stay hidden deep within the forest. But the sound of Kṛṣṇa's flute drew them out into the open, where they came near Kṛṣṇa and, beholding His beauty, were bewildered by Cupid. In that condition, they could think of nothing but Him. They simply gazed at Him in great love, as if worshiping Him. And their husbands also reacted the same way to the song of Kṛṣṇa's flute. The doe and bucks — those most exalted of animals — were endowed with such deep love for the Supreme Lord that they could never become proud of their good fortune; they always behaved like innocent creatures.

As the *gopīs* meditate on the devotional service of the deer, they cannot help but think, "These deer are fortunate because they can worship Kṛṣṇa along with their husbands. But our foolish husbands cannot tolerate our worship of Kṛṣṇa. Therefore, despite being born as human beings, fully able to understand and act, we are unfortunate. In fact, we are most unfortunate, even though born in the very virtuous and clever cowherd caste, because we cannot follow Kṛṣṇa and listen to His flute while He wanders about in His forest dress. We cannot gaze at Him with wide-open eyes filled with love and serve Him with pleasing glances. And even if a few of us can occasionally perform such service for Him, our husbands object." The word *kṛṣṇa-sāra* means "the black deer." But the word *sāra* also means "important." So the *gopīs* think, "The husbands of the deer are called *kṛṣṇa-sāras* because only Kṛṣṇa is important to them; the attitude of our husbands, however, is just the opposite." Actually, the cowherd men are also most fortunate Vaiṣṇavas, exclusively devoted to Kṛṣṇa; still, the *gopīs,* as subordinates, as wives, feel shy to disclose to their husbands their worship of Kṛṣṇa. Constrained by the husband-and-wife relationship, the *gopīs* have to worship Kṛṣṇa secretly as a paramour. This unique style of worship enables the *gopīs* to achieve the extreme limit of success — the highest degree of pure love for Kṛṣṇa.

## TEXT 117

गावश्च कृष्णमुखनिर्गतवेणुगीत-
पीयूषमुत्तभितकर्णपुटैः पिबन्त्यः ।
शावाः स्नुतस्तनपयःकवलाः स्म तस्थुर्
गोविन्दमात्मनि दृशाश्रुकलाः स्पृशन्त्यः ॥

*gāvaś ca kṛṣṇa-mukha-nirgata-veṇu-gīta-*
*pīyūṣam uttabhita-karṇa-puṭaiḥ pibantyaḥ*
*śāvāḥ snuta-stana-payaḥ-kavalāḥ sma tasthur*
*govindam ātmani dṛśāśru-kalāḥ spṛśantyaḥ*

*gāvaḥ* — the cows; *ca* — and; *kṛṣṇa-mukha* — from the mouth of Lord Kṛṣṇa; *nirgata* — emitted; *veṇu* — of the flute; *gīta* — of the song; *pīyūṣam* — the nectar; *uttabhita* — raised high; *karṇa* — with their ears; *puṭaiḥ* — which were acting as vessels; *pibantyaḥ* — drinking; *śāvāḥ* — the calves; *snuta* — exuding; *stana* — from their udders; *payaḥ* — of the milk; *kavalāḥ* — whose mouthfuls; *sma* — indeed; *tasthuḥ* — stood still; *govindam* — Lord Kṛṣṇa; *ātmani* — within their minds; *dṛśā* — with their vision; *aśru-kalāḥ* — their eyes full of tears; *spṛśantyaḥ* — touching.

**"Using their upraised ears as vessels, the cows are drinking the nectar of the flute-song flowing out of Kṛṣṇa's mouth. The calves, their mouths full of milk from their mothers' moist nipples, stand still as they take Govinda within themselves through their tear-filled eyes and embrace Him within their hearts."**

COMMENTARY: By far superior to the deer of the Vṛndāvana forest are the cows personally tended by Śrī Gopāladeva. In this verse (*Bhāgavatam* 10.21.13) other *gopīs* glorify Kṛṣṇa's cows. To the cows, the sound of Kṛṣṇa's flute was just like *pīyūṣa,* the nectar created on the moon. This means that Kṛṣṇa's face seemed to them like the moon. Anxious not to spill a drop of that nectar, they used their ears like cupped palms to drink it carefully. In other words, they listened to the flute with rapt attention. Despite the cowherds' vigilance, the *śāvas,* or calves, some of them newly born, had somehow joined their mothers and were busy drinking their mothers' milk. But as soon as the calves heard Kṛṣṇa's flute, they forgot what they were doing; they simply kept their mothers' milk in their mouths without swallowing it.

Or else it may be that the calves were not present and the word *śāvāḥ* refers to the cows themselves. The cows were so absorbed in drinking the nectar from Kṛṣṇa's moonlike face that they became motionless like corpses (*śavāḥ*). As love for Kṛṣṇa swelled in the hearts of the cows, milk spontaneously flowed from their udders, and the grass they were eating remained in their mouths because they were unable to chew.

The cows were raised to the highest platform of love of God by seeing Kṛṣṇa with their eyes and embracing Him within their hearts. They were so moved that drops (*kalāḥ*) of tears (*aśru*) appeared in their eyes. Or, taking *kalāḥ* to mean "producing," the cows were shedding profuse tears. Hearing this description, the *gopīs* commented, "Dear friends, if the cows act like this, then we *gopīs,* as human beings, should be excused for being driven to extremes by the force of *prema.*"

## TEXT 118

वृन्दशो व्रजवृषा मृगगावो
वेणुवाद्यहृतचेतस आरात् ।
दन्तदष्टकवला धृतकर्णा
निद्रिता लिखितचित्रमिवासन् ॥

*vṛndaśo vraja-vṛṣā mṛga-gāvo*
*veṇu-vādya-hṛta-cetasa ārāt*
*danta-daṣṭa-kavalā dhṛta-karṇā*
*nidritā likhita-citram ivāsan*

*vṛndaśaḥ* — in groups; *vraja* — kept in the pasture; *vṛṣāḥ* — the bulls; *mṛga* — the deer; *gāvaḥ* — and the cows; *veṇu* — of the flute; *vādya* — by the playing; *hṛta* — stolen away; *cetasaḥ* — their minds; *ārāt* — at a distance; *danta* — by their teeth; *daṣṭa* — bitten; *kavalāḥ* — whose mouthfuls; *dhṛta* — holding up; *karṇāḥ* — their ears; *nidritāḥ* — asleep; *likhita* — drawn; *citram* — an illustration; *iva* — as if; *āsan* — they were.

**"When Kṛṣṇa vibrates His flute, Vraja's bulls, deer, and cows, standing in groups at a great distance, are all captivated by the sound, and they stop chewing the food in their mouths and cock their ears. Stunned, they appear as if asleep, or like figures in a painting."**

COMMENTARY: This verse (*Bhāgavatam* 10.35.5) describes the rare good fortune shared by the cows and the bulls and the other animals that were with them. "Dear friends, please now hear something wonderful! When the bulls, deer, and cows hear Kṛṣṇa's flute, they feel the urge to approach Him. They all come from far away and stand nearby Him, fully enchanted. They forget about the grass in their mouths, and it either stays there unchewed or else falls from their mouths to the ground. Their ears standing upright, the animals remain still, as if asleep or as if not living beings but painted images." Thus these animals, bewildered by *prema,* lose their powers of thought and activity.

Or, explaining what happens in another way, at first the cows hear Kṛṣṇa's flute from a distance as an indistinct murmur, without embellishments or even a discernable melody. But simply that faint sound is enough to capture their hearts and completely agitate them. After a short time, when the cows, bulls, and deer hear the song of Kṛṣṇa's flute more clearly, they feel fear that death might intervene and separate them from Kṛṣṇa. So to prevent themselves from hearing any more, they lift their front legs and forcibly cover the holes of their ears. When that fails to stop the sound, they come closer to Kṛṣṇa, holding blades of grass in their mouths as a sign of humble entreaty. And when that also fails to stop Kṛṣṇa from playing, they all become stunned.

The word *citram* in this verse is in the singular form because as these animals fell into a stupor they came together into a densely packed group, like figures posed together in a painting.

## TEXT 119

पूर्णाः पुलिन्द्य उरुगायपदाब्जराग-
श्रीकुंकुमेन दयितास्तनमण्डितेन ।
तद्दर्शनस्मररुजस्तृणरूषितेन
लिम्पन्त्य आननकुचेषु जहुस्तदाधिम् ॥

*pūrṇāḥ pulindya urugāya-padābja-rāga-*
*śrī-kuṅkumena dayitā-stana-maṇḍitena*
*tad-darśana-smara-rujas tṛṇa-rūṣitena*
*limpantya ānana-kuceṣu jahus tad-ādhim*

*pūrṇāḥ* — fully satisfied; *pulindyaḥ* — the wives of the Śabara tribe; *urugāya* — of Lord Kṛṣṇa; *pada-abja* — from the lotus feet; *rāga* — of reddish color; *śrī-kuṅkumena* — by the transcendental *kuṅkuma* powder; *dayitā* — of His girlfriends; *stana* — the breasts; *maṇḍitena* — which had decorated; *tat* — of that; *darśana* — by the sight; *smara* — of Cupid; *rujaḥ* — feeling the torment; *tṛṇa* — upon the blades of grass; *rūṣitena* — attached; *limpantyaḥ* — smearing; *ānana* — upon their faces; *kuceṣu* — and breasts; *jahuḥ* — they gave up; *tat* — that; *ādhim* — mental pain.

**"The aborigine women of the Vṛndāvana area become disturbed by lust when they see the grass marked with reddish kuṅkuma powder. Endowed with the color of Kṛṣṇa's lotus feet, this powder originally decorated the breasts of His beloveds, and when the aborigine women smear it on their faces and breasts, they feel fully satisfied and give up all their anxiety."**

COMMENTARY: The human beings in Vraja, of course, are more exalted than the lower forms of life. In this verse (*Bhāgavatam*

10.21.17) one *gopī* first glorifies the outcaste women who dwell in the forest. The Pulindas are an aborigine tribe living in Vraja. They are also known as Śabaras. Referring to them also implies other tribes of Vraja, including the Bhilla tribe. The low-class Pulinda women felt fully satisfied (*pūrṇāḥ*) when they smeared themselves with the effulgently red *kuṅkuma* that came from the lotus feet of Śrī Kṛṣṇa, Urugāya, who plays His flute (*gāyati*) in many wonderful ways (*urudhā*). As soon as they smeared this cosmetic powder on their faces and breasts, the Pulindīs felt relief from the piercing arrows of Cupid.

How was this *kuṅkuma,* usually found on the breasts of women, found on the grass by the Pulindīs? Out of shyness, the *gopīs* do not explain the reason in so many words, but the fact is that this *kuṅkuma* came from the breasts of some of the *gopīs.* Those particular *gopīs,* who had succumbed to the allure of *kṛṣṇa-saṅkīrtana* and the song of Kṛṣṇa's flute, had allowed Him to seduce them. During their intimate pastimes, the *kuṅkuma* had been transferred from their breasts to His lotus feet. Later, as Kṛṣṇa walked through the forest, the same *kuṅkuma* fell from His feet onto the grass and stones on the path. Apparently Kṛṣṇa was walking vigorously, because the *kuṅkuma* became firmly attached to the grass and stones. And when the aborigine women, foraging for wood and wild herbs, came to the same part of the forest, they discovered the *kuṅkuma.*

Why were the Pulindīs disturbed by lust? Seeing the *kuṅkuma* on the ground reminded them first of Kṛṣṇa and then of His intimate affairs with the *gopīs.* Thinking about these things agitated their minds. (The word *smara* can be understood to mean either "remembrance" or "Cupid.") And how were the aborigine women relieved of this agitation? By picking up the red powder and smearing it on their faces and breasts, which were burning with lust. Having done this, the Pulindīs felt completely satisfied. In contrast, the *gopīs* speaking and hearing this account lament that they will never feel so satisfied.

As implied by the words *śrī* ("splendid") and *maṇḍita* ("adorned"), the *kuṅkuma* became more beautiful by being smeared on the breasts of Kṛṣṇa's beloved *gopīs,* and even more effulgent by contact with Kṛṣṇa's lotus feet. Though the Pulindīs normally have no beauty or glow in their faces, when they decorated their own bodies with this *kuṅkuma* from the grass and stones they became beautiful, effulgent, and free from the pain of lust. The *gopī* speaking means to say, "We are condemned because we cannot become exalted like the aborigine women!" Or, looking at the situation another way, because the blessed *gopīs* are always immersed in the torment of separation from Kṛṣṇa, they tend to presume that everyone else must also be suffering the same way. And so the Pulindīs too, they think, must now be suffering the pain of separation from Kṛṣṇa.

The limbs of the Pulindīs were covered (*pūrṇāḥ*) with *kuṅkuma* that looked exactly like the color of the soles of Śrī Urugāya's lotus feet. So when the *gopīs* saw the Pulindīs, the *gopīs* remembered how for Kṛṣṇa's pleasure they themselves had first decorated their own breasts with that same *kuṅkuma.* Because the color of that *kuṅkuma* resembled the hue of Kṛṣṇa's feet, the *gopīs* liked to use it.

Another explanation is also possible. The wonderful music of Kṛṣṇa's flute had drawn the *gopīs* into the forest to wander about searching for Him, and when they couldn't find Him anywhere, in the anguish of *viraha-bhāva* they rolled on the ground, smearing the grass with the *kuṅkuma* from their breasts. Later, when the Pulindīs came, simply seeing the red powder made them remember Kṛṣṇa and His dealings with the *gopīs,* and they were stung by the arrows of Cupid.

Thinking about the great love the *gopīs* have for Kṛṣṇa and recalling that this *kuṅkuma* had been in contact with the *gopīs'* bodies, the aborigines picked up some of the powder with great reverence and applied it to their faces. Then their own lust impelled them to smear it also on their breasts. But then they wiped this *kuṅkuma* off their bodies and threw it away. Why? Because it caused them intense pain. They were already disturbed by lust just by seeing the *kuṅkuma,* and when they touched it their minds became thoroughly agitated. Then when they smeared it on their faces and breasts the pain became so extreme that they quickly wiped the *kuṅkuma* off and threw it away, afraid that otherwise they would come to a bad end.

"Alas!" the *gopī* speaking complains. "Just like those Pulindīs, we too are most unfortunate, cast into an ocean of intolerable pain. But just see how especially unlucky we *gopīs* are! Just by touching the cosmetics from our bodies, people feel such misery that they throw the stuff away to protect their lives!"

### TEXT 120

यदि दूरं गतः कृष्णो वनशोभेक्षणाय तम् ।
अहं पूर्वमहं पूर्वमिति संस्पृश्य रेमिरे ॥

*yadi dūraṁ gataḥ kṛṣṇo*
*vana-śobhekṣaṇāya tam*
*ahaṁ pūrvam ahaṁ pūrvam*
*iti saṁspṛśya remire*

*yadi* — if; *dūram* — to a distant place; *gataḥ* — went; *kṛṣṇaḥ* — the Supreme Personality of Godhead; *vana-śobhā* — the beauty of the forest; *īkṣaṇāya* — for visiting and enjoying; *tam* — Him (Kṛṣṇa); *aham* — I; *pūrvam* — first; *aham* — I; *pūrvam* — first; *iti* — in this way; *saṁspṛśya* — by touching; *remire* — they enjoyed life.

**"Sometimes Kṛṣṇa would go to a somewhat distant place to see the beauty of the forest. Then all the other boys would run to accompany Him, each one saying, 'I shall be the first to run and touch Kṛṣṇa! I shall touch Kṛṣṇa first!' In this way they enjoyed life by repeatedly touching Kṛṣṇa."**

COMMENTARY: The cowherd boys who constantly accompany Kṛṣṇa are certainly superior to the aborigine forest women. Parīkṣit Mahārāja now recites six verses to praise those cowherd boys, or *gopa-kumāras*. The first three verses are spoken by Śukadeva Gosvāmī in the Tenth Canto, Chapter Twelve (texts 6,

11, and 12). They describe how those boys joined Kṛṣṇa in tending the cows. Very early in the morning, the Supreme Lord, eager to enjoy the day's countless pastimes, like killing Aghāsura and eating lunch on the grass, called out to His friends by bugling on His buffalo horn, and they came out of their houses by the thousands. Tending thousands, millions, and billions of calves, they all set out to the forest. They decorated themselves with forest ornaments of fruits, twigs, and other items and sported by playing their flutes, blowing their horns, imitating animals, and playing "keep away" with one another's lunches. They played all these games simply for Kṛṣṇa's enjoyment. They had a chance to touch Kṛṣṇa and embrace Him, which gave them the highest happiness. In their eagerness, they competed to see who would be first to touch Kṛṣṇa. Sometimes the beauty of Vṛndāvana and other forests would so beguile Kṛṣṇa that He wanted to go alone to explore them. But He was so attached to the company of His friends that He would leave them only for a short time. Then the boys would run after Him, trying to follow Him on His solitary side trips. The cowherd boys were not satisfied unless they could be right there with Kṛṣṇa and able to touch Him.

## TEXT 121

इत्थं सतां ब्रह्मसुखानुभूत्या
दास्यं गतानां परदैवतेन ।
मायाश्रितानां नरदारकेण
साकं विजह्रुः कृतपुण्यपुञ्जाः ॥

*ittham satāṁ brahma-sukhānubhūtyā*
*dāsyaṁ gatānāṁ para-daivatena*
*māyāśritānāṁ nara-dārakeṇa*
*sākaṁ vijahruḥ kṛta-puṇya-puñjāḥ*

*ittham* — in this way; *satām* — for the transcendentalists; *brahma-sukha* — of the joy of the impersonal Supreme; *anubhūtyā* — with Kṛṣṇa, who appears in the form of their experience; *dāsyam* — servitorship; *gatānām* — for the devotees who have accepted; *para-daivatena* — with the Supreme Personality of Godhead; *māyā-āśritānām* — for those in the clutches of material energy; *nara-dārakeṇa* — with Him who is like an ordinary child; *sākam* — together; *vijahruḥ* — (the cowherd boys) enjoyed; *kṛta-puṇya-puñjāḥ* — who had accumulated the results of life after life of pious activities.

**"In this way, all the cowherd boys, having accumulated the results of pious activities for many lives, used to play with Kṛṣṇa, who for impersonalist jñānīs is realization of the bliss of Brahman, who for devotees in eternal servitorship is the Supreme Personality of Godhead, and who for ordinary persons is but another ordinary child.**

COMMENTARY: Amazed by the incomparable good fortune of the cowherd boys, Śrī Bādarāyaṇi continues to praise them for joining Kṛṣṇa in His cow-tending and other such pastimes. By associating so intimately with Kṛṣṇa, these boys were directly experiencing the transcendental happiness of Brahman realization. Kṛṣṇa is the supreme worshipable Deity of saints (*satām*) who have been given the privilege to enter His service. *Satām* also means "liberated souls." Kṛṣṇa's friends in Vraja are liberated persons who take part in the happiness of knowing Brahman, the Absolute Truth. Most people, however, are not liberated. They are *māyāśrita,* bewildered by the Supreme Lord's power of illusion, and therefore they consider Kṛṣṇa an ordinary cowherd boy (*nara-dāraka*). *Satām* can also be understood to indicate the seekers of spiritual knowledge, who realize Kṛṣṇa in His impersonal Brahman feature and enjoy the happiness of knowing Brahman in that way. But to the Vaiṣṇava devotees who consider themselves Kṛṣṇa's servants (*dāsyaṁ gatānām*), Kṛṣṇa, the supreme master (*para-daivata*), gives Himself, submitting Himself to their control. Material nature bewilders the entire creation, but Kṛṣṇa's pure servants bewilder Him by the strength of their pure love and thus defeat material nature.

Taken in another sense, *māyāśritānām* refers to Kṛṣṇa's

beloved *gopīs,* who worshiped the goddess Māyā with choice *mantras:*

*kātyāyani mahā-māye*
*mahā-yoginy adhīśvari*
*nanda-gopa-sutaṁ devi*
*patiṁ me kuru te namaḥ*
*iti mantraṁ japantyas tāḥ*
*pūjāṁ cakruḥ kumārikāḥ*

"Each of the young unmarried girls performed her worship while chanting the following *mantra.* 'O goddess Kātyāyanī, O great potency of the Lord, O possessor of great mystic power and mighty controller of all, please make the son of Nanda Mahārāja my husband. I offer my obeisances unto you.'" (*Bhāgavatam* 10.22.4)

These *gopīs* could see Kṛṣṇa only as an attractive youth (*nara-dāraka*). They gave no thought to His godly omnipotence. As if ordinary girls, they simply focused their attention on Him as the sole object of their desire and affection. Or — another reading — the same Kṛṣṇa who is the constant companion of the cowherd boys is also amorous appeal personified for all human females (*nara-dārāḥ*). Or else Kṛṣṇa figuratively tears apart all persons (*narān dārayati*) by filling their hearts with unique love for Him. Of course, Kṛṣṇa's attraction in the conjugal *rasa* is most appropriately described in relation to women, but because the *gopīs* presume every human being to be like themselves, they think that Kṛṣṇa tears apart the heart of everyone and fills it with love. This presumption is suggested by the use of the masculine form *nara-dārakeṇa,* which can be grammatically understood to include both males and females.

Accepting that *māyāśritānām* refers to the *gopīs,* in this verse we have a hierarchy in which the devotees in eternal servitorship are higher than the *jñānīs,* and the *gopīs* are still higher. Thus in this verse, which glorifies the cowherd boys, the greatness of the *gopīs* is also to be seen.

The cowherd boys of Vraja, to become eligible to play as they do with Kṛṣṇa, must have performed heaps of pious deeds in their previous lives. The word *puñja* ("great quantity") implies that these boys must have had an inexhaustible stock of pious credits. And the word *kṛta* in *kṛta-puṇya-puñjāḥ,* as in the similar expression *kṛtārtha* ("having achieved the success of one's life"), indicates that their past pious works were of a very special quality — pure acts of sacrifice offered to the Supreme Lord for His pleasure. Or the word *puṇya* in this context can be interpreted to mean activities of pure devotional service, for Kṛṣṇa Himself says, *dharmo mad-bhakti-kṛt proktaḥ,* "Actual religious principles are stated to be those that lead one to My devotional service." (*Bhāgavatam* 11.19.27) Or else *kṛta* can mean the ancient Satya-yuga (Kṛta-yuga), when the great souls who were later to become Kṛṣṇa's friends performed faultless meditation on the Personality of Godhead and became all-around perfect Vaiṣṇavas.

Although the darling son of Nanda Mahārāja is the Supreme Personality of Godhead, very few persons are fortunate enough to know Him as He is. The knowers of the impersonal Supreme realize Him in the form of *brahma-sukha;* in other words, within their hearts they can enjoy only the perception of His existence as pure spirit. And even most Vaiṣṇava devotees realize Kṛṣṇa only as the embodiment of eternity, knowledge, and bliss — the Supreme Truth, the Supreme Soul, the Supreme Lord. Burdened by a sense of reverence for Him, they worship accordingly and experience a corresponding quality of bliss. But Kṛṣṇa's beloved *gopīs* in Vraja realize Him as Śrī Nanda's young son. Freed from theoretical knowledge and reverence that would damage the treasure of their most exalted love, they experience the highest *prema.* This truth has been stated repeatedly in *Śrī Bṛhad-bhāgavatāmṛta,* but it cannot be overstressed.

The *gopīs* are always beside themselves with transcendental anxiety due to the excessive love they feel for Kṛṣṇa. They usually cannot be with Him during the day, and even in their nocturnal meetings they do not feel as completely free to enjoy with Him as they would like, because of the constant threat of opposition from their husbands and families. The cowherd boys, on the other hand, are always free to play with Kṛṣṇa in varieties of pastimes, both at home and in the forest. Therefore their good fortune is most exceptional.

This does not contradict the many statements of *Śrīmad-Bhāgavatam* that confirm that the blessed *gopīs* are more exalted and fortunate than all other beings; rather, it indicates that the revered Śukadeva, in the core of his heart, is a follower of the *gopīs'* mood of devotion and therefore while elaborating on the wonderful pastimes of Kṛṣṇa and the cowherd boys and glorifying the boys for being able to play constantly with Kṛṣṇa in the forest he speaks like the *gopīs* themselves. Śukadeva's style of praising the *gopa-kumāras* as supremely fortunate is nondifferent from the way the *gopīs* themselves describe as the perfection of vision the sight of Śrī Kṛṣṇa's face while He sports within the forest:

*akṣaṇvatāṁ phalam idaṁ na paraṁ vidāmaḥ*
*sakhyaḥ paśūn anuviveśayator vayasyaiḥ*
*vaktraṁ vrajeśa-sutayor anu-veṇu-juṣṭaṁ*
*yair vā nipītam anurakta-kaṭākṣa-mokṣam*

"O friends, the eyes that see the beautiful faces of the sons of Mahārāja Nanda are certainly fortunate. As these two sons, surrounded by Their friends, enter the forest, driving the cows before Them, They hold Their flutes to Their mouths and glance lovingly upon the residents of Vṛndāvana. For those who have eyes, we think there is no greater object of vision." (*Bhāgavatam* 10.21.7)

## TEXT 122

यत्पादपांशुर्बहुजन्मकृच्छ्रतो
धृतात्मभिर्योगिभिरप्यलभ्यः ।
स एव यद् दृग्विषयः स्वयं स्थितः
किं वर्ण्यते दिष्टमतो व्रजौकसाम् ॥

*yat-pāda-pāṁśur bahu-janma-kṛcchrato*
*dhṛtātmabhir yogibhir apy alabhyaḥ*

*sa eva yad-dṛg-viṣayaḥ svayaṁ sthitaḥ*
*kiṁ varṇyate diṣṭam ato vrajaukasām*

*yat* — whose; *pāda-pāṁśuḥ* — dust of the lotus feet; *bahu-janma* — in many births; *kṛcchrataḥ* — from undergoing severe austerities and penances; *dhṛta-ātmabhiḥ* — who are able to control the mind; *yogibhiḥ* — by *yogīs; api* — even; *alabhyaḥ* — unachievable; *saḥ* — the Supreme Personality of Godhead; *eva* — indeed; *yat* — of whom (the Vraja-vāsīs); *dṛk-viṣayaḥ* — the object of direct vision, face to face; *svayam* — personally; *sthitaḥ* — present in front of them; *kim* — what; *varṇyate* — can be described; *diṣṭam* — about the fortune; *ataḥ* — therefore; *vraja-okasām* — of the inhabitants of Vraja-bhūmi.

**"Yogīs may undergo severe austerities and penances for many births. Yet in due course of time, when these yogīs attain the perfection of controlling the mind, they will still be unable to taste even a particle of dust from the lotus feet of the Supreme Personality of Godhead. What then can we describe about the great fortune of the inhabitants of Vraja-bhūmi, with whom the Supreme Personality of Godhead personally lived and who saw the Lord face to face?"**

COMMENTARY: The good fortune of the cowherd boys in being able to see Kṛṣṇa face to face defies description, what to speak of how blessed they must be to be able to play with Kṛṣṇa constantly. The cowherd boys and all the residents of Vraja-bhūmi are the most fortunate beings in creation because they can look directly on the beauty of Kṛṣṇa. Dedicated *yogīs* endeavor for lifetimes to approach Kṛṣṇa, but for all their labor they can never hope to become as fortunate as the Vraja-vāsīs. Even one particle of dust from Kṛṣṇa's feet is impossible to achieve for *yogīs* who do not follow humbly in the footsteps of the devotees of Vraja.

The meaning of "the dust from Kṛṣṇa's feet" may be understood in several ways. It can mean a single atom of His feet. It can mean the marks of His footprints in the dust of Vraja-bhūmi. It can mean dust that has been in contact with His feet and then shaken off somewhere in His wanderings. It can refer to anything that has been even indirectly in contact with His feet, no matter from how far away. Or the words *pāda-pāṁśu* — "the dust from Kṛṣṇa's feet" — can be redivided and modified to *pādapa-aṁśu,* meaning the effulgence (*aṁśu*) emanating from Kṛṣṇa's favorite *kadamba* trees and the other trees (*pādapa*) of the Vṛndāvana forest. Even the most distant contact with Kṛṣṇa's *pāda-pāṁśu* in any of these senses is for mystic *yogīs* a rare accomplishment.

Determined *yogīs,* in their attempts to succeed, practice severe disciplines, such as *brahmacarya* and other austerities. For many lifetimes they struggle to steady themselves by withdrawing the mind and senses from material objects. But even if they achieve the success of *samādhi,* they cannot achieve Kṛṣṇa, who is the full embodiment of spiritual perfection, *sac-cid-ānanda-ghana-mūrti.* He is beyond the purview of the senses. Only the Vraja-vāsīs can see Him as He is. The form of the Supreme Lord visible in Vraja is not a *vibhūti,* one of God's opulent expansions, nor is He a partial incarnation of Godhead, nor is He even Lord Nārāyaṇa. He is the original source of all forms of God yet viewable by the cowherds like any other perceptible object and constantly fixed (*sthitaḥ*) in their sight. In other words, He never leaves the path of their eyes. How then can the exalted fortune of the Vraja-vāsīs ever be adequately described?

Or, translating Śukadeva's question in a different way, *kiṁ varṇyate diṣṭam* asks whether the condition of the Vraja-vāsīs is the result of their fate. The answer, of course, is that the Vraja-vāsīs' situation is not the karmic effect of pious works done in previous lifetimes. It is solely the result of Kṛṣṇa's mercy. Or, dividing words another way, the fortunate condition of the Vraja-vāsīs is a perpetual festival (*diṣṭa-maho*). Or the power of their good fortune is inconceivable (*adiṣṭa-* or *adṛṣṭa-maho*). The pure devotional service of the Vraja-vāsīs displays all these features.

A discriminating reader may question the placement of this verse — which tells of the good fortune of merely seeing Kṛṣṇa — after the verse depicting the special fortune of the cowherd boys in being able to always play with Kṛṣṇa. The good fortune of playing with Kṛṣṇa automatically includes the good fortune of seeing Him and goes beyond it, the reader may argue, so placing these items out of the natural logical order of lesser to greater, general to specific, is a fault in poetic style.

To accommodate this reasonable doubt, we may construe Śukadeva's statements in yet another way: The boys who enjoy playing with Kṛṣṇa are indeed extremely fortunate, and this verse amplifies that assertion by showing that actually all creatures living in Vraja are fortunate beyond description. It is easy to prove that any resident of Vraja is greater than the most accomplished *yogī.* So it naturally follows that the boys who live so closely with the Personality of Godhead and are so uniquely dear to Him are, of all living beings, the most exalted.

Or we can say that Śukadeva is continuing to glorify the cowherd boys in particular — *these* inhabitants of Vraja-bhūmi — because Kṛṣṇa is the constant object of their vision. The eyes of the *gopa-kumāras* see Kṛṣṇa and nothing else. As a general rule, each individual sense has its own proper object. The sense of sight perceives only visible forms, not tastes, smells, or other sensations. But the attention of the boys is so engrossed in Kṛṣṇa that they are disregardful of whatever else is present before them. The eyes of other people perceive various objects like pots and cloths, but wherever the cowherd boys turn their eyes they see only Kṛṣṇa — that is to say, they see everything in relationship to Kṛṣṇa. The poetry of Śrī Jayadeva Kavi illustrates this kind of special vision: *paśyati diśi diśi rahasi bhavantam,* "In every direction, in every secret corner, She sees only You." (*Gīta-govinda* 12.1) Thus it is appropriate for Śukadeva to speak this verse after the previous one, since even greater than the cowherd boys' good fortune of always playing with Kṛṣṇa is their being always able to see Him everywhere. This marks their love for Kṛṣṇa as being almost as good as that of the *gopīs.*

## TEXT 123

क्वचित्पल्लवतल्पेषु नियुद्धश्रमकर्शितः ।
वृक्षमूलाश्रयः शेते गोपोत्सङ्गोपबर्हणः ॥

*kvacit pallava-talpeṣu*
*niyuddha-śrama-karśitaḥ*
*vṛkṣa-mūlāśrayaḥ śete*
*gopotsaṅgopabarhaṇaḥ*

*kvacit* — sometimes; *pallava* — made from new twigs and buds; *talpeṣu* — upon beds; *niyuddha* — from the fighting; *śrama* — by fatigue; *karśitaḥ* — worn out; *vṛkṣa* — of a tree; *mūla* — at the base; *āśrayaḥ* — taking shelter; *śete* — He lay down; *gopa-utsaṅga* — the lap of a cowherd boy; *upabarhaṇaḥ* — as His pillow.

**"Sometimes Lord Kṛṣṇa grew tired from fighting and lay down at the base of a tree, resting upon a bed made of soft twigs and buds and using the lap of a cowherd friend as His pillow.**

COMMENTARY: Texts 123 through 125 are from *Śrīmad-Bhāgavatam* (10.15.16–18). Here Śukadeva Gosvāmī describes some of the services the cowherd boys did for Kṛṣṇa while He rested in the forest. These pastimes were a part of Kṛṣṇa's *paugaṇḍa-līlā* of tending His cows in Śrī Vṛndāvana forest. Kṛṣṇa would enjoy lying down to rest at various times (when fatigued after wrestling with His friends, for instance) and in various places, such as the cool, breezy shore of the Yamunā. To rest comfortably, He would choose the base of a *kadamba, tamāla,* or other tree with ample shade. Anticipating Kṛṣṇa's daily pastimes, the goddess Vṛndā would have beds of leaves, flowers, and young soft twigs waiting at the bases of those trees, or sometimes Kṛṣṇa's *gopa* friends would arrange this bedding when they arrived. Even though Kṛṣṇa lay down on only one bed at a time, Śrīla Śukadeva refers to the beds in the plural, either because many devotees were involved in making them, or simply out of great respect for the paraphernalia of Kṛṣṇa's pastimes, or else because the cowherd boys would compete to make several different beds and Kṛṣṇa would expand His universal form to please all the boys by simultaneously lying down on each bed, unseen by the makers of the others. Kṛṣṇa would accept as His pillow the lap of His most intimate friend, Śrīmatī Rādhārāṇī's brother Śrīdāmā.

## TEXT 124

पादसंवाहनं चक्रुः केचित्तस्य महात्मनः ।
अपरे हतपाप्मानो व्यजनैः समवीजयन् ॥

*pāda-saṁvāhanaṁ cakruḥ*
*kecit tasya mahātmanaḥ*
*apare hata-pāpmāno*
*vyajanaiḥ samavījayan*

*pāda-saṁvāhanam* — the massaging of the feet; *cakruḥ* — did; *kecit* — some of them; *tasya* — of Him; *mahā-ātmanaḥ* — great souls; *apare* — others; *hata-pāpmānaḥ* — who were free from all sins; *vyajanaiḥ* — with fans; *samavījayan* — perfectly fanned Him.

**"Some of the cowherd boys, who were all great souls, free of all sin, would then massage His lotus feet, and others would expertly fan Him.**

COMMENTARY: When Kṛṣṇa's cowherd friends, who loved Him so much, saw that He was fatigued, many of them responded immediately, doing whatever they could to relieve His discomfort. In this flurry of activity, the boys were overcome by ever-increasing affection for Him. Many boys would massage His legs, either one boy at a time in turns or else all the boys massaging various places at once. It may also be that to please His beloved friends, who all wanted to serve Him in this way, the Supreme Lord manifested His all-pervasive form — without leaving aside His form as the son of Śrī Nanda — and allowed a huge crowd of cowherd boys to massage His feet simultaneously, each unseen by the others. Thus Kṛṣṇa displayed His supreme powers even in His childhood pastimes, as expressed in a later verse of the

*Bhāgavatam* (10.15.19) by the words *īśa-ceṣṭitaḥ* ("exhibiting feats only God can perform"). With this in mind, instead of taking the word *mahātmanaḥ* in this verse to refer to Kṛṣṇa's friends, we can take it as referring to Kṛṣṇa ("the Supreme Soul"). In these pastimes, Kṛṣṇa demonstrates the greatness of the Supreme Being even more convincingly than in God's typical activities like creation. In these childhood pastimes, Kṛṣṇa shows His power to enchant the entire world with His sweetness.

Śukadeva Gosvāmī speaks of Kṛṣṇa's friends as *hata-pāpmānaḥ,* "persons who have had their sins destroyed." For ordinary pious persons, whatever contradicts the principles of religion is sin, but for devotees of the Supreme Lord, sin is anything that obstructs pure devotional service, and that is the sense that applies here; the cowherd boys of Vraja have not the slightest inclination to do anything that does not please Kṛṣṇa. Kṛṣṇa Himself is also called *hata-pāpmānaḥ* in the sense that He destroys the sins of all the worlds by displaying His glories for everyone to hear and chant.

## TEXT 125

अन्ये तदनुरूपाणि मनोज्ञानि महात्मनः ।
गायन्ति स्म महाराज स्नेहक्लिन्नधियः शनैः ॥

*anye tad-anurūpāṇi*
*mano-jñāni mahātmanaḥ*
*gāyanti sma mahā-rāja*
*sneha-klinna-dhiyaḥ śanaiḥ*

*anye* — others; *tat-anurūpāṇi* — suitable for the occasion; *manaḥ-jñāni* — attractive to the mind; *mahā-ātmanaḥ* — of the great personality (Lord Kṛṣṇa); *gāyanti sma* — they would sing; *mahā-rāja* — O King Parīkṣit; *sneha* — by love; *klinna* — melted; *dhiyaḥ* — their hearts; *śanaiḥ* — slowly.

**"My dear king, other boys would sing songs, appropriate**

**to the occasion, that would enchant Kṛṣṇa, and the hearts of the boys would melt out of love for Him."**

COMMENTARY: Some of Kṛṣṇa's friends sang songs with sweet, gentle melodies, just right for His nap time. This encouraged Him to fall asleep quickly. Kṛṣṇa is the most exalted of persons, graver than the combined depth of millions of oceans, but these songs fascinated Him because they described His loving dealings with the *gopīs*. And His mind was strongly attracted even to the parts of those songs that merely glorified His devotional service in general ways.

It may be that here Śukadeva Gosvāmī uses the word *mahātmanaḥ* ironically. Unable to control his ecstasy, Śukadeva calls Kṛṣṇa a "great soul" with the understanding that Kṛṣṇa is actually the prince of womanizers, who shamelessly indulges His lusty propensities by stealing the clothes of the cowherds' daughters, making them appear naked before Him.

The songs sung by Kṛṣṇa's friends for His pleasure inspired intensified *prema,* which melted the boys' hearts. They sang softly, their voices choked with tears of ecstasy. From this we can know that even though pure love for Kṛṣṇa arises in the course of all kinds of devotional service, it appears most quickly and fully when one performs *saṅkīrtana* by singing songs dear to Kṛṣṇa and otherwise glorifying His name and fame.

As stated in the previous verse, the boys who served Kṛṣṇa while He rested were *hata-pāpmānaḥ,* "free from all sin." They were great souls, extremely advanced in devotional service, each capable of purifying the entire universe. Thus as they performed their individual services for Kṛṣṇa they felt more and more love for Him, and their hearts melted in ecstasy. And again, the word *mahātmanaḥ* applies equally well to both Kṛṣṇa and His friends.

In this verse Śrīla Śukadeva addresses King Parīkṣit as *mahārāja*. This may mean that the pastime of Kṛṣṇa's being served in royal style is fit to be heard by a king. Or it may imply that kings like Parīkṣit Mahārāja can hardly expect such luxurious comforts. Or describing to Parīkṣit the supreme fortune of the cowherd boys creates an upsurge of loving feelings in Śrī Śukadeva's heart that makes him address Parīkṣit as *mahā-rāja* to attract the attention of the king, who is also overwhelmed by the bewilderment of pure *prema*. Or Śukadeva calls Parīkṣit *mahā-rāja*, the best of the royal class, because only King Parīkṣit is competent to understand the sublime good fortune of these cowherd boys. Or else the term may indicate that the fondness cherished by the cowherd boys for Kṛṣṇa is supremely splendid; it is the *mahā-rāja* of loving sentiments. Although this *sneha*, or love, is always present within the boys, in this setting of intimate service it now rises to the peak of its potency. It radiates with infinite brilliance, leaving all contamination far behind.

TEXT 126

नन्दः किमकरोद् ब्रह्मञ्छ्रेय एवं महोदयम् ।
यशोदा वा महाभागा पपौ यस्याः स्तनं हरिः ॥

*nandaḥ kim akarod brahman*
*śreya evaṁ mahodayam*
*yaśodā vā mahā-bhāgā*
*papau yasyāḥ stanaṁ hariḥ*

*nandaḥ* — Mahārāja Nanda; *kim* — what; *akarot* — performed; *brahman* — O learned *brāhmaṇa; śreyaḥ* — auspicious activities, like performing penances and austerities; *evam* — thus (as exhibited by him and Yaśodā); *mahā-udayam* — from which they achieved the greatest perfection; *yaśodā* — Mother Yaśodā; *vā* — also; *mahā-bhāgā* — most fortunate; *papau* — drank; *yasyāḥ* — of whom; *stanam* — the breast milk; *hariḥ* — the Supreme Personality of Godhead.

**"O learned brāhmaṇa, Mother Yaśodā's breast milk was sucked by the Supreme Personality of Godhead. What past auspicious activities did she and Nanda Mahārāja perform to thus achieve such perfection in ecstatic love?"**

COMMENTARY: Texts 126 through 130 are dedicated to the supreme glories of Goparāja Nanda and his wife, Śrī Yaśodā. After Śukadeva explains to Parīkṣit Mahārāja the special way Kṛṣṇa favored Mother Yaśodā, Parīkṣit speaks the current verse (*Bhāgavatam* 10.8.46). By showing the universal form and by displaying other exceptional pastimes, Kṛṣṇa made Himself known to all the Vraja-vāsīs as the Supreme Lord. But then, to show His most extreme mercy especially to His mother, He again covered her consciousness with His unique potency so that she could think of Him only as her son. Thus Kṛṣṇa made the highest degree of pure affection pervade His mother's mind and all her senses.

Parīkṣit addresses the son of Badarāyaṇa Vyāsa with the word *brahman,* "O direct embodiment of the Supreme Absolute Truth," because Parīkṣit is asking a question that only the Lord Himself can answer: What special pious acts could Nanda and Yaśodā have done to achieve such a blessed state, unattainable in this material world?

The devotional success of Nanda and Yaśodā is *mahodayam,* "the greatest perfection," unequaled by other devotees, including Vasudeva and Devakī. In the very next *Bhāgavatam* verse (10.8.47), Śrī Parīkṣit states:

*pitarau nānvavindetāṁ*
*kṛṣṇodārārbhakehitam*
*gāyanty adyāpi kavayo*
*yal loka-śamalāpaham*

"Although Kṛṣṇa was so pleased with Vasudeva and Devakī that He descended as their son, they could not enjoy Kṛṣṇa's magnanimous childhood pastimes, which are so great that simply chanting about them vanquishes the contamination of the material world." Vasudeva and Devakī were Kṛṣṇa's true parents, but they were less fortunate than Nanda and Yaśodā, who witnessed Kṛṣṇa's childhood pastimes, in which He generously bestowed upon the world sense enjoyment, liberation, devotional service, and ecstatic love.

*Gāyanty adyāpi kavayaḥ:* Even today, in the Kali-yuga, great poets like Brahmā and Vyāsadeva sing about these pastimes because this is the means for uprooting all the evils of the modern age. Without glorifying Kṛṣṇa's pastimes, no one can eradicate the faults of Kali-yuga. Pure devotees have always chanted these glories of Kṛṣṇa, and continue to do so up to the present day.

The phrase *loka-śamalāpaham* can be explained in several ways. One is that this glorification, or *saṅkīrtana,* removes (*apaha*) the misery (*śamala*) of all living beings. Or, taking *śama* to mean "peace of mind," *lāpa* to mean "speech," and *ha* to mean "killing," another explanation is that by engaging in this hearing and chanting one develops the highest quality of *prema,* which in turn disturbs the equilibrium of the mind and brings the faculty of speech to a complete halt. Or, reading *śama* as "well-being" and *lāpa* as "discussion," another idea is that engaging in *saṅkīrtana* transforms the attitude of all who take part, leaving no scope for further discussion of impersonal self-contentment.

*Śrīmad-Bhāgavatam* (10.8.21–45) describes some of the wonderful pranks the infant Kṛṣṇa shared with Nanda and Yaśodā by His special mercy. Were it not for this unprecedented mercy, Mother Yaśodā would be on the same level as Devakī, who also fed Kṛṣṇa with her breast milk. Later in the Tenth Canto (*Bhāgavatam* 10.85.55), while narrating how Kṛṣṇa recovered His dead elder brothers, Śukadeva says:

*pītvāmṛtaṁ payas tasyāḥ*
*pīta-śeṣaṁ gadā-bhṛtaḥ*
*nārāyaṇāṅga-saṁsparśa-*
*pratilabdhātma-darśanāḥ*

"By drinking Devakī's nectarean milk, the remnants of what Kṛṣṇa Himself had drunk, the six sons touched the transcendental body of the Lord, Nārāyaṇa, and this contact awakened them to their original identities." This verse confirms that Kṛṣṇa once drank from Devakī's breast. Right after Kṛṣṇa's birth in Kaṁsa's prison, Devakī begged four-armed Kṛṣṇa to become an ordinary baby, and at that time He must have sat on her lap for a few minutes and drunk from her breast. Later, too, when Brahmā stole Kṛṣṇa's calves and friends, Kṛṣṇa took on their forms and drank the milk of all their mothers. Therefore, in the verse quoted as the present text of *Śrī Bṛhad-bhāgavatāmṛta,* Parīkṣit takes care to distinguish Yaśodā's special good fortune from that of Kṛṣṇa's other mothers. It is for this reason that he uses the word *evam* ("thus").

Parīkṣit here calls Kṛṣṇa by the name Hari, indicating that by the motherly love Kṛṣṇa kindled in Yaśodā through His childhood *līlās* He constantly stole her mind. And by speaking of her as *mahā-bhāga,* Parīkṣit implies that she is even more fortunate than Nanda Mahārāja. It is common knowledge that children are more strongly bound by affection to their mothers than to their fathers. This general truth applies to Kṛṣṇa also, as shown in the Tenth Canto by the descriptions of Kṛṣṇa's infant behavior, especially in the pastime of His being tied up with rope. We will hear some of these descriptions in the verses recited next by King Parīkṣit.

Although Vasudeva and Devakī worshiped Kṛṣṇa with devotion for the duration of four *yugas* and underwent severe austerities to gain Him as their son, they could not achieve a trace of the blessings Kṛṣṇa showered upon Nanda and Yaśodā. Vasudeva and Devakī could not directly enjoy Kṛṣṇa's pastimes of crawling about and otherwise acting as an infant, pastimes great poets headed by Śrī Brahmā praise in song.

## TEXT 127

ततो भक्तिर्भगवति पुत्रीभूते जनार्दने ।
दम्पत्योर्नितरामासीद् गोपगोपीषु भारत ॥

*tato bhaktir bhagavati*
*putrī-bhūte janārdane*
*dam-patyor nitarām āsīd*
*gopa-gopīṣu bhārata*

*tataḥ* — thereafter; *bhaktiḥ* — devotion; *bhagavati* — for the Supreme Personality of Godhead; *putrī-bhūte* — who became their son; *janārdane* — Lord Kṛṣṇa; *dam-patyoḥ* — in both husband and wife; *nitarām* — perfectly fixed; *āsīt* — there was; *gopa-gopīṣu* — in all the inhabitants of Vṛndāvana, the *gopas* and the *gopīs; bhārata* — O Mahārāja Parīkṣit.

**"Thereafter, O Mahārāja Parīkṣit, best of the Bhāratas, when the Supreme Personality of Godhead became the son of Nanda Mahārāja and Yaśodā, they attained perfectly fixed devotional love for Him, and so also did all the other inhabitants of Vṛndāvana, the gopas and gopīs."**

COMMENTARY: To explain why Nanda and Yaśodā were able to drink so fully from the nectar ocean of Śrī Kṛṣṇa's all-auspicious childhood pastimes, Śukadeva Gosvāmī answered the question from Parīkṣit Mahārāja by recounting how in a previous birth Nanda and Yaśodā were blessed by Lord Brahmā to achieve the highest devotion for Kṛṣṇa. In this verse (*Bhāgavatam* 10.8.51), Śukadeva concludes that description. Because Brahmā is a first-class devotee, by his benediction Nanda and Yaśodā developed perfect love for the Supreme Personality of Godhead Janārdana, the annihilator of demons and other wicked persons, and the Lord assumed the role of their son. Kṛṣṇa is also called Janārdana because all people (*janāḥ*) hanker with ardor (*ardanti*) to achieve from Him what they imagine to be important in life. Nanda and Yaśodā, who considered Kṛṣṇa alone important, were able to obtain Him as their son.

Here the grammatical form of the expression *putrī-bhūte* indicates something that has become what it wasn't before. He who is the Supreme Truth, Supreme Soul, and Supreme Lord cannot be the born son of anyone, yet because He understood that the highest mode of devotion to Him cannot develop unless He becomes the son of His devotees, He became the child of Nanda and Yaśodā. By doing this, He displayed His superexcellent qualities, especially His selfless concern for His devotees.

By Brahmā's benediction, the devotion of Nanda and Yaśodā

became irrevocably fixed (*nitarām āsīt*). All the *gopas* and *gopīs* of Vraja have great love for Kṛṣṇa, but the love shown by Nanda and Yaśodā is greater than that of everyone else, at least in the context of Kṛṣṇa's early childhood. Later, of course, when Kṛṣṇa reaches the *paugaṇḍa* age, and especially the *kaiśora* age, the ultimate form of love for Him becomes revealed in the young *gopīs*. The *gopīs' mādhurya-rasa,* the most precious of all devotional jewels, begins manifesting itself slightly even during Kṛṣṇa's *bālya* years. As Parīkṣit Mahārāja continues reciting verses from *Śrīmad-Bhāgavatam,* he gradually comes to this point of realization, in particular when he speaks the verses describing Uddhava's visit to Vṛndāvana.

In the present verse, Śrī Śukadeva addresses Parīkṣit as a descendant of the eminent Bhārata dynasty, implying that Parīkṣit himself should now be able to answer his own question as to how Nanda and Yaśodā attained the perfection of having Kṛṣṇa as their son. The answer to that question is as follows: In a previous life, Śrī Devakī and Vasudeva worshiped the Supreme Lord with the desire to obtain a son like Him. The Lord bestowed upon them that specific blessing by pledging to become their son in three births. Śrī Nanda and Yaśodā, however, prayed to render the best devotional service to Kṛṣṇa, and it was Brahmā who awarded the fulfillment of their prayer. Thus the Personality of Godhead demonstrated that a benediction from His devotee is more valuable than one directly from Him.

By descending to earth in Vraja-bhūmi, Kṛṣṇa expanded His supremely attractive childhood pastimes for the benefit of His parents Nanda and Yaśodā, and for the benefit of everyone related to them. The ecstatic devotion for Kṛṣṇa those pastimes evoked eclipses the importance of the four great goals of life. Nanda and the other Vraja-vāsīs are Kṛṣṇa's eternal companions and most dear devotees; they only seem to obtain devotion for Kṛṣṇa by Brahmā's blessing, just as Kṛṣṇa only apparently obtains Sāmba as His son by the blessing of Śrī Rudra. The address "O Bhārata" also implies that Parīkṣit Mahārāja should already be aware of this.

TEXT 128

नन्दः स्वपुत्रमादाय प्रोष्यागतमुदारधीः ।
मूर्ध्न्यवघ्राय परमां मुदं लेभे कुरूद्वह ॥

*nandaḥ sva-putram ādāya*
*proṣyāgatam udāra-dhīḥ*
*mūrdhny avaghrāya paramāṁ*
*mudaṁ lebhe kurūdvaha*

*nandaḥ* — Mahārāja Nanda; *sva-putram* — his son Kṛṣṇa; *ādāya* — taking on his lap; *proṣya* — having traveled away from home; *āgatam* — and returned; *udāra-dhīḥ* — because he was always liberal and simple; *mūrdhni* — on Kṛṣṇa's head; *avaghrāya* — formally smelling; *paramām* — the highest; *mudam* — bliss; *lebhe* — achieved; *kuru-udvaha* — O Mahārāja Parīkṣit.

**"O Mahārāja Parīkṣit, best of the Kurus, Nanda Mahārāja was very liberal and simple. On returning home from his trip, he at once took his son Kṛṣṇa on his lap, and by formally smelling Kṛṣṇa's head he undoubtedly enjoyed transcendental bliss."**

COMMENTARY: Vasudeva may also be able to claim Kṛṣṇa as his son, but Nanda has an even greater right to consider Kṛṣṇa *sva-putra,* his own son. This verse (*Bhāgavatam* 10.6.43) tells of Nanda Mahārāja's special glories.

After Nanda paid taxes to Kaṁsa and returned home from Madhupurī, he discovered that Kṛṣṇa had killed the demoness Pūtanā. Nanda was overjoyed to see his son alive and safe from near calamity. Though the Vraja-vāsīs, astonished to see the great Rākṣasī killed by Kṛṣṇa, couldn't help but wonder what kind of powerful being Kṛṣṇa really was, this heightened awareness of Kṛṣṇa's greatness did not at all undermine Nanda Mahārāja's firm conviction that Kṛṣṇa was nothing more or less than his own dependent son. His affection for Kṛṣṇa was too pure to be weakened by any distraction.

When Nanda arrived home, he met Kṛṣṇa, took Him on his lap, and embraced Him with enthusiasm. In ecstasy, Nanda smelled the hair on his son's head and felt the highest limit of happiness (*paramāṁ mudām*). Or, if we split the first of these words as *para-mām,* the happiness Nanda felt at that moment was greater than the joy felt by the goddess Lakṣmī (Mā) when she serves her Lord. Nanda Mahārāja deserves such pleasure because he is *udāra-dhīḥ,* a very saintly and generous devotee. On the occasion of Kṛṣṇa's name-giving ceremony, for example, he gave away vast amounts of charity. The word *udāra-dhīḥ* also means that he is very intelligent. After all, didn't he disregard all other possible benedictions and ask Brahmā only for the boon of exclusive devotion for Kṛṣṇa?

One might question why this verse singles out the good fortune of Nanda Mahārāja, since Mother Yaśodā had also prayed for devotion to Kṛṣṇa and had shared equally in Lord Brahmā's blessing. In a previous life, as Droṇa and Dharā, Nanda and Yaśodā had requested Brahmā:

*jātayor nau mahā-deve*
*bhuvi viśveśvare harau*
*bhaktiḥ syāt paramā loke*
*yayāñjo durgatiṁ taret*

"Please permit us to be born on the planet earth so that after our appearance the Supreme Lord, the Personality of Godhead, the supreme controller and master of all planets, will appear also and spread devotional service, the ultimate goal of life. Thus those born in this material world may very easily be delivered from the miserable condition of materialistic life by accepting devotional service." (*Bhāgavatam* 10.8.49)

Since both Nanda and Yaśodā, in a previous life, had together offered the same prayer, shouldn't they both have the same ecstasy? The verse above from *Bṛhad-bhāgavatāmṛta* highlights the ecstasy shown by Nanda Mahārāja after the killing of Pūtanā, but wasn't Mother Yaśodā's ecstasy just like his? Or since a mother normally loves her son even more than the child's father does, shouldn't her love have been even greater than his?

Yes, although Nanda and Yaśodā both have extraordinary love for Kṛṣṇa, her love for Kṛṣṇa is greater. The special ecstasy shown here by Nanda Mahārāja was occasioned by special circumstances. Nanda had just returned from an extended trip to Mathurā City. Upon coming home from a distant journey, one only naturally feels special love for dear ones he has not seen for some time and feels extra eagerness and happiness. Śrī Yaśodā always felt that high level of ecstatic affection.

Actually, the love of great devotees of the Lord like Nanda and Yaśodā is always fully developed to its ultimate limit; it can never diminish or increase. Thus the constant love Nanda Mahārāja has for Kṛṣṇa could not have changed into something new on his return from Mathurā. Only in imitation of ordinary family relationships does it appear to have changed. Or, looking at this a different way, the rare treasure of pure *prema* constantly gives rise to all varieties of endearing emotions, perceived as newer and newer at every moment. This distinguishes the ecstasy of *prema* from the joy of mere liberation. Nanda Mahārāja's apparent momentary increase in love for his son was simply a special ecstasy occasioned by the circumstance of his coming home.

## TEXT 129

स मातुः स्विन्नगात्राया विस्रस्तकबरस्रजः ।
दृष्ट्वा परिश्रमं कृष्णः कृपयासीत्स्वबन्धने ॥

*sa mātuḥ svinna-gātrāyā*
*visrasta-kabara-srajaḥ*
*dṛṣṭvā pariśramaṁ kṛṣṇaḥ*
*kṛpayāsīt sva-bandhane*

*saḥ* — He (Kṛṣṇa); *mātuḥ* — of His mother (Yaśodā-devī); *svinna-gātrāyāḥ* — who was perspiring all over; *visrasta* — falling down; *kabara* — from the braids of whose hair; *srajaḥ* —

the flower garlands; *dṛṣṭvā* — seeing; *pariśramam* — the fatigue; *kṛṣṇaḥ* — the Supreme Personality of Godhead; *kṛpayā* — by His causeless mercy; *āsīt* — was (agreeable); *sva-bandhane* — for His being bound.

**"Because of Mother Yaśodā's hard labor, her whole body became covered with perspiration, and the flowers were falling from the braids of her hair. When child Kṛṣṇa saw His mother thus fatigued, He became merciful to her and agreed to be bound."**

COMMENTARY: This verse and the next (*Bhāgavatam* 10.9.18, 20) glorify Mother Yaśodā, who is more advanced in Kṛṣṇa consciousness than even Nanda Mahārāja. One morning she wanted to churn butter herself for her son Kṛṣṇa, who was very fond of fresh butter. With great love in her heart, she set about the laborious task of churning from the previous day's yogurt. Just then, however, Kṛṣṇa rose from His sleep and demanded her breast milk. She began to feed Him while continuing to churn, but He again interfered by grabbing the churning rod. And then she noticed that the milk she had put on the stove was boiling over. So although Kṛṣṇa had not finished drinking, she quickly put Him aside to run to the kitchen. When she came back, after a moment, she found that the churning pot had a hole in its bottom, obviously made by the nearby grinding stone. And Kṛṣṇa had disappeared.

She looked around and found Him inside the house, and as she watched unseen from the corridor she saw Him sitting on a large upturned mortar, stealing butter and feeding it to young monkeys. She picked up a stick and came up to Him from behind, but He ran away, making her chase Him around before she finally caught up to Him. Seizing her crying son, she scolded Him sharply, but then, not wanting to frighten Him too much, she threw the stick away. Still, she wanted to do the right thing for His benefit, so she decided to punish Him by tying Him up. She tied a rope around His waist, but as people know throughout the world, the rope was too short by just two finger-widths.

She tried tying together all the ropes she could find in the house, but still the rope remained short by the same length. Seeing this astonished her. Finally Kṛṣṇa, choosing to reward His mother for her strenuous devotional effort, agreed to let her bind Him.

Although Kṛṣṇa's all-spiritual body is beyond the limitations of time and space and the individuality of objects, He responded mercifully to the strenuous labor of His mother. He cannot be bound by anyone, but in His exceptional mercy He allowed Himself to be tied. Taking the alternative reading *sva-mātuḥ* ("His own mother") instead of *sa mātuḥ,* we get the idea that Yaśodā is eternally established in this intimate relationship with Him and so she certainly deserves His special mercy. When she tried to bind Him, Kṛṣṇa submitted to her effort because of her exalted love, which was evident externally by the perspiration on her limbs and by the falling of the flowers from her hair.

## TEXT 130

नेमं विरिञ्चो न भवो न श्रीरप्यङ्गसंश्रया ।
प्रसादं लेभिरे गोपी यत्तत्प्राप विमुक्तिदात् ॥

*nemaṁ viriñco na bhavo*
*na śrīr apy aṅga-saṁśrayā*
*prasādaṁ lebhire gopī*
*yat tat prāpa vimukti-dāt*

*na* — not; *imam* — this (exalted position); *viriñcaḥ* — Lord Brahmā; *na* — nor; *bhavaḥ* — Lord Śiva; *na* — nor; *śrīḥ* — the goddess of fortune; *api* — indeed; *aṅga-saṁśrayā* — although she always takes shelter of His body; *prasādam* — mercy; *lebhire* — obtained; *gopī* — the cowherd woman (Mother Yaśodā); *yat tat* — as that which; *prāpa* — obtained; *vimukti-dāt* — from Kṛṣṇa, who gives deliverance from this material world.

**"Neither Lord Brahmā, nor Lord Śiva, nor even the goddess of fortune, who always seeks refuge at the chest of the Supreme Lord, can obtain from the Supreme Personality of**

**Godhead, the deliverer from this material world, such mercy as received by Mother Yaśodā."**

COMMENTARY: While describing the good fortune of Mother Yaśodā, Śrīla Śukadeva Gosvāmī became more and more amazed, and the hairs on his body stood on end. Although many devotees of Kṛṣṇa obtain Kṛṣṇa's favor, the mercy received by Yaśodā was most wonderful. While thinking of this, Śukadeva Gosvāmī spoke this verse (*Bhāgavatam* 10.9.20).

Śukadeva affectionately refers to Mother Yaśodā as *gopī,* alluding to her privileged status as the wife of the king of the *gopas*. The favor she obtained from Kṛṣṇa was never achieved by Kṛṣṇa's son Brahmā, by Kṛṣṇa's friend Śiva, or by His dear consort Lakṣmī, who always resides on His chest. How then could lesser persons than these ever receive as much favor as Yaśodā? Yaśodā is a better devotee than Lord Brahmā, Lord Śiva, and the goddess Lakṣmī because all three of them merely worship Kṛṣṇa with reverence as the Supreme Godhead but she has pure affection for Him as her son. The Dāmodara pastime, in which Yaśodā tied Kṛṣṇa with rope, demonstrated the power of God to resist all attempts to capture Him, but when Yaśodā witnessed Kṛṣṇa's omnipotence her pure maternal love only increased.

To emphasize the unique position of Mother Yaśodā, in this verse Śrīla Śukadeva repeats three times the negation *na*. The three greatest personages of the material world may obtain great favor from Kṛṣṇa, but they are unable to please Kṛṣṇa or obtain as much favor as Yaśodā. Most people living in this material world are much less fortunate than Brahmā, Śiva, and Lakṣmī and cannot even imagine the sublime position of Mother Yaśodā. To sincere aspirants for spiritual perfection, Kṛṣṇa gives liberation from the bondage of birth and death, but His love for His mother is so special that He lets her bind Him with ropes meant for tying cows. To some pure Vaiṣṇavas, Kṛṣṇa grants *vimukti,* the superior liberation of elevation to His own world to live in His proximity in transcendental bliss. Let Him grant this *vimukti* to fortunate souls, but even such Vaiṣṇavas cannot expect the favor shown to Mother Yaśodā.

## TEXTS 131–132

पयांसि यासामपिबत्पुत्रस्नेहस्नुतान्यलम् ।
भगवान्देवकीपुत्रः कैवल्याद्यखिलार्थदः ॥

तासामविरतं कृष्णे कुर्वतीनां सुतेक्षणम् ।
न पुनः कल्पते राजन्संसारोऽज्ञानसम्भवः ॥

*payāṁsi yāsām apibat*
*putra-sneha-snutāny alam*
*bhagavān devakī-putraḥ*
*kaivalyādy-akhilārtha-daḥ*

*tāsām aviratam kṛṣṇe*
*kurvatīnāṁ sutekṣaṇam*
*na punaḥ kalpate rājan*
*saṁsāro 'jñāna-sambhavaḥ*

*payāṁsi* — milk; *yāsām* — of all of whom; *apibat* — Lord Kṛṣṇa drank; *putra-sneha-snutāni* — that milk coming from the bodies of the *gopīs,* not artificially but because of maternal affection; *alam* — sufficiently; *bhagavān* — the Supreme Personality of Godhead; *devakī-putraḥ* — who appeared as the son of Devakī; *kaivalya-ādi* — like liberation, or merging into the Brahman effulgence; *akhila-artha-daḥ* — the bestower of all blessings; *tāsām* — of all of them (the *gopīs*); *aviratam* — constantly; *kṛṣṇe* — unto Lord Kṛṣṇa; *kurvatīnām* — making; *suta* — as at their own child; *īkṣaṇam* — glances; *na* — never; *punaḥ* — again; *kalpate* — can be imagined; *rājan* — O King Parīkṣit; *saṁsāraḥ* — the material bondage of birth and death; *ajñāna* — from ignorance; *sambhavaḥ* — which is created.

**"The Supreme Personality of Godhead, Kṛṣṇa, is the bestower of many benedictions, including liberation, or oneness with the Brahman effulgence. For that son of Devakī, the gopīs always felt maternal love. They looked at**

**Him as if He were their own son, and Kṛṣṇa with full satisfaction sucked the milk that by maternal affection flowed freely from their breasts. Therefore one should never think that after leaving their bodies they returned to material existence, which arises as a result of ignorance."**

COMMENTARY: Parīkṣit is now coming to the point of glorifying Kṛṣṇa's supermost devotees, the young *gopīs*. But first he takes the opportunity to praise the elder *gopīs*, the mothers of Kṛṣṇa's cowherd friends. While narrating the history of Pūtanā's attempt to kill Kṛṣṇa, Śukadeva spoke these two verses (*Bhāgavatam* 10.6.39–40) comparing Pūtanā's good fortune to that of these elder *gopīs*, from whose breasts Kṛṣṇa drank when He assumed the forms of His friends after Lord Brahmā had kidnapped the friends and calves.

The son of Devakī drank the breast milk of these *gopīs* plentifully (*alam*) because He took the role of their sons for an entire year. He bestowed this favor on them even though He is the Supreme Personality of Godhead, complete and self-satisfied in all respects. Because of the motherly relationship these *gopīs* had with Him, they were freed from the prospect of future suffering in the cycle of birth and death; their material existence was finished once and for all, in that very lifetime. Conditioned living beings are trapped in *saṁsāra* due to their ignorance, but the elder *gopīs* were steeped in the highest spiritual knowledge. They were the most perfect *jñānīs* because they constantly thought of Kṛṣṇa as their son. Indeed, all transcendental knowledge and its corollary benefits are automatically included in pure Kṛṣṇa consciousness. Other devotees might feed Kṛṣṇa without identifying Him as their son, but these women had already attained such a high realization of love of Godhead that they thought of Kṛṣṇa with intense parental affection. They loved Kṛṣṇa so much that milk would spontaneously flow from their breasts.

Kṛṣṇa is the giver of liberation and all other goals of life. But as the word *alam* implies, Kṛṣṇa, not satisfied with the milk of only His mother Devakī, was eager to drink from the *gopīs* also. He had every right to the breast milk of Devakī, but He abandoned her to drink extensively from these *gopīs* instead. His love for them was that great. Therefore, since He gives desired goals like liberation to other persons, why shouldn't He grant liberation to these women, whom He favored over His own mother by drinking their milk for one whole year? How could they remain entangled in material existence?

*pūtanā loka-bāla-ghnī*
*rākṣasī rudhirāśanā*
*jighāṁsayāpi haraye*
*stanaṁ dattvāpa sad-gatim*

*kiṁ punaḥ śraddhayā bhaktyā*
*kṛṣṇāya paramātmane*
*yacchan priya-tamaṁ kiṁ nu*
*raktās tan-mātaro yathā*

"Pūtanā was always hankering for the blood of human children, and with that desire she came to kill Kṛṣṇa; but because she offered her breast to the Lord, she attained the greatest achievement. What then is to be said of those who had natural devotion and affection for Kṛṣṇa as mothers and who offered Him their breasts to suck or offered something very dear, as a mother offers something to a child?" (*Bhāgavatam* 10.6.35–36)

*yātudhāny api sā svargam*
*avāpa jananī-gatim*
*kṛṣṇa-bhukta-stana-kṣīrāḥ*
*kim u gāvo 'nu-mātaraḥ*

"Although Pūtanā was a great witch, she attained the position of a mother in the transcendental world and thus achieved the highest perfection. What then is to be said of the cows whose nipples Kṛṣṇa sucked with great pleasure and who offered their milk very jubilantly with affection exactly like that of a mother?" (*Bhāgavatam* 10.6.38)

Pūtanā attained a destination possible only for saintly devotees of the Personality of Godhead. She became a mother of

Kṛṣṇa like Devakī in the highest heaven, Śrī Vaikuṇṭha. *Svarga,* or heaven, is commonly conceived as the world of unlimited happiness, but true happiness — in freedom from birth and death — is found only in the kingdom of God. There Pūtanā achieved liberation and was established in *vātsalya-rasa.* So how can the elder *gopīs* of Vraja be expected to attain anything less? The word *saṁ-sāra* may be taken to refer to liberation as the "complete essence" of the four goals of life, and this liberation may be understood to be *jñāna-sambhavaḥ,* indicating that it is achieved by the discipline of philosophical knowledge. But these *gopīs* deserve more than this inadequate reward. For these *gopīs,* liberation is inadequate because they possess pure devotion for Kṛṣṇa, which includes knowledge, liberation, and everything else desirable. Liberation, therefore, is meaningless for the *gopīs* because they are already liberated.

To devotees unconditionally surrendered to Him, Kṛṣṇa never gives mere liberation. And from devotees full of material desires He withholds it. Thus Śukadeva Gosvāmī calls Kṛṣṇa *kaivalyādy-akhilārtha-daḥ,* He who destroys (*dyati*) all the inferior goals of life (*arthas*), headed by liberation (*kaivalya*), which in comparison to attainment of Śrī Vaikuṇṭha are insignificant. Since Kṛṣṇa is so kind even to materialistic devotees, why should He give mere liberation to absolutely selfless devotees like the *gopīs*? The great achievement, even for the residents of Vaikuṇṭha, is the attainment of Goloka.

In the Sixth Canto of *Śrīmad-Bhāgavatam* (6.11.23) the demon Vṛtra says:

*trai-vargikāyāsa-vighātam asmat-*
*patir vidhatte puruṣasya śakra*
*tato 'numeyo bhagavat-prasādo*
*yo durlabho 'kiñcana-gocaro 'nyaiḥ*

"Our Lord, who is the Supreme Personality of Godhead, forbids His devotees to endeavor uselessly for religion, economic development, and sense gratification. O Indra, one can thus infer how kind the Lord is. Such mercy is obtainable only by unalloyed devotees, not by persons who aspire for material gains." Because efforts to attain *dharma, artha,* and *kāma* can achieve little more than the pain of the endeavor, the supreme protector of His devotees ruins a devotee's attempts to achieve these goals. This should be understood as the greatest mercy of the all-compassionate Lord.

But don't some devotees of the Lord succeed in obtaining the three goals *dharma, artha,* and *kāma*? Yes, but we should understand who is eligible to receive the Lord's mercy in full. The Personality of Godhead gives full protection to devotees who are *akiñcana* (free from false identifications), who renounce everything material for His sake, who offer their very bodies and all bodily possessions for His service, and who have no support but Him. For others His full mercy is very difficult to obtain. To devotees distracted by material desires, who fall short of the *akiñcana* standard, Kṛṣṇa sometimes gives the benefits of *dharma, artha,* and *kāma*.

Even neophyte Vaiṣṇavas, being more or less free from material desires, can at least aspire for the special mercy of the Lord, but nondevotees can never come near it. Nondevotees have no hope of gaining the Supreme Lord's favor, by which material entanglement is destroyed. Vṛtrāsura therefore tells Indra that being king of heaven is useless because Indra is not a pure devotee of the Personality of Godhead. Vṛtra disdains Indra's heaven because Vṛtra has his eyes set on Śrī Vaikuṇṭha.

A similar statement is found in the Fifth Canto of *Śrīmad-Bhāgavatam* (5.19.27):

*satyaṁ diśaty arthitam arthito nṛṇāṁ*
*naivārtha-do yat punar arthitā yataḥ*
*svayaṁ vidhatte bhajatām anicchatām*
*icchāpidhānaṁ nija-pāda-pallavam*

"The Supreme Personality of Godhead fulfills the material desires of a devotee who approaches Him with material motives, but He does not bestow benedictions that will cause the devotee to demand more benedictions again. However, the Lord willingly gives the devotee shelter at His own lotus feet, even when the devotee does not aspire for it, and that shelter satisfies all desires. That is the Supreme Personality's special mercy." For God no request is impossible to fulfill. He is the root of the tree that can satisfy all desires. Still, though people pray to Him for liberation and other perfections, He often refuses to give what is asked. This means that when granting a request will result in the devotee's being impelled by still more desires, the Lord protects His devotee by withholding the desired object.

A person whom the Lord allows to become proficient in religious formularies may become greedy for the fruits of religiosity. Elevated by piety and endowed with such fruits, the person may then become attracted to sense gratification. Addicted to sense gratification, he may turn again to religiosity, just to get more of the same sense gratification. Only rarely does anyone take proper advantage of the cycle of *puruṣārthas,* or goals in human life, by experiencing *dharma, artha,* and *kāma,* evaluating them realistically, and then redirecting his aim to *mokṣa.* Then, if such a rare person is truly fortunate, after achieving liberation he may come in contact with pure devotees of the Supreme Lord, learn the insignificance of liberation, and strive for *bhakti.* As stated in *Śrī Padma Purāṇa, muktaiḥ prārthyā harer bhaktiḥ:* "Lord Hari's devotional service is prayed for by those who are liberated." But even in this most unlikely set of fortunate circumstances, the candidate for spiritual advancement has to go through so much trouble to aspire after various goals, one after another, and achieve them. Therefore the Personality of Godhead prefers to cut short the involvement of His devotees in *dharma, artha, kāma,* and *mokṣa.*

But when the Supreme Lord refuses to give His devotees what they beg, doesn't that spoil His reputation as "the wish-fulfilling cow who can satisfy countless desires"? The demigods speaking the above verse from the Fifth Canto answer this doubt by referring to the Lord as *artha-da,* the giver of what is of real value. In other words, the Lord never gives His devotees what is *anartha,* or not good for them. As a good father refuses a son's demand for some unwholesome food or drink, the Supreme

Lord refuses to give His devotees anything that will cause them harm. This behavior only enhances the Lord's reputation as the well-wisher of His servants.

What higher *artha,* then, does the Lord prefer to give? And how will this *artha* satisfy the Lord's devotee in the face of unfulfilled personal desires? The demigods answer that the Personality of Godhead gives away His own lotus feet — or, in other words, pure devotion to His feet. He gives this even to those who don't want it or who harbor desires for other things, such as liberation, and therefore don't consider pure devotion their exclusive goal. By the gift of devotion to His lotus feet, the Lord obliterates those other desires, because in pure devotional service all possible desires are automatically fulfilled.

In devotional service there is such an abundance of pure ecstasy that a devotee loses all interest in inferior pleasures. Thus even though before attaining *prema-bhakti* pure devotees may have asked something from Kṛṣṇa and now may not have gotten it, they do not feel at all slighted or dissatisfied. They are too absorbed in the sheer bliss of Kṛṣṇa consciousness to even notice the discrepancy. Kṛṣṇa is so extremely merciful that He shows this kindness even to devotees who don't want it, just as a father entices his child to take a nice sweetball when he sees the child trying to eat dirt. The child may not want the sweet, but the father forces it on him to take the child's mind away from eating dirt. Thus the father gives the child real happiness. This is Kṛṣṇa's way of reciprocating with His devotees for the service they have done at His lotus feet.

As Śrī Śukadeva told Mahārāja Parīkṣit:

*rājan patir gurur alaṁ bhavatāṁ yadūnāṁ*
*daivaṁ priyaḥ kula-patiḥ kva ca kiṅkaro vaḥ*
*astv evam aṅga bhajatāṁ bhagavān mukundo*
*muktiṁ dadāti karhicit sma na bhakti-yogam*

"My dear king, the Supreme Person, Mukunda, is actually the maintainer of all the members of the Pāṇḍava and Yadu dynasties. He is your spiritual master, your worshipable Deity, your friend, and the director of your activities. To say nothing of this, He sometimes serves your family as a messenger or servant. This means He works just like an ordinary servant. Those engaged in getting the Lord's favor attain from the Lord liberation very easily, but He does not very easily give the opportunity to render direct service unto Him." (*Bhāgavatam* 5.6.18)

Paraphrasing this verse and taking the last line in a different way, Śrīla Sanātana Gosvāmī gives this meaning: "My dear King Parīkṣit, for the Pāṇḍavas and Yadus the Supreme Lord Mukunda is very much absorbed in acting in roles like that of master. And for you, the sons of Pāṇḍu, He sometimes even acts as a menial servant. Even though bestowing *bhakti-yoga* makes the Lord subordinate to His devotees, He still gives this *bhakti-yoga* to those who worship Him." In the context of this reading, *bhakti-yoga* means not only perfect love of God but also devotional service in practice, which enables one to achieve that love, mainly through association with pure devotees. As Kṛṣṇa explained to Śrī Uddhava in the Eleventh Canto (11.3.31), *bhaktyā sañjātayā bhaktyā:* the one kind of *bhakti* awakens the other.

The Supreme Lord never gives liberation to His surrendered devotees. Because liberation is achievable by the seekers of impersonal knowledge, He thinks that to give liberation to His pure devotees would devalue their devotional service.

Parīkṣit Mahārāja has glorified the other mothers of Kṛṣṇa in Vraja after Śrī Yaśodā, but this does not mean that they are greater devotees than she. After all, they fed Kṛṣṇa their milk for only one year, and their love for Kṛṣṇa never equaled hers. We should understand, therefore, that praise of the other *gopīs* has been placed here just to underscore the glories of Mother Yaśodā. If these other *gopīs* are so great, how great must be Yaśodā's unique motherly affection.

## TEXT 133

गोपीनां परमानन्द आसीद्गोविन्ददर्शने ।
क्षणं युगशतमिव यासां येन विनाभवत् ॥

*gopīnāṁ paramānanda*
*āsīd govinda-darśane*
*kṣaṇaṁ yuga-śatam iva*
*yāsāṁ yena vinābhavat*

*gopīnām* — for the young cowherd girls; *parama-ānandaḥ* — the greatest happiness; *āsīt* — arose; *govinda-darśane* — in seeing Govinda; *kṣaṇam* — a moment; *yuga-śatam* — a hundred millenniums; *iva* — just as; *yāsām* — for whom; *yena* — whom (Kṛṣṇa); *vinā* — without; *abhavat* — became.

**"The young gopīs took the greatest pleasure in seeing Govinda come home, since for them even a moment without His association seemed like a hundred ages."**

COMMENTARY: In texts 133 through 152, Parīkṣit Mahārāja praises the supremely glorious *gopīs*. He begins by quoting this verse from *Śrīmad-Bhāgavatam* (10.19.16), in which Śrī Bādarāyaṇi describes the *gopīs'* ecstasy at seeing Kṛṣṇa return home in the evening after saving His friends from a fire in the Muñja forest. Just to catch a glimpse of Govinda would raise all the *gopīs* to the highest limit of ecstasy. Who can describe, then, what they felt later when they enjoyed talks and various sports with Him? If for even the shortest time they couldn't see Kṛṣṇa, to them that small portion of the day would seem like a hundred *yugas*. In their own words:

*aṭati yad bhavān ahni kānanaṁ*
*truṭi yugāyate tvām apaśyatām*
*kuṭila-kuntalaṁ śrī-mukhaṁ ca te*
*jaḍa udīkṣatāṁ pakṣma-kṛd dṛśām*

"When You go off to the forest during the day, a tiny fraction of a second becomes like a millennium for us because we cannot see You. And even when we *can* eagerly look upon Your beautiful face, so lovely with its adornment of curly locks, our pleasure is hindered by our eyelids, which were fashioned by the foolish creator." (*Bhāgavatam* 10.31.15)

Of course the days spent without Kṛṣṇa didn't literally last hundreds of *yugas,* but, as indicated by the word *iva,* such was the *gopīs'* subjective experience while in the pain and anxiety of separation. And it makes perfect sense that these same *gopīs* who would suffer intensely from a moment's separation from Kṛṣṇa would conversely enjoy the topmost bliss from but a moment's sight of Him. Though the *gopīs* passed every day with such ecstasies, the description given here is especially appropriate for the day Kṛṣṇa saved His cowherd friends from the fire in the Muñja forest, because on that same day He saved His girlfriends from the forest fire of *viraha-bhāva* in their hearts.

## TEXT 134

तन्मनस्कास्तदालापास्तद्विचेष्टास्तदात्मिकाः ।
तद्गुणानेव गायन्त्यो नात्मागाराणि सस्मरुः ॥

*tan-manaskās tad-ālāpās*
*tad-viceṣṭās tad-ātmikāḥ*
*tad-guṇān eva gāyantyo*
*nātmāgārāṇi sasmaruḥ*

*tat-manaskāḥ* — their minds filled with thoughts of Him; *tat-ālāpāḥ* — conversing about Him; *tat-viceṣṭāḥ* — imitating His activities; *tat-ātmikāḥ* — filled with His presence; *tat-guṇān* — about His qualities; *eva* — simply; *gāyantyaḥ* — singing; *na* — not; *ātma* — their own; *āgārāṇi* — homes; *sasmaruḥ* — remembered.

**"Their minds absorbed in thoughts of Him, they conversed about Him, acted out His pastimes, and felt themselves filled with His presence. They completely forgot about their homes as they loudly sang the glories of Kṛṣṇa's transcendental qualities."**

COMMENTARY: This verse (*Bhāgavatam* 10.30.43) describes how the force of love for Kṛṣṇa made the *gopīs* forget everything else. At the beginning of the *rāsa* dance, when Kṛṣṇa disappeared, leaving the *gopīs* in total distress, they searched everywhere but couldn't find Him. By the time they gave up their search, they had wandered far into the thickest part of the forest, where even the light of the autumn moon couldn't go. Under the circumstances, one would have expected them to go home in disappointment, but they couldn't even remember that they had homes. In this condition, instead of complaining about Kṛṣṇa's cruelty, the surrendered *gopīs* continued to sing His glories. All their faculties were fixed on Him: their minds, with which they could only accept Him, never reject Him; their power of speech, by which they called out plaintively to Him and performed His *saṅkīrtana;* and their other working senses, by which they made garlands and beds from flowers and leaves. Mind, body, and words, the *gopīs* were fully absorbed in Kṛṣṇa; their whole existence was dedicated to Him. Even at home the *gopīs* were so focused on Kṛṣṇa in thought, word, and deed that they went about their household duties oblivious of what was going on around them. Now that they were outside, why should they give any thought to their homes? Abandoned by Kṛṣṇa in the forest in the midst of the night, they simply went on chanting His glories.

Another meaning of the words *tan-manaskās tad-ālāpās tad-viceṣṭās tad-ātmikāḥ* is that in the anxiety of separation the *gopīs* became so intense in their remembrance of Kṛṣṇa, the enthusiastic enjoyer of wonderful pastimes, that they began to assume the unique characteristics of His personality. Their minds, just like His, became free from fear and suffering. Their speech became grave, articulate, and charming, just like His. They started to behave just like Him, embracing and kissing one another. Their bodies even appeared like His, as they emulated His threefold-bending posture. But unlike impersonal *yogīs* who forget devotion to God as they begin to develop His qualities, the *gopīs* only increased in their natural devotion for Kṛṣṇa more and more, and they went on singing His glories. In this utter absorption in Kṛṣṇa, they forgot themselves, what to speak of the homes and other things they were meant to enjoy.

## TEXT 135

गोप्यस्तपः किमचरन्यदमुष्य रूपं
लावण्यसारमसमोर्ध्वमनन्यसिद्धम् ।
दृग्भिः पिबन्त्यनुसवाभिनवं दुरापम्
एकान्तधाम यशसः श्रिय ऐश्वरस्य ॥

*gopyas tapaḥ kim acaran yad amuṣya rūpaṁ*
*lāvaṇya-sāram asamordhvam ananya-siddham*
*dṛgbhiḥ pibanty anusavābhinavaṁ durāpam*
*ekānta-dhāma yaśasaḥ śriya aiśvarasya*

*gopyaḥ* — the *gopīs; tapaḥ* — austerities; *kim* — what; *acaran* — performed; *yat* — from which; *amuṣya* — of such a one (Lord Kṛṣṇa); *rūpam* — the form; *lāvaṇya-sāram* — the essence of loveliness; *asama-ūrdhvam* — unparalleled and unsurpassed; *ananya-siddham* — not perfected by any other ornament (self-perfect); *dṛgbhiḥ* — by the eyes; *pibanti* — they drink; *anusava-abhinavam* — constantly new; *durāpam* — difficult to obtain; *ekānta-dhāma* — the only abode; *yaśasaḥ* — of fame; *śriyaḥ* — of beauty; *aiśvarasya* — of opulence.

**"What austerities must the gopīs have performed! With their eyes they always drink the nectar of Lord Kṛṣṇa's form, which is the essence of loveliness and is not to be equaled or surpassed. That loveliness is the only abode of beauty, fame, and opulence. It is self-perfect, ever fresh, and extremely rare.**

COMMENTARY: Texts 135 though 137 (*Bhāgavatam* 10.44.14–16) are spoken by the women of Mathurā who watch Kṛṣṇa as He enters Kaṁsa's arena to wrestle with Cāṇūra. The ladies of Mathurā praise the *gopīs* of Vṛndāvana because the *gopīs* can always enjoy seeing Kṛṣṇa and chanting His glories, in all circumstances.

First the ladies praise the *gopīs* for being always able to see the beauty of Kṛṣṇa's transcendental form. The Vedic scriptures explain various benefits to be gained by a variety of disciplines, but the women of Mathurā have never heard of anyone receiving such a benefit as bestowed upon the *gopīs*. What penances, religious duties, or meditation could enable one to attain such perfection? What *tapas* could the *gopīs* of Vraja have performed to earn the privilege of drinking Kṛṣṇa's beauty with their mortal eyes, directly relishing His beauty the way one relishes nectar with the tongue? Out of reverence for Kṛṣṇa, at this moment the city women cannot utter His name, but can only refer to the son of Nanda as "Him."

According to the description of the Mathurā women, Kṛṣṇa is the most charming of persons. Indeed, He embodies the very essence of charm. Even those who consider Him an *avatāra* of Viṣṇu cannot find any *avatāra* equal to Him; and persons who know that He is in fact the source of all *avatāras* can understand that no one is greater. Moreover, His supreme excellence is not created by anyone or anything else. His excellence is not lent to Him by His ornaments; it is innately His own. As Śrī Uddhava states in the Third Canto of *Śrīmad-Bhāgavatam* (3.2.12):

*yan martya-līlaupayikaṁ sva-yoga-*
*māyā-balaṁ darśayatā gṛhītam*
*vismāpanaṁ svasya ca saubhagarddheḥ*
*paraṁ padaṁ bhūṣaṇa-bhūṣaṇāṅgam*

"The Lord, by His internal potency, Yogamāyā, appeared in the mortal world in His eternal form, just suitable for His pastimes. Those pastimes were wondrous for all, even for those who were proud of their own opulence, including the Lord Himself in His form as the Lord of Vaikuṇṭha. Thus Śrī Kṛṣṇa's transcendental body is the ornament of all ornaments."

*Ananya-siddham* can also be understood in another way, as meaning that these excellences of Kṛṣṇa are not realized anywhere else but in Vraja. Furthermore, persons who taste Kṛṣṇa's glories are never satiated; rather, they always experience those glories as newer and newer at every moment. As the poet Māgha says, *kṣaṇe kṣaṇe yan navatām upaiti/ tad eva rūpaṁ ramaṇīyatāyāḥ:* "The true form of attractiveness is that which appears newer at every moment." Therefore the full glories of Kṛṣṇa are very difficult to realize; other than the *gopīs,* no one can ever expect to know them directly. And only the *gopīs* have Kṛṣṇa completely under their control.

Kṛṣṇa is the most charming of persons, and He possesses all supreme qualities. He is the only constant reservoir of fame, splendor, and the six divine opulences indicated by the word *bhagavān*. Thus both His form and His personality are in all ways supremely attractive.

In stating that the *gopīs* of Vraja always enjoy the sight of Kṛṣṇa's beauty, the women speaking in the wrestling arena use the present tense (*pibanti*). By this they mean to say that the beauty of Kṛṣṇa never actually abandons the *gopīs,* for the *gopīs* never fail to see Him, even when He is physically absent. "The *gopīs* are the most fortunate of women. We ladies of Mathurā are not at all pious, because we can see Him only at inauspicious times and places. There is no chance of our ever drinking the nectar of His beauty with the same love and respect as the *gopīs*."

## TEXT 136

या दोहनेऽवहनने मथनोपलेप-
प्रेङ्खेङ्खनार्भरुदितोक्षणमार्जनादौ ।
गायन्ति चैनमनुरक्तधियोऽश्रुकण्ठ्यो
धन्या व्रजस्त्रिय उरुक्रमचित्तयानाः ॥

*yā dohane 'vahanane mathanopalepa-*
*preṅkheṅkhanārbha-ruditokṣaṇa-mārjanādau*
*gāyanti cainam anurakta-dhiyo 'śru-kaṇṭhyo*
*dhanyā vraja-striya urukrama-citta-yānāḥ*

*yāḥ* — who (the *gopīs*); *dohane* — while milking; *avahanane* — threshing; *mathana* — churning; *upalepa* — smearing; *preṅkha* — on swings; *iṅkhana* — swinging; *arbha-rudita* — (taking care of) crying babies; *ukṣaṇa* — sprinkling; *mārjana* — cleaning; *ādau* — and so on; *gāyanti* — they sing; *ca* — and; *enam* — about Him; *anurakta-dhiyaḥ* — whose minds are very much attached; *aśru-kaṇṭhyaḥ* — whose throats are full of tears; *dhanyāḥ* — fortunate; *vraja-striyaḥ* — the ladies of Vraja; *urukrama* — on Kṛṣṇa; *citta-yānāḥ* — whose minds were fixed.

**"The ladies of Vraja are the most fortunate of women. Their minds fully attached to Kṛṣṇa, their throats always choked with tears, they constantly sing about Him while milking the cows, winnowing grain, churning butter, gathering cow dung for fuel, riding on swings, caring for their crying babies, sprinkling the ground with water, cleaning their houses, and so on. Their minds are fixed on Kṛṣṇa alone.**

COMMENTARY: Even if in the course of Kṛṣṇa's infinitely varied pastimes the *gopīs* are sometimes unable to see that most clever Kṛṣṇa, they can remain submerged in an ocean of transcendental pleasure by chanting His glories. The *gopīs* do not engage in *saṅkīrtana* only when circumstances are conducive — when performing special services for Him like making garlands. They chant His names and glories always, in all situations. While describing the autumn *rāsa* dance, Parāśara Muni says in the *Viṣṇu Purāṇa* (5.13.52, 56):

*kṛṣṇaḥ śarac-candramasaṁ*
*kaumudī-kumudākaram*
*jagau gopī-gaṇās tv ekaṁ*
*kṛṣṇa-nāma punaḥ punaḥ*

"Kṛṣṇa sang about the autumn moon and its light upon the lotus ponds, while the *gopīs* simply sang Kṛṣṇa's name over and over again."

*rāsa-geyaṁ jagau kṛṣṇo*
*yāvat tārāyata-dhvaniḥ*
*sādhu kṛṣṇeti kṛṣṇeti*
*tāvat tā dvi-guṇaṁ jaguḥ*

"While Kṛṣṇa sang a *rāsa*-dance song in a resonant voice, the *gopīs* congratulated Him and redoubled their chanting of 'Kṛṣṇa! Kṛṣṇa!' "

In the verse Parīkṣit Maharaja recites here, the phrase *vraja-striyaḥ* ("the women of Vraja") indicates not just the *gopīs* but also women who live in the forest. The city ladies who are speaking are not careful to distinguish between the *gopīs* of Nanda's community and the other women of Vraja, who are mostly aborigines. All the women who come in contact with Kṛṣṇa in the forest, whether children, young girls, or old women, become rich in the highest favor of the goddess of fortune. And only the women of Vraja have this kind of excellent luck, not the women of any other place.

Why are the women of Vraja so fortunate? Because they always engage in *kṛṣṇa-saṅkīrtana,* no matter what else they do. They sing while they milk the cows and churn butter for their husbands and children, while they apply *kuṅkuma, candana,* and other cosmetics to their bodies, while they swing on swings, while they comfort their babies, while they clean their houses with water and cow dung. They sing Kṛṣṇa's names while cooking, grinding grains, smearing the courtyards with auspicious pastes, and beautifying the walls of their houses with painted designs. Thus the *gopīs'* unavoidable duties in taking care of their families and maintaining their own bodies do not at all obstruct the ecstasy the *gopīs* feel in worshiping Kṛṣṇa; rather, these contribute to it by giving suitable occasions for *saṅkīrtana.*

The *gopīs* are so absorbed in Kṛṣṇa's glories that they are hardly aware of the effort they expend while working. And so intense is their singing that they actually see Kṛṣṇa. Either by the power of meditation they see Him in their hearts as He plays all around Vraja-bhūmi, or else they make excuses to take their work out into the pastures and so directly see Him playing there. Sometimes the presence of their elders makes them too shy to sing about Kṛṣṇa, and then they fly to where Kṛṣṇa is by the inner vehicle of their minds, helplessly attracted by the power of Lord Urukrama, who intrudes by stealth into the minds of His best devotees. As the *gopīs* chant about Kṛṣṇa, their minds are more and more attracted to Him, and gradually they are unable to think coherently about anything else. Shedding tears of love, they sob uncontrollably, and their hearts go swiftly (*uru-kramena*) to join Kṛṣṇa, wherever He is. In short, they are the most fortunate of women because they always see Kṛṣṇa, always chant His glories, always think about Him, and always feel completely attracted to Him in pure love.

The words *anurakta-dhiyo 'śru-kaṇṭhyaḥ,* which describe how the *gopīs* sing, can be understood to be a response to the following doubt: "Isn't it true that a woman does what she does only because she is attracted to doing it? The *gopīs* must have some attraction for household work, otherwise why would they be so busy doing it? How then can they be said to be merged totally, exclusively in love for Kṛṣṇa?" The Mathurā women respond by commenting that such symptoms as tears in the eyes prove that the *gopīs'* minds are full of loving attraction for Kṛṣṇa. The *gopīs* do their household duties only for His sake.

But then another doubt might arise: "With such distracted minds, how could the *gopīs* maintain their bodies and fulfill their family responsibilities?" The answer is that Kṛṣṇa is Urukrama, the Supreme Lord who possesses amazing energies and accomplishes wonderful feats. The *gopīs,* by fixing their hearts on Him, are easily able to carry out all their duties and obtain whatever is needed. Even though the *gopīs* think only of Kṛṣṇa, to the exclusion of everything else, they are free from anxiety over the many duties they are obliged to fulfill. Everything they do is for His satisfaction, so they can do everything expertly simply by the force of Kṛṣṇa consciousness.

This verse also describes the *gopīs'* singing about Kṛṣṇa as most prominent. Their remembrance and visions of Him come as natural consequences of this primary service of singing His glories. Therefore the *gopīs'* meditating on Kṛṣṇa and envisioning Him are not explicitly mentioned. The ladies of Mathurā conclude, "These women alone are the most fortunate, and in ways for which we can never aspire. How sad!"

## TEXT 137

प्रातर्व्रजाद् व्रजत आविशतश्च सायं
गोभिः समं क्वणयतोऽस्य निशम्य वेणुम् ।
निर्गत्य तूर्णमबलाः पथि भूरिपुण्याः
पश्यन्ति सस्मितमुखं सदयावलोकम् ॥

*prātar vrajād vrajata āviśataś ca sāyaṁ*
*gobhiḥ samaṁ kvaṇayato 'sya niśamya veṇum*
*nirgatya tūrṇam abalāḥ pathi bhūri-puṇyāḥ*
*paśyanti sa-smita-mukhaṁ sadayāvalokam*

*prātaḥ* — in the early morning; *vrajāt* — from Vraja; *vrajataḥ* — of Him who is going; *āviśataḥ* — entering; *ca* — and; *sāyam* — in the evening; *gobhiḥ samam* — together with the cows; *kvaṇayataḥ* — who is playing; *asya* — His; *niśamya* — hearing; *veṇum* — the flute; *nirgatya* — coming out; *tūrṇam* — quickly; *abalāḥ* — the women; *pathi* — on the road; *bhūri* — extremely; *puṇyāḥ* — pious; *paśyanti* — they see; *sa* — with; *smita* — smiling; *mukham* — face; *sa-daya* — merciful; *avalokam* — with glances.

**"When the young gopīs hear Kṛṣṇa playing His flute as He leaves Vraja in the morning with His cows or returns with them at sunset, they quickly come out of their houses to see Him. They must have performed many pious activities to be able to see Him as He walks on the road, His smiling face mercifully glancing upon them."**

COMMENTARY: "We ladies of Mathurā may also have the privilege of seeing Kṛṣṇa in all His glory, and we too may be able to glorify Him in *saṅkīrtana* while we engage in our activities — at least after He kills Kaṁsa and remains here with us. But the experience will never be the same for us as for the *gopīs* of Vraja. For only they can watch Kṛṣṇa in the morning as He leaves for the forest and in the evening as He returns home. Only they can see Him surrounded by His cows and His cowherd friends. As soon as the *gopīs* hear His flute, they come outside, onto the road on which He will walk. They may be powerless women (*abalāḥ*), devoid of independent strength, but still they are the most fortunate and pious of human beings."

When Kṛṣṇa comes into view, the *gopīs* not only see Him but also hear His flute song and the jingling of His foot bells as He walks with the grace of a skilled dancer. Kṛṣṇa's face is always adorned with merciful glances, and no one ever sees it not smiling. The *gopīs,* however, even while gazing on Kṛṣṇa's beauty, are in anxiety because they know that He will soon be out of sight. What is so fortunate about seeing Kṛṣṇa go off to the forest? What is so auspicious about being left in the anguish of separation? In fact, however, anything in connection with Kṛṣṇa is auspicious, even when it superficially appears to be a cause for suffering. The *gopīs* may see Him leave in the morning, but they also see Him return in the late afternoon. Having languished in their homes during the day, like lotuses almost dead from being overexposed to sunlight, the *gopīs* rush out of their houses as soon as the nectar of Kṛṣṇa's flute song enters their ears. Each time they see Kṛṣṇa is like a festival for them. Every morning they make various excuses to come early to Mother Yaśodā's house to see Kṛṣṇa and follow Him as He leaves for the forest. They are completely absorbed, morning and evening, in meditating on how to get out of their houses to be near Kṛṣṇa — but when they hear Him playing His flute they at once run outside, for the sound of the flute arouses in them the urges of Cupid, rendering them helpless and weak (*abalāḥ*).

As repeatedly explained in *Śrī Bṛhad-bhāgavatāmṛta,* the *gopīs* receive the greatest mercy of the Personality of Godhead when they are immersed in the mood of separation. Nonetheless, the women of Mathurā limit themselves to describing the ecstasy of seeing Kṛṣṇa, because the sublime subject of the *gopīs'* feelings of separation is beyond their grasp. And they dare not even mention the supreme glories of Kṛṣṇa's *rāsa-līlā*. Since the wonder of merely seeing Kṛṣṇa is difficult for the Mathurā women to describe, what can they tell about the *gopīs'* greatest fortune — being able to dance with Kṛṣṇa in the *rāsa-līlā*? The

Mathurā women lament, "Because our stock of pious credits is so meager, we will never be able to see Kṛṣṇa in this same way."

## TEXT 138

न पारयेऽहं निरवद्यसंयुजां
स्वसाधुकृत्यं विबुधायुषापि वः ।
या माभजन्दुर्जरगेहशृङ्खलाः
संवृश्च्य तद्वः प्रतियातु साधुना ॥

*na pāraye 'haṁ niravadya-saṁyujāṁ*
*sva-sādhu-kṛtyaṁ vibudhāyuṣāpi vaḥ*
*yā mābhajan durjara-geha-śṛṅkhalāḥ*
*saṁvṛścya tad vaḥ pratiyātu sādhunā*

*na* — not; *pāraye* — am able to make; *aham* — I; *niravadya*— faultlessly; *saṁyujām* — who have allied with Me; *sva-sādhu-kṛtyam* — proper compensation; *vibudha-āyuṣā* — with a lifetime as long as that of the demigods; *api* — even; *vaḥ* — to you; *yāḥ* — who; *mā* — Me; *abhajan* — have worshiped; *durjara* — difficult to overcome; *geha-śṛṅkhalāḥ* — the chains of household life; *saṁvṛścya* — cutting; *tat* — that; *vaḥ* — of you; *pratiyātu* — let it be returned; *sādhunā* — by the good activity itself.

**"I am not able to repay My debt for your spotless service, even within a lifetime of Brahmā. Your connection with Me is beyond reproach. You have worshiped Me, cutting off all domestic ties, which are difficult to break. Therefore please let your own glorious deeds be your compensation."**

COMMENTARY: This verse (*Bhāgavatam* 10.32.22) describes the most exalted position of the *gopīs,* earned by their pure love for the Personality of Godhead. When Kṛṣṇa suddenly disappeared at the beginning of the *rāsa* dance, the *gopīs* cried in great pain. But then He reappeared, sat comfortably in their midst, and listened to their eager questions. The present verse is Kṛṣṇa's answer to those questions.

Texts 138 through 146 tell of the Supreme Lord's special love for the *gopīs*. In these nine verses the Lord Himself, from His own lotus mouth, explains this wonderful aspect of His own glories.

The *gopīs* are faultless in their love for Kṛṣṇa. Neglecting all considerations other than making Him happy, they submerge their minds in thoughts of Him in spotless *prema*. Surely these girls should not be criticized for approaching Kṛṣṇa with lust, even though followers of the *smṛti-śāstras* may want to criticize them. Their "lust" for Kṛṣṇa is in fact a great virtue, since it is the cause of their faultless association with Him. As previously shown in this book, the *gopīs'* attraction to Kṛṣṇa is an exceptional development of their fully matured love of God. In fact, Kṛṣṇa considers Himself unable to repay the *gopīs* for their devotion, even in a lifetime of the intelligent demigods or sages or the supremely intelligent Lord Brahmā. If we read *sva-sādhu-kṛtyam* to mean "proper compensation," the Lord says that He is unable to repay the *gopīs* for their devotion. And if we read it, alternatively, to mean "one's own saintly behavior," the Lord says that He cannot act with the same exceptionally saintly devotion for them as they have for Him.

Kṛṣṇa is amazed by how strongly committed to Him the *gopīs* are. They have cut the insurmountable knots of attachment to home and husband and children and the multitude of duties centered on them. Severing these attachments, the *gopīs* have worshiped Kṛṣṇa fully, whereas Kṛṣṇa, because He has ties of love to so many devotees, feels He can never be as exclusively dedicated. Therefore He can only suggest to the *gopīs* that their own saintliness might repay His debt to them. There is nothing He can do in kind to reciprocate.

Dividing the phrase *sva-sādhu-kṛtyam* differently yields yet another understanding. *Su-asādhu-kṛtyam* (which changes to *sv-asādhu-kṛtyam*) means "very unvirtuous acts." Thus Kṛṣṇa indicates that even the things the *gopīs* do that lack virtue, such as behaving cruelly toward Him, are glorious. Even those acts, Kṛṣṇa suggests, contribute to absolving His debt, so what then of the pious things the *gopīs* do? Kṛṣṇa says this to the *gopīs* out of greed to enjoy with them in all situations, no matter how they treat Him.

Unfortunately, Kṛṣṇa cannot properly repay the service of the *gopīs,* who have offered Him their faultless bodies (*niravadya-saṁyujām*). Kṛṣṇa is encumbered by various household duties of His own, like His constant duty to tend the cows. He cannot abandon His responsibilities and serve the *gopīs* properly (*mā bhajan*). And Kṛṣṇa's other obligations are unbreakable (*durjarāḥ*), like strong metal chains (*śṛṅkhalāḥ*). As implied by the prefix *sam* ("completely") in the word *saṁvṛścya* ("completely cutting off"), Kṛṣṇa might be able to put aside His inner attachment to these other engagements, but He cannot avoid being externally involved in them.

Kṛṣṇa thinks that unless He offers Himself to the *gopīs* completely, as they have offered themselves to Him — unless He worships them in absolutely exclusive devotion, disregarding everything else — He cannot requite their love. He remains in debt because in His dealings with them He has broken the vow He made in *Bhagavad-gītā* (4.11) *ye yathā māṁ prapadyante tāṁs tathaiva bhajāmy aham:* "As all surrender unto Me, I reward them accordingly."

In all humility, Kṛṣṇa sweetly requests the *gopīs* that for their saintly behavior they agree to be repaid by their own saintly qualities (*sādhunā*). Or, if we take the word *sādhunā* to mean "by a saintly devotee," Kṛṣṇa suggests that although He Himself cannot reciprocate adequately, perhaps in the future some of His devotees will become followers of the *gopīs* and serve them faithfully.

## TEXT 139

गच्छोद्धव व्रजं सौम्य पित्रोर्नः प्रीतिमावह ।
गोपीनां मद्वियोगाधिं मत्सन्देशैर्विमोचय ॥

*gacchoddhava vrajaṁ saumya*
*pitror naḥ prītim āvaha*

*gopīnāṁ mad-viyogādhiṁ*
*mat-sandeśair vimocaya*

*gaccha* — please go; *uddhava* — O Uddhava; *vrajam* — to Vraja; *saumya* — O gentle one; *pitroḥ* — to the parents; *naḥ* — Our; *prītim* — satisfaction; *āvaha* — bring; *gopīnām* — of the *gopīs; mat* — from Me; *viyoga* — caused by separation; *ādhim* — of the mental pain; *mat* — brought from Me; *sandeśaiḥ* — by messages; *vimocaya* — relieve them.

**"Dear gentle Uddhava, go to Vraja and give pleasure to Our parents. And also relieve the gopīs, suffering in separation from Me, by giving them My message.**

COMMENTARY: Texts 139 through 146 were spoken by Śrī Kṛṣṇa to His dear servant and best of advisors, Uddhava. What we say about another person when that person is absent usually indicates our true feelings more reliably than what we say in his presence. Therefore Kṛṣṇa's confidential statements to Uddhava about the *gopīs* confirm that Kṛṣṇa does indeed feel as indebted to them as He claimed while speaking with them. Kṛṣṇa wanted to do what would most help the *gopīs* obtain His full mercy, so instead of going to Vṛndāvana Himself, He dispatched Uddhava. He hoped that the message Uddhava was to convey would pacify the Vraja-vāsīs, whose feelings of separation were burning them like an uncontrolled forest fire. Kṛṣṇa's message was meant to sprinkle on them the nectar of His company and give them some hope that they might see Him again.

This verse and the three that follow come from the Tenth Canto of *Śrīmad-Bhāgavatam* (10.46.3–6). In the first half of this verse, Kṛṣṇa follows the way of ordinary dealings by asking Uddhava to console His mother and father. In the second half, He directs Uddhava to give special attention to the *gopīs*.

The name Uddhava means "festival," so by using this name Kṛṣṇa implies that just by meeting Uddhava the Vraja-vāsīs should feel very much encouraged. And Kṛṣṇa refers to Himself by using the plural pronoun *naḥ* either because He feels proud to be the son of Nanda and Yaśodā or else because He thinks that since Nanda and Yaśodā accept Balarāma also as their son, they should accept Uddhava the same way. Surely Uddhava deserves this treatment. He is amply endowed with saintly humility and with pure devotion for Kṛṣṇa, so he should give Nanda and Yaśodā great satisfaction by his uncontrived skill in delivering Kṛṣṇa's message.

Uddhava is *saumya,* very mild by nature. Or else *saumya* indicates that since Uddhava is as beautiful as the moon (*soma*), Nanda and Yaśodā will be very much pleased just by seeing Him. To pacify the *gopīs,* however, will require more than merely Uddhava's finesse. The *gopīs* feel the pain of separation from Kṛṣṇa so deeply that to relieve them His own words must be conveyed. Or else Kṛṣṇa is saying that nothing less than His own words, with their pleasing tone and special connotations, will pacify both His parents and the *gopīs*. Still, though by hearing His message His mother and father will become happy, the *gopīs* will feel only limited relief. So great is their love for Him that they can never feel content in His absence.

## TEXT 140

ता मन्मनस्का मत्प्राणा मदर्थे त्यक्तदैहिकाः ।
ये त्यक्तलोकधर्माश्च मदर्थे तान्बिभर्म्यहम् ॥

*tā man-manaskā mat-prāṇā*
*mad-arthe tyakta-daihikāḥ*
*ye tyakta-loka-dharmāś ca*
*mad-arthe tān bibharmy aham*

*tāḥ* — they (the *gopīs*); *mat* — absorbed in Me; *manaskāḥ* — their minds; *mat* — fixed upon Me; *prāṇāḥ* — their lives; *mat-arthe* — for My sake; *tyakta* — abandoning; *daihikāḥ* — everything on the bodily platform; *ye* — who (the *gopīs,* or anyone); *tyakta* — giving up; *loka* — this world; *dharmāḥ* — religiosity;

*ca* — and; *mat-arthe* — for My sake; *tān* — them; *bibharmi* — sustain; *aham* — I.

**"The minds of those gopīs are always absorbed in Me, and their very lives are ever devoted to Me. For My sake they have abandoned everything related to their bodies, including ordinary happiness in this life and the religious duties needed for happiness in the next. Therefore I take it upon Myself to sustain those gopīs in all circumstances.**

COMMENTARY: In this verse Kṛṣṇa tells Uddhava why the *gopīs* need to be so carefully consoled. He also explains why He feels so obliged to them and what attributes set them apart as His greatest devotees. Because the *gopīs* always think about Kṛṣṇa, they appear as if possessed by insanity. And because Kṛṣṇa is their very life and soul, whenever He goes any distance away from them they seem on the verge of death. In the past they expressed their unalloyed devotion for Him by making great sacrifices. For His sake they gave up the company of their husbands, children, and homes. But now that they live in Vraja without Him they feel desolate, because they cannot resort to any other shelter than Him.

If the *gopīs* have actually sacrificed everything for Kṛṣṇa, why don't they just go to Mathurā to be with Him? They don't because He promised He would soon return to Vraja. That promise, as well as their concern for Kṛṣṇa's happiness, keeps them from abandoning their physical responsibilities to their husbands, children, and so on and keeps them nicely dressing and ornamenting themselves. Otherwise the *gopīs* would simply walk away from their families and cast aside their fine clothing and the jewelry Kṛṣṇa sent them from Mathurā. The *gopīs* have no attachment to any of these.

For the sake of Kṛṣṇa, the *gopīs* have put aside all hopes for success in this life and the next. They have abandoned all expectations of material happiness (*loka*) and spiritual happiness (*dharma*). Kṛṣṇa confesses that because the *gopīs* are so perfectly surrendered to Him, He takes it as His duty to maintain them, give them strength, and assure their happiness. Kṛṣṇa alone is the real source of happiness for the *gopīs,* and He is their real protector, much more than their husbands. Therefore Uddhava should agree to carry Kṛṣṇa's message to Vraja.

Here Kṛṣṇa uses the masculine forms of the pronouns *ye* and *tān* because, man or woman, any devotee who has such pure love deserves His protection. Nonetheless, the *gopīs,* through their womanly nature, manifest unique qualifications: they have made what for women is the supreme sacrifice by abandoning for Kṛṣṇa's sake their social connections (*loka*) and their feminine virtues of shyness and chastity (*dharma*).

Uddhava may worry that the *gopīs,* having abandoned everything, must be wandering aimlessly in the wilderness. How then will he be able to find them? And furthermore, since they have rejected all social ties, they must have become like madwomen haunted by ghosts. How then will he be able to reason with them? Kṛṣṇa assures Uddhava that even though the *gopīs* have for His sake abandoned *loka* and *dharma,* He watches over them and protects them. He continues to provide them the same worldly and superworldly benefits they have rejected. Thus when Uddhava reaches Vṛndāvana he will find the *gopīs* at home with their husbands and children, and of sane mind. What's more, Kṛṣṇa personally continues to provide even for the husbands and children the *gopīs* have mentally abandoned. There is no need to worry that the families of the *gopīs* might be uncared for, or that the community might have ostracized the husbands for having wives who have abandoned religious principles. Kṛṣṇa is protecting the *gopīs'* families, and of course He is protecting the *gopīs* themselves and their religious principles. Through His personal energies, Kṛṣṇa provides for the needs of the husbands and children, so what doubt can there be that He maintains the *gopīs*? He supplies their worldly needs (*loka*), maintains the integrity of their religious duties as women (*strī-dharma*), and keeps them strongly engaged in their primary interest and highest *dharma* — *nāma-saṅkīrtana* and the other essential aspects of devotional service to Him.

According to the rules for Sanskrit euphony, *ye tyakta* may be read as the elided form of *ye atyakta,* and when we take the liberty to restore the prefix *a-* ("not"), another meaning of the last two lines of this verse comes out: "Only for My sake have the *gopīs* not abandoned their worldly responsibilities [*loka-dharma*]. Therefore, dear Uddhava, since you are virtually equal to Me, you should go to Vraja, make the *gopīs* happy, protect their sanity and natural humility, and do the same for their husbands, their children, and everyone else in Vraja."

## TEXT 141

मयि ताः प्रेयसां प्रेष्ठे दूरस्थे गोकुलस्त्रियः ।
स्मरन्त्योऽङ्ग विमुह्यन्ति विरहौत्कण्ठ्यविह्वलाः ॥

*mayi tāḥ preyasāṁ preṣṭhe*
*dūra-sthe gokula-striyaḥ*
*smarantyo 'ṅga vimuhyanti*
*virahautkaṇṭhya-vihvalāḥ*

*mayi* — I; *tāḥ* — they; *preyasām* — of all objects of endearment; *preṣṭhe* — the most dear; *dūra-sthe* — being far away; *gokula-striyaḥ* — the women of Gokula; *smarantyaḥ* — remembering; *aṅga* — dear (Uddhava); *vimuhyanti* — become stunned; *viraha* — of separation; *autkaṇṭhya* — by the anxiety; *vihvalāḥ* — overwhelmed.

**"My dear Uddhava, for those women of Gokula I am the most cherished object of love. Thus when they remember Me, who am so far away, they are overwhelmed by the anxiety of separation.**

COMMENTARY: Here Kṛṣṇa speaks to His friend Uddhava with deep concern for the *gopīs*. Never, He tells Uddhava, has He seen in anyone such distress as the *gopīs* now suffer, nor has He ever heard of such misery in any historical or literary account. At every moment the *gopīs* are so beside themselves in the bewilderment of separation that they seem ready to leave their bodies for the abode of Death.

In this world one's spouse, children, and friends are generally very dear. Yet more dear is one's own body, and still more dear the vital air of life. More dear than life is *dharma,* still more dear is *mokṣa,* and even more dear is *kṛṣṇa-bhakti,* pure devotional service to Kṛṣṇa. *Kṛṣṇa-bhakti* finds its perfect culmination in unalloyed *prema,* and because the *gopīs* are more advanced in *kṛṣṇa-prema* than anyone else, they are most dear to the Supreme Lord and His devotees.

For the *gopīs,* Kṛṣṇa Himself is the most dear object of attraction. When He goes far away to Mathurā and remains there, the *gopīs* nearly drown in the anxiety of separation, and stay alive only by the faint hope that He will come back to them. Unable to think and act coherently, they become as if insane. They fall into obsessive remembrance of Kṛṣṇa, thinking about how they used to associate with Him. And they become so confused and distant from reality that it becomes difficult to verify that they are still alive. The *gopīs* suffer greatly when Kṛṣṇa leaves them for even a moment, but when He leaves Vṛndāvana for Mathurā they approach the extreme limit of distress. Yet even though the greatness of their pain often overwhelms their minds, the *gopīs* cannot help but remember Kṛṣṇa.

Kṛṣṇa calls Uddhava *aṅga,* "dear friend," to remind Uddhava, "I am depending on your skills as a messenger and counselor to save the lives of the *gopīs* by delivering My message."

## TEXT 142

धारयन्त्यतिकृच्छ्रेण प्रायः प्राणान्कथञ्चन ।
प्रत्यागमनसन्देशैर्बल्लव्यो मे मदात्मिकाः ॥

*dhārayanty ati-kṛcchreṇa*
*prāyaḥ prāṇān kathañcana*
*pratyāgamana-sandeśair*
*ballavyo me mad-ātmikāḥ*

*dhārayanti* — they hold on; *ati-kṛcchreṇa* — with great difficulty; *prāyaḥ* — barely; *prāṇān* — to their lives; *kathañcana* — somehow; *prati-āgamana* — about return; *sandeśaiḥ* — by the messages; *ballavyaḥ* — the cowherd women; *me* — My; *mat-ātmikāḥ* — who are fully dedicated to Me.

**"Simply because I have promised to return to them, My fully devoted cowherd girlfriends struggle to somehow or other maintain their lives."**

COMMENTARY: In the previous verse, Kṛṣṇa described the condition of *gokula-striyaḥ,* which can be taken to mean all the ladies of Vraja, old as well as young. Now He focuses His attention on the *vraja-gopīs* who are most dear to Him — the young *gopīs,* such as Śrī Rādhikā. As improbable as it seems to Kṛṣṇa, these dear *gopī* girlfriends, including Candrāvalī, even though on the constant verge of death from the pain of separation, manage somehow to survive.

Kṛṣṇa is ashamed to confess that He intends to lie to the *gopīs,* yet He must explain the contents of the message He is asking Uddhava to carry. Uddhava must assure the *gopīs* that Kṛṣṇa will come back to them very soon. This should save the *gopīs* from the grips of death, just as such a message saved them once before, when Akrūra had taken Kṛṣṇa and Balarāma away from Gokula. At that time Kṛṣṇa sent a messenger with the promise that He would return after only a few days, and since the simple *gopīs* had full faith in Kṛṣṇa's words, they found in this promise the strength to tolerate the disappointment of losing Him. The anticipation of soon again enjoying the beauty of Kṛṣṇa gave them solace.

Aware of how daunting the task must appear, Kṛṣṇa explains to Uddhava that the *gopīs,* headed by Śrī Rādhikā, have dedicated themselves life and soul to Him alone. Only by Kṛṣṇa's special efforts to keep them alive do their souls stay in their bodies. The *gopīs* are burning in a fire of *viraha-bhāva,* but Kṛṣṇa is still struggling to save them.

As Kṛṣṇa indicates by the word *prāyaḥ,* most of the *gopīs* have somehow managed to survive, but some of them have already died, and others, sad to say, will also be lost. As the fire of separation grows in intensity, for the *gopīs* to stay alive becomes more and more difficult. In truth, only by the shelter of Kṛṣṇa's personal power, provided secretly, are the *gopīs* surviving at all. Kṛṣṇa doesn't want to admit this to Uddhava, who might rebuke Him for preserving the *gopīs'* lives. Were Kṛṣṇa to allow the *gopīs* to leave their bodies, their suffering would end, but by keeping them alive He is only prolonging and intensifying their torment. Yet there is something else for Uddhava to consider: Kṛṣṇa will share the *gopīs'* fate. Kṛṣṇa needs to be saved as much as they do. Therefore Uddhava should take most seriously his mission of bringing the *gopīs* a message of renewed hope.

For devotees too pained by the account of the *gopīs'* inner torment, this fourth verse of instruction to Uddhava can be interpreted in a different way, one that places more emphasis on how Kṛṣṇa plans to maintain the *gopīs'* lives. Two verses before, Kṛṣṇa gave His assurance that He sustains the *gopīs* through all difficulties (*tān bibharmy aham*). Kṛṣṇa thus promised to arrange, somehow or other, for the *gopīs'* happiness. And now Kṛṣṇa tells just how Uddhava can help. The way to keep the *gopīs* alive is to bring them Kṛṣṇa's message promising His return. Although to save them is practically impossible, this message may keep the breath of life barely flowing in the *gopīs'* throats. Uddhava should visit the *gopīs* and convince them: "Śrī Nanda-nandana is returning very soon. He is already on the way. He is practically here already."

## TEXT 143

रामेण सार्धं मथुरां प्रणीते
श्वाफल्किना मय्यनुरक्तचित्ताः ।
विगाढभावेन न मे वियोग-
तीव्राधयोऽन्यं ददृशुः सुखाय ॥

*rāmeṇa sārdhaṁ mathurāṁ praṇīte*
*śvāphalkinā mayy anurakta-cittāḥ*
*vigāḍha-bhāvena na me viyoga-*
*tīvrādhayo 'nyaṁ dadṛśuḥ sukhāya*

*rāmeṇa* — with Balarāma; *sārdham* — together; *mathurām* — to the city of Mathurā; *praṇīte* — when brought; *śvāphalkinā* — by Akrūra; *mayi* — I; *anurakta* — constantly attached; *cittāḥ* — those whose consciousness was; *vigāḍha* — extremely deep; *bhāvena* — by love; *na* — not; *me* — than Me; *viyoga* — of separation; *tīvra* — intense; *ādhayaḥ* — who were experiencing mental distress, anxiety; *anyam* — anything other; *dadṛśuḥ* — they saw; *sukhāya* — that could make them happy.

**"The residents of Vṛndāvana, headed by the gopīs, were always completely attached to Me with deepest love. Therefore, when My uncle Akrūra brought My brother Balarāma and Me to the city of Mathurā, the residents of Vṛndāvana suffered extreme mental distress in separation from Me and could not find any other source of happiness.**

COMMENTARY: The next four verses recited by Parīkṣit Mahārāja to his mother (texts 143 through 146) come from Kṛṣṇa's discussion with Uddhava in the Eleventh Canto of *Śrīmad-Bhāgavatam* (11.12.10–13). When Kṛṣṇa and Uddhava were together in Dvārakā, Kṛṣṇa explained to Uddhava the great value of associating with saintly devotees of the Lord. Discussing this topic reminded Kṛṣṇa of the most exalted of all saintly Vaiṣṇavas, His own beloved *gopīs,* and this so overwhelmed Kṛṣṇa's heart that He digressed to speak these four verses.

King Kaṁsa engaged Akrūra, the son of Śvaphalka, to bring Kṛṣṇa to Mathurā, whatever it took. Kṛṣṇa was reluctant to make the trip, but Akrūra used His wits to convince Vasudeva and Balarāma that going to Mathurā was unavoidable. By referring to Akrūra as the noble son of Śvaphalka (Śvaphalka being a worthy descendant of Yadu), Kṛṣṇa is telling Uddhava that the Vraja-vāsīs, including Kṛṣṇa Himself, have to excuse Akrūra. After all,

Akrūra was only doing what he thought necessary to protect his dynasty from the wrath of Kaṁsa. Lord Balarāma, who was present when Akrūra came to Vṛndāvana, could have expertly pacified the Vraja-vāsīs, as He had done previously when Kṛṣṇa seemed imperiled in the grip of Kāliya; but this time, somehow, He made no such attempt. And when Akrūra approached Balarāma to present the plight of Vasudeva, Devakī, and the other Yadus, who were living in fear and misery under the rule of Kaṁsa, it was Balarāma who gave His consent for taking Kṛṣṇa from Vṛndāvana to Mathurā. Had it not been for this, Kṛṣṇa might never have left Vṛndāvana.

After Kṛṣṇa departed, the *gopīs* could find no other object of delight for their eyes. Whatever they saw reminded them that Kṛṣṇa was gone, and this only made them more miserable. With the supreme desirable object removed from their sight, everything else appeared worthless. Separation from Kṛṣṇa was like a persistent throbbing in the head that made enjoying anything in life impossible. Even before Kṛṣṇa left, the *gopīs'* attraction to Him had been obsessive, but now it was utterly out of control, and it tormented them like a raging fever in the brain. They entered the rarest state of ecstasy, in which nothing around them seemed able to give any happiness.

Uddhava might wonder why the *gopīs,* whose wisdom is praised by the most learned sages, continued to be attracted to Kṛṣṇa even after He had caused them so much anguish. Kṛṣṇa's answer is that the *gopīs'* love for Him was so extremely intense that nothing, not even His mistreatment of them, could impede it. As the sage Parāśara describes,

*sa tathā saha gopībhī*
*rarāma madhusūdanaḥ*
*yathābda-koṭi-pratimaḥ*
*kṣaṇas tena vinābhavat*

"Madhusūdana gave so much delight to the *gopīs* that later, when He was absent, a moment seemed to them like ten million years." (*Viṣṇu Purāṇa* 5.13.58) Parāśara was describing to Maitreya, some years after the fact, the separation the *gopīs* felt, and thus he used the past tense.

The word *gopī* can here be understood to derive from *gāḥ pānti,* "they protect their senses." The *gopīs* protected their senses by keeping them away from material objects. In truth the *gopīs* were the greatest of self-controlled *yogīs.* But Kṛṣṇa's charms so entranced them that they became entangled in loving affairs with Him and therefore suffered. Madhusūdana is the name of a particular bee well known for his rapacious nature of greedily collecting honey from many lotus flowers. And another Madhusūdana, known as Kṛṣṇa, took from the *gopīs* and ruined (*sūdayati*) all their honey (*madhu*), all their attractive, enjoyable qualities. He stole everything they had.

Kṛṣṇa here confesses to Uddhava that it is simply His nature to attract all sorts of people, exploit them for His own pleasure, enjoy them to His full, and then go away and leave them miserable. In the message Kṛṣṇa was instructing Uddhava to carry, Kṛṣṇa might have said that He Himself endured as much torment in separation from the *gopīs* as they did in separation from Him. But the facts prove otherwise. The *gopīs* surrendered to Kṛṣṇa with absolute dedication, as He Himself will describe in the next two verses; Kṛṣṇa, however, as He confesses to Uddhava, is not nearly as surrendered to them. Kṛṣṇa may have a high reputation as the most exalted of saintly persons, but in His own opinion, expressed in these verses, the *gopīs* are much more virtuous. In them there is not a trace of cruelty or ingratitude, and pure love for Him like theirs is not to be found anywhere else.

## TEXT 144

तास्ताः क्षपाः प्रेष्ठतमेन नीता
मयैव वृन्दावनगोचरेण ।
क्षणार्धवत्ताः पुनरङ्ग तासां
हीना मया कल्पसमा बभूवुः ॥

*tās tāḥ kṣapāḥ preṣṭha-tamena nītā*
*mayaiva vṛndāvana-gocareṇa*
*kṣaṇārdha-vat tāḥ punar aṅga tāsāṁ*
*hīnā mayā kalpa-samā babhūvuḥ*

*tāḥ tāḥ* — all those; *kṣapāḥ* — nights; *preṣṭha-tamena* — with the most dearly beloved; *nītāḥ* — spent; *mayā* — with Me; *eva* — indeed; *vṛndāvana* — in Vṛndāvana; *go-careṇa* — who was present; *kṣaṇa* — a moment; *ardha-vat* — like half; *tāḥ* — those very nights; *punaḥ* — again; *aṅga* — dear Uddhava; *tāsām* — for the *gopīs; hīnāḥ* — bereft; *mayā* — of Me; *kalpa* — a day of Brahmā (4,320,000,000 years); *samāḥ* — equal to; *babhūvuḥ* — became.

**"Dear Uddhava, all of those nights the gopīs spent with Me, their most dearly beloved, when I was present in Vṛndāvana seemed to them to pass in less than a moment. But when bereft of My association, the gopīs felt those same nights drag on forever, as if each night were equal to a day of Brahmā.**

COMMENTARY: Here Kṛṣṇa acknowledges the terrible agony the *gopīs* endure on His account. He addresses Uddhava as *aṅga* to indicate that Uddhava is as dear to Him as His own body. And He describes how the pleasure of the *rāsa* dance He shared with His beloved *gopīs* passed swiftly, as if in a single moment, even though the *rāsa-līlā* lasted several nights. As certain *smṛti-śāstras* explain, the word "nights" can also mean "days and nights." By the Supreme Lord's special energies, the *rāsa* dance did not end in a single night, but lasted many nights and days. Although outsiders were unaware, Kṛṣṇa and the *gopīs* celebrated the *rāsa-līlā* for a long time, without interruption. That such an extended festival seemed to the *gopīs* to last only a moment proves how happy Kṛṣṇa's pure devotees become in His intimate association.

The moonlit autumn nights when Kṛṣṇa danced with the *gopīs* passed quickly for the *gopīs,* but not other nights. On other nights the suffering they underwent from Kṛṣṇa's absence seemed to last millions of years. Or if we accept that Kṛṣṇa, almost every night, would find ways to sneak out of the house to meet the *gopīs,* then every night passed quickly, not just the nights of the *rāsa-līlā* season. Only the daytimes were excruciatingly long.

Kṛṣṇa admits that the *gopīs'* great love for Him has cast them into utter misery. This thought might prompt a friend to suggest that Kṛṣṇa bring the *gopīs* to Dvārakā and again make them happy. But this idea, Kṛṣṇa answers, is not feasible. The *rāsa* dance was a source of delight for Him and the *gopīs* because they enjoyed it together in Vṛndāvana. Neither Kṛṣṇa nor the *gopīs* can feel the same ecstasy anywhere else. Only in Vṛndāvana does Kṛṣṇa wander among His cows and dress Himself as a cowherd. Only in the atmosphere of Vṛndāvana is the highest ecstasy perceived. Unfortunately, Kṛṣṇa confesses, He is no longer the same person as in Vṛndāvana. He has become ungrateful and hard-hearted. Yet the original virtues of the *gopīs* have not degraded at all, and therefore Kṛṣṇa considers the *gopīs* much more exalted than Himself.

## TEXT 145

ता नाविदन्मय्यनुसङ्गबद्ध-
धियः स्वमात्मानमदस्तथेदम् ।
यथा समाधौ मुनयोऽब्धितोये
नद्यः प्रविष्टा इव नामरूपे ॥

*tā nāvidan mayy anusaṅga-baddha-*
*dhiyaḥ svam ātmānam adas tathedam*
*yathā samādhau munayo 'bdhi-toye*
*nadyaḥ praviṣṭā iva nāma-rūpe*

*tāḥ* — they (the *gopīs*); *na* — not; *avidan* — were aware of; *mayi* — in Me; *anusaṅga* — by intimate contact; *baddha* — bound; *dhiyaḥ* — their consciousness; *svam* — their own; *ātmānam* — body or self; *adaḥ* — the next life; *tathā* — as well as; *idam* — this life; *yathā* — just as; *samādhau* — in *yoga-samādhi; munayaḥ* — great sages; *abdhi* — of the ocean; *toye* — in the water; *nadyaḥ* — rivers; *praviṣṭāḥ* — having entered; *iva* — like; *nāma* — names; *rūpe* — and forms.

**"My dear Uddhava, just as great sages in yoga trance merge into self-realization, like rivers merging into the ocean, and are thus unaware of material names and forms, the gopīs of Vṛndāvana were so completely attached to Me within their minds that they could not think of their own bodies, or of this world, or of their future lives. Their entire consciousness was simply bound up in Me.**

COMMENTARY: The *gopīs* are married women with husbands, children, and household responsibilities. How can they be considered superior to renounced, self-contented sages who have given up all material attachments? Here Kṛṣṇa answers this doubt. After sages who follow the *aṣṭāṅga-yoga* system become advanced in the practice of *yama, niyama, āsana, prāṇāyāma, pratyāhāra, dhyāna,* and *dhāraṇā,* they realize the Absolute Truth as Lord Viṣṇu in their perfected trance, or *samādhi.* In that perfect consciousness, they forget the temporary names and forms of the material world, including the names and forms of their own bodies.

The *gopīs* resemble such perfect sages, for the activities of the *gopīs'* minds are all fixed on Kṛṣṇa in a highly developed trance, achieved by virtue of their constant connection with Kṛṣṇa, their natural relationship with Him in pure love. Like sages adept in *aṣṭāṅga-yoga,* the *gopīs* have forgotten everything of this world — their husbands and children, their own bodies (the normal objects of self-centered attachment), their individual identities as proprietors and enjoyers of the material body, and all their hopes for success in this life and the next.

As rivers abandon themselves to the waves of the ocean, the *gopīs* have merged their hearts in thought of Kṛṣṇa. Thus, being fully dedicated to Kṛṣṇa, they should be recognized as even greater than *munis* perfect in the *aṣṭāṅga-yoga* system. Even while standing in the midst of a blazing fire, the *gopīs* are not burned; rather, all their desires are fulfilled. Furthermore, simply by remaining always in Kṛṣṇa consciousness, the *gopīs* have gained the spiritual strength to easily turn away from everything material. Their hearts are irrevocably attracted to Kṛṣṇa in all circumstances, whereas *munis* have to struggle hard to progress through the successive methods of *aṣṭāṅga-yoga*. The *munis* must deeply concentrate to bring their minds under subjugation, and only after long endeavor can they possibly reach the goal — *samādhi,* in which they can forget material names and forms. The *gopīs* are much greater because they easily achieve *samādhi.*

But aren't self-contented sages like the four Kumāras considered the most advanced of saintly persons? In ordinary circles that opinion may prevail, but in truth the *gopīs* are more saintly than self-contented sages. The *gopīs* differ from sages whose minds flow like rivers into the ocean of *samādhi,* oblivious of names and forms. Though the *gopīs* forget everything material, including their own bodies, they never forget Kṛṣṇa's names, forms, and qualities. The lives of the *gopīs* are practical and real, full of variety, and imbued with the spirit of devotion to Kṛṣṇa. The *gopīs,* fixing their intelligence completely on Kṛṣṇa, never forget His names and forms. Thus they excel all *munis* by easily realizing the highest limit of happiness in full love of God.

In the Ninth Canto of *Śrīmad-Bhāgavatam* (9.4.64) Lord Nārāyaṇa tells the *muni* Durvāsā:

*nāham ātmānam āśāse*
*mad-bhaktaiḥ sādhubhir vinā*
*śriyam ātyantikīṁ vāpi*
*yeṣāṁ gatir ahaṁ parā*

"O best of the *brāhmaṇas,* without saintly persons for whom I am the only destination, I do not desire to enjoy My transcendental bliss or even the association of My consort Śrī, the supreme goddess of fortune." In other words, the Supreme Lord is more attracted to His pure devotees than to the goddess Śrī.

Here a doubt may arise: The *gopīs* of Vṛndāvana are also said to be goddesses of fortune. Doesn't that put them in the same category with Śrī? How then can they be considered Kṛṣṇa's dearmost devotees? Kṛṣṇa dispels this doubt here in His discussion with Uddhava in the Eleventh Canto by disclosing a confidential aspect of the *gopīs'* glories, an aspect that establishes the *gopīs* beyond all doubt as the greatest of saints, and greater even than the goddess Śrī. Earlier, in the Tenth Canto, while giving Uddhava the message to convey to the *gopīs,* Kṛṣṇa glorified them. But at that time Kṛṣṇa did not reveal that He Himself was distressed by being separated from them. Had He done so, Uddhava might have told this to the *gopīs,* and their condition would only have worsened. But now, in the Eleventh Canto, Kṛṣṇa wishes to refute the popular misconception that He is hard-hearted, and He wishes to satisfy Uddhava, and so, revealing the greatness of His own ecstasy, He discloses His feelings for the *gopīs*. In so doing, He describes how it is that the *gopīs* are more saintly than everyone else.

To understand the hidden meaning of what Kṛṣṇa is saying here, we have to read the word *avidan* as a present participle ("being unaware") instead of a past-tense verb ("were unaware"). The rules of Sanskrit grammar allow this. As a participle, *avidan* is a masculine form in the nominative case, and so it must refer to the speaker, Kṛṣṇa Himself. *Avidan* can therefore be translated as "if I am unaware." Kṛṣṇa's being the subject of the previous verse, which includes the word *mayā* ("by Me"), further justifies such a reading. The sages (*munayaḥ*) are another subject in the current verse, and thus, by extension, the participle can also refer to the sages.

Kṛṣṇa is saying, then, "Sages are not really sages if in their *samādhi* they become like rivers flowing into the ocean and forget My names and forms. Because the activities of their senses completely stop, such forgetful sages become as if dead, for they are devoid of the living soul's defining quality of thought and unable to experience transcendental ecstasy. In the same way, were I ever to forget My *gopīs,* were I ever to fail to think of them constantly, I would no longer be Śrī Kṛṣṇa, the Personality of Godhead." Or, understanding this idea in an even more radical sense: "Then My life would come to an end; I would no longer exist." Kṛṣṇa refrains from openly speaking this last thought, because He wants to spare Uddhava the pain of hearing something so distasteful.

Kṛṣṇa, divulging why He feels the way He does, says to Uddhava, "I am obliged to the *gopīs* because their minds are absolutely fixed on Me. The *gopīs* always think exclusively of Me, and their attraction to Me is most sublime. Therefore, dear brother, for them I have the greatest love. I must confess to not having the same kind of love for anything or anyone else — not for My parents, My brothers, My queens, My children, not for My own transcendental body, not for My Vaikuṇṭha abode with all its paraphernalia and associates, nor My special abodes here in Dvārakā and Mathurā. All of them I could forget and still be Myself, Śrī Kṛṣṇa, and not feel as much pain as if I were ever to forget the *gopīs* of Vraja. I am always thinking of the *gopīs* with supreme love and attachment."

In another verse, found in Śrīla Rūpa Gosvāmī's *Padyāvalī* (135), Uddhava tells the *gopīs:*

*viyoginīnām api paddhatiṁ vo*
*no yogino gantum api kṣamante*
*yad dhyeya-rūpasya parasya puṁso*
*yūyaṁ gatā dhyeya-padaṁ durāpam*

"The path you women traverse who feel separation from Kṛṣṇa, even great *yogīs* cannot approach. You have realized the goal of meditation that others can hardly achieve — the Supreme Personality of Godhead, whose form is the most worthy object of meditation." Real *yogīs,* engaged in eternal devotional service to the Supreme Lord, know only Kṛṣṇa as the object of their meditation. But the *gopīs* have surpassed even such genuine *yogīs* because the *gopīs* are the constant object of Kṛṣṇa's meditation. Therefore they are greater than everyone else.

## TEXT 146

मत्कामा रमणं जारमस्वरूपविदोऽबलाः ।
ब्रह्म मां परमं प्रापुः सङ्गाच्छतसहस्रशः ॥

*mat-kāmā ramaṇaṁ jāram*
*asvarūpa-vido 'balāḥ*
*brahma māṁ paramaṁ prāpuḥ*
*saṅgāc chata-sahasraśaḥ*

*mat* — Me; *kāmāḥ* — those who desired; *ramaṇam* — charming; *jāram* — the lover of another's wife; *asvarūpa-vidaḥ* — not knowing My actual situation; *abalāḥ* — women; *brahma* — the Absolute; *mām* — Me; *paramam* — supreme; *prāpuḥ* — they achieved; *saṅgāt* — by association; *śata-sahasraśaḥ* — by the hundreds of thousands.

**"All those hundreds of thousands of women, knowing Me as their most charming lover and ardently desiring Me that way, were unaware of My actual position. Yet by intimately associating with Me, they attained Me, the Supreme Absolute Truth."**

COMMENTARY: The *gopīs* fulfilled their highest ambitions by achieving Kṛṣṇa as their lover. Those cowherd women were so exalted that by personal contact with them thousands of the outcaste women of Vraja — Pulindīs and other aborigines — achieved the same rarest goal of life. The word *abalā* ("women") in its literal sense means "not strong," indicating that the aborigine women lacked the assets of knowledge, good birth, good behavior, and devotion to God. They were ignorant of their own eternal identities as spirit souls, and because they had never come close enough to Nanda Mahārāja's village to see Kṛṣṇa with their own eyes, they were also ignorant of Kṛṣṇa's all-attractive beauty. Nonetheless, in the forest the aborigine women of Vraja accidentally came in contact with grass and leaves smeared with *kuṅkuma* from the bodies of the *gopīs* and in this way gained the transcendental association of the *gopīs* and also became infected with the desire to have Kṛṣṇa as their lover. Or if we presume that the Pulindīs and other aborigine women, simply by being born in Kṛṣṇa's holy *dhāma,* must have known that they were eternal souls, their association with the *gopīs,* even though indirect, infused them with sublime devotion for

Kṛṣṇa and made them forget whatever spiritual knowledge they had. They were also ignorant of who they were in another sense: taking no heed of their own dirtiness and their dingy complexions, they were helplessly impelled toward Kṛṣṇa by the conjugal attraction they contracted from the *gopīs.*

The Pulindīs and others may have been low-class tribal women, but they had the greatest fortune of being attracted to the Supreme Absolute Truth, the darling son of Nanda Mahārāja. And that attraction was extraordinary. They accepted Him as the absolute master of their lives, and that too in the special mood that He was their unmarried lover. They had to keep their love for Kṛṣṇa secret because as outcastes they had little hope of ever meeting Him and if they did chance to meet Him that contact would be considered altogether illicit. Thus they privately cherished the treasure of *prema* within the cores of their hearts. At every moment they tasted newer and newer sweetness in the highest possible limits of blissful satisfaction. Having had some contact with the *gopīs,* the aborigine women of Vraja all attained a perfection similar to theirs, if not in this life then in the next.

## TEXT 147

एताः परं तनुभृतो भुवि गोपवध्वो
गोविन्द एव निखिलात्मनि रूढभावाः ।
वाञ्छन्ति यद्भवभियो मुनयो वयं च
किं ब्रह्मजन्मभिरनन्तकथारसस्य ॥

*etāḥ paraṁ tanu-bhṛto bhuvi gopa-vadhvo*
*govinda eva nikhilātmani rūḍha-bhāvāḥ*
*vāñchanti yad bhava-bhiyo munayo vayaṁ ca*
*kiṁ brahma-janmabhir ananta-kathā-rasasya*

*etāḥ* — these women; *param* — alone; *tanu* — their bodies; *bhṛtaḥ* — maintain successfully; *bhuvi* — on earth; *gopa-vadhvaḥ* — the young cowherd women; *govinde* — for Lord Kṛṣṇa; *eva* — exclusively; *nikhila* — of all; *ātmani* — the Soul; *rūḍha-bhāvāḥ* — who have perfected their ecstatic loving attraction; *vāñchanti* — they desire; *yat* — which (ecstatic attraction); *bhava* — material existence; *bhiyaḥ* — those who fear; *munayaḥ* — sages; *vayam* — we; *ca* — also; *kim* — what use; *brahma* — as a *brāhmaṇa* or as Lord Brahmā; *janmabhiḥ* — with births; *ananta* — of the unlimited Lord; *kathā* — for the topics; *rasasya* — for one who has a taste.

**"Among all persons on earth, these cowherd women alone have actually perfected their embodied lives, for they have achieved the perfection of unalloyed love for Lord Govinda. Their pure love is hankered after by those who fear material existence, by great sages, and by ourselves as well. For one who has tasted the narrations of the infinite Lord, what is the use of taking birth as a high-class brāhmaṇa, or even as Lord Brahmā himself?**

COMMENTARY: Texts 147 through 152 (*Bhāgavatam* 10.47.58–63) were spoken by Śrī Uddhava during his visit to Vṛndāvana. Because of his own solid reputation as an exalted Vaiṣṇava, his testimony that the devotional service of the *gopīs* is supreme is extremely credible. Uddhava is a favorite student of Bṛhaspati, the spiritual master of the demigods, and he is a trusted advisor to Kṛṣṇa in Dvārakā. Kṛṣṇa Himself praises Uddhava with enthusiasm:

*athaitat paramaṁ guhyaṁ*
*śṛṇvato yadu-nandana*
*su-gopyam api vakṣyāmi*
*tvaṁ me bhṛtyaḥ suhṛt sakhā*

"My dear Uddhava, O beloved of the Yadu dynasty, because you are My servant, well-wisher, and friend, I shall now speak to you the most confidential knowledge. Please hear as I explain these great mysteries to you." (*Bhāgavatam* 11.11.49)

*vāsudevo bhagavatāṁ*
*tvaṁ tu bhāgavateṣv aham*

"Among those entitled to the name Bhagavān I am Vāsudeva. And among the devotees, you indeed, Uddhava, represent Me." (*Bhāgavatam* 11.16.29)

*na tathā me priya-tama*
*ātma-yonir na śaṅkaraḥ*
*na ca saṅkarṣaṇo na śrīr*
*naivātmā ca yathā bhavān*

"My dear Uddhava, neither Lord Brahmā, Lord Śiva, Lord Saṅkarṣaṇa, nor the goddess of fortune, nor indeed My own self is as dear to Me as you." (*Bhāgavatam* 11.14.15)

When Uddhava met with the *gopīs* in Vṛndāvana, he used all his diplomatic skill to deliver Kṛṣṇa's message in a way that would relieve the agony the *gopīs* felt in separation from Kṛṣṇa. But after hearing the message, the *gopīs* became even more deeply immersed in the ocean of their distress. Uddhava was astonished by the extraordinary intensity of the *gopīs'* attachment to Kṛṣṇa. He had never seen or even heard of such pure devotional surrender. Therefore, just before leaving Vṛndāvana, Uddhava spoke these six verses, in homage to the *gopīs* and their pure devotion for Kṛṣṇa.

Here, in the first of these verses, Uddhava declares the *gopīs* greater than all aspirants for liberation, greater than all self-realized liberated saints, and greater than all other devotees of the Personality of Godhead. Only the *gopīs* — the goddesses of fortune who reside in the cowherd village of Śrī Nanda — have realized the full potential of human life (*tanu-bhṛto bhuvi*). That these greatest of all Vaiṣṇavas are human beings and residents of earth is fitting because on higher planets like Svarga, the abode of Indra, the residents enjoy so much power and sense gratification that such love for Kṛṣṇa is practically impossible for them to achieve. In other words, the demigods and sages living in the higher regions of the universe can hardly ever perfect their lives like the *gopīs* of Vraja.

The words *tanu-bhṛto bhuvi* ("perfecting their lives on earth") can also be understood in another way: By sharing the rare gift of *prema-bhakti,* the *gopīs* deliver the fallen conditioned souls of this earth. In other words, the devotional lives of the inhabitants of earth are nourished by the *gopīs.* The influence of the natural compassion and other virtues of the *gopīs* is supremely beneficial for everyone because the *gopīs* possess the greatest possible love for the inner Lord of all souls, the son of the king of the cowherds, the Lord who is famous as Govinda because He is "the Indra of the cows." Moreover, the *gopīs* disregard everything else and love Govinda as the Lord of their hearts, their lover, their paramour. They enjoyed with Kṛṣṇa the unprecedented *rāsa-līlā* festival, and then, by displaying the all-attractive transformations of their *viraha-bhāva,* they deprived Uddhava of his wisdom by vanquishing his sobriety. For a long time the *gopīs* had quietly endured within their hearts the pain of separation from Kṛṣṇa; but after hearing Kṛṣṇa's message from Uddhava they could no longer hold themselves back. Uddhava then became a witness to the uncontrollable waves of their complete distress. The ecstasy the *gopīs* feel in separation from Kṛṣṇa makes the whole world cry in sympathy and brings Vaiṣṇavas to the verge of death.

In the obvious sense, Kṛṣṇa is *nikhilātmā* in that He is "the soul of all beings," but in this verse the phrase *nikhilātmani* has another, confidential meaning. He is also *nikhilātmā* in that each *gopī* cherishes Him as her very life and soul (literally, "her entire self"), in a way that other devotees cannot imitate. No one loves Kṛṣṇa as unconditionally as do the *gopīs.*

*Mumukṣus,* renounced aspirants for liberation, fear material existence; and self-satisfied Vaiṣṇava devotees of the Lord, who are liberated souls (*muktas*), are free from such fear. And both, in their own ways, understand Kṛṣṇa to be the supreme goal and the supreme fruit of spiritual endeavors. The liberated Vaiṣṇavas and the aspirants for liberation who have the good fortune to get the mercy of those Vaiṣṇavas admire the love the *gopīs* have for Kṛṣṇa, but rarely do they attain it. Uddhava considers Himself to be in the same category — a sincere servant of Kṛṣṇa who can only admire the *gopīs' prema* from a distance.

But isn't Lord Brahmā, rather than the *gopīs,* the greatest of all Vaiṣṇavas? Since he is the original *guru* for the path of devotional service, isn't he superior to all aspirants for liberation and to all liberated devotees? He sits on the seat of highest sovereignty in this universe, and he is endowed with many excellences. If the *gopīs* are so exalted, then why didn't they accept births like his, in which they would have been worshiped by the whole world, rather than come to the earth as lowly cowherd women? Uddhava answers these questions by saying *kiṁ brahma-janmabhir ananta-kathā-rasasya.* The term *ananta-kathā* refers to topics about the unlimited Lords — Śrī Kṛṣṇa and Śrī Balarāma. Uddhava simply states that a *rasika-bhakta,* a person who has a taste for hearing *ananta-kathā,* sees no use in being born as Lord Brahmā, even numerous times. Such *rasika-bhaktas* regard birth as Brahmā as an obstacle to cultivating the taste for *ananta-kathā* because such a birth creates various distractions, such as pride. Therefore the *gopīs,* intent on tasting the honey found at Śrī Govinda's lotus feet, would rather be born as simple daughters of cowherds than as such an exalted being as Lord Brahmā.

Alternatively, the rules of Sanskrit grammar allow *kathā-rasasya* to be split as *kathā-arasasya,* meaning "for one who has no taste for hearing these topics." If someone has no interest in *ananta-kathā,* what can he gain by taking birth as the creator of the universe? Nothing of real value. Attraction to *ananta-kathā* is the real fruit of renunciation, liberation, and devotional practice. Thus a person who lacks this taste cannot honestly be called a renunciant, a liberated sage, or a Vaiṣṇava.

Another way of looking at Uddhava's words is that he is explaining why the *gopīs,* though on the highest level of self-realization, chose to abandon the norms of civilized behavior, the principles of *dharma* taught in the *Vedas.* In this context, *brahma-janma* can be interpreted to mean "the appearance of Vedic knowledge within." For the *gopīs,* or indeed for anyone who has a taste for the topics of the unlimited Lord, the presence of Vedic knowledge on the lips and in the heart is less important than attraction to *kṛṣṇa-kathā.*

*Brahma* can also be taken to signify "knowledge of the pure self," and *janma* to signify "the means to generate this knowledge," namely the *Vedas.* In other words, a person who has realized *ananta-kathā-rasa* has nothing to gain by Vedic study or theoretical knowledge that he is spirit distinct from matter. And to a person who has no *ananta-kathā-rasa,* of what use is Vedic study or knowledge of the self? *Ananta-kathā-rasa* is the only substantial result to be gained from studying the *Vedas* and inquiring into the identity of the self. Vedic study and self-realization are only means toward that final goal. Once one has reached the goal, one can put aside the means by which one got there, just as a person who has lit a lamp to find something in his room before going to sleep can put out the lamp and lay down to rest once he has found what he was looking for, or just as one who has paid to take a boat across a river can forget about the boat after crossing. And, conversely, when a person never attains the goal but remains stubbornly attached to the means, all he accomplishes is useless effort, as in beating empty husks of grain.

A devotee situated in *ananta-kathā-rasa* is therefore a superior person. Whether practicing the regulations of *vaidhī-bhakti* or helplessly submerged in the ocean of *rasa,* he can never give up hearing and chanting about Kṛṣṇa, and doing whatever promotes that hearing and chanting. What to speak, then, of the *gopīs,* those most fortunate of all women, who have the rarest quality of love for Śrī Govinda? For them, ordinary Vedic cultural standards and the dry realizations of selfish meditation are of no value whatsoever.

## TEXT 148

क्वेमाः स्त्रियो वनचरीर्व्यभिचारदुष्टाः
कृष्णे क्व चैष परमात्मनि रूढभावः ।
नन्वीश्वरोऽनुभजतोऽविदुषोऽपि साक्षाच्
छ्रेयस्तनोत्यगदराज इवोपयुक्तः ॥

*kvemāḥ striyo vana-carīr vyabhicāra-duṣṭāḥ*
*kṛṣṇe kva caiṣa paramātmani rūḍha-bhāvaḥ*

*nanv īśvaro 'nubhajato 'viduṣo 'pi sākṣāc*
*chreyas tanoty agada-rāja ivopayuktaḥ*

*kva* — where, in comparison; *imāḥ* — these; *striyaḥ* — women; *vana* — in the forests; *carīḥ* — who wander; *vyabhicāra* — by wayward behavior; *duṣṭāḥ* — contaminated; *kṛṣṇe* — for Kṛṣṇa; *kva ca* — and where; *eṣaḥ* — this; *parama-ātmani* — for the Supreme Soul; *rūḍha-bhāvaḥ* — stage of perfect love (known technically as *mahā-bhāva*); *nanu* — certainly; *īśvaraḥ* — the Personality of Godhead; *anubhajataḥ* — to one who constantly worships Him; *aviduṣaḥ* — not learned; *api* — even though; *sākṣāt* — directly; *śreyaḥ* — the highest good; *tanoti* — bestows; *agada* — of medicines; *rājaḥ* — the king (namely, the nectar which the demigods drink for long life); *iva* — as if; *upayuktaḥ* — taken.

**"How amazing it is that these simple women who wander about the forest, seemingly spoiled by wayward behavior, have achieved the perfection of unalloyed love for Kṛṣṇa, the Supreme Soul! Indeed, it is true that the Supreme Lord Himself awards His blessings even to an ignorant worshiper, just as the best medicine works even when taken by a person ignorant of its ingredients.**

COMMENTARY: It is obviously with irony that Uddhava speaks these words. He considers himself unqualified to have the company of the *gopīs,* which he has achieved only by the undeserved mercy of the Supreme Personality of Godhead, Śrī Kṛṣṇa. Contrasting himself with the *gopīs,* Uddhava thinks that they are Kṛṣṇa's dearmost devotees whereas he has deviated in so many ways from the path of devotion: he has committed serious *aparādhas,* refused to carry out Kṛṣṇa's instructions, and failed to develop confidence in the process of *bhakti-yoga.* According to him, compared to the *gopīs* he is especially fallen.

The *gopīs* are "roamers of the forest." In other words, their intense love for Kṛṣṇa impels them to wander about the Vṛndāvana forest, where so many of His pastimes took place. And in the agony of separation from Kṛṣṇa they live in the most secluded part of the Vṛndāvana forest, where they wander about in the impassable wilderness. These transcendental goddesses of fortune in Śrī Nanda's cowherd community are now totally helpless under the sway of their incomparable *prema.*

Uddhava's life is nothing like that of the *gopīs:* He is male and lives in a bustling metropolis, where his residence is fixed; he enjoys all comforts and is therefore unfit to wander about the Vṛndāvana forest; he is proud of knowing philosophically who Kṛṣṇa is and so cannot gain the topmost treasure, the *gopīs'* love for Kṛṣṇa. Thus Uddhava judges himself a most fallen wretch compared with the *gopīs,* whose saintly qualities are inexhaustible. He thinks he will never deserve their association.

Uddhava refers to himself in the plural (*duṣṭāḥ*) either because of the honor he gained by the slight association he had with the *gopīs* in Vṛndāvana or else because he speaks on behalf of Śrī Nārada and Akrūra also. He does not refer to the *gopīs* directly but simply calls them "these women" (*imāḥ*), thus indicating the awe he feels in their presence. Certainly nowhere but in the hearts of the *gopīs* can such elevated pure love for Kṛṣṇa be seen. And certainly, Uddhava thinks, only by the special power of devotional service to Kṛṣṇa could such a foolish person as himself have had the privilege of witnessing the glories of the *gopīs.*

Kṛṣṇa is *īśvara,* the independent supreme controller, free to give suitable rewards for any service done for Him. He can reciprocate with His devotees however He wishes. He can shower His kindness even on an ignorant person who knows nothing of His greatness and the greatness of His servants, a person who sees devotees and devotional service with material vision but who somehow has rendered a little service to one of His devotees. If any person, by approaching Kṛṣṇa's devotee, takes even a slight step toward accepting service to Kṛṣṇa, Kṛṣṇa at once reciprocates with all kinds of assistance and blessings. Just as a powerful medicine is effective even on patients completely ignorant of its properties, the Lord's mercy acts on anyone who comes in touch with Him.

The word *nanu* ("certainly") can alternatively be understood as two separate words, *na* ("not") and *nu* ("indeed"). Indeed, because Kṛṣṇa is the Supreme Personality of Godhead, whatever He wants to do He can, and whatever He does not want to do He can refrain from. Or He can transform reality; in other words, He can undo any situation to change it to whatever He prefers. He has unlimited, all-powerful energies, by which He fulfills all His desires. Thus He can award the highest perfection of life to anyone — to the wise saint who worships Him constantly without deviation (*anubhajataḥ*), to someone who has worshiped Him irregularly (*na anubhajataḥ*), or even to someone who has never worshiped Him but has by some good fortune or other come in touch with His devotees. And if Kṛṣṇa wants, He can award this causeless mercy without delay (*sākṣāc chreyas tanoti*). He can make His mercy visible to all, not just a select few. He can make His mercy so obvious that one need not search for it by speculative philosophical conjectures. Kṛṣṇa's mercy thus acts like a rare, most potent medicine, effective even if not swallowed and digested but merely brought near the patient and smelled.

## TEXT 149

नायं श्रियोऽङ्ग उ नितान्तरतेः प्रसादः
स्वर्योषितां नलिनगन्धरुचां कुतोऽन्याः ।
रासोत्सवेऽस्य भुजदण्डगृहीतकण्ठ-
लब्धाशिषां य उदगाद् व्रजसुन्दरीणाम् ॥

*nāyaṁ śriyo 'ṅga u nitānta-rateḥ prasādaḥ*
*svar-yoṣitāṁ nalina-gandha-rucāṁ kuto 'nyāḥ*
*rāsotsave 'sya bhuja-daṇḍa-gṛhīta-kaṇṭha-*
*labdhāśiṣāṁ ya udagād vraja-sundarīṇām*

*na* — not; *ayam* — this; *śriyaḥ* — for the goddess of fortune; *aṅge* — on the chest; *u* — alas; *nitānta-rateḥ* — who is very intimately related; *prasādaḥ* — the favor; *svaḥ* — of the heavenly planets; *yoṣitām* — for the women; *nalina* — of the lotus flower;

*gandha* — having the aroma; *rucām* — and bodily luster; *kutaḥ* — much less; *anyāḥ* — others; *rāsa-utsave* — in the festival of the *rāsa* dance; *asya* — of Lord Śrī Kṛṣṇa; *bhuja-daṇḍa* — by the arms; *gṛhīta* — embraced; *kaṇṭha* — their necks; *labdha-āśiṣām* — who achieved such a blessing; *yaḥ* — which; *udagāt* — became manifest; *vraja-sundarīṇām* — for the beautiful *gopīs,* the transcendental girls of Vraja-bhūmi.

**"When Lord Śrī Kṛṣṇa was dancing with the beautiful gopīs of Vraja in the rāsa-līlā, the gopīs were embraced by the arms of the Lord. This transcendental favor was never bestowed upon the goddess of fortune or other consorts in the spiritual world. Indeed, never was such a thing even imagined by the most beautiful girls in the heavenly planets, girls whose bodily luster and aroma resemble the beauty and fragrance of the lotus. And what to speak of worldly women who are very beautiful by mundane estimation?**

COMMENTARY: Uddhava is astonished that although Mahā-lakṣmī, the consort of Lord Nārāyaṇa, is famous as His beloved, she cannot enjoy the Supreme Lord's favor in the same way as the *gopīs* of Vraja. If the supreme goddess of fortune is less fortunate than these *gopīs,* what can be said of everyone else?

This verse has already been explained by Śrī Nārada Muni in an earlier chapter of *Śrī Bṛhad-bhāgavatāmṛta* (2.5.189–191).

TEXT 150

आसामहो चरणरेणुजुषामहं स्यां
वृन्दावने किमपि गुल्मलतौषधीनाम् ।
या दुस्त्यजं स्वजनमार्यपथं च हित्वा
भेजुर्मुकुन्दपदवीं श्रुतिभिर्विमृग्याम् ॥

*āsām aho caraṇa-reṇu-juṣām ahaṁ syāṁ*
*vṛndāvane kim api gulma-latauṣadhīnām*

*yā dustyajaṁ sva-janam ārya-pathaṁ ca hitvā*
*bhejur mukunda-padavīṁ śrutibhir vimṛgyām*

*āsām* — of the *gopīs; aho* — oh; *caraṇa-reṇu* — the dust of the lotus feet; *juṣām* — who are devoted to; *aham syām* — let me become; *vṛndāvane* — in Vṛndāvana; *kim api* — any one; *gulma-latā-oṣadhīnām* — among the bushes, creepers, and herbs; *yāḥ* — (the *gopīs*) who; *dustyajam* — very difficult to give up; *sva-janam* — family members; *ārya-patham* — the civilized path of chastity; *ca* — and; *hitvā* — giving up; *bhejuḥ* — worshiped; *mukunda-padavīm* — the lotus feet of Mukunda, Kṛṣṇa; *śrutibhiḥ* — by the *Vedas; vimṛgyām* — which are to be searched for.

**"The gopīs of Vṛndāvana have given up the association of their husbands, sons, and other family members, who are very difficult to give up, and have forsaken the path of chastity, to take shelter of the lotus feet of Mukunda, Kṛṣṇa, which one should search for by Vedic knowledge. Oh, let me be so fortunate as to be one of the bushes, creepers, or herbs in Vṛndāvana, because the gopīs trample them and bless them with the dust of their lotus feet.**

COMMENTARY: By observing the glories of the *gopīs,* by describing those glories in his own words, and by meeting the *gopīs* in person, Uddhava is now completely absorbed in the *gopīs'* special mood of loving Kṛṣṇa. In this exalted state, he has now discovered his true heart's desire, which in this verse he prays to achieve as the final fruit of all the service he has done for Kṛṣṇa. In his next life, he hopes to become any of the plants in Vṛndāvana who receive the dust from the *gopīs'* feet.

The enthusiasm Uddhava gains from expressing this wish inspires him to say more about the greatness of the *gopīs.* For the service of Śrī Mukunda's lotus feet, the *gopīs* have abandoned things impossible for young women to give up — husbands, children, and other relatives, and the Vedic standards of behavior. Casting aside everything ordinarily precious, they have chosen to devote themselves utterly to *mukunda-padavīm,* the lotus feet of Kṛṣṇa. Or, understanding *padavīm* in its more literal sense of "footpath," every day the *gopīs* eagerly go out, morning and evening, to watch the path Kṛṣṇa will use to go to the forest and return. Or else *mukunda-padavīm* is the spiritual path of *bhakti-yoga.* The *gopīs* have abandoned their families and religious principles just to engage in Kṛṣṇa's service, even without expecting to obtain Him. For such unique surrender, they should be acknowledged as supremely glorious.

But why have these *gopīs,* whose feet are worshiped by all respectable persons, set a bad example by abandoning the noble life of dedication to their husbands and fathers? Why have they defied the authority of the *Vedas* in that way? Uddhava answers that the *Vedas* themselves consider devotional service to Kṛṣṇa the most important goal in life and aspire for the service of Śrī Mukunda's lotus feet. The word *vimṛgyām* indicates that the *Vedas* can only strive to achieve the *prema* of the *gopīs,* not achieve it. Therefore, even though the *Vedas* are the teachers of all principles of religion and spiritual knowledge, it is perfectly fitting that the *gopīs* take no heed of Vedic authority and in fact abandon the Vedic principles for the sake of obtaining the most precious thing — something the *Vedas* themselves can hardly obtain. Indeed, for the *gopīs* to observe the religious principles upon which their families insist would only prevent the *gopīs* from properly worshiping the lotus feet of Mukunda.

On this matter, Lord Kṛṣṇa has given His own opinion:

*trai-guṇya-viṣayā vedā*
*nistrai-guṇyo bhavārjuna*

"The *Vedas* deal mainly with the subject of the three modes of material nature. O Arjuna, become transcendental to those three modes." (*Bhagavad-gītā* 2.45) And here in *Bṛhad-bhāgavatāmṛta* we have just read, in Text 147, Uddhava's own words from *Śrīmad-Bhāgavatam* (10.47.58), *kiṁ brahma-janmabhir ananta-kathā-rasasya:* "For one who has tasted the narrations of the infinite Lord, what is the use of taking birth as a high-class *brāhmaṇa,* or even as Lord Brahmā himself?" In other words, any real attraction to the topics of Lord Ananta exempts one from having to follow the Vedic injunctions that regulate thought and behavior. The *gopīs,* moreover, have earned this exemption even more certainly than have others because the only desire the *gopīs* have is to follow the path of their beloved Mukunda.

Alternatively, Uddhava's statement may be understood as his answer to another doubt. The *Vedas,* the *śrutis,* are the supreme object of reverence even for Brahmā and the other demigods, who receive their knowledge from the *Vedas.* This we hear from the very words of the *śrutis* themselves. How then are the *gopīs* justified in disregarding the Vedic instructions? In response to this query, Uddhava says that the scope of Vedic authority is limited to the field of ordinary religious life whereas the *gopīs* have completely transcended that jurisdiction by taking exclusive shelter of Kṛṣṇa. The *Vedas* can merely seek Kṛṣṇa, but the *gopīs* already possess Him. In the opinion of some authorities, the *Upaniṣads* earned the right to become *gopīs* out of intense hankering to worship Kṛṣṇa in the *gopīs'* special mode of *prema.* But this should be rejected as an untenable theory. Why? Because the *Upaniṣads* are inferior in devotion even to the goddess Lakṣmī. Thus the *Upaniṣads,* on their own merit, do not deserve the good fortune of becoming *gopīs.* Only on the strength of Kṛṣṇa's special mercy could any of them ever attain that perfection.

## TEXT 151

या वै श्रियार्चितमजादिभिराप्तकामैर्
योगेश्वरैरपि सदात्मनि रासगोष्ठ्याम् ।
कृष्णस्य तद्भगवतः प्रपदारविन्दं
न्यस्तं स्तनेषु विजहुः परिरभ्य तापम् ॥

*yā vai śriyārcitam ajādibhir āpta-kāmair*
*yogeśvarair api sad-ātmani rāsa-goṣṭhyām*
*kṛṣṇasya tad bhagavataḥ prapadāravindaṁ*
*nyastaṁ staneṣu vijahuḥ parirabhya tāpam*

*yāḥ* — who (the *gopīs*); *vai* — indeed; *śriyā* — by the goddess of fortune; *arcitam* — worshiped; *aja* — by the unborn (Brahmā); *ādibhiḥ* — and other demigods; *āpta-kāmaiḥ* — who have already realized all desires; *yoga-īśvaraiḥ* — masters of mystic power; *api* — even though; *sat-ātmani* — in the pure mind; *rāsa* — of the *rāsa* dance; *goṣṭhyām* — in the gathering; *kṛṣṇasya* — of Lord Kṛṣṇa; *tat* — those; *bhagavataḥ* — of the Supreme Lord; *prapada-aravindam* — the tip of His lotus feet; *nyastam* — placed; *staneṣu* — on their breasts; *vijahuḥ* — they gave up; *parirabhya* — by embracing; *tāpam* — their torment.

**"Although the goddess of fortune herself and Lord Brahmā and all the other demigods have realized all their desires and are masters of yogic perfection, they can worship the lotus feet of Kṛṣṇa only within their purified minds. But during the rāsa dance Lord Kṛṣṇa placed His feet upon these gopīs' breasts, and by embracing those feet the gopīs gave up all sorrow.**

COMMENTARY: Aren't all devotees of Kṛṣṇa equally glorious for renouncing their families and whatever else prevents them from approaching Kṛṣṇa? Yes, but the intimacy of the *gopīs'* surrender makes them special. Kṛṣṇa's lotus feet are worshiped by the goddess of fortune with all the opulence at her command; she serves her Lord's feet by massaging them, and she attends Him in various other ways. Brahmā, Rudra, Indra, and other demigods also worship Kṛṣṇa's feet, and so do the *mahat-tattva* and the other elements of creation; the demigods and the elements over which the demigods preside worship Kṛṣṇa's feet by performing Vedic sacrifices and carrying out His orders. Self-satisfied liberated sages also worship with devotion those same feet, aiming at them as the supreme goal of life. The great masters of *bhakti-yoga* worship His lotus feet within their purified hearts by hearing and chanting Kṛṣṇa's glories with pure love. But the worship performed by all these elevated souls (with the exception of the goddess Lakṣmī) is for the most part only mental; rarely does

Kṛṣṇa grant His *darśana* to these demigods, sages, and devotees. The *gopīs'* worship of Kṛṣṇa's lotus feet is much more intimate.

The words *kṛṣṇasya tad bhagavataḥ* indicate this intimacy. The pronoun *tat* ("that") implies that even before the *rāsa* dance the *gopīs* were already intimately familiar with the supreme beauty of Kṛṣṇa's feet. And after Kṛṣṇa left the *gopīs* at the very beginning of the *rāsa-līlā,* they spent some time vividly remembering those very feet in the ecstasy of separation. Though these were the same lotus feet worshiped by Śrī, the goddess of fortune, the *gopīs* realized them in a special way, as the feet of the darling young son of Yaśodā and Nanda. The lotus feet the *gopīs* repeatedly held to their breasts during the *rāsa* dance were thus the most excellent embodiment of all beauty. By holding Kṛṣṇa's feet in this way, the *gopīs* were completely relieved of the pain of separation. Certainly, then, the *gopīs* are the greatest devotees, because they worshiped Kṛṣṇa's feet not merely by meditating on them but by holding them physically in their embrace. Because the feet they worshiped were the feet of the Supreme Lord in the form of Kṛṣṇa, the *gopīs* are superior to the demigods, headed by Brahmā. Because the *gopīs* touched those feet directly, the *gopīs* are superior to the self-satisfied sages. Because the *gopīs* held those feet to their breasts, the *gopīs* are superior to the masters of *yoga.* And because the association of the *gopīs* with Kṛṣṇa occurred during the *rāsa-līlā,* the *gopīs* are superior even to Mahā-lakṣmī.

As Uddhava describes how the *gopīs,* during the *rāsa* dance, obtained relief from the distress of separation, he harbors the concern that the feelings of separation the *gopīs* suffer now are much more serious. Now that Kṛṣṇa has left them to go to Mathurā, Uddhava doubts whether even a skillfully delivered message from Kṛṣṇa can do much to console them. Although Uddhava has done his best, the effect will most likely be negligible. But in any case, he himself has been deeply affected by his meeting with the *gopīs.* He has imbibed the spirit of their special *prema,* and in that mood he has prayed to take birth in Vraja in any form of life, be it a bush or other plant, that may be touched by the dust of the *gopīs'* divine feet. Because Uddhava could properly value and learn from the love of the *gopīs,* it was him Kṛṣṇa chose to carry the message to Vṛndāvana.

Like Uddhava, Śrīla Śukadeva Gosvāmī took to his own heart the *gopīs'* mood of devotion to Kṛṣṇa. At the end of the Tenth Canto, Śrīla Śukadeva expresses this mood when he praises Kṛṣṇa's Dvārakā queens:

*yāḥ samparyacaran premṇā*
*pāda-saṁvāhanādibhiḥ*
*jagad-guruṁ bhartṛ-buddhyā*
*tāsāṁ kim varṇyate tapaḥ*

"How could one possibly describe the great austerities performed by these women who perfectly served Him, the spiritual master of the universe, in pure ecstatic love? Thinking of Him as their husband, they rendered such intimate services as massaging His feet." (*Bhāgavatam* 10.90.27) Even though Śrīla Śukadeva, while speaking this verse, uses the term *bhartṛ* ("husband") rather than *jāra* ("paramour"), he is actually thinking of the *gopīs* of Vraja and burning in the fire of their ecstasy. But he dares not mention this, out of fear that in ecstasy he would lose his self-control.

Even in modern times, and even among men, there are great devotees who are known to have attained pure love for Kṛṣṇa in the mood of the *gopīs.* No one should doubt this, thinking that for male devotees the mood of the *gopīs* is incompatible. Anyone well versed in the epics and *Purāṇas* will know the example of the austere sages of the Daṇḍaka forest. When the sages saw the beauty of Śrī Raghunātha (Lord Rāmacandra), they became attracted in the conjugal mood and wanted to enjoy having Him as their husband. In the *Uttara-khaṇḍa* of *Śrī Padma Purāṇa,* Lord Śiva, speaking to his wife Pārvatī, describes that history:

*dṛṣṭvā rāmaṁ hariṁ tatra*
*bhoktum aicchan su-vigraham*
*te sarve strītvam āpannāḥ*
*samudbhūtāś ca gokule*

*hariḥ samprāpya kāmena*
*tato muktā bhavārṇavāt*

"When they saw Lord Hari in the beautiful form of Rāmacandra, they at once wanted to enjoy Him. Thus they all took birth as women in Gokula and, by their lusty attraction to Lord Hari, obtained Him as their husband. In this way they gained liberation from the ocean of material existence."

The *Kūrma Mahā-purāṇa* also states:

*agni-putrā mahātmānas*
*tapasā strītvam āpire*
*bhartāraṁ ca jagad-yoniṁ*
*vāsudevam ajaṁ vibhum*

"By performing austerities, the wise sons of Agni took birth as women and obtained as their husband Lord Vāsudeva, the unborn and unlimited source of creation."

TEXT 152

वन्दे नन्दव्रजस्त्रीणां पादरेणुमभीक्ष्णशः ।
यासां हरिकथोद्गीतं पुनाति भुवनत्रयम् ॥

*vande nanda-vraja-strīṇāṁ*
*pāda-reṇum abhīkṣṇaśaḥ*
*yāsāṁ hari-kathodgītaṁ*
*punāti bhuvana-trayam*

*vande* — I offer my respects; *nanda-vraja* — of the cowherd village of Nanda Mahārāja; *strīṇām* — of the women; *pāda* — of the feet; *reṇum* — to the dust; *abhīkṣṇaśaḥ* — perpetually; *yāsām* — whose; *hari* — of Lord Kṛṣṇa; *kathā* — about the topics; *udgītam* — loud chanting; *punāti* — purifies; *bhuvana-trayam* — the three worlds.

**"Again and again I offer my respects to the dust from the feet of the women of Nanda Mahārāja's cowherd village.**

**When these gopīs loudly chant the glories of Śrī Kṛṣṇa, the vibration purifies the three worlds."**

COMMENTARY: After thus taking great satisfaction from sweetly singing the glories of the *gopīs,* Uddhava falls flat on the ground, on the very path their lotus feet have touched. Picking up a speck of dust from the path, he places it on his head as if it were the rarest treasure in the universe. And after offering again his prostrate obeisance, he recites this final prayer.

Uddhava is absorbed in ecstasy, so much so that even though he can see the *gopīs,* he speaks and offers homage to them with deep reverence as if they were not present. Obviously, he feels sublime pleasure in chanting their glories. The most ecstatic kind of *saṅkīrtana,* however, is that chanted by the *gopīs* themselves; their loud songs purify all the worlds, including the upper, lower, and middle planetary systems. Śrī Śukadeva Gosvāmī has described this earlier in his narration of Uddhava's visit to Vṛndāvana:

*udgāyatīnām aravinda-locanaṁ*
*vrajāṅganānāṁ divam aspṛśad dhvaniḥ*
*dadhnaś ca nirmanthana-śabda-miśrito*
*nirasyate yena diśām amaṅgalam*

"As the ladies of Vraja loudly sang the glories of lotus-eyed Kṛṣṇa, their songs blended with the sound of their churning, ascended to the sky, and dissipated everything inauspicious in every direction." (*Bhāgavatam* 10.46.46)

Uddhava also implies that any suitable praise of the *gopīs,* such as the prayers he has just sung, is in fact the most excellent form of *hari-kathā*. Such glorification can easily purify the three worlds, as Uddhava hoped to do by speaking these verses.

TEXT 153

गोप्यः किमाचरदयं कुशलं स्म वेणुर्
दामोदराधरसुधामपि गोपिकानाम् ।

भुङ्क्ते स्वयं यदवशिष्टरसं ह्रदिन्यो
हृष्यत्त्वचोऽश्रु मुमुचुस्तरवो यथार्याः ॥

*gopyaḥ kim ācarad ayaṁ kuśalaṁ sma veṇur*
*dāmodarādhara-sudhām api gopikānām*
*bhuṅkte svayaṁ yad avaśiṣṭa-rasaṁ hradinyo*
*hṛṣyat-tvaco 'śru mumucus taravo yathāryāḥ*

*gopyaḥ* — O *gopīs; kim* — what; *ācarat* — performed; *ayam* — this; *kuśalam* — auspicious activities; *sma* — certainly; *veṇuḥ* — flute; *dāmodara* — of Kṛṣṇa; *adhara-sudhām* — the nectar of the lips; *api* — even; *gopikānām* — which is owed to the *gopīs; bhuṅkte* — enjoys; *svayam* — independently; *yat* — from which; *avaśiṣṭa* — remaining; *rasam* — the taste only; *hradinyaḥ* — the rivers; *hṛṣyat* — feeling jubilant; *tvacaḥ* — whose bodies; *aśru* — tears; *mumucuḥ* — shed; *taravaḥ* — the trees; *yathā* — exactly like; *āryāḥ* — old forefathers.

**"My dear gopīs, what auspicious activities must the flute have performed to enjoy the nectar of Kṛṣṇa's lips independently and leave only a taste for us gopīs, for whom that nectar is actually meant! The forefathers of the flute, the bamboo trees, shed tears of pleasure. His mother, the river on whose bank the bamboo was born, feels jubilation, and therefore her blooming lotus flowers are standing like hair on her body."**

COMMENTARY: Now that Parīkṣit Mahārāja has sung the praises of the young *gopīs* of Vraja, he turns his attention to the most excellent of those *gopīs,* the blessed Śrī Rādhā, whose ecstatic love for Kṛṣṇa is so deep that mere words cannot do it justice. King Parīkṣit remembers how Śrīmatī Rādhārāṇī constantly hankers to drink the nectar of Śrī Kṛṣṇa's lips, so much so that when She hears Kṛṣṇa's flute-song from a distance as He enters the Vṛndāvana forest She imagines the flute to be tasting that nectar as it touches His lips. Thinking like that, She begins to envy the flute as if it were a rival lover. As Her girlfriends stand and talk about Kṛṣṇa, Śrīmatī Rādhādevī then interjects this comment of Her own (*Bhāgavatam* 10.21.9), which Parīkṣit Mahārāja now chooses to recite.

Śrī Rādhā, addressing Her friends, headed by Lalitā, asks what good deeds this flute, this lifeless piece of wood, could have done to earn the blessing of enjoying the nectar from Kṛṣṇa's lips? If She could find out what the flute has done, the *gopīs* could also do it and obtain the same favor. After all, the nectar of Kṛṣṇa's lips belongs to them, not the flute. Śrī Rādhikā doesn't specifically say that the nectar is "theirs to enjoy," but says only that the nectar is "theirs," because She feels too shy to speak so explicitly. The flute may have the right to rest in the hand of his master, Dāmodara, or be held to Dāmodara's chest or even His lips, but when that flute dares drink as much as he likes of the intoxicating nectar of Kṛṣṇa's lips, that flute is being too bold. Because Śrī Rādhā and Her friends are members of the cowherd community and therefore have a close relationship with Kṛṣṇa, they can claim ownership of the nectar from Kṛṣṇa's lips. The flute is an outsider. If he continues the audacity of drinking this nectar, the *gopīs* will have to steal him and take him to some secret place for safekeeping. Otherwise the flute will take all the nectar himself, leaving only the remnants of its fragrance for the *gopīs*.

The rivers are like the flute's mothers because their milklike water enabled the flute to grow to his present size. When the rivers contemplate the success of their son, the groves of lotuses growing in their waters bloom, like hair on their bodies standing jubilantly erect. And the bamboo trees in whose family the flute was born are so proud of him that they shed a downpour of ecstatic tears in the form of sweet sap. Their skin erupts in goose bumps, and they cry profusely, like venerable elders of a clan who see one of their children become a servant of the Personality of Godhead.

The phrase *avaśiṣṭa-rasam* has several possible meanings. One is that the flute enjoys all the nectar of Kṛṣṇa's lips, leaving not a drop for anyone else. Another is that as much as the flute drinks, his thirst (*rasa* or *rāga*) remains unquenched, and being frustrated he cannot stop drinking more and more. A third meaning is that the *gopīs,* having rejected all material tastes (*rasa*) and having thus lost all interest in sense gratification in this life and the next, are attracted only to the taste of the nectar from Kṛṣṇa's lips — and the flute, knowing this well, still deprives them of that nectar by drinking it himself.

A more complex explanation of *avaśiṣṭa-rasam* may be understood as follows. How fortunate this flute must be! The Yamunā and the other rivers of Vraja, who purify all the worlds by providing arrangements for bathing and other auspicious activities, are satisfied to partake of the mere remnants of nectar that Kṛṣṇa's flute has left behind as dry pulp. Connoisseurs of devotional poetry know very well how the rivers of Vraja, during the water sports enjoyed by Kṛṣṇa and the *gopīs,* obtain some of the nectar from Kṛṣṇa's lips (*adharāmṛta*). Or perhaps only one of the rivers, Śrī Kālindī-devī (Yamunā), is allowed to drink that *adharāmṛta* directly, and the other rivers in Śrī Vṛndāvana-dhāma receive remnants from her, an opportunity they have earned by residing in the abode of Kṛṣṇa's pastimes. After tasting even the smallest drop of the nectar that remains, all the rivers feel transcendental bliss, and their bodily hairs stand on end. And since the rivers become ecstatic just to have a drop of that nectar, how pious must be Kṛṣṇa's flute to be able to drink as much as he wants.

By providing shade and fruits for everyone, the *pippala* and other trees on the banks of Vraja's rivers are like the elders of a noble family who perform auspicious service for others. Those trees cry unhappy tears because they cannot receive the nectar from Kṛṣṇa's lips. We may wonder why the trees cannot share this nectar or may doubt whether trees should be crying in disappointment when they don't receive it. After all, a beggar may be sorry to have nothing to eat, but he shouldn't lament that he can't rule a kingdom. This doubt is dispelled by knowledge that the trees of Vraja are Āryans, great saints. As exalted devotees of Śrī Kṛṣṇa, the trees are moved to tears by sadness when they don't obtain Kṛṣṇa's *adharāmṛta,* even though they have no right to claim it. Or, taking another meaning of the word *āryāḥ,* the ones crying in frustration are the mothers-in-law and other respectable elders of Śrī Rādhā.

## TEXT 154

जयति जननिवासो देवकीजन्मवादो
यदुवरपरिषत्स्वैर्दोर्भिरस्यन्नधर्मम् ।
स्थिरचरवृजिनघ्नः सुस्मितश्रीमुखेन
व्रजपुरवनितानां वर्धयन्कामदेवम् ॥

*jayati jana-nivāso devakī-janma-vādo*
*yadu-vara-pariṣat svair dorbhir asyann adharmam*
*sthira-cara-vṛjina-ghnaḥ su-smita-śrī-mukhena*
*vraja-pura-vanitānāṁ vardhayan kāma-devam*

*jayati* — eternally lives gloriously; *jana-nivāsaḥ* — He who lives among human beings and is the ultimate resort of all living entities; *devakī-janma-vādaḥ* — known as the son of Devakī; *yadu-vara-pariṣat* — served by the exalted members of the Yadu dynasty; *svaiḥ dorbhiḥ* — by His own arms; *asyan* — expelling; *adharmam* — irreligion; *sthira-cara* — of all living entities, moving and not moving; *vṛjina-ghnaḥ* — the destroyer of all the ill fortune; *su-smita* — always smiling; *śrī-mukhena* — by His beautiful face; *vraja-pura-vanitānām* — of the damsels of Vṛndāvana; *vardhayan* — increasing; *kāma-devam* — the lusty desires.

**"Lord Śrī Kṛṣṇa, the ultimate resort of all living entities, is also known as Devakī-nandana or Yaśodā-nandana, the son of Devakī and Yaśodā. He is the guide of the Yadu dynasty, and with His mighty arms He kills everything inauspicious, and every man who is impious. By His presence He destroys all misfortune for all living entities, moving and inert. His blissful smiling face always increases the lusty desires of the gopīs of Vṛndāvana. May He be all glorious and happy!"**

COMMENTARY: Śrī Parīkṣit Mahārāja recited several verses of *Śrīmad-Bhāgavatam* to glorify, generally and specifically, the residents of Gokula. Now, to conclude properly and invoke auspiciousness, he glorifies the supremacy of the Personality of Godhead by again repeating the words of his own spiritual master, Śukadeva Gosvāmī. Just as Agastya Ṛṣi drank from his palm the entire salt ocean, the divine Śukadeva spoke this verse in an effort to drink from his own palm the entire ocean of Śrī Kṛṣṇa's pastimes described in the *Bhāgavatam's* Tenth Canto. Śrīla Śukadeva places this verse (10.90.48) near the very end of the canto as a complete synopsis of the pastimes discussed in several thousand verses. The verse that immediately precedes this in the *Bhāgavatam* mentioned Kṛṣṇa explicitly, and Kṛṣṇa's glories are the focus of this part of Śukadeva's narrative. Thus even though the present verse does not mention Kṛṣṇa by name, it is obviously about Him. Just as Parīkṣit Mahārāja sang the praises of different Vraja-vāsīs in order of their relative importance, Śukadeva here tells of six special aspects of Śrī Kṛṣṇa's super-excellence, in order of increasing importance.

First, Kṛṣṇa is the *nivāsa* — the residence, shelter, and foundation — of all living beings. He also resides as the Supersoul within their hearts. And He is manifest externally, especially among His *janas,* or favorite devotees, in the forms of His numerous incarnations. Thus He is the Supreme Brahman, the Supreme Ātmā, the Lord of all, the seed of all *avatāras.*

Second, Kṛṣṇa displayed the extreme limit of His manifold opulence in the respectful words He spoke to His father and mother at the time of His birth, when He described the reason for His birth as their son and His desire to be carried to Gokula. By this unprecedented revelation of the purpose of His descent, He proved Himself the most generous bestower of benedictions and the most compassionate protector of His parents. And by ordering Vasudeva to carry Him to Gokula, Kṛṣṇa showed His intention to distribute far and wide the most precious treasure of *prema.*

Third, by having the most excellent Yadus as His companions and servants, Kṛṣṇa further demonstrates the supreme opulence of His appearance. As Śrī Yādavendra, Kṛṣṇa puts to an end the distress of His dear servants the Yadus and secures their happiness by killing wicked enemies of their clan, like Kaṁsa and Jarāsandha. Thus He shows His absolute concern for His devotees. The phrase *yadu-vara-pariṣat* indicates that Kṛṣṇa is served by the exalted members of the Yadu dynasty. Or, since the word *pariṣat* carries the meaning "assembly," we can understand the phrase to mean that Kṛṣṇa brought down to the earth the Sudharmā assembly hall of the demigods, making it the court of the king of the Yadus, Ugrasena. The Sudharmā hall is but one of many treasures of heaven, including the *pārijāta* tree, that Kṛṣṇa brought to the earth. Thus Kṛṣṇa, by defeating the demigods on several occasions, displayed His supreme power and opulence. And by giving the royal assembly hall to Ugrasena, the father of His archenemy Kaṁsa, the Lord displayed His causeless unequaled kindness.

Fourth, although Kṛṣṇa could have effortlessly done away with the causes of irreligion simply by using His supreme will, to create pleasurable pastimes for His devotees He killed the demonic opponents of religion by using His mighty arms, arms long, well developed, beautifully shaped, adorned with armlets and other ornaments, and bearing weapons like His Sudarśana disc. As described in *Śrī Hari-vaṁśa's* narration of Kṛṣṇa's battle with Bāṇāsura, when fighting such enemies Kṛṣṇa would sometimes, for the special delight of select devotees, manifest four arms instead of two. Therefore Śukadeva uses the plural form *dorbhiḥ* instead of the dual form *dorbhyām,* which is normally used to indicate only two arms. Or, understanding the word "arms" another way, devotees who assisted Kṛṣṇa, such as the Pāṇḍavas, acted as His arms. Kṛṣṇa used these *kṣatriyas,* originally born from His arms, to kill envious enemies and uproot the power of irreligion. Of course, Kṛṣṇa by His mere desire could have killed Jarāsandha and all the other wicked kings who opposed Him, but out of fatherly compassion He chose to share His fame with His devotees.

Fifth, while enjoying His pastimes in Gokula, Kṛṣṇa expanded the fullness of His loving devotional service. Although the pastimes Kṛṣṇa performed in Mathurā and Dvārakā occurred after His pastimes in Gokula, here they are mentioned in inverse order because Kṛṣṇa's excellences are most completely manifest in Gokula. Kṛṣṇa generously bestowed His *prema-bhakti* on all the residents of Vṛndāvana, including even the nonmoving beings, such as creepers, bushes, and trees, what to speak of the moving creatures, down to even the insects and microbes. Disregarding their lack of qualifications, He gave them the gift of loving devotion to Himself, which automatically destroys all the troubles of material existence.

Or, from another angle, just as the happiness available in heaven is an impediment for those who want liberation, the happiness of liberation is an impediment for those who want loving devotional service to Kṛṣṇa. That distressful obstacle — that so-called happiness — Kṛṣṇa effortlessly destroys for all the devotees spontaneously attracted to Him in Vṛndāvana and elsewhere in Vraja-bhūmi. Simply by expanding His *prema-bhakti* throughout Vraja-bhūmi, Kṛṣṇa delivers the moving and nonmoving residents of Vraja from the miseries of both material entanglement and impersonal liberation. Indeed, when Kṛṣṇa expanded the flood of love of God in Vraja, all moving and nonmoving living beings in the three worlds were relieved of the unhappiness of material existence. Just as a fire lit for the sake of cooking also dispels cold and darkness, the spread of *kṛṣṇa-bhakti* automatically freed all living beings from material miseries as a secondary result. In fact, when Kṛṣṇa descended to Gokula on earth, He freed all His devotees throughout the universe from attraction to liberation, which they may obtain as easily as *yogīs* obtain wonderful *siddhis.* This freedom was an automatic by-product of the unalloyed *prema* displayed in Vraja-bhūmi. But even though all devotees in the universe were thus freed, the devotees living in Vraja during Kṛṣṇa's pastimes gained the fullest relief from the dangers of liberation and material entanglement.

Finally, sixth, Kṛṣṇa most fully reveals His greatest glories — His fascinating beauty, charm, and cleverness — in His pastimes with the young *gopīs* of Vraja. During Kṛṣṇa's presence Vraja-bhūmi becomes like an opulent city (*pura*), bustling with Kṛṣṇa's many different pastimes and romantic dalliances. Kṛṣṇa's lovely smiling face, decorated by His flute and various ornaments, enchants the women living in Vraja. The god of love, Kāmadeva, is called *deva* because he is brilliantly radiant (*dīvyati*). The beauty of Kṛṣṇa's face gives Kāmadeva unlimited power over the *gopīs,* a power that conquers the attractions of material life and transcends even the attraction of liberation.

Cupid is famous for spoiling the self-interests of everyone he influences, but for the *gopīs* of Vraja Cupid destroys the bonds of material existence. He helps the *gopīs* bring Śrī Kṛṣṇa under their control and assumes for them the forms of *mukti* and *bhakti.* Thus Cupid arranges for the *gopīs* to realize Kṛṣṇa in His full glory and enjoy His company as ever fresh at every moment.

Attraction to Kṛṣṇa in the mood of the *gopīs* may itself be called *kāma-deva* — the god of all love — because the most excellent form of desire is that which focuses unconditionally on the Supreme Personality of Godhead. Only such single-pointed desire evolves into the most exalted state of pure love.

The word *deva* also indicates the idea of play. Taken in that sense, it indicates that in pastimes of intimate enjoyment the beauty of Kṛṣṇa's face expands the play of Cupid among the *gopīs.* The beauty of Kṛṣṇa's face has a powerful effect on the *gopīs,* much to His delight. It makes them forget the four goals of life and raises them to the highest level of pure *prema,* which is the mature fruit of all devotional endeavors. In this way, Kṛṣṇa's smiling face represents the ultimate greatness of the Supreme Person — the magnificence of His charm, His beauty, and His expertise in loving affairs.

It is not without reason that Śukadeva Gosvāmī uses the word *vardhayan* ("increasing") in the present tense. It expresses the fact that Kṛṣṇa's pastimes go on eternally in Vraja-bhūmi. In *Śrīmad-Bhāgavatam* (10.44.13) the women of Mathurā also use the present tense to describe Kṛṣṇa's sporting in Vṛndāvana even after He has moved to Mathurā. *Vikrīḍayāñcati giritra-ramārcitāṅghriḥ:* "He whose feet are worshiped by Lord Śiva and the goddess Ramā is wandering about in Vṛndāvana, enacting His many pastimes." The fact of Kṛṣṇa's eternal presence in Vṛndāvana is upheld by many statements of scripture and by the personal experience of many unalloyed devotees. As stated in *Śrīmad-Bhāgavatam* (10.1.28), *mathurā bhagavān yatra nityaṁ sannihito hariḥ:* "Mathurā is very intimately connected with Kṛṣṇa, for Lord Kṛṣṇa lives there eternally."

The word *pura* suggests the city of Mathurā. And indeed Kṛṣṇa increases the influence of Cupid for both the women of Vraja and the women of Mathurā City. But the mention of the city more confidentially implies that when Kṛṣṇa goes away to Mathurā the *gopīs* become immersed in the agony of separation. It is then that they achieve the highest limit of *prema,* and therefore Śrīla Śukadeva, even while glorifying Kṛṣṇa's sports with the *gopīs* in Gokula, has alluded to His going to Mathurā.

In summary, the same Supersoul who resides in the hearts of all living beings took up residence in the womb of Devakī. As the Supersoul He is only the passive indwelling supervisor, but as the son of Devakī He speaks and reciprocates with her in many loving ways. The mighty heroes of the Yādava dynasty are the Supreme Lord's servants, and they are able to defeat all the forces of evil. Still, the Lord chooses to use His own two arms to kill opposing kings. He also destroys the sins and miseries of all moving and nonmoving creatures. But with the *gopīs* He acts in a seemingly contrary way. Although they are married to other men, He incites in them the influence of Cupid and becomes their paramour. Thus He only increases their shame and misery. The *gopīs* themselves are not at fault in this, because it is the beauty of Kṛṣṇa's face that causes their predicament.

By thus presenting so many alternative understandings, Śrīla Śukadeva Gosvāmī proves beyond any doubt the superexcellence of Kṛṣṇa and His wonderful qualities, such as His compassionate concern for His devotees.

## TEXT 155

श्रीजनमेजय उवाच
कृतार्थोऽस्मि कृतार्थोऽस्मि निश्चितो भगवन् गुरो ।
गुह्यं गोलोकमाहात्म्यं यदहं सेवितस्त्वया ॥

*śrī-janamejaya uvāca*
*kṛtārtho 'smi kṛtārtho 'smi*
*niścito bhagavan guro*
*guhyaṁ goloka-māhātmyaṁ*
*yad ahaṁ sevitas tvayā*

*śrī-janamejayaḥ uvāca* — Śrī Janamejaya said; *kṛta-arthaḥ* — all-successful; *asmi* — I am; *kṛta-arthaḥ* — all-successful; *asmi* — I am; *niścitaḥ* — undoubtedly; *bhagavan* — O lord; *guro* — O spiritual master; *guhyam* — the secret; *goloka* — of Goloka; *māhātmyam* — the glories; *yat* — because; *aham* — I; *sevitaḥ* — provided; *tvayā* — by you.

**Śrī Janamejaya said: I am all-successful! I am all-successful! For you, O lord, O spiritual master, have given me the opportunity to relish the secret glories of Goloka.**

COMMENTARY: King Janamejaya, having received from Jaimini Ṛṣi everything he asked, is fully satisfied. He repeats Himself — *kṛtārtho 'smi kṛtārtho 'smi* — out of extreme joy and the firm conviction that he has achieved his goal. Addressing Śrī Jaimini, he uses the word *bhagavan* because he reveres Jaimini, his *guru,* as equal to God and is grateful for the mercy Jaimini has shown him.

## TEXT 156

श्रीजैमिनिरुवाच
तातात्थ सत्यं यद्भक्त्या श्रवणादपि कीर्तनात् ।
अस्याख्यानस्य वा ध्यानात्तत्पदं लभते नरः ॥

*śrī-jaiminir uvāca*
*tātāttha satyaṁ yad bhaktyā*
*śravaṇād api kīrtanāt*
*asyākhyānasya vā dhyānāt*
*tat padaṁ labhate naraḥ*

*śrī-jaiminiḥ uvāca* — Śrī Jaimini said; *tāta* — dear boy; *āttha* — you say; *satyam* — true; *yat* — that which; *bhaktyā* — with devotion; *śravaṇāt* — by hearing; *api* — also; *kīrtanāt* — by chanting; *asya* — of this; *ākhyānasya* — narrative; *vā* — or; *dhyānāt* — by contemplation; *tat* — His; *padam* — abode; *labhate* — achieves; *naraḥ* — a person.

**Śrī Jaimini said: My dear boy, what you say is true. Anyone who hears or chants or meditates upon this narrative with devotion will achieve the abode of the Supreme.**

COMMENTARY: Śrī Jaimini is also very much satisfied to hear his disciple's words, filled as they are with the pure spirit of *prema*. From what Janamejaya has said, Śrī Jaimini can discern that this disciple has properly assimilated what he has heard. Thus Jaimini answers him affectionately, calling him *tāta* ("my dear boy").

Janamejaya was correct to say that now his life was successful, because he had listened carefully to Jaimini's narrative about the glories of Goloka. Simply by hearing or chanting this narrative with devotion, or thinking about it deeply, anyone can achieve that most inaccessible of divine abodes. And if one engages seriously in the regulative practice meant for attaining Goloka, then certainly one will achieve success.

Jaimini is confident, therefore, that the disciple has now fulfilled his goal in life by having heard these glories, and that he himself has fulfilled his own goal by having recited them. The auspicious fruits of hearing and chanting this narrative have thus been definitely assured.

## TEXT 157

तस्मै नमोऽस्तु निरुपाधिकृपाकुलाय
श्रीगोपराजतनयाय गुरूत्तमाय ।
यः कारयन्निजजनं स्वयमेव भक्तिं
तस्यातितुष्यति यथा परमोपकर्तुः ॥

*tasmai namo 'stu nirupādhi-kṛpākulāya*
*śrī-goparāja-tanayāya gurūttamāya*
*yaḥ kārayan nija-janaṁ svayam eva bhaktiṁ*
*tasyātituṣyati yathā paramopakartuḥ*

*tasmai* — to Him; *namaḥ* — obeisances; *astu* — let there be; *nirupādhi* — causeless; *kṛpā* — with compassion; *ākulāya* — who is agitated; *śrī-gopa-rāja* — of the blessed king of the cowherds; *tanayāya* — the son; *guru-uttamāya* — the highest *guru;* *yaḥ* — who; *kārayan* — causing; *nija-janam* — for His own devotee; *svayam* — on His own initiative (not considering the devotee's qualifications); *eva* — indeed; *bhaktim* — pure devotion; *tasya* — with him (the devotee); *atituṣyati* — He is extremely satisfied; *yathā* — as; *parama* — supreme; *upakartuḥ* — for a benefactor.

**Obeisances to Him, the son of the blessed king of the cowherds, who is always astir with causeless compassion, who on His own initiative impels His servant to develop devotion for Him, and who then becomes fully satisfied, as if His devotee were being very kind to Him.**

COMMENTARY: Coming to the end of his narration, Śrī Jaimini Ṛṣi remembers the supreme kindness of the Personality of Godhead and offers at His feet this entire effort. *Nirupādhi-kṛpākulāya* can be understood in two ways: Kṛṣṇa is full of many different kinds of causeless compassion (*kṛpā-kula*), or Kṛṣṇa, without any selfish motive, is always keen to do something beneficial (*kṛpā-ākula*). Śrī Jaimini calls Kṛṣṇa "the son of the king of the cowherds" either out of great respect or out of shyness. Since Jaimini now shares the mood of the *gopīs,* he is shy to mention Nanda Mahārāja, a respectable elder, by name.

Kṛṣṇa is the best of all spiritual instructors. Both internally as the Supersoul and externally as a Vaiṣṇava spiritual master, He bestows knowledge and everything else required for advancing on the path of devotional service. As Uddhava described to Kṛṣṇa in the Eleventh Canto (*Bhāgavatam* 11.29.6):

*naivopayanty apacitiṁ kavayas taveśa*
*brahmāyuṣāpi kṛtam ṛddha-mudaḥ smarantaḥ*
*yo 'ntar bahis tanu-bhṛtām aśubhaṁ vidhunvann*
*ācārya-caittya-vapuṣā sva-gatiṁ vyanakti*

"O my Lord! Transcendental poets and experts in spiritual science would not be able to fully express their indebtedness to You, even if they were endowed with the prolonged lifetime of Brahmā, for You appear in two features — externally as the *ācārya* and internally as the Supersoul — to deliver the embodied living being by directing him how to come to You."

Whatever Jaimini has spoken to Janamejaya, therefore, has been inspired by Kṛṣṇa, either directly or on the strength of instructions imparted by Kṛṣṇa's representative, the spiritual master. Thus it is fitting for Jaimini to offer the fruits of his labor to Kṛṣṇa, the Supreme Soul. Because Kṛṣṇa is the most compassionate friend of all living beings and is their original spiritual master, Kṛṣṇa, without regard for spiritual qualifications and abilities, tries to engage everyone in devotional service to Him. He tries to engage all the senses of everyone in devotional practices, beginning with hearing and chanting of His glories. And when He sees some positive response from a conditioned soul, Kṛṣṇa becomes extremely pleased. He then showers all favors on the candidate for His service. The gratitude is mutual: Just as people in general are satisfied with someone who significantly helps them, all of Kṛṣṇa's devotees are ever thankful to the Lord; and when Kṛṣṇa sees His devotees practicing devotional service, He considers them His most gracious benefactors.

To end the *Dig-darśinī* commentary on *Śrī Bṛhad-bhāgavatāmṛta,* Śrīla Sanātana Gosvāmī offers this prayer:

*svayaṁ pravartitaiḥ kṛtsnair*
*mamaital-likhana-śramaiḥ*
*śrīmac-caitanya-rūpo 'sau*
*bhagavān prīyatāṁ sadā*

"May the Supreme Lord in His form of Śrī Caitanya, who

personally made me take up the labor of this writing, be always pleased." The Lord renowned by the name Caitanya is *śrīmān,* the possessor of all divine opulences. He is Lord Kṛṣṇa Himself appearing as the son of Śacīdevī. Or *śrīmac-caitanya-rūpa* can refer to the most fortunate servant of Lord Caitanya, Śrīla Rūpa Gosvāmī. Describing Śrīla Rūpa Gosvāmī as *bhagavān* is appropriate according to this definition of the term:

*āyatiṁ niyatiṁ caiva*
*bhūtānām āgatāgatim*
*vetti vidyām avidyāṁ ca*
*sa vācyo bhagavān iti*

"One is called *bhagavān* who knows the future and fortune, the birth and rebirth, the ignorance and enlightenment, of all beings." Thus, both to the Lord and to that best of Vaiṣṇavas, Śrīla Rūpa Gosvāmī, Śrīla Sanātana offers his respects.

*Thus ends the seventh chapter of Part Two of Śrīla Sanātana Gosvāmī's Bṛhad-bhāgavatāmṛta, entitled "Jagad-ānanda: The Bliss of the Worlds."*

THUS ENDS PART TWO

This translation was completed at Śrī Puruṣottama-kṣetra on June 30, 1999, on the occasion of Lord Jagannātha's Snāna-yātrā.

# Appendixes

# *Expanded* TABLE *of* CONTENTS

## PART TWO
*Śrī-goloka-māhātmya*
The Glories of Goloka
(concluded)

### FIVE
### PREMA: *Love of* GOD

SIX

## ABHĪṢṬA-LĀBHA: *The* ATTAINMENT *of* ALL DESIRES

SEVEN

## JAGAD-ĀNANDA: *The* BLISS *of the* WORLDS

# *My own remarks* WITHIN *the* COMMENTARY

THE COMMENTARY GIVEN in this edition of *Śrī Bṛhad-bhāgavatāmṛta* closely follows that of Śrīla Sanātana Gosvāmī, variously summarizing his statements, paraphrasing them, or translating them word for word. In a few places, however, I have added remarks of my own. In Volume One those places are few and obvious. They especially occur where I praise Sanātana Gosvāmī, who obviously wouldn't write in praise of himself. In Volume Three (as in Volume Two) my comments are more numerous and not readily evident. This appendix, therefore, records what they are.

I first indicate the number of the chapter and verse being commented upon, then the paragraph in which my comments occur or begin, and finally the first words of my comments. A dash appears in the "paragraph starting" column when the commentary has only one paragraph.

Where I have indicated that the number of my own sentences includes or consists of ½, I am speaking phrasally, not mathematically. That is, the ½ indicates a clause.

Where the sentence just before my remarks seems a poor fit with the one that comes after, this is an artifact of writing and editing. Both sentences, after all, are meant to fit with the ones between them. Allow for this and the parts match.

For a further discussion of how my commentary derives from Śrīla Sanātana Gosvāmī's *Dig-darśinī-ṭīkā,* please see the first appendix in Volume One.

| VERSE | PARAGRAPH STARTING | TEXT STARTING | SENTENCES |
|---|---|---|---|
| 5.7 | — | Since the devotees | 1 |
| 5.24 | This Rohiṇī is | This Rohiṇī is | 1 |
| 5.29 | — | But He also wanted | 1 |

| | | | |
|---|---|---|---|
| 5.31 | — | Since Gopa-kumāra was | 1 |
| 5.40 | — | Still, they felt that | 1 |
| 5.42 | — | To him, more important | 1 |
| 5.43 | — | To maintain his | 1 |
| 5.45 | — | By the power of the | 1 |
| 5.46 | — | Being unable for even | 1 |
| 5.61 | — | Although time and space | ½ |
| 5.62 | — | Nārada had just told | 1 |
| 5.65 | — | The positions of | 1 |
| 5.72 | — | Since nouns in Sanskrit | ½ |
| 5.76 | After hearing what | In this prayer Vasudeva | 1 |
| 5.95 | — | The earthly Gokula | 1 |
| 5.99–100 | The great sages | The great sages | ½ |
| 5.99–100 | Yet other sages | Śrī Rūpa Gosvāmī, | 3 |
| 5.107 | When Mother Yaśodā | When Mother Yaśodā | 1 |
| 5.108 | Beauty is next | no one was able | ½ |
| 5.112 | Although Nārada here | Although Nārada here | 1 |
| 5.116 | After His miraculous | once while drinking | ½ |
| 5.122 | On what began | On what began | 1 |
| 5.122 | On what began | they were looking | ½ |
| 5.123 | In fact, Kṛṣṇa was | In fact, Kṛṣṇa was | 2 |
| 5.125 | Brahmā's defeat | Brahmā's defeat | ½ |
| 5.127 | Because the cowherd | Because the cowherd | 1 |
| 5.131 | — | Kṛṣṇa, defeated in | ½ |
| 5.133 | The most expert | The most expert | 1 |
| 5.133 | The *gopīs,* in their | The *gopīs,* in their | 1 |
| 5.133 | It was particularly | It was particularly | 1 |
| 5.135 | In the course of | In the course of | 1 |
| 5.136 | Kṛṣṇa's intention | Kṛṣṇa's intention | 1½ |
| 5.136 | Kṛṣṇa's miraculous | Kṛṣṇa's miraculous | 1 |
| 5.137 | — | Kṛṣṇa proved Himself | 1 |
| 5.140 | The sound of Kṛṣṇa's | The sound of Kṛṣṇa's | 1 |
| 5.140 | Glorifying Kṛṣṇa's | One can understand | 1 |
| 5.143 | Flying over the | and their wives | ½ |
| 5.147 | Nārada speaks of | affecting not only | ½ |
| 5.150 | — | but all the austerities | ½ |
| 5.152 | Śukadeva Gosvāmī | Śukadeva Gosvāmī | 1 |
| 5.153 | — | and inquired from | ½ |
| 5.153 | — | the devotional ecstasy | ½ |
| 5.154 | — | Nārada considers | 1½ |
| 5.158 | — | Here Nārada mentions | 1 |
| 5.161 | — | The residents of Vraja | 2 |
| 5.172 | On this path, not | On this path, not | 1 |
| 5.172 | On this path, not | The highest perfection | 1 |
| 5.181 | — | Nārada considers Uddhava | 1 |
| 5.183 | — | The words he speaks | 1 |
| 5.187 | — | This is another verse | 1 |
| 5.195 | — | And therefore, because | 1 |
| 5.199 | Here the word | Thus Viśvāmitra became | 1 |

| | | | |
|---|---|---|---|
| 5.199 | Kṛṣṇa blessed the *gopīs* | Kṛṣṇa blessed the *gopīs* | 1 |
| 5.204 | — | As it was, he was | ½ |
| 5.216 | — | Similarly, most aspiring | 1 |
| 5.218 | — | By *nāma-saṅkīrtana* | 1 |
| 5.229 | — | The purpose of | 1 |
| 5.229 | — | The symptoms of | 1 |
| 5.234 | — | To protect the hope | 2 |
| 5.247 | — | He wanted only the | 1 |
| 6.3 | — | and now all his | ½ |
| 6.22 | — | but what they actually | ½ |
| 6.30 | — | The other realms | ½ |
| 6.31 | — | Even though he was | ½ |
| 6.36 | — | But being kindly | 1 |
| 6.50 | — | This was evidence of | 1 |
| 6.52 | — | The *gopīs* had no need | 2½ |
| 6.60 | — | Gopa-kumāra was already | 2 |
| 6.68 | — | The men, women, and | 1 |
| 6.97 | — | In any event, His taste | 1 |
| 6.103 | — | She could never actually | 1 |
| 6.104 | — | They couldn't carry | 1 |
| 6.124 | — | The *Rāja-nighaṇṭu* | 2 |
| 6.125 | — | Everything the Supreme | 1 |
| 6.134 | — | Without arousing suspicion | ½ |
| 6.137 | — | He is *akhila-rasāmṛta-mūrti* | 1 |
| 6.142 | — | The *gopīs* are always | 1 |
| 6.143 | — | Kṛṣṇa is more eager | 1 |
| 6.154 | — | If those silly girls | 1 |
| 6.155 | — | The *gopīs* arrived at | 1 |
| 6.166 | — | Mother Yaśodā, however, | 1 |
| 6.176 | — | All this He had to do | 1 |
| 6.193 | Texts 192 and 193 | And the word *iva* | 1 |
| 6.196 | — | For all its sweetness, | 1 |
| 6.202–203 | Alternatively, the word | Both a reflection and | 4 |
| 6.217 | — | Caring nothing for their | 1 |
| 6.220 | — | The lake in which | 1 |
| 6.224 | — | And now to see Kāliya | 1 |
| 6.229 | — | The shock of hearing | 1 |
| 6.231 | — | Balarāma couldn't believe | 1½ |
| 6.236 | — | It had taken all of | 1 |
| 6.239 | — | His devotees are driven | ½ |
| 6.244 | — | Even though Kṛṣṇa was | 1 |
| 6.265 | — | The Vraja-vāsīs all knew | 1 |
| 6.267 | — | Nanda had no choice but | 1 |
| 6.269 | — | In the civil law | 3 |
| 6.282 | — | Akrūra is trying to | 1 |
| 6.290 | — | And besides, the *gopīs* | 1 |
| 6.293 | — | If You leave us we | 1 |
| 6.294 | — | Only for at best | 2 |

| | | | |
|---|---|---|---|
| 6.315 | — | Now that he was finally | 1 |
| 6.322 | — | Therefore in the company | 1 |
| 6.330 | — | Nanda should have no | 1 |
| 6.333 | — | and curiously reverses roles | ½ |
| 6.337 | — | As the *Dharma-śāstras* | 2 |
| 6.340 | — | And they persisted in | 1 |
| 6.343 | — | Since no one told the | 2 |
| 6.350 | — | Even in their dreams | 1 |
| 6.359 | — | In pure devotional life | 1 |
| 6.361 | — | Yes, to one who has | 1 |
| 6.364 | — | And since he is attached | 1 |
| 6.370 | — | As already revealed in | ½ |
| 6.371 | — | as in the famous aphorism | ½ |
| 6.375 | — | The journey is no more | 1 |
| 6.378 | — | Śrī Sarūpa's vision is | 1 |
| | | | |
| 7.2 | — | Sarūpa's disciple, on the | 2 |
| 7.14 | The prefix *upa-* | This implies that one | 1 |
| 7.14 | Thus Kṛṣṇa always makes | Thus Kṛṣṇa always makes | 1 |
| 7.14 | The unlimited ways the | The unlimited ways the | 1 |
| 7.14 | Impersonalists conceive | To reciprocate with them | ½ |
| 7.23 | — | The five tender parts | 6 |
| 7.24 | — | Kṛṣṇa is lionlike | ½ |
| 7.28 | — | Kṛṣṇa is the transcendental | 1½ |
| 7.30 | — | Śrī Yamunā took birth | 1½ |
| 7.33 | — | In this situation, both | 1 |
| 7.37 | — | From Śrī Kṛṣṇa's mouth | 1 |
| 7.43 | Lord Kapiladeva similarly | In the liberated state, | ½ |
| 7.43 | As the queens reveal | That the *gopīs* of Vraja | 1 |
| 7.46 | — | He values the "attacks" | ½ |
| 7.73 | — | So that Janaśarmā would | 1 |
| 7.74 | At the beginning of | At the beginning of | 2 |
| 7.74 | And at the beginning | And at the beginning | 2 |
| 7.77 | — | he wants to remind her | ½ |
| 7.78 | — | And since that love | 1 |
| 7.80 | Consequently, Śrī | In other words, Brahmaloka | 1 |
| 7.80 | If the word *jyotiṣām* | The word *jyotiṣām,* therefore, | 1 |
| 7.92 | Kṛṣṇa is the Supersoul | yet He also lives eternally | ½ |
| 7.93 | — | This is Verse 43 of the | 1 |
| 7.94–95 | Here *Śrī Brahma-saṁhitā* | Brahmā calls Goloka by | ½ |
| 7.94–95 | The cows of Goloka | Sequences of events may | ½ |
| 7.96 | Starting with this verse, | Starting with this verse, | 1 |
| 7.101 | Lord Brahmā is amazed | Baka and Agha were | 1 |
| 7.102 | Here Brahmā responds | Successful *sannyāsīs* deserve | 1 |
| 7.103 | Kṛṣṇa comes to the | His attempts to bestow the | 1 |
| 7.104 | According to the third | For this purpose the | 1 |
| 7.105 | Or Kṛṣṇa might be | After all, isn't Brahmā | 1 |
| 7.105 | And suppose Kṛṣṇa | What difference should | 1 |
| 7.106 | And while describing | And while describing | ½ |

| | | | |
|---|---|---|---|
| 7.106 | As Brahmā indicates | In His expanded forms | ½ |
| 7.107 | After reciting for His | And we can understand | 1 |
| 7.107 | The word *dhanyā* most | The word *dhanyā* most | ½ |
| 7.108 | The words *avaratānya-* | The words *avaratānya-* | 1 |
| 7.110 | The *gopīs* single out | The *gopīs* single out | 1 |
| 7.112 | The devotees of the | *Prema* should not be | 1 |
| 7.114 | Or, understanding the | They too must be | 1 |
| 7.115 | Another *gopī,* enchanted | sages are not so | ½ |
| 7.116 | In this verse | *Dhanyāḥ sma* means | 1 |
| 7.117 | By far superior | To the cows, the sound | 1 |
| 7.119 | As implied by the words | And so the Pulindīs | 1 |
| 7.119 | Another explanation is | Another explanation is | 1 |
| 7.121 | Amazed by the | Most people, however, | 1 |
| 7.121 | Accepting that | Thus in this verse, | 1 |
| 7.122 | The good fortune of | The cowherd boys and | 3 |
| 7.122 | Determined *yogīs,* | Only the Vraja-vāsīs | 1 |
| 7.124 | When Kṛṣṇa's cowherd | even more convincingly | 1½ |
| 7.126 | Parīkṣit addresses the | because Parīkṣit is | ½ |
| 7.128 | After Nanda paid taxes | Nanda was overjoyed | 1 |
| 7.128 | Yes, although Nanda | Yes, although Nanda | 2 |
| 7.130 | To emphasize the | The three greatest | 1 |
| 7.131–132 | The son of Devakī | Indeed, all transcendental | 2 |
| 7.131–132 | A person whom the | Therefore the Personality | 1 |
| 7.131-132 | Paraphrasing this verse | Paraphrasing this verse | 1 |
| 7.134 | This verse (*Bhāgavatam* | Abandoned by Kṛṣṇa in | 1 |
| 7.135 | First the ladies praise | The Vedic scriptures | ½ |
| 7.137 | When Kṛṣṇa comes into | What is so auspicious | 2 |
| 7.137 | When Kṛṣṇa comes into | Each time they see | 1 |
| 7.138 | Kṛṣṇa is amazed by how | Kṛṣṇa is amazed by how | 1 |
| 7.139 | Texts 139 through 146 | Therefore Kṛṣṇa's confidential | 1 |
| 7.139 | The name Uddhava | Surely Uddhava deserves | 1 |
| 7.143 | The word *gopī* can here | He stole everything they | 1 |
| 7.145 | But aren't self-contented | In ordinary circles that | 1 |
| 7.145 | Here a doubt may | Had He done so, Uddhava | 1 |
| 7.145 | To understand the | *Avidan* can therefore be | 1 |
| 7.146 | The Pulindīs and others | They had to keep their | 1 |
| 7.147 | Texts 147 through 152 | Because of his own | 1 |
| 7.147 | A devotee situated in | A devotee situated in | 2 |
| 7.148 | It is obviously with | It is obviously with | 1 |
| 7.148 | The word *nanu* | He can make His mercy | 1 |
| 7.151 | Aren't all devotees | Yes, but the intimacy | 1 |
| 7.151 | Aren't all devotees | The *gopīs'* worship of | 1 |
| 7.151 | The words *kṛṣṇasya* | The words *kṛṣṇasya* | 1 |
| 7.151 | As Uddhava describes | Although Uddhava has | 2½ |
| 7.152 | Uddhava is absorbed | The most ecstatic kind | ½ |
| 7.154 | Third, by having the | The phrase *yadu-vara-pariṣat* | 1 |
| 7.154 | It is not without | In *Śrīmad-Bhāgavatam* | 1 |
| 7.157 | To end the *Dig-darśinī* | To end the *Dig-darśinī* | 1 |
| 7.157 | To end the *Dig-darśinī* | Thus, both to the Lord | 1 |

# *Variant Readings of* ŚRĪ BṚHAD-BHĀGAVATĀMṚTA

IN PREPARING THIS EDITION of *Śrī Bṛhad-bhāgavatāmṛta,* I consulted three printed editions, published by the Caitanya Maṭha, by Purīdāsa Mahāśaya, and by the Saurī Prapannāśrama (see the Bibliography for details). All three editions were published in Bengali script. Listed below are the variants found among those editions. Purīdāsa additionally cites variant readings from a manuscript he identifies only as being located in Vṛndāvana, and he occasionally cites variants without identifying their source. Apart from a few variants and several corrected typographical errors, the readings of the Purīdāsa edition notably match those of the Saurī edition, first published nineteen years earlier.

The editions and manuscripts are identified in this appendix by the following letters:

| | |
|---|---|
| C | Caitanya Maṭha edition |
| P | Purīdāsa edition |
| S | Saurī-prapannāśrama edition |
| V | Vṛndāvana manuscript |
| U | unidentified manuscript |
| * | corroborated by the *Dig-darśinī* commentary |

The first column of the listing gives the number for the chapter and verse of the variant, followed by a letter (a, b, c...) to indicate the *pāda* (usually, the quarter verse). ("*Uvāca*" lines are not counted.) The next column gives the reading chosen for this edition, preceded by an asterisk when the choice is shown correct by the author's *Dig-darśinī* commentary. The last column gives the variant, preceded by one or more letters indicating its source or sources. When the variant is obviously wrong grammatically or syntactically, it is given in brackets.

Before considering variants, I have first transliterated the Sanskrit into roman characters according to the following standards used by the Bhaktivedanta Book Trust: Pāṇini's options for doubling consonants are never applied, the optional conversion of *anusvāra* to nasal stops is applied always inside words and never at the end of words, *avagrahas* are indicated only at the beginning of words and only when they stand for a deleted short *a,* and hyphens are added to indicate compounded words. After transliteration, any texts that don't match count as variants.

## LISTING OF VARIANTS

| | | | | |
|---|---|---|---|---|
| 5.5C | | *tūlī-* | S | *tulī-* |
| 5.8B | | *upariṣṭād* | CPS | [*upariṣṭāt*] |
| 5.14B | | *utthāpya* | V | *utthāya* |
| 5.21A | | *bahir* | S | [*bahi*] |
| 5.21B | | *tāmbūla-* | S | [*tāmbula-*] |
| 5.34B | | *vilokayan* | S | [*vilokayam*] |
| 5.46B | | *me vyatheta* | P | *vyatheta* |
| 5.49C | | *vismayenāpi* | S | [*vismayeṇāpi*] |
| 5.49D | | *īdṛśam* | S | [*īdṛśyam*] |
| 5.79C | * | *vṛndāvanādi-* | C | *vṛndāvanādri-* |
| 5.85B | | *-vardhanaḥ* | S | [*-vardhvanaḥ*] |
| 5.106C | * | *aghāsurādikān* | C | [*akhāsurādikān*] |
| 5.107A | | *-vīthībhir* | S | [*-vīthābhir*] |
| 5.110A | | *pakṣma-* | S | [*pakṣmā-*] |
| 5.111A | * | *mahimā sa tasyā* | U | *mahimātra kasyā* |
| 5.116C | | *dvi-vārau* | U | *dvau vārau* |
| 5.130D | | *-arcane* | S | [*-arcaṇe*] |
| 5.131B | * | *muñja-* | PS | *mañju-* |
| 5.150B | * | *-paripāka-* | S | [*-pāripāka-*] |
| 5.158B | * | *vidanti* | S | *vadanti* |
| 5.159A | | *tad-goṣṭha-* | C | [*tad-agoṣṭha-*] |
| 5.166C | | *nāma* | C | *nāma nāma* |
| 5.172B | * | *yādṛgbhis* | C | [*yadṛgbhis*] |
| 5.176A | * | *bahavas* | PS | [*bahvas*] |
| 5.188C | | *nirīkṣamāṇo* | CPS | *nirīkṣyamāṇo* |
| 5.189D | | *-janim* | C | [*-janīm*] |
| 5.192D | | *dhairyaṁ na rakṣati* | U | *dhairya-vighātinī* |
| 5.197A | * | *yad arcitaṁ* | C | *yadārcitaṁ* |

| | | | | |
|---|---|---|---|---|
| 5.198A | | *vibhuḥ* | V | *prabhuḥ* |
| 5.201B | | *-praṇaya-* | P | [*-prāṇaya-*] |
| 5.204C | * | *daṣṭvā* | P | *dṛṣṭvā* |
| 5.210D | | *kalindajā-* | S | [*kalindājā-*] |
| 5.219C | * | *prayāsyad* | C | [*prajāsyad*] |
| 5.237D | * | *-pūrārdra-* | P | [*-pūrvārdra-*] |
| 5.239A | | *tasmiñ* | CPS | [*tasmin*] |
| 5.242C | | *chūnyam* | P | [*chanyam*] |
| 5.246B | * | *bhavān* | S | *bhagavān* |
| 5.246D | | *tyaktvā* | CPS | [*tyaktā*] |
| | | | | |
| 6.13B | * | *tam ito* | U | *gamito* |
| 6.15A | | *tasmiñ* | CPS | [*tasmin*] |
| 6.25A | | *-durlabhaiḥ* | C | [*-dulabhaiḥ*] |
| 6.25B | | *-bharaiḥ* | S | [*-bharaiṁ*] |
| 6.25C | * | *-pateḥ* | C | [*-pate*] |
| 6.31C | | *-ghoṣāḍhyaṁ* | S | [*-ghoṣācyaṁ*] |
| 6.33A | | *rudantaṁ* | S | [*rudantam ntaṁ*] |
| 6.44D | | *vyalokayam* | PS | [*vyalokayan*] |
| 6.45A | | *-bhāreṇa* | C | [*-bhareṇa*] |
| 6.48A | | *-rasaṁ* | PS | [*-rasam*] |
| 6.48C | * | *-uṣṇo jvalita-* | P | *-uṣṇojjvalita-* |
| 6.49C | | *vraja-* | P | [*vaja-*] |
| 6.55A | * | *athāpaśyam* | CPS | [*athāpaśyan*] |
| 6.56B | | *bārha-* | S | [*bāha-*] |
| 6.58C | * | *javād* | CS | *javad-* |
| 6.66C | | *praskhalat-* | S | [*praṅkhalat-*] |
| 6.71B | | *-mūḍhaḥ* | S | [*-mūḍha*] |
| 6.73B | | *kṣaṇād dhairyam* | C | [*kṣaṇā-airyam*] |
| 6.77D | | *nayantaḥ* | C | [*niyantaḥ*] |
| 6.80B | * | *dhautāmbarāṅgyā* | PS | *dhautāmbarāṅgā* |
| 6.81C | | *vetti* | PS | *veti* |
| 6.93B | | *-kautukato* | S | *-kautūkato* |
| 6.96C | | *āsū* | CS | [*āsa*] |
| 6.98A | | *kiñcid* | CPS | [*kiñcit*] |
| 6.98B | | *dadhus* | CS | [*dadhyus*] |
| 6.99B | | *-kasturī-* | P | *-kastūrī-* |
| 6.101D | | *ratim* | S | [*rātim*] |
| 6.103D | | *ruṣeva* | S | [*rumeva*] |
| 6.109B | | *nārhati* | S | [*nāhati*] |
| 6.105A | | *nirīkṣamāṇānāṁ* | CS | *nirīkṣyamāṇānāṁ* |
| 6.116B | | *-purandaram* | CPS | [*purandaraḥ*] |
| 6.117D | | *bhṛśam* | S | [*bhūśam*] |
| 6.119D | | *pibañ* | CPS | [*piban*] |
| 6.120D | | *-yutam* | S | [*-ṣutam*] |
| 6.121A | | *-pakvāni* | S | [*-pakkāni*] |
| 6.123C | | *-cūrṇānvitair* | S | [*-cūrṇānvatair*] |
| 6.125B | | *-vilāsa-* | C | [*-vilasa-*] |

| | | | |
|---|---|---|---|
| 6.131D | * *bhuktvāhaṁ* | P | [*bhuktāhaṁ*] |
| 6.134C | *paśyañ* | CPS | [*paśyan*] |
| 6.134D | *carvitaṁ* | C | *cakitaṁ* |
| 6.134D | * *man-mukhe* | CPS | *sammukhe* |
| 6.137D | *-tūlike* | CS | [*-tulike*] |
| 6.138A | * *niraṅka-* | C | [*nīraṅka-*] |
| 6.140B | *tāmbūla-* | S | [*tāmbula-*] |
| 6.141B | *tāmbūla-* | S | [*tāmbula-*] |
| 6.142A | *-chrotra-* | CPS | [*-chotra-*] |
| 6.149 | *śrī-yaśodovāca* | C | [*śrī-yaśodā uvāca*] |
| 6.149A | * *bālo* | S | *balo* |
| 6.152B | * *tato 'vidan* | CPS | *tato vidan* |
| 6.161C | * *utthāpya* | CPS | [*tathāpya*] |
| 6.163D | *vādayan* | S | *vādayam* |
| 6.180D | *nirīkṣamāṇāḥ* | CPS | *nirīkṣyamāṇāḥ* |
| 6.188D | * *nivavarta* | V | *nivṛtto 'bhūd* |
| 6.190A | *tasya* | S | [*tāsya*] |
| 6.194D | * *nirūpayet* | S | [*nirupayet*] |
| 6.195B | *tanayāmbu nipāyayaṁs* | PS | *tanayāmbunipāyayaṁs* |
| | | C | *tanayāmbūnipāyayaṁs* |
| 6.203D | * *prītaye* | CS | *prīyate* |
| 6.208C | *evaita* | CPS | [*evaite*] |
| 6.221C | *kūrditvā* | S | [*kūditvā*] |
| 6.227B | *dhāvañ* | CPS | [*dhāvan*] |
| 6.223D | * *hradam* | PS | [*hadam*] |
| 6.230A | *sa gṛhe* | U | *sva-gṛhe* |
| 6.259D | *baddhvāśu* | PS | [*baddhāśu*] |
| 6.260B | * *samutplutya* | PS | *samupatya* |
| 6.270B | *nyasto* | S | [*nyāsto*] |
| 6.281A | *āvṛtaṁ* | S | [*āvṛtaḥ*] |
| 6.282A | *nityaṁ* | PS | [*nityam*] |
| 6.286A | *-jātān* | S | [*-jyatān*] |
| 6.286D | *parirakṣatām ū* | CS | *parirakṣatām* |
| 6.291 | *śrī-gopya ūcuḥ* | C | has this line missing |
| 6.291D | *nayasva* | CPS | *na yasya* |
| 6.292A | * *'bhavad ālayo* | CPS | *bhavad-ālayo* |
| 6.296B | *kiyāñ* | CPS | [*kiyān*] |
| 6.303A | * *tāṁ* | S | *tāḥ* |
| 6.310B | *nyapatañ* | CPS | [*nyapatan*] |
| 6.315D | * *mohena* | S | [*mohana*] |
| 6.318D | *'krūraḥ* | C | [*'kraraḥ*] |
| 6.320A | *ārūḍhā* | S | [*āruḍhā*] |
| 6.329 | — | P | *śrī-bhagavānuvāca* (added) |
| 6.344A | *-nādair* | S | [*-nādaiḥr*] |
| 6.344C | *prāpur* | S | [*prāpyur*] |
| 6.348D | * *'cirād* | CPS | *cirād* |
| 6.349A | *-maṇiḥ* | S | [*-maṇiṁ*] |
| 6.357B | * *manyante* | PS | [*manyate*] |

| | | | |
|---|---|---|---|
| 6.370D | *yujyeta* | S | [*yujyete*] |
| 6.371A | *tiṣṭhan* | S | [*tiṣṭham*] |
| 6.378D | * *paśyāmi* | S | *paśyāpi* |
| 7.3A | *yad* | [CPS] | *yat* |
| 7.3C | *vīkṣe* | CS | *vīkṣye* |
| 7.11C | * *apekṣe* | CPS | *upekṣe* |
| 7.19A | *madhurā* | S | [*mathurā*] |
| 7.22D | * *-bhṛtam* | CP | *-bhūtam* |
| 7.23B | *-piccha-* | S | [*-picchā-*] |
| 7.23C | *-kambu-* | S | [*-kambū-*] |
| 7.33D | *-naipuṇau* | C | [*-naipuṇyau*] |
| 7.36B | *dayālur* | S | [*dayālar*] |
| 7.38A | * *kṣemaṁ* | S | *kṣepaṁ* |
| 7.40 | *śrī-parīkṣid uvāca* | S | has this line missing |
| 7.47A | *kīlāla-* | C | [*kālāla-*] |
| 7.47B | *vādayañ chrī-* | CPS | [*vādayan śrī-*] |
| 7.50C | * *sa-kūrdanaṁ* | PS | *sa-kūrdanas* |
| 7.51B | *hārāñ* | CPS | [*hārān*] |
| 7.54C | *eva* | U | *amba* |
| 7.56C | *kharjūra-* | C | *kharjura-* |
| 7.59C | * *paricarvaṁs* | CS | *paricaryaṁs* |
| 7.59D | *hāsayitvā* | P | [*hasayitvā*] |
| 7.67C | *cānyaiḥ* | C | [*cānyaiṁ*] |
| 7.68C | *vinirmite* | P | [*vinimite*] |
| 7.70A | * *nānānukāra-* | C | *nānānukara-* |
| 7.73B | * *apūrva-yātam* | C | *apūrva-jātam* |
| 7.75D | * *saṅghaṭante* | C | [*saṅghante*] |
| 7.86 | *kiṁ ca* | C | has these words missing |
| 7.90 | *śrī-jaiminir uvāca* | CS | have this line missing |
| 7.94A | * *kāntāḥ kāntaḥ* | C | [*kāntaḥ*] *kāntaḥ* |
| 7.107D | *bhujayor* | C | [*bhūjayor*] |
| 7.108A | *vṛndāvanaṁ* | S | [*vṛndāvanaḥ*] |
| 7.108D | *prekṣyādri-* | S | [*prekṣyadri-*] |
| | | C | *prekṣādri-* |
| 7.109A | *adrir* | P | [*ādrir*] |
| 7.113D | *jahaty* | CS | [*jahāty*] |
| 7.116A | *-matayo* | U | *-gatayo* |
| 7.119C | *-rūṣitena* | PS | [*-ruṣitena*] |
| 7.126AB | *brahmañ / chreya* | CPS | [*brahman / śreya*] |
| 7.129C | * *kṛṣṇaḥ* | P | *tatra* |
| 7.135C | *durāpam* | S | [*durapim*] |
| 7.136B | *-ruditokṣaṇa-* | V | *-ruditotsava-* |
| | | C | *-ruditokṣaṇe* |
| 7.136B | *-mārjanādau* | C | [*mārjanadeau*] |
| 7.139C | *gopīnāṁ* | S | [*gopīnāḥ*] |
| 7.146C | *prāpuḥ* | S | [*prāpaḥ*] |
| 7.151D | *nyastaṁ* | S | [*nyāstaṁ*] |

# *Readings of* ŚRĪMAD-BHĀGAVATAM
# *Verses that Differ from the BBT Edition*

FOR EACH VARIANT READING, column 1 lists the number of the *Bhāgavatam* verse and (in parentheses) the *Bṛhad-bhāgavatāmṛta* text (or texts) in whose commentary the variant is cited. (A citation given in the text itself is numbered in bold.) Column 2 gives the first words of the cited verse, column 3 the variant words according to *Bṛhad-bhāgavatāmṛta,* and column 4 the corresponding words in the BBT edition of *Śrīmad-Bhāgavatam.*

| VERSE | STARTING | BṚHAD-BHĀG. | BBT EDITION |
|---|---|---|---|
| 4.9.10 (7.14) | *yā nirvṛtis tanu-* | *kiṁ v* | *kiṁ tv* |
| 5.6.18 (7.131–132) | *rājan patir gurur* | *bhajatāṁ bhagavān* | *bhagavān bhajatāṁ* |
| 5.12.13 (7.14) | *yatrottamaḥ-śloka-* | *yatrottamaḥ-śloka-* | *yatrottamaśloka-* |
| 9.4.64 (7.145) | *nāham ātmānam* | *śriyam ātyantikīṁ vāpi* | *śriyaṁ cātyantikīṁ brahman* |
| 10.2.2 (6.18) | *anyaiś cāsura-* | *vṛtaḥ* | *yutaḥ* |
| 10.2.17 (7.106) | *sa bibhrat pauruṣaṁ* | *rājamāno durvisaho* | *bhrājamāno 'ti-durdharṣo* |
| 10.6.39 (**7.131**) | *payāṁsi yāsām* | *akhilārtha-daḥ* | *akhila-pradaḥ* |
| 10.6.43 (**7.128**) | *nandaḥ sva-putram* | *proṣyāgatam avaghrāya* | *pretyāgatam upaghrāya* |
| 10.8.46 (**7.126**) | *nandaḥ kim akarod* | *yaśodā vā* | *yaśodā ca* |
| 10.9.18 (**7.129**) (5.107) | *sa mātuḥ svinna-* | *sa mātuḥ sva-mātuḥ** | *sva-mātuḥ* |
| 10.11.7 (5.107) | *gopībhiḥ stobhito* | *nṛtyan* | *'nṛtyad* |
| 10.11.8 (5.107) | *bibharti kvacid* | *udvahan* | *āvahan* |
| 10.11.9 (5.107) | *darśayaṁs tad-vidāṁ* | *bhakta-* | *bhṛtya-* |
| 10.12.12 (**7.122**) | *yat-pāda-pāṁśur* | *-pāṁśur* | *-pāṁsur* |
| 10.13.11 (5.30) | *bibhrad veṇuṁ* | *madhye tiṣṭhan* | *tiṣṭhan madhye* |
| 10.14.31 (**7.97**) | *aho 'ti-dhanyā* | *'dyāpy atha nālam* | *'dyāpi na cālam* |

* This reading matches that of the BBT *Bhāgavatam* but varies from the reading in the text of *Bṛhad-bhāgavatāmṛta* itself.

| VERSE | STARTING | BṚHAD-BHĀG. | BBT EDITION |
|---|---|---|---|
| 10.14.39 (**7.105**) | *anujānīhi māṁ* | *jagac caitat* | *jagad etat* |
| 10.21.11 (**7.116**) | *dhanyāḥ sma* | *mūḍha-matayo* | *mūḍha-gatayo* |
| | | *-veṣam* | *-veśam* |
| 10.21.12 (5.143) | *kṛṣṇaṁ nirīkṣya* | *-vicitra-* | *-vivikta-* |
| 10.21.14 (**7.115**) | *prāyo batāmba* | *munayo vihagā* | *vihagā munayo* |
| 10.22.19 (5.134) | *yūyaṁ vivastrā* | *baddhāñjaliṁ* | *baddhvāñjaliṁ* |
| 10.23.22 (5.135) | *śyāmaṁ hiraṇya-* | *-veśam* | *-veṣam* |
| 10.23.31 (5.135) | *patayo nābhyasūyeran* | *anumanyate* | *anumanvate* |
| 10.38.8 (**5.197**) | *yad arcitaṁ brahma-* | *-kuṅkumācitam* | *-kuṅkumāṅkitam* |
| 10.44.16 (**7.137**) | *prātar vrajād* | *nirgatya* | *nirgamya* |
| 10.46.4 (**7.140**) | *tā man-manaskā* | after *-daihikāḥ* | *mām eva*… (extra couplet) |
| 10.47.60 (5.150, **7.149**) | *nāyaṁ śriyo 'ṅga* | *-sundarīṇām* | *-vallabhīnām* |
| 10.47.62 (**7.151**) | *yā vai śriyārcitam* | *sad-ātmani prapadāravindaṁ* | *yad ātmani caraṇāravindaṁ* |
| 10.51.53 (7.14) | *bhavāpavargo* | *ratiḥ* | *matiḥ* |
| 10.60.24 (5.190) | *tasyāḥ su-duḥkha-* | *-vihatā* | *-vihato* |
| 10.83.41 (7.43) | *na vayaṁ sādhvi* | *pārameṣṭhyaṁ vā* | *pārameṣṭhyaṁ ca* |
| 11.12.12 (**7.145**) | *tā nāvidan mayy* | *anusaṅga-* | *anuṣaṅga-* |
| 11.13.36 (7.14) | *dehaṁ ca naśvaram* | *parihitaṁ* | *parikṛtaṁ* |

# SANSKRIT
# *Pronunciation* GUIDE

THROUGHOUT THE CENTURIES, the Sanskrit language has been written in a variety of alphabets. The mode of writing most widely used throughout India, however, is called *devanāgarī,* which means, literally, the writing used in "the cities of the demigods." The *devanāgarī* alphabet consists of forty-eight characters: thirteen vowels and thirty-five consonants. Ancient Sanskrit grammarians arranged this alphabet according to practical linguistic principles, and this order has been accepted by all Western scholars. The system of transliteration used in this book conforms to a system that scholars have accepted to indicate the pronunciation of each Sanskrit sound.

## VOWELS

अ **a**  आ **ā**  इ **i**  ई **ī**  उ **u**  ऊ **ū**  ऋ **ṛ**

ॠ **ṝ**  ऌ **ḷ**  ए **e**  ए **ai**  ओ **o**  औ **au**

## CONSONANTS

| | | | | | |
|---|---|---|---|---|---|
| Gutturals: | क **ka** | ख **kha** | ग **ga** | घ **gha** | ङ **ṅa** |
| Palatals: | च **ca** | छ **cha** | ज **ja** | झ **jha** | ञ **ña** |
| Cerebrals: | ट **ṭa** | ठ **ṭha** | ड **ḍa** | ढ **ḍha** | ण **ṇa** |
| Dentals: | त **ta** | थ **tha** | द **da** | ध **dha** | न **na** |
| Labials: | प **pa** | फ **pha** | ब **ba** | भ **bha** | म **ma** |
| Semivowels: | य **ya** | र **ra** | ल **la** | व **va** | |
| Sibilants: | | श **śa** | ष **ṣa** | स **sa** | |
| Aspirate: | ह **ha** | Anusvara: ं **ṁ** | | Visarga: ः **ḥ** | |

NUMERALS

**०–0 १–1 २–2 ३–3 ४–4 ५–5 ६–6 ७–7 ८–8 ९–9**

The vowels are written as follows after a consonant:

**ा ā ि i ी ī ु u ू ū ृ ṛ ॄ ṝ े e ै ai ो o ौ au**

For example: **क ka का kā कि ki की kī कु ku कू kū**
**कृ kṛ कॄ kṝ कॢ kḷ के ke कै kai को ko कौ kau**

Generally two or more consonants in conjunction are written together in a special form, as for example: **क्ष kṣa त्र tra**
The vowel **"a"** is implied after a consonant with no vowel symbol.
The symbol *virāma* (्) indicates that there is no final vowel: क्

THE VOWELS ARE PRONOUNCED AS FOLLOWS:

**a** — as in b**u**t
**ā** — as in f**a**r but held twice as long as **a**
**i** — as in p**i**n
**ī** — as in p**i**que but held twice as long as **i**
**u** — as in p**u**sh
**ū** — as in r**u**le but held twice as long as **u**

**ṛ** — as in **ri**m
**ṝ** — as in **ree**d but held twice as long as **ṛ**
**ḷ** — as in hapi**lly**
**e** — as in th**ey**
**ai** — as in **ai**sle
**o** — as in g**o**
**au** — as in h**ow**

THE CONSONANTS ARE PRONOUNCED AS FOLLOWS:

**Gutturals**
(pronounced from the throat)
**k** — as in **k**ite
**kh** — as in E**ckh**art
**g** — as in **g**ive
**gh** — as in di**g-h**ard
**ṅ** — as in si**ng**

**Palatals**
(pronounced with the middle of the tongue against the palate)
**c** — as in **ch**air
**ch** — as in staun**ch-h**eart
**j** — as in **j**oy
**jh** — as in he**dgeh**og
**ñ** — as in ca**ny**on

**Cerebrals**
(pronounced with the tip of the tongue against the roof of the mouth)

**ṭ** — as in **t**ub
**ṭh** — as in ligh**t-h**eart
**ḍ** — as in **d**ove
**ḍh** — as in re**d-h**ot
**ṇ** — as in si**n**g

**Dentals**
(pronounced like the cerebrals but with the tongue against the teeth)

**t** — as in **t**ub
**th** — as in ligh**t-h**eart
**d** — as in **d**ove
**dh** — as in re**d-h**ot
**n** — as in **n**ut

**Labials**
(pronounced with the lips)

**p** — as in **p**ine
**ph** — as in u**p-h**ill
**b** — as in **b**ird
**bh** — as in ru**b-h**ard
**m** — as in **m**other

**Semivowels**

**y** — as in **y**es
**r** — as in **r**un
**l** — as in **l**ight
**v** — as in **v**ine, except when preceded in the same syllable by a consonant, then as in s**w**an

**Sibilants**

**ś** — as in the German word ***s**prechen*
**ṣ** — as in **sh**ine
**s** — as in **s**un

**Aspirate**

**h** — as in **h**ome

**Anusvara**

**ṁ** — a resonant nasal sound as in the French word *bo**n***

**Visarga**

**ḥ** — a final h-sound: **aḥ** is pronounced like **aha**; **iḥ** like **ihi**.

There is no strong accentuation of syllables in Sanskrit, or pausing between words in a line, only a flowing of short and long syllables (the long twice as long as the short). A long syllable is one whose vowel is long (**ā**, **ī**, **ū**, **ṝ**, **e**, **ai**, **o**, **au**) or whose short vowel is followed by more than one consonant. The letters **ḥ** and **ṁ** count as consonants. Aspirated consonants (consonants followed by an **h**) count as single consonants.

# GLOSSARY

**abhiṣeka** A ceremonial bath performed in the worship of a Deity or the coronation of a king.

**ādi-guru** The first spiritual master of a disciplic succession.

**Aditi** Dakṣa's oldest daughter, a wife of Kaśyapa. She gave birth to twelve sons, including the eleven principal demigods (such as Sūrya, Varuṇa, and Indra) and the Supreme Personality of Godhead Lord Vāmana.

**Āgamas** See *tantras*.

**Agha (-asura)** A demon who assumed the form of a huge python, swallowed Kṛṣṇa and the cowherd boys, but was killed by Kṛṣṇa.

**Akrūra** A distant relative whom Kṛṣṇa considered His uncle and who on Kaṁsa's order brought Kṛṣṇa and Balarāma from Vraja to Mathurā.

**Ananta (Ananta Śeṣa, Śeṣa Nāga)** An expansion of God who appears as a serpent with thousands of heads and who serves as the bed of Lord Viṣṇu. Ananta Śeṣa holds all the planets of the universe on His hoods and constantly sings the glories of Viṣṇu from all His mouths.

**aparādha** An offense, especially against the Supreme Lord or His devotees.

**ārati** A standard ceremony of worship with offerings of lamps, fans, incense, flowers, bathing water, and other items. Its origin is the custom of greeting a guest to one's home at night (*ā-rātrikam*) with a lamp.

**Arjuna** The third of the five Pāṇḍava brothers. A great bowman, he figured prominently in winning the Kurukṣetra battle, with Kṛṣṇa driving his chariot. It was to Arjuna that Kṛṣṇa spoke the *Bhagavad-gītā* just before the battle.

**artha** Economic development, one of the four standard goals of human life.

**ārya** A civilized human being, one who lives according to the standards of the Vedic culture.

**Āryāvārta** The "home of the Āryans," comprising the part of India bounded by seas on the west and east, by the Himālaya Mountains on the north, and by the Vindhyā Mountains on the south.

**āsanas** Postures assumed in *yoga* practice to purify the body and mind.

**āśrama** 1. The hermitage of a sage or teacher. 2. One of the four stages of spiritual development in the *varṇāśrama* social system: *brahmacarya* (celibate student life), *gṛhastha* (marriage), *vānaprastha* (retirement), and *sannyāsa* (the renounced order).

**aṣṭāṅga-yoga** The eight-phase system of *yoga* practice taught by the sage Patañjali in his *Yoga-sūtras*.

**avatāra** A "descent" of the Supreme Lord to the material world in one of His many forms.

**Ayodhyā** The capital of the Kośala kingdom, inherited by Lord Rāmacandra from His ancestors. It is located in south-central Uttar Pradesh. The original Ayodhyā in the eternal kingdom of God lies above the other Vaikuṇṭha worlds and below Goloka Vṛndāvana.

**Badarāyaṇa** See *Dvaipāyana Vyāsa*.

**Bādarāyaṇi** Śukadeva, the son of Badarāyaṇa (Dvaipāyana Vyāsa). Śukadeva heard *Śrīmad-Bhāgavatam* from his father and later repeated it to Mahārāja Parīkṣit.

**Baka (-asura)** A demon friend of Kaṁsa's who assumed the form of a gigantic bird, a crane, and entered Vraja with the intention of killing Kṛṣṇa. Kṛṣṇa killed him by bifurcating his beak.

**Bāla-gopāla** The infant cowherd Kṛṣṇa.

**Balarāma (Baladeva, Balabhadra)** Kṛṣṇa's elder brother, son of Vasudeva and Rohiṇī.

**Bali** King of the Daitya demons, son of Virocana, and grandson of the great Vaiṣṇava Prahlāda. When Lord Vāmana tricked

Bali into donating three paces of land and then with two steps covered the universe, Bali achieved perfection by surrendering everything he had to the Lord.

**bālya** Childhood.

**bhagavad-bhakti** Devotional service to the Supreme Lord.

**Bhagavad-gītā** The essential teachings on progressive spiritual life and pure devotion to the Supreme Lord spoken by the Supreme Lord Himself, Kṛṣṇa, to His friend Arjuna at Kurukṣetra in the last moments before the great battle. Vyāsadeva included the *Bhagavad-gītā* in the *Bhīṣma-parva* of the *Mahābhārata*.

**Bhagavān** The Personality of Godhead, who possesses in full the six opulences (*bhagas*) of perfection—strength, fame, beauty, knowledge, renunciation, and power to control.

**Bhāgavatam** See *Śrīmad-Bhāgavatam*.

**bhakta** A devotee of the Supreme Lord.

**bhakti** Devotional service to the Supreme Lord. *Bhakti* in practice is the prime means of spiritual success, and perfected *bhakti,* pure love of God, is the ultimate goal of life.

**bhakti-rasa** The ecstatic taste of personal reciprocation with the Supreme Lord in pure devotional service.

**bhakti-yoga** The spiritual discipline of linking to the Supreme Lord through pure devotional service.

**Bharata**. 1. The second brother of Lord Rāmacandra. When Bharata's mother, Kaikeyī, obliged her husband to send Rāma into exile and give the throne to Bharata instead, Bharata placed Rāma's shoes on the throne and ruled as His representative until Rāma returned.

2. The eldest son of Ṛṣabhadeva. He was close to achieving pure love of God but became attracted to a helpless deer and so himself had to be born a deer. Then once again he was born, as the seemingly dull *brāhmaṇa* Jaḍa Bharata. In this third life he instructed King Rahūgaṇa and achieved ultimate perfection.

3. The son of Duṣmanta (Duṣyanta) and Śakuntalā.

**Bhāratas** The royal descendants of Bharata the son of Duṣmanta. The Kurus belong to this dynasty.

**Bhārata-varṣa** The planet earth, named after Bharata the son of Ṛṣabhadeva. In a more restricted sense, greater India.

**Bhauma (-asura)** A demon born of Lord Viṣṇu's incarnation Varāha and Bhūmi, the goddess earth. He is also known as Narakāsura. After causing havoc in Indra's heaven and on earth, he was killed by the original Viṣṇu, Kṛṣṇa.

**Bhīṣma** The son of Śantanu and the sacred Gaṅgā. He was one of the twelve Mahājanas, the great authorities on Vedic knowledge. As the elder of the Kuru warriors, he led Duryodhana's forces in battle until felled by the arrows of Arjuna. He passed away gloriously at his own chosen moment in the presence of Kṛṣṇa.

**Bhūmi** The earth, and the goddess who presides over it.

**Bhūr (Bhū-loka)** The middle region of the universe, which includes the planet earth.

**Brahmā** The first finite living being in the material creation. He was born from the lotus growing from the navel of Garbhodaka-śāyī Viṣṇu. At the beginning of creation, and again at the start of each day of his life, Brahmā engineers the appearance of all the species and the planets on which they reside. He is the first teacher of the *Vedas* and the final material authority to whom the demigods resort when belabored by their opponents.

**brahmacārī** A celibate boy in the student phase of spiritual life, receiving education at the residence of a spiritual master.

**Brahmaloka** The highest material planet, the residence of Lord Brahmā and his associates. Also known as Satyaloka.

**brahma-muhūrta** The hour and a half just before sunrise, a time-span considered the most auspicious for daily spiritual practices.

**Brahman** The impersonal, all-pervasive aspect of the Supreme Truth. Another meaning of the word *brahman* is the transcendental sound of the *Vedas*.

**brāhmaṇa** A member of the most intelligent class among the four occupational divisions in the *varṇāśrama* social system.

**brahmānanda** The bliss of impersonal realization of the Supreme.

**brahmarṣi** A sage among *brāhmaṇas.*

**brahma-vādī** A seeker of impersonal realization of the Supreme.

**Bṛhaspati** The spiritual master of Indra and the demigods, and ruler of the planet Jupiter. He is a son of the sage Aṅgirā and grandson of Brahmā. His son is Uddhava, the great devotee of Kṛṣṇa.

**Caitanya Mahāprabhu (Caitanyadeva)** The form in which the Personality of Godhead Kṛṣṇa made His advent in 1486 at Māyāpura, West Bengal, and acted in the guise of His own devotee. He taught the pure worship of Rādhā and Kṛṣṇa, primarily by *saṅkīrtana,* the congregational chanting of Their names.

**cāmara** A fan made from the hairs of a yak's tail, usually bleached white. Used in worship and the attendance of kings, it also has the practical purpose of driving away flies.

**candana** Sandalwood, which may be ground into a cooling paste.

**Candra** The moon and its presiding demigod, a son of the sage Atri.

**Candrāvalī** The leader of the *gopīs* who are rivals of Śrīmatī Rādhārāṇī.

**dāl** Any of several varieties of pulses and beans used in soups and other preparations in Indian cooking.

**Dānavas** Demons descended from the children of Danu, a wife of Kaśyapa.

**darśana** "Viewing," an auspicious audience with a Deity or holy person.

**Devahūti** The daughter of Svāyambhuva Manu, wife of the sage Kardama, and mother of the Supreme Lord's incarnation Kapiladeva. Lord Kapila taught Devahūti the science of pure devotional service through a study of the elements of creation.

**Devakī** The wife of Vasudeva and mother of Kṛṣṇa.

**devas** The demigods who reside in Svarga, led by Indra. They rule the universe and administer the necessities of life for its inhabitants.

**Devī** "The goddess," Durgā, Lord Śiva's consort.

**dhāma** A domain where the Supreme Lord personally resides and enjoys eternal pastimes with His loving devotees.

**Dhanvantari** The incarnation of Viṣṇu who appeared from the churning of the Ocean of Milk and then delivered to the demigods the nectar of immortality. He is the first teacher of the *Āyur-veda,* the Vedic medical science.

**dhāraṇā** Fixed concentration of the mind, one step of the *aṣṭāṅga-yoga* system.

**dharma** "Religious principles," or, more properly, individual duty. In another sense, *dharma* is the inseparable nature of a thing that distinguishes it, like the heat of fire or the sweetness of sugar.

**dharma-śāstras** The scriptures, supplementary to the *Vedas,* that teach the proper behavior for civilized human society. Some *dharma-śāstras* are in the form of concise codes (*sūtras*), and others in the form of common verse. Best known of this second group is the *Manu-smṛti* (*Manu-saṁhitā*).

**Dhruva** The younger son of Uttānapāda, and grandson of Svāyambhuva Manu, and great-grandson of Brahmā. Insulted by his stepmother, Dhruva left home at the age of five and achieved perfection in six months. Lord Vāsudeva gave Dhruva his own spiritual planet at the top of the universe, called Dhruvaloka or the polestar.

**dhyāna** The yogic practice of meditation.

**Draupadī** The daughter of Drupada and wife of all five Pāṇḍava brothers. Her abusive treatment at the hands of Duryodhana and his sons led to the destruction of the Kuru dynasty.

**Durgā** Lord Śiva's eternal consort, of many names and forms, who joins him in his incarnations. She is the creator and controller of the material world.

**Dvaipāyana Vyāsa** The empowered editor of the *Vedas.* A different Vyāsa appears at the end of each Dvāpara age, when understanding of the *Vedas* becomes helplessly confused. The current Vyāsa, Kṛṣṇa Dvaipāyana, is an incarnation of the Supreme Lord. The *Vedānta-sūtra* and *Mahābhārata* are his personal compositions, and the culmination of his literary effort is the *Śrīmad-Bhāgavatam.*

**Dvāpara (-yuga)** The third of four repeating ages that form the basic cycles of universal time. During its 864,000 years, the mode of passion becomes dominant. The latest Dvāpara-yuga ended about five thousand years ago, at the time of the *avatāras* of Kṛṣṇa and Dvaipāyana Vyāsa and the Battle of Kurukṣetra.

**Dvārakā (-purī, Dvāravatī)** The eternal abode in which Kṛṣṇa fully displays the opulence of God. While descended on earth, Kṛṣṇa resettled the entire population of Mathurā in the city of Dvārakā, which He manifested by constructing it on the coast of the western Ānarta province.

**Dvārakā-vāsīs** The residents of Dvārakā.

**Gada** Kṛṣṇa's younger brother.

**Gandharvas** Singers of the heavenly planets. Capricious by nature, they often distract meditators.

**Garga** A sage who served as family priest of the Yadus. He performed the name-giving ceremony for the infant Kṛṣṇa.

**Garuḍa** The eternal companion of the Supreme Lord who serves as His personal carrier in the form of a large bird. He appeared as the son of Kaśyapa and Vinatā.

**ghāṭa** Steps built for bathing in a river or lake.

**Gokula** The first home of the infants Kṛṣṇa and Balarāma in Vraja, before Nanda's cowherds moved to Nanda-grāma. It is located in the Mahāvana forest, on the eastern shore of the Yamunā, seven miles south of Mathurā City. The name Gokula is also sometimes used to distinguish Kṛṣṇa's abode on earth from Goloka in the spiritual world.

**Goloka** The eternal abode of the Supreme Lord in His original form of Kṛṣṇa. It is located above all the other Vaikuṇṭha planets. It has three parts—Vṛndāvana, Mathurā, and Dvārakā.

**Gopāla** Kṛṣṇa the cowherd.

**gopas** Cowherds, especially those of the community led by Nanda Mahārāja in Vraja.

**Gopīnātha** Kṛṣṇa, the Lord of the *gopīs.*

**gopīs** Cowherd girls or women, especially Kṛṣṇa's young girlfriends in Vraja, who are His most intimate devotees.

**Gopīśvara Mahādeva** The *liṅga* Deity of Lord Śiva in Vṛndāvana who protects the site of Kṛṣṇa's *rāsa* dance with the *gopīs*.

**Govardhana** Girirāja, "the king of mountains," a large hill located fifteen miles west of Mathurā City. For seven days, Kṛṣṇa lifted Govardhana like a huge umbrella to protect the residents of Vraja from a devastating storm caused by the jealous Indra. Sometimes the name Govardhana refers to the village in the center of the hill.

**Govardhana-dhārī** Kṛṣṇa, the "lifter of Govardhana."

**Govardhana-pūjā** The worship of Govardhana Hill by offering mountains of food and circumambulating the hill. This *pūjā* was first initiated by Kṛṣṇa to establish that worship of Him is superior to worship of even the king of heaven, Indra.

**Govinda** Kṛṣṇa, the Lord of the cows, the earth, and everyone's senses.

**gṛhastha** A member of the household order of life, the third stage of spiritual progress in the *varṇāśrama* social system.

**guṇa-avatāras** The empowered incarnations of the Supreme Lord who preside over the three modes of nature. Brahmā, the secondary creator, directs the mode of passion. Śiva, the destroyer, directs ignorance. And Viṣṇu, the maintainer, primary creator, and Supreme Lord Himself, directs goodness.

**guṇas** The three modes, or controlling principles, of material creation—goodness, passion, and ignorance.

**guñjā** A small berry that is strung into garlands and worn by Kṛṣṇa and His friends for decoration. Garlands of *guñjā* are considered especially sacred by Lord Caitanya and His followers.

**guru** A spiritual master. The *gurus* who initiate one and instruct one in pure Kṛṣṇa consciousness are to be honored equally with the Supreme Lord.

**gurukula** "The *guru's* family," a teacher's *āśrama* where traditional education is given.

**Haṁsa** Lord Viṣṇu's incarnation as a swan, who gave instructions to Brahmā and his sons.

**Hanumān** Lord Rāmacandra's most faithful eternal servant, who has the body of a *kimpuruṣa*, a humanlike monkey. Hanumān, son of Añjanā, was minister to Sugrīva in the monkey kingdom Kiṣkindha.

**Hari** The Supreme Lord, Kṛṣṇa or Viṣṇu.

**Hastināpura** The capital of the Kurus, located on the banks of the Gaṅgā, east of what is now Delhi.

**Hṛṣīkeśa** Kṛṣṇa or Viṣṇu, the master of the senses.

**Indra (Mahendra)** The king of the demigods, ruler of Svargaloka. In each *manv-antara* there is a different Indra. The name of the current Indra is Purandara.

**Jaḍa Bharata** See *Bharata*.

**Jagannātha (-deva)** "Lord of the universe," an ancient Deity of Kṛṣṇa. He was established along with His brother Balarāma and sister Subhadrā in the holy city of Purī, on the coast of Orissa. Caitanya Mahāprabhu resided in Purī and worshiped Lord Jagannātha.

**Jaimini** A prominent sage, a disciple of Dvaipāyana Vyāsa. Jaimini wrote the Mīmāṁsā-sūtras, which established the philosophical school of Vedic textual interpretation.

**jalebī** A syrupy fried pastry in the shape of a tubular swirl.

**Jāmbavatī** The daughter of Jāmbavān. After Kṛṣṇa fought Jāmbavān over the Syamantaka jewel, Jāmbavān surrendered to Kṛṣṇa and offered Him Jāmbavatī, who became one of Kṛṣṇa's eight principal queens.

**Janaloka** The planet above Svarga and Mahar that is inhabited by altruistic celibates.

**Janamejaya** Parīkṣit's eldest son, the next emperor of the Kuru dynasty. After Parīkṣit died, Janamejaya heard the *Mahābhārata* from Dvaipāyana Vyāsa's disciple Vaiśampāyana.

**Janārdana** Lord Viṣṇu, the protector of His devotees and destroyer of their enemies.

**japa** Chanting of a *mantra* quietly to oneself.

**Jarāsandha** A powerful enemy of Kṛṣṇa's, the emperor of the

Māgadha kingdom. Yudhiṣṭhira could not perform the Rājasūya sacrifice without first neutralizing Jarāsandha's opposition, so Kṛṣṇa arranged for Jarāsandha to be killed by Bhīma.

**jīva** An eternal finite spirit soul, qualitatively equal with the Supreme Soul.

**jñāna** Knowledge.

**jñānī** A practitioner of *jñāna-yoga,* or, more generally, any learned person.

**Kali (-yuga)** The fourth of four repeating ages that form the basic cycles of universal time. In each Kali-yuga the world degrades into quarrel and dishonesty. The present Kali-yuga began 5,000 years ago and will continue for another 427,000 years. Kali is also the name of the ruler of the *yuga.*

**Kālindī** The River Yamunā appearing in human form to become one of Kṛṣṇa's eight chief queens in Dvārakā.

**Kāliya** A many-headed serpent who poisoned a lake within the Yamunā. Kṛṣṇa subdued the serpent by dancing on his hoods and then banished him from Vraja.

**kāma** Sense gratification.

**Kaṁsa** The king of Bhoja and son of Ugrasena who usurped the throne of Mathurā. After sending many demons to Vraja to kill Kṛṣṇa and Balarāma, he finally brought the brothers to Mathurā for a rigged wrestling tournament, where Kṛṣṇa killed him.

**Kapila (-deva)** A white-complexioned incarnation of the Supreme Lord who appeared in the Satya-yuga as the son of Kardama and Devahūti. He taught His mother *sāṅkhya-yoga,* the path of devotional service through systematic study of the material creation.

**karma** Material action and its reactions.

**karma-bhūmi** Bhārata-varṣa, the land where men work in accordance with the Vedic system of sacrifice.

**Kaśyapa** One of the original Prajāpatis, the populators of the universe. Son of Brahmā's first mind-born son, Marīci, he married thirteen of Dakṣa's daughters and fathered many demigods, demons, and species of animals.

**Kauravas** See *Kurus.*

**Kaustubha** A jewel worn by Lord Viṣṇu on His chest. It is one of the few marks visibly distinguishing Him from His devotees in Vaikuṇṭha.

**Keśī** A demon who assumed the form of a wild horse and attacked Vraja. Kṛṣṇa thrust His hand into the demon's mouth and killed him.

**kiśora** The age between eleven and fifteen years.

**Kṛṣṇa (-candra)** The Supreme Personality of Godhead in His original form, enjoying as a youthful cowherd with His family and friends in Vṛndāvana and later as a valiant prince in Mathurā and Dvārakā.

**kṛṣṇa-kathā** Discussions about Kṛṣṇa.

**kṛṣṇa-prema** Pure ecstatic love for Kṛṣṇa. It is the perfection of life.

**kṣatriyas** Members of the second of the four occupational classes in the *varṇāśrama* social system. The *kṣatriyas* are the political and military leaders of society. They are expected to be heroic, charitable, selflessly dedicated to the welfare of all citizens, respectful of the spiritual authority of the *brāhmaṇas,* and ready to use force to stop wrongdoing.

**Kṣīrodaka-śāyī Viṣṇu** The third of the three Puruṣas, incarnations of the Supreme Lord for the creation of the material universe. Kṣīrodaka-śāyī Viṣṇu resides on the island of Śvetadvīpa in the Milk Ocean and expands into the heart of every materially embodied being as the Supersoul.

**Kuntī (Pṛthā)** One of King Pāṇḍu's two wives. By union with various demigods, she became the mother of Karṇa, Yudhiṣṭhira, Bhīma, and Arjuna.

**Kurukṣetra** "The holy field of the Kurus," where in ancient times the members of that dynasty performed sacrifices. The battle fought there decided the fate of the dynasty and so ushered in the beginning of the Kali-yuga.

**Kurus (Kauravas)** The descendants of the ancient king Kuru. They ruled in north-central India, but five thousand years ago they suffered a fratricidal conflict between two groups among them—the sons of Pāṇḍu and those of Dhṛtarāṣṭra.

**Kuvera** The demigod who looks after the vast treasures of heaven.

**Lakṣmī (-devī)** The eternal consort of the Supreme Lord Viṣṇu. She presides over the infinite opulences of Vaikuṇṭha, and her partial expansion dispenses opulences in the material world.

**Lalitā** Śrīmatī Rādhārāṇī's slightly older friend, Her chief companion.

**līlā** "Pastimes," the eternal activities of the Supreme Lord in loving reciprocation with His devotees. Unlike the affairs of materially conditioned souls, the Lord's *līlās* are not restricted by the laws of nature or impelled by the reactions of past deeds. Finite souls who enter those *līlās* also become completely free.

**lotus feet** With the lotus regarded as an emblem of beauty in the material world, the term "lotus" is accepted to describe the all-pure and all-attractive feet of the Supreme Lord or His pure devotee.

**Madana-gopāla** Kṛṣṇa, the transcendental Cupid appearing as a young cowherd.

**Madhupurī** See *Mathurā.*

**mādhurya-rasa** Devotional service to Kṛṣṇa in conjugal love.

**mahā-bhāva** The ultimate limit of devotional ecstasy, found only in Śrī Rādhā and some of Her intimate servants. Śrī Caitanya Mahāprabhu, who was Śrī Kṛṣṇa in the mood of Śrī Rādhā, also displayed such ecstasy.

**Mahādeva** "The great god," Śiva.

**Mahā-lakṣmī** See *Lakṣmī.*

**mahā-prasāda** Food directly from the plate that has been offered to the Supreme Lord. Such food from Lord Jagannātha at Purī is especially known as *mahā-prasāda,* but Śrīla Sanātana Gosvāmī uses the term to refer to Kṛṣṇa's *prasāda* in general.

**Mahar (-loka)** The first of the planets where sages reside above the heaven of Indra. The residents of Maharloka are sages who have not renounced family life.

**Mahārāja** "Great ruler," a term of address to kings and renounced holy men.

**mahātmā** A "great soul," a saint who has broad intelligence by dint of his full Kṛṣṇa consciousness.

**mahat-tattva** The first transformation of primordial nature. It contains all the other elements in their subtle, unmanifest forms.

**Maheśa** The "great Lord," Śiva.

**Maitreya** A sage who was a friend of Dvaipāyana Vyāsa. Maitreya heard Kṛṣṇa's discussions with Uddhava just before Kṛṣṇa's disappearance and passed on what he learned to Vidura. The conversations of Maitreya and Vidura comprise the Third and Fourth Cantos of *Śrīmad-Bhāgavatam.*

**Mānasī-gaṅgā** The most sacred of lakes, located at the midpoint of Govardhana Hill. Kṛṣṇa created it from His mind and filled it with the waters of the Gaṅgā and all other holy rivers and lakes to dissuade His father from leaving Vraja to go on pilgrimage.

**mantra** A short expression in sacred language chanted to purify the mind and fulfill various aspirations.

**Manus** The original progenitors and lawgivers of the human race. In each day of Brahmā there are fourteen Manus. The current Manu is Vaivasvata, son of the sun-god Vivasvān.

**manv-antara** The period of a Manu's reign, lasting 306,720,000 years.

**Mathurā (-dhāma, -maṇḍala, -purī)** The eternal abode in which Kṛṣṇa manifests Himself as the Lord of the Yādavas. During His descent to earth, Kṛṣṇa reclaimed Mathurā for the Yādavas by killing Kaṁsa and installing Ugrasena on the throne. Kṛṣṇa resided in Mathurā for thirty-three years before relocating the Yādavas to Dvārakā.

**Māyā** The Supreme Lord's inferior, material energy. She creates and controls the material world, keeping its inhabitants in countless varieties of illusion.

**Milk Ocean** See *Ocean of Milk.*

**mokṣa** Liberation from the cycle of birth and death.

**Mukunda** Kṛṣṇa or Viṣṇu, the "giver of liberation."
**muni** A thoughtful sage.
**Murāri** Kṛṣṇa, the enemy of the demon Mura.
**Nāga-patnīs** The wives of "the serpent," Kāliya.
**nāma-saṅkīrtana** Chanting of the names of the Supreme Lord in pure love.
**Nanda (Gopa)** The king of the cowherds of Vraja. He and his wife Yaśodā, the greatest of devotees in the mood of parents, raised Kṛṣṇa from His infancy until He left Vraja for Mathurā.
**Nanda-gokula** The cowherd community of Nanda Mahārāja.
**Nanda-kiśora** Kṛṣṇa, "the young son of Nanda."
**Nanda-nandana** Kṛṣṇa, "the darling son of Nanda."
**Nandīśvara Hill** The hill, nondifferent from Lord Śiva, on which Nanda Mahārāja's capital stands.
**Nārada** One of the principal associates of Lord Nārāyaṇa. He travels freely throughout the spiritual and material worlds, preaching pure devotional service and delivering news to various parties to advance the Supreme Lord's pastimes.
**Nara-Nārāyaṇa** The incarnation of the Supreme Lord as the twin sons of Dharma and Mūrti. Nara is an empowered *jīva,* and Nārāyaṇa is directly the Personality of Godhead. They live at Badarikā, practicing severe austerities and meditation for the welfare and instruction of the world. Nārada Muni is among their disciples.
**Nārāyaṇa** The Personality of Godhead as the Lord of Vaikuṇṭha, the infinitely opulent spiritual world.
**nārāyaṇa-bhakta** A devotee of Lord Nārāyaṇa.
**niyamas** The eight secondary regulations observed from the start of the *aṣṭāṅga-yoga* system.
**Nṛsiṁha (-deva)** The pastime incarnation of the Supreme Lord Viṣṇu as half-man half-lion. He appeared in order to deliver the saintly child Prahlāda from the persecutions of his father, Hiraṇyakaśipu. When Hiraṇyakaśipu demanded of Prahlāda, "If your God is everywhere, is He also in this pillar?" Lord Nṛsiṁha burst out of the pillar and ripped Hiraṇyakaśipu apart.
**Ocean of Milk** One of the seven oceans that surround the

"islands" of Jambūdvīpa, the earthly planetary system. Within the Ocean of Milk lies an eternal spiritual planet, Śvetadvīpa, the abode of Kṣīrodaka-śāyī Viṣṇu.

**Pān** Betel nut prepared with lime and spices and wrapped in a leaf for chewing.

**Pañcarātras** Vaiṣṇava *tantras* that teach one to worship the Supreme Lord by serving His Deity forms and chanting *mantras* addressed to Him.

**Pāṇḍavas** The five sons of Pāṇḍu. The three older Pāṇḍavas—Yudhiṣṭhira, Bhīma, and Arjuna—were born to Pāṇḍu's wife Kuntī by the three demigods Yamarāja, Vāyu, and Indra. The other two sons, Nakula and Sahadeva, were born of Pāṇḍu's other wife Mādrī by the Aśvinī-kumāras.

**Para-brahman (paraṁ brahma)** The supreme personal form of the Absolute Truth.

**paramahaṁsa** "Perfect swan," a completely pure devotee of the Supreme Lord, beyond any influence of material illusion.

**Paraśurāma** One of the *daśa-avatāras,* the ten most famous incarnations of Lord Viṣṇu. He appeared as a *brāhmaṇa* but had the qualities of a warrior. When Paraśurāma's father was murdered by the wicked King Kārtavīrya, Paraśurāma vowed to exterminate all the *kṣatriyas* on earth, and he fulfilled that vow twenty-one times.

**Parīkṣit** The son of Abhimanyu who inherited the Kuru throne from Yudhiṣṭhira. Kṛṣṇa personally saved him in his mother's womb, and thus the child was named Parīkṣit because he was searching (*parīkṣeta*) for the person who had protected him.

**Pātālas** The seven subterranean heavenly planets.

**paugaṇḍa** The age between five and ten years.

**Pippalāyana** A son of Ṛṣabhadeva who became a prominent sage on Tapoloka.

**Pradyumna** A son of Kṛṣṇa in Dvārakā. He appears in Dvārakā and Mathurā as the transcendental Cupid, the third of the original quadruple *vyūha* expansions of the Supreme Lord. He again expands from Lord Nārāyaṇa in Vaikuṇṭha, in the second quadruple, as the ruler of mind.

**Prahlāda** One of the greatest devotees of Lord Viṣṇu. As the five-year-old son of the mighty demon Hiraṇyakaśipu, he openly dared to worship the Personality of Godhead and preach His glories. Hiraṇyakaśipu tried many ways to kill the boy, but failed to harm him. Finally Lord Viṣṇu appeared as Lord Nṛsiṁha, killed Hiraṇyakaśipu, and enthroned Prahlāda as king of the demons.

**prāṇa** The vital air of life. It causes all movement in the body, physical and mental, and at death carries the soul into the next body.

**prāṇāyāma** The breath control exercises in the *aṣṭāṅga-yoga* system.

**prasāda** The remnants of food and other items offered to the Supreme Lord. By accepting Kṛṣṇa's *prasāda* one can rapidly become purified and achieve pure love of God.

**pratyāhāra** In the *aṣṭāṅga-yoga* system, the practice of withdrawing the senses.

**prema** Pure ecstatic love of God.

**prema-bhakti** Devotional service to the Supreme Lord in pure love.

**Pṛśni** Kṛṣṇa's mother Devakī in an earlier life, when Krsna appeared as Pṛśnigarbha. Even earlier, she appeared as Aditi, the mother of Lord Vāmana.

**Purāṇas** The histories of the universe, supplements to the *Vedas*. There are eighteen major *Purāṇas* and many secondary ones. The major *Purāṇas* are divided into three groups of six, meant for readers in each of the three modes of material nature.

**Purī** See *Puruṣottama-kṣetra*.

**Puruṣa** The Supreme Lord in a Viṣṇu expansion for the creation of the material world.

**puruṣārtha** The four standard goals of human life: *dharma* (religiosity), *artha* (economic development), *kāma* (sense gratification), and *mokṣa* (liberation).

**Puruṣottama** See *Jagannātha*.

**Puruṣottama (-kṣetra, Purī, Nīlācala, Nīlādri)** The holy city (in Orissa on the Bay of Bengal) where Lord Jagannātha resides.

**Pūtanā** An infanticidal witch who entered Vraja disguised as a beautiful woman and offered the child Kṛṣṇa her poisoned breast milk, which He sucked out along with her life. Thus killed by Kṛṣṇa, Pūtanā was elevated to Kṛṣṇa's eternal service in the mood of a mother.

**Rādhā (-rāṇī, Rādhikā)** Kṛṣṇa's original pleasure potency, from whom all His internal energies expand. She is His eternal consort in Vṛndāvana and the most dedicated and beloved of His devotees.

**rāgānuga-bhakti** The stage of *sādhana-bhakti* in which one's practice of devotional service to Kṛṣṇa becomes spontaneous and follows in the mood of one of Kṛṣṇa's eternal associates in Vraja.

**Raghunātha (Raghupati)** Lord Rāmacandra, "the Lord of the Raghus."

**Raghus** The dynasty of the Kośala kingdom, descended from King Raghu, the great-great-grandfather of Lord Rāmacandra.

**Rākṣasī** A female type of man-eating demon.

**Rāma (-candra)** An incarnation of the Supreme Lord as a perfect righteous king, born as the son of Daśaratha and Kauśalyā. Rāma is also a name of Lord Kṛṣṇa, meaning "the source of all pleasure," and a name of Lord Balarāma and Lord Paraśurāma.

**Ramā** Lakṣmī, the "giver of pleasure" to Lord Nārāyaṇa.

**rasa** "Transcendental taste." The five primary *rasas* are the primary moods in relationship with the Supreme Lord—reverence, servitude, friendship, parental affection, and conjugal love. *Rasa* also indicates the boundless pleasure enjoyed in such reciprocations.

**rāsa (-līlā)** Kṛṣṇa's divine dance with the *gopīs,* the grand celebration of their conjugal love.

**rasāyana** An Āyurvedic tonic.

**Ṛṣabha (-deva)** An empowered incarnation of the Supreme Lord who set the standard of an ideal king, gave valuable instructions to his one hundred sons, and then became an exemplar of complete renunciation.

**ṛṣi** A Vedic sage. The first *ṛṣis* were the "seers" of the Vedic hymns, who perceived the eternal *mantras* in their meditation and passed them on to human society.

**Rudra** Lord Śiva.

**Rukmiṇī (-devī)** Kṛṣṇa's first wife, the mother of Pradyumna, nine other illustrious sons, and one daughter.

**Rūpa Gosvāmī** One of the six Gosvāmīs of Vṛndāvana, principal followers of Caitanya Mahāprabhu. Śrīla Rūpa is the prime authority on the science of *rasa,* loving exchanges with God, which he explained in his *Bhakti-rasāmṛta-sindhu* and *Ujjvala-nīlamaṇi.* He was also an eminent playwright and poet. Most Gauḍīya Vaiṣṇavas consider themselves *rūpānugas,* followers of Rūpa Gosvāmī. See the essay entitled "Śrīla Sanātana Gosvāmī" in the front matter of Volume One of this work.

**sac-cid-ānanda** "Eternal existence, full consciousness, and complete bliss," the constitutional nature of the Supreme Lord and the finite living beings. The Supreme Lord's *sac-cid-ānanda* nature is always manifest, but that of the *jīvas* is liable to be covered by material illusion when they rebel against the Lord.

**sādhaka** A practitioner of devotional service or some other authorized spiritual discipline.

**sādhana** Practices for achieving pure devotional service; more generally, the means for achieving any goal.

**sādhana-bhakti** Pure devotional service in practice, which purifies the heart and brings one toward spontaneous loving service to the Supreme Lord.

**sakhīs** The girlfriends of Śrīmatī Rādhārāṇī.

**samādhi** Fully matured meditation, the last of the eight steps of the *yoga* system taught by Patañjali. A perfected devotee of the Supreme Lord also achieves the same *samādhi.*

**Sāmba** One of Kṛṣṇa's favorite sons, the first son of Jāmbavatī.

**saṁsāra** The cycle of repeated birth and death, which continues until one gives up one's rebellion against the Supreme Lord.

**Sanaka (-kumāra)** The oldest of the first four sons of Lord Brahmā. Sanaka and his three brothers are great masters of *yoga* who teach the science of pure Kṛṣṇa consciousness. His brothers are named Sanat, Sanandana, and Sanātana.

**Sanat (-kumāra)** See *Sanaka*.

**Sanātana Gosvāmī** The author of *Śrī Bṛhad-bhagavatāmṛta*. See the essay entitled "Śrīla Sanātana Gosvāmī" in Volume One of this work.

**Sāndīpani** A sage residing in Avantī who was the teacher of Kṛṣṇa and Balarāma, after they moved to Mathurā. They learned from him the *Vedas* and all the sixty-four traditional arts in sixty-four days.

**saṅkīrtana** Congregational chanting of the names and glories of Kṛṣṇa, which is the prime means for spiritual success in the current age of Kali.

**sannyāsa** The renounced order of life. See *sannyāsī*.

**sannyāsī** A man in the renounced order, the final stage of spiritual progress in the *varṇāśrama* system. *Sannyāsīs* take a vow of lifetime celibacy.

**śāstra** Revealed scripture, or an authorized textbook in any subject.

**sāttvika ecstasy (bhāva)** An estasy that spontaneously appears in the heart of a devotee who has realized a particular loving relationship with Kṛṣṇa.

**Satya (-loka)** Lord Brahmā's planet, the topmost and purest region within the material creation.

**Satyabhāmā** One of Kṛṣṇa's eight principal queens, the daughter of Satrājit. At her request Kṛṣṇa brought the *pārijāta* flower by force from heaven.

**Satya-yuga** The first of four repeating ages that form the basic cycles of universal time. During its 1,728,000 years, purity and spiritual competence are prominent.

**Śeṣa** See *Ananta Śeṣa*.

**śikṣā-guru** An instructing spiritual master.

**Śiva** The special expansion of the Supreme Lord who is uniquely neither God nor *jīva*. He energizes the material creation and, as the presiding deity of the mode of ignorance, controls the forces of destruction.

**Śivaloka** The personal abode of Lord Śiva in the last shell that covers the material universe, the shell of false ego.

**smṛti** "What is remembered," the secondary Vedic literatures, which need not be passed down verbatim but may be reworded by the sages who transmit them in each age. The *Purāṇas* and *dharma-śāstras* are among the *smṛtis*.

**Śrīdāmā** One of Kṛṣṇa's closest friends, the brother of Śrīmatī Rādhārāṇī.

**Śrīdhara Svāmī** The author of the oldest existing commentary on *Śrīmad-Bhāgavatam*.

**Śrīmad-Bhāgavatam** The "spotless *Purāṇa*," which teaches unalloyed devotional service to Kṛṣṇa, the Supreme Personality of Godhead.

**Śrīmān** "Having the favors of the goddess of fortune," an honorific used with the names of respected males.

**śruti** "What has been heard," the original *Vedas*, meant to be passed on orally from generation to generation without change. They are considered coexistent with the Supreme Lord Himself and so in need of no author.

**Sudarśana cakra** The disc weapon of Kṛṣṇa or Viṣṇu, which the Lord uses to dispatch those who dare to attack Him or His devotees.

**Sudharmā** The royal assembly hall of the Yādavas, which Kṛṣṇa brought by force from Indra's heaven.

**Śuka (-deva)** A great renounced sage, son of Dvaipāyana Vyāsa. He heard *Śrīmad-Bhāgavatam* from his father and later repeated it to Mahārāja Parīkṣit.

**Sūrya (-deva)** The sun-god, currently Vivasvān.

**Sutapā** The husband of Pṛśni and father of the Supreme Lord's incarnation Pṛśnigarbha. Sutapā in his previous life had been Kaśyapa, the father of Lord Vāmana, and after his life as Sutapā he became Vasudeva, Kṛṣṇa's father.

**Svarga (-loka, Svar)** The heavenly domain (above Bhuvarloka) of Indra, king of the demigods.

**Śvetadvīpa** "The white island," the abode of Lord Kṣīrodakaśāyī Viṣṇu. It is a spiritual planet manifest within the material world, in the Ocean of Milk.

**śyāma** The dark-blue color, not seen in the material world, that is the hue of Kṛṣṇa's body.

**Śyāmasundara** Kṛṣṇa, who is dark-blue in complexion (*śyāma*) and beautiful (*sundara*).

**tantras** Scriptures that teach *mantra* chanting and Deity worship, especially for persons not initiated into study of the original *Vedas*. There are separate *tantras* for Vaiṣṇavas and Śaivites. The most important Vaiṣṇava *tantras* are the *Pañcarātra Āgamas*.

**tapas** Literally, the heat of concentration. Austerity, or trouble undertaken voluntarily for a higher purpose.

**tilaka** Auspicious marks, of sacred clay and other substances, applied daily on the forehead and various limbs to dedicate one's body to God.

**tīrtha** Literally, the ford of a river. A holy place, especially one at which pilgrims bathe for purification.

**Tṛṇāvarta** A demon friend of Kaṁsa's who assumed the form of a whirlwind and entered Vraja to kill Kṛṣṇa but instead was killed by Him.

**tulasī** The sacred plant most beloved of Kṛṣṇa. *Tulasī* is a form of the *gopī* Vṛndā, the expansion of Śrīmatī Rādhārāṇī who owns the Vṛndāvana forest. Without the leaves of the *tulasī* plant, no offering of food is accepted by Lord Viṣṇu, and no worship to Him is complete.

**Uddhava** One of Kṛṣṇa's closest friends, His most confidential adviser in Mathurā and Dvārakā.

**Ugrasena** The Bhoja king of Mathurā whose throne was usurped by his son Kaṁsa but restored by Kṛṣṇa after Kṛṣṇa killed Kaṁsa.

**upanayana** A boy's investiture with the sacred thread, a ceremony that marks the beginning of his Vedic education.

**Upaniṣads** The philosophical chapters of the *Vedas*, organized into 108 books. They are also called *Vedānta*, meaning "the culmination of Vedic knowledge," and were explained systematically by Dvaipāyana Vyāsa in his *Vedānta-sūtra.*

**Uttarā** King Virāṭa's daughter, the wife of Arjuna's son Abhimanyu. Kṛṣṇa entered her womb to save her son, Parīkṣit, the last heir to the Kuru throne.

**vaidhī-bhakti** The regulative practice of devotional service.

**Vaikuṇṭha (-loka)** Literally, the place free from anxiety. The kingdom of God, full of all opulences and unlimited by time and space.

**Vaiśampāyana** The disciple of Dvaipāyana Vyāsa who narrated the *Mahābhārata* to King Janamejaya.

**Vaiṣṇava** A devotee of the Supreme Lord Viṣṇu. Since Kṛṣṇa and Viṣṇu are different aspects of the same Supreme Person, devotees of Kṛṣṇa are also Vaiṣṇavas.

**Vāmana (-deva)** Lord Viṣṇu's form as a young *brāhmaṇa* boy, one of the *daśa-avatāras,* the ten most famous incarnations of the Lord. After begging three steps of land from Bali Daityarāja, Vāmanadeva covered with His first two steps the entire universe, and for the third step Bali offered his own head. Pleased with Bali's surrender, Lord Vāmana offered to become the guard at Bali's door.

**vānaprastha** A man in the retired order of life, the third stage of spiritual progress in the *varṇāśrama* social system. In this order a married man leaves home and travels to the forest and holy places of pilgrimage, either with or without his wife, to prepare himself for full renunciation, *sannyāsa.*

**Varāha (-deva)** Lord Viṣṇu's incarnation as a huge boar, who killed the demon Hiraṇyākṣa and lifted the earth from the depths of the Garbha Ocean.

**varṇa** In the *varṇāśrama* social system, the four occupational divisions: *brāhmaṇas* (teachers and priests), *kṣatriyas* (rulers and warriors), *vaiśyas* (businessmen and farmers), and *śūdras* (workers).

**varṇāśrama** The Vedic social system, consisting of four occupational divisions (*varṇas*) and four stages of spiritual development (*āśramas*).

**Varuṇa** The demigod who presides over water and the oceans.

**-vāsīs** Residents.

**Vasus** A group of eight major demigods born from Kaśyapa and Aditi.

**Vasudeva** Kṛṣṇa's father in Mathurā and Dvārakā. He and his wife Devakī were persecuted by Kaṁsa for many years before Kṛṣṇa delivered them by killing Kaṁsa.

**Vāsudeva** Kṛṣṇa, the son of Vasudeva. Vāsudeva is also the name of Kṛṣṇa's first expansion outside Vraja, and of the first of the quadruple expansions in Vaikuṇṭha.

**Vatsa (-asura)** A demon friend of Kaṁsa's who entered Vraja in the form of a calf and was killed by Kṛṣṇa.

**Vedānta-sūtra** A concise systematic explanation of the Vedic *Upaniṣads.* It was written by Dvaipāyana Vyāsa and has been commented on by the impersonalist Śaṅkara and by great Vaiṣṇava *ācāryas* like Rāmānuja, Madhva, and Baladeva Vidyābhūṣaṇa.

**Vedas** The original revealed scriptures, eternal like the Supreme Lord and thus in need of no author. Because in Kali-yuga the *Vedas* are difficult to understand or even study, the *Purāṇas* and epic histories, especially *Śrīmad-Bhāgavatam,* are essential for gaining access to the teachings of the *Vedas.*

**Vidura** The Pāṇḍavas' uncle who was the son of Dvaipāyana Vyāsa by the maidservant of the deceased Vicitravīrya. Vidura was an incarnation of Yama, who had been cursed to be born a *śūdra.*

**viraha-bhāva** The ecstasy of separation from Kṛṣṇa.

**Viṣṇu** The Supreme Lord in His opulent feature as the Lord of Vaikuṇṭha, who expands into countless forms and incarnations.

**Viśrāma-ghāṭa (Viśrānti-tīrtha)** The main bathing *ghāṭa* in the city of Mathurā on the river Yamunā. It is famous for being the place where Lord Varāha rested after killing the first demon in the universe, Hiraṇyākṣa.

**Vraja (-bhūmi)** The eternal place of Kṛṣṇa's pastimes with the cowherds, manifest on earth in the district of Mathurā.

**vraja-bhakti** The pure devotion for Kṛṣṇa of the residents of Vraja.

**Vrajanātha** Kṛṣṇa, the Lord of Vraja.

**Vraja-vāsīs** The residents of Vraja.

**Vṛndāvana (-dhāma)** Kṛṣṇa's most beloved forest in Vraja-bhūmi, where He enjoys pastimes with the cowherd boys and the young *gopīs.*

**vṛndāvana-līlā** Kṛṣṇa's pastimes in Vṛndāvana.

**Vṛṣṇis** See *Yādavas.*

**Vyāsa (-deva)** See *Dvaipāyana Vyāsa.*

**Yādavas (Yadus)** The royal dynasty led by Kṛṣṇa in Mathurā and Dvārakā, descended from the ancient King Yadu, son of Yayāti. The dynasty included hundreds of thousands of valiant warriors and princes, all fully devoted to Kṛṣṇa.

**Yādavendra** Kṛṣṇa, the Lord of the Yādavas.

**yajña** Vedic sacrifice, or any work done for the pleasure of the Supreme Lord Viṣṇu.

**Yakṣas** A militant class of celestial beings, obedient to the treasurer of the demigods, Kuvera. Although frequently grouped with the man-eating Rākṣasas, they are also called the *puṇya-janas* ("righteous men").

**yamas** The first eight regulations observed from the beginning of the *aṣṭāṅga-yoga* system.

**Yamunā** The holiest of rivers, flowing through Vraja-bhūmi and thus touched by the dust of Kṛṣṇa's feet. The Yamunā personified is also known as Kālindī. After Kṛṣṇa established his capital at Dvārakā, she became one of His eight principal queens.

**Yaśodā (-devī)** Kṛṣṇa's mother in Vraja. She raised Him from infancy until He moved to Mathurā. She is the most exalted of all of Kṛṣṇa's devotees in the mood of parental love.

**yoga** Spiritual discipline to link oneself with the Supreme. There are various kinds of *yoga,* including *karma-yoga* (the offering of the fruits of one's work for the pleasure of the Supreme), *jñāna-yoga* (the cultivation of spiritual knowledge of the soul and Supersoul), *aṣṭāṅga-yoga* (the eightfold process of meditation taught by Patañjali), and *bhakti-yoga* (pure devotional service to the Personality of Godhead).

**Yogamāyā (Mahāyogā)** The aspect of Kṛṣṇa's personal energy who enhances His loving pastimes with His devotees by putting the devotees in benign illusion, making them forget that He is God. When Kṛṣṇa descended to earth, Yogamāyā appeared as His sister, Subhadrā. Mahāmāyā, the material energy of illusion, is her partial expansion.

**yogī** A practitioner of *yoga.*

**Yudhiṣṭhira** The eldest of the five sons of Pāṇḍu. He was actually begotten in Pāṇḍu's wife Kuntī by Yamarāja, the maintainer of religious principles. Thus Yudhiṣṭhira strictly performed religious duties all his life and could never say anything untrue. He was installed as emperor of the world at the end of the Battle of Kurukṣetra.

**yugas** Ages in the cycle of universal history. See *Kṛta, Tretā, Dvārapa,* and *Kali.*

# BIBLIOGRAPHY

## IN SANSKRIT

*Śrī Bhāvārtha-dīpikā,* commentary on *Śrīmad-Bhāgavatam* by Śrīla Śrīdhara Svāmī. Included in the Kṛṣṇa-śaṅkara and Rāmanārāyaṇa editions of *Śrīmad-Bhāgavatam.*

———. Edited by Purīdāsa Mahāśaya. Dhaka: Śrī Śacīnātha Rāya Caturdharī, 1947.

*Brahmavaivartapurāṇa.* Edited by Jagadīśa-lāl Śāstrī. Delhi: Motilal Barnasidass, 1996.

*Chāndogya Upaniṣad.* In *Upaniṣat-saṅgraha,* edited by J. L. Shastri. Delhi: Motilal Barnasidass, 1996.

*Śrī Bṛhad-bhāgavatāmṛtam,* by Śrīla Sanātana Gosvāmī. Edited by Bhaktivilāsa Tīrtha Mahārāja. Māyāpura, W. Bengal: Śrī Caitanya Maṭha, 1969.

———. Edited by Purīdāsa Mahāśaya. Dhaka: Śrī Śacīnātha Rāya Caturdharī, 1946.

———. Edited by Bhaktiśāstrī Gosvāmī. 1927. Reprint, Medinīpura, W. Bengal: Saurī Prapannāśrama, 1995.

*Chāndogya Upaniṣad.* In *Upaniṣat-saṅgraha,* edited by J. L. Shastri. Delhi: Motilal Barnasidass, 1996.

*Gīta-govinda,* by Jayadeva Kavi. Edited by Yamunāvallabha Gosvāmī. Vṛndāvana: Śrī Rādhā-Mādhava Mandira, 1969.

*The Harivaṁśapurāṇam.* Edited by Nageshnath Sharma. Delhi: Nag Publishers, 1995.

*The Kūrmamahāpurāṇam.* Edited by S. R. Swaminath. Delhi: Nag Publishers, 1996.

*Śrī Laghu-bhāgavatāmṛtam,* by Śrīla Rūpa Gosvāmī. Edited by Bhaktivilāsa Tīrtha Mahārāja. Māyāpura: Śrī Caitanya Maṭha, 1962.

*Mahābhārata*. Edited by Vishnu S. Sukthankar et al. Pune: Bhandarkar Oriental Research Institute, 1942.

*The Padmamahāpurāṇam*. Edited by Cārudeva Śāstrī. Delhi: Nag Publishers, 1996.

*Padyāvalī,* by Śrīla Rūpa Gosvāmī. Edited by Vanamālidāsa Śāstrī. Vṛndāvana: Rāghava Caitanya Dāsa, 1959.

*Śabda-kalpadruma,* by Rādhākāntadeva Bāhādura. Delhi: Motilal Barnasidass, 1961.

*The Śivamahāpurāṇam*. Edited by Nāgaśaraṇa Siṁha. Delhi: Nag Publishers, 1996.

*The Skandamahāpurāṇam*. Delhi: Nag Publishers, 1995.

*Śrīmad-Bhāgavatam*. Edited by Śrī Kṛṣṇa-śaṅkara Śāstrī with commentaries. Ahmedabad, Gujarat: Śrī Bhāgavata Vidyāpīṭha, 1965–1997.

———. Edited by Śrī Rāmanārāyaṇa Vidyāratna with commentaries. Berhampur (now in West Bengal): Rāmadeva Miśra, 1904–11.

*The Viṣṇumahāpurāṇam*. Edited by Rājendranātha Śarma. Delhi: Nag Publishers, 1995.

*Yogavāsiṣṭha Mahārāmāyaṇa* of Valmiki. Edited by Thakur Prasad Dwivedi. Delhi: Chaukamba Sanskrit Pratisththan, 1992.

## IN BENGALI

*Śrī Śrī Gauḍīya-vaiṣṇava-abhidhāna,* by Śrī Haridāsa Dāsa. Navadvīpa, W. Bengal: Śrī Haribol-kuṭīra, 1988.

## IN SANSKRIT AND ENGLISH

*Bhagavad-gītā As It Is*. English translation and commentary by His Divine Grace A. C. Bhaktivedanta Swami Prabhupāda. Second Edition. Los Angeles: The Bhaktivedanta Book Trust, 1983.

*Brahma-saṁhitā* (Fifth Chapter), with commentary by Śrī Jīva Gosvāmī, translation and purport by Śrīla Bhaktisiddhānta Sarasvatī Gosvāmī. Madras: Shree Gaudiya Math, 1932.

*Śrīmad-Bhāgavatam* (Cantos 1–9). English translation and commentary by His Divine Grace A. C. Bhaktivedanta Swami Prabhupāda. Los Angeles: The Bhaktivedanta Book Trust, 1972–1977.

*Śrīmad-Bhāgavatam* (Cantos 10–12). English translation and commentary by His Divine Grace A. C. Bhaktivedanta Swami Prabhupāda, completed by his disciples. Los Angeles: The Bhaktivedanta Book Trust, 1980–1987.

IN ENGLISH

*Hari-bhakti-sudhodaya.* English translation by Bhakti Prajnan Yati Maharaj. Madras: Sri Gaudiya Math, 1989.

*Purāṇic Encyclopedia,* by Vettam Mani. Delhi: Motilal Barnarsidass, 1993.

# INDEX *of* VERSES QUOTED

THE VERSES QUOTED in the text and commentary for this volume are listed here, in English alphabetical order. An entry appears for each set of two *pādas* (that is, usually for each half verse). In each entry, first comes the first few words. Then comes the source from which the verse has been cited. (The verse number is included except in the few instances where we have been unable to locate it. When we have been unable to find the source of a verse, we have left the space for it blank. A list of abbreviations for source scriptures is given below.) Finally comes the chapter-verse reference for the *Bṛhad-bhāgavatāmṛta* text or texts in whose commentary the verse is quoted. Numbers in bold indicate verses quoted in the text.

| | |
|---|---|
| *Bhagavad-gītā* | *Bg* |
| *Brahma-saṁhitā* | *Bs* |
| *Brahma-vaivarta Purāṇa* | *BvP* |
| *Bṛhad-bhāgavatāmṛta* | *Bb* |
| *Chandogya Upaniṣad* | *ChU* |
| *Hari-bhakti-sudhodaya* | *Hbs* |
| *Hari-vaṁśa* | *Hv* |
| *Kūrma Purāṇa* | *KP* |
| *Mahābhārata* | *Mb* |
| *Padma Purāṇa* | *PP* |
| *Skanda Purāṇa* | *SkP* |
| *Śrīmad-Bhāgavatam* | *Bhāg.* |
| *Viṣṇu Purāṇa* | *VP* |
| *Yoga-vāsiṣṭha-rāmāyaṇa* | *Yv* |


| VERSE QUOTED | SOURCE | LOCATION IN COMMENTARY |
|---|---|---|
| *adya-prabhṛti gopānāṁ* | *Hv* 2.12.46 | 5.145 |
| *agni-putrā mahātmānas* | *KP* | 7.151 |
| *aham ātmā guḍākeśa* | *Bg* 10.20 | 7.80 |

# GENERAL INDEX

NUMERALS IN BOLDFACE type indicate translations to the verses of *Śrī Bṛhad-bhāgavatāmṛta.*

# G

# H



# I



# J

# K

Kṛṣṇa
in Goloka (*continued*)
deeds of as wonderful, **5.113**
Dhenuka killed by, **5.127**
dressed and decorated by *gopīs,* **6.97**
driven by compassion for His suffering devotees, **6.349**
eager to enjoy with the *gopīs,* **6.84–85**
eats with friends, 5.30
embarrassed, **6.75**
embraces and kisses Gopa-kumāra, **6.75**
enters His village, **7.73**
enters Vṛndāvana forest, **6.192**
entrusts Janaśarmā to Sarūpa, **7.73**
eternally present, 7.154
exiles Kāliya, **6.253**
expert in dance and song, **5.156**
expert in pastimes of separation, **5.153–155**
faints out of love for devotees, **7.34**
as family member for Vraja-vāsīs, 5.136
feeds cowherd boys with *yajña* offering, 5.135
feeds Sarūpa with His own hand, **6.127**
feet of, on Gopa-kumāra's head, **6.71**
flute of. *See* Flute of Kṛṣṇa
forces Sarūpa to speak, **7.5–7**
forest dress of, **5.133**
friends and family, gives Himself to, **5.159**
garlands for, **7.63–66**
glories, shows or conceals them, 5.111
goes to Mathurā again, **6.354**
Gopa-kumāra first sees, **6.55–59**
*gopīs,* gives *pān* to, **6.143**
*gopīs'* fatigue removed by, **5.199**
Govardhana held by, **5.136**
grazes animals at Govardhana, **7.71**
greeted by His family and friends, 5.127
held by Akrūra, **6.315**

Kṛṣṇa
in Goloka (*continued*)
indebted to *gopīs,* **5.155**
influenced by Yogamāyā, **6.361**
*kaiśora* age entered by, 5.112
Kaṁsa killed again by, **6.354**
Keśī mounted by, **6.260**
on Keśī with friends, **6.261**
kindness displayed by, **5.106**
known especially as Hari, 5.88
*laḍḍu* pastime of, **6.129–131**
leaves for Mathurā, **6.302**
leaves the grove, **6.288**
as life and soul of His friends, **7.49**
lifts *gopīs* onto Kāliya's hoods, **6.242**
lunch of, **6.113–135, 7.52–62**
makes Vraja-vāsīs forget misery, **6.349**
means of achieving, pure love as, 5.214
melts with compassion, **7.35**
night pastimes of, Sarūpa does not describe, **6.146**
opulences not always displayed by, **5.105**
orders His animals by His flute, **7.44–45**
pained, apparently, **6.93**
pained by devotees' sorrow, **6.314**
pastimes of, described by Nārada, **5.116–137**
pastimes of, repeated again and again by, **6.355–356**
plays outside after lunch, **6.136–137**
pleases His friends, **7.70**
promises to return soon, **6.299–330**
puts *pān* into Sarūpa's mouth, **6.134**
rainy season pastimes of, **5.132**
Rādhā, shows special favor to, 6.144
*rāsa* dance of on Kāliya's hoods, **6.243**
relaxes in the forest, **7.70**
rescues Nanda from Varuṇa's realm, **5.137**
resides eternally in, **5.165**
rests after playing, **6.137**
returns to Vraja, **6.348**
returns to Vraja again, **6.354**

# Q



# R



# S

# T



# U

# V

# W



# Y

# INDEX *of* SANSKRIT VERSES

THIS INDEX CONSTITUTES a complete listing of the Sanskrit texts of this volume of *Śrī Bṛhad-bhāgavatāmṛta,* arranged in English alphabetical order. A listing is included for each half verse (that is, for each set of two *pādas*). The Sanskrit transliteration is followed by the chapter-verse reference.